Oracle® Performance Tuning for 10gR2
Second Edition

Oracle Database Related Book Titles:

Oracle 9iR2 Data Warehousing, Hobbs, et al,
ISBN: 1-55558-287-7, 2004

Oracle 10g Data Warehousing, Hobbs, et al,
ISBN 1-55558-322-9, 2004

Oracle High Performance Tuning for 9i and 10g, Gavin Powell,
ISBN: 1-55558-305-9, 2004

Oracle SQL Jumpstart with Examples, Gavin Powell,
ISBN: 1-55558-323-7, 2005

Implementing Database Security and Auditing, Ben Natan,
ISBN 1-55558-334-2, 2005

Oracle Real Applications Clusters, Murali Vallath,
ISBN: 1-55558-288-5, 2004

Oracle 10g RAC Grid, Services & Clustering, Murali Vallath,
ISBN 1-55558-321-0, 2006

Oracle Database Programming Using Java and Web Services, Kuassi Mensah
ISBN 1-55558-329-6, 2006

Oracle® Performance Tuning for 10gR2
Second Edition

Gavin Powell

ELSEVIER
DIGITAL
PRESS

Amsterdam · Boston · Heidelberg · London · New York · Oxford
Paris · San Diego· San Francisco · Singapore · Sydney · Tokyo

Elsevier Digital Press
30 Corporate Drive, Suite 400, Burlington, MA 01803, USA
Linacre House, Jordan Hill, Oxford OX2 8DP, UK

∞ Recognizing the importance of preserving what has been written, Elsevier prints its books on acid-free paper whenever possible.

Library of Congress Cataloging-in-Publication Data
Application Submitted.

British Library Cataloguing-in-Publication Data
A catalogue record for this book is available from the British Library.

ISBN-13: 978-1-55558-345-3

ISBN-10: 1-55558-345-8

For information on all Elsevier Digital Press publications visit our Web site at www.books.elsevier.com

Printed and bound by CPI Group (UK) Ltd, Croydon, CR0 4YY
Transferred to Digital Print 2011

Working together to grow
libraries in developing countries

www.elsevier.com | www.bookaid.org | www.sabre.org

ELSEVIER   BOOK AID International   Sabre Foundation

Contents at a Glance

Contents

Preface

This book is about tuning Oracle databases. Three areas of Oracle Database tuning are data model tuning, SQL code tuning, and physical and configuration tuning. The author began his career as an applications developer, not as a systems or network administrator. As a result, this book is written from an applications rather than an operating system perspective.

The objective of this book is to cover all three areas of Oracle database tuning. Currently, no title on the market completely covers all of these areas. This book will cover all three by explaining both problem detection and resolution.

The approach in this book is to present something that appears to be immensely complex in a simplistic and easy-to-understand manner. Both reference material and examples are utilized appropriately in order to expedite understanding for the reader.

Reference material is not overused. Oracle software has been in general use commercially for many years and is intended to provide for a very large and diverse customer base. Features are often not removed from Oracle software between versions, and new features are continuously being added. The result is that Oracle software contains a plethora of available options and features. Using only reference information to explain Oracle Database tuning would therefore be difficult to read, contrary to the approach of this book, and would not provide the reader with much practical advice. This book contains a lot of examples, with realistic databases and data, sometimes even very large amounts of data. After all, if your production database needs tuning, you probably have more data than you first expected.

A broad-based tutorial on the subject of tuning Oracle Database is much needed. Most database administrators have operating system administration experience, and little SQL code or data modeling experience. On the other hand, developers have the opposite. This book targets both developers and database administrators because it includes all three areas essential to tuning Oracle installations effectively. The important factor is that all tuning skills—both administration and development skill sets—are required for best performance.

Being a broad-based tutorial, this title is written to reach the widest possible audience, including data modelers, developers, database administrators, and system administrators. Each of these audiences is very specialized, but all are related and interdependent. No existing titles include tuning for data models, tuning of SQL code, and physical and configuration tuning all in one book.

People who would benefit from reading this book are database administrators, developers, data modelers, systems or network administrators, and technical managers. Technical people with these different skills are often ignorant of the skills of each other. This is a great pity because all skill sets are very much dependent on each other for well-constructed databases and applications. Let's take a common example situation. Developers cannot simply hand off SQL code tuning to database administrators when application coding is complete. Database administrators, more often than not, know absolutely nothing about SQL code tuning. The result is that no SQL code tuning is ever done, and too much time is spent squeezing out an extra 10% of performance, with the database administrator doing physical and configuration tuning. Targeting a few hard-hitting SQL statements will probably result in much more than a 10% performance improvement, which is much more productive.

What is in this book?

Data Model Tuning

What is the data model?

The data model is the table structure and the relationships between those tables. Tuning the data model for performance involves normalization and denormalization. Different approaches are required depending on the type of database installation, such as OLTP (the focus of this book) or data warehouse–type databases. Inappropriate database design can make SQL code impossible to tune. If the data model is poor, changing the data model can have the most profound effect on database performance. All SQL code is constructed from the underlying tables. The big problem is that altering the data model after completion of development is expensive because application code may require extensive rework.

Note: OLTP refers to online transaction processing. OLTP generally implies the Internet. Within the scope of this book, OLTP is used to represent both OLTP architectures and perhaps client/server architectures as well.

What in the data model causes problems, and what is data model tuning?

Data model tuning is most effectively performed by a combination of both database administrators and developers. It is seldom the case that both skill sets are involved, however. The result is that table structures are often either development-centric (top-down), or administration-centric (bottom-up) in design. Java development is often top-down and attempts to impose an object structure over a relational framework. Bottom-up design often results in overnormalization and too much granularity. People with different skills should be working together.

What are the benefits of data model tuning?

Tuning the data model can often provide performance improvements in excess of 100%, but it is expensive because application code can be drastically affected.

SQL Code Tuning

What is SQL code?

SQL code is the code directly accessing the database, embedded either in applications or in stored procedures. Sometimes generic SQL code is used, which is SQL code generated by an application on an ad hoc basis. Generic SQL code can cause serious performance issues.

What causes SQL code performance problems, and what is SQL code tuning?

As with data modeling, it is often confusing to determine which personnel skill sets are responsible for SQL code tuning. This is one of the causes of poorly performing SQL code. Performance is served most effectively when developers and database administrators work together to a certain extent.

Poorly written SQL code is often the biggest culprit of performance problems, because it is expensive to rectify, but it is cheaper than changing the data model. SQL code tends to be contained inside independent blocks within applications or stored procedures. This containment is commonly known as embedded SQL code. Tuning SQL code is in general a two-step process, as follows:

1.   Isolation and recoding of the worst-performing SQL statements, perhaps the slowest-performing 10% of SQL code.

2.   General tuning of SQL code involving changes to SQL statements throughout applications and the database, plus adjustments to alternate (secondary) indexing. Alternate indexing is not specifically part of the steps of normalization and denormalization but can be designated as data modeling or SQL code tuning. It is important that database administrators have some involvement with respect to alternate indexing, at the very least in an advisory capacity. Too many or inappropriately constructed alternate indexes can completely destroy performance.

What are the benefits of SQL code tuning?

SQL code tuning can increase performance between 25% and 100%, sometimes much more. In rare situations, I have seen enormous performance improvements when tuning SQL code. One or two projects I have worked on in the past have been sped up 30 to 500 times, for both individual SQL code statements and sometimes even the applications in general. Additionally, SQL code is often embedded in applications in such a way that changing the SQL code does not affect application functionality.

Physical Database and Configuration Tuning

What is physical and configuration tuning?

Physical database tuning involves hardware resource usage, networking, and various other administration tasks, such as configuration and file distribution.

What causes physical and configuration performance problems?

Physical configuration is usually a culprit of poor performance where Oracle software is installed with defaults and never altered by an expert. Developers often build table structures and SQL code. In this case, physical tuning is relied on to solve performance problems. This is usually a mistake because physical configuration tuning usually only provides at most 10% to 20% performance improvement.

What are the benefits of physical and configuration tuning?

Physical and configuration tuning usually only results in at most a 25% performance improvement—and usually a lot less. The relative cost of using physical and configuration tuning only is usually not cost effective. Hardware upgrades are common in these situations.

Hardware Upgrades

As a side issue, there are always potential hardware upgrades, which are sometimes a short-term solution because this approach does not necessarily tackle the real problems. Sometimes a combination of hardware upgrades and Oracle installation tuning is the most cost-effective option. Hardware upgrades can often be more expensive than tuning. Three months of SQL code tuning by an expert may be much more cost effective than purchasing new machines, RAID arrays, and all the other bits and pieces that go with it. Additionally, an expert can teach developers and database administrators to build properly tuned databases and applications in the first place.

Tuning with the Database Control

Oracle Enterprise Manager has now reached its maturity in Oracle Database 10*g*, with the introduction of the Database Control. The Database Control runs in a browser, across a network. The Database Control is a magnificent tool that is useful for administration, maintenance, and performance tuning.

Sample Databases Used in This Book

Several sample databases are utilized in this publication. Some are simple and some are highly complex, depending on their use when explaining aspects of tuning. All details and diagrams are included in full in Appendix A.

Please note that this book does not cover operating system tuning or data warehouse tuning, even though they may be mentioned or alluded to in many places. I do not claim to know everything about Oracle Database performance tuning. However, I do have 18 years of custom applications development and database administration experience. What I do know is shared in this book.

Note: Multiple versions of Oracle Database are covered in this book, up to and including Oracle Database 10*g*, Release 2.

I received a few complaints from the first edition of this book with respect to it not being up to date with Oracle Database 10*g*. This second edition is written with the most recent production release of Oracle Database 10*g* Release 2.

Note: The statements and opinions expressed in this book are often my own and do not necessarily represent the opinion of any corporation, company, or anyone else. And don't run anything without testing it first!

Let's get started.

Introduction

Let's begin by looking at what we need to examine in order to tune Oracle installations:

- A tuning environment
- When to tune
- What to tune
- When to stop tuning
- Tuning from development through to production

Finally, we will briefly describe how this book is organized.

A Tuning Environment

What is a tuning environment? A tuning environment is an environment in which your tuning efforts can be productive.

What Is Required When Tuning Oracle Database?

- Good software tools
- Skilled personnel
- Staging (testing) environments
- A realistic duplication of the production environment:
  - *Actual and expected production environments*. These can often be different if growth is rapid or requirements change.

■ *If possible, databases should be of the same size and content.* If this is impractical, then at least development and testing databases should be proportionate to production.

■ *Are the statistics the same?* Statistics can be copied or executed using the same time intervals as production.

What Tools Are Available?

Excellent software tools for tuning and monitoring Oracle databases are numerous. Oracle Enterprise Manager has many very useful bells and whistles. Spotlight is excellent for visual and informative real-time monitoring of busy production systems. Both Oracle Enterprise Manager and Spotlight are very useful as tuning aids for physical and SQL code performance analysis.

Many other tools are available. The most important tools in the tuning process are the developers and the administrators. That is why you are reading this book. The best software tools are usually the most expensive, but that does not mean that the less expensive tools are useless. In general, the more expensive tools tend to do more for you. However, when something is being done for you automatically and you do not understand the internals, it is unlikely that your tool set can do better than well-trained, experienced database administrators and developers.

Skilled Personnel

Good skills have their correct places. Database administrators tend to have roots as either system administrators or developers. Each skill set has its pros and cons. Developers tend to know a lot more about coding SQL and building data models. System administrators have extensive knowledge of operating systems such as UNIX and tend to concentrate tuning efforts on the physical aspects of Oracle Database. Developers tend to concentrate on tuning the data model and building efficiently performing SQL code. Unfortunately, this is not always the case, because there is sometimes a tendency for developers to place the burden of tuning SQL code and the data model into the database administrators' responsibility. Confusion can result, and perhaps nothing gets done.

Staging (Testing) Environments

You need as many testing and staging environments as you can get. As the resident DBA, you should not be expected to perform database tuning on an active production database that is required to be up and usable 24x7x365. Tuning on a production database in this situation will limit your scope and could cost you your job! Insist on at least one extra machine and always test anything you do, no matter how trivial. This is the most important difference between production and development. Developers do everything quickly because they have to. Production database administrators are expected to get their tasks done just as fast, but additionally, everything must be perfect all the time. So make sure you insist on extra hardware and extra time.

Duplicating Production Databases for Effective Tuning

It is absolutely essential to have the most recent and most realistic copy of a production database for tuning purposes. Tuning on a production database is risky, and using a development database for tuning can be completely useless. It is extremely rare that development and production databases are alike. Testing databases can be useful when development and production databases cannot be made the same.

Statistics are also important. In a production environment such as an online transactional database, the data in that production database could be changing constantly. Even if your database is not changing too much, statistics could change or rapidly become out of date. The more dynamic the data is, the more often statistics should be updated. The SQL code optimizer utilizes statistics to compile the most efficient methods of executing SQL statements. Statistics are measurements of the data itself, such as how large a table is and how useful an index is. When a SQL statement accesses a table, both the table and index states are important. States of database objects such as tables and indexes are contained within statistics. If statistics are out of date, the optimizer is not functioning realistically. Out-of-date statistics would have the same effect on all types of databases. It is very important to duplicate statistics from production to tuning environments, either by copying or by executing statistics gathering on a tuning database, consistent with the production database.

Making a copy of a production database to a development database is not an issue when the production database is small. When the production database is large, however, continuous copying to a development database could be very time consuming. Be aware that using the database import utility for even single-schema imports on even a small database can take a lot longer than the production database export.

Note: The DBMS_STATS package can be used to copy statistics between databases.

When to Tune

When should you tune? Constantly and throughout the life cycle of your product, perhaps only when performance is a problem. On the other hand, the database should be configured and organized properly in the first place to avoid having to continuously put out fires. If you are always putting out fires, the chances are you will make little progress with anything else. It is much better to be proactive and preempt potential problems rather than to react when they occur. It is preferable to tune your database during development rather than after development in production.

Tuning during development will lengthen the life cycle of any system. Why is this the case? If different tasks can be compartmentalized during distinctly separate phases of a project, such that those phases do not overlap each other, then a better product will result. For instance, any developer knows that changing code in order to tune SQL code, after completion of development, could change the integrity and neatness of that code. This may not seem too important, but the more times a piece of code is altered, the more it will deteriorate, not only because the code is changing but also because different coders may be changing that code. Every coder has a different style and approach, and subsequent coding is often confused by code written by other people and vice versa. Errors can be introduced into application code when it is changed. The more changes, the more potential errors.

We do not live in a perfect world. Distinct lines cannot be drawn between development and production. Changing requirements often cause changes in different project phases, making gray areas. There is often overlap between development and production.

It is best to tune during development, particularly data models and SQL code. When tuning after development in a postdevelopment requirements change phase, or in production, tuning should be done carefully, especially when it comes to changing application code. If tuning cannot be done fully in the development cycle, which it probably cannot, take the following approach when tuning in production:

- Set performance targets.
- Use test environments.
- Use test environments that match production as closely as possible.
- Tune with care.

What to Tune in Production

There are five general stages in tuning an Oracle production database:

1.   Resolve obvious bottlenecks.

2.   Examine basic configuration. Configuration is often inappropriate as a result of initial Oracle installation and database creation.

3.   Physical space can be wasted. Often a database can be better organized and become much smaller, even as much as one-tenth of current size, and sometimes more.

Note: (10g) Oracle Database is becoming more automated with respect to physical configuration.

---

4.   Poorly written SQL code in both applications and in the database can only be counteracted partially by physical and configuration tuning. SQL code tuning can help performance immensely but should be performed in development and testing environments first.

5.   Data model tuning may be required if SQL code tuning does not resolve production performance problems. As with SQL code tuning, data model tuning should be done in development and testing environments first.

The easiest approach to tuning during production is Oracle Database physical and configuration tuning. In general, tuning the data model is the most expensive because it will require changes to SQL code, application code, and the production database. If SQL code is not tunable, then your data model may be too granular or not properly normalized. Physical and configuration tuning on your database server will not require SQL code and data model tuning changes. However, the purely database-oriented tuning approach may eventually lead to expensive hardware upgrades, which can often be the best tuning option. However, costs can sometimes be greater when the hardware becomes so complex that highly skilled, expensive administrators are required. Hardware upgrades are often a short-term solution, and their cost effectiveness can be appropriate if the software life cycle is short or money is tight, assuming the hardware is reusable or sellable.

When to Stop Tuning During Production

When do you stop tuning? This is always debatable. You could stop tuning when performance targets are met, depending on what needs to be tuned. The resolution of obvious bottlenecks is a clear indicator that no more tuning is required. Physical tuning (i.e., configuration, physical database structure, networking, and hardware bottleneck issues) can often only amount to as little as 10% of total effective tuning activity, both in development and production.

The simple approach to when to stop tuning is to teach your developers to build properly tuned SQL code from the outset, and make sure that the data model is sound before you do even that. This is probably impossible, but the more SQL code tuning that is done during the development process, the fewer problems you will have later on. Many software projects are discarded because they take too long to develop. However, many other software projects are thrown out or rewritten because they do not meet acceptable performance standards, rendering them useless. Tuning data models and SQL code after completion of development can sometimes simply be too expensive.

When to stop tuning depends on your situation and the skills you have. If the company and your database size and activity grow, you will have performance problems anyway, but you can be better prepared. Let us examine the steps in tuning production databases in order to decide when to stop tuning the different areas.

Bottlenecks

Solving performance bottlenecks is usually reactive rather than proactive. The term *bottleneck* is technical computer jargon that usually deals with a particular facet of your environment, which is overloaded, be it within or outside of your database.

Note: Stop tuning when the bottleneck is removed.

Configuration

If there are immense configuration and physical problems, some downtime may be required. Configuration issues are easier to resolve than physical problems, and both are easier than tuning data models and SQL code.

Configuration can be as simple as setting parameters correctly in the Oracle Database configuration parameters file and Oracle networking software configuration files. Make absolutely sure that configuration parameters are completely understood before changing them. First, incorrectly formed configuration can prevent the database from starting and perhaps cause a crash. Second, some parameters have very specific functions; incorrect settings can cause a totally different and probably undesired effect.

Stop tuning when configuration parameters are correct. Experimenting with changing configuration parameters on a production database is risky, so test, test, test!

Physical Space Usage

Physical space usage and growth tuning for performance includes tuning of datafiles, redo logs, archive logs, and rollback segments.

Note: (10*g*) Manual rollback is deprecated. Use automated undo.

Resolving physical problems with space usage and growth can cause a lot of downtime but may be the only solution. Small databases have small initial configuration parameter settings. If those small databases suddenly start to get very busy, then immense problems can occur. The sooner the physical issues are resolved for a rapidly growing database, the better. If the database continues growing, the temptation is often to spend enormous amounts of money on hardware. Organizing a database physically can essentially save a lot of disk space.

Note: (10*g*) The current trend in Oracle Database is veering toward automated management of physical space. As a result, physical space management to save disk space is becoming less important.

The smaller a database is, the less disk space is needed to search through when finding data, thus the faster your data searches will be. Additionally, highly fragmented data can cause a lot of "bouncing around" when retrieving data.

Stop tuning when performance is acceptable, as long as requirements for uptime are not compromised. Only extreme situations of database growth cause problems with use of physical space.

SQL Code Tuning

Poorly constructed SQL code usually causes most database performance problems. When SQL code is poorly tuned, database administrators can do little to improve performance using physical and configuration tuning alone. Database administrators can tune SQL code contained in PL/SQL stored procedures. The most ideal approach to SQL code tuning is to teach your developers to tune SQL code as they build applications.

Sometimes developers will build applications rapidly without much consideration for building efficient SQL code. Developers do not really have extra time to make sure the SQL code is as efficient as possible. Most production database administrators tend to have roots as either operating system or network administrators. These skills are essential for production database administration, and there's the rub! The administrators sometimes do not know how to tune SQL code, and they cannot change the application code because the code belongs to the developers. The developers do not have the time or the skills to produce efficient SQL code. Most Oracle Database tuning experts perform physical tuning on the database and the operating system, not SQL code tuning. The result is often only a 10% performance improvement. I have seen SQL code tuned for an application in its entirety and performance increases of 30 to 500 times. That is 500 times faster. One hundred percent is twice as fast. This is an extreme from a consulting job I worked on a few years ago. There were other projects in the past with similar performance issues.

Stop tuning SQL code when development stops, if you can. Teach and encourage your developers to write efficient SQL code during development. It is much more difficult and expensive to tune SQL in production, especially when SQL is embedded in applications.

Data Model Tuning

SQL code performance depends largely on the data model, especially if the data model is poorly structured. Beware of copying older, previously invented data models or using a data model because it is the accepted standard for a particular application. Relational databases, normalization, and denormalization have existed for many years. However, the structure of the applications overlaying those relational databases has changed recently and is still changing. What in the past was COBOL and C is now C++, Java, Perl, and even object Perl.

Object-oriented design application development languages such as Java tend to confuse what used to be accepted relational database design. Object applications tend to impose an unwilling structure on top of a relational database. The result is a data model that is a hybrid between relational and object database methodologies. This hybrid structure can be an advantage for OLTP and client/server transactional applications but a performance hog for any type of reporting or data warehouse applications.

I have seen many OLTP applications with Java object structures imposed onto relational databases. Sometimes this top-down application to data model approach works extremely well, sometimes very poorly. Object methodology promotes breaking things down into their smallest manageable parts. This approach can be a complete disaster for efficiency in a relational database. Imposing an object structure onto a relational database in its purest form is relational database normalization in its extreme. In these situations, third, fourth, and fifth normal forms are common. A partial solution is often two databases—one OLTP and the other a data warehouse—doubling costs. The second database is a denormalized data warehouse database. Denormalizing a database can enhance performance from a reporting perspective.

Tuning the data model is the most difficult and most expensive option because SQL code depends on the structure of the data model; extensive application code changes can result. Tuning the data model is more effective than physical and configuration tuning but can easily escalate into a full rewrite.

If further data model tuning is required after production release, you may want to look at data warehouse–type options. Tuning the data model for an OLTP database after production release will generally involve a partial or complete rewrite. A data warehouse–type approach generally involves duplicating a database and restructuring that duplicate for output performance in terms of processing many rows at once. Transactional databases in OLTP and client/server environments are often required to be tuned for small-response reaction time to keep your customers happy—very few rows retrieved at a time. If a Web page takes more than seven seconds to load, then your customers may lose interest and go elsewhere, straight to the competition. Data warehouse databases, however, are designed for rapid throughput of large amounts of information for analytical and reporting purposes.

Stop tuning your data model, preferably before development starts or before the first production release. Do not build your relational database to mimic the object structure of a Java application because

relational and object methodologies are completely opposed to each other with respect to methodology. Object structures break down for simplicity, and relational structures are efficient when summarizing information into groupings. These structural types are completely contrary to each other.

So when should you stop tuning in general? As long as there are problems or if users are not satisfied—never! Tune whenever something changes if there are problems or when you have not reached a performance target. There is no harm in going past a target level of performance. Then again, time might be better utilized doing other tasks. You should stop tuning the data model before SQL code development starts. You should stop tuning SQL code when development finishes and the code goes into production.

Tuning from Development to Production

Remember this: Probably most Oracle client installations are very small databases, even for some large companies. For instance, many databases for a lot of the Silicon Valley–based dot-com companies of the late 1990s were well under 10 gigabytes, sometimes even as small as being less than a single gigabyte. They expected growth. The point is this: Many databases are small. A lot of Oracle clients are small companies. The result is that Oracle installation software and database creation tools tend to cater to those small companies. Oracle Corporation's strategy in this respect is perfectly sensible because the smaller companies lack the funds for highly skilled staff. The smaller companies need more done for them. Large end-user software vendor companies often take this approach. The result is that in the Oracle installation software, most of the configuration parameters and physical settings for files are much too small for any database that experiences a reasonable amount of growth. If a database is over 10 Gb, is highly active, or is growing rapidly, then configuration created by Oracle installation software and database creation tools is probably inappropriate.

Tuning an Oracle database is not just tuning the database. As we can see from the stages of tuning already discussed, tuning the database also includes tuning the data model, SQL code, and thus applications. Tuning Oracle Database is a combination of tuning both the Oracle database server and the applications accessing that database. There is a process of tuning an Oracle Database environment including a large number of separate steps or phases. These phases are repetitive but should be performed as closely as possible to the sequential order as shown in Figure I.1.

The Steps in Tuning

Tuning is a set of distinct steps, which can be repeated in any order but are preferably completed in the order shown in Figure I.1. The order and existence of these steps could vary depending on the application type, skills resources, time for development, and capacity of available hardware.

Figure I.1

The steps in tuning an Oracle installation

➡ **Physical tuning**
   ➡ Initial check of configuration parameters
➡ **Data model tuning**
   ➡ Normalization
   ➡ Denormalization
   ➡ Alternate (secondary) indexing
   ➡ Constraints, procedures, event and state change triggers
   ➡ Implementing referential integrity
➡ **SQL code tuning**
   ➡ PL/SQL embedded SQL in the database
   ➡ Applications embedded SQL
   ➡ Alternate (secondary) indexing
➡ **Physical tuning**
   ➡ Configuration parameters
   ➡ I/O contention
   ➡ Space usage
➡ **Operating system and network tuning**

The steps in tuning an Oracle installation should more or less follow the same path as in the development cycle of software development, namely analyze, design, build, test, implement, and verify.

Data Model Tuning

■ A data model is used to represent a set of business rules. Business rules are implemented using entities (tables) and the enforcement of relationships between those entities. Additionally, business rules can be implemented using database-encapsulated stored procedures plus event or state change triggers.

Note: Using triggers can cause serious performance problems.

- Business rules can be tuned into a more mathematically correct design using normalization and referential integrity. Referential integrity ensures that relationships between data items are conformed to.

- Denormalization is the removal of the more granular results of normalization. Granularity causes complex mutable multiple table joins. Multiple table joins can be difficult to tune effectively.

- Alternate or secondary indexing to cater for SQL code not complying directly with a normalized structure can cause problems. This is common for object applications. This step is part of both the data modeling and the applications coding stages, not either. Alternate indexing is generally enhanced in the applications development stage but should be strictly controlled. Creating too many indexes can cause as many problems as it resolves.

- Constraints, PL/SQL stored procedures, functions, and event or state change triggers should be tuned for performance in accordance with entities, relationships, and alternate indexing structures. Triggers are best avoided. Database-level coded PL/SQL will perform better in some situations than others. PL/SQL can be compiled into binary, stored in the database as BLOB objects, possibly increasing PL/SQL execution performance. PL/SQL should only cover business rule functionality and database access code, not applications functionality. Business rules sometimes match relational database structure, whereas applications functionality often does not.

- Implementing referential integrity:

  - *Should referential integrity be implemented?* Not necessarily. Referential integrity can ensure the correctness of data, but it will slow down data changes somewhat because of verification.
  - *How should referential integrity be implemented?* It can be implemented using constraints or triggers. Constraints are the faster and much more reliable method. All sorts of things can go wrong with triggers, and their performance is highly questionable.
  - *Can referential integrity be partially implemented?* Yes, it can. Very small tables containing static, referential data can often have their foreign keys removed. Additionally, noncritical tables or highly used tables can avoid referential integrity to help performance. Generic static tables, when used, probably should avoid referential integrity as well. An example of a generic static table is shown in Figure I.2. These types of tables, in the interests of performance at the database level, are best avoided.

■ *Where should referential integrity be implemented?* Referential integrity can be enforced in the database or at the application level. The benefit of implementing referential integrity at the database level is simple implementation in one place and one place to change in the future. Developers may not necessarily agree with this philosophy, but database administrators generally would.

Figure I.2
Using static generic entities

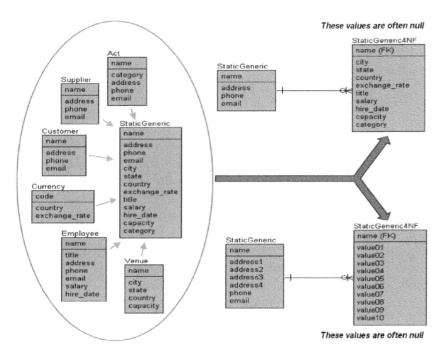

SQL Code Tuning

SQL coding requirements should fit the specifications of the data model based on entities, relationships, and alternate indexing. SQL code can be in both database-based PL/SQL coding and applications-embedded SQL code. What are the steps in tuning SQL code?

■ Identify the worst-performing SQL code and tune only those SQL statements.

■ When the worst-performing code is tuned, SQL code can be tuned in general if there is still a problem.

■ Create, remove, and tune alternate indexing to suit SQL code performance requirements without jeopardizing the data model. When matching SQL code to indexing, it is best to attempt to map SQL code filtering, sorting, and joining to primary and foreign index structures (referential integrity). Using already existing referential integrity keys will reduce the number of alternate indexes. More indexes on tables will speed up data selection but will slow down data updates, sometimes drastically. The fact is that if SQL code is not utilizing referential integrity indexing, there may be a mismatch between the data model and application requirements, or the data model is simply inappropriate.

- How are individual SQL code statements tuned in Oracle Database?

  - Often the most effective method is to examine the SQL code by hand and make sure that the SQL statements conform to indexing in the database, namely in selecting, filtering, sorting, and grouping clauses. The more complex SQL code is, the more difficult it will be to tune in this manner. In fact, complex SQL code is sometimes beyond the capabilities of the optimizer.

  - Use the Oracle Database EXPLAIN PLAN command to examine the optimizer's best execution path for SQL code. EXPLAIN PLAN will show where potential improvement can be made. A simple query plan is shown in Figure I.3.

Figure I.3
A simple query plan using EXPLAIN PLAN

Query Plan from EXPLAIN PLAN

Cost = 102 SELECT STATEMENT on
        HASH JOIN on
            TABLE ACCESS FULL on CUSTOMER
        HASH JOIN on
            TABLE ACCESS FULL on CURRENCY
        HASH JOIN on
        HASH JOIN on
        HASH JOIN on
            TABLE ACCESS FULL on CURRENCY
        INLIST ITERATOR on
            TABLE ACCESS BY INDEX ROWID on INVOICE
            INDEX RANGE SCAN on ADX_INVOICE_1
            TABLE ACCESS FULL on ORDER
            TABLE ACCESS FULL on ORDERLINE

- Trace files and TKPROF can be used to tune SQL code, but tracing produces excessive amounts of information. Tracing should be a last-resort method of tuning SQL code.

- Make sure coders use bind variables in both PL/SQL and applications-embedded SQL code. Bind variables are not as significant after Oracle Database 8*i* Release 1 (8.1.6) because of the cursor-sharing configuration parameter, but forcing cursor sharing lowers statistical accuracy and deteriorates optimizer performance.

- Beware of generic or generated SQL code, which is common at the applications level. This type of embedded SQL code can be very difficult to tune.

Configuration and Physical Tuning

Configuration Tuning

Possibly one of the most effective tuning practices, especially as far as configuration tuning is concerned, is proper initial Oracle installation and configuration of your databases. Do not leave your Oracle installation as Oracle installation software and database creation tools create it. It might be expedient to use the Oracle Database creation tool for a first experimental database creation only.

Note: (10*g*) The database creation tool (Database Configuration Assistant) has become more sophisticated over time. However, most database administrators still prefer to use scripting because it can be modified at will and executed in parts. This approach is no longer necessary except for highly complex installations.

The database creation tool creates a fairly well-organized physical and configured structure, but its default settings are geared toward very small databases. Take the time to properly organize the database and its configuration initially, and you will be less likely to have large amounts of downtime later on.

Physical Tuning

Physical tuning involves the removal of competition for resources. Physical tuning covers the following areas:

- Physical space usage and proper storage structure usage in terms of how blocks are used and reused. Tuning at the block level depends on the application type.

- Growth management of the database and capacity planning must be monitored.

- Setting files such as log files and rollback segments to sizes and frequencies as appropriate to database usage.

Note: (10*g*) Manual rollback is deprecated. Use automated undo.

- There can be contention between processes, memory usage, and data. Some of this type of tuning falls within the scope of both configuration and physical tuning.
- I/O contention can be dealt with in the file system by spreading the I/O load using multiple disks or RAID arrays. RAID arrays are most efficiently used with random access on data spaces and sequential access on index spaces. In non-RAID systems, it is sensible to separate data and index spaces because both are read more or less concurrently. Oracle partitioning is a classic example of this type of tuning.

How Is This Book Organized?

This book is broken into four parts: relational data model tuning in Part I, SQL code tuning in Part II, physical and configuration tuning in Part III, and tuning everything at once in Part IV. The object in this book is to cover all aspects of tuning and Oracle installation. Each chapter focuses on a particular aspect of tuning Oracle Database. As you read through each part, each chapter will build on the preceding chapter, digging deeper step by step.

Part I. Data Model Tuning

Chapters 1 and 2 introduce and offer tuning solutions for relational data modeling. Chapter 3 looks at alternative data modeling methodologies, and Chapter 4 provides some historical background.

Chapter 1.   The Relational Database Model

    Introduces normalization and referential integrity.

Chapter 2.   Tuning the Relational Database Model

    Tuning using efficient normalization, referential integrity indexing, alternate indexing, denormalization, and some useful tricks.

Chapter 3.   Different Forms of the Relational Database Model

This chapter provides a contrast of relational, object, and object-relational concepts.

Chapter 4.   A Brief History of Data Modeling

This is a brief history of relational data modeling and the roots of SQL.

Part II. SQL Code Tuning

The format in Part II is to first describe problems and then offer solutions and tools to help find those solutions. Chapters 5 to 7 present SQL and describe how to tune SQL code without having to dig into the depths of the Oracle optimizer. Chapter 8 looks at indexing. Chapters 9 to 11 dig into the Oracle optimizer, statistics, and hints. Chapters 12 and 13 present tools used to help find SQL code performance problems. Solving as opposed to finding SQL code problems is in preceding chapters of Part II.

Chapter 5.   What Is SQL?

A brief description of SQL and the basics that Oracle SQL can accomplish. Everything is explained in detail and using practical examples.

Chapter 6.   The Basics of Efficient SQL

This chapter is the most important chapter in Part II: SQL Code Tuning. This chapter will teach you step by step how to write properly tuned SQL code. Robust realistic data sets and Oracle Database schemas are used to prove all aspects of tuning. Some tables in schemas are in excess of 1 million rows. There is plenty of data to tune with.

Note: The number of rows in tables varies as the book progresses.

Chapter 7.   Advanced Concepts of Efficient SQL

This chapter expands on the details learned in Chapter 6, by introducing more complex concepts, such as joins and subqueries.

Chapter 8.   Common-Sense Indexing

Teaches how to build indexes properly, building on tuning of SQL code taught in preceding chapters. Indexing and index types are analyzed, explained, and compared for speed in relation to various database activities.

Chapter 9.   Oracle SQL Optimization and Statistics

Covers very deep-level tuning of SQL code in Oracle with an emphasis on using the optimizer, without wasting time on too many nitty-gritty details. This chapter describes how the Oracle SQL code optimizer functions and what can be done to influence the optimizer. If you have read, understood, and implemented the advice and pointers made in previous chapters, you may never need to understand the optimizer on this level.

Chapter 10. How Oracle SQL Optimization Works

This chapter examines and explains the ways in which Oracle Database internally accesses data. An understanding of the various access methods will help when deciphering query plans.

Chapter 11. Overriding Optimizer Behavior Using Hints

This chapter examines and explains the ways in which Oracle Database internally accesses data. An understanding of the various access methods will help when deciphering query plans.

Chapter 12. How to Find Problem Queries

Describes the ins and outs of optimizer query plans using EXPLAIN PLAN, Tracing, and TKPROF. Additional details covering Oracle V$ performance views for SQL code tuning are also provided.

Chapter 13. (10g) Automated SQL Tuning

A brief picture of automated SQL code tuning tools, contained within the Database Control.

Part III. Physical and Configuration Tuning

As in Part II, the format in Part III is to first describe problems and then offer solutions and tools to help find those solutions. Part III describes how to build cleanly structured Oracle installations.

Chapter 14. Tuning Oracle Database File Structures

Tuning Oracle Database file structures encompasses both the physical and logical layers of tuning from the Oracle Instance and

Oracle Database file system layers through to logical layers and tablespaces.

Chapter 15. Object Tuning

Object tuning covers database objects such as tables, indexes, sequences, and synonyms. Numerous tweaks can be made to various database objects to tune for performance.

Chapter 16. Low-Level Physical Tuning

This chapter covers physical block and extent structures and how to build a physical structure from the ground up.

Chapter 17. Hardware Resource Usage Tuning

Hardware resource usage tuning is introduced, covering tuning CPU usage, Oracle Database memory cache buffers, and finally tuning of I/O activity.

Chapter 18. Tuning Network Usage

This chapter covers the Listener, network naming methods, and shared server configuration. There are numerous ways in which Oracle network connectivity can be tuned for better performance, depending on requirements.

Chapter 19. Oracle Partitioning and Parallelism

Oracle Partitioning allows for breaking up of large tables into separate objects, which can have SQL code executed on them in parallel for excellent performance improvements.

Part IV. Tuning Everything at Once

This is where you get to see all aspects of tuning put together and into practice.

Chapter 20. Ratios: Possible Symptoms of Problems

Traditionally, Oracle Database practitioners use large numbers of ratios to assess and provide pointers as to what and where to tune. The secret is to not tune the ratios themselves. Use the ratios as indicators of and pointers to potential problems.

Chapter 21. Wait Events

A wait event occurs when a process or session is forced to wait for another to finish using something both processes require.

Chapter 22. Latches

> Latches are used to protect Oracle Database memory cache buffers from simultaneous access.

Chapter 23. Tools and Utilities

> There are many tools usable for physical and configuration tuning, including Oracle Enterprise Manager and the most important: the Database Control. There are numerous non-Oracle vendor tools, such as Spotlight. Various tuning aspects with utilities are briefly mentioned.

Chapter 24. Tuning with the Wait Event Interface

> This *interface* is a group of interrelated statistical performance views, which can be used to isolate bottlenecks. The Database Control is the best tool to use when drilling down into the Oracle Database Wait Event Interface, when trying to isolate the source of performance problems.

Chapter 25. (9i) Tuning with STATSPACK

Note: As of Oracle Database 9*i*, STATSPACK was currently the official Oracle Corporation–recommended tuning and performance monitoring tool.

Appendices

The appendices contain sample database entity relationship diagrams, scripting examples, and some reference material. Please note that one particular database, the Accounts schema, had active processing executing on it throughout the writing of this book. As a result, the quantities of data in the tables are not constant. If row numbers in tables vary between different chapters and sometimes within chapters, it is nothing to be concerned about.

Some Final Points

Oracle software is highly complex, fully featured, fully loaded, and an excellent piece of software. There are many options and different ways of doing things in Oracle Database software. The result is that the right way to do something in Oracle Database can sometimes be a matter of opinion among different database administrators, designers, and developers.

Because Oracle Database is so large and versatile, many aspects of Oracle Database can sometimes be subject to those opinions.

Perhaps one of the most important things to note about tuning Oracle installations is that there is no hard-and-fast set of rules for tuning. On the other hand, it is sometimes best to plan a set number of steps and follow those guidelines when tuning in order to avoid a random approach to tuning. Guesswork should never be the order of the day. When tuning Oracle installations, focus on critical problem areas. How can critical areas be found? Talk to the users. Talk to developers. Talk to everyone. Find out what problems exist before attempting to solve anything.

Numerous elements discussed in this book have been desupported from Oracle software or deprecated or both. *Desupported* is a term Oracle Corporation uses for an option that is soon to be removed. *Deprecated* is a term used to describe something that is no longer available in Oracle software. Desupported and deprecated elements have been retained in this book for two reasons: (1) multiple versions of Oracle Database are installed out in industry at present, and (2) it is sometimes necessary to include details of older less-favored options within Oracle software in order to facilitate explaining differences between old and new facets of the database.

What Is Oracle Database 10*g*?

Oracle Database 8 and before were just Oracle Database. Oracle Database 8*i* and OracleDatabase 9*i* were Oracle *Internet* Databases. Oracle Database 10*g* is Oracle 10 *grid* Database. Oracle Database 10*g* is designed for use on computer grids, incorporating all sorts of different types of applications, including integrated messaging, enhanced scalability and performance, plus automated storage management.

This book can be read in part or in whole by reading each of the separate parts. However, it is not a reference manual, so it is best read from start to finish because there is a lot of crossover between the three different disciplines. To start learning from a development perspective and pass through to a production perspective later on, I would suggest starting with data model tuning in Part I. Let's get started with relational data model tuning.

Part I
Data Model Tuning

The Relational Database Model

Describing how to tune a relational database model would not be complete without a description of normalization. I have attempted to simplify normalization. When I attended university, I found myself somewhat befuddled by the complexity of the rules of normalization. Before returning to university as a computer science undergraduate, I had worked with relational databases for the three years before, so I had a good basic understanding of how to build relational database models. I worked with a relational database dictionary-based application. Moreover, I found the rules of the five normal forms to be obtuse, overcomplicated, and simply impossible to decipher at first glance. The usual response of a college student's first reading of the descriptions of each normal form is usually, "Huh?" These descriptions have a tendency to cause immense confusion for both the trained and the untrained eye alike. I probably read those rules two or three times and wondered what all the fuss was about. [1]

Before we examine my off-the-wall interpretation of normalization, let's look briefly at how normalization and normal forms are formally defined.

1.1   The Formal Definition of Normalization

Normalization is the sequence of steps by which a relational database model is both created and improved upon. The sequence of steps involved in the normalization process is called *normal forms*. Essentially, normal forms applied during a process of normalization allow creation of a relational database model as a step-by-step progression.

Tuning of a database installation, and particularly, making SQL coding perform well, is heavily dependent on effective entity design. So a good understanding of normalization is essential.

The most commonly applied normal forms are first, second, and third normal forms. Additionally, there are the rarely commercially implemented Boyce-Codd, fourth, fifth, and Domain Key normal forms. The normal forms steps are cumulative upon each other. In other words, each one is applied to the previous step, and the next step cannot be applied until the previous one is implemented. The following examples apply:

- A database model can only have third normal applied when it is in second normal form.

- If a database model is only in first normal form, then third normal form cannot be applied.

That is what is meant by cumulative. The overall result of normalization is removal of duplication and minimizing on redundant chunks of data. The result is better organization and more effective use of physical space, among other factors.

Normalization is not always the best solution. In data warehouses, there is often a completely different approach to database mode design. Normalization is not the only solution. The formal approach to normalization insists on expecting a designer to apply every normal form layer, in every situation. In a commercial environment this is often overzealous application of detail. The trouble with the deeper and more precisely refined aspects of normalization is that normalization tends to overdefine itself simply for the sake of defining itself further.

Before going into the details of normalization, some specifics should be covered briefly, because they are used in the process of explaining normalization and the different normal forms. These specifics include the concepts of anomalies, dependence, and determinance.

1.1.1   Anomalies

Relational database modeling eliminates what are called anomalies from occurring in a database. Anomalies can potentially occur during changes to a database. An anomaly is a bad thing because data can become logically corrupted. An *anomaly*, with respect to relational database design, is essentially an erroneous change to data, more specifically to a single record.

Anomalies apply to any changes to data. Thus insert, delete, and update anomalies can occur as follows:

- *Insert Anomaly.* This is caused when a record is added to a detail table, with no related record existing in a master table. For example, adding a new book first, as written by a specific author, creates a book written by nobody. This is senseless.

- *Delete Anomaly.* This is caused when a record is deleted from a master table, without first deleting all sibling records from detail tables. For example, deleting authors without deleting books first will result in *authorless* books. A special case is a cascade deletion, where deletion of a master record automatically deletes all child records in all related detail tables, before deleting the parent record in the master table.

- *Update Anomaly.* This anomaly is similar to deletion in that both master and detail records must be updated, in order to avoid orphaned detail records. When cascading, it needs to be ensured that any primary key updates are propagated to related child table foreign keys.

1.1.2   Dependence and Determinance

Dependence implies that a value is dependent on another value. Determinance implies that a value will help to determine the value of another value. These are the details:

- *Functional Dependence.* Y is functionally dependent on X, if the value of Y is determined by X. In other words, if Y = X + 1, then the value of X will help to determine the value of Y. Thus, Y is dependent on X as a function of the value of X.

- *Determinant.* A determinant is the inversion (opposite) of functional dependency. Therefore, if Y = X + 1, then X is a determinant of Y. This is because X determines the value Y, at least partially because 1 is added to X as well.

- *Transitive Dependence.* Z is transitively dependent on X when X determines Y, and Y determines Z. Therefore, Z is indirectly dependent on X through its relationship with Y.

- *Candidate Key.* A candidate key is any column or combination of columns that can be used as a primary key for an entity. A primary key uniquely identifies each record in an entity.

- *Full Functional Dependence.* This situation occurs where X determines Y, but X combined with Z does not determine Y. In other words, Y depends on X and X alone. If Y depends on X with anything else, then there is not full functional dependence. Thus, following on from the description of what a candidate key is, if X is the determinant, it cannot be a composite key because a composite key contains more than one column (the equivalent of X with Z).

- *Multivalued Dependence.* A column containing a comma-delimited list (a collection) is a multivalued dependency. All values are dependent as a whole on the primary key.

- *Trivial Multivalued Dependence.* This occurs between two columns when they are the only two columns in the entity. One is the primary key and the other a multivalued list.

- *Nontrivial Multivalued Dependence.* This occurs when there are other columns in an entity in addition to the primary key and a collection.

- *Cyclic Dependence.* This is when X is dependent on Y, which in turn is also dependent on X, directly or indirectly. Cyclic dependence, therefore, indicates a logically circular pattern of interdependence. Cyclic dependence typically occurs with entities containing a composite primary key of three or more columns. For example, three columns in an entity are related in pairs to each other. In other words, X relates to Y, Y relates to Z, and X relates to Z. Ultimately, Z relates back to X.

That covers the definitions of anomalies, dependence, and determinance. Now let's examine the definitions of normal forms from a formal perspective.

1.1.3   First Normal Form (1NF)

First normal form eliminates repeating groups where all records in all entities are identified uniquely by a primary key in each entity. All columns other than the primary key must be dependent on the primary key. First normal form achieves the following:

- Eliminates repeating groups
- Defines primary keys
- All records must be uniquely identified by a primary key. The primary key is unique, prohibiting duplicate values.

- All columns other than the primary key must depend on the primary key, either directly or indirectly.

- All columns must contain a single value.

- All values in each column must be of the same datatype.

- Creates a new entity and moves repeating groups to the new entity, removing them from the original entity.

1.1.4 Second Normal Form (2NF)

Second normal form requires that all nonkey values must be fully functionally dependent on the primary key. No partial dependencies are allowed. A partial dependency will exist when a column is fully dependent on a part of a composite primary key. A composite primary key is a primary consisting of more than one column in an entity. Second normal form achieves the following:

- The entity must be in first normal form.

- Removes columns to other entities that are independent of the primary key.

- All nonkey values must be fully functionally dependent on the primary key. In other words, nonkey columns that are not completely and individually dependent on the primary key are not allowed.

- Partial dependencies must be removed. A partial dependency is a special type of functional dependency that exists when a column is fully dependent on a part of a composite primary key.

- Creates a new entity to separate the partially dependent part of the primary key and its dependent columns.

1.1.5 Third Normal Form (3NF)

Third normal form eliminates transitive dependencies where a column is indirectly determined by the primary key. This is because the column is functionally dependent on another column, whereas the other column is dependent on the primary key. Third normal form achieves the following:

- The entity must be in second normal form.

- Eliminates transitive dependencies, where a column is indirectly determined by the primary key. This is because that column is functionally dependent on a second column, where that second column is dependent on the primary key.

- Creates a new entity to contain any separated columns.

1.1.6   Boyce-Codd Normal Form (BCNF)

In Boyce-Codd normal form, every determinant in an entity is a candidate key. If there is only one candidate key, then third normal form and BCNF are the same. Boyce-Codd normal form achieves the following:

- An entity must be in third normal form.

- An entity can have only one candidate key, where all potential primary keys are separated into separate entities.

1.1.7   Fourth Normal Form (4NF)

Fourth normal form eliminates multiple sets of multivalued dependencies. Fourth normal form achieves the following:

- An entity must be in third normal form or Boyce-Codd normal form.

- Multivalued dependencies must be transformed into functional dependencies. This implies that a single value is dependent on the primary key, as opposed to multiple values (a collection) being dependent on the primary key.

- Eliminates multiple sets of multivalued dependencies, sometimes described as nontrivial multivalued dependencies.

1.1.8   Fifth Normal Form (5NF)

Fifth normal form eliminates cyclic dependencies. 5NF is also known as Projection normal form (PJNF). The term *projection* is used to describe new entities containing subsets of data from the original entity. A cyclic dependency is a form of circular dependency, where three pairs result as a combination of a single three-column composite primary key entity, those three pairs being column 1 with column 2, column 2 with column 3, and column 1 with column 3. In other words, everything is related to everything else, including itself. If normalized entities are joined again using a three-entity join, the resulting records will be the same as that present in the original entity. Fifth normal form achieves the following:

- An entity must be in fourth normal form.

- Cyclic dependencies must be eliminated, where a *cyclic dependency* is a column that depends on a second column, where the first column is either directly or indirectly dependent on itself.

- The post-transformation join must match records for a query on the pretransformation entity.

1.1.9   Domain Key Normal Form (DKNF)

Domain key normal form is the ultimate application of normalization and is more a measurement of a conceptual state of a database model, as opposed to a transformation process in itself. DKNF is the ultimate normal form and describes how a completely normalized database model should be structured:

- Anomalies are not allowed, including insertion, update, or deletion.

- Every record in the database must be directly accessible in all manners, such that no errors can result.

- Every record in every entity must be uniquely identifiable and directly related to the primary key in its entity. Therefore, all columns in all entities are directly determined by the primary keys in their respective entities.

- All validation of data is done within the database model. From a practical perspective, it is prudent to split functionality between database and front-end applications.

Now let's take a step sideways and try to simplify normalization.

1.2   A Layperson's Approach to Normalization

Many existing commercial relational databases do not go beyond the implementation of third normal form. This is often true of online transaction processing (OLTP) databases and nearly always true in properly designed data warehouse databases. Application of normal forms beyond third normal form can tend to produce too many entities, resulting in too many entities in SQL query joins. Too many entities in SQL query joins can reduce system performance for any type of database. The more entities in a join, the more difficult queries are to tune. Also, more query complexity makes it more difficult for a database query optimizer to make a best guess at the fastest execution path for a query. The result is poor performance.

From a purely commercial perspective, good performance is much more important than granular perfection in relational database design. It's not about the design but more about satisfied customers and end users. Poor response time from a computer system will upset people. In fact, poor response time can be much more than simply upsetting because it can impact business and the bottom line for a company.

How can normalization be made simple? Why is it easy? I like to offer a simplified interpretation of normalization to get the novice started. In a perfect world, most relational database model designs are very similar. As a result, much of the basic database design for many applications, such as accounting or manufacturing, is all more or less the same. Some of the common factors are separating repeated columns in master-detail relationships using first normal form, pushing static data into new entities using my version of second normal form, and doing various interesting things with third normal form and beyond.

Normalization is for the most part easy, and largely common sense, with some business knowledge experience thrown in. There are, of course, numerous exceptional circumstances and special cases where my basic interpretation of normalization does not fill all needs up to 100 percent. In these situations, parts of the more refined formal interpretation can be used.

The result is that I have partially redefined the normal forms of normalization, slightly different from what I like to call the *formal* form of normalization. I have thus redefined normalization into fewer normal forms, which I consider practical for use in a commercial environment. If you find any of my definitions to be contrary to the accepted definitions of normalization, that is because I have deliberately attempted to simplify the various normal form layers for the layperson.

Application of the relational database model to a data set involves the removal of duplication, which is performed using a process called normalization. Normalization consists of a set of rules called Normal Forms. Normalization is applied to a set of data in a database to form entities. Entities are for placing directly associated data into. Entities can be related or linked to each other through the use of key or index identifiers, which describe a row of data in an entity much like an index is used in a book. An index in a book is used to locate an item of interest without having to read the entire book from cover to cover.

In my version of normalization, there are four levels or layers of normalization I like to call first, second, third, and beyond third normal forms. Each normal form may be a refinement of the previous normal form, although that is not strictly a requirement. In other words, my simple method does not necessarily require cumulative normal forms, although, in most cases, cumulative application of each successive layer makes sense. In designing entities for performance, it is common practice for designers to ignore the steps of normalization and jump directly to second normal form. Third normal form is often not applied either unless many-to-many joins cause an absolute need for unique values at the application level.

Experienced designers make it more of an instinctive process because they have seen similar patterns in data, time and again. This is why I think it is possible to partially rewrite and simplify the normal forms of normalization. My intention is by no means to be bombastic, but only to try to make this process a little easier to understand, and in the context of this book, to allow for ultimately better-performing SQL queries, by reducing the granularity and complexity of the underlying data structures.

Note: Overnormalization using third normal forms and beyond can lead to poor performance in both OLTP and data warehouse type databases. Overnormalization is more commercially in top-down designed Java object applications. In this situation, an object structure is imposed onto a relational database. Object and relational data structures are completely different methodologies, because the fine details of granularity are inherent in object modeling. The same is true of extreme application of normal forms, but that creates too many entities, too much processing built into a database model, and ultimately highly complex SQL coding and poor performance as a result.

So I am assuming that normalization in its strictest form is generally impractical because of its adverse effect on performance in a commercial environment, especially fourth normal form and beyond. The simplest way to describe what normalization attempts to achieve can be explained in three ways:

1.   Divide the whole into smaller, more manageable parts.

Note: The key phrase is manageable parts. There is a sensible balance somewhere between placing detailed granularity in both the database and front-end applications. The most practical form is basic structures in the database model (first, second, and third normal forms), and all other normal forms applied in applications, using application coding.

---

2.   Remove duplicated data into related subsets.

3.   Link two indirectly related entities by creating a new entity. The new entity contains indexes (keys) from the two indirectly related entities. This is commonly known as a many-to-many join.

These three points are meaningless without further explanation of normalization, so let's go through the rules and try to explain normalization in an informal fashion. Let's start with some relational database buzzwords.

- An *entity* contains many repetitions of the same row. An entity defines the structure for a row. An example of an entity is a list of customer names and addresses.

Note: An entity is also known as a table.

- A *row* is a line of data. Many rows make up the data in an entity. An example of a row is a single customer name and address within an entity of many customers. A row is also known as a record or a tuple.

- The structure of a row in an entity is divided up into *columns*. Each column contains a single item of data such as a name or address. A column can also be called a field or attribute.

- *Referential integrity* is a process of validation between related entities where references between different entities are checked against each other. A *primary key* is placed on a parent or superset entity as the primary identifier or key to each row in the entity. The primary key will always point to a single row only, and it is unique within the entity. A *foreign key* is a copy of a primary key value in a subset or child entity. An example of a function of referential integrity is that it will not allow the deletion of a primary key entity row where a foreign key value exists in a child entity. Primary keys are often referred to as PK and foreign keys as FK. Note that both primary and foreign keys can consist of more than one column. A key consisting of more than one column is known as a composite key.

- An ***index*** is used to gain fast access to an entity. A key is a special form of an index used to enforce referential integrity relationships between entities. An index allows direct access to rows by duplicating a small part of each row to an additional (index) file. An index is a copy of the contents of a small number of columns in an entity, occupying less physical space and therefore faster to search through than an entity. The most efficient unique indexes are usually made up of single columns containing integers. There are many other types of indexes of various shapes and forms, but specialized indexes such as bitmap indexes have very specific applications.

Note: Primary and foreign keys are special types of indexes applying referential integrity. Oracle Database automatically indexes primary keys but not foreign keys.

1.2.1   First Normal Form

First normal form removes repetition by creating one-to-many relationships. Data repeated many times in one entity is removed to a subset entity, which becomes the container for the removed repeating data. Each row in the subset entity will contain a single reference to each row in the original entity. The original entity will then contain only nonduplicated data. This one-to-many relationship is commonly known as a master-detail relationship, where repeating columns are removed to a new entity. The new entity gets a primary key consisting of a composite of the primary key in the master entity and a unique identifier (within each master primary key) on the detail entity.

In the example in Figure 1.1, a first normal form transformation is shown. The sales order entity on the left contains customer details, sales order details, and descriptions of multiple items on the sales order. Application of first normal form removes the multiple items from the sales order entity by creating a one-to-many relationship between the sales order and the sales order item entities. This has three benefits:

1.   Saves space

2.   Reduces complexity

3.   Ensures that every sales order item will belong to a sales order

In Figure 1.1, the crow's foot pointing to the sales order item entity indicates that for a sales order to exist, the sales order has to have at least one sales order item. The line across the pointer to the sales order entity signifies that at least one sales order is required in this relationship. The crow's foot is used to denote an inter-entity relationship.

Note: Inter-entity relationships can be zero, one, or many to zero, one, or many.

The relationship shown in Figure 1.1 between the sales order and sales order item entity is that of one to one-or-many.

Figure 1.1
First normal form

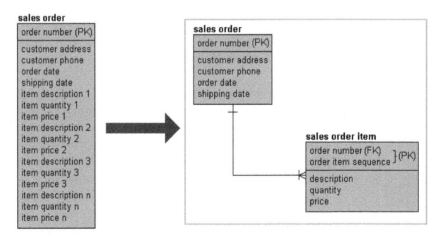

Example rows for the first normal form structure in Figure 1.1 are shown in Figure 1.2. Notice how the master and detail rows are now separated.

1.2.2   Second Normal Form

Second normal form creates not one-to-many relationships but many-to-one relationships, effectively separating static from dynamic information. Static information is potentially repeatable. This repeatable static information is moved into separate entities. In Figure 1.3, the customer information is removed from the sales order entity. Customer information

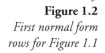

Figure 1.2
*First normal form
rows for Figure 1.1*

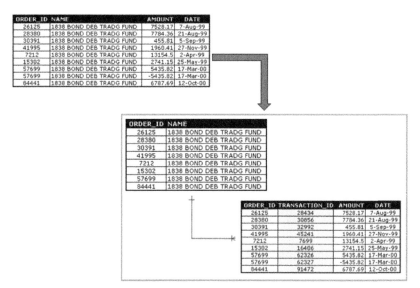

can be duplicated for many sales orders or have no sales orders, thus the one-and-only-one to zero-one-or-many relationship between customers and sales orders. This many-to-one relationship, as opposed to the one-to-many relationship created by a first normal form transformation, is commonly known as a dynamic-static relationship where repeating values, rather than repeating columns (first normal form), are removed to a new entity. The new entity, containing static data, gets a single column primary key, which is copied to a foreign key in the dynamic entity.

Figure 1.3
*Second normal
form*

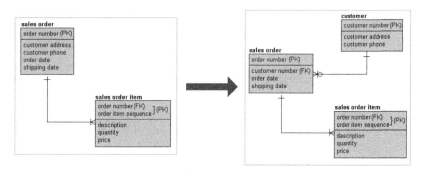

Example rows for the second normal form structure in Figure 1.3 are shown in Figure 1.4. Now we have separation of master and detail rows and a single entry for our customer name; there is no duplication of information. On creation of the Customer entity, one would create a primary key on the

CUSTOMER_NUMBER column, as shown on the right side of the diagram in Figure 1.3. Figure 1.4 does not show a CUSTOMER_NUMBER, but merely a customer name for explanatory purposes. In Figure 1.4, a primary key would be created on the name of the Customer entity. One of the most significant realistic benefits of excessive normalization is saving physical space. However, with the low prices of disk space in the modern world, this is not really too much of an important factor anymore. Processor and memory costs are relatively much more expensive than the costs of storage on disk.

Figure 1.4
Second normal form rows for Figure 1.2

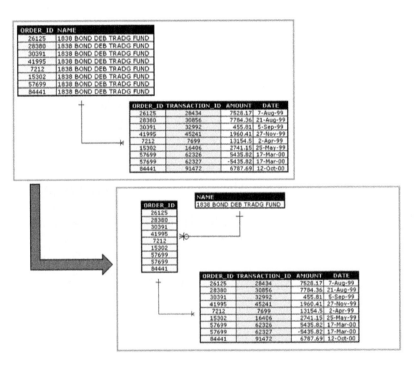

Note: In the previous edition of this book, one of the readers pointed out that the normal form transformation shown in Figures 1.3 and 1.4 is actually a second to third normal form transformation, rather than a first to second normal form transformation. This is because the transformation splits a composite key into two entities. I am attempting to simplify the process of normalization, not rewrite it. Separating static and dynamic data into separate entities is looking at the process from a business operational perspective. The objective is not to contradict the accepted process of normalization, but to make it a little easier for the layperson. This is a simplified interpretation.

1.2.3 **Third Normal Form**

Third normal form is used to resolve many-to-many relationships into unique values. In Figure 1.5, a student can be enrolled in many courses, and a course can have many students enrolled. It is impossible to find a unique course-student item without joining every student with every course. Therefore, each unique item can be found with the combination of values. Thus the CourseStudent entity in Figure 1.5 is a many-to-many join resolution entity. In a commercial environment, it is very unlikely that an application will ever need to find this unique item, especially not a modern-day Java object Web application, where the tendency is to drill down through list collections rather than display individual items. Many-to-many join resolutions should *only* be created when they are specifically required by the application. It can sometimes be better to resolve these joins in the application to improve database performance and not create new entities at all.

Note: Be very careful using third normal form and beyond.

Figure 1.5
Third normal form

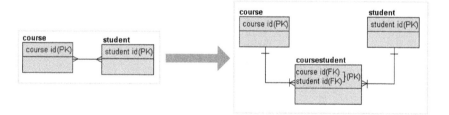

Example rows for the third normal form structure in Figure 1.5 are shown in Figure 1.6. Notice how the containment of both students within courses, and courses within students, is provided by the application of third normal form. The question you should ask yourself when using third normal form is this: Does your application need both of these one-to-many relationships? If not, then do not create the new entity, because more entities lead to more complex joins, and thus slower SQL statements. Theoretically, application of third normal form under these circumstances is correct. However, in a commercial application, you will not necessarily need to access the information in both orders.

Now let's understand this a little further. Look at Figure 1.7. That many-to-many relationship we had between the two entities on the left in

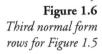

Figure 1.6
*Third normal form
rows for Figure 1.5*

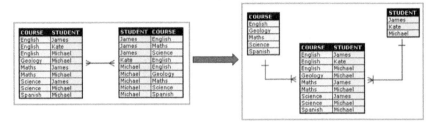

Figure 1.6 has disappeared, because the two entities on the left in Figure 1.6 are the same entity; they contain the same data, only in a different order. The courses and students with the contained intra-relationships can be retrieved from a single entity simply by applying a different sort order. Figure 1.7 shows the entities and the number of rows increasing with the application of third normal form. So, not only will we have more complex joins, but we will also have more rows and thus more physical space usage, also leading to slower SQL statements.

Figure 1.7
*A more concise
version of rows in
Figure 1.6*

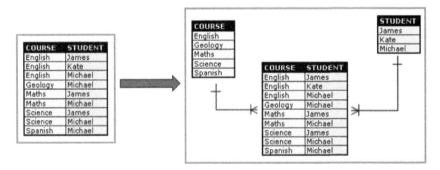

There are other applications of the formal method of third normal form, which I have not included here. My simplified interpretation of normalization allows me to push these other applications of third normal form into the realm of beyond third normal form. For example, the formal version of third normal form can be used to extract common columns from two similar entities and create a third entity containing the common columns, including a reference back to the original two entities. Those common columns are then removed from the first two entities. A second example of third normal form application is removal of a transitive dependency. A transitive dependency exists where one column is not completely dependent on the primary key of an entity, perhaps dependent on another column. In other words, an entity contains three columns: column 1 is the primary key; column 2 depends on column 1; and column 3 depends on column 2.

Therefore, column 3 is indirectly dependent on column 1. Thus, column 3 is transitively dependent on column 1 (the primary key), through its dependence on column 2. A third example of third normal form application is that of calculated columns removed altogether from an entity, because they can be recalculated by the columns in the entity that comprise the expression for the calculation. There are also other possibilities.

1.2.4 Beyond Third Normal Form

Many modern relational database models do not extend beyond third normal form. Sometimes, not even third normal form is used, because of the generation of too many entities and resulting complex SQL code joins. The result is poor database response times. This approach applies not only to devolved data warehouse models, but also to very busy OLTP databases, where even in highly accurate, single-record update environments, the extra functionality and accuracy given by beyond third normal form structures can usually be better provided by application coding.

On the contrary, maintenance of data with respect to accessing of individual records in a database can be more effectively and easily managed using beyond third normal form layers. However, any form of querying can be so adversely affected by too many entities that, in most cases, it is better to make single row access work a little bit harder than to cause even the smallest of queries to take an unacceptable amount of time to execute.

Once again, application software development kits (SDKs) are far more powerful as number crunchers than database engine structural and functional capabilities. Extreme implementation of normalization using layers beyond third normal forms can tend to place too much functionality into the database. Often, the most effective approach is to utilize the best of both worlds—combining the benefits of both database and application capabilities. Use the database to mostly just store data, perhaps with some manipulation capabilities. Allow applications to manipulate and verify data to a large extent.

Extreme levels of granularity in relational database modeling are a form of mathematical perfection. It looks nice and feels good to the trained mind. These extremes rarely apply in fast-paced commercial environments. Commercial operations require that a job is done efficiently and cost effectively. Perfection in database model design is a side issue to that of making a profit.

What I like to do with beyond third normal form is to present several cases, where those cases very likely slot into the formal definitions of fourth normal form, Boyce-Codd normal form, and fifth normal form. Domain key normal form is more a measure of perfection rather than a transformation in itself, so it does not apply in this simplified explanation. In essence, these beyond third normal form transformations should be applied when application requirements make them necessary, rather than for the sake of applying all possible normal forms to a database model.

1.2.4.1   One-To-One NULL Separation Relationships

It is possible to remove potentially NULL-valued fields into a separate entity, creating a one-to-one or zero relationship between parent and child entity. This implies that the child row does not always have to exist. This is usually done to save space in the parent entity. Oracle Database permits variable row lengths because NULL values occupy almost zero physical space. This makes the reduction in physical space usage negligible. This type of normalization therefore does not save any physical space and is pointless. The overall effect of creating these one-to-one NULL separation relationships is yet one more entity to join in queries. Also, because the child entity does not have to contain every row in the parent entity, outer joins will probably result. In my experience, outer joins are often the result of poor entity design, or in this case overgranular (overdetailed) entity design. Disk space is cheap and, as already stated, increased numbers of entities lead to bigger SQL joins and poorer performance.

Figure 1.8 shows an example where it is assumed that because not all customers' addresses and phone numbers are known, the CUSTOMER_ADDRESS and CUSTOMER_PHONE columns can be moved to a separate entity. Note in this extreme case how the new entity is actually exactly the same structurally as the pretransformation entity, although it could contain fewer rows. In this situation, the amount of data has likely been increased, rather than decreased.

Figure 1.8
A one-to-one NULL separation relationship

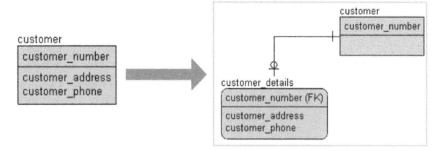

Figure 1.9 shows an even further extreme of one-to-one NULL separation where the CUSTOMER_ADDRESS and CUSTOMER_PHONE columns can be separated into two new entities, resulting in three entities. This can be done because (1) either CUSTOMER_ADDRESS or CUSTOMER_PHONE can be NULL, and (2) the two fields are not directly related to each other, but they are individually dependent on the CUSTOMER_NUMBER primary key column.

Figure 1.9
*Figure 1.8
normalized even
further*

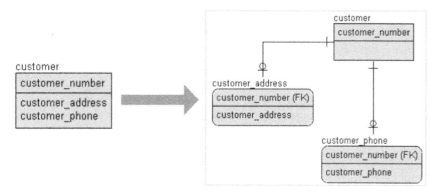

Example rows for the diagram shown in Figure 1.8 are shown in Figure 1.10. The amount of data to be stored has actually increased in this case because addresses and phone numbers for all customers are known and stored in the database. Figure 1.9 would be worse given that there would be three tables, instead of two.

Figure 1.10
*One-to-one NULL
separation rows for
Figure 1.8*

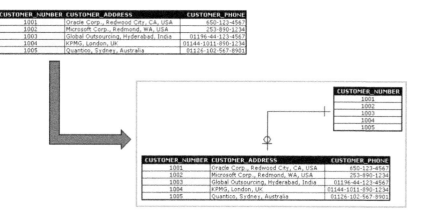

1.2.4.2   Separating Object Collections in Entities

Object collections in entities imply multivalued lists, or comma-delimited lists, of same datatype values repeated within a single column of an entity. They are all directly dependent on the primary key as a whole, but not as individual collection elements. In Figure 1.11, employee skill and certification collections are removed into separate entities. An employee could have skills or certifications or both. Thus, there is no connection between the attributes of the Employees entity, other than the employee number, and the details of skills or certifications for each employee.

Figure 1.11
*Removing
contained object
collections*

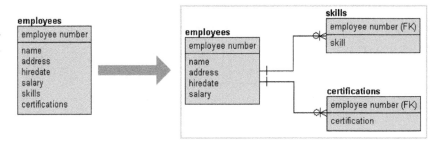

Example rows for the normalized structure Figure 1.11 are shown in Figure 1.12. The rows are divided from one into three separate entities. Because skills and certifications are duplicated in the normalization of the Employees entity, further normalization is possible but not advisable. Once again, creation of too many entities creates a propensity for complex and slow SQL statements.

Note: Oracle Database will allow creation of object collections within entities. The skills and certifications attributes shown on the left of Figure 1.11 are candidates for a contained object collection structure, namely a TABLE, VARRAY, or associated array object datatypes. However, because object and relational structures do not always mix well using an Oracle collection object datatype, this is not necessarily the most efficient storage method for later fast SQL access, even if it is an elegant solution.

1.2.4.3   Multicolumn Composite Keys

Multicolumn composite primary keys normalization divides related columns into separate entities based on those relationships. In Figure 1.13, products, managers, and employees are all related to each other. Thus, three

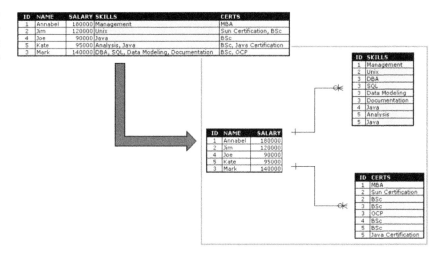

Figure 1.12
Contained object collection rows for Figure 1.11

separate entities can be created to explicitly define those interrelationships. The result is information that can be reconstructed from smaller parts.

Note: All of the columns in the transformed entities on the right side of the diagram in Figure 1.13 consist of composite primary keys.

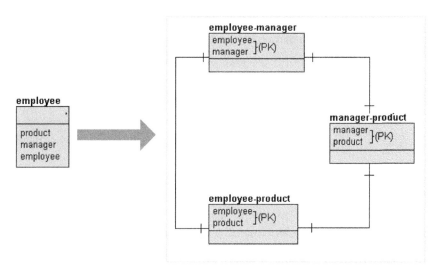

Figure 1.13
Removing multicolumn composite keys

Example rows for the normalized structure in Figure 1.13 are shown in Figure 1.14. Note how there are two one-to-many relationships on the right side of Figure 1.14; the nature of the data has caused this. In Figure 1.14, it should be clear that entities divide up data in an elegant and logical way. Once again, this level of normalization will be detrimental to SQL performance because of more complex SQL statement joins and more physical storage space used. There are just too many entities created. Once again, more entities in a data model result in larger and more complex SQL join queries. The more entities in a join there are, the less efficient a query will be, not only because the database optimizer can be overloaded, but also simply because bigger joins are more difficult to write coding for.

Figure 1.14
Multicolumn composite key rows for Figure 1.13

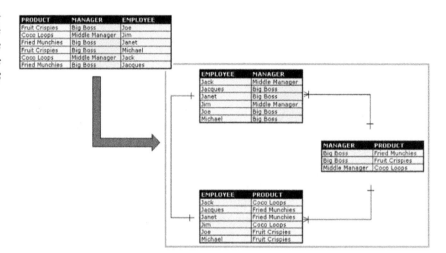

1.2.4.4   Summarizing a Layperson's Form of Normalization

- ***First normal form removes repetition by creating one-to-many relationships***, separating duplicated columns into a master-detail relationship between two entities.

- ***Second normal form creates not one-to-many relationships but many-to-one relationships***, dividing static from dynamic information by removing duplicated values (not columns), into a dynamic-static relationship between two entities.

- ***Third normal form is used to resolve many-to-many relationships into unique values***. Third normal form allows for uniqueness of information by creating additional many-to-many join resolution entities. These entities are rarely required in modern-day applications.

- My representation of beyond third normal form is intended to show various specific scenarios that I have seen repeatedly in the past. There are likely many other situations not covered here. Those covered are one-to-one NULL separation relationships, separating object collections in entities, and multicolumn composite keys.

1.3 Referential Integrity

We know that referential integrity is a mechanism used to validate data between primary and foreign key columns in related entities. The primary key is placed on the parent table, and the foreign key is placed on a child table. The primary and foreign key values must be the same. Referential integrity is a set of rules that a relational database uses to ensure that data does not go missing.

What is all this in plain language? That is very simple to explain. What happens if we have a customer database with associated or *related* invoices? Now let's assume that we have no referential integrity and a customer is deleted from the database. Because we cannot physically get inside the bits and electronics of our database, the invoices are essentially electronically lost! Why? Because it is highly likely that our applications will only ever find invoices by looking at the customers first. Even if this is not the case, the invoices will only have a reference to the customer, and we won't know who to mail the invoices to. We also won't know who we should bill. Not billing is likely to persuade the customer not to pay, perhaps not on time at least, but certainly a sorry state of affairs. It is important to get paid! Also, regulations can incur huge financial penalties for lost data. That is what referential integrity is and why we should use it.

There is a small but distinct difference between normalization and referential integrity. Normalization is a process of building entities to represent organized data and joining them together with relationships. Referential integrity is the process of enforcing entity relationships using constraints or rules. Oracle Database rules are called triggers. Triggers are *fired* based on the occurrence of an event. The next chapter examines how to tune with the relational database model.

1.4 Endnotes

1. Beginning Database Design (Gavin Powell, Wiley, Dec 2005, ISBN: 0764574906)

2

Tuning the Relational Database Model

So how do we go about tuning a relational database model?

2.1 Normalization and Tuning

What does normalization have to do with tuning? There are a few simple guidelines to follow and things to watch out for:

- *Too little normalization can lead to too much duplication.* The result could be a database that is bigger than it should be. Too much data could slow access times, again, more than should be for the given set of data. A database that is physically much larger than it should be will be searching more disk space than it should.

- *Incorrect normalization should be obvious.* Convoluted and complex application code with nowhere to go but a rewrite or the garbage pile, the final resting place of many failed commercial applications.

- *Too much normalization leads to overcomplex SQL code, which can be difficult, if not impossible, to tune.* I tend to pass on the application of fourth, Boyce-Codd, and fifth normal forms. Additionally, I think very carefully about the usefulness of third normal form– derived entities.

- *Databases are often designed without knowledge of applications.* The data model could be built on a purely theoretical basis. Later in the development cycle, the application not only has difficulty using a highly granular data model but the data may also be structured totally different from the application. One possible answer is that both development and administration people should be involved in data modeling. Another possibility is that the data model supports the application, and thus should be built with all knowledge in hand. This is a best-case scenario and not impossible, but busy commercial development projects rarely have spare time to ensure that absolutely everything is taken into account; it's just too expensive. Thus it should be acceptable to alter the data model at least during the development process, possibly substantially. Most of the problems with relational database model tuning are normalization related. Normalization should be simple because it is simple!

Note: This is why I attempt to simplify normalization. Many data models are designed and built from a theoretical perspective. Theory often does not work perfectly commercially. Normalization is based on simple set theory. Normalization in its most basic form is akin to those little circles and intersections, and things you used to draw and color in at school.

■ *Watch out for excessive use of outer joins in SQL code.* If you have a lot of outer joins, it could mean that your data model is too granular; you could have overused the higher normal forms beyond third normal form. The higher normal forms are rarely needed in the name of efficiency, but rather preferred in the name of perfection, and possibly over application of business rules as database structure. Sometimes excessive use of outer joins might be akin to: *Go and get this. Oh! Go and get that too because this doesn't quite cover it.*

The other side of normalization is denormalization. In many cases, denormalization is the undoing of normalization. Normalization is performed by the application of normal form transformations. In other cases, denormalization is performed through the application of numerous specialized tricks. We will get into some of those tricks later on in this chapter. Let's begin by looking at referential integrity.

2.2   Referential Integrity and Tuning

How referential integrity and tuning are related is twofold. First, decide whether to use or implement referential integrity at all, and second, if implementing referential integrity, how should it be implemented?

2.2.1 Using Referential Integrity or Not

Should referential integrity be implemented? If so, how? The question should be: *Should you implement referential integrity at all?* You should, but for the sake of performance, sometimes it is not needed. For the sake of maintaining the integrity or correctness of your data, you should implement referential integrity. It is always advisable to partially implement referential integrity, at least on critical relationships. For instance, some static entities do not necessarily need to have referential integrity checks even if it is advisable. Continual referential integrity checking will affect performance. On the contrary, there are cases where not implementing referential integrity can hurt performance in unexpected ways.

Use referential integrity where and when it is needed. When data is changing constantly, we continually need to check that the data changes are valid. This is where referential integrity comes into play. Consider, for instance, a data warehouse. Typically, data warehouse databases or reporting databases are used to report data, or store large amounts of data, and they mostly require high-speed throughput. Throughput implies large amounts of processing and database access at once. Reporting databases report; they read data. If they are updated, they are often mass updated in batches that can be recovered and executed all over again, assuming the database is not extremely large.

Is referential integrity required in data warehouse databases with no OLTP or client/server updating activity? From a purely data modeling perspective, the answer might very often be a resounding *No*! However, this is not the case. Data warehouses can become extremely poor performers with no primary and foreign keys, and, might I add, no indexes on those foreign keys. Data warehouses use highly specialized queries and optimization techniques that do require referential integrity.[1] Referential integrity is not just required to validate changes to the database.

One case of problematic application of referential integrity is where a database uses generic static entities, such as a centralized system entity. The centralized system entity contains counters for the entire database. If generic static entities are used, referential integrity is inadvisable on these entities. A generic static entity includes multiple types of static data items, which are unrelated to each other in any way other than structurally. Repeating the diagram from the introduction, as shown in Figure 2.1, we can see an example of a generic static entity. Please be aware that the creation of generic static entities does not have anything to do with normalization. Generic static entities allow for more modular application coding and not referential integrity. In other words, they are application-centric, help-ing application coding. They are not database-centric. Efficient data model-ing and normalization do not always benefit when created from the perspective of creating better application code. If you have generic static entities, get rid of them if possible!

Note: Generic static entities are often created to allow for ease of program-ming. Structuring the data model from the perspective of creating generic application code does not necessarily lend itself to an efficient data model. Keep generic code in the application and out of the database if possible. If some aspect of a data model makes application coding easier, it is probably detrimental to database performance.

Figure 2.1
Static generic entities

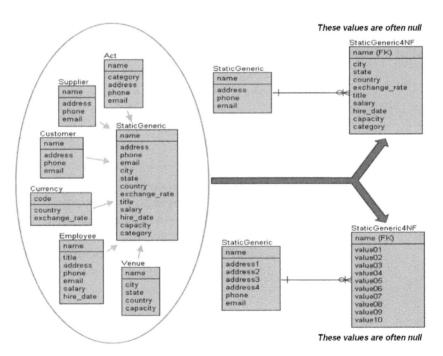

If generic static entities must be used, it might be best to enforce refer-ential integrity in the application and not in the database, because those generic aspects stem from the application.

2.2.2 How to Implement Referential Integrity

Referential integrity can be implemented at the database level or in the application. The chances are that coding referential data checks in the application will produce messier code, which is less granular or modular than is desirable. The functionality of an application can sometimes have little to do with normalization of data. Including referential integrity in application code might perform better than at the database level because processing is distributed. However, distribution does not necessarily mean better response time for the customer, because client or middle-tier machines will be performing extra processing.

At the database level, referential integrity can best be implemented using primary and foreign key constraints. Using triggers should be avoided like the plague! Triggers are notoriously slow. Oracle Database triggers have a reputation of usually performing at speeds up to at least ten times slower than using constraints for referential integrity. This might be caused by improper or poor coding practices. Then again, triggers are written in interpretive PL/SQL code, which is slow to execute. Additionally, triggers do not allow COMMIT or ROLLBACK commands because they are event driven and can drive other events; therefore, they can produce large transactions. Referential integrity is sometimes implemented using triggers, when an organization has a lack of data modeling skills, and programming skills are abundant. In other words, programmers know how to write code but are not necessarily expert in the fine art of data modeling. Obviously, the reverse will be true when programming skills are lacking, and thus problems in other areas could arise. I have seen some absurdly overcomplicated data models when the company had a proliferation of data architects and modelers but not enough programmers. These things happen. Such is the way of the world.

Changes later on, such as disabling some referential checks, will be much easier to find and make in the database when implemented with constraints. Sifting through a lot of trigger code or application code in order to change referential integrity constraints could be very time consuming. Also, any technical manager knows that each programmer has an individual style and approach to writing code. Because personnel in the computer industry are notorious for job-hopping, having new coders working on someone else's code can be problematic, especially if the original coder was very messy. This can be incredibly frustrating for the programmers as well. Building referential integrity with constraints is much more manageable. Skills required are an understanding of normalization plus simple constraint creation using DDL administration commands or a front-end tool, such as Oracle Enterprise Manager. These skills are easily learned with a little practice.

To summarize, changing application code will always introduce new bugs, some completely unexpected. Trigger code is less likely to cause problems than application code in this respect because it is centralized and in one place in the database, not in multiple applications. Changing constraints involves simple changes to Oracle Database metadata. What could be easier? In short, the more referential integrity is implemented without using constraints, the more problems you are likely to have. Changes to the data model, for instance, will probably not be possible if referential integrity is implemented at the application level. On the other hand, changing simple database-level constraints will not affect the application in any way. The only possible effect on the application is if the application is using the tables in a way that violates referential integrity or attempts to circumvent a well-normalized data model. This is positive because data integrity errors will be detectable and can be corrected, probably in development and testing.

Note: Every form of implementation depends on the current situation and circumstances, from both technical and business perspectives. In other words, everything is relative to the resources available, time plus personnel, and financial resources. If changes cannot be made easily to poorly built software, then try resolving potentially business-threatening problems in little steps. You do not have to do everything at once.

So what's the skinny on implementing referential integrity?

- *Implement referential integrity at the database level using primary and foreign key constraints.* This is usually the best way for both the short term and the long term.

- *Avoid placing referential integrity code into the application because later changes for the purposes of helping performance could be problematic, for both tuning the data model and tuning SQL code.* The result is likely to be application bugs and little potential for tuning. Coding referential integrity into application code will not only overcode applications but also introduce more complexity into application code, ultimately hurting speed and maintainability.

■ *Remove or disable any referential integrity constraints from the database at a later stage as required and if necessary.* Much can be done to keys, indexes, tables, and all sorts of other things in the database, easily and in one place. Or better still, if loading a database, simply load tables in the order in which existing referential integrity rules dictate. In other words, load data in a parent entity before loading a child table, and so on down the hierarchy of data model relations.

2.2.2.1 Using Constraints (Primary and Foreign Keys)

Now we want to examine using constraints to implement referential integrity. Referential integrity establishes relationships between entities. In the case of the relational database model, those relationships are most commonly one-to-many in nature. The result is what could be perceived as a hierarchical structure, where an entity could contain links to collections of other entities, such as that shown in Figure 2.2.

In Figure 2.2, note that many divisions are in a company, many departments are in each division, and each department has many employees. Each successive child entity, passing from companies down to employees, inherits the primary key of its parent entity. Thus the Company entity has a primary key called Company, the Division entity has a primary key made up of a concatenation of both the company name and the division name, and so on.

Figure 2.2
A hierarchy of relational entities

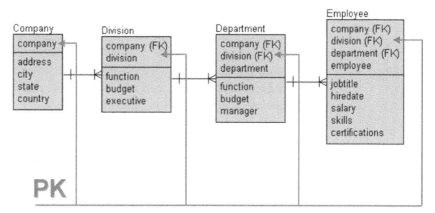

The primary and foreign keys, denoted in Figure 2.2 as PK and FK respectively, are what apply referential integrity. Thus in Figure 2.2, in order for a division to exist, it must be part of a company. Additionally, a company cannot be removed if it has an existing division. Referential integrity verifies that these conditions exist whenever changes are attempted to any of these entities. If a violation occurs, an error will be returned. It is also possible to cascade or pass changes down through the hierarchy. In other words, when cascade-deleting a company, then all divisions, departments, and employees for that company will be removed from the database all together.

Tuning the structure of the keys will be covered in a later chapter. However, it will suffice at this stage to state that the primary key structures represented in Figure 2.2 are not as efficient as they could be. How would we make these primary keys more efficient?

2.2.2.1.1   Efficient Keys

In a purist's or traditional relational data model, keys are created on actual values, such as those shown in Figure 2.2. The primary key for the Company entity is created on the name of the company, a variable-length string. Try to create keys on integer values. Integer values make for more efficient keys than do alphanumeric values, because both range and exact searches, using numbers, are mathematically much easier than using alphanumeric values. There are only 10 possible digits to compare (0 to 9), but many more alphanumeric characters. Sorting and in particular hashing is much more efficient with numbers.

Always try to avoid creating keys on large fixed- or variable-length strings, such as Oracle Database VARCHAR2 datatypes. Dates can also cause problems because of implicit conversion requirements and differences between dates and timestamps. Numbers require less storage and thus shorter byte lengths. Oracle Database NUMBER field values occupy a maximum number of bytes based on the number of digits in a value. The only negative aspect is that as the numbers grow, predicting space occupied becomes more difficult. Sometimes it may be useful to create keys using short fixed-length character strings. An Oracle Database CHAR(3) datatype will use exactly three bytes, a known and predictable value. However, short fixed-length character strings were often used in the past as substitute coded values for large variable-length strings. This is rare in modern relational data models because of the object nature of application development tools such as Java. Coded pick lists are no longer the rage.

Some applications create primary and foreign key structures using alphanumeric object pointer representations. This is generally not efficient because the representations of these pointers will require variable-length strings using Oracle Database VARCHAR2 datatypes. This approach should be avoided in a relational data model, being more appropriate to an object data model.

A possibly more efficient key structure for the data model in Figure 2.2 would be as shown in Figure 2.3, where all variable-length strings are relegated as details of the entity, by the introduction of integer primary keys. Integer primary keys are known as surrogate keys, the term *surrogate* meaning substitute value or key.

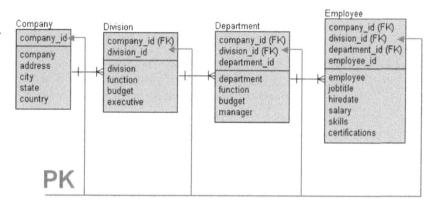

Figure 2.3
A hierarchy of relational entities using integer keys

Another variation on the data models in both Figure 2.2 and Figure 2.3 would be the data model shown in Figure 2.4, where the relationships become what is known as *nonidentifying*. In Figure 2.4, each entity contains its own unique integer identifier (surrogate key) as a primary key, and all parent unique integer identifiers are removed from the primary key, becoming foreign keys where applicable. Foreign keys not directly related to immediate parent entities are removed altogether. Thus entities in Figure 2.4 allow unique identification of every row within each entity based on the primary key. This is a little closer to the object model and is more consistent with modern object application development environments, such as Java. Consistency is always beneficial. However, the Employee entity in Figure 2.4 could additionally include the COMPANY_ID and DIVISION_ID columns as foreign keys, to allow for better flexibility. The same would apply by including the COMPANY_ID column into the Department entity.

Unique integer identifiers are most efficiently created in Oracle Database using sequence number generators. Never create unique identifiers for new rows in tables using something like *SELECT MAX(identifier) FROM table*. This approach will execute a full table scan whenever a new row is added, which is extremely inefficient. Maximum integer identifier values

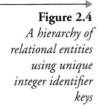

Figure 2.4
A hierarchy of relational entities using unique integer identifier keys

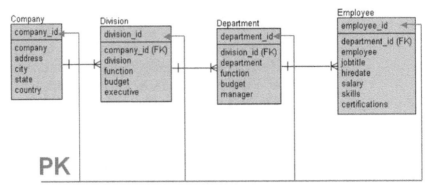

stored in a separate central entity of sequence numbers would create hot blocks and concurrency issues (locking), but might be more efficient than using a MAX function for every new row required, especially for large tables. Oracle Database sequence objects are by far the most efficient method for integer identifier value generation.

Note: In referential integrity, primary keys and foreign keys are known as keys. Keys are not explicitly called indexes because the two are not identical.

2.2.2.1.2 *Indexing Foreign Keys and Locking Issues*

Oracle Database automatically creates indexes on primary keys but not on foreign keys. An index is automatically created on a primary key because it is required to be unique. Uniqueness implies that when a new primary key is inserted into an entity, the whole entity must be searched to make sure the new insertion is not duplicating an already existing key.

Foreign keys are not required to be unique, and they can even contain NULL values. If indexes are required on foreign keys, they must be created manually. Generally, it is essential to create indexes on foreign keys to avoid locking problems. These locking problems occur as a result of full table scans and potential shared or exclusive locks on the child entity, when doing updates or deletes in the primary key entity. Also, specialized data warehouse structures and queries live and breathe by foreign key indexes.

In a highly concurrent environment, when changes constantly occur to rows in parent and child entities, serious wait times for lock releases on the child entity could result when changing primary key parent entities. Why?

Oracle Database searches child entity foreign keys for existence when update or deletion occurs on a parent entity.

Note: Updates should not occur to primary keys because they are static in nature, especially in the case of surrogate primary keys. Primary key updates are more likely in more traditionally designed relational databases that do not use surrogate keys.

When Oracle Database searches into a child entity, if no key exists on a foreign key, a full table scan will result on the child entity because every foreign key must be checked. This can cause locking on the child entity. Other concurrent DML activity occurring on the child entity would exacerbate the problem. Concurrency issues can be addressed, but only up to a point.

The result of creating indexes on foreign keys will be much better performance, particularly in highly concurrent environments. It reduces locking and contention on the child entity, because only the index on the foreign key is checked. SQL, which is continuously table scanning as a result of no foreign key indexes, could kill the performance of your system altogether. This is a common problem.

The more sound your data model is, the more foreign key indexes will help performance, because the data model key structure should match application requirements. Build indexes on foreign keys to prevent locking issues, not only for referential integrity constraint checking but also for SQL performance.

New primary key insertions do not require indexes on child entity foreign keys because no activity occurs on the child entity. Figure 2.5 attempts to show a picture of potential foreign key locking activity.

2.2.2.1.3 *Sacrificing Referential Integrity for Performance*

Can performance be increased by removing primary and foreign keys, plus foreign key indexes? Yes, sometimes, but it is extremely risky in relation to maintaining the integrity of rows between parent and child entities.

Creating indexes on foreign keys is required when parent entities are updated or deleted from, not inserted into. It may be difficult for a database administrator to be certain of this, given limited knowledge of applications and any future changes. In fact, the database administrator's knowledge is probably limited to being outside the scope of development. Database administrators are often not included in the development process. Some

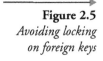

Figure 2.5
Avoiding locking
on foreign keys

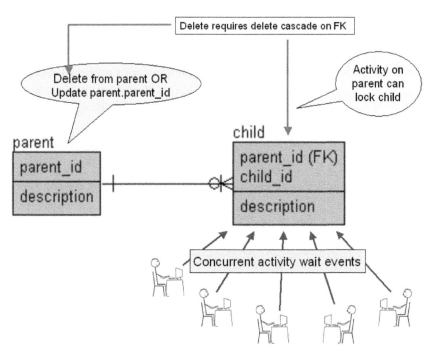

companies may not even hire a database administrator until the development process is complete, or perhaps nearing completion.

In cases where child entities are static and very small, perhaps referential integrity checks between the parent and child entities are less necessary. In this case, one must assume applications always validate the existence of foreign key child rows when adding or changing primary keys. Again, the child entity has to be small! The optimizer will usually perform a full table scan on small tables, regardless of the presence of indexes. This further builds the case that small static entities can simply be excluded from referential integrity checks, by removing or disabling any child entity foreign key constraints. Under these rare circumstances, it may also be expedient to remove or disable the primary key constraint from the child entity as well. Because the entity is static, there may never be a need to ensure that the primary key remains unique.

Once again, this strategy is risky and inadvisable but could be utilized under extreme circumstances, when creating indexes on foreign keys has not fully resolved concurrency and locking performance issues. The full strategy is one of two options:

1.   Always create indexes on foreign keys for all types of entities.

2.   For small static entities, if indexes are not created on foreign keys, it may be best to exclude a child entity from referential integrity altogether, by disabling child entity foreign key constraints. If this is acceptable, the child entity primary key constraint may be disabled as well.

2.2.2.2   Coding Business Rules in the Database

We have already established that referential integrity can be implemented in the database by using either constraints or triggers. Constraints are usually more easily maintained than triggers, depending on the skills available. Using triggers to implement referential integrity *will* very likely be much slower. Triggers may be more easily maintainable during development, especially if the data model is continually changing. Constraints are more easily maintainable in production because changes are less likely to cause errors. Code changes are always likely to introduce unexpected bugs. If constraints are continuously being changed, then the system *should* still be under development. If the data model is not correct at the time of your first production release, then you may have all sorts of other problems too.

So what are business rules? This term is often used vaguely where it could have different meanings. Some technical people will insist on placing all business rules into the database, whereas others require the opposite. This is often because of a lack of skilled personnel in development, database administration, or data modeling. Many development projects are top heavy with developers and lacking in people with administration and modeling skills. A technical manager will often sensibly tend to guide system development in the direction of the skill sets available, be those skills development or otherwise. An ideal situation is having all of the necessary skills. Coding business rules in the database or not is often a problem with terminology, namely the term *business rules*. Therefore, let's categorically avoid a definition for the meaning of that term. We will concentrate not on what should, or should not, be in the database, but on what could be in the database.

There are two important areas:

1.   ***Referential integrity***: Referential integrity can be implemented in the database using constraints or triggers.

2.   ***General database access using SQL code***: Stored procedures and functions.

2.2.2.2.1   *Using Triggers for Referential Integrity*

The case often made for triggers rather than constraints is that triggers are more easily managed. This is often the case when programmers rather than database administrators, or data modelers, are building those constraints. Programmers are usually frustrated with having to enable, disable, and perhaps even temporarily drop constraints, in order to change entities. In fact, most entity changes do not require constraint changes unless primary or foreign keys are being changed directly; primary and foreign keys restrict data in entities, not the structure of those entities. Where a database administrator would carefully alter an entity and *never* drop an entity, it is normal for developers, during the development process, to simply drop entities. Dropping entities and recreating entities in a production environment is risky. This sort of practice is fine and common during the development process. The point I am making is that different people have different skills, mindsets, and approaches to resolving issues. As a manager, understanding the strong and weak points of the people working for you can help you decide who does what.

Note: Older relational databases and perhaps ancient versions of Oracle Database required dropping entities in order to make structural columnar changes: adding, changing, or deleting columns. For many years, Oracle Database has been extravagantly equipped with both object CREATE and ALTER commands, allowing more or less any change to an entity even when entities are online and actively being used.

Programmers generally make poor database administrators, because the approach to database administration is generally a slower and more careful one. In defense of the programming community, database administrators often make terrible programmers. I have seen some database administrators with UNIX backgrounds construct and write entire systems using UNIX scripting, even avoiding a primitive programming language such as PL/SQL. I hope this little story makes it more palatable for a developer to understand that database administration is a much more meticulous process, particularly in production. The skills of coding and administration are very different in approach, but both are required, even during the development process. In fact, database administrators tend to subdivide themselves into one of two camps: Production DBAs and Development DBAs.

So what does all this mean? It means triggers are a hopeless substitute for constraints as a method of enforcing referential integrity. Triggers make implementation easier for a programmer but will seriously affect performance in the long run, perhaps even making your application as much as 10 times slower than it could be.

2.2.2.2.2 *Using Triggers for Event Trapping*

In some relational databases, triggers can be used to trap specific database events, in addition to SQL insert, update, and delete events. In Oracle Database, this is not the case. Triggers are a less efficient substitute for constraints when implementing referential integrity.

Trigger code is slow because coded PL/SQL will execute much slower than Oracle Database internal constraint checks. Trigger code must be parsed and compiled before execution and uses explicit SQL. Explicit SQL competes with all other SQL in the database for use of parsing and execution resources.

Note: $\widehat{(10g)}$ Compiled PL/SQL coding is now stored in binary objects, implying that PL/SQL is now a compiled, rather than an interpreted, execution. However, because PL/SQL uses the optimizer and the shared pool in the same manner as SQL code, for preparsing and optimization, I have yet to see any improvement in PL/SQL performance.

Triggers may require too much coding maintenance. Constraints should be created when the data model is first built, such that a database administrator is in a position during production to be able to switch off specific constraints, in order to help performance. This type of tuning can be difficult with triggers if individual triggers contain multiple aspects of functionality, such as a trigger detecting all of the insert, update, and deletion events for an entity. A better approach could be a set of three triggers on that same table: one for each of insert, update, and delete event detection. Coders tend to amalgamate functionality and make things generic. Generic code is not consistent with an efficient data model, as demonstrated in the case of the static generic entity shown in Figure 2.1.

I have worked with an application in the past where replacement of triggers with constraints gave a general performance increase of between five and tenfold. It is also unlikely that a single trigger can deal with all potential problems. The simple fact is that the more code an application has, the more convoluted and difficult to maintain it will become over time. If you are creating triggers because they are easier to maintain, then the data model is probably being built during the coding phase, which has its disadvantages.

2.2.2.2.3   Using Stored Procedures and Functions

Stored procedures and functions can be used for SQL activity as opposed to embedding SQL code in applications. I have encountered varying opinions on this subject and have seen both work and both fail. Stored procedures can include only SQL code, or they can include some processing, either in the form of groups of SQL statements, to form transactional blocks, or even as far as including application logic, which could probably be at the application level but not necessarily.

In short, PL/SQL is not a fully capable programming language. PL/SQL has extensive programming language capabilities, a few bells and whistles, and even some object and abstraction capability. However, PL/SQL is not the equivalent of C or Java when it comes to applications-level programming.

From my experience, my recommendation is this: PL/SQL can be used to store database SQL code in one place. This has the effect of only allowing people with PL/SQL and Oracle Database administration skills to build and change that code. However, because PL/SQL may essentially be primitive as a programming language, and because developers make better programmers than database administrators, there is a strong case for minimizing use of PL/SQL. In other words, using PL/SQL extensively is one of those things that might require a mix of skills. Most techies are either programmers or DBAs, but rarely both. If you have both skill sets, then you are lucky.

Note: A reader of the first edition of this book complained about my opinion of PL/SQL and its uses. I feel the urge to apologize if I cause any offense with my possibly opinionated comments. I don't intend to cause offense, only to point out potential pitfalls. Otherwise, there are always exceptions, which is becoming more likely as all I am expressing are experienced opinions. Please be aware that only my opinions are expressed in this book, and they are not necessarily opinions that are shared by others. If you disagree, then by all means please voice your opinions by e-mailing me. I can only quote from my personal experience of working in database administration and software development, in numerous companies, for the last 20 years or so. That doesn't mean that I am always correct! Not all situations are the same.

Note: One of the biggest dangers with any programming language or software tool is misuse or inappropriate use. Time and again I have seen various tools misused and abused, with resulting poor performance of databases and applications. Therefore, my instinct is to always consider that if I am stretching a programming language to its limits, then I am probably exceeding its capabilities and pushing it too far. The opposite consideration to use multiple development tools is that it is far, far easier and faster (thus more cost effective) to write programming code using PL/SQL, rather than using C or Java. Additionally, using multiple programming languages on one particular project tends to overcomplicate everything as well.

I would advise against writing your entire system using PL/SQL. It can be done, but it might be better to build at least some of your number-crunching into a front-end SDK tool such as Java. When using PL/SQL to create database access SQL code, perhaps think of simple maintenance and central control as good reasons for using PL/SQL, rather than in terms of granularity. Modern application environments are very effective at managing and allowing creation of embedded SQL code. Using stored database procedures is probably faster, but not always. Use of stored procedures depends largely on the skills available to the company (or development team) and the function of applications. Programmers should not be doing too much database administration and modeling, because that is not their area of expertise. Similarly, programmers might want to attempt to discourage database administrators from indulging in too much programming. The skill sets and approach are completely different. In terms of overcoding and perhaps overloading a database with stored procedures, you may also overload your database administrators. Do programmers write the PL/SQL code or do the database administrators write PL/SQL code? Do you have someone who knows how to do both? Additionally, most Oracle database administrators have UNIX backgrounds and will probably write PL/SQL stored procedures that look like scripts. HTML and JavaScript are scripting languages. Java is a programming language, as PL/SQL is supposed to be.

Oracle Database will allow the creation of stored procedures using Java with a JVM embedded in the Oracle Database kernel. There is also a compiler called the Java Accelerator, which will allow compilation of Java-coded stored procedures into binary, allowing for fast execution times. Performance of Java-coded stored procedures is unknown to myself because I have never used Java in Oracle Database as such. Java is an extremely rich coding environment. If even more complexity is required, then external binary compilations can be used, coded in high execution performance languages such as C.

2.3   **Optimizing with Alternate Indexes**

Alternate indexes are sometimes known as secondary indexes. The meaning of the terms alternate and secondary is somewhat confusing because they mean different things in English. In the context of a relational database, they are the same. Alternate implies *another option* and secondary implies *in addition to*. This means the same thing. So now we are all completely confused. The precise meaning of the terms in this context is immaterial.

The problem is this: We create alternate indexes because the primary and foreign key indexes in our data model do not allow for everything our applications require for filtering and sorting. Filtering and sorting SQL statements is what uses indexes, in order to access the database quickly, by scanning over much smaller amounts of physical disk space, in a required sorted order.

Having a lot of alternate indexes means that your database has a lot of indexes to maintain. Whenever an entity is changed, every index created on that entity must be changed as well. Thus inserting a single row into an entity with four indexes actually requires five additions, not one addition. That will hurt performance, sometimes very badly. If your database has many alternate indexes, several possibilities could be responsible:

- *The most obvious is imposition of reporting-type functionality on top of OLTP-type functionality.* More traditional relational database structures, such as those shown in Figure 2.2 and Figure 2.3, include composite primary keys and are more compatible with reporting efficiency. Structures such as that shown in Figure 2.4 do not have composite primary keys. Imposition of reporting requirements on the structure in Figure 2.4 would probably require composite alternate indexes.

- *When creating alternate indexing essential to reporting, SQL statements may require filtering and sorting, different from that provided by primary composite keys*, such as those shown in Figure 2.2 and Figure 2.3. When existing composite primary keys do not allow for requirements, then perhaps either further normalization or denormalization is a possibility. Or perhaps current structures simply do not match application requirements. However, changing the data model at a late stage is difficult, and further normalization can cause other problems, particularly with recoding of application and stored procedure code.

- *A less obvious and often overlooked possibility is that the database has been ported directly from development to production.* Developers have a habit of creating a lot of indexes while coding, as they should do. They are building and testing after all. Indexes are often not cleaned up, and they may not be removed when no longer in use.

- *Sometimes in object structures*, such as that shown in Figure 2.4, since abstract unique identifiers are used for primary keys, *items such as names of people or departments may be required to be unique*. These unique keys are not part of referential integrity, but they can be important and are most easily maintained at the database level using constraints.

In summary, there is no easy answer to which alternate keys should be allowed and how many should be created. The only sensible approach is to control the creation of what are essentially *extra* keys. These keys were not thought about in the first place, or an application designed for one purpose has been expanded to include new functionality, such as reporting.

Alternate indexing is not part of the normalization process. It should be somewhat included at the data model design stage, if only to avoid difficulties when coding. Programmers may swamp database administrators with requests for new indexes if they were not added in the data modeling process. Typically, alternate keys added in the data modeling stage are those most obvious as composites, where foreign keys are inherited from parent entities, such as the composite primary keys shown in Figure 2.2 and Figure 2.3. Note that this does not apply in the object-like hierarchical structure represented in Figure 2.4 because the parent of the parent is not present on the child entity as a foreign key; it is not required to be.

Note: Not all composite indexing on all possible columns is always required. Sometimes it is better to index fewer than all of the columns for a composite index. Remember to examine data as well as data structures. For example, if an entity contains 1 million rows, and the first column in a composite index contains only 10 unique values, would it really help to create an index? Indexing in a case like this is unlikely to always be beneficial because any one of those index values, read by itself, will probably result in 100,000 rows read. As a result, the index will probably be ignored anyway because so many indexes must be read. A BTree index is good for exact searches, and limited-range searches, but is pointless for reading 100,000 rows.

The structure in Figure 2.4 is typical of modern Java object application environments, where every table's primary key is unique to the entire database, within that table. In other words, a row in a child entity can be accessed using its primary key without the necessity for obtaining the parent entity primary key first; no direct dependency exists between the parent and child entities, at least in an abstract sense. Figure 2.4 is more like an object database than a relational database. Figure 2.4 represents an *object-to-relational* mapping solution and functions very well with OLTP systems and very poorly for reporting. This is one reason why Java application-driven Oracle database designs often result in two databases: an OLTP database and a data warehouse. The data warehouse database takes care of the reporting and contains all of the alternate and composite indexing required for reporting. The only likely composite indexes sometimes in existence in OLTP, object-like, relational databases are the primary keys of many-to-many join resolution entities, something like the Actor entity shown in Figure 2.7.

Figure 2.6
An object-like many-to-many join resolution entity

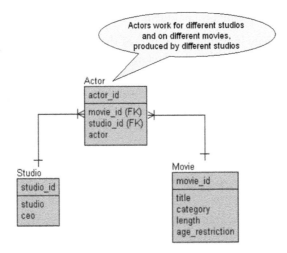

Figure 2.7 contains an equivalent traditional, non-object-like representation of the schema snippet shown in Figure 2.6.

The sheer scale and size of OLTP Internet databases can sometimes be horrifying to even the most seasoned database administrators. Many hundreds of gigabytes are common (and even terabytes for really large organizations), and with OLTP and reporting, processing is mixed in the same database. Enormous amounts of money can be spent on expensive hardware to maintain performance at a level acceptable to customer satisfaction. Additionally, development cannot possibly be coded and tested against

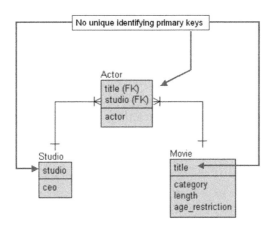

Figure 2.7
A traditional relational version of Figure 2.6

databases of such magnitude. The result is often applications coded to small-scale databases and unexpected, if not disappointing, performance in production. Extensive tuning is often required. The larger the database, the more likely that a dual database architecture has to be adopted. That dual database architecture would be OLTP plus data warehouse architecture in separate databases on different computers.

2.4   Undoing Normalization

Undoing normalization, or removal of too much data model granularity, is essential to the performance of data retrieval from a relational data model. This is true not only for reporting and data warehouse databases but also quite significant even for OLTP, small transactional unit databases.

I am calling removal of normalization for performance a process of undoing because denormalization in its purest form, being normalization in reverse, does not cover all practical possibilities. The following are areas of interest when it comes to undoing granularity:

- *Denormalization*: undoing various normal forms, some more than others

- *Some useful tricks*: various tricks to speed up data access

- *Denormalization using unusual Oracle Database objects*: creation of special types of database objects used to cluster, presort and precon-struct data, avoiding excessive amounts of complex repetitive SQL

The reason for removal or degradation of normalization is to improve performance. As already stated, it is very important to note that removal of normalization granularity is usually a necessity in data warehousing and sometimes even smaller-scale reporting environments. It has often been the case, in my experience, that even OLTP transactional data models have required reduction in granularity produced by overnormalization. Any application retrieving data from an overnormalized database can potentially have performance problems. A very deeply normalized database is only most effective for single-row insert, update, and deletion transactions, changing single data items.

In the past, I have even seen some very poorly performing OLTP applications, even those with small transactional units. The reason for this poor performance is often the result of severely granular data models. Some of these systems did not contain large numbers of rows or occupy a lot of physical space. Even so, brief data selection listings into one page of a browser, usually performed join queries comprising many entities. These types of applications sometimes fail, their creators fail, or both. In these cases, a data model must be designed with the functionality of the application in mind, not just the beauty of the granularity of an enormously overnormalized relational data model structure.

One particular project I have in mind had some queries with joins containing in excess of 15 entities, a database under 10 megabytes in size, and some query return times of over 30 seconds on initial testing. These time tests were reduced to mere seconds after extensive application code changes of embedded SQL code. However, it was too late to change the data model without untenable amounts of application recoding, and thus some very highly tuned and convoluted embedded SQL code remained. Maintenance for this particular application will probably be a nightmare, if it is even possible. It might even be more cost effective to rewrite.

The conclusion is as follows: normalization granularity can often be degraded in order to speed up SQL data retrieval performance. How? The easiest and often the most effective method, from the perspective of the data model, is a drastic reduction to the number of entities in joins. It is possible to tune SQL statements joining 15 entities, but it is extremely difficult, not only to write SQL code in this case, but also for the database optimizer to perform at its best. If the data model can possibly be changed, then begin with that data model. Changing the data model obviously affects any SQL code, be it in stored procedures or embedded in applications. So now we know why we might need to do the unexpected with a nicely normalized data model. Let's begin with describing what denormalization is.

2.4.1 Denormalization

What is denormalization? In most cases, denormalization is the opposite of normalization. Where normalization is an increase of granularity removing duplication, denormalization is an attempt to remove granularity by reintroducing duplication, previously removed by normalization. Denormalization is usually required in order to assist performance because a highly granular structure is only useful for retrieving precise, small amounts of information, rather than large amounts of information. Denormalization is used to analyze and report and not to facilitate changing specific data items. In simple terms, denormalize to decrease the number of entities in joins; joins are *slow!* Simple SQL statements are fast and easy to tune, being the order of the day wherever possible.

Entity structure is sometimes much too granular or possibly even incompatible with structure imposed by applications. This particular situation can occur when the data model is designed with the perfection of normalization in mind, without knowledge of or perhaps even consideration for realistic application requirements. It is a lucky development team that understands application requirements completely, when the data model is being built. Denormalization is one possible solution in this type of situation.

Denormalization is not rocket science. Denormalization is antonymic with normalization. In other words, the two are completely opposite. Both are common sense.

2.4.1.1 Reminding Ourselves about Normalization

A relational database relates subsets of a data set to each other. How do we relate these subsets? What do we mean by a subset and what is a data set?

- A data set is the equivalent of a database in Sybase or Ingres, and a schema in Oracle Database. A data set is a set of entities.

- A subset is an entity. An entity defines the structure and contains the row and column data for each subset.

- Entities are related to each other by linking them, based on common items and values between two entities. The common links are primary and foreign keys.

At this point, if you have not yet read the previous chapter on normalization, it might provide better clarity for you when reading the next sections. I have an unorthodox approach to normalization, and much of that approach is simply reversed in my approach to denormalization. My perspective of normalization is one of it being a little too complex and detailed for what is often the generic nature of development in a commercial environment.

2.4.1.2 Why Denormalize?

Denormalize to speed up a poorly performing database by removing the potential for mutable and complex SQL table joins. Joins are difficult and can sometimes even be impossible to tune.

2.4.1.3 What to Look for to Denormalize

2.4.1.3.1 Mutable and Complex Joins

A mutable join is a join of more than two entities. A complex join is a mutable join including filtering. The more entities in a join, the slower it will execute and the more difficult it will be to tune. If these types of joins are heavily executed, simplification by denormalizing offending entities could help performance. Following is an ANSI format SQL statement showing a mutable join of eight entities, in the Accounts data model (see Appendix A). This query is completely ridiculous, but it is the sort of complexity that you might want to search for:

```
SELECT cu.customer_id, o.order_id, ol.seq#, ca.category_id
FROM customer cu JOIN orders o ON (cu.customer_id = o.customer_id)
 JOIN transactions t ON (o.order_id = t.order_id)
  JOIN transactionsline tl ON (t.transaction_id = tl.transaction_id)
   JOIN ordersline ol ON (o.order_id = ol.order_id)
    JOIN stockmovement sm ON (tl.stockmovement_id =
sm.stockmovement_id
    AND ol.stockmovement_id = sm.stockmovement_id)
     JOIN stock s ON  (s.stock_id = sm.stock_id)
      JOIN category ca ON (ca.category_id = s.category_id)
WHERE ca.text = 'Software';
```

The WHERE clause adds filtering, making the mutable join a complex mutable join. The ANSI format of this query is no more difficult to tune than the Oracle Proprietary format. This example shows the number of entities joined very clearly.

2.4.1.3.2   Mutable Joins to Find Few Columns

When constructing SQL statement joins, are you finding many entities in joins, where those entities are scattered throughout the entity relationship diagram? When finding those columns, are you passing through one or more entities, from which no columns are retrieved? This is inefficient because every entity passed through adds another entity to the join. This problem can be resolved in two ways: (1) by denormalization, which may be difficult, because there could possibly be so much denormalization that it may affect functionality in too much application code, or (2) by maintaining copies of the offending column values in both entities. Refer to the section later in this chapter entitled "Copying Columns between Entities."

Note: This type of joining is a potential indicator that a single data model services multiple loosely connected applications, which should not always be placed into the same data set (Oracle Database schema). Sometimes this is unavoidable, though.

Following is the same ANSI format query as before but with a small change, where only the CUSTOMER_ID and CATEGORY_ID columns are retrieved. The join is still ridiculous and probably would never be a requirement for an application, but this is the only way that the stock category can be linked to a customer. This is definitely a problem. In this example, denormalization would be nonsensical, but some type of a relationship could possibly be established between the Customer and the Stock entities. On the other hand, new entity relationships would only further complicate the data model:

```
SELECT cu.customer_id, ca.category_id
FROM customer cu JOIN orders o ON (cu.customer_id =
o.customer_id)
 JOIN transactions t ON (o.order_id = t.order_id)
  JOIN transactionsline tl ON (t.transaction_id =
tl.transaction_id)
   JOIN ordersline ol ON (o.order_id = ol.order_id)
    JOIN stockmovement sm ON (tl.stockmovement_id =
sm.stockmovement_id
     AND ol.stockmovement_id = sm.stockmovement_id)
      JOIN stock s ON  (s.stock_id = sm.stock_id)
       JOIN category ca ON (ca.category_id = s.category_id)
WHERE ca.text = 'Software';
```

2.4.1.3.3 Adding Composite Keys

Do entities have composite keys? It is possible to partially denormalize by adding composite key elements to the primary keys of subset entities. Composite keys are totally contrary to object structure and more compatible with reporting. Java applications may perform poorly when data is accessed using composite keys. Object applications perform best when accessing precise objects containing collections of other precisely defined objects.

Note: Composite indexes not constructed as primary keys fall into the realm of alternate indexing. Refer to the section previously in this chapter entitled "Optimizing with Alternate Indexes."

A purist's relational database structure will contain composite primary key columns in subset entities, for all parent entities above in the hierarchy. Java applications typically add a single-column unique identifier to each entity as a primary key and exclude parent entity foreign key columns from the primary key. The only problem with this type of object-to-relational mapping, top-down Java design is as follows: reporting and even on-screen listings of less than a page can result in mutable joins, which could be extremely hard-hitting SQL join statements.

Note: A mutable join is simply a join of more than two tables.

This is where those 15 entity joins start to appear. The root cause and reason for the existence of these types of mutable joins is usually extreme overnormalization, particularly with normalization of fourth normal form and beyond. Normal forms are a relational and not an object methodology. Figure 2.2 and Figure 2.3 contain composite primary keys. Figure 2.4 contains a Java top-down object-relational mapping structure.

2.4.1.3.4 One-to-One Relationships

Look for one-to-one relationships. These may be unnecessary if the required removal of NULL values causes costly joins. Disk space is cheap. Mutable SQL join statements can destroy performance. These one-to-one relationships are typical of fourth normal form and beyond. An example of this problem is shown in Figure 2.8.

2.4.1.3.5 Many-to-Many Join Resolution Entities

Do you have many-to-many join resolution entities? Are they all necessary? Are they all used by applications? Many-to-many join resolution entities are typical of third normal form. When a data set is first designed, there often may be overusage of third normal form, leaving some superfluous, performance-hitting entities, which can become more difficult to remove because of required application code changes. Two things are important about these types of third normal form–created entities:

1. *Are the new entities used by the application?* These entities are often created from the perspective of the data model and may never be used by the application, and they may not need to be used either.

2. *A clue as to the usefulness of these new entities is: Do they have meaning?* Are the names of these entities a combination of the parent entity names? Or do they have a name, which is distinct only to the new entity? The Assignment entity in Figure 2.10 is a good example of a meaningful many-to-many relationship entity. The CourseStudent entity in Figure 2.9 is a good example of a potentially meaningless many-to-many join resolution entity.

2.4.1.3.6 Application Functions versus Entities

Compare the number of functions in the application versus the number of entities. If you have far more entities than functional units, you might want to denormalize or simply remove some of the entities, because some entities may have become redundant.

2.4.1.3.7 Static Data in Multiple Entities

When searching for static data items, such as customer details, are you querying a single entity or multiple entities? Querying a single entity is much more efficient than multiple entities. Static data does not need to be normalized into separate entities unless said separate entities are accessed individually, using separate SQL statements. Even so, static entities are often small and generally will have a full table scan performed by the optimizer anyway, regardless of any indexing. A good example of this is represented by the Listing and Exchange entities in Figure 2.11, which do not need to be separate entities.

2.4.1.3.8 **Intermediary Entities Covering Summary Groupings and Calculations**

Extra entities, or even materialized views, can be created and perhaps regenerated periodically to contain summaries of larger entities. These types of entities are more akin to reporting and data warehouse read-only functionality but can sometimes be useful in OLTP applications. These entities are useful as long as less than real-time response is acceptable for the summarized information. The script shown following creates an entity in the Accounts schema (see Appendix A), which is a grouping summary of a join between the COA and GeneralLedger entities:

```
CREATE TABLE ChartOfAccounts AS
  SELECT coa.coa#, coa.type, coa.subtype, coa.text,
    sum(gl.dr), sum(gl.cr)
  FROM coa, generalledger gl
  WHERE coa.coa# = gl.coa#
  GROUP BY coa.coa#, coa.type, coa.subtype, coa.text;
```

2.4.1.4 **Denormalizing by Reversing Normal Forms**

You should balk at denormalizing first and second normal forms, at least the formal versions. Then again, if the difference between the number of rows in master and detail entities is extremely small (first normal form application), you could conceivably denormalize first normal form. However, this strategy is not advisable in an OLTP database model. In some cases, my simplified version of second normal form can be denormalized.

Do denormalize third normal form many-to-many join resolution entities, if they are not used. Pay special attention to introduced entities with meaningless entity names, such as CourseStudent, used to represent unique combinations of courses and students, as shown in Figure 1.5. Renaming the CourseStudent entity to Enrollment is meaningful, showing that the combination of courses and students has a specific purpose. When considering removal of meaningless named entities, verify that applications do not use what might appear to be a meaningless many-to-many join resolution entity. Other types of third normal form created entities, such as those created to remove common columns, resolve transitive dependencies, or removal of calculated columns, among others, can all be denormalized. Anything beyond third normal form probably should be denormalized for the sake of performance, but not always!

The easiest way to approach denormalization of previously applied normalization is to describe the process in reverse. In other words, begin with the most detailed normal form layers, such as fifth normal form, and work backward to third or perhaps even second normal form. In the case of including my simplified interpretation of normalization, we will begin with the beyond third normal form application of normalization and then mix in denormalizing some interesting examples of formal versions of normalization.

2.4.1.4.1 Denormalizing Beyond Third Normal Form

Chapter 1 covered beyond third normal form transformations, including the following:

- One-to-one NULL separation relationships
- Separating object collections in entities
- Multicolumn or composite keys

Note: The term composite key is often used to describe a key that contains more than one column.

This chapter covers more denormalization possibilities, including some not included in Chapter 1, because these forms of extreme normalization should probably not be used in a commercial environment at all:

- Extra entities for common columns
- Formal third normal form transitive dependencies
- Calculated columns
- Formal Boyce-Codd normal form

2.4.1.4.2 Denormalizing One-to-One NULL Separation Relationships

A very common cause of performance problems is the overapplication of transformations, which have removed NULL values from entities. Examine the diagram in Figure 2.8. Note the two one-to-one or zero relationships, between the Customer to Listed entities and the Customer to Address entities. The zero part of these relationships implies that a customer does not have to have either a stock ticker symbol or an address. Thus the transformation has allowed the removal of these two sections to new entities, the Listed and Address entities.

Removal of NULL values from entities to new entities can save space, but this issue is debatable. Because NULL values are empty and Oracle Database has variable record lengths, the space-saving element may be negligible. SQL statements to retrieve customer details from these three entities would require a three-entity join to retrieve all of the customer information. When it is taken into account that other information will be retrieved with customers, such as orders and invoices, very large joins could result. The overnormalized detail shown in the top part of Figure 2.8 could cause complex mutable joins, which are difficult to tune. The result could be severe performance problems. These types of performance problems are often detected only when applications are placed onto realistically sized production databases at the end of the development cycle. Making data model changes in the production maintenance cycle can be so costly as to make them impossible. It is best not to do this sort of thing in the first place.

Figure 2.8
*Denormalizing
one-to-one NULL
separation
relationships*

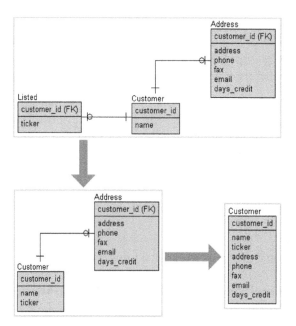

2.4.1.4.3   Denormalizing Contained Object Collections

Figure 1.11 shows the removal of contained object collections from a single entity, separated into multiple normalized entities. Figure 1.12 shows an example set of data created by normalizing out the collections. In terms of physical space, it is likely that the normalized version uses more physical space, because the normalized version has more columns. Additionally, the normalized version shown in Figure 1.11 and Figure 1.12 has three entities, as opposed to the denormalized version with only a single entity.

Once again, queries against a single entity will be far more efficient and also far more easily tunable using a single entity, rather than three entities. Using an application programming language to split and merge the collection comma-delimited list is likely to be a lot more efficient than relying on SQL code to perform the same task. Splitting and merging of comma-delimited lists is not really a function of database access, but more one of number crunching, using a more appropriate language, such as Java or C. Thus the normalization transformation shown in Figure 1.11 is very likely best reversed by denormalizing it as shown in Figure 2.9.

Figure 2.9
Denormalizing contained object collections

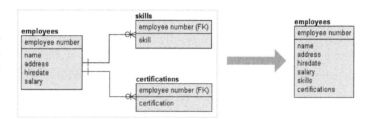

Note: Normalization of contained object collections is equivalent to the formal version of fourth normal form. Fourth normal form transformations eliminate multiple sets of multivalued dependencies.

2.4.1.4.4 Denormalizing Multicolumn Composite Keys

Figure 1.13 shows normalization of multicolumn composite primary keys, normalizing to divide related columns into separate entities, based on those relationships. In Figure 1.13, products, managers, and employees are all related to each other. Thus three separate entities are created to explicitly define those interrelationships. The result is information that can be reconstructed from smaller parts. The negative aspects of this form of normalization are as follows:

- Three entities instead of one, which is inefficient for SQL code queries.

- The point of this form of normalization (usually the formal fifth normal form) is that the resulting normalized structures must produce a join query, which is identical to a query on the original single denormalized rows. Again, this points the way to efficient single-row access and inefficient query access. Do most applications produce more output to their end users, in the form of multirow queries? Even only a few rows at a time in queries may be significant for joins containing many entities. Or do most end users continually add, change, and delete single rows, through an application into a database? As I am writing this book, I am searching on a Web site for parts on construction of a new bass speaker I am building. I find myself becoming frustrated with the response time of searching for parts, when browsing through one or two Web pages at a time. It takes each page between 10 and 15 seconds to load. I am now becoming impatient when having selected a single item, which I am intending to place into my shopping basket. That's too much time for most people to wait.

So the denormalization process shown in Figure 1.13 is something I would reverse, denormalizing in exactly the opposite direction, as shown in Figure 2.10.

Figure 2.10
Denormalizing
multicolumn
composite keys

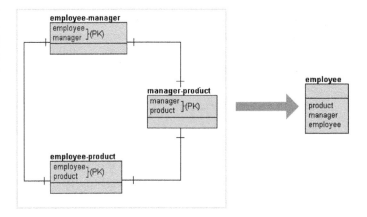

Note: Normalization of multicolumn composite keys is equivalent to an application of the formal version of fifth normal form. Fifth normal form transformations remove cyclic dependencies.

2.4.1.4.5   Denormalizing Extra Entities for Common Columns

Formal third normal form can be used to remove columns, common to two or more entities, into a new entity. The result is as shown on the left side of

Figure 2.11, where common columns are shared between multiple entities, using an extra entity. Once again, the denormalized version of this transformation, as shown on the right side of Figure 2.11, is possibly a more efficient form. The common columns are duplicated across all entities that use those columns. This is deduced on the basis of reducing the number of entities in SQL code join queries. The denormalized structure shown on the right side of Figure 1.11 is neither an elegant nor even a mathematically clean solution. However, it might be a more prudent option based on an objective of improved join query performance. Additionally, if you count the numbers of columns, the denormalized individual entities on the right side of Figure 2.11 contain fewer columns than the normalized entities on the left side. Thus the denormalized structure occupies less physical space.

Figure 2.11
Denormalizing common columns by duplicating into a single shared entity

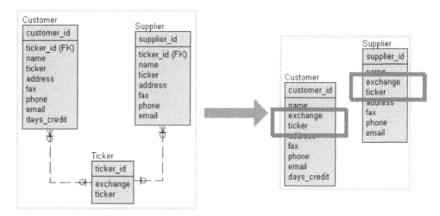

2.4.1.4.6 Denormalizing Formal Third Normal Form Transitive Dependencies

A formal third normal form transformation can remove a transitive dependency, as shown on the left side of Figure 2.12. A transitive dependency is when a third column is dependent on a second column, where the second column is dependent on the primary key, but the third column is not fully dependent on the primary key. Thus the third column can be removed to a new entity, as shown on the left side of Figure 2.12, such that the second column becomes the primary key of the new entity. In other words, on the left side of Figure 2.12, DEPARTMENT depends on DIVISION, which in turn depends on COMPANY, but DEPARTMENT does not absolutely depend on COMPANY.

Once again, in the interests of efficient join queries and saving physical space to be traversed, the denormalized form, as shown on the right side of Figure 2.12, might be the most prudent option.

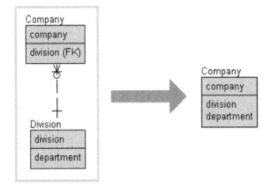

Figure 2.12
*Denormalizing
formal third
normal form
transitive
dependencies*

2.4.1.4.7 Denormalizing Calculated Columns

Formal third normal form transformations require that any calculated columns (calculated on columns in the same entity and perhaps across multiple entities) be removed from the data model all together. The result of this type of normalization is that any future calculations must be performed whenever a calculation is required by SQL coding. Obviously, retaining expression results (calculated columns) within entities increases physical space use. This is somewhat unimportant as a result of the efficiency and low prices of modern disk storage. The real issue with denormalized storage of calculated columns is how they are updated. If columns are calculated based on columns in the same entity, then potential concurrency locking issues are seldom a problem. However, when calculated columns are stored in parent entities (the one side of a one-to-many relationship), and particularly where those parent entities are static entities, with the child being a dynamic entity, then there could be serious concurrency locking issues when updating the calculated columns in the static parent entities.

Note: Static entities contain data that does not change often, such as customer names and addresses. Dynamic entities, also known as transactional entities, are entities containing data that changes frequently, such as invoices. Invoices are updated frequently relative to customer names and addresses. Changing customers' outstanding balances every time they buy something could cause monumental concurrency locking issues.

The right side of Figure 2.13 shows how the denormalization process places calculated columns into entities in order to remove continual expression calculations from queries. However, note that those calculations must occur when data is changed, row per row, or on a regular basis, using batch processing. If the calculations are to be real time, then they have to be changed on a row-per-row basis every time a row is inserted into, changed, or deleted. Changes could be implemented in application coding, in stored procedures (lumped together with the target entity INSERT, UPDATE and DELETE commands), or even using triggers. The right side of Figure 2.13 shows a normalized form with entities with no calculated columns.

Figure 2.13
Denormalizing
expression
constituents into
calculated columns

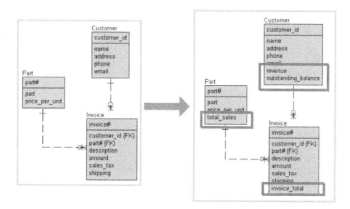

2.4.1.4.8 Denormalizing Formal Boyce-Codd Normal Form

The formal Boyce-Codd normal form is intended to separate candidate keys into separate entities. In other words, any column in an entity, which has potential as a primary key (is capable of representing a row uniquely), should not be allowed to be dependent on the primary key. It should be its own primary key, in its own entity, and link back to the parent entity through a one-to-one relationship. As shown on the left side of Figure 2.14, I have created a rather absurdly overnormalized form of Boyce-Codd normal form. This shows how far one can really stretch Boyce-Codd normal form. This is not a sensible approach to take, and if this type of normalization must be applied, then perhaps not all candidate keys should be removed to new entities. The right side of Figure 2.14 shows a fully denormalized version of entities shown on the left side of Figure 2.14.

2.4.1.4.9 Denormalizing Third Normal Form Many-to-Many Join Resolution Entities

Figure 2.15 shows a sensible application of a third normal form many-to-many join resolution entity, because each row in the Assignment entity will be a unique assignment of a task to an employee. In other words, the Assignment entity makes realistic and useful sense.

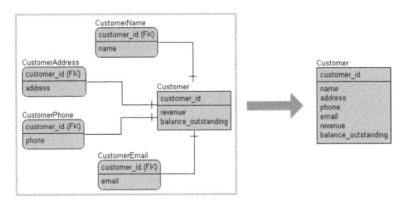

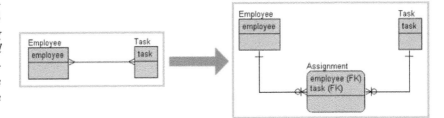

Figure 2.16, on the other hand, shows an insensible application of a third normal form many-to-many join resolution entity, because each row in the CourseStudent entity is meaningless for each separate row. In other words, there is no such thing as a CourseStudent. There is such a thing as enrollment of students in courses, but the entity has not been named to contain enrollments of students in specific courses. That is the kind of thing I look for with these types of entities. If I do not find a sensible name, I might start digging into code. I would ask developers if they actually use an entity like the CourseStudent table. In the past, nine out of ten times, I have found that this type of misnamed entity is generally not used in applications. However, make sure you check first before you remove it from the model.

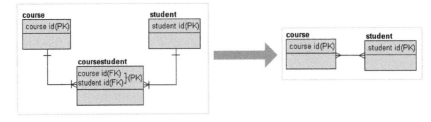

2.4.1.4.10 Denormalizing Second Normal Form

Can second normal form be denormalized? Let's backtrack a little to answer that particular question. Go back to the one-to-one NULL separation denormalization shown in Figure 2.8. Now look at Figure 2.17, except this time, include an extra entity. The new entity is the Exchange entity, with the addition to the Listing entity of the EXCHANGE_ID foreign key column. The relationship between the Listing and Exchange entities is a many-to-one relationship, placing the entities into second normal form. Why is this second normal form? Because the Exchange entity will contain items such as NYSE (New York Stock Exchange) or NASDAQ. The names of exchanges are static relative to the companies listed on those exchanges. Ticker symbols are used to represent companies on stock exchanges. This is my simplified version of second normal form.

The big arrow in Figure 2.17 shows the removal of the Exchange entity by placing the name of the exchange into the Listed entity. This is effective denormalization because there is no information on the Exchange entity other than its unique identifier (EXCHANGE_ID) and the name of the exchange. In short, the Exchange entity in this situation is completely unnecessary and will ultimately hurt performance, requiring more entities in join queries.

Figure 2.17
Second normal form denormalization of static entities

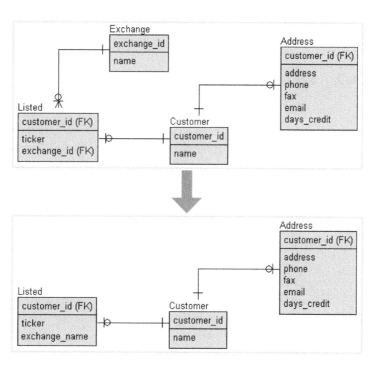

Normalization versus denormalization can be determined somewhat on the ultimate target of performance you want to achieve out of both your database and applications. There are two questions you can ask yourself in this situation:

- How do join queries function in relation to static and dynamic entities?

    - **Answer**: *Join queries will use static entities heavily,* in order to retrieve readable data into query results.

- How do single-row insertions, updates, and deletions function with respect to static data?

    - **Answer**: *The data is static, and thus changes to data do not occur.* If changes do occur, they are rare in relation to changes to dynamic data. The term *static* implies that the data does not change very often, if ever. In other words, static data, such as a list of customers, changes a lot less frequently than a transactional (dynamic) entity containing all invoices against all customers. To reiterate, the answer to this question is that the data is static, and thus changes to static entities are irrelevant. Therefore, why be concerned about single-row insertions, changes, and deletions on a static data table? There is no reason to be concerned. Denormalize in this situation.

2.4.2   Some Useful Tricks

There are many tricks to denormalizing data, which are not necessarily reversals of any of the steps of normalization, but they could be similar to denormalization steps already mentioned in this chapter. Here are some of those tricks:

- *Copying columns between entities*. Making copies of columns between unrelated entities to avoid too many entities in joins. You don't necessarily want a situation where a join between two entities passes through several other entities, just to retrieve columns from two entities that are distantly related. It may well be that the overnormalization is the reason for these large joins. One possible solution is to copy column values to the two distantly related entities, thereby avoiding a join altogether.

- *Placing summary columns into parent entities*. Avoids large summarizing joins, but there will be continual real-time updating of these types of columns. The result can cause hot block issues, which are sometimes better updated in batch mode during low activity cycles. A hot block is a very busy part of the database that is accessed much too often by many different sessions.

- *Separating active and inactive data*. Avoiding frequent unnecessary searching through data that is no longer used. The intention is to reduce the amount of physical space being searched through. Separation of active and inactive data is the purpose of a data warehouse, by storing the inactive data.

- *Separating heavily and lightly accessed columns*. Similar to separating active and inactive data, but the separation applies to heavily and lightly accessed columns, split into separate entities, avoiding unnecessary access to rarely used data.

- *Focus on heavily used functionality*. Tune specific areas of a data model.

- *Using views*. Often useful for application coding but can be detrimental to database performance, especially where views are overused or misused.

- *Local application caching*. Store static values on client or middle-tier levels. This will help avoid repetitive database access.

Note: Any other related useful denormalization tricks that readers would like to see added to this section can be included in the next edition of this book. Please e-mail the author with details.

2.4.2.1 Copying Columns between Entities

This is a case where two entities, generally somewhat disassociated from each other in a data model, can be made to contain a copy of the same value. This would be done in order to avoid joining between multiple entities, through a hierarchy, to obtain a single value.

Figure 2.18 shows a section of the Accounts data model (see Appendix A). The date field DTE should be maintained only in the StockMovement entity, but it is duplicated on the Orders and Transactions entities as well. This helps avoid joins from Orders and Transactions, through StockMovement entries, simply to retrieve the date.

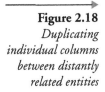

Figure 2.18
Duplicating individual columns between distantly related entities

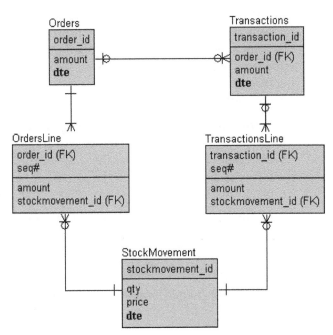

One could use event triggers to copy column values between entities, but this activity might be better implemented at the application level. Use of triggers can have a dire effect on performance in highly active concurrent databases.

2.4.2.2   Placing Summary Columns into Parent Entities

Summary columns can be used to add up or aggregate a repetitive value from a child entity into a parent entity. These aggregates can be placed into parent entities to summarize information held in child entities. Obviously, these summaries would be commonly accessed summary amounts, but we would not want to be continually joining many entities and re-executing grouping functions to find a simple summary. The problem with using summary columns is potential locking and concurrency hot block problems on the summary column entity rows. This applies especially if those summary columns are updated in real time. Typically, these types of denormalized structures are batch updated at times of low activity.

Note: Materialized views can be used to solve these types of problems.

Figure 2.19 shows another section of the Accounts data model (see Appendix A). The BALANCE column on the Customer and Supplier entities summarizes their respective transaction and cashbook entity amount entries. Maintenance of summary columns of this nature in real time may be best updated in batch mode. Using event triggers on child entities will cause even greater performance problems.

Figure 2.19
Summary columns in parent entities

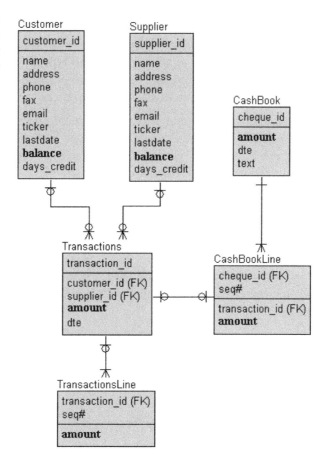

The duplication shown in Figure 2.19 is similar to that shown in Figure 2.13. In Figure 2.13, both the Part and Customer entities have parent entity summary columns. The Part entity has a TOTAL_SALES figure, calculated from all INVOICE_TOTAL values, for all invoices for a specific part. Similarly, the Customer entity contains REVENUE and BALANCE_OUTSTANDING columns, representing total invoice amounts for each customer.

2.4.2.3   Separating Active and Inactive Data

Separation of active and inactive data effectively creates further granularity, but it also ensures that unused data does not interfere with highly accessed data. This can help immensely with performance, especially when the amount of historical or archived data far outweighs that of current data, as is often the case. This tactic is a primitive form of partitioning or data warehousing without the data warehouse. A prime candidate for this type of separation in the Accounts schema (see Appendix A) would be the GeneralLedger entity. General ledger entries in accounting systems can often become large very rapidly. Splitting this type of entity into active and archived entities would be based on some sort of accounting period, such as years or quarters. Even months would be expedient.

Separation of active and inactive data could affect application design. Because data is separated, the application could have to be constructed such that it can access both types of data separately or together. Obviously, if data is being accessed together at the application level, then there is probably not much point in separating it in the first place. An effective application-level solution is having multiple layers of functionality, and thus multiple programs. As an example, the GeneralLedger entity in the Accounts schema could have separate reporting programs for dealing with current and previous periods, when reports are executed against the GeneralLedger table. At the application level, a report such as this could be written with date or year input parameters, allowing access to active or archived data (or both).

Note: The GeneralLedger entity would be a perfect example for Oracle partitioning, which is covered in Part III on physical and configuration tuning.

2.4.2.4   Mixing Heavily and Lightly Accessed Columns

Mixing heavily and lightly accessed columns in SQL statements can cause problems. Perhaps separate those columns into different entities. However, be very careful with this type of solution. This variation on data model tuning is more or less the same as one-to-one NULL separation relationships (sometimes occurring as fourth normal form normalization), which can cause problems as well.

2.4.2.5   Focus on Heavily Used Functionality

Focusing on the heavily used functionality section of a data model is merely one approach to data model tuning. In this situation, I would stress focusing on specific areas of the data model or to provide better performance in areas of a data model that are heavily used by applications. Therefore, attempt more focused tuning of particular entities or indexing. Sometimes this approach can involve use of exotic object types, such as clusters, index organized tables, partitioning, and materialized views, among other Oracle software bells and whistles.

2.4.2.6 Using Views

Views are frequently used by developers to simplify application design and coding, a similar approach to that of using generic static entities, as shown in Figure 2.1. Any type of simplification of application coding can lead to a poor data model structure. This is what could be called an application-centric or top-down approach. Performance design considerations for both data model and applications must be taken into account. Similarly, the same is true of a bottom-up approach, where applications and data models are built from the data model upward. In other words, designing and building applications and data models with too much emphasis on either can both cause problems. Views are often overutilized by developers because they can make prototyping much easier. Views can also often lead to too many database objects, and thus too much data model complexity. Views are effectively overlays, producing more complexity than is necessary at the database level because of the constant resolving of view contents. Some applications even use multiple layers of views, making problems even worse. In this respect, views absolutely do not help SQL code and database performance.

A reader made a comment in the previous edition of this book as follows:

> "A view should be used not so much for ad-hoc SQL, but to hide complexity in code. Views are not evil, views are good, views do not *kill performance* anymore than SQL kills performance, for all a view is, is a stored SQL query!"

The point I am trying to make here is that views are not a problem, but time and again I have seen them used incorrectly, or moreover, overused. In other words, views are not a problem. Yes, from an application perspective they can be used to hide complexity. No, views are not evil in themselves. The problem arises where developers use views like base tables and begin to place WHERE clauses against views and embed layer upon layer of views to build all the SQL code for an application. I call this abuse of views, and it is asking for trouble, with respect to overall database and application performance. Thus views are not the issue. The misuse of views is the issue.

Another reader responded with this comment:

> "Agreed. I worked on a student system, where engineers had built layer upon layer of views, all on top of each other. The views were very slow. They then based materialized views on these views, and wondered why processing took half a day to complete. I believe they are still looking at the problem, although they know at the engineering level what is wrong."

So make your own choice. This is only a friendly warning based on specific uses of views that I have seen repeatedly in the past. In other words, views are a convenience. Just don't overuse them, because it could cause problems further down the development path.

2.4.2.7   Local Application Caching

Heavily used data, which is not constantly changing, can be cached on client or middle-tier machines. For instance, a date, such as today's date, not requiring a time as well, only requires refreshing every 24 hours. Some of the highest execution quantities of SQL code are often for statements performing the simplest tasks, such as retrieving today's date. A common SQL statement of this type in Oracle SQL is a SELECT SYSDATE FROM DUAL statement. Even the simplest SQL statements can affect performance if they are executed often enough. With Java object applications, application-level caching is often effectively utilized. Object-relational mappings can function best using preloading of static data at application startup.

2.4.3   Using Special-Purpose Oracle Database Objects

Denormalization using unusual Oracle Database objects allows creation of special types of database objects used to cluster, presort, and preconstruct data, avoiding excessive amounts of complex repetitive SQL. In effect, denormalization of a relational data model is a way of undoing granular complexity. The reason for this undoing process is to increase performance by minimizing hard-hitting SQL statements. There are numerous types of logical data objects available in Oracle Database, which do what could be called a form of denormalization into preconstructed physically organized data sets. These objects are often used to precreate data sets to be retrieved at a later date, in the structure and form required by an application. These object types are generally as follows:

- **Clusters**: Places most commonly accessed indexed columns, and some data columns, together in the same place physically, in the desired order. Clusters will allow physical copies of heavily accessed columns and tables, in join queries, allowing for faster access to data with more precise I/O.

- **Index-organized tables**: Sorts both the index and the data columns of a table into a required sorted order. An index-organized table builds all the columns in the table into the form of a BTree index.

- **Materialized views**: Preconstructs and stores the results of an SQL statement. This avoids repetitive SQL code execution. A materialized view *materializes* the data. In other words, it stores data physically separate from the source tables. Unlike a materialized view, a view is simply an overlay of another entity or entities, re-executing an SQL statement every time the view is accessed. Views are sometimes not helpful for performance, depending on how they are used. Materialized views are often helpful for performance and are often used in data warehouses. Additionally, in Oracle Database, materialized views can be accessed both by direct SQL coding and automatically by the optimizer, when the optimizer thinks it's a good idea. This is called *query rewrite* because queries can be automatically rewritten by the Oracle Database optimizer. Materialized views are commonly used in data warehouses for precalculated aggregation queries, which contain a summary of rows, from one or more tables, using a GROUP BY clause. The result is much less I/O activity and much better performance.

- **Temporary tables**: Can be used to form intermediary functions per session (at the session level, for a connected user). Temporary tables can sometimes help eliminate intermediary functionality and duplication. The result is less I/O activity.

Note: These items can all be found in my data warehouse tuning book. [2]

All of these solutions are a physical rather than a logical form of denormalization. These specialized objects do not reduce logical complexity, but they can very well do the opposite by increasing complexity, simply because more database objects are being created. What specialized objects do accomplish is to place data sets into purpose-built constructs, which can be used to access data in the required order, without jeopardizing access speed to the underlying tables.

The next chapter briefly discusses various different forms of the relational database model.

2.5   Endnotes

1.   *Oracle Data Warehouse Tuning for 10g* (Gavin Powell, Digital Press, Aug 2005, ISBN: 1555583350)

2.   *Oracle Data Warehouse Tuning for 10g* (Gavin Powell, Digital Press, Aug 2005, ISBN: 1555583350)

3

Different Forms of the Relational Database Model

Over the years since the relational database model was first invented, the art of data modeling in relational databases has evolved somewhat. From the perspective of commercial applications, this evolving process has often been the result of the changing methodologies used by software application development kits (SDKs).

The most significant change in recent years to the way relational database models are built has been the advent of objects. Data structures most efficiently used by object-oriented Java and C++ are generally very different, from those that would have been used by a procedural programming language, such as C or Modula-2. Let's start from the first ideas of relational database modeling and work our way up to data models used by modern online Java object applications.

3.1 The Purist's Relational Database Model

What I like to call the purist's relational data model is what the relational database looked like in its original, most pure form. Figure 3.1 shows a purist's form of a schema used to represent the employees of a company. Note how all of the primary keys are composite indexes. All of these composite indexes are concatenations of all keys inherited (passed down) from all parent tables above in the hierarchy. The unique identifying key in the entity concerned is placed at the end of each primary key.

The type of primary key structure shown in Figure 3.1 provides effective performance for reporting or retrieval of groups of rows, where it is assumed that the report output is sorted based on primary key values. SQL was originally designed to retrieve sets of rows, not single rows. Note that the size of the keys is large, and in some cases, the indexes would occupy almost as much physical space as the tables themselves. If tables were to be joined, the tables would be joined on the basis of all the elements of each primary key. Following is an example script of a join, which selects rows from four tables; note the size of the WHERE clause used to execute the join:

```
SELECT de.name, pr.name, pt.name, prd.revenue - prd.cost
FROM department de, project pr, projecttype pt, product prd
WHERE de.division = pr.division
AND de.department = pr.department
AND pr.projecttype = pt.projecttype
AND pr.division = prd.division
AND pr.department = prd.department
AND pr.projecttype = prd.projecttype
AND pr.project = prd.project;
```

Figure 3.1
A purist's form of the Employees schema

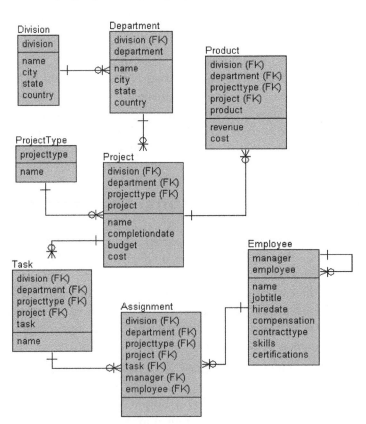

Large WHERE clauses would be used for SQL statements using a data model as shown in Figure 3.1. The primary keys would be shortened coded versions of the NAME columns in each entity. Thus, if Division.NAME values are *North East*, *South East*, *Mid-West*, and *Pacific Coast*, then their related division code values could be *NE*, *SE*, *MW*, and *PC*, respectively. Without the coded values, indexes would be created based on the name of each row, such as Division.NAME. Coded values were used to make coding easier and to reduce the physical size of indexes.

So that is the purist's form of the relational database model. Let's now look at how object SDKs have affected how relational database models have changed and evolved as a result.

3.2   Object Applications and the Relational Database Model

How do object applications affect the structure of relational database models? The point is that object application SDKs do not have to change the structure of a data model, but in general they probably should. In order to impose an object-oriented architecture on top of a relational database, certain small changes can be made to a relational data model. We will examine these in due course. Let us first look at a simple description of the object database model in order to help explain recent trends in relational data modeling.

3.2.1   The Object Database Model

The object model is somewhat different from the relational model. Object databases are much more capable of handling complex data structures. What are the parts and rules that make up the object model?

- **Class**: Defines a structure, the equivalent to a relational entity

- **Attribute**: Specific slots within classes, the equivalent to a relational entity column or field

- **Methods**: Code is attached to classes in methods, which are chunks of localized coding. A method is vaguely equivalent to a relational database stored procedure, except that it executes on the data contents of an object, within the bounds of that object. A method is far more powerful than a relational database stored procedure.

- **Object**: A copy of a class made at run-time where multiple object copies can be made from a single class. The process of creating an object from a class is known in computer jargon as *instantiation*.

- **Inheritance**: A special term applying to types or specializations in an object model, where one class can inherit, and override, attributes and behavior, passed down from a parent class. In some object models, multiple inheritance is allowed. Multiple inheritance can create a dual-direction hierarchical structure, which is flexible, but can also be exceedingly complicated. Retrieving attributes and behavior of a class of object in a hierarchy is known as *typecasting*, where the specifics of one particular class are extracted from an object.

For the sake of simplicity, I assume for the purposes of this explanation that multiple inheritance is not permitted in the object model. Unlike a relational model, an object model supports relationships between objects, through the structure of objects, and the classes defining those objects. Classes are defined as containing collections of pointers to other classes, as being inherited from other classes above in a hierarchy, or as being abstractions of other classes below in the hierarchy. This leads us to observe that classes can be both specialized and abstracted. A specialized class is a more specific form of a class, inheriting everything from its parent class, but allowing local overriding changes and additions. An abstracted class is a more general form of a class, containing common aspects of inherited classes. The abstracted class is the *inheritee*—an abstracted parent class.

Figure 3.2 shows an object database class structure on the left and a relational database entity structure on the right. Note the following differences:

- The object model has no types (TypeCode). Types are represented by the specializations of the Person class, Employee class, and Manager class.

- The relationships between the different classes in the object model are represented in the actual class structure, those relationships being both collection inclusion and inheritance. Thus, the object model contains objects containing pointers to other contained objects.

- An invisible difference is the power of black-box processing using methods in an object database. PL/SQL can perform some of these tasks but does them inadequately.

Figure 3.2
The object versus the relational model

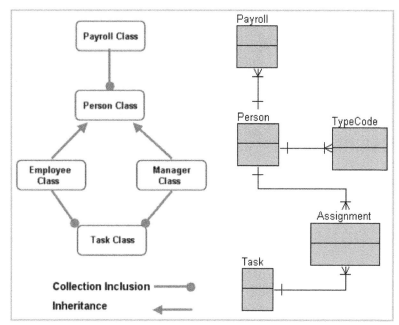

The Person class is a collection included within the Payroll class, as is the Task class in both the Employee class and the Manager class. The Employee class and the Manager class are both specializations of the Person class. The Person class is an abstraction, where the Employee class and the Manager class are inherited from the Person class. The run-time object structure is shown in Figure 3.3, for the object model shown in Figure 3.2. As you can see, the object structure in Figure 3.3 is not the same as the object model class structure in Figure 3.2.

Figure 3.3
The run-time objects

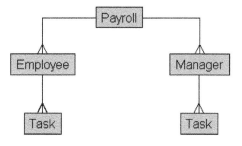

The object model uses data abstraction to conceptualize both data and encapsulated functionality using methods. Inheritance allows the passing of data definition and functionality onto specialized objects and extensive coding reuse. The crux and greatest benefit of objects is in their simplicity. The more that objects are broken down, the more powerful and efficient the structure becomes. A relational database cannot be broken down to the level of an object structure. A relational structure can only be made more granular using normalization, a certain distance, before the amount of normalization becomes detrimental to performance. An object structure can be broken down into an extreme of granularity, and it is therefore highly efficient at handling small, precise transactions. However, an object structure is dreadful at handling any kind of reporting. A relational structure can do both fairly well.

So what is the answer? Perhaps the object-relational model is the solution.

3.2.2   The Object-Relational Database Model

The object-relational model attempts to combine the relational and the object worlds. The problem is that the underlying storage structure of an object database is totally different from that of a relational database. The relational database storage method uses tables and rows (tuples) and is not particularly compatible with an object structure. An object structure allows containment of objects within other objects in a hierarchy, allowing exact searching anywhere into the entire object database.

The best product of the object-relational model is the ability to store and reference large binary objects, such as multimedia. Most of the collection aspects, such as table-contained array types, are often complex and inefficient. Methods can be created using PL/SQL, whose coding implementation is often too complex and convoluted. So the object-relational model simply includes some aspects of the object model, which is more successful in some areas than in others.

My experience of working with both multiple relational and object databases is that the two should not be mixed to any great extent. Relational and object methodologies are completely opposed to each other, and the two simply do not mix very easily.

3.2.3   The Benefits of Overlaying Objects onto Relations

So far in this chapter we have examined an example object model and briefly discussed what the object-relational model attempts to achieve. Many ideas have been put forward in attempting to map object structures from an SDK, such as Java onto a relational model. The best option I have come across has been that shown in Figure 3.4. The data model in Figure 3.4 is a partially abstracted form of the data model shown in Figure 3.1. In

Figure 3.4, every entity has a unique identifier, generated using Oracle Database sequences. Those unique identifiers are actually surrogate primary keys or surrogate keys. The only problem with a structure of the form in Figure 3.4 is that, as with an object database, reordering the data to generate reports can be exceedingly slow, without extensive alternate indexing. There is little point in reporting in the order of a meaningless surrogate key. Too much indexing uses too much physical space and will slow down database change activity.

Figure 3.4
The Employees schema

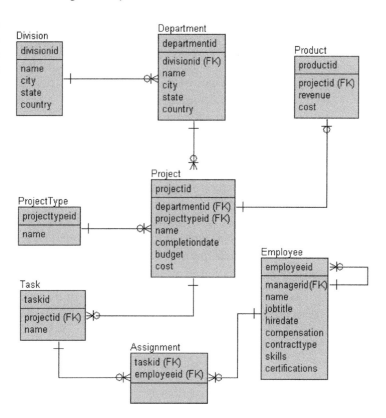

The data model shown in Figure 3.4 would allow a different version of the join statement shown previously in this chapter. Note how this SQL join statement has a much smaller WHERE clause because fewer matching conditions are required:

```
SELECT de.name, pr.name, pt.name, prd.revenue - prd.cost
FROM department de, project pr, projecttype pt, product prd
WHERE de.department_id = pr.department_id
```

```
AND pr.projecttype_id = pt.projecttype_id
AND pr.project_id = prd.project_id;
```

That covers just about everything we need to look at for relational data model tuning, including a brief glimpse at the object data model. Overall, not much can be said about tuning a relational data model, other than changes to granularity. You can increase granularity using normalization and decrease granularity using denormalization, among some other simple tricks. The secret about relational data model design is that it is probably simpler than it appears. The wording in the normal forms layers of normalization might make normalization seem a lot more complicated than it really is. The object model, however, allows inclusion of extensive functionality in an object database directly. As a result, the object model is probably much more difficult to design. Objects by their very nature demand more upfront design and planning work. It should be said, however, that most of the work required in building a relational data model is analysis and understanding of requirements, particularly with regards to potential applications. You should understand applications fully prior to sitting down and drawing out entity relationship diagrams. Putting more time into data model design, prior to beginning coding, will absolutely benefit performance immensely in later stages. ***The data model is the most important part in the development of any custom application, because every other piece of the puzzle depends on it.*** Applications rely on the integrity, applicability to application usage, and serviceability of the data model.

The next chapter presents a brief history of data modeling and gradually leads up to using and tuning of SQL, to be presented in Part II.

4

A Brief History of Data Modeling

A brief history of data modeling is important because it will lead us into the introduction to and tuning of SQL code in the next part of this book. With respect to Oracle software, it is important to understand the roots and reasons for the existence of both the relational and object data models. SQL was created in the very beginnings of the relational data model. Additionally, Oracle Database is effectively an object-relational database, and object-relational databases attempt to meld aspects of object data modeling into the relational data model. It is fundamental to the tuning of SQL to understand how SQL was devised, in order to comprehend how SQL can be tuned in its most simplistic forms.

We will start our short history of data modeling with a look at all types of data models, progressing on to the history of relational databases and the Oracle Database. Finally, we will examine the roots of SQL. As already stated, this will lead us into the next major part of this book, SQL code tuning.

4.1 The History of Data Modeling

A database is a term used to describe an ordered set of information stored on a computer. This ordered set of data (or data set) is often structured using a data modeling solution, in order to make the retrieval of that data more efficient. Depending on the type of applications using the database, the database structure can be modified to allow for efficient changes to that data as well. It is appropriate to discover how different data modeling techniques have developed over the past 50 years, in order to accommodate efficiency in terms of both data retrieval and data changes.

Databases started out stored quite simply in a file system and have evolved through hierarchical, network, relational, object, and object-relational data models, as shown in Figure 4.1.

Figure 4.1
The history and evolution of data modeling

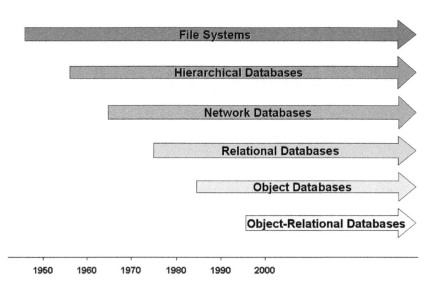

4.1.1 The Different Types of Data Models

- A database stored as a ***file system*** structure simply utilizes the structure of an operating system file system.

- A ***hierarchical*** data model, as shown in Figure 4.2, is a tree-like structure where child tables can have only a single parent. In a hierarchical data model, child tables are completely dependent on the existence of parent tables, supporting one-to-many but not many-to-many relationships.

Figure 4.2
A hierarchical model of company employees

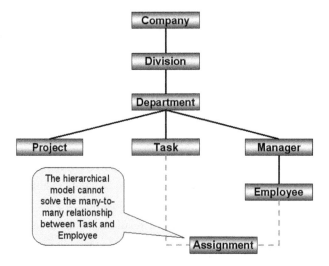

- In a ***network*** data model, as shown in Figure 4.3, the hierarchical model is refined. Now many-to-many relationships are catered for, by allowing a child table to have more than one parent, effectively creating a networked structure of tables.

Figure 4.3
A network model of company employees

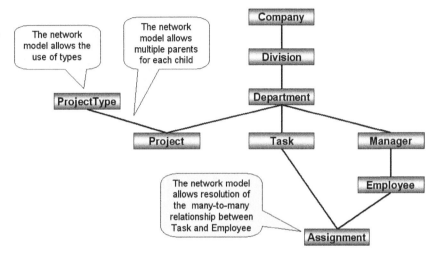

- A ***relational*** data model, as shown in Figure 4.4, allows links between any two tables in the data model, regardless of position in any hierarchy. There is also direct possible access to any table without having to access parent tables first. A relational database is essentially a two-dimensional structure of loosely linked tables containing rows, helping to remove duplication, and allowing for easy access to groups of data. A relational data model is intended for data throughput and is thus most efficient for retrieving sets of data.

- An ***object*** data model is shown on the left side of Figure 4.5. The object model applies an object collection and unique pointer structure, giving a somewhat three-dimensional or spherical structure to data. Object databases are best used for high-speed access to very small and precise amounts of data within a larger data set. Unlike a relational database, an object database is not efficient for reporting. Figure 3.2 in Chapter 3 shows a good demonstration of a comparison between a relational and an object model. This diagram is repeated in this chapter in Figure 4.5 for convenience.

- An ***object-relational database*** is a relational database with some object database aspects added, with varying degrees of success.

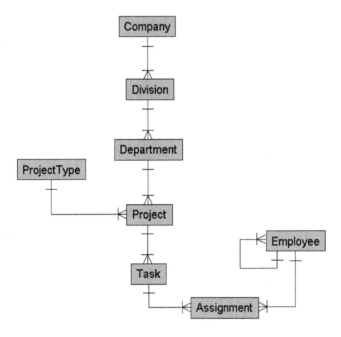

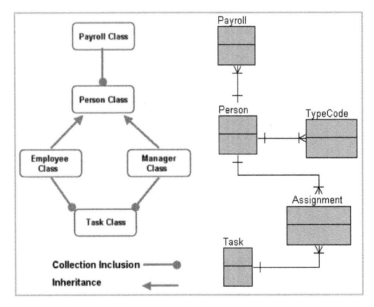

4.2   The History of Relational Databases

The diagram in Figure 4.6 shows the evolution of relational databases. Notice on the left how SQL was first devised as a data access language, with the development of System R from IBM, used today as SQL or Structured Query Language.

Figure 4.6
The evolution of the relational databases

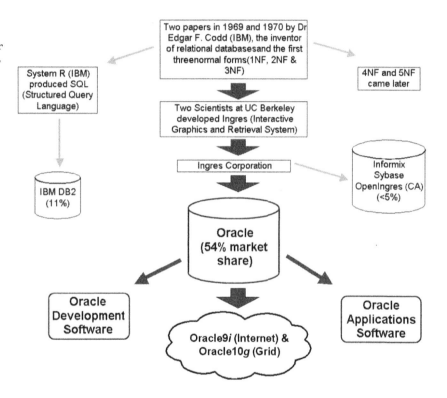

Note: Arrows in Figure 4.6 represent both a flow of development and a flow of people and their skills. Oracle Corporation created Oracle software. Ingres Corporation did not create Oracle Database. Oracle Corporation also did not invent the relational database. However, the skills and personnel were passed between the different database vendor software companies. Ingres Corporation is now defunct and owned by Computer Associates.

4.3   The History of the Oracle Database

Now let's take a more detailed look at the history of the Oracle Database. Examine the diagram in Figure 4.7. Many of the items listed are relevant to tuning Oracle installations. Many items are specifically relevant to SQL code tuning, some physical and configuration tuning, and some both:

- Most of the hardware distribution elements–such as clustering, client/ server, thin client, and multiple-tier environments–using application servers, helped performance with respect to distribution of processing.

- The 4GL and PL/SQL programming tools and languages helped with creation of better, more efficient, and more maintainable source code. It could be said that the easier code is to write, the more time will be available for tuning. However, in relation to coding of fast-performing C code, this theory is probably complete hogwash! Then again, planning and coding efficiency may very well be relative to how much time is spent building code. C code development is notoriously slow and complex.

- Cost-based optimization and statistics help with SQL code tuning in relation to actual data space utilization. Statistics allows for two aspects of physical tuning: (1) better use of space. Statistics help to assess space usage and storage structure from datafiles down to the block level. (2) better analytical information for using in capacity planning. Capacity planning is the process of estimating physical space usage and growth rates.

- A multitude of aspects are introduced in both the OracleDatabase 8*i* and Oracle Database 9*i* Internet versions of Oracle Database software. These releases helped the performance of modern-day Internet and Intranet database environments.

- (10*g*) Oracle Database 10*g* has better performance and scalability, is more highly available, is easier to manage, is better automated, and has tighter security, among other aspects. Where 8*i* and 9*i* represented the Internet database, 10*g* now represents one step further, the Grid database.

Figure 4.7

*The history of
Oracle Database*

1979	RSI released the first version of Oracle using SQL
Early	RSI renamed to Oracle Corp.
	Cross-platform compatibility
	Portable toolsets
Mid 80's	Client/server environments
	4GL
Late 80's	Financials (the first application)
	Oracle6
	PL/SQL
Early	Oracle7
	Referential Integrity
	Cost-based statistics and optimization
	Clustering
Mid 90's	Oracle8 (the object-relational database)
	The thin client
	Application server
Late 90's	Oracle8*i* (the internet database)
	Database kernel Java stored procedures
Y2K+	Oracle9*i* (the internet database)
	Middle tier Oracle9*i* Application Server
	Middle tier Oracle tools integration
2003	Oracle10*g* (the grid database)

4.4   **The Roots of SQL**

Why are we going backward in time looking at data models and relational databases that are no longer in use? In order to tune SQL code effectively, we need to understand the most basic forms of SQL and why newer data modeling techniques are better. In short, database access coding (SQL coding, in the case of a relational database) has evolved with data modeling techniques. Object database data access coding has been called ODQL (Object Definitional Query Language). ODQL was developed for object database access.

SQL stems from an idea of a reporting language devised in theory by the inventor of the relational database. It is very important to remember that the roots of SQL lie in retrieval of sets of data. In other words, SQL is originally intended as a language to retrieve many rows, from one or many tables at once, as a result set. Retrieval of sets or groups of rows is consistent with the original relational data model. SQL was not originally intended to retrieve individual rows from a relational database as exact row matches (access single rows). SQL can now be used to do exactly that (exact row matches), and fairly efficiently.

The next chapter is the first chapter in Part II of this book, SQL code tuning. We will begin the process of explaining SQL code tuning by introducing the very basics of SQL. In subsequent chapters of Part II, we will progress on to the most fundamental aspects of SQL code tuning, and then later to specifics of using and tuning Oracle SQL, specifically for Oracle Database SQL coding.

Part II
SQL Code Tuning

5

What Is SQL?

Let's start the examination of tuning SQL with descriptions of the various basic SQL statements used in relational databases, leading to the Oracle Database specifically.

Note: Oracle texts use the terms statement and command when referring to Oracle SQL syntax. In the context of this book, the terms statement and command mean the same thing.

SQL is pronounced "Ess-Queue-Ell" or "Sequel," depending on the source and location of your training. The meaning of the acronym SQL is Structured Query Language. SQL is the language used to access data from a relational database, such as Oracle Database. SQL was originally devised as a computer language with the development of the IBM relational database called System R. The idea of SQL originates from the relational data model. SQL is used to access subsets of data, in the form of rows or tuples from a larger data set. A data set is represented by a related group of entities, in a data model of a set of tables, in an Oracle Database schema.

5.1   DML and DDL

Unlike other relational databases, Oracle Database classifies and separates SQL statements into two distinct groups, as shown in Figure 5.1. These two groups are Data Manipulation Language (DML) statements and Data Definition Language (DDL) statements. There are two differences between DML and DDL statements, as shown in Figure 5.1.

DML statements manipulate data. A DML statement changes column values in rows, in tables. The INSERT, UPDATE, DELETE, and MERGE statements are by definition DML statements because they change data.

Figure 5.1
DML versus DDL

DML (*data manipulation language*)	DDL (*data definition language*)
Change data in tables	Change metadata or the tables containing data (*the definitional data*)
Under transactional control (*can be undone*)	Automatically execute a COMMIT statement (*COMMIT terminates any previously non-COMMITED DML statements*)

The SELECT and TRUNCATE statements are not DML statements. The SELECT statement is not a DML statement because it does not change data. The SELECT statement also does not produce rollback or redo log entries. The TRUNCATE statement, on the other hand, does change data but automatically executes a COMMIT statement. The TRUNCATE statement is therefore a DDL statement.

Now let's take a quick look at syntax for all the Oracle SQL DML statements.

5.1.1 DML Statement Syntax

The first thing is to make some changes and expand the Employees schema, as shown in Figure 5.2. The previous version of the Employees schema is shown in Figure 3.4.

Figure 5.2
The Employees schema

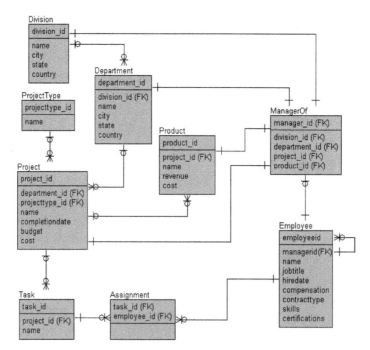

Now we will describe the syntax for all of the Oracle SQL DML statements with explanatory examples of each, using the schema in Figure 5.2.

5.1.1.1   The SELECT Statement

Here is a simplistic form of the Oracle SQL syntax for the SELECT statement (the (10g) MODEL clause[1] is excluded):

```
SELECT { [alias.]column | expression | [alias.]* [ , … ] }
FROM [schema.]table [alias]
[ WHERE [ [schema.]table.|alias.] { column | expression }
   comparison { … }
      [ { AND | OR } [ NOT ] … ]
]
[ GROUP BY
   { expression | rollup-cube | grouping-sets }
      [, { expression | rollup-cube | grouping-sets } ... ]
   [ HAVING condition ]
]
[ ORDER BY
   { { column | expression | position }
      [ ASC | DESC ] [ NULLS { FIRST | LAST } ]
    [, … ] }
]
;


rollup-cube: ROLLUP | CUBE ( expression [, expression ... ] )
grouping-sets: GROUPING SETS
( rollup-cube | expression [, expression ... ])
```

The WHERE clause is used to filter out or remove unwanted rows. The GROUP BY clause is used to generate a summary of rows. The ORDER BY clause is used to sort rows that a query returns. ROLLUP, CUBE, and GROUPING SETS clauses are specialized extensions to the GROUP BY clause.

5.1.1.1.1   Logical Operators

Logical operators allow for Boolean logic in WHERE clause filtering and various other places. Mathematically, the sequence of precedence is NOT, followed by AND, and finally OR. Precedence can be altered using parentheses.

This first query finds the CEO (the CEO is *top dog* and the buck stops with him, therefore, the CEO does not have a manager) and the second employee. The CEO has no manager, and thus his Employee.MANAGER_ ID is NULL. The CEO's EMPLOYEE_ID value happens to be 2:

```
SELECT * FROM employee WHERE employee_id = 2 OR manager_id IS
NULL;
```

This query returns no rows because EMPLOYEE_ID is unique, and the MANAGER_ID of that employee is not NULL; that person is not the CEO:

```
SELECT * FROM employee WHERE employee_id = 2 AND manager_id IS
NULL;
```

This next query returns a spurious result because precedence of executing AND in conjunction with OR is not implemented using parentheses. Parentheses are otherwise known as round brackets. Using parentheses would force either AND or OR to execute first:

```
SELECT employee_id, manager_id FROM employee
WHERE manager_id IS NULL AND employee_id = 1 OR employee_id =
2;
```

This query enforces precedence using parentheses:

```
SELECT employee_id, manager_id FROM employee
WHERE manager_id IS NULL AND (employee_id = 1 OR employee_id =
2);
```

5.1.1.1.2   Comparison Conditions

Comparison conditions allow for different methods of comparison between expressions:

- expression { [!]= | > | < | >= | <= } expression:

```
SELECT * FROM projecttype WHERE projecttype_id = 1;
```

```
SELECT * FROM projecttype WHERE projecttype_id != 1;
```

```
SELECT * FROM projecttype WHERE projecttype_id < 5;

SELECT * FROM projecttype WHERE projecttype_id >= 8;
```

- expression [NOT] LIKE expression

  LIKE is a pattern matcher:

```
SELECT name FROM projecttype WHERE name LIKE '%a%';

SELECT name FROM projecttype WHERE name LIKE 'R%';

SELECT name FROM projecttype WHERE name LIKE 'R%'
OR name LIKE 'S%';

SELECT name FROM projecttype WHERE name LIKE 'R%'
AND name LIKE '%a%';
```

- expression [NOT] IN expression

  IN is used to check for set inclusion:

```
SELECT projecttype_id FROM projecttype
WHERE projecttype_id IN (1,2,3,4,5);

SELECT projecttype_id FROM projecttype
WHERE projecttype_id NOT IN (1,2,3,4,5);
```

- [NOT] EXISTS (subquery)

  EXISTS checks for *existence of*, giving a Boolean as a TRUE or FALSE result:

```
SELECT projecttype_id FROM projecttype
WHERE EXISTS (SELECT * FROM DUAL);

SELECT p.projecttype_id FROM projecttype p
WHERE EXISTS
        (SELECT projecttype_id FROM projecttype
WHERE projecttype_id < 10
AND projecttype_id = p.projecttype_id);
```

```
SELECT p.projecttype_id FROM projecttype p
WHERE EXISTS
    (SELECT project_id FROM project
    WHERE projecttype_id = p.projecttype_id);
```

- expression [NOT] BETWEEN expression AND expression

  BETWEEN does a range check much the same as x >= 1 and x <= 10.

```
SELECT projecttype_id FROM projecttype
WHERE projecttype_id BETWEEN 1 AND 5;
```

- expression [= | != | > | < | >= | <=] [ANY | SOME | ALL] expression

  ANY and SOME verify if any items match, and ALL verifies if all items match.

```
SELECT name FROM projecttype
WHERE projecttype_id = ANY (SELECT projecttype_id FROM
project);
```

```
SELECT name FROM projecttype
WHERE projecttype_id = SOME (SELECT projecttype_id FROM
project);
```

The two queries following will produce no rows because every item must match or not match respectively:

```
SELECT name FROM projecttype
WHERE projecttype_id = ALL (SELECT projecttype_id FROM
project);
```

```
SELECT name FROM projecttype
WHERE projecttype_id != ALL (SELECT projecttype_id FROM
project);
```

5.1.1.1.3 Types of SELECT Statements

There are numerous ways in which the SELECT statement can be used. Let's begin with simple queries:

5.1.1.1.4   Simple Query

```
SELECT * FROM projecttype;
```

5.1.1.1.5   Filtering Queries Using the WHERE Clause

```
SELECT * FROM projecttype WHERE name LIKE 'R%';
```

5.1.1.1.6   Sorting Queries Using the ORDER BY Clause

```
SELECT * FROM projecttype ORDER BY name;
```

5.1.1.1.7   Joining Tables

The ANSI (American National Standards Institute) format was introduced in order to comply with ANSI standards. Tuning ANSI standard format SQL join statements is covered in a later chapter.

The syntax of the Oracle SQL proprietary join format is as shown:

```
SELECT { [ [schema.]table. | [alias.] ]
   { column | expression [, ... ] } | * }
FROM [schema.]table [alias] [, …]

[ WHERE
   [ [schema.]table.|alias.] { column | expression [(+)] }
     comparison condition
   [ [schema.]table.|alias.] { column | expression [(+)] }
   [ { AND | OR } [ NOT ] … ]
]
[ GROUP BY … ]
[ ORDER BY … ];
```

As shown in the previous syntax diagram, the (+) or outer join operator is always placed on the side deficient in information.

```
SELECT di.name, de.name
FROM division di, department de
WHERE di.division_id = de.division_id(+);
```

The Department table is the table deficient in information. Thus rows in the Division table, without entries in the Department table, will be included in the returned result as a left outer join. The term left outer join implies that if the table on the left (the first table in the FROM clause) contains rows that are not in the table on the right (the second table in the

FROM clause), then rows from the first table will be returned in addition to the intersection.

This next syntax diagram shows the syntax for the ANSI standard join format:

```
SELECT {{[[schema.]table.|alias.] {column|expression} [, … ]}|*}
FROM [schema.]table [alias]


[
      CROSS JOIN [schema.]table [alias]

   | NATURAL [INNER | [ LEFT | RIGHT | FULL] OUTER]
         JOIN [schema.]table [alias]

   |{
      [INNER | [LEFT | RIGHT | FULL] OUTER] JOIN [schema.]table
[alias]

      {
          ON (column = column [{AND | OR} [NOT] column = column … ])
        | USING (column [, column … ])
      }
   }
]
[ WHERE … ]
[ GROUP BY … ]
[ ORDER BY … ];
```

The next query is the equivalent ANSI standard syntax for the Oracle SQL proprietary format of the left outer join query shown previously:

```
SELECT di.name, de.name
FROM division di LEFT OUTER JOIN department de USING
(division_id);
```

5.1.1.1.8   Types of Joins

- *Cross-Join*. A cross-join (or Cartesian product) is a merge of all rows in both tables, where each row in one table is matched with every other row in the second table:

```
SELECT * FROM division, managerof;
```

- **Inner or Natural Join**. An inner join is an intersection between two tables, joining based on a column or column names:

```
SELECT * FROM division NATURAL JOIN managerof;
```

- **Outer Join**. An outer join joins rows from two tables. Rows joined are those both in the intersection plus rows in either or both tables, and not in the other table. It is important to remember that for an outer join, rows found in one table, and not in the other, have their columns replaced with NULL values in the joined rows.

- **Left Outer Join**. A left outer join joins all intersecting rows plus rows only in the left table:

```
SELECT * FROM division NATURAL LEFT OUTER JOIN managerof;
```

- **Right Outer Join**. A right outer join is the opposite of a left outer join: the intersection plus all rows in the right table only:

```
SELECT * FROM division NATURAL RIGHT OUTER JOIN managerof;
```

- **Full Outer Join**. A full outer join retrieves all rows from both tables:

```
SELECT * FROM division NATURAL FULL OUTER JOIN managerof;
```

- **Self-Join**. A self-join joins a table to itself:

```
SELECT manager.name, employee.name
FROM employee manager JOIN employee employee
ON (employee.manager_id = manager.employee_id);
```

- **Equi-/Anti-/Range Joins**. These joins use the appropriate comparison conditions to join rows in tables:

```
SELECT * FROM division di JOIN department de
ON(di.division_id = de.division_id);
```

- *Mutable and Complex Joins*. A mutable join is a join of two or more tables. A complex join is a mutable join with extra filtering:

```
SELECT di.name, de.name, prj.name
FROM division di
JOIN department de ON(di.division_id = de.division_id)
JOIN project prj ON(de.department_id = prj.department_id)
WHERE di.division_id = 5;
```

5.1.1.1.9   Subqueries

There are specific types of subqueries:

- *Single-Row Subquery*. A single-row subquery returns a single row from the subquery. Some comparison conditions require a single row with a single column:

```
SELECT * FROM project
WHERE projecttype_id =
(SELECT projecttype_id FROM projecttype
WHERE projecttype_id = 1);
```

- *Multiple-Row Subquery*. A multiple-row subquery returns one or more rows from the subquery back to the calling query:

```
SELECT project_id FROM project
WHERE projecttype_id IN
(SELECT projecttype_id FROM projecttype);
```

- *Multiple-Column Subquery*. A multiple-column subquery returns many columns:

```
SELECT COUNT(*) FROM(SELECT * FROM project);
```

- *Regular Subquery*. A regular subquery executes a subquery in its entirety where there is no communication between calling query and subquery:

```
SELECT * FROM department WHERE division_id IN
(SELECT division_id FROM division);
```

- *Correlated Subquery.* A correlated subquery can use a value passed from a calling query as a parameter, to filter specific rows in the subquery. Values can only be passed from calling to subquery, not the other way around:

```
SELECT * FROM division WHERE EXISTS
(SELECT division_id FROM department
WHERE division_id = division.division_id);
```

There are numerous places where subqueries can be used:

- In a SELECT clause:

```
SELECT p.project_id,
    (SELECT projecttype_id FROM projecttype
WHERE projecttype_id = p.projecttype_id)
FROM project p;
```

- In a WHERE clause (filtering):

```
SELECT project_id FROM project
WHERE projecttype_id IN
(SELECT projecttype_id FROM projecttype);

SELECT division_id FROM division
WHERE division_id IN
  (SELECT division_id FROM department
  WHERE department_id IN
    (SELECT department_id FROM department));
```

- In an ORDER BY clause (sorting):

```
SELECT name FROM projecttype
ORDER BY (SELECT 'name' FROM DUAL);
```

- In a HAVING clause (filtering groups):

```
SELECT name, COUNT(name) FROM projecttype
GROUP BY name
HAVING name = ANY (SELECT name FROM projecttype);
```

- In a FROM clause:

```
SELECT COUNT(*) FROM (
SELECT di.name, de.name, pr.name
FROM division di
JOIN department de ON (di.division_id = de.division_id)
  JOIN project pr ON (de.department_id = pr.department_id));
```

- In an INSERT statement VALUES clause:

```
INSERT INTO projecttype(projecttype_id, name)
VALUES((SELECT MAX(projecttype_id)+1 FROM projecttype)
  ,'A new project type');
```

- In an UPDATE statement SET clause as SET = (subquery):

```
UPDATE department SET name = (SELECT name FROM division
WHERE division_id = department.division_id);
```

- In a CASE statement expression:

    There is no example for a CASE statement expression because it is PL/SQL. PL/SQL syntax is not part of tuning Oracle SQL code.

- As a function parameter:

```
SELECT LPAD('xxx',10,(SELECT * FROM DUAL)) FROM DUAL;
```

5.1.1.1.10   Table and View Creation

This example uses a subquery to create a new table:

```
CREATE TABLE namesTable AS
    SELECT di.name AS Division, de.name AS Department,
pr.name AS Project
    FROM division di
    JOIN department de ON (di.division_id = de.division_id)
      JOIN project pr ON (de.department_id = pr.department_id);
```

This example uses a subquery to create a new view:

```
CREATE VIEW namesView AS
    SELECT di.name AS Division, de.name AS Department,
pr.name AS Project
    FROM division di
    JOIN department de ON (di.division_id = de.division_id)
      JOIN project pr ON (de.department_id = pr.department_id);
```

5.1.1.1.11 Hierarchical Query

A hierarchical query allows display of hierarchical data in a single table:

```
SELECT name, employee_id, manager_id FROM employee
  CONNECT BY PRIOR employee_id = manager_id;
```

5.1.1.1.12 Set Operators and Composite Queries

Set operators are used to combine two separate queries into a composite query. Both queries must have the same datatypes for each column:

- UNION ALL retrieves all rows from both queries including duplicates. Duplicate rows are rows returned by both queries.

- UNION returns on distinct rows and UNION ALL returns all rows, including any duplicate rows.

- INTERSECT returns distinct rows from both queries. An intersection is a little like an inner join.

- MINUS returns one query less the other, a little like a left outer join without the intersection, where only distinct rows in the first query are returned.

In order to demonstrate sensible use of set operators and composite queries, Figure 5.3 shows a split of the Employees schema, Employee table, into two tables.

Using the two Manager and Employee tables, we can use a set operator to join the two tables together into a composite query:

```
SELECT manager_id, name FROM manager
UNION ALL
SELECT employee_id, name FROM employee;
```

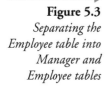

Figure 5.3
*Separating the
Employee table into
Manager and
Employee tables*

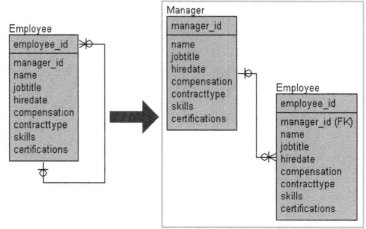

This next query will not work because the sequence of column datatypes is different between the two queries (the columns are in opposite sequence between the two queries):

```
SELECT name, manager_id FROM manager
UNION ALL
SELECT employee_id, name FROM employee;
```

5.1.1.1.13   Flashback

Flashback queries are not particularly relevant to tuning but are important enough to include, simply so that you know that they exist as an option for a quick and easy way of examining older data, or for recovery. Flashback simply returns rows at a particular point in time, using a System Change Number (SCN) or a timestamp. The syntax is as follows:

```
SELECT … AS OF { SCN | TIMESTAMP } expression
```

5.1.1.1.14   (10g) Flashback Versions Queries

Flashback queries are improved upon in Oracle Database 10*g*, such that they can be used to return multiple versions of a query. A flashback version query can return multiple iterations of the same rows, within a period of time.

```
SELECT … [ VERSIONS BETWEEN { SCN | TIMESTAMP }
{ expression | MINVALUE } AND { expression | MAXVALUE }
AS OF { SCN | TIMESTAMP } expression
```

5.1.1.1.15   (10*g*) **Flashback Database**

The FLASHBACK DATABASE has little to do with tuning, apart from the fact that it might make restoration of a previous database state much easier and faster. The FLASHBACK DATABASE statement allows database recovery by allowing the undoing of all changes back to an SCN or timestamp.

5.1.1.1.16   **Using DISTINCT**

DISTINCT retrieves the first value from a repeating group. When there are multiple repeating groups, DISTINCT will retrieve the first row from each repeating group. A repeating group is a term applied to duplicate rows. DISTINCT can operate on one or more columns:

```
SELECT COUNT ( [ DISTINCT | ALL ] expression ) ...
SELECT DISTINCT column [, column ... ] ...
SELECT DISTINCT (column [, column ... ]) ...
```

5.1.1.1.17   **The DUAL Table**

Every DML statement creates an implicit cursor. A cursor is an area in memory allocated for the results of an SQL statement. SELECT statements require a source table for the implicit cursor to operate on. The DUAL table is required as a dummy table, to allow the SELECT statement to retrieve data not stored in a table, view, or other database object. The DUAL table is a repository for an expression result applied to a single value. The DUAL table acts as a temporary repository for the result of an expression. The result of the expression is selected from the DUAL table, as in the following examples:

```
SELECT * FROM DUAL;
SELECT a.*, b.* FROM DUAL a, projecttype b;
SELECT 'This is a string' FROM DUAL;
```

The DUAL table also can be used to retrieve Oracle Database settings (constant, variable, or pseudocolumn) in a SELECT statement:

```
SELECT SYSDATE FROM DUAL;
SELECT USER FROM DUAL;
```

5.1.1.1.18   **NULLs**

There are several things to remember about NULL:

- NULL represents nothing.

- Not even a space character is NULL.

- NULL is not the same as zero.

- NULL values are not always created in indexes.

- Most functions return NULL when passed a NULL value.

- Test for NULL using IS [NOT] NULL.

- An expression containing a NULL returns NULL.

- Use the NVL(value, replace) function to account for NULL values in expressions.

- NULL values sort as the highest value.

5.1.1.1.19   *Pseudocolumns*

A pseudocolumn is a virtual column producing a specific value when used in DML and queries. A pseudocolumn is essentially an expression calculator or a window into some part of an Oracle database.

- ***Sequences***:
    - CURRVAL (sequence.CURRVAL)
    - NEXTVAL (sequence.NEXTVAL)
- ***ROWID*** provides the fastest access method but can change because it is a relative address. A ROWID is unique across a table and used as the pointer in an index, pointing to a table row. A ROWID is made up of the following:
    - Tablespace identifier
    - Datafile block
    - Data block row
    - Tablespace datafile number
- ***ROWNUM*** is an order sequence number of rows returned by a SELECT statement.
- ***LEVEL*** provides a hierarchical level number in a hierarchical query.
- ***XMLDATA*** allows access to XMLTYPE datatypes.

5.1.1.1.20 Using Functions

Functions can be used in most parts of different DML statements. Using functions can affect performance because they add processing time. Functions can be divided into the following general categories:

- Single-row functions
- Datatype conversion functions
- Group functions
- Object reference functions
- User-defined functions

5.1.1.2 The INSERT Statement

There are two forms of the INSERT statement, which can be used to add rows to a single table or multiple tables. There are various syntax options:

```
INSERT INTO [schema.]table [ ( column [, column …] ) ]
VALUES ( { expression | DEFAULT | (subquery) }
    [, { expression | DEFAULT | (subquery) } ... ] )
[ RETURNING expression [, expression ] INTO variable [,
variable ]  ];
```

The specified columns are optional if the VALUES clause specifies columns in existing physical column order (the same as in the table):

```
INSERT INTO projecttype
VALUES (projecttype_seq.NEXTVAL, 'A new project type');
```

The RETURNING clause is PL/SQL (too advanced for this chapter) and will be covered later in this book.

5.1.1.2.1 Multiple-Table INSERT Statements

A multiple-table INSERT statement means that a single row can be added to more than one table in the same statement. The syntax is as follows:

```
INSERT { FIRST | ALL }
[ WHEN condition THEN ] INTO table [ VALUES (…) ]
[ WHEN condition THEN ] INTO table [ VALUES (…) ]
```

```
ELSE INTO table [ VALUES (…) ]
subquery;
```

All WHEN conditions are executed on every row of the table. The WHEN condition determines if an INTO table VALUES clause is executed. The ELSE option is executed if all WHEN conditions have failed. Processing is moved to the next row retrieved after processing of a successful WHEN condition.

FIRST will cause only the first WHEN condition to add rows. ALL will cause all successful WHEN conditions to be executed, potentially adding a row to more than a single table (a multiple-table insertion).

5.1.1.3   The UPDATE Statement

The syntax for the UPDATE statement is as shown here:

```
UPDATE [schema.]table
SET column = expression | (subquery) | DEFAULT
   | ( column [, column … ] ) = (subquery)
[ WHERE ... ]
[ RETURNING expression [, expression ] INTO variable [,
variable ] ) ];
```

5.1.1.4   The DELETE and TRUNCATE Statements

This is the syntax for the DELETE statement:

```
DELETE [ FROM ] [schema.]table
[ WHERE ... ]
[ RETURNING expression [, expression ] INTO variable [,
variable ] ) ];
```

The TRUNCATE statement is a DDL statement, which executes an automatic COMMIT statement and is therefore not undoable. The TRUNCATE statement is as follows:

```
TRUNCATE TABLE [schema.]table;
```

Note: Truncating a table drops the contents of a table without producing rollback information. Deleting all rows from a table using the DELETE statement does produce rollback, and thus TRUNCATE can be much faster than DELETE.

5.1.1.5 (10g) The MERGE Statement

The MERGE statement is used to add new rows and update existing rows between two tables, as shown in Figure 5.4.

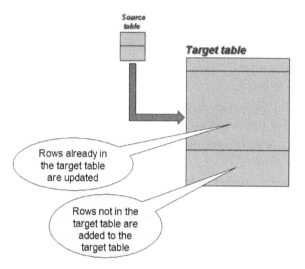

Figure 5.4
The MERGE statement

The MERGE statement is upgraded in Oracle Database 10*g*, as shown by the highlighted lines in the following syntax:

```
MERGE [ hint ] INTO [schema.]table [alias]
USING { [schema.] table | view | (subquery) } [ alias ]
ON ( column = column [, column = column ... ] )
{
 WHEN MATCHED THEN
  UPDATE SET { column = { column | expression | DEFAULT }
  [ , column = ... ]}
  [ WHERE filter ]
  [ DELETE WHERE filter ]
|
 WHEN NOT MATCHED THEN
  INSERT ( column [, column ... ] )
   VALUES ( { column | expression | DEFAULT } [ , column ...
] )
  [ WHERE filter ]
|
 both UPDATE and INSERT
};
```

The changes for the MERGE statement for Oracle Database 10*g* can be described as follows:

1. WHERE filtering clauses have been added.

2. Updated rows can be optionally deleted after updating of each row is complete. In other words, rows are filter-deleted based on updated values, rather than before the merging operation takes place.

3. Oracle Database 9*i* syntax required that both INSERT and UPDATE clauses must exist. Both INSERT and UPDATE are now partially optional, where at least one or both must be specified.

Note: (10*g*) The MERGE statement is now much more flexible and can help performance simply by gluing inserts and updates into a single statement.

5.2   Transaction Control

SQL DML can be controlled for rollback. DDL statements cannot be rolled back (undone). A transaction is a sequence of SQL DML statements. This sequence of statements can be stored using a COMMIT statement or undone using a ROLLBACK statement. A SAVEPOINT statement can be used to execute a partial rollback on a transaction, back to that SAVEPOINT label:

```
SAVEPOINT label;
...
sql commands
...
ROLLBACK TO SAVEPOINT label;
```

The SET TRANSACTION statement is used to set certain aspects for a transaction or sequence of SQL statements, as shown by the following syntax:

```
SET TRANSACTION
{
```

```
        NAME 'transaction'
    | {
            READ { WRITE | ONLY }
          | ISOLATION LEVEL { READ COMMITTED | SERIALIZABLE }
          | USE ROLLBACK SEGMENT rollback segment
      } [ NAME 'transaction' ]
};
```

The defaults for the SET TRANSACTION statement are READ WRITE and ISOLATION LEVEL READ COMMITTED. The default command ISOLATION LEVEL READ COMMITTED will cause the transaction to wait for any competing locks to be released, before a transaction is allowed to complete. ISOLATION LEVEL SERIALIZABLE will cause a transaction to immediately fail if a lock is encountered.

5.2.1   COMMIT versus ROLLBACK

COMMIT stores changes made in a transaction to the database. ROLLBACK will undo those changes. A quick examination of exactly what the COMMIT and ROLLBACK statements do is warranted, because COMMIT is generally a faster process than a ROLLBACK operation. The reason for this is that it is assumed, and quite sensibly so, that COMMIT is executed much more often than ROLLBACK. Therefore, COMMIT has been deliberately designed to execute much faster.

The question to ask is: Why is a COMMIT statement faster than a ROLLBACK statement? What occurs in the database during the processing of these statements?

- Before COMMIT or ROLLBACK
    - Redo logs are written.
    - The database is changed.
    - Rollback is written.

- On COMMIT
    - Rollback is deleted.

- On ROLLBACK
    - Rollback is recorded in the redo logs.
    - Rollback is applied to the database.
    - Rollback is deleted.

Note: Redo log entries are always written first in order to ensure subsequent possible recoverability.

Before COMMIT or ROLLBACK statements are executed, changes are physically stored in the database. The COMMIT statement simply removes any recourse to undoing the changes. ROLLBACK executes everything in reverse. Figure 5.5 shows a vague relationship between the database, logs, and rollback.

Figure 5.5
COMMIT versus
ROLLBACK

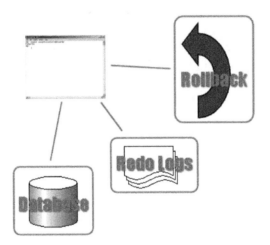

Note: (10g) Various options have been newly introduced in the COMMIT statement, allowing processing to continue before redo log entries are copied from log buffer to redo log files, and also even allowing redo log entries to write after database buffer cache writes.

The default options are executed simply by executing a COMMIT statement. Adding the WRITE clause to a COMMIT statement (COMMIT WRITE) allows a transaction to complete before the log buffer has completed writing out to the current log file group. This can improve performance of the database in general, for very high-response-time environments.

Note: Default behavior can be centrally controlled by setting the COMMIT_WRITE parameter.

5.2.2 Transaction Control between Multiple Sessions

Locking can occur between different sessions when changes are made to the same data, by different sessions. If one user changes a row using an UPDATE or DELETE statement, without terminating the transaction, then that row or rows will be locked until a COMMIT or ROLLBACK statement is executed. A second session attempting to change the same row or rows will not respond until the first session terminates the transaction. Multiple sessions can access the database, as shown in Figure 5.6.

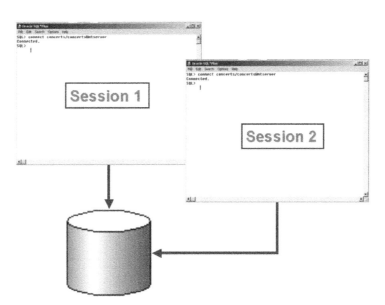

Figure 5.6
*Locking rows before
transaction
completion*

5.3 Parallel Queries

In an ideal world, parallel queries are useful on multiple CPU platforms when Oracle partitioning is being used, with separate disks or RAID arrays. Parallel queries are often only an advantage for very large tables (but not always), or in very large databases, such as data warehouses. Using parallel queries on small, highly active, concurrent OLTP databases can sometimes cause rather than solve performance problems. There will be more on parallel queries and Oracle partitioning later in this book. Certain types of SQL can be executed in parallel:

- Any query with at least a single table scan using SELECT, INSERT, UPDATE, and DELETE statements

- The CREATE INDEX and ALTER INDEX REBUILD statements

- Using the CREATE TABLE statement generating a table from a SELECT statement

- Partitions with local indexes, which are created on each separate partition

Those are the basics of Oracle SQL queries and DML for changing data in a database. In the next chapter, we will start to examine the concepts of creating efficient SQL code.

5.4   Endnotes

1.   Oracle SQL: Jumpstart with Examples (Gavin Powell, Digital Press, Sep 2004, ISBN: 1555583237)

6

The Basics of Efficient SQL

In the previous chapter, we examined the basic syntax of SQL in Oracle Database. This chapter and the next chapter (which covers more advanced topics) will attempt to detail the most simplistic aspects of SQL code tuning. In other words, we are going to discuss what in SQL statements is good for performance and what is not. The approach to performance in this chapter will be one of focusing purely on the SQL coding. The objective is to avoid the nitty-gritty and internal processing occurring in Oracle Database at this stage. Therefore, this chapter focuses on tuning SQL code and ignores performance factors, such as I/O, cache, and configuration parameters. It is essential to understand the basic facts about how to write well-performing SQL code first, without considering specific details of Oracle Database and hardware configuration.

The most important rule of thumb with SQL statements, and particularly SELECT statements (those most subject to tuning), is what is commonly known as the *KISS* rule or *Keep It Simple, Stupid!* The simpler your SQL statements are, then the faster they will likely be. There are two reasons for this: (1) simple SQL statements are much more easily tuned because there is less code to consider; and (2) the optimizer will function a lot better when assessing less complex SQL code. The negative effect of this is granularity, but this negative effect depends on how the application is coded. For instance, connecting to and disconnecting from the database for every SQL code statement is extremely inefficient. That's far too much granularity.

Part of the approach in this chapter and the next is to present SQL performance examples, without bombarding the reader with the details of too much theory and reference material. Any reference items, such as explanations of producing query plans, will be covered later in this book.

Note: The note on the whole next page is the MOST IMPORTANT note in this entire book!

Note: There is a lot of talk out there, in the big wide world of Oracle Database tuning, about LIOs (Logical I/O to cache), and not using cost to estimate query plan execution. I know about the cost thing. This is why I using timing estimates in addition to query plan cost estimates. And LIOs? Well, using LIOs as a way of estimating execution times, for anything in Oracle Database, has also been subject to seriously conflicting opinions in the recent past.

When considering LIOs versus PIOs (physical I/O to disk), there is much evidence to support the fact that using the database buffer cache exorbitantly, is not nearly as efficient as we are lead to believe. Tuning an Oracle database quite often has very, very little to do with tuning the database buffer cache—usually making it bigger. This just uses more resources. Using more resources is not necessarily a problem but managing larger cache sizes gets more difficult the more they are used. Unless of course in the case of a data warehouse where I/O activity is so heavy that perhaps a database buffer cache might be best to be as small as possible. My approach in this book is hopefully scientific. What I am trying to do is present possibilities. I am not trying to provide exact instructions because there aren't any; at least I don't think so. I am sure there are some who will disagree with me.

For every database, every server, and every set of applications—they are all different from one installation to another. I am simply trying to provide methods and a general approach to tuning Oracle databases. Perhaps my overall message should be that I find that breaking things down into smaller parts, is usually much more effective in the long run. When readers send me queries that are pages long, saying they have no idea how to tune this. My response is—Nor do I. I then suggest that they try to tune something in small sections first, and it might get a little easier. And the Oracle optimizer is good, but don't expect it to be a magician!

The issue with using costs to compare potential query execution times is a delicate matter, so it seems. Essentially the cost of a query plan is a guess at what the optimizer might do when executing a query. No it is not 100% correct. And it is quite likely the query might behave completely differently to that of the suggestion of the optimizer, when executing. The point about using query plan costs to estimate the potential execution times for queries, is that using cost is a best guess, and is probably the only guess that is straightforward to use, and easy to access.

The reason why I re-execute a query again and again in this book, is in order to temporarily discount any effects (even the beneficial ones), gained by utilizing special I/O and cache features (mostly the database buffer cache, which is covered later on in this book.

This chapter covers a general type of SQL code tuning. Thus the title of this chapter: *The Basics of Efficient SQL.* Let's start with a brief look at the SELECT statement.

6.1   The SELECT Statement

It is always faster to SELECT exact column names. Thus, using the Employees schema:

```
SELECT division_id, name, city, state, country FROM division;
```

Is faster than:

```
SELECT * FROM division;
```

Also, since there is a primary key index on the Division table:

```
SELECT division_id FROM division;
```

This query will only read the index file and should completely ignore the table. Because the index contains only a single column and the table contains five columns, reading the index is faster because there is less physical space to traverse.

In order to prove these points, we need to use the EXPLAIN PLAN command. Oracle Database's EXPLAIN PLAN command allows a quick peek into how the Oracle Database optimizer will execute a SQL statement, displaying a query plan devised by the optimizer.

The EXPLAIN PLAN command creates entries in the PLAN_TABLE for a SELECT statement. The resulting query plan for the SELECT statement following is shown after it. Various versions of the query used to retrieve rows from the PLAN_TABLE, a hierarchical query, can be found in Appendix B. In order to use the EXPLAIN PLAN command, statistics must be generated. Both the EXPLAIN PLAN command and statistics will be covered in detail later in this book:

```
EXPLAIN PLAN SET statement_id= 'TEST' FOR SELECT * FROM
division;
```

Query	Cost	Rows	Bytes
SELECT STATEMENT on	1	10	460
TABLE ACCESS FULL on DIVISION	1	10	460

Note: The (10g) Database Control and the (9i) Oracle Enterprise Manager console can also be used to view query plans. These tools will be explained in later chapters, specifically dedicated to describing available tools and their specific uses. For now, simple command-line tools will suffice.

One thing that is important to remember about the EXPLAIN PLAN command is that it produces a listed sequence of events, a query plan. Examine the following query and its query plan. The *Pos* or positional column gives a rough guide to the sequence of events that the optimizer will follow. In general, events will occur listed in the query plan from bottom to top, where additional indenting denotes containment. In other words, examining the following example output, the step *SELECT STATEMENT on* occurs last:

```
EXPLAIN PLAN SET statement_id= 'TEST' FOR
    SELECT di.name, de.name, prj.name, SUM(prj.budget-prj.cost)
    FROM division di JOIN department de USING(division_id)
        JOIN project prj USING(department_id)
GROUP BY di.name, de.name, prj.name
HAVING SUM(prj.budget-prj.cost) > 0;
```

Query	Pos	Cost	Rows	Bytes
SELECT STATEMENT on	97	97	250	17500
FILTER on	1			
SORT GROUP BY on	1	97	250	17500
HASH JOIN on	1	24	10000	700000
TABLE ACCESS FULL on DIVISION	1	1	10	170
HASH JOIN on	2	3	100	3600
TABLE ACCESS FULL on DEPARTMENT	1	1	100	1900
TABLE ACCESS FULL on PROJECT	2	13	10000	340000

Now let's use the Accounts schema, which has some very large tables. Large tables show differences between the costs of data retrievals more easily. The GeneralLedger table contains more than 700,000 rows at this point in time.

In the next example, we explicitly retrieve all columns from the table using column names, similar to using SELECT * FROM GeneralLedger. Using the asterisk probably involves a small overhead in reinterpretation into a list of all column names, but this is internal to Oracle Database, and unless there are a huge number of these types of queries, this is probably negligible:

```
EXPLAIN PLAN SET statement_id='TEST' FOR
SELECT generalledger_id,coa#,dr,cr,dte FROM generalledger;
```

The cost of retrieving 752,740 rows is 493, and the GeneralLedger table is read in its entirety, indicated by *TABLE ACCESS FULL*:

Query	Cost	Rows	Bytes
SELECT STATEMENT on	**493**	752740	**19571240**
TABLE ACCESS FULL on GENERALLEDGER	493	752740	19571240

Now we will retrieve only the primary key column from the GeneralLedger table:

```
EXPLAIN PLAN SET statement_id='TEST' FOR
SELECT generalledger_id FROM generalledger;
```

For the same number of rows, the cost is reduced by about half, to 217, because the byte value is reduced, reading the index only, using a form of a full index scan. This means that only the primary key index, not the table, is being read:

Query	Cost	Rows	Bytes
SELECT STATEMENT on	**217**	752740	**4516440**
INDEX FAST FULL SCAN on XPKGENERALLEDGER	217	752740	4516440

Here is another example using an explicit column name, but this one has a greater difference in cost from that of the full table scan, because the column retrieved uses an index, which is physically smaller than the index for the primary key. The index on the COA# column is consistently of five bytes in length for all rows. For the primary key index, only the first 9,999 rows have an index value of less than five bytes in length:

```
EXPLAIN PLAN SET statement_id='TEST' FOR
SELECT coa# FROM generalledger;
```

Query	Cost	Rows	Bytes
SELECT STATEMENT on	5	752740	4516440
INDEX FAST FULL SCAN on XFK_GL_COA#	5	752740	4516440

Following are two interesting examples utilizing a composite index. The structure of the index is built as the SEQ# column contained within the CHEQUE_ID column (CHEQUE_ID + SEQ#) and not the other way around. In older versions of Oracle Database, this probably would have been a problem. In the Oracle 10*g* Database, the optimizer is now much improved when matching poorly ordered SQL statement columns to existing indexes.

Both of the following examples use the same index. The order of columns is not necessarily a problem in Oracle 10*g* Database:

```
EXPLAIN PLAN SET statement_id='TEST' FOR
SELECT cheque_id, seq# FROM cashbookline;
```

Query	Cost	Rows	Bytes
SELECT STATEMENT on	65	188185	1505480
INDEX FAST FULL SCAN on XPKCASHBOOKLINE	65	188185	1505480

As can be seen following, even with the columns selected in the reverse order of the index, the index is still used:

```
EXPLAIN PLAN SET statement_id='TEST' FOR
SELECT seq#,cheque_id FROM cashbookline;
```

```
Query                                    Cost    Rows     Bytes
-------------------------------------   ------  -------  ---------
SELECT STATEMENT   on                     65   188185   1505480
  INDEX FAST FULL SCAN on XPKCASHBOOKLINE  65   188185   1505480
```

The GeneralLedger table has a large number of rows. Now let's examine the idiosyncrasies of very small tables. There are some differences between the behavior of SQL when dealing with large and small tables.

In the next example, the Stock table is small, and thus the cost of reading the table or the index is the same. The first query, doing the full table scan, reads approximately 20 times more physical space, but the cost is the same. When tables are small, the processing speed may not be better when using indexes. Additionally, when joining tables, the optimizer may very well choose to perform a full scan on a small static table rather than read both index and table. The optimizer may select the full table scan as being quicker. This is often the case with generic static tables containing multiple types because they typically are read more often:

```
EXPLAIN PLAN SET statement_id='TEST' FOR SELECT * FROM stock;
```

```
Query                             Cost    Rows     Bytes
------------------------------   ------  -------  ---------
SELECT STATEMENT   on              1       118      9322
  TABLE ACCESS FULL on STOCK       1       118      9322
```

```
EXPLAIN PLAN SET statement_id='TEST' FOR SELECT stock_id FROM stock;
```

```
Query                             Cost    Rows     Bytes
------------------------------   ------  -------  ---------
SELECT STATEMENT   on              1       118      472
  INDEX FULL SCAN on XPKSTOCK      1       118      472
```

That is a brief look into how to tune simple SELECT statements. Try to *use explicit columns, and try to read columns in index orders if possible, even to the point of reading indexes and not tables.*

6.1.1 A Count of Rows in the Accounts Schema

I want to show a row count of all tables in the Accounts schema that I have in my database. If you remember, we have already stated that larger tables are more likely to require use of indexes, and smaller tables are less likely to need them. The Accounts schema has both large and small tables. As a result, SELECT statements and various clauses executed against different tables will very much affect how those different tables should be accessed in the interest of good performance. Current row counts for all tables in the Accounts schema are shown in Figure 6.1.

Note: Accounts schema row counts vary throughout this book because the database is continually actively adding rows, and they are occasionally recovered to the initial state shown in Figure 6.1. Row counts between tables remain relatively constant.

Figure 6.1
Row counts of
Accounts schema
tables

Table	Rows
CASHBOOK	188,185
CASHBOOKLINE	188,185
CATEGORY	13
COA	55
CUSTOMER	2,694
GENERALLEDGER	752,740
ORDERS	172,304
ORDERSLINE	540,827
PERIOD	60
PERIODSUM	0
POSTING	8
STOCK	118
STOCKMOVEMENT	570,175
STOCKSOURCE	12,083
SUBTYPE	4
SUPPLIER	3,874
TRANSACTIONS	188,185
TRANSACTIONSLINE	570,175
TYPE	6

6.1.2 Filtering with the WHERE Clause

Filtering the results of a SELECT statement using a WHERE clause implies retrieving only a subset of rows from a larger set of rows. The WHERE clause can be used to include wanted rows, exclude unwanted rows, or both.

Once again using the Employees schema, in the SQL statement following we filter rows to include only those rows we want, retrieving only those rows with ProjectType values starting with the letter *R*:

```
SELECT * FROM projecttype WHERE name LIKE 'R%';
```

Now we do the opposite and filter out rows we do not want. We get everything with values not starting with the letter *R*:

```
SELECT * FROM projecttype WHERE name NOT LIKE 'R%';
```

How does the WHERE clause affect the performance of a SELECT statement? If the sequence of expression comparisons in a WHERE clause can match an index, then it should affect performance. The WHERE clause in the previous SELECT statement does not match an index, and thus the whole table will be read. This is unimportant because the Employees schema ProjectType table is small, containing only 11 rows. However, in the case of the Accounts schema, where many of the tables have large numbers of rows, avoiding full table scans and forcing reading of indexes where possible is important.

Note: (10*g*) Query rewrite is switched on by default (using the QUERY_REWRITE_ENABLED parameter), so queries may not execute as expected.

Following is a single WHERE clause comparison condition, example SELECT statement. We will once again show the cost of the query using the EXPLAIN PLAN command. This query does an exact match on a very large table, applying an exact value to find a single row. Note the unique index scan and the low cost of the query:

```
EXPLAIN PLAN SET statement_id='TEST' FOR
SELECT * FROM stockmovement WHERE stockmovement_id = 5000;
```

Query	Cost	Rows	Bytes
SELECT STATEMENT on	3	1	24
TABLE ACCESS BY INDEX ROWID on STOCKMOVEMENT	3	1	24
INDEX UNIQUE SCAN on XPKSTOCKMOVEMENT	2	1	

Now let's compare this query with an example that uses another single-column index, searching for many more rows rather than a single row. This example consists of two queries. The first query gives us the WHERE clause literal value for the second query. The result of the first query is displayed here:

```
SQL> SELECT coa#, COUNT(coa#) "Rows" FROM generalledger GROUP
BY coa#;

COA#        Rows
-----   -----------
30001       310086
40003        66284
41000       173511
50001       169717
60001        33142
```

Now let's look at a query plan for the second query with the WHERE clause filter applied. The second query shown next finds all of the rows in one of the groups listed in the result shown earlier:

```
EXPLAIN PLAN SET statement_id='TEST' FOR
SELECT * FROM generalledger WHERE coa# = 40003;
```

Query	Cost	Rows	Bytes
SELECT STATEMENT on	493	150548	3914248
TABLE ACCESS FULL on GENERALLEDGER	493	150548	3914248

This query has an interesting result because the table is fully scanned. This is because the optimizer considers it more efficient to read the entire table rather than use the index on the COA# column, to find specific columns in the table. This is because the WHERE clause will retrieve over 60,000 rows, just shy of 10% of the entire GeneralLedger table. Over 10% in this case is enough to trigger the optimizer to execute a full table scan.

In comparison to the previous query, the two queries following read a very small table, the first with a unique index hit and the second with a full table scan as a result of the range comparison condition (<). In the second query, if the table were much larger, possibly the Optimizer would have executed an index range scan, reading the index file. However, because the table is small, the optimizer considers reading the entire table as being faster than reading the index to find what could be more than a single row:

```
EXPLAIN PLAN SET statement_id='TEST' FOR
SELECT * FROM category WHERE category_id = 1;
```

```
Query                                       Cost    Rows     Bytes
---------------------------------------- ------ ------- ---------
SELECT STATEMENT   on                        1       1        12
  TABLE ACCESS BY INDEX ROWID on CATEGORY    1       1        12
    INDEX UNIQUE SCAN on XPKCATEGORY                 1
```

The costs of both index use and the full table scan are the same because the table is small:

```
EXPLAIN PLAN SET statement_id='TEST' FOR
SELECT * FROM category WHERE category_id < 2;

Query                                     Cost    Rows     Bytes
-------------------------------------- ------ ------- ---------
SELECT STATEMENT   on                      1       1        12
  TABLE ACCESS FULL on CATEGORY            1       1        12
```

So far, we have looked at WHERE clauses containing single comparison conditions. In tables where multiple-column indexes exist, there are other factors to consider. The two queries following produce exactly the same result. Note the unique index scan on the primary key for both queries. As with the ordering of index columns in the SELECT statement, in previous versions of Oracle it is possible that the same result would not have occurred for the second query, because in the past the order of table column comparison conditions absolutely had to match the order of columns in an index. In the past, the second query shown would probably have resulted in a full table scan. The Optimizer is now more intelligent in Oracle 10*g* Database.

We had a similar result previously in this chapter, using the CHEQUE_ID and SEQ# columns on the CashbookLine table. The same applies to the WHERE clause:

```
EXPLAIN PLAN SET statement_id='TEST' FOR
SELECT * FROM ordersline WHERE order_id = 3137 AND seq# = 1;

Query                                        Cost    Rows     Bytes
----------------------------------------- ------ ------- ---------
SELECT STATEMENT   on                         3       1        17
  TABLE ACCESS BY INDEX ROWID on ORDERSLINE   3       1        17
    INDEX UNIQUE SCAN on XPKORDERSLINE        2       1
```

```
EXPLAIN PLAN SET statement_id='TEST' FOR
SELECT * FROM ordersline WHERE seq# = 1 AND order_id = 3137;
```

Query	Cost	Rows	Bytes
SELECT STATEMENT on	3	1	17
TABLE ACCESS BY INDEX ROWID on ORDERSLINE	3	1	17
INDEX UNIQUE SCAN on XPKORDERSLINE	2	1	

Let's now try a different variation. The next example query should use only the second column, in the composite index, on the STOCK_ID and SUPPLIER_ID columns, of the StockSource table. What must be done first is to find a StockSource row that is uniquely identified by both the STOCK_ID and SUPPLIER_ID columns. Let's simply create a unique row. I have not used sequences in the INSERT statements shown because I want to preserve the values of the sequence objects:

```
INSERT INTO stock(stock_id, category_id, text, min, max)
VALUES((SELECT MAX(stock_id)+1 FROM stock),1,'text',1,100);

INSERT INTO supplier(supplier_id, name, ticker)
VALUES((SELECT MAX(supplier_id)+1 FROM supplier)
,'name','TICKER');

INSERT INTO stocksource
VALUES((SELECT MAX(supplier_id) FROM supplier)
,(SELECT MAX(stock_id) FROM stock),100.00);
```

Note: The names of the columns in the Stock table (Stock.MIN and Stock.MAX) refer to minimum and maximum Stock item values required to be in stock (recorded in the Stock table), not the MIN and MAX Oracle SQL functions.

The three INSERT statements created a single row in the StockSource table such that the primary key composite index uniquely identifies the first column, the second column, and the combination of both columns. We can find those unique values by finding the maximum values for them:

```
SELECT COUNT(stock_id), MAX(stock_id)
FROM stocksource
```

```
WHERE stock_id = (SELECT MAX(stock_id) FROM stocksource)
GROUP BY stock_id;


COUNT(STOCK_ID) MAX(STOCK_ID)
--------------- -------------
              1           119


SELECT COUNT(supplier_id), MAX(supplier_id)
FROM stocksource
WHERE supplier_id = (SELECT MAX(supplier_id) FROM supplier)
GROUP BY supplier_id;


COUNT(SUPPLIER_ID) MAX(SUPPLIER_ID)
------------------ ----------------
                 1             3875
```

Now let's attempt that unique index hit on the second column of the composite index in the StockSource table, among other combinations:

```
EXPLAIN PLAN SET statement_id='TEST' FOR
SELECT * FROM stocksource WHERE supplier_id = 3875;
```

Something very interesting happens. The foreign key index on the SUPPLIER_ID column is range scanned because the WHERE clause is matched. The composite index is ignored:

Query	Cost	Rows	Bytes
SELECT STATEMENT on	2	3	30
TABLE ACCESS BY INDEX ROWID on STOCKSOURCE	2	3	30
INDEX RANGE SCAN on XFK_SS_SUPPLIER	1	3	

The query following uses the STOCK_ID column, the first column in the composite index. Once again, even though the STOCK_ID column is the first column in the composite index, the optimizer matches the WHERE clause against the nonunique foreign key index on the STOCK_ID column. Again the result is a range scan:

```
EXPLAIN PLAN SET statement_id='TEST' FOR
SELECT * FROM stocksource WHERE stock_id = 119;
```

```
Query                                          Cost    Rows     Bytes
---------------------------------------------- ----  -------  ---------
SELECT STATEMENT  on                             8      102      1020
  TABLE ACCESS BY INDEX ROWID on STOCKSOURCE     8      102      1020
    INDEX RANGE SCAN on XFK_SS_STOCK             1      102
```

The next query executes a unique index hit on the composite index because the WHERE clause exactly matches the index:

```
EXPLAIN PLAN SET statement_id='TEST' FOR
SELECT * FROM stocksource
WHERE stock_id = 119 AND supplier_id = 3875;
```

```
Query                                          Cost    Rows     Bytes
---------------------------------------------- ----  -------  ---------
SELECT STATEMENT  on                             2        1        10
  TABLE ACCESS BY INDEX ROWID on STOCKSOURCE     2        1        10
    INDEX UNIQUE SCAN on XPK_STOCKSOURCE         1    12084
```

Let's clean up and delete the unique rows we created with the INSERT statements. My script executing queries (see Appendix B) on the PLAN_TABLE contains a COMMIT command, because ROLLBACK will not work:

```
DELETE FROM StockSource WHERE supplier_id = 3875 and stock_id
= 119;
DELETE FROM supplier WHERE supplier_id = 3875;
DELETE FROM stock WHERE stock_id = 119;
COMMIT;
```

Now let's do something slightly different. The purpose of creating unique stock and supplier items in the StockSource table was to get the best possibility of producing a unique index hit. If we were to select from the StockSource table, where more than a single row existed, we would once again not get unique index hits. Depending on the number of rows found, we could get index range scans or even full table scans.

First, find maximum and minimum counts for stocks duplicated on the StockSource table:

```
SELECT * FROM(
SELECT supplier_id, COUNT(supplier_id) AS suppliers
FROM stocksource GROUP BY supplier_id
ORDER BY suppliers DESC)
WHERE ROWNUM = 1
UNION
SELECT * FROM(
SELECT supplier_id, COUNT(supplier_id) AS suppliers
FROM stocksource GROUP BY supplier_id
ORDER BY suppliers)
WHERE ROWNUM = 1;
```

There are nine suppliers with a SUPPLIER_ID column value of 2,711 and one with SUPPLIER_ID column value 2:

```
SUPPLIER_ID  SUPPLIERS
-----------  ----------
          2           1
       2711           9
```

Both of the next two queries perform index range scans. If one of the queries retrieved enough rows, as in the COA# = 40003 previously shown in this chapter, the optimizer would force a read of the entire table:

```
EXPLAIN PLAN SET statement_id='TEST' FOR
SELECT * FROM stocksource WHERE supplier_id = 2;
```

Query	Cost	Rows	Bytes
SELECT STATEMENT on	2	3	30
TABLE ACCESS BY INDEX ROWID on STOCKSOURCE	2	3	30
INDEX RANGE SCAN on XFK_SS_SUPPLIER	1	3	

```
EXPLAIN PLAN SET statement_id='TEST' FOR
SELECT * FROM stocksource WHERE supplier_id = 2711;
```

Query	Cost	Rows	Bytes
SELECT STATEMENT on	2	3	30
TABLE ACCESS BY INDEX ROWID on STOCKSOURCE	2	3	30
INDEX RANGE SCAN on XFK_SS_SUPPLIER	1	3	

Try to always do two things with WHERE clauses: (1) *try to match comparison condition column sequence with existing index column sequences (although it is not strictly necessary)*, and (2) always *try to use unique, single-column indexes wherever possible*. A single-column unique index is much more likely to produce exact hits, and an exact hit is the fastest access method.

6.1.3   Sorting with the ORDER BY Clause

The ORDER BY clause sorts the results of a query. The ORDER BY clause is always applied after all other clauses are applied, such as the WHERE and GROUP BY clauses. Without an ORDER BY clause in a SQL statement, rows will often be retrieved in the physical order in which they were added to the table. Also, rows are not always appended to the end of a table because space can be reused. Therefore, physical row order is often useless. Additionally, the sequence and content of columns in the SELECT statement, WHERE and GROUP BY clauses, can help determine returned sort order to a certain extent.

In the example following, we are sorting based on the content of the primary key index. There is no use of the index because the entire table is being read. Note the sorting applied to rows retrieved from the table, represented as a number of bytes of sorted data, as a result of re-sorting applied by the ORDER BY clause:

```
EXPLAIN PLAN SET statement_id='TEST' FOR
    SELECT customer_id, name FROM customer ORDER BY customer_id;
```

Query	Cost	Rows	Bytes	Sort
SELECT STATEMENT on	25	2694	67350	
SORT ORDER BY on	25	2694	67350	**205000**
TABLE ACCESS FULL on CUSTOMER	9	2694	67350	

In the next example, the NAME column is removed from the SELECT statement, and thus the primary key index is used. Specifying only the CUSTOMER_ID column in the SELECT statement forces use of the index. The ORDER BY clause does not force use of the index. Additionally, there is no sorting because the index is already sorted in the required order. In this case, the ORDER BY clause is unnecessary because an identical result would be obtained without it:

```
EXPLAIN PLAN SET statement_id='TEST' FOR
    SELECT customer_id FROM customer ORDER BY customer_id;
```

Query	Cost	Rows	Bytes	Sort
SELECT STATEMENT on	6	2694	10776	
INDEX FULL SCAN on XPKCUSTOMER	6	2694	10776	

The next example re-sorts the result by NAME. Again the whole table is read, so no index is used. The results are the same as for the query before the previous one. Again, there is physical sorting of the rows retrieved from the table:

```
EXPLAIN PLAN SET statement_id='TEST' FOR
    SELECT customer_id, name FROM customer ORDER BY name;
```

Query	Cost	Rows	Bytes	Sort
SELECT STATEMENT on	25	2694	67350	
SORT ORDER BY on	25	2694	67350	**205000**
TABLE ACCESS FULL on CUSTOMER	9	2694	67350	

The ORDER BY clause will re-sort results.

Note: (10g) Queries and sorts are now less case sensitive than in previous versions of Oracle Database.

6.1.3.1 Overriding WHERE with ORDER BY

The example following is interesting because the primary key composite index is used. Note that there is no sorting in the query plan. It is unnecessary to sort because the index scanned is being read in the order required by the ORDER BY clause. In this case, the optimizer ignores the ORDER BY clause:

```
EXPLAIN PLAN SET statement_id='TEST' FOR
SELECT * FROM ordersline WHERE order_id < 10
ORDER BY order_id, seq#;
```

```
Query                                      Cost    Rows     Bytes
----------------------------------------- ------- ------- ---------
SELECT STATEMENT   on                         4       3        51
  TABLE ACCESS BY INDEX ROWID on ORDERSLINE   4       3        51
    INDEX RANGE SCAN on XPKORDERSLINE         3       3
```

The second example excludes the overriding ORDER BY clause. Note how the index specified in the WHERE clause is utilized for an index range scan (there is a nonunique foreign key index on the ORDER_ID column). Thus, in the absence of the ORDER BY clause, which is present in the previous example, the optimizer sorts according to the index specified in the WHERE clause; the ORDER BY clause is apparently not needed:

```
EXPLAIN PLAN SET statement_id='TEST' FOR
SELECT * FROM ordersline WHERE order_id < 10;
```

```
Query                                      Cost    Rows     Bytes
----------------------------------------- ------- ------- ---------
SELECT STATEMENT   on                         3       3        51
  TABLE ACCESS BY INDEX ROWID on ORDERSLINE   3       3        51
    INDEX RANGE SCAN on XFK_ORDERLINE_ORDER   2       3
```

The next example adds the WHERE clause back into the query, containing the first column in the primary key index. It also uses an ORDER BY clause containing only the second column in the composite primary key index. This query has a higher cost than both the first and second queries shown before. Why? The optimizer is retrieving rows based on the WHERE clause and then being overridden by the ORDER BY clause. What is happening is that the ORDER BY clause is re-sorting the results of the WHERE clause:

```
EXPLAIN PLAN SET statement_id='TEST' FOR
SELECT * FROM ordersline WHERE order_id < 10
ORDER BY seq#;
```

```
Query                                      Cost    Rows     Bytes
----------------------------------------- ------- ------- ---------
SELECT STATEMENT   on                         5       3        51
  SORT ORDER BY on                            5       3        51
```

```
TABLE ACCESS BY INDEX ROWID on ORDERSLINE    3    3    51
  INDEX RANGE SCAN on XFK_ORDERLINE_ORDER     2    3
```

In general, it is difficult to demonstrate the performance tuning aspects of the ORDER BY clause, because re-sorting is executed after everything else has completed. The ORDER BY clause should not be allowed to conflict with the best optimizer performance choices of previous clauses. An ORDER BY clause can be used as a refinement of previous clauses, rather than used to replace those previous clauses. The WHERE clause will filter rows and the ORDER BY re-sorts those filtered rows. The ORDER BY clause can sometimes persuade the optimizer to use a less efficient key.

In some older relational databases, it was always inadvisable to apply any sorting in the ORDER BY clause that was already sorted in the WHERE clause. In Oracle Database, this is not the case, because the optimizer is now intelligent enough to often be able to utilize the best index for searching regardless. Leaving columns out of the ORDER BY clause, because they are already covered in the WHERE clause, is not necessarily a sound approach. Additionally, various other SELECT statement clauses execute sorting automatically. The GROUP BY and DISTINCT clauses are two examples that perform inherent sorting. Use inherent sorting if possible rather than doubling up with an ORDER BY clause.

Note: In the previous edition of this book, this section was more or less the same as is presented above. Now I will add to this by contradicting myself from the first edition. I considered it better for repeat readers to understand that I was partially incorrect in my assumption that an ORDER BY clause was sometimes not required (perhaps when integer surrogate primary keys are used). I feel more comfortable in contradicting myself from the first edition, rather than simply deleting this section, and pretending I never put it into the first edition. Technically speaking, this concept is not always 100% incorrect.

The reason why the ORDER BY clause is catered for by other clauses in the previous examples is because I have used surrogate keys in my database, and all the data was generated in the order of the primary key generated sequences. In other words, the data is largely already in the required sorted order physically. Figure 6.2 shows an example of some unsorted rows. Rows are sorted in the order of increasing population value.

Figure 6.2
*Rows are returned
in physical order*

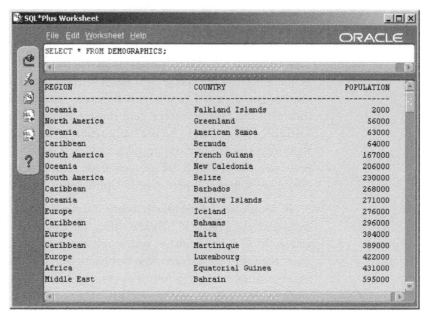

In Figure 6.3, I have attempted to force a sort using the WHERE clause, with the obvious negative result, as can be seen by the full table scan in the EXPLAIN PLAN and a slight lack of sorting of rows in Figure 6.3.

```
EXPLAIN PLAN SET statement_id='TEST' FOR
SELECT * FROM demographics WHERE country < 'D';
```

Query	Pos	Cost	Rows	Bytes
SELECT STATEMENT on	0	5	41	2009
TABLE ACCESS FULL on DEMOGRAPHICS	1	5	41	2009

The next and most obvious step is to create an index on the COUNTRY column of the table queried in Figure 6.3:

```
CREATE INDEX XAK_DEMOGRAPHICS_1 ON DEMOGRAPHICS(COUNTRY);
```

The result is as shown in Figure 6.4 and the preceding query plan. The WHERE clause allows the query to be read in the order of the index, which is sorted in the order of that index. In this case, an ORDER BY clause is not required to sort the rows in order of the name of the country. However, if too many rows were returned such that the optimizer re-sorted

Figure 6.3
*Filtered sorting
may occur on
an index*

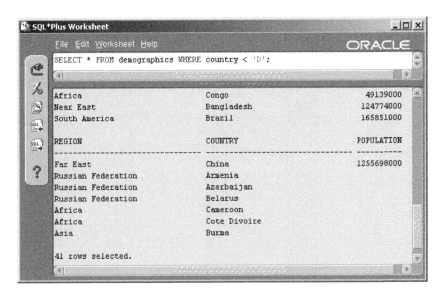

to a full table scan, then the rows would be read from the table and not the index, and as a result would no longer be sorted in the order of the COUNTRY column.

```
EXPLAIN PLAN SET statement_id='TEST' FOR
SELECT * FROM demographics WHERE country < 'D';
```

Query	Pos	Cost	Rows	Bytes
SELECT STATEMENT on	0	2	41	2009
TABLE ACCESS BY INDEX ROWID on DEMOGRAPHICS	1	2	41	2009
INDEX RANGE SCAN on XAK_DEMOGRAPHICS_1	1	1	41	

Attempting to avoid using an ORDER BY clause when it is required is risky to say the least. Contrary to my comments in the previous edition of this book, don't do it!

6.1.4 Grouping Result Sets

The GROUP BY clause can perform some inherent sorting. As with the SELECT statement, WHERE, and ORDER BY clauses, matching of GROUP BY clause column sequences with index column sequences is relevant to SQL code performance.

Figure 6.4
*Rows may be read
in index order*

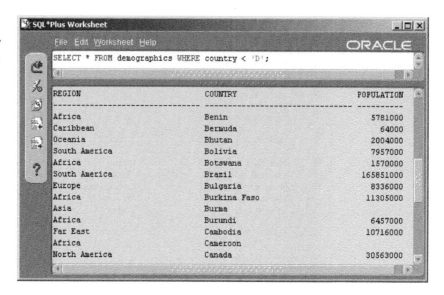

The first example aggregates based on the nonunique foreign key on the ORDER_ID column. The aggregate is executed on the ORDER_ID column into unique values for that ORDER_ID. The foreign key index is the best-performing option. The foreign key index is already sorted in the required order. The NOSORT content in the *SORT GROUP BY NOSORT on* clause implies no sorting is required using the GROUP BY clause:

```
EXPLAIN PLAN SET statement_id='TEST' FOR
SELECT order_id, COUNT(order_id) FROM ordersline
GROUP BY order_id;
```

Query	Cost	Rows	Bytes
SELECT STATEMENT on	26	172304	861520
SORT GROUP BY NOSORT on	26	172304	861520
INDEX FULL SCAN on XFK_ORDERLINE_ORDER	26	540827	2704135

The next example uses both columns in the primary key index because the composite index is a better option. However, because the composite index is much larger in both size and rows, the cost is much higher:

```
EXPLAIN PLAN SET statement_id='TEST' FOR
SELECT order_id, seq#, COUNT(order_id) FROM ordersline
GROUP BY order_id, seq#;
```

```
Query                                Cost    Rows      Bytes
----------------------------------   ------  -------   ---------
SELECT STATEMENT   on                1217    540827    4326616
  SORT GROUP BY NOSORT on            1217    540827    4326616
    INDEX FULL SCAN on XPKORDERSLINE 1217    540827    4326616
```

In the next case, we reverse the order of the columns in the GROUP BY sequence. As you can see, there is no effect on cost. The optimizer manages to match against the primary key composite index:

```
EXPLAIN PLAN SET statement_id='TEST' FOR
SELECT order_id, seq#, COUNT(order_id) FROM ordersline
GROUP BY seq#, order_id;
```

```
Query                                Cost    Rows      Bytes
----------------------------------   ------  -------   ---------
SELECT STATEMENT   on                1217    540827    4326616
  SORT GROUP BY NOSORT on            1217    540827    4326616
    INDEX FULL SCAN on XPKORDERSLINE 1217    540827    4326616
```

6.1.4.1   Sorting with the **GROUP BY** Clause

The next example uses a nonindexed column to aggregate, and the whole table is accessed. Now *NOSORT* is no longer included in the *SORT GROUP BY on* section of the query plan. The GROUP BY clause is now performing sorting on the AMOUNT column:

```
EXPLAIN PLAN SET statement_id='TEST' FOR
SELECT amount, COUNT(amount) FROM ordersline
GROUP BY amount;
```

```
Query                              Cost   Rows     Bytes       Sort
--------------------------------   -----  -------  ---------   ---------
SELECT STATEMENT   on              4832   62371    374226
  SORT GROUP BY on                 4832   62371    374226      7283000
    TABLE ACCESS FULL on ORDERSLINE 261   540827   3244962
```

Let's examine GROUP BY clause sorting a little further. Sometimes it is possible to avoid sorting forced by the ORDER BY clause, by ordering column names in the GROUP BY clause. Rows will be sorted based on the contents of the GROUP BY clause:

```
EXPLAIN PLAN SET statement_id='TEST' FOR
SELECT amount, COUNT(amount) FROM ordersline
GROUP BY amount
ORDER BY amount;
```

In this case the ORDER BY clause is ignored:

Query	Cost	Rows	Bytes
SELECT STATEMENT on	6722	62371	374226
SORT GROUP BY on	6722	62371	374226
TABLE ACCESS FULL on ORDERSLINE	1023	540827	3244962

Inherent sorting in the GROUP BY clause can sometimes be used to avoid extra sorting when using an ORDER BY clause.

As you can see in the following example, without the GROUP BY clause aggregation, the query plan contains the step *SORT ORDER BY on*, as opposed to *SORT GROUP BY on* (in the previous example), proving that the GROUP BY clause does perform some sorting:

```
EXPLAIN PLAN SET statement_id='TEST' FOR
SELECT amount FROM ordersline
ORDER BY amount;
```

Query	Pos	Cost	Rows	Bytes
SELECT STATEMENT on	0	3865	540827	2704135
SORT ORDER BY on	1	3865	540827	2704135
TABLE ACCESS FULL on ORDERSLINE	1	1847	540827	2704135

6.1.4.2 Using DISTINCT

DISTINCT retrieves the first value from a repeating group. When there are multiple repeating groups, DISTINCT will retrieve the first row from each group. DISTINCT will always require a sort in order to return all repeating groups in the correct sequence. DISTINCT can operate on a single or on multiple columns.

For example, the following query executes a sort in order to find the first value in each group:

```
EXPLAIN PLAN SET statement_id='TEST' FOR
SELECT DISTINCT(stock_id) FROM stockmovement;
```

Query	Cost	Rows	Bytes
SELECT STATEMENT on	704	118	472
SORT UNIQUE on	**704**	118	472
INDEX FAST FULL SCAN on XFK_SM_STOCK	4	570175	2280700

This second example has the DISTINCT clause removed and does not execute a sort. As a result, this query has a much lower cost. DISTINCT will sort regardless:

```
EXPLAIN PLAN SET statement_id='TEST' FOR
SELECT stock_id FROM stockmovement;
```

Query	Cost	Rows	Bytes
SELECT STATEMENT on	4	570175	2280700
INDEX FAST FULL SCAN on XFK_SM_STOCK	4	570175	2280700

As far as performance tuning is concerned, ***DISTINCT will always require a sort***, which slows performance.

6.1.4.3   The HAVING Clause

Using the COUNT function as shown in the first two examples following, there is little difference in performance. The slight difference is caused by the application of the filter on the HAVING clause, allowing return of fewer rows. First we exclude the HAVING clause:

```
EXPLAIN PLAN SET statement_id='TEST' FOR
   SELECT customer_id, COUNT(order_id) FROM orders
GROUP BY customer_id;
```

Query	Cost	Rows	Bytes
SELECT STATEMENT on	**298**	2693	5386
SORT GROUP BY on	298	2693	5386
TABLE ACCESS FULL on ORDERS	112	172304	344608

Second, the mere act of using the HAVING clause to return fewer rows helps performance:

```
EXPLAIN PLAN SET statement_id='TEST' FOR
    SELECT customer_id, COUNT(order_id) FROM orders
GROUP BY customer_id
HAVING customer_id < 10;
```

Query	Cost	Rows	Bytes
SELECT STATEMENT on	**296**	10	20
FILTER on			
SORT GROUP BY on	296	10	20
TABLE ACCESS FULL on ORDERS	112	172304	344608

On the contrary, the next two examples use the SUM function as opposed to the COUNT function and have a much bigger difference in cost. This is because the COUNT function is faster, especially when counting on indexes or using the asterisk option (COUNT(*)).

Note: The COUNT function will be demonstrated in detail later in this chapter. The SUM function does a lot of processing that the COUNT function does not.

Once again, we begin by excluding the HAVING clause:

```
EXPLAIN PLAN SET statement_id='TEST' FOR
    SELECT customer_id, SUM(order_id) FROM orders
GROUP BY customer_id;
```

Query	Cost	Rows	Bytes	Sort
SELECT STATEMENT on	**1383**	2693	18851	
SORT GROUP BY on	1383	2693	18851	2827000
TABLE ACCESS FULL on ORDERS	112	172304	1206128	

Using the HAVING clause to return fewer rows helps performance again, as indicated by the *FILTER on* clause:

```
EXPLAIN PLAN SET statement_id='TEST' FOR
    SELECT customer_id, SUM(order_id) FROM orders
GROUP BY customer_id
HAVING customer_id < 10;
```

Query	Cost	Rows	Bytes	Sort
SELECT STATEMENT on	**366**	10	70	
FILTER on				
SORT GROUP BY on	366	10	70	
TABLE ACCESS FULL on ORDERS	112	172304	1206128	

6.1.4.3.1   (10g) *The MODEL Clause*

The MODEL clause extends the GROUP BY clause, allowing display of data into multiple dimensions, including calculations between rows. It is very similar to a spreadsheet program such as Excel. The MODEL clause provides additional OLAP-type functionality and is more applicable to data warehousing as opposed to Internet OLTP databases. However, using the MODEL clause can possibly reduce the number of tables in mutable joins and remove the need for set operators such as UNION, INTERSECT, and MINUS. Set operators can help merge multiple queries together.

The HAVING clause filter can help performance because it filters, allowing the return and processing of fewer rows. The ***HAVING clause filtering*** shown in the query plans shows that HAVING clause filtering ***is always executed after the GROUP BY sorting process***.

6.1.4.4   **ROLLUP, CUBE, and GROUPING SETS**

The ROLLUP, CUBE, and GROUPING SETS clauses can be used to create breaks and subtotals for groups. The GROUPING SETS clause can be used to restrict the results of ROLLUP and CUBE clauses. Before the advent of the ROLLUP and CUBE clauses, producing the same types of results would involve extremely complex SQL statements. These queries involved extensive use of temporary tables, or perhaps even of PL/SQL. ROLLUP, CUBE, and GROUPING SETS clauses are more applicable to reporting and data warehouse functionality, but they can have significant benefits to performance.

The following examples simply show the use of the ROLLUP, CUBE, and GROUPING SETS clauses:

```
SELECT type, subtype, SUM(balance+ytd)FROM coa
GROUP BY type, subtype;

SELECT type, subtype, SUM(balance+ytd)FROM coa
GROUP BY ROLLUP (type, subtype);

SELECT type, subtype, SUM(balance+ytd)FROM coa
GROUP BY CUBE (type, subtype);

SELECT type, subtype, SUM(balance+ytd)FROM coa
GROUP BY GROUPING SETS ((type, subtype), (type), (subtype));
```

Let's take a simple example using a ROLLUP clause. In the following example, the ROLLUP clause creates subtotals for each grouped change, based on the GROUP BY clause columns. The result is shown in Figure 6.5.

Figure 6.5
A ROLLUP clause can be used to produce subtotals for each GROUP BY clause grouping change

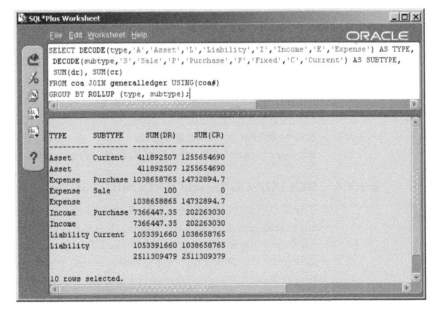

This is the query plan for the query including the ROLLUP clause, as shown in Figure 6.5:

```
EXPLAIN PLAN SET statement_id='TEST' FOR
SELECT DECODE(type,'A','Asset','L','Liability','I','Income','E','Expense') AS
TYPE,
```

```
    DECODE(subtype,'S','Sale','P','Purchase','F','Fixed','C','Current') AS
    SUBTYPE,
     coa#, SUM(dr), SUM(cr)
    FROM coa JOIN generalledger USING(coa#)
    GROUP BY type, subtype, coa#;
```

Query	Pos	Cost	Rows	Bytes
SELECT STATEMENT on	0	**3979**	12	288
SORT GROUP BY ROLLUP on	1	3979	12	288
HASH JOIN on	1	3472	739469	17747256
TABLE ACCESS FULL on COA	1	6	55	550
TABLE ACCESS FULL on GENERALLEDGER	2	3408	739469	10352566

One method of reproducing the query shown in Figure 6.5, without the benefit of the ROLLUP clause, is to use a UNION clause to merge the various required queries together. Even though this query does not need resorting, an ORDER BY clause is sometimes required to ensure that rows are sorted properly. The ORDER BY clause is applied to the rows resulting from the UNION, not each or either of the two merged queries. Not using a ROLLUP clause for the previous query results in a hugely costly query plan like the following, reading all of the rows in both tables three times to retrieve all the equivalent totals:

Query	Pos	Cost	Rows	Bytes
SELECT STATEMENT on	0	**17466**	17	396
SORT UNIQUE on	1	17466	17	396
UNION-ALL on	1			
HASH GROUP BY on	1	4485	12	288
HASH JOIN on	1	3472	739469	17747256
TABLE ACCESS FULL on COA	1	6	55	550
TABLE ACCESS FULL on GENERALLEDGER	2	3408	739469	10352566
HASH GROUP BY on	2	4482	4	88
HASH JOIN on	1	3469	739469	16268318
VIEW on index$_join$_004	1	3	55	440
HASH JOIN on	1			
INDEX FAST FULL SCAN on XFK_COA_TYPE	1	1	55	440
INDEX FAST FULL SCAN on XPK_COA	2	1	55	440
TABLE ACCESS FULL on GENERALLEDGER	2	3408	739469	10352566
SORT AGGREGATE on	3	8499	1	20

HASH JOIN on	1	3467	739469	14789380
INDEX FULL SCAN on XPK_COA	1	1	55	330
TABLE ACCESS FULL on GENERALLEDGER	2	3408	739469	10352566

Note: One of my other books covering Oracle Database data warehouse tuning[1] covers the topic of GROUP BY clause extensions in great detail.

In general, *the GROUP BY clause can perform some sorting* if it matches indexing. *Filtering aggregate results with the HAVING clause can help increase performance* by filtering aggregated results of the GROUP BY clause.

6.1.5 The FOR UPDATE Clause

The FOR UPDATE clause is a nice feature of SQL because it allows locking of selected rows during a transaction. Rarely, rows selected should be locked if there are dependent following changes in a single transaction, requiring selected data to remain the same during the course of that transaction.

```
SELECT ...
   FOR UPDATE OF [ [schema.]table.]column [, ... ] ] [ NOWAIT |
WAIT n ]
```

Note the two WAIT and NOWAIT options in the preceding syntax. When a lock is encountered, NOWAIT forces an abort. The WAIT option will force a wait for a number of seconds. The default simply waits until a row is available.

With respect to tuning and concurrent multiuser capability of applications, the FOR UPDATE clause should be avoided if possible. Perhaps the data model could be too granular, necessitating the need to lock rows in various tables during the course of a transaction across multiple tables. Using the FOR UPDATE clause is not good for the efficiency of SQL code in general because of potential locks and possible resulting waits for and by other concurrently executing transactions.

6.2   Using Functions

The most relevant thing to say about functions is that they should not be used where you expect a SQL statement to use an index. There are function-based indexes of course, which contain the resulting value of an expression. An index search against that function-based index will search the index for the value of the expression.

Let's take a quick look at a few specific functions.

6.2.1   The COUNT Function

For older versions of Oracle Database, the COUNT function has been recommended as performing better when used in different ways. Prior to Oracle Database 10*g*, the COUNT(*) function using the asterisk was the fastest form, because the asterisk option was specifically tuned to avoid any sorting. Let's look at each of four different methods and show that they are all the same using both the EXPLAIN PLAN command and time testing. We will use the GeneralLedger table in the Accounts schema because it has the largest number of rows.

Notice how all of the query plans for all four following COUNT function options are identical. Additionally, there is no sorting on anything but the resulting single row produced by the COUNT function, the sort on the aggregate.

Using the asterisk:

```
EXPLAIN PLAN SET statement_id='TEST' FOR
    SELECT COUNT(*) FROM generalledger;
```

Query	Cost	Rows
SELECT STATEMENT on	382	1
SORT AGGREGATE on		1
INDEX FAST FULL SCAN on XPK_GENERALLEDGER	382	752825

Forcing the use of a unique index:

```
EXPLAIN PLAN SET statement_id='TEST' FOR
    SELECT COUNT(generalledger_id) FROM generalledger;
```

```
Query                                              Cost      Rows
------------------------------------------ ---------- --------
SELECT STATEMENT   on                               382         1
  SORT AGGREGATE on                                             1
    INDEX FAST FULL SCAN on XPK_GENERALLEDGER       382    752825
```

Using a constant value:

```
EXPLAIN PLAN SET statement_id='TEST' FOR
    SELECT COUNT(1) FROM generalledger;
```

```
Query                                              Cost      Rows
------------------------------------------ ---------- --------
SELECT STATEMENT   on                               382         1
  SORT AGGREGATE on                                             1
    INDEX FAST FULL SCAN on XPK_GENERALLEDGER       382    752825
```

Using a nonindexed column:

```
EXPLAIN PLAN SET statement_id='TEST' FOR
    SELECT COUNT(dr) FROM generalledger;
```

```
Query                                              Cost      Rows
------------------------------------------ ---------- --------
SELECT STATEMENT   on                               382         1
  SORT AGGREGATE on                                             1
    INDEX FAST FULL SCAN on XPK_GENERALLEDGER       382    752825
```

Now with time testing, in the following example, I have simply executed the four COUNT function options with SET TIMING set to ON in SQL*Plus. Executing these four SQL statements twice will ensure that all data is loaded into memory and that consistent results are obtained:

```
SQL> SELECT COUNT(*) FROM generalledger;

  COUNT(*)
----------
    752741
```

Elapsed: 00:00:01.01

```
SQL> SELECT COUNT(generalledger_id) FROM generalledger;

COUNT(GENERALLEDGER_ID)
-----------------------
                 752741
```

Elapsed: 00:00:01.01

```
SQL> SELECT COUNT(1) FROM generalledger;

  COUNT(1)
----------
    752741
```

Elapsed: 00:00:01.01

```
SQL> SELECT COUNT(dr) FROM generalledger;

  COUNT(DR)
----------
    752741
```

Elapsed: 00:00:01.01

As you can see from these time tests, the COUNT function will perform the same no matter which method is used. In the latest version of Oracle Database, different forms of the COUNT function will perform identically. It is apparent that no form of the COUNT function is better tuned than any other. ***All forms of the COUNT function perform the same; using an asterisk, a constant or a column, regardless of column indexing, the primary key index is always used***.

6.2.2 **The DECODE Function**

The DECODE function can be used to replace composite SQL statements using a set operator such as UNION (the DECODE function was used previously in this chapter to describe a ROLLUP clause query). The Accounts Stock table has a QTYONHAND column, which denotes how many items of a particular stock item are currently in stock. Negative QTYONHAND values indicate that items have been ordered by customers but not yet received from suppliers.

The first example uses four full reads of the Stock table and concatenates the results together using UNION set operators:

```
EXPLAIN PLAN SET statement_id='TEST' FOR
SELECT stock_id||' Out of Stock' FROM stock WHERE qtyonhand <=0
UNION
SELECT stock_id||' Under Stocked' FROM stock
WHERE qtyonhand BETWEEN 1 AND min-1
UNION
SELECT stock_id||' Stocked' FROM stock
WHERE qtyonhand BETWEEN min AND max
UNION
SELECT stock_id||' Over Stocked' FROM stock
WHERE qtyonhand > max;
```

Query	Pos	Cost	Rows	Bytes
SELECT STATEMENT on	12	12	123	1543
SORT UNIQUE on	1	12	123	1543
UNION-ALL on	1			
TABLE ACCESS FULL on STOCK	1	1	4	32
TABLE ACCESS FULL on STOCK	2	1	1	11
TABLE ACCESS FULL on STOCK	3	1	28	420
TABLE ACCESS FULL on STOCK	4	1	90	1080

This second example replaces the UNION set operators (four full table scan reads) with a single full table scan using nested DECODE functions. DECODE can be used to improve performance:

```
EXPLAIN PLAN SET statement_id='TEST' FOR
SELECT stock_id||' '||
DECODE(SIGN(qtyonhand)
      ,-1,'Out of Stock',0,'Out of Stock'
      ,1,DECODE(SIGN(qtyonhand-min)
      ,-1,'Under Stocked',0,'Stocked'
      ,1,DECODE(sign(qtyonhand-max)
      ,-1,'Stocked',0,'Stocked',1,'Over Stocked'
      )
   )
) FROM stock;
```

```
Query                          Pos   Cost    Rows    Bytes
----------------------------  -----  ------  ------  ---------
SELECT STATEMENT   on            1      1     118     1770
   TABLE ACCESS FULL on STOCK    1      1     118     1770
```

Using the DECODE function as a replacement for multiple query set operators is good for performance but should only be used in extreme cases, such as in the UNION clause joining SQL statements shown previously.

6.2.3 Datatype Conversions

Datatype conversions are a problem and will conflict with existing indexes, unless function-based indexes are available and can be created. Generally, if a function is executed in a WHERE clause, or anywhere else that can utilize an index, a full table scan is likely. This leads to inefficiency. There is some capability in Oracle SQL for implicit datatype conversion. However, use of functions in SQL statements will often cause the optimizer to miss the use of indexes and perform poorly.

The most obvious datatype conversion concerns dates. Date fields in all of the databases I have used are stored internally as Julian numbers. A Julian number or date is an integer value, measured from a database-specific date in seconds. When retrieving a date value in a tool such as SQL*Plus, there is usually a default date format. The internal date value is converted to that default format. The conversion is implicit, automatic, and transparent:

```
SELECT SYSDATE, TO_CHAR(SYSDATE,'J') "Julian" FROM DUAL;


  SYSDATE    Julian
  ---------  -------
  03-MAR-03  2452702
```

Now for the sake of demonstration, I will create an index on the GeneralLedger DTE column:

```
CREATE INDEX ak_gl_dte ON GENERALLEDGER(DTE);
```

It is difficult to demonstrate an index hit with a key such as this because the date is a datestamp, as well as a simple date. A simple date format such as MM/DD/YYYY excludes a timestamp. Simple dates and datestamps (timestamps) are almost impossible to match, so I will use SYSDATE to avoid a check against a simple formatted date. Both the GeneralLedger DTE column and SYSDATE are timestamps because the date column in the table was created using values generated by SYSDATE. We are only trying to show optimizer query plans without finding rows.

The first example hits the new index I created and has a very low cost:

```
EXPLAIN PLAN SET statement_id='TEST' FOR
  SELECT * FROM generalledger WHERE dte = SYSDATE;
```

Query	Cost	Rows	Bytes
SELECT STATEMENT on	**2**	593	15418
TABLE ACCESS BY INDEX ROWID on GENERALLEDGER	2	593	15418
INDEX RANGE SCAN on AK_GL_DTE	1	593	

This second example does not hit the index because the TO_CHAR datatype conversion is completely inconsistent with the datatype of the index. As a result, the cost is much higher:

```
EXPLAIN PLAN SET statement_id='TEST' FOR
   SELECT * FROM generalledger
WHERE TO_CHAR(dte, 'YYYY/MM/DD') = '2002/08/21';
```

Query	Cost	Rows	Bytes
SELECT STATEMENT on	**493**	7527	195702
TABLE ACCESS FULL on GENERALLEDGER	493	7527	195702

Another factor to consider with datatype conversions is making sure that they are not placed onto columns. Convert literal values that are not a part of the database if possible. In order to demonstrate this, I am going to add a zip code column to my Supplier table, create an index on that zip code column, and then regenerate statistics for the Supplier table. I do not need to add values to the zip code column to prove my point.

```
ALTER TABLE supplier ADD(zip NUMBER(5));
CREATE INDEX ak_sp_zip ON supplier(zip);
ANALYZE TABLE supplier COMPUTE STATISTICS;
```

Now we can show two examples. The first example uses an index because there is no datatype conversion on the column in the table:

```
EXPLAIN PLAN SET statement_id='TEST' FOR
    SELECT * FROM supplier WHERE zip = TO_NUMBER('94002');
```

Query	Cost	Rows	Bytes
SELECT STATEMENT on	1	1	142
TABLE ACCESS BY INDEX ROWID on SUPPLIER	1	1	142
INDEX RANGE SCAN on AK_SP_ZIP	1	1	

The second example reads the entire table because the conversion is on the column:

```
EXPLAIN PLAN SET statement_id='TEST' FOR
    SELECT * FROM supplier WHERE TO_CHAR(zip) = '94002';
```

Query	Cost	Rows	Bytes
SELECT STATEMENT on	13	1	142
TABLE ACCESS FULL on SUPPLIER	13	1	142

Oracle SQL does not generally allow implicit type conversions, but there is some capacity for automatic conversion of strings to integers, if a string contains an integer value. Using implicit type conversions is very bad programming practice, and as a programmer I do not recommend it. Programmers should never rely on another tool to do their job for them. Explicit coding is less likely to meet with potential errors in the future. It is better to be precise because computers are always precise, doing exactly as you instruct them to. Implicit type conversion is included in Oracle SQL for ease of programming. Ease of program coding is a top-down application to database design approach, totally contradictory to database tuning. Using a database from the point of view of how the application can most easily be coded is not favorable to eventual production performance. Do not use implicit type conversions. As can be seen in the following integer conversion examples, implicit type conversions do not appear to make any difference to optimizer costs:

```
EXPLAIN PLAN SET statement_id='TEST' FOR
```

```
SELECT * FROM supplier WHERE supplier_id = 3801;
```

Query	Cost	Rows	Bytes
SELECT STATEMENT on	**2**	1	142
TABLE ACCESS BY INDEX ROWID on SUPPLIER	2	1	142
INDEX UNIQUE SCAN on XPK_SUPPLIER	1	3874	

```
EXPLAIN PLAN SET statement_id='TEST' FOR
    SELECT * FROM supplier WHERE supplier_id = '3801';
```

Query	Cost	Rows	Bytes
SELECT STATEMENT on	**2**	1	142
TABLE ACCESS BY INDEX ROWID on SUPPLIER	2	1	142
INDEX UNIQUE SCAN on XPK_SUPPLIER	1	3874	

In short, ***try to avoid using any type of data conversion function in any part of a SQL statement, which could potentially match an index***, especially if you are trying to assist performance by matching appropriate indexes.

6.2.4   Using Functions in Queries

Now let's expand on the use of functions by examining their use in all of the clauses of a SELECT statement.

6.2.4.1   Functions in the **SELECT** Statement

First, let's put a datatype conversion into a SELECT statement, which uses an index. As we can see in the two examples following, use of the index is not affected by the datatype conversion placed into the SELECT statement:

```
EXPLAIN PLAN SET statement_id='TEST' FOR
    SELECT customer_id FROM customer;
```

Query	Cost	Rows	Bytes
SELECT STATEMENT on	1	2694	10776
INDEX FAST FULL SCAN on XPKCUSTOMER	1	2694	10776

And here's the datatype conversion:

```
EXPLAIN PLAN SET statement_id='TEST' FOR
    SELECT TO_CHAR(customer_id) FROM customer;
```

Query	Cost	Rows	Bytes
SELECT STATEMENT on	1	2694	10776
INDEX FAST FULL SCAN on XPKCUSTOMER	1	2694	10776

6.2.4.2   Functions in the WHERE Clause

Now let's examine the WHERE clause. In the two examples, the only difference is in the type of index scan utilized. Traditionally, the unique index hit produces an exact match, and it should be faster. A later chapter will examine the difference between these two types of index reads:

```
EXPLAIN PLAN SET statement_id='TEST' FOR
    SELECT customer_id FROM customer WHERE customer_id = 100;
```

Query	Cost	Rows	Bytes
SELECT STATEMENT on	1	1	4
INDEX UNIQUE SCAN on XPKCUSTOMER	1	1	4

And here's the datatype conversion:

```
EXPLAIN PLAN SET statement_id='TEST' FOR
    SELECT customer_id FROM customer
WHERE TO_CHAR(customer_id) = '100';
```

Query	Cost	Rows	Bytes
SELECT STATEMENT on	1	1	4
INDEX FAST FULL SCAN on XPKCUSTOMER	1	1	4

6.2.4.3   Functions in the ORDER BY Clause

The ORDER BY clause can utilize indexing well, as already seen in this chapter, as long as WHERE clause index matching is not compromised. Let's keep it simple. Looking at the two following examples, it should suffice to say that it might be a bad idea to include functions in ORDER BY clauses:

```
EXPLAIN PLAN SET statement_id='TEST' FOR
SELECT * FROM generalledger ORDER BY coa#;
```

Query	Cost	Rows	Bytes	Sort
SELECT STATEMENT on	**826**	752740	19571240	
TABLE ACCESS BY INDEX ROWID on GL	826	752740	19571240	
INDEX FULL SCAN on XFK_GL_COA#	26	752740		

An index is not used in the second query, and consequently the cost is much higher:

```
EXPLAIN PLAN SET statement_id='TEST' FOR
   SELECT * FROM generalledger ORDER BY TO_CHAR(coa#);
```

Query	Cost	Rows	Bytes	Sort
SELECT STATEMENT on	**19070**	752740	19571240	
SORT ORDER BY on	19070	752740	19571240	60474000
TABLE ACCESS FULL on GENERALLEDGER	493	752740	19571240	

The next query shows an interesting twist to using the same datatype conversion in these two examples, but with the conversion in the SELECT statement, and setting the ORDER BY clause to sort by position rather than using the TO_CHAR(COA#) datatype conversion. This third example is lower in cost than the second example because the conversion is done on selection, and ORDER BY resorting is executed after data retrieval. In other words, in this example the ORDER BY clause does not affect the data access method:

```
EXPLAIN PLAN SET statement_id='TEST' FOR
   SELECT TO_CHAR(coa#), dte, dr cr FROM generalledger ORDER BY 1;
```

Query	Cost	Rows	Bytes	Sort
SELECT STATEMENT on	**12937**	752740	13549320	
SORT ORDER BY on	12937	752740	13549320	42394000
TABLE ACCESS FULL on GENERALLEDGER	493	752740	13549320	

6.2.4.4 Functions in the GROUP BY Clause

Using functions in GROUP BY clauses will slow performance, as shown in the following two examples:

```
EXPLAIN PLAN SET statement_id='TEST' FOR
SELECT order_id, COUNT(order_id) FROM ordersline
GROUP BY order_id;
```

Query	Cost	Rows	Bytes
SELECT STATEMENT on	**26**	172304	861520
SORT GROUP BY **NOSORT** on	26	172304	861520
INDEX FULL SCAN on XFK_ORDERLINE_ORDER	26	540827	2704135

And here's the function:

```
EXPLAIN PLAN SET statement_id='TEST' FOR
SELECT TO_CHAR(order_id), COUNT(order_id) FROM ordersline
GROUP BY TO_CHAR(order_id);
```

Query	Cost	Rows	Bytes	Sort
SELECT STATEMENT on	**3708**	172304	861520	
SORT GROUP BY on	3708	172304	861520	8610000
INDEX FAST FULL SCAN on XFK_ORDERLINE_ORDER	4	540827	2704135	

> *When using functions in SQL statements, it is best to keep the functions away from any columns involving index matching.*

6.3 Pseudocolumns

Pseudocolumns can be used to increase performance.

6.3.1 Sequences

A sequence is often used to create unique integer identifiers as primary keys for tables (surrogate keys). A sequence is an Oracle Database object accessed as sequence.NEXTVAL and sequence.CURRVAL. Using the Accounts

schema Supplier table, we can show how a sequence is an efficient method
in this case:

```
EXPLAIN PLAN SET statement_id='TEST' FOR
INSERT INTO supplier (supplier_id, name, ticker)
VALUES(supplier_seq.NEXTVAL,'A new supplier', 'TICK');
```

Query	Cost	Rows	Bytes
INSERT STATEMENT on	1	11	176
SEQUENCE on SUPPLIER_SEQ			

And now without using the sequence object:

```
EXPLAIN PLAN SET statement_id='TEST' FOR
INSERT INTO supplier (supplier_id, name, ticker)
VALUES((SELECT MAX(supplier_id)+1
FROM supplier), 'A new supplier', 'TICK');
```

Query	Cost	Rows	Bytes
INSERT STATEMENT on	1	11	176

This query plan is the same but missing details on the subquery. That is
a problem. Notice in the previous query that a subquery is used to find the
next SUPPLIER_ID value, using the MAX function. This subquery is not
evident in the query plan. Let's do a query plan for the subquery as well:

```
EXPLAIN PLAN SET statement_id='TEST' FOR
   SELECT MAX(supplier_id)+1 FROM supplier;
```

Query	Cost	Rows	Bytes
SELECT STATEMENT on	2	1	3
SORT AGGREGATE on		1	3
INDEX FULL SCAN (MIN/MAX) on XPK_SUPPLIER	2	3874	11622

We can see that the subquery will cause extra work. The query plan containing the subquery seems to have difficulty with subqueries, so it is diffi-

cult to tell the exact cost of using the subquery. *Use sequences for unique integer identifiers: they are centralized, more controllable, more easily maintained, and very likely to perform better than other methods of counting.*

6.3.2   ROWID Pointers

A ROWID is a logically unique database pointer to a row in a table. When a row is found using an index, the index is searched to find its ROWID value. After the row is found in the index, the ROWID is extracted from the index and used to find the exact logical location of the row in its respective table. Accessing rows using the ROWID pseudocolumn is probably the fastest row-access method in Oracle Database, because it is a direct pointer to a unique address. The downside about ROWID pointers is that they do not necessarily point at the same rows in perpetuity because they are relative to datafile, tablespace, block, and row. These values can change. Never store a ROWID in a table column as a pointer to other tables or rows if data or structure will be changing in the database. If ROWID pointers can be used for data access, they can be blindingly fast, but this is not recommended by Oracle Corporation.

6.3.3   ROWNUM

A ROWNUM is a row number or a sequential counter representing the order in which a row is returned from a query. ROWNUM can be used to restrict the number of rows returned. ROWNUM can be used in numerous interesting ways. The example following allows creation of a new table from another table, including all constraints, but excluding any rows. This is a useful and fast method of making an empty copy of a very large table:

```
CREATE TABLE tmp AS SELECT * FROM generalledger WHERE ROWNUM <
1;
```

One point to note is as in the following example. A ROWNUM restriction is applied in the WHERE clause. The ROWNUM restriction is not applied to the sorted output because the ORDER BY clause occurs after the WHERE clause:

```
SELECT * FROM customer WHERE ROWNUM < 25 ORDER BY name;
```

This is the solution to this problem:

```
SELECT * FROM (SELECT * FROM customer ORDER BY name) WHERE
ROWNUM < 25;
```

6.4   Comparison Conditions

Different comparison conditions can sometimes have vastly different effects on the performance of SQL statements. Let's examine each in turn, with various options and recommendations for potential improvement. These are the comparison conditions:

- Equi-, anti-, and range

    - expr { [!]= | > | < | <= | >= } expr
    - expr [NOT] BETWEEN expr AND expr

- LIKE pattern matching

    - expr [NOT] LIKE expr

- Set membership

    - expr [NOT] IN expr
    - expr [NOT] EXISTS expr

Note: (10g) IN is now called an IN rather than a set membership condition in order to limit confusion with object collection MEMBER conditions.

- Groups

    - expr [= | != | > | < | >= | <=] [ANY | SOME | ALL] expr

6.4.1   Equi-, Anti-, and Range

Using an equals sign (equi) is the fastest comparison condition if a unique index exists. Any type of anti comparison, such as != or NOT, is looking for what is *not* in a table, so the entire table must be read regardless (sometimes full index scans can be used). Range comparisons scan indexes for ranges of rows. Let's look at some examples.

This example performs a unique index hit; using the equals sign, an exact hit single row is found:

```
EXPLAIN PLAN SET statement_id='TEST' FOR
   SELECT * FROM generalledger WHERE generalledger_id = 100;
```

Query	Cost	Rows	Bytes
SELECT STATEMENT on	3	1	26
TABLE ACCESS BY INDEX ROWID on GENERALLEDGER	3	1	26
INDEX UNIQUE SCAN on XPKGENERALLEDGER	2	1	

The anti (!=) comparison finds everything but the single row specified and reads the entire table:

```
EXPLAIN PLAN SET statement_id='TEST' FOR
   SELECT * FROM generalledger WHERE generalledger_id != 100;
```

Query	Pos	Cost	Rows	Bytes
SELECT STATEMENT on	493	493	752739	19571214
TABLE ACCESS FULL on GENERAL	1	493	752739	19571214

In the next case, using the range (<) comparison searches a range of index values rather than a single unique index value:

```
EXPLAIN PLAN SET statement_id='TEST' FOR
   SELECT * FROM generalledger WHERE generalledger_id < 10;
```

Query	Cost	Rows	Bytes
SELECT STATEMENT on	4	1	26
TABLE ACCESS BY INDEX ROWID on GENERALLEDGER	4	1	26
INDEX RANGE SCAN on XPKGENERALLEDGER	3	1	

In the next example, the whole table is read rather than using an index range scan because most of the table will be read. The optimizer considers reading the table as being faster:

```
EXPLAIN PLAN SET statement_id='TEST' FOR
   SELECT * FROM generalledger WHERE generalledger_id >= 100;
```

Query	Pos	Cost	Rows	Bytes
SELECT STATEMENT on	493	493	752740	19571240
TABLE ACCESS FULL on GENERALLEDGER	1	493	752740	19571240

In this next example, the BETWEEN comparison causes a range scan on an index because the range of rows is small enough to not warrant a full table scan:

```
EXPLAIN PLAN SET statement_id='TEST' FOR
SELECT * FROM generalledger
WHERE generalledger_id BETWEEN 100 AND 200;
```

Query	Cost	Rows	Bytes
SELECT STATEMENT on	4	1	26
TABLE ACCESS BY INDEX ROWID on GENERALLEDGER	4	1	26
INDEX RANGE SCAN on XPKGENERALLEDGER	3	1	

6.4.2 LIKE Pattern Matching

The approach in the query plan used by the optimizer will depend on how many rows are retrieved and how the pattern match is constructed.

This query finds a single row:

```
EXPLAIN PLAN SET statement_id='TEST' FOR
SELECT * FROM supplier WHERE name like '24/7 Real Media, Inc.';
```

Query	Cost	Rows	Bytes
SELECT STATEMENT on	2	1	142
TABLE ACCESS BY INDEX ROWID on SUPPLIER	2	1	142
INDEX UNIQUE SCAN on AK_SUPPLIER_NAME	1	1	

This next query also retrieves a single row, but there is a wildcard pattern match. A full table scan is the result:

```
EXPLAIN PLAN SET statement_id='TEST' FOR
    SELECT * FROM supplier WHERE name LIKE '21st%';
```

```
Query                                   Cost    Rows    Bytes
-----------------------------------   ------  -------  ---------
SELECT STATEMENT    on                   13     491     69722
  TABLE ACCESS FULL on SUPPLIER          13     491     69722
```

The next query finds almost 3,000 rows. A full scan of the table results regardless of the exactness of the pattern match:

```
SQL> SELECT COUNT(*) FROM supplier WHERE name LIKE '%a%';


  COUNT(*)
----------
      2926


EXPLAIN PLAN SET statement_id='TEST' FOR
    SELECT * FROM supplier WHERE name LIKE '%a%';
```

```
Query                                   Cost    Rows    Bytes
-----------------------------------   ------  -------  ---------
SELECT STATEMENT    on                   13     194     27548
  TABLE ACCESS FULL on SUPPLIER          13     194     27548
```

Note: A pattern match using a percentage full wild card pattern-matching character anywhere in the pattern-matching string will usually produce a full table scan.

In general, LIKE will often read an entire table because LIKE usually matches patterns that are in no way related to indexes.

6.4.3 Set Membership

IN should be used to test against literal values and EXISTS to create a correlation between a calling query and a subquery. IN will cause a subquery to be executed in its entirety before passing the result back to the calling query. EXISTS will stop once a result is found. IN is best used as a preconstructed set of literal values:

```
EXPLAIN PLAN SET statement_id='TEST' FOR
SELECT * FROM coa WHERE type IN ('A', 'L', 'I', 'E');
```

Query	Cost	Rows	Bytes
SELECT STATEMENT on	1	38	950
TABLE ACCESS FULL on COA	1	38	950

There are two advantages to using EXISTS over using IN. The first advantage is the ability to pass values from a calling query to a subquery, never the other way around, creating a correlated query. The correlation allows EXISTS the use of indexes between calling query and subquery, particularly in the subquery.

Note: (10g) IN can also be used to create correlated queries and in some circumstances can be more efficiently utilized than EXISTS.

The second advantage of EXISTS is that, unlike IN, which completes a subquery regardless, EXISTS will halt searching when a value is found. Thus the subquery can be partially executed, reading fewer rows:

```
EXPLAIN PLAN SET statement_id='TEST' FOR
SELECT * FROM coa WHERE EXISTS
(SELECT type FROM type WHERE type = coa.type);
```

Query	Cost	Rows	Bytes
SELECT STATEMENT on	1	55	1485
NESTED LOOPS SEMI on	1	55	1485
TABLE ACCESS FULL on COA	1	55	1375
INDEX UNIQUE SCAN on XPKTYPE		6	12

Now let's compare the use of IN versus the use of EXISTS. The next two examples both use indexes and have the same result. IN is the same cost as EXISTS because the query contained within the IN subquery matches an index based on the single column it selects:

```
EXPLAIN PLAN SET statement_id='TEST' FOR
SELECT stock_id FROM stock s WHERE EXISTS
```

```
(SELECT stock_id FROM stockmovement WHERE stock_id =
s.stock_id);
```

Query	Cost	Rows	Bytes
SELECT STATEMENT on	**119**	118	944
NESTED LOOPS SEMI on	119	118	944
INDEX FULL SCAN on XPKSTOCK	1	118	472
INDEX RANGE SCAN on XFK_SM_STOCK	1	570175	2280700

And in comparison to using IN:

```
EXPLAIN PLAN SET statement_id='TEST' FOR
SELECT stock_id FROM stock WHERE stock_id IN
(SELECT stock_id FROM stockmovement);
```

Query	Cost	Rows	Bytes
SELECT STATEMENT on	**119**	118	944
NESTED LOOPS SEMI on	119	118	944
INDEX FULL SCAN on XPKSTOCK	1	118	472
INDEX RANGE SCAN on XFK_SM_STOCK	1	570175	2280700

Now let's perform some different queries to show a distinct difference between IN and EXISTS. Note how the first example is much lower in cost than the second:

```
EXPLAIN PLAN SET statement_id='TEST' FOR
SELECT * FROM stockmovement sm WHERE EXISTS
(SELECT * FROM stockmovement
WHERE stockmovement_id = sm.stockmovement_id);
```

Query	Cost	Rows	Bytes	Sort
SELECT STATEMENT on	**8593**	570175	16535075	
MERGE JOIN SEMI on	8593	570175	16535075	
TABLE ACCESS BY INDEX ROWID on SM	3401	570175	13684200	
INDEX FULL SCAN on XPKSTOCKMOVEMENT	1071	570175		

```
SORT UNIQUE on                           5192   570175   2850875   13755000
  INDEX FAST FULL SCAN on XPKSTMOVE        163   570175   2850875
```

This second example is higher in cost because it cannot match indexes, and as a result executes two full table scans:

```
EXPLAIN PLAN SET statement_id='TEST' FOR
SELECT * FROM stockmovement sm WHERE qty IN
(SELECT qty FROM stockmovement);
```

Query	Cost	Rows	Bytes	Sort
SELECT STATEMENT on	**16353**	570175	15964900	
MERGE JOIN SEMI on	16353	570175	15964900	
SORT JOIN on	11979	570175	13684200	45802000
TABLE ACCESS FULL on STOCKMOVEMENT	355	570175	13684200	
SORT UNIQUE on	4374	570175	2280700	13755000
TABLE ACCESS FULL on STOCKMOVEMENT	355	570175	2280700	

Now let's go yet another step further and restrict the calling query to a single-row result. This ensures that EXISTS has the best possible chance of passing a single-row identifier into the subquery, thus ensuring a unique index hit in the subquery. The StockMovement table has been joined to itself to facilitate the demonstration of the difference between using EXISTS and IN. Note how the IN subquery executes a full table scan and the EXISTS subquery does not:

```
EXPLAIN PLAN SET statement_id='TEST' FOR
    SELECT * FROM stockmovement sm
    WHERE EXISTS(
SELECT qty FROM stockmovement
      WHERE stockmovement_id = sm.stockmovement_id)
    AND stockmovement_id = 10;
```

Query	Cost	Rows	Bytes
SELECT STATEMENT on	**2**	1	29
NESTED LOOPS SEMI on	2	1	29
TABLE ACCESS BY INDEX ROWID on STOCKMOVEMENT	2	1	24
INDEX UNIQUE SCAN on XPK_STOCKMOVEMENT	1	570175	
INDEX UNIQUE SCAN on XPK_STOCKMOVEMENT		1	5

And now using IN:

```
EXPLAIN PLAN SET statement_id='TEST' FOR
SELECT * FROM stockmovement sm
WHERE qty IN
(SELECT qty FROM stockmovement)
AND stockmovement_id = 10;
```

Query	Cost	Rows	Bytes
SELECT STATEMENT on	**563**	1	28
NESTED LOOPS SEMI on	563	1	28
TABLE ACCESS BY INDEX ROWID on STOCKMOVEMENT	2	1	24
INDEX UNIQUE SCAN on XPK_STOCKMOVEMENT	1	570175	
TABLE ACCESS FULL on STOCKMOVEMENT	**561**	570175	2280700

The benefit of using EXISTS rather than IN for a subquery comparison is that EXISTS can potentially find much fewer rows than IN. *IN is best used with literal values, and EXISTS is best used as applying a fast-access correlation between a calling and a subquery.*

6.4.4 Groups

ANY, SOME, and ALL comparisons are generally not conducive to SQL tuning. In some respects, they are best not used.

That ends this chapter on examining the basics of how to create efficient SQL. In the next chapter, we will look into some more advanced concepts behind coding of efficient SQL, such as joins, subqueries in more detail, other database objects, and use of PL/SQL.

6.5 Endnotes

1. Oracle Data Warehouse Tuning for 10g (Gavin Powell, Digital Press, Aug 2005, ISBN: 1555583350)

7

Advanced Concepts of Efficient SQL

The previous chapter examined the basics of efficient SQL, including basic queries, using functions, pseudocolumns, and comparison conditions. This chapter explores more advanced facets of efficient SQL, including joins, subqueries, and various other objects and methods. It might seem a little odd that this chapter and the next are not a single chapter. In the previous edition of this book that was the case, but that single chapter was just too long. In this chapter we will begin with joins.

7.1 Joins

A join is a combination of rows extracted from two or more tables. Joins can be very specific, for instance, an intersection between two tables, or they can be less specific, such as an outer join. An outer join is a join returning an intersection plus rows from either or both tables, not in the other table.

This discussion on tuning joins is divided into three sections: join syntax formats, efficient joins, and inefficient joins. It seems sensible to divide joins between efficient joins and inefficient joins because this book is all about tuning. First, let's look at the two different available join syntax formats in Oracle SQL.

7.1.1 Join Formats

Two different syntax formats are available for SQL join queries: Oracle Corporation's proprietary format and the ANSI standard format. Let's test the two formats to see if either can be tuned to perform faster than the other.

The Oracle SQL proprietary format places join specifications into the WHERE clause of a SQL query. The only syntactical addition to the standard SELECT statement syntax is the use of the (+) or outer join operator. We will deal with tuning outer joins later in this chapter. Following is an example Oracle SQL proprietary join formatted query with its query plan, using the Employees schema. All tables are fully scanned because there is joining but no filtering. The optimizer forces full table reads on all tables because it is the fastest access method to read all the data:

```
EXPLAIN PLAN SET statement_id='TEST' FOR
SELECT di.name, de.name, prj.name
FROM division di, department de, project prj
WHERE di.division_id = de.division_id
AND de.department_id = prj.department_id;
```

Query	Cost	Rows	Bytes
SELECT STATEMENT on	23	10000	640000
HASH JOIN on	23	10000	640000
HASH JOIN on	3	100	3600
TABLE ACCESS FULL on DIVISION	1	10	170
TABLE ACCESS FULL on DEPARTMENT	1	100	1900
TABLE ACCESS FULL on PROJECT	13	10000	280000

The next example shows the same query except using the ANSI standard join format. Notice how the query plan is identical:

```
EXPLAIN PLAN SET statement_id='TEST' FOR
SELECT di.name, de.name, prj.name
FROM division di JOIN department de USING(division_id)
JOIN project prj USING (department_id);
```

Query	Cost	Rows	Bytes
SELECT STATEMENT on	23	10000	640000
HASH JOIN on	23	10000	640000
HASH JOIN on	3	100	3600
TABLE ACCESS FULL on DIVISION	1	10	170
TABLE ACCESS FULL on DEPARTMENT	1	100	1900
TABLE ACCESS FULL on PROJECT	13	10000	280000

What is the objective of showing these two queries, including their query plan details? The task of this book is performance tuning. Is either the Oracle SQL proprietary or ANSI join format inherently faster? Let's try to prove it either way. Once again, the Oracle SQL proprietary format is shown following but with a filter added, finding only a single row in the join:

```
EXPLAIN PLAN SET statement_id='TEST' FOR
SELECT di.name, de.name, prj.name
FROM division di, department de, project prj
WHERE di.division_id = 5
AND di.division_id = de.division_id
AND de.department_id = prj.department_id;
```

Query	Cost	Rows	Bytes
SELECT STATEMENT on	4	143	9152
TABLE ACCESS BY INDEX ROWID on PROJECT	2	10000	280000
NESTED LOOPS on	4	143	9152
NESTED LOOPS on	2	1	36
TABLE ACCESS BY INDEX ROWID on DIVISION	1	1	17
INDEX UNIQUE SCAN on XPKDIVISION		1	
TABLE ACCESS FULL on DEPARTMENT	1	10	190
INDEX RANGE SCAN on XFKPROJECT_DEPARTMENT	1	10000	

Next is the ANSI standard equivalent of the previous join, including the filter. Two of the most important aspects of tuning SQL join queries is the ability to apply filtering prior to joining tables, plus specifying the table with the largest filter applied as being the first table in the FROM clause, especially for very large tables. The question is this: Does the ANSI format allow for tuning of joins down to these levels of detail? Is the ANSI format a faster and more tunable option?

```
EXPLAIN PLAN SET statement_id='TEST' FOR
SELECT di.name, de.name, prj.name
FROM division di JOIN department de
ON(di.division_id = de.division_id)
JOIN project prj ON(de.department_id = prj.department_id)
WHERE di.division_id = 5;
```

In the previous join query, filtering is visibly applied after the specification of the join. Also note that with the addition of filtering, the ON clause, rather than the USING clause, is required. In the query plan following, note that the optimizer has not changed its plan of execution between the Oracle SQL proprietary and ANSI join formats. There is no difference in performance between the Oracle SQL proprietary and ANSI standard join formats:

Query	Cost	Rows	Bytes
SELECT STATEMENT on	4	**143**	**9152**
TABLE ACCESS BY INDEX ROWID on PROJECT	2	10000	280000
NESTED LOOPS on	4	143	9152
NESTED LOOPS on	2	1	36
TABLE ACCESS BY INDEX ROWID on DIVISION	1	1	17
INDEX UNIQUE SCAN on XPKDIVISION		1	
TABLE ACCESS FULL on DEPARTMENT	1	10	190
INDEX RANGE SCAN on XFKPROJECT_DEPARTMENT	1	10000	

A more visibly tunable join could be demonstrated by retrieving a single row from the largest rather than the smallest table. Here is the Oracle SQL proprietary format:

```
EXPLAIN PLAN SET statement_id='TEST' FOR
SELECT di.name, de.name, prj.name
FROM project prj, department de, division di
WHERE prj.project_id = 50
AND de.department_id = prj.department_id
AND di.division_id = de.division_id;
```

Notice in the query plan following that the cost is the same, but the number of rows and bytes read are substantially reduced; only a single row is retrieved. The Project table is placed first in the FROM clause because it is being reduced in size more than any other table. The same applies to the Department table because it is larger than the Division table:

Query	Cost	Rows	Bytes
SELECT STATEMENT on	4	1	67
NESTED LOOPS on	4	1	67
NESTED LOOPS on	3	1	50
TABLE ACCESS BY INDEX ROWID on PROJECT	2	1	31
INDEX UNIQUE SCAN on XPKPROJECT	1	1	
TABLE ACCESS BY INDEX ROWID on DEPARTMENT	1	100	1900

```
     INDEX UNIQUE SCAN on XPKDEPARTMENT                          100
   TABLE ACCESS BY INDEX ROWID on DIVISION               1      10        170
     INDEX UNIQUE SCAN on XPKDIVISION                            10
```

Now let's do the same query but with the ANSI join format. From the query plan following, we can once again see that use of either the Oracle SQL proprietary or ANSI join format does not appear to make any difference to performance and capacity for tuning:

```
EXPLAIN PLAN SET statement_id='TEST' FOR
SELECT di.name, de.name, prj.name
FROM project prj JOIN department de
ON(prj.department_id = de.department_id)
JOIN division di ON(de.division_id = di.division_id)
WHERE prj.project_id = 50;
```

Query	Cost	Rows	Bytes
SELECT STATEMENT on	**4**	**1**	**67**
NESTED LOOPS on	4	1	67
NESTED LOOPS on	3	1	50
TABLE ACCESS BY INDEX ROWID on PROJECT	2	1	31
INDEX UNIQUE SCAN on XPKPROJECT	1	1	
TABLE ACCESS BY INDEX ROWID on DEPARTMENT	1	100	1900
INDEX UNIQUE SCAN on XPKDEPARTMENT		100	
TABLE ACCESS BY INDEX ROWID on DIVISION	1	10	170
INDEX UNIQUE SCAN on XPKDIVISION		10	

Let's take this further and do some time testing. We will use the Accounts schema because the Employees schema does not have much data. We want to retrieve more rows to give a better chance of getting a time difference, and thus we will not filter on the largest table first. As can be seen from the results following, the timing is identical. Perhaps changing the join orders could make subtle differences, but there is no reason why the ANSI join format should be considered less tunable:

```
SQL> SELECT COUNT(*) FROM (
  2  SELECT t.text, st.text, coa.text, gl.dr, gl.cr
  3  FROM type t, subtype st, coa, generalledger gl
  4  WHERE t.type = 'A'
```

```
5   AND coa.type = t. type
6   AND coa.subtype = st.subtype
7   AND gl.coa# = coa.coa#);

COUNT(*)
----------
   239848
```

Elapsed: 00:00:04.06

```
SQL> SELECT COUNT(*) FROM (
  2   SELECT t.text, st.text, coa.text, gl.dr, gl.cr
  3   FROM type t JOIN coa ON(t.type = coa.type)
  4   JOIN subtype st ON(st.subtype = coa.subtype)
  5   JOIN generalledger gl ON(gl.coa# = coa.coa#)
  6   WHERE t.type = 'A');

COUNT(*)
----------
   239848
```

Elapsed: 00:00:04.06

7.1.2 Efficient Joins

What is an efficient join? An efficient join is a join SQL query that can be tuned to an acceptable level of performance. Certain types of join queries are inherently easily tuned and can give good performance. In general, a join is efficient when it can use indexes on large tables or is reading only very small tables. Moreover, any type of join will be inefficient if coded improperly.

7.1.2.1 Intersections

An inner or natural join is an intersection between two tables. In *mathematical set* parlance, an intersection contains all elements occurring in both of the sets (elements common to both sets). An intersection is efficient when index columns are matched together in join clauses. Intersection matching not using indexed columns will be inefficient. In that case, you may want to create alternate indexes. On the other hand, when a table is very small the optimizer may conclude that reading the whole table is faster than reading an associated index plus the table. How the optimizer makes this decision will be discussed in later chapters, because this subject matter delves into indexing and physical file block structure in Oracle Database datafiles.

In the following example, both the Type and COA tables are so small that the optimizer does not bother with the indexes, simply reading both of the tables fully:

```
EXPLAIN PLAN SET statement_id='TEST' FOR
SELECT t.text, coa.text FROM type t JOIN coa USING(type);
```

Query	Cost	Rows	Bytes
SELECT STATEMENT on	3	55	1430
HASH JOIN on	3	55	1430
TABLE ACCESS FULL on TYPE	1	6	54
TABLE ACCESS FULL on COA	1	55	935

In the next example, the optimizer has done something a little odd by using a unique index on the Subtype table. Why is this odd? The Subtype table has only four rows and is extremely small:

```
EXPLAIN PLAN SET statement_id='TEST' FOR
SELECT t.text, coa.text FROM type t JOIN coa USING(type)
JOIN subtype st USING(subtype);
```

Query	Cost	Rows	Bytes
SELECT STATEMENT on	3	55	1650
NESTED LOOPS on	3	55	1650
HASH JOIN on	3	55	1540
TABLE ACCESS FULL on TYPE	1	6	54
TABLE ACCESS FULL on COA	1	55	1045
INDEX UNIQUE SCAN on XPKSUBTYPE		4	8

Once again, in the example following the optimizer has chosen to read the index for the very small Subtype table. However, the GeneralLedger table has its index read because it is very large, and the optimizer considers that more efficient because the GeneralLedger does have an index on the COA# column and thus the index is range scanned:

```
EXPLAIN PLAN SET statement_id='TEST' FOR
SELECT t.text, coa.text
FROM type t JOIN coa USING(type)
  JOIN subtype st USING(subtype)
  JOIN generalledger gl ON(gl.coa# = coa.coa#);
```

Query	Cost	Rows	Bytes
SELECT STATEMENT on	58	752740	31615080
NESTED LOOPS on	58	752740	31615080
NESTED LOOPS on	3	55	1980
HASH JOIN on	3	55	1870
TABLE ACCESS FULL on TYPE	1	6	54
TABLE ACCESS FULL on COA	1	55	1375
INDEX UNIQUE SCAN on XPKSUBTYPE		4	8
INDEX RANGE SCAN on XFK_GL_COA#	1	752740	4516440

The most efficient type of inner join will generally be one retrieving very specific rows, such as in the next example. Most SQL is more efficient when retrieving very specific, small numbers of rows:

```
EXPLAIN PLAN SET statement_id='TEST' FOR
SELECT t.text, st.text, coa.text, gl.dr, gl.cr
FROM generalledger gl JOIN coa ON(gl.coa# = coa.coa#)
JOIN type t ON(t.type = coa.type)
JOIN subtype st ON(st.subtype = coa.subtype)
WHERE gl.generalledger_id = 100;
```

Note how all tables in the query plan are accessed using unique index hits:

Query	Pos	Cost	Rows	Bytes
SELECT STATEMENT on	0	6	1	62
NESTED LOOPS on	1	6	1	62
NESTED LOOPS on	1	5	1	54
NESTED LOOPS on	1	4	1	45
TABLE ACCESS BY INDEX ROWID on GENERALLEDGER	1	3	1	20
INDEX UNIQUE SCAN on XPK_GENERALLEDGER	1	2	1	
TABLE ACCESS BY INDEX ROWID on COA	2	1	55	1375
INDEX UNIQUE SCAN on XPK_COA	1	0	1	
TABLE ACCESS BY INDEX ROWID on SUBTYPE	2	1	4	36
INDEX UNIQUE SCAN on XPK_SUBTYPE	1	0	1	
TABLE ACCESS BY INDEX ROWID on TYPE	2	1	6	48
INDEX UNIQUE SCAN on XPK_TYPE	1	0	1	

7.1.2.2   Self-Joins

A self-join joins a table to itself. Sometimes self-joining tables can be handled with hierarchical queries. Otherwise, a self-join is applied to a table containing columns within each row, which link to each other. The Employee table in the Employees schema is such a table. It would be fairly efficient to join the tables using the MANAGER_ID and EMPLOYEE_ID columns because both columns are indexed:

```
EXPLAIN PLAN SET statement_id='TEST' FOR
SELECT manager.name, employee.name
FROM employee manager, employee employee
WHERE employee.manager_id = manager.employee_id;
```

In the query plan, the Employee table is fully scanned twice because all the data is read, and the optimizer considers this faster because the Employee table is small:

Query	Cost	Rows	Bytes
SELECT STATEMENT on	3	110	2970
HASH JOIN on	3	110	2970
TABLE ACCESS FULL on EMPLOYEE	1	111	1554
TABLE ACCESS FULL on EMPLOYEE	1	111	1443

7.1.2.3   Equi-Joins and Range Joins

An equi-join uses the equals sign (=), and a range join uses range operators (<, >, <=, >=, and the BETWEEN operator). In general, the = operator will execute an exact row hit on an index, and thus use unique index hits. The range operators will usually require the optimizer to execute index range scans. BTree (binary tree) indexes, the most commonly used indexes in Oracle Database, are highly amenable to range scans. A BTree index is a little like a limited-depth tree and is optimized for both unique hits and range scans.

Going back into the Accounts schema, this first query uses two unique index hits. The filter helps that happen:

```
EXPLAIN PLAN SET statement_id='TEST' FOR
SELECT coa.*, gl.*
FROM generalledger gl JOIN coa ON(gl.coa# = coa.coa#)
```

```
WHERE generalledger_id = 10;
```

Query	Cost	Rows	Bytes
SELECT STATEMENT on	4	1	51
NESTED LOOPS on	4	1	51
TABLE ACCESS BY INDEX ROWID on GENERALLEDGER	3	1	26
INDEX UNIQUE SCAN on XPKGENERALLEDGER	2	1	
TABLE ACCESS BY INDEX ROWID on COA	1	55	1375
INDEX UNIQUE SCAN on XPKCOA		55	

This second query uses a range index scan on the GeneralLedger table as a result of the range operator in the filter. Did you notice that the join clause inside the ON clause is where the range join operator is placed? There isn't really much point in joining *ON(gl.coa# >= coa.coa#)*. I do not think I have ever seen a SQL join joining using a range operator. The result would be a very unusual type of outer join perhaps. Thus there is no need for a query plan:

```
EXPLAIN PLAN SET statement_id='TEST' FOR
SELECT coa.*, gl.*
FROM generalledger gl JOIN coa ON(gl.coa# >= coa.coa#)
WHERE generalledger_id = 10;
```

Note: Cartesian products and range joins are often useless in OLTP databases. Cartesian products are sometimes used in data warehouses.

7.1.3   Inefficient Joins

What is an inefficient join? An inefficient join is a SQL query joining tables, which is difficult to tune, or it cannot be tuned to an acceptable level of performance. Certain types of join queries are inherently both poor performers and difficult, if not impossible, to tune. Inefficient joins are best avoided.

7.1.3.1   Cartesian Products

The ANSI join format calls a Cartesian product a cross-join. A cross-join is only tunable as far as columns selected match indexes, such that rows are retrieved from indexes and not tables.

I have left the Rows and Bytes columns in the following query plans as overflowed numbers, replaced with a string of # characters. This is done to stress the pointlessness of using a Cartesian product in an OLTP database:

```
EXPLAIN PLAN SET statement_id='TEST' FOR
SELECT * FROM coa, generalledger;
```

Query	Cost	Rows	Bytes
SELECT STATEMENT on	27116	######	########
MERGE JOIN CARTESIAN on	27116	######	########
TABLE ACCESS FULL on COA	1	55	1375
BUFFER SORT on	27115	752740	19571240
TABLE ACCESS FULL on GENERALLEDGER	493	752740	19571240

The second query has a lower cost than the first because the selected columns match indexes on both tables:

```
EXPLAIN PLAN SET statement_id='TEST' FOR
SELECT coa.coa#, gl.generalledger_id FROM coa, generalledger gl;
```

Query	Cost	Rows	Bytes
SELECT STATEMENT on	11936	######	########
MERGE JOIN CARTESIAN on	11936	######	########
INDEX FULL SCAN on XPKCOA	1	55	330
BUFFER SORT on	11935	752740	4516440
INDEX FAST FULL SCAN on XPKGENERALLEDGER	217	752740	4516440

7.1.3.2 Outer Joins

Tuning an outer join requires the same approach to tuning as with an inner join. The only point to note is that if applications require a large quantity of outer joins, there is likely to be a potential for data model tuning. The data model could be too granular. Outer joins are probably more applicable to reporting and data warehouse–type applications.

An outer join is not always inefficient. The performance—and to a certain extent the indication of a need for data model tuning—depends on the ratio of rows retrieved from the intersecting joins, in comparison to rows retrieved outside of intersecting joins. The more rows retrieved from the intersection, the better. My question is this: Why are outer joins needed?

Examine the data model first to see if outer joins are a result of poor data model design (data warehouses excepted, of course).

7.1.3.3 Anti-Joins

An anti-join is always a problem. An anti-join simply does the opposite of a requirement. The result is that the optimizer must search for everything not meeting a condition. An anti-join will generally always produce a full table scan, as seen in the example following. Again, the Rows and Bytes columns are left as overflowing, showing the possibly folly of using anti-joins:

```
EXPLAIN PLAN SET statement_id='TEST' FOR
SELECT t.text, coa# FROM type t, coa WHERE t.type != coa.type;
```

Query	Cost	Rows	Bytes
SELECT STATEMENT on	7	275	4675
NESTED LOOPS on	7	275	4675
TABLE ACCESS FULL on TYPE	1	6	54
TABLE ACCESS FULL on COA	1	55	440

The second example uses one index because indexed columns are being retrieved from one of the tables:

```
EXPLAIN PLAN SET statement_id='TEST' FOR
SELECT coa.coa#, gl.generalledger_id FROM coa, generalledger gl
WHERE coa.coa# != gl.coa#;
```

Query	Pos	Cost	Rows	Bytes
SELECT STATEMENT on	27116	27116	######	########
NESTED LOOPS on	1	27116	######	########
INDEX FULL SCAN on XPKCOA	1	1	55	330
TABLE ACCESS FULL on GENERALLEDGER	2	493	752740	9032880

7.1.3.4 Mutable and Complex Joins

A mutable join is a join of more than two tables. A complex join is a mutable join with added filtering. We have already examined a complex mutable join in the section on intersection joins, and various other parts of this chapter.

7.1.4 How to Tune a Join

So how can a join be tuned? There are several factors to consider:

- Use equality first.

- Use range operators where equality does not apply.

- Avoid use of negatives in the form of != or NOT.

- Avoid LIKE pattern matching.

- Try to retrieve specific rows, and in small numbers.

- Filter from large tables first to reduce the number of rows joined. Retrieve tables in order from the most highly filtered table downward, preferably the largest table, which has the most filtering applied.

Note: The most highly filtered table is the largest table with the smallest percentage of its rows retrieved.

- Use indexes wherever possible, except for very small tables.

- Let the optimizer do its job.

- Materialized views and query rewrite.[1] Materialized views are somewhat out of the scope of OLTP databases, but perhaps not so in the future.

Note: (10*g*) Query rewrite is enabled automatically, but materialized views are not recommended in highly active OLTP databases.

7.2 Using Subqueries for Efficiency

Tuning subqueries is a highly complex topic. Subqueries can often be used to partially replace subset parts of very large mutable joins, with possible enormous performance improvements.

7.2.1 Correlated versus Noncorrelated Subqueries

A correlated subquery allows a correlation between a calling query and a subquery. A value for each row in the calling query is passed into the subquery to be used as a constraint by the subquery. A noncorrelated or regular subquery does not contain a correlation between calling query and subquery. The subquery is executed in its entirety, independently of the calling query, for each row in the calling query. Tuning correlated subqueries is easier because values in subqueries can be precisely searched for in relation to each row of the calling query.

A correlated subquery will access a specified row or set of rows for each row in the calling query. Depending on circumstances, a correlated subquery is not always faster than a noncorrelated subquery. Use of indexes or small tables inside a subquery, even for noncorrelated subqueries, does not necessarily make a subquery perform poorly.

7.2.2   IN versus EXISTS

We have already seen substantial use of IN and EXISTS in the section on comparison conditions in Chapter 6. We know already that IN is best used for small tables or lists of literal values. EXISTS is best used to code queries in a correlated fashion, establishing a link between a calling query and a subquery. To reiterate, it is important to remember that using EXISTS is not always faster than using IN.

7.2.3   Nested Subqueries

Subqueries can be nested where a subquery can call another subquery. The following example using the Employees schema shows a query calling a subquery, which in turn calls another subquery:

```
EXPLAIN PLAN SET statement_id='TEST' FOR
SELECT * FROM division WHERE division_id IN
(SELECT division_id FROM department WHERE department_id IN
(SELECT department_id FROM project));
```

Notice in the query plan how the largest table is scanned using an *INDEX FAST FULL SCAN*. The optimizer is intelligent enough to analyze this nested query and discern that the Project table is much larger than both of the other two tables. The other two tables are so small that the only viable option is a full table scan:

Query	Cost	Rows	Bytes
SELECT STATEMENT on	14	10	590
HASH JOIN SEMI on	14	10	590
TABLE ACCESS FULL on DIVISION	1	10	460
VIEW on VW_NSO_1	8	10000	130000
HASH JOIN on	8	10000	60000
TABLE ACCESS FULL on DEPARTMENT	1	100	400
INDEX FAST FULL SCAN on XFKPROJECT_DEPT	4	10000	20000

Nested subqueries can be difficult to tune but can often be a viable and sometimes highly effective tool for tuning mutable complex joins, with three and sometimes many more tables in a single join. There is a point when there are so many tables in a join that the optimizer can become less effective. This leads us to the following section.

7.2.4 Replacing Joins with Subqueries

Before beginning this discussion, there is a very important point to make about replacing joins with nested subqueries. Nesting of joins into semi-joined nested layers of subqueries does not necessarily result in faster execution, when compared to an equivalent single-layer hierarchy join (with no subqueries). However, the nested subquery structure is going to be alot easier on both the eye and the mind, when it comes to tuning. Once again, this returns to my approach of *Keep it simple, stupid* (KISS) by breaking everything down into smaller, more manageable, and thus far more easily tunable parts.

For very large complex mutable joins, it is often possible to replace joins or parts of joins with subqueries. Very large joins can benefit the most because they are difficult for programmers to decipher and just as difficult to tune. Very large joins, and even some not so very large joins, are beyond the intelligence of the optimizer to assess in the best possible way. Large joins with four or more tables are usually poor performers because the optimizer is overwhelmed and there is only so much a programmer can do. Huge joins can be made easier in all respects by using subqueries in two ways, replacing complex mutable joins as follows:

1. **A table in the join that is not returning a column in the primary calling query can be removed from the join, and checked using a subquery.** The table is not really part of the join, so why retain it in the data being returned for display?

2. **FROM clauses can contain nested subqueries to break up joins much in the way that PL/SQL would use nested looping cursors.** This gives better control to programmers, allowing breaking queries into simplified parts. And a FROM clause subquery is not actually a semi-join (returns no columns) because it can return columns. This is why a FROM clause subquery is known as an inline view, which is a little like a view, just *inline*, or within a query.

Certain aspects of SQL coding placed in subqueries can cause problems:

- **An ORDER BY clause is always applied to a final result and should not be included in subqueries if possible.** Why sort a subquery when sorting is usually required by the final result? The final result is returned by the query returning the rows and columns for display. A calling query does not need to see a subquery in sorted order because no human eyes are looking at its results; only the calling query is using the results of the subquery.

- **DISTINCT will always cause a sort and is not always necessary.** Perhaps a parent table could be used where a unique value is present.

- **When testing against subqueries, retrieve, filter, and aggregate on indexes, not tables.** Indexes usually offer better performance.

- **Do not be too concerned about full table scans on very small static tables.**

Note: Instances where joins can be replaced with subqueries often involve databases with heavy outer join requirements. Excessive use of SQL outer joins is possibly indicative of an overgranular data model structure. However, it could also indicate orphaned child table rows or the opposite: redundant static data. Cleaning out redundant or orphaned rows can sometimes help performance immensely by negating the need for complex and expensive outer joins.

7.2.4.1 Remove Tables without Returned Columns Using EXISTS

Going back to the Accounts schema once again, look at the following complex mutable join. We are joining four tables and selecting a column from only one of the tables:

```
EXPLAIN PLAN SET statement_id='TEST' FOR
SELECT c.name
FROM customer c JOIN orders o USING(customer_id)
JOIN ordersline ol USING(order_id)
JOIN transactions t USING(customer_id)
JOIN transactionsline tl USING(transaction_id)
WHERE c.balance > 0;
```

The query plan using Oracle Database 9*i* is a little scary. There are three full table scans and two full index scans. The objective is to remove full table scans and change as many index scans as possible into unique index scans:

Query	Cost	Rows	Bytes
SELECT STATEMENT on	#####	######	########
MERGE JOIN on	#####	######	########
SORT JOIN on	#####	######	########
MERGE JOIN on	4988	######	########
SORT JOIN on	3209	100136	3805168
HASH JOIN on	762	100136	3805168
TABLE ACCESS FULL on CUSTOMER	9	2690	69940
MERGE JOIN on	316	100237	1202844
INDEX FULL SCAN on XFK_ORDERLINE_ORDER	26	540827	2704135
SORT JOIN on	290	31935	223545
TABLE ACCESS FULL on ORDERS	112	31935	223545
SORT JOIN on	1780	188185	1317295
TABLE ACCESS FULL on TRANSACTIONS	187	188185	1317295
SORT JOIN on	5033	570175	2850875
INDEX FAST FULL SCAN on XFK_TRANSLINE_TRANS	4	570175	2850875

Note: (10*g*) On the contrary, the query plan using an equivalent Oracle Database 10*g* is much different and much better. The Transactions table is twice as large in the Oracle 10*g* database. Several highly inefficient sort-merge joins are avoided here, but that is most likely because of more effective parameter settings and automated memory management in Oracle Database 10*g*.

Query	Pos	Cost	Rows	Bytes
SELECT STATEMENT on	0	**5696**	15310	673640
HASH JOIN on	1	5696	15310	673640
HASH JOIN on	1	2704	3070	122800
NESTED LOOPS on	1	1087	125	4250
HASH JOIN on	1	1038	24	720
TABLE ACCESS FULL on CUSTOMER	1	60	1	24
TABLE ACCESS FULL on ORDERS	2	973	64674	388044
INDEX RANGE SCAN on XPK_ORDERSLINE	2	2	5	20
TABLE ACCESS FULL on TRANSACTIONS	2	1612	65881	395286
INDEX FAST FULL SCAN on XPK_TRANSACTIONSLINE	2	2904	1111780	4447120

Note: (10g) Any examples not repeated for both Oracle Database 9*i* and Oracle Database 10*g* are produced in Oracle 10*g*.

Now let's remove tables from the join, which do not return columns in the main query. Also, EXISTS comparisons can be placed into the WHERE clause to force index access. Following on with the same example, only the Customer.NAME column is selected. So I can ultimately remove three tables from the join. The next query removes every table from the join, except the Customer table. Let's show this in two stages. First, I will remove the transaction tables from the join:

```
EXPLAIN PLAN SET statement_id='TEST' FOR
SELECT c.name
FROM customer c JOIN orders o ON(c.customer_id =
o.customer_id)
JOIN ordersline ol USING(order_id)
WHERE c.balance > 0
AND EXISTS(
SELECT t.transaction_id FROM transactions t
WHERE t.customer_id = c.customer_id
AND EXISTS(
        SELECT transaction_id FROM transactionsline
        WHERE transaction_id = t.transaction_id
    )
);
```

In the following query plan, run on my Oracle Database 9*i*, I have now reduced the full table scans to two, have a single full index scan, and most important, have index range scans on both of the transaction tables:

Query	Cost	Rows	Bytes
SELECT STATEMENT on	**359**	5007	190266
FILTER on			
HASH JOIN on	359	5007	190266
TABLE ACCESS FULL on CUSTOMER	9	135	3510
MERGE JOIN on	316	100237	1202844
INDEX FULL SCAN on XFK_ORDERLINE_ORDER	26	540827	2704135
SORT JOIN on	290	31935	223545
TABLE ACCESS FULL on ORDERS	112	31935	223545
NESTED LOOPS on	72	212	2544
TABLE ACCESS BY INDEX ROWID on TRANSACTIONS	2	70	490
INDEX RANGE SCAN on XFX_TRANS_CUSTOMER	1	70	
INDEX RANGE SCAN on XFK_TRANSLINE_TRANS	1	570175	2850875

Comparing with Oracle 10*g*, the improvement is unfortunately not as good. According to the query plan, the cost should theoretically be better because there are more index scans than for the Orace Database 9*i* example. It is possible that default settings in Oracle 10*g* are less conducive to this type of coding. Obviously, configuration parameters can be tweaked, but this chapter is about SQL coding, not configuration parameter tuning. Also, changing parameters can affect other things—and usually unexpectedly:

Query	Pos	Cost	Rows	Bytes
SELECT STATEMENT on	0	**555**	37	1258
FILTER on	1			
NESTED LOOPS on	1	176	125	4250
NESTED LOOPS on	1	127	24	720
TABLE ACCESS FULL on CUSTOMER	1	60	1	24
TABLE ACCESS BY INDEX ROWID on ORDERS	2	67	24	144
INDEX RANGE SCAN on XFK_ORDERS_CUSTOMER	1	1	77	
INDEX RANGE SCAN on XFK_ORDERLINE_ORDER	2	2	5	20
NESTED LOOPS SEMI on	2	6	2	20
TABLE ACCESS BY INDEX ROWID on TRANSACTIONS	1	2	83	498
INDEX RANGE SCAN on XFX_TRANS_CUSTOMER	1	1	24	
INDEX RANGE SCAN on XPK_TRANSACTIONSLINE	2	2	1111780	4447120

Now let's get completely ridiculous and remove every table from the join but the Customer table:

```
EXPLAIN PLAN SET statement_id='TEST' FOR
SELECT c.name FROM customer c
WHERE c.balance > 0
AND EXISTS(
      SELECT o.order_id FROM orders o
      WHERE o.customer_id = c.customer_id
      AND EXISTS(
          SELECT order_id FROM ordersline
          WHERE order_id = o.order_id
      )
)
AND EXISTS(
SELECT t.transaction_id FROM transactions t
WHERE t.customer_id = c.customer_id
AND EXISTS(
          SELECT transaction_id FROM transactionsline
WHERE transaction_id = t.transaction_id
)
);
```

This is about the best that can be done with this query, which is now no longer a join. This final result has full table access on the Customer table only, along with four index range scans. We could possibly improve the query further by decreasing the number of Customer rows retrieved using filtering:

Query	Cost	Rows	Bytes
SELECT STATEMENT on	9	7	182
FILTER on			
TABLE ACCESS FULL on CUSTOMER	9	7	182
NESTED LOOPS on	66	201	2412
TABLE ACCESS BY INDEX ROWID on ORDERS	2	64	448
INDEX RANGE SCAN on XFK_ORDERS_CUSTOMER	1	64	
INDEX RANGE SCAN on XFK_ORDERLINE_ORDER	1	540827	2704135
NESTED LOOPS on	72	212	2544
TABLE ACCESS BY INDEX ROWID on TRANSACTIONS	2	70	490

```
INDEX RANGE SCAN on XFX_TRANS_CUSTOMER          1      70
INDEX RANGE SCAN on XFK_TRANSLINE_TRANS         1  570175   2850875
```

> **Note:** (10*g*) Using EXISTS and semi-joins to remove nonretrieved columns from joins will produce better performance gains in Oracle Database 9*i* than it will in Oracle Database 10*g*. The reason why this is so is unknown, but it is important to note that this type of SQL coding can simplify the process of a person trying to tune great big horrible complex queries by breaking those queries down into smaller, more manageable, more tunable parts.

7.2.4.2 FROM Clause Subquery Nesting

Now we want to retrieve columns from different tables. Columns cannot be retrieved from an EXISTS comparison in the WHERE clause. We have to use another method. Nested subqueries in the FROM clause allow retrieval of columns.

In this example, I am adding extra filtering to the TransactionsLine table. At more than 500,000 rows, it is the largest table in the query. The TransactionsLine table is filtered first because it is larger than the Customer table:

```
EXPLAIN PLAN SET statement_id='TEST' FOR
SELECT c.name, tl.amount FROM customer c
 JOIN orders o USING(customer_id)
  JOIN ordersline ol USING(order_id)
   JOIN transactions t USING(customer_id)
    JOIN transactionsline tl USING(transaction_id)
WHERE tl.amount > 3170
AND c.balance > 0;
```

We start with three full table scans, one index range scan, and a unique index hit:

Query	Cost	Rows	Bytes
SELECT STATEMENT on	**1860**	605	33880
NESTED LOOPS on	1860	605	33880
HASH JOIN on	1667	193	9843

TABLE ACCESS FULL on ORDERS	112	31935	223545
MERGE JOIN CARTESIAN on	436	43804	1927376
NESTED LOOPS on	292	16	288
TABLE ACCESS FULL on TRANSACTIONSLINE	276	16	176
TABLE ACCESS BY INDEX ROWID on TRANSACTIONS	1	188185	1317295
INDEX UNIQUE SCAN on XPKTRANSACTIONS		188185	
BUFFER SORT on	435	2690	69940
TABLE ACCESS FULL on CUSTOMER	9	2690	69940
INDEX RANGE SCAN on XFK_ORDERLINE_ORDER	1	540827	2704135

First, we'll do some simple tuning. The TransactionsLine table should be selected from first because it is the largest table, containing the smallest relative filtered result.

> **Note:** The first table to be processed should be the largest table with the largest relative row reduction filter or the biggest table with the lowest number of rows retrieved from it. This applies to both the FROM clause and the WHERE clause. Always reduce rows to be joined first before they are joined.

```
EXPLAIN PLAN SET statement_id='TEST' FOR
SELECT c.name, tl.amount FROM transactionsline tl
 JOIN transactions t USING(transaction_id)
  JOIN customer c USING(customer_id)
   JOIN orders o USING(customer_id)
    JOIN ordersline ol ON(ol.order_id = o.order_id)
WHERE tl.amount > 3170
AND c.balance > 0;
```

Appropriate simple tuning yields one full table scan, two index range scans, and two unique index hits:

Query	Cost	Rows	Bytes
SELECT STATEMENT on	**1381**	3267	182952
NESTED LOOPS on	1381	3267	182952
NESTED LOOPS on	340	1041	53091
NESTED LOOPS on	308	16	704
NESTED LOOPS on	292	16	288
TABLE ACCESS FULL on TRANSACTIONSLINE	276	16	176
TABLE ACCESS BY INDEX ROWID on TRANSACTIONS	1	33142	231994

INDEX UNIQUE SCAN on XPKTRANSACTIONS		33142	
TABLE ACCESS BY INDEX ROWID on CUSTOMER	1	2690	69940
INDEX UNIQUE SCAN on XPKCUSTOMER		2690	
TABLE ACCESS BY INDEX ROWID on ORDERS	2	172304	1206128
INDEX RANGE SCAN on XFK_ORDERS_CUSTOMER	1	172304	
INDEX RANGE SCAN on XFK_ORDERLINE_ORDER	1	540827	2704135

Now let's use the FROM clause to create nested subqueries. The trick is to put the largest table, with the most severe filter, at the deepest nested level. The idea is to force it to execute first. Even though this can be done using an unnested join query, it's a lot easier to see it and to control the execution path of SQL coding by doing it this way. Don't you think? Thus we start with the TransactionsLine table:

```
EXPLAIN PLAN SET statement_id='TEST' FOR
SELECT c.name, b.amount
FROM customer c,
(
SELECT t.customer_id, a.amount
FROM transactions t,(
SELECT transaction_id, amount FROM transactionsline
WHERE amount > 3170
) a
WHERE t.transaction_id = a.transaction_id
) b, orders o, ordersline ol
WHERE c.balance > 0
AND c.customer_id = b.customer_id
AND o.customer_id = c.customer_id
AND ol.order_id = o.order_id;
```

The cost is reduced further with the same combination of scans because fewer rows are being joined:

Query	Cost	Rows	Bytes
SELECT STATEMENT on	**533**	605	33880
NESTED LOOPS on	533	605	33880
NESTED LOOPS on	340	193	9843
NESTED LOOPS on	308	16	704
NESTED LOOPS on	292	16	288

TABLE ACCESS FULL on TRANSACTIONSLINE	276	16	176
TABLE ACCESS BY INDEX ROWID on TRANSACTIONS	1	33142	231994
INDEX UNIQUE SCAN on XPKTRANSACTIONS		33142	
TABLE ACCESS BY INDEX ROWID on CUSTOMER	1	2690	69940
INDEX UNIQUE SCAN on XPKCUSTOMER		2690	
TABLE ACCESS BY INDEX ROWID on ORDERS	2	31935	223545
INDEX RANGE SCAN on XFK_ORDERS_CUSTOMER	1	31935	
INDEX RANGE SCAN on XFK_ORDERLINE_ORDER	1	540827	2704135

Now let's combine WHERE clause comparison subqueries and FROM clause embedded subqueries:

```
EXPLAIN PLAN SET statement_id='TEST' FOR
SELECT c.name, b.amount
FROM customer c,
(
SELECT t.customer_id, a.amount
FROM transactions t,(
SELECT transaction_id, amount FROM transactionsline
WHERE amount > 3170
) a
WHERE t.transaction_id = a.transaction_id
) b
WHERE c.balance > 0
AND EXISTS(
        SELECT o.order_id FROM orders o
        WHERE o.customer_id = c.customer_id
        AND EXISTS(
            SELECT order_id FROM ordersline
            WHERE order_id = o.order_id
        )
);
```

Using EXISTS makes the query just that little bit faster with lower cost because the number of tables joined is reduced:

Query	Cost	Rows	Bytes
--	------	-------	---------
SELECT STATEMENT on	**420**	2190	91980
FILTER on			

NESTED LOOPS on	420	2190	91980
MERGE JOIN CARTESIAN on	420	2190	81030
TABLE ACCESS FULL on TRANSACTIONSLINE	276	16	176
BUFFER SORT on	144	135	3510
TABLE ACCESS FULL on CUSTOMER	9	135	3510
INDEX UNIQUE SCAN on XPKTRANSACTIONS		188185	940925
NESTED LOOPS on	66	201	2412
TABLE ACCESS BY INDEX ROWID on ORDERS	2	64	448
INDEX RANGE SCAN on XFK_ORDERS_CUSTOMER	1	64	
INDEX RANGE SCAN on XFK_ORDERLINE_ORDER	1	540827	2704135

7.3   Using Synonyms

A synonym is what its name implies: another name for a known object. Synonyms are typically used to reference tables between schemas. Public synonyms make tables contained within schemas available to all schemas. Apart from the obvious security issues, there can be potential performance problems when overusing synonyms in highly concurrent environments. Don't create too many synonyms, because with enormous numbers of database objects, Oracle just has more to manage. More specifically, too many metadata objects can cause problems with the shared pool. Oracle has to manage the shared pool. Of course, you can increase the size of the shared pool. That can have the same effect, making a large shared pool more difficult and time consuming for Oracle Database software to manage. It may not necessarily be effective to divide functionality between different schemas, only to allow users global or semi-global access to all of the underlying schemas. Simplicity in development for the purpose of hiding or burying complexity, using objects like synonyms, can often lead to complexity and performance problems in production.

7.4   Using Views

Views are application friendly and security friendly. Views can also be used to reduce, hide, or bury complexity. This is particularly the case in development environments. In general, views are not conducive to good performance because they are often overused or even misused.

Note: Please refer back to the section entitled "Using View" in Chapter 2 for more information.

A view is a logical overlay on top of one or more tables. A view is created using a SQL statement. A view does not contain data. The biggest problem with a view is that whenever it is queried, its defining SQL statement is re-executed. It is common in applications for a developer to query a view and add additional filtering. The potential results are views containing large queries, where programmers will then execute small row number retrievals from the view. The result is that two queries are executed, commonly with the view query selecting all the rows in the underlying table or join.

Let's try to prove that views are inherently slower than direct table queries. First, I create a view on my largest Accounts schema table:

```
CREATE VIEW glv AS SELECT * FROM generalledger;
```

Now let's do some query plans. I have four queries and query plans listed over the following pages. The first two retrieve a large number of rows from the view and then a large number of rows from the table. It is apparent that the query plans are identical in cost between retrieving from table or view, which makes perfect sense. First, selecting from the view:

```
EXPLAIN PLAN SET statement_id='TEST' FOR
SELECT * FROM glv WHERE coa# = '40003';
```

Query	Cost	Rows	Bytes
SELECT STATEMENT on	**165**	150548	3914248
TABLE ACCESS BY INDEX ROWID on GENERALLEDGER	165	150548	3914248
INDEX RANGE SCAN on XFK_GL_COA#	5	150548	

And second, selecting from the table:

```
EXPLAIN PLAN SET statement_id='TEST' FOR
SELECT * FROM generalledger WHERE coa# = '40003';
```

Query	Cost	Rows	Bytes
SELECT STATEMENT on	**165**	150548	3914248
TABLE ACCESS BY INDEX ROWID on GENERALLEDGER	165	150548	3914248
INDEX RANGE SCAN on XFK_GL_COA#	5	150548	

Now let's filter and return much fewer rows. Once again, the query plans are the same. First, selecting from the view:

```
EXPLAIN PLAN SET statement_id='TEST' FOR
SELECT * FROM glv WHERE generalledger_id = 500000;
```

Query	Cost	Rows	Bytes
SELECT STATEMENT on	**3**	1	26
TABLE ACCESS BY INDEX ROWID on GENERALLEDGER	3	1	26
INDEX UNIQUE SCAN on XPKGENERALLEDGER	2	1	

And second, selecting from the table:

```
EXPLAIN PLAN SET statement_id='TEST' FOR
SELECT * FROM generalledger WHERE generalledger_id = 500000;
```

Query	Cost	Rows	Bytes
SELECT STATEMENT on	**3**	1	26
TABLE ACCESS BY INDEX ROWID on GENERALLEDGER	3	1	26
INDEX UNIQUE SCAN on XPKGENERALLEDGER	2	1	

So now let's try some time tests, because we can't really have confidence in query plan cost figures.

Note: Query plan cost figure values have so many different dependencies that they can only really be used as a vague estimate to possible query execution speeds.

The COUNT function is used as a wrapper, and each query is executed twice to ensure no conflict exists between reading from disk and memory. Part II of this book focuses on SQL coding tuning, not configuration parameters tuning, which is covered in Part III:

```
SELECT COUNT(*) FROM(SELECT * FROM glv WHERE coa# = '40003');
SELECT COUNT(*) FROM(SELECT * FROM generalledger WHERE coa# =
'40003');
SELECT COUNT(*) FROM(SELECT * FROM glv
```

```
WHERE generalledger_id = 500000);
SELECT COUNT(*) FROM(SELECT * FROM generalledger
WHERE generalledger_id = 500000);
```

In the first two instances, retrieving from the view is slightly faster than reading from the table:

```
SQL> SELECT COUNT(*) FROM(SELECT * FROM glv WHERE coa# =
'40003');
  COUNT(*)
----------
     66287
```
Elapsed: 00:00:04.04

```
SQL> SELECT COUNT(*) FROM(SELECT * FROM generalledger WHERE
coa# = '40003');
  COUNT(*)
----------
     66287
```
Elapsed: 00:00:04.09

```
SQL> SELECT COUNT(*) FROM(SELECT * FROM glv WHERE
generalledger_id = 500000);
  COUNT(*)
----------
         1
```
Elapsed: 00:00:00.00

```
SQL> SELECT COUNT(*) FROM(SELECT * FROM generalledger WHERE
generalledger_id = 500000);
  COUNT(*)
----------
         1
```
Elapsed: 00:00:00.00

For a single table and a view on that table, there appears to be no difference in query plan or execution time.

Now let's re-create our view with a join, rather than just a single table. This code drops and re-creates the view I created previously:

```
DROP VIEW glv;
CREATE VIEW glv AS
SELECT gl.generalledger_id, coa.coa#, t.text AS type,
st.text AS subtype, coa.text as coa, gl.dr, gl.cr, gl.dte
FROM type t JOIN coa USING(type)
    JOIN subtype st USING(subtype)
        JOIN generalledger gl ON(gl.coa# = coa.coa#);
```

When retrieving a large percentage of rows in the two following queries, the cost in the query plan is much better when retrieving using the tables join rather than the view. First, selecting from the view:

```
EXPLAIN PLAN SET statement_id='TEST' FOR
    SELECT * FROM glv WHERE coa# = '40003';
```

Note: The WHERE clause filtering predicate in the previous query is executed against the view. A reader of the first edition of this book complained about this, thus I am clarifying the purpose of these examples.

Query	Cost	Rows	Bytes
SELECT STATEMENT on	**168**	30110	2107700
NESTED LOOPS on	168	30110	2107700
NESTED LOOPS on	3	1	44
NESTED LOOPS on	2	1	34
TABLE ACCESS BY INDEX ROWID on COA	1	1	25
INDEX UNIQUE SCAN on XPKCOA		1	
TABLE ACCESS BY INDEX ROWID on TYPE	1	6	54
INDEX UNIQUE SCAN on XPKTYPE		6	
TABLE ACCESS BY INDEX ROWID on SUBTYPE	1	4	40
INDEX UNIQUE SCAN on XPKSUBTYPE		4	
TABLE ACCESS BY INDEX ROWID on GENERALLEDGER	165	150548	3914248
INDEX RANGE SCAN on XFK_GL_COA#	5	150548	

And second, selecting from the table join (using the query stored in the view):

```
EXPLAIN PLAN SET statement_id='TEST' FOR
SELECT gl.generalledger_id, coa.coa#, t.text AS type,
```

```
st.text AS subtype, coa.text as coa, gl.dr, gl.cr, gl.dte
FROM type t JOIN coa USING(type)
     JOIN subtype st USING(subtype)
       JOIN generalledger gl ON(gl.coa# = coa.coa#)
WHERE gl.coa# = '40003';
```

Note: In the previous view called GLV, the WHERE clause filtering predicate was executed against the view. Now the predicate is executed against the table. Yes, this could cause the optimizer to do something a little different by filtering within the join somewhere. The objective in this situation is to show that filtering against a view is risky because a view could contain filtering as well. I agree that it is unfair to perform a comparison of this nature, but I don't see a better way to demonstrate this point.

Query	Cost	Rows	Bytes
SELECT STATEMENT on	5	30110	2107700
NESTED LOOPS on	5	30110	2107700
NESTED LOOPS on	3	1	44
NESTED LOOPS on	2	1	34
TABLE ACCESS BY INDEX ROWID on COA	1	1	25
INDEX UNIQUE SCAN on XPKCOA		1	
TABLE ACCESS BY INDEX ROWID on TYPE	1	6	54
INDEX UNIQUE SCAN on XPKTYPE		6	
TABLE ACCESS BY INDEX ROWID on SUBTYPE	1	4	40
INDEX UNIQUE SCAN on XPKSUBTYPE		4	
TABLE ACCESS BY INDEX ROWID on GENERALLEDGER	2	150548	3914248
INDEX RANGE SCAN on XFK_GL_COA#	1	150548	

Let's try some more timing tests. The first timing test retrieves a large set of rows from the view:

```
SQL> SELECT COUNT(*) FROM(SELECT * FROM glv WHERE coa# =
'40003');

  COUNT(*)
----------
     66287
```

Elapsed: 00:00:04.02

The second timing test retrieves the same large set of rows from the table join and is obviously much faster:

```
SQL> SELECT COUNT(*) FROM(
  2  SELECT gl.generalledger_id, coa.coa#, t.text AS type,
st.text AS subtype, coa.text as coa, gl.dr, gl.cr, gl.dte
  3  FROM type t JOIN coa USING(type)
  4    JOIN subtype st USING(subtype)
  5     JOIN generalledger gl ON(gl.coa# = coa.coa#)
  6  WHERE gl.coa# = '40003');

  COUNT(*)
----------
     66287
```

Elapsed: 00:00:00.07

Comparing with a single row retrieved, there is no time difference between the view and the retrieval from the join. In a highly active concurrent environment, this might not be the case:

```
SQL> SELECT COUNT(*) FROM(SELECT * FROM glv WHERE
generalledger_id = 500000);

  COUNT(*)
----------
         1
```

Elapsed: 00:00:00.00

```
SQL> SELECT COUNT(*) FROM (SELECT gl.generalledger_id,
coa.coa#, t.text AS type, st.text AS subtype, coa.text as coa,
gl.dr, gl.cr,
gl.dte
  2  FROM generalledger gl JOIN coa ON(gl.coa# = coa.coa#)
  3   JOIN type t USING(type)
  4    JOIN subtype st USING(subtype)
  5  WHERE generalledger_id = 500000);
```

```
        COUNT(*)
      ----------
               1
```

Elapsed: 00:00:00.00

Views can now have constraints, including primary and foreign key constraints. These may help performance of data retrieval from views. However, assuming that views are created for coding development simplicity and not security, adding complexity to a view could negate the simplification issue and perhaps hurt performance if views are overused.

The exception to views re-executing every time they are queried is a materialized view, which is a separate database object in Oracle Database, storing the results of a query. Thus, when a materialized view is queried, data is extracted from the materialized view and not the underlying objects in the query. Materialized views are traditionally used as read-only data source in data warehouses and sometimes for replication. However, with the default setting of query rewrite in Oracle Database 10*g*, it is likely that updatable materialized views will be utilized in OLTP databases in the future.

Views are often not performance friendly! For the sake of performance, be careful about overusing views or even using views at all. Some applications are built with multiple layers of views. This type of application design is often application convenient and can produce disappointing results with respect to database performance. There is simply too much metadata in the shared pool and often too much filtering complexity across multiple layers of views. A brute-force method of resolving selection of rows, from multiple layered sets of views, is to use a form of the FROM clause in the SELECT statement, including the ONLY clause as shown in the following syntax. The ONLY clause will not retrieve rows from subset views:

```
SELECT … FROM ONLY (query) …
```

7.5   Temporary Tables

In years past, temporary tables were created in traditional relational databases as shell structures. These shell structures contained temporarily generated data, usually for the purposes of reporting. Oracle Database has the ability to create tables containing temporary rows. Rows created in temporary table objects are created locally to a session, somewhat managed by the database. It is more efficient to use Oracle Database temporary table objects in some circumstances. Creating traditional temporary tables, filling them, emptying them, and storing or deleting their rows is unlikely to perform better than Oracle Database temporary table objects.

7.6 Resorting to PL/SQL

PL/SQL is a mnemonic for Programming Language for SQL. From a purely programming perspective, PL/SQL is really SQL with programming logic wrapper controls, among numerous other bells and whistles. Compared with C or Java, PL/SQL is a primitive programming language at best. Beware of writing entire applications using PL/SQL. SQL is designed to retrieve sets of data from larger sets and is not procedural, sequential, or object-like in nature. Programming languages are required to be one of those or a combination thereof. PL/SQL has its place as a relational database access language and not as a number-crunching programming language like C or Java. Additionally, PL/SQL is interpretive, which means it is slow!

Note: (10*g*) PL/SQL objects are now stored in compiled form in binary object variables or BLOB objects. This could help PL/SQL procedure execution performance.

Does PL/SQL allow for faster performance? The short answer is no. The long answer may be that PL/SQL allows much greater control over SQL coding than simple SQL does. However, modern Oracle SQL is much more sophisticated than it was years ago. Some of the aspects of PL/SQL used in the past, allowing better performance in PL/SQL than SQL, are effectively redundant, particularly with retrieval of data. This is because basic Oracle SQL is now so much more versatile and sophisticated in Oracle Database 10*g*.

Note: Once again, as described in Chapter 2, "Coding Business Rules in the Database", my opinions of PL/SQL as a programming language are merely my opinions from past experience. Your experiences might be different from mine.

There are several reasons for resorting to PL/SQL:

- *PL/SQL may not provide better performance but can allow a breakdown of SQL coding complexity.* Breaking down complexity can allow easier tuning of SQL statements, through better control of cursors.

- *An obvious benefit of PL/SQL is the ability to build stored procedures and triggers.* Triggers should be used sparingly and avoided for implementation of referential integrity; constraints are much faster. In the case of stored procedures, the obvious benefits are centralized control and potential performance increases. Stored procedure code is executed on the server. Execution on a database server reduces network traffic. The result is improved performance.

- *There are some situations where it is impossible to code SQL code using SQL alone, and thus PL/SQL has to be resorted to.* This is becoming less frequent as basic Oracle SQL is becoming more sophisticated.

- *Some exceedingly complex SQL code can benefit from the use of PL/SQL instead of SQL.* Some SQL code can become so complex that it is impossible to tune or even code in SQL. PL/SQL becomes the faster option. For example, using the DECODE function is similar to control structures such as IF and CASE statements. PL/SQL allows all the appropriate control structures.

- PL/SQL packages can be cached into memory to avoid reparsing.

PL/SQL can provide better program coding control of cursors plus execution and maintenance from a central, single point. Perhaps the most significant benefit of resorting to PL/SQL is a potential reduction in complexity. Once again, as with views, reducing complexity is not necessarily conducive to performance tuning. In fact, simplicity, as with overnormalization, can often hurt performance in a relational database. Thus, further discussion of tuning SQL retrieval code using PL/SQL is largely irrelevant at this stage.

Tuning PL/SQL is a programming task that has little to do with coding well-performing SQL code. The obvious programming points to note are as follows:

- *Do not process more in a loop or a cursor than is necessary.* Break out of loops when no more processing is required.

- *Large IF statements should be replaced with CASE statements or appropriate breaks should be used.* Traditionally, CASE statements are faster than IF statements.

- *Recursion using embedded procedures creates very elegant code but in PL/SQL can cause performance problems,* especially where transactions are not completed within a recursion.

- *PL/SQL used to be executed as interpretive code, meaning it was read as text, not binary information.* PL/SQL objects are now stored in compiled form, stored in binary object variables (BLOB objects) in the database. Is this a compiled code in the sense that compiled C code is? The answer to this question is unknown. In fact, Oracle documentation is somewhat vague on the storage of compiled PL/SQL code into binary objects. Also, this newfangled way calls into question how PL/SQL uses the shared pool in Oracle Database 10*g*. The shared pool is acted on by both SQL and PL/SQL for re-execution, searching for, reparsing, and so on.

- *The WHERE CURRENT OF clause can refer to a cursor ROWID, giving direct pointer access to a cursor row in memory.* The RETURNING INTO clause can help with reducing the need for subsequent SELECT statements, further on in a procedure by returning values into variables.

- Explicit cursors can be faster than implicit cursors but are more difficult to code.

- *PL/SQL has three parameter formats for passing variables in and out of procedures.* IN and OUT pass values in and out of procedures, respectively. IN OUT passes a pointer both in and out of a procedure. Use only what is needed.

- *As with SQL code embedded in applications, PL/SQL procedures of any kind can use bind variables.* Using bind variables can have a profound effect on increasing performance by lowering parsing requirements in the library cache.

7.6.1 Tuning DML in PL/SQL

There are two interesting points to note in relation to performance of DML statements in PL/SQL. Other than what has already been covered in this chapter, little else can be done to tune DML (INSERT, UPDATE, DELETE, MERGE) or SELECT statements in PL/SQL.

7.6.1.1   The **RETURNING INTO** Clause

In the following example, the RETURNING INTO clause prevents the coder from having to code an extra SELECT statement, in order to find the identifier value required for the second INSERT statement. The same applies similarly to the second INSERT statement, returning a second value for the DBMS_OUTPUT.PUT_LINE procedure:

```
DECLARE
    division_id division.division_id%TYPE;
    division_name division.name%TYPE;
    department_name department.name%TYPE;
BEGIN
    INSERT INTO division(division_id, name)
    VALUES(division_seq.NEXTVAL, 'A New Division')
    RETURNING division_id, name
INTO division_id, division_name;

    INSERT INTO department(department_id, division_id, name)
        VALUES(department_seq.NEXTVAL, division_id,
'A New Department')
        RETURNING name INTO department_name;

    DBMS_OUTPUT.PUT_LINE('Added : '||
division_name||', '||department_name);
    END;
    /
```

Note: Remember that to see DBMS_OUTPUT display results in SQL*Plus, you must first execute the DBMS_OUTPUT.ENABLE (1000000) procedure (1,000,000 is the maximum byte value possible). To switch off output, again execute the DBMS_OUTPUT.DISABLE procedure.

Note: (10*g*) The RETURNING INTO clause can be used to return collections.

7.6.2   **When to Resort to PL/SQL and Cursors**

In general, SQL in Oracle Database is now powerful enough to deal with almost any requirement. Some occasions do call for substituting SQL code nested loop–type queries using PL/SQL. PL/SQL provides better programming control and allows much easier management of highly complex SQL code. Better performance can sometimes be gained using PL/SQL to control nested SQL statements.

PL/SQL can sometimes be faster when compiled, pinned, and executed on the database server, depending on the application. One of the original goals of stored procedures was to minimize on-network traffic. With the speed of modern network connections available, this is not necessarily an issue anymore. So what do I mean by resorting to PL/SQL and cursors? After all, I did not just state *Resorting to PL/SQL*. So what am I talking about? Look at this example:

```
EXPLAIN PLAN SET statement_id='TEST' FOR
    SELECT * FROM coa NATURAL JOIN generalledger;
```

This query plan shows the COA table in the outer loop and the GeneralLedger table in the inner loop:

Query	Cost	Rows	Bytes
SELECT STATEMENT on	1642	1068929	50239663
HASH JOIN on	1642	1068929	50239663
TABLE ACCESS FULL on COA	2	55	1320
TABLE ACCESS FULL on GENERALLEDGER	1128	1068929	24585367

To convert the SQL statement shown previously to PL/SQL, I would need PL/SQL code similar to that shown here:

```
DECLARE
    CURSOR cCOA IS SELECT * FROM coa;
    TYPE tGL IS REF CURSOR RETURN generalledger%ROWTYPE;
    cGLs tGL;
    rGL generalledger%ROWTYPE;
BEGIN
    FOR rCOA IN cCOA LOOP
```

```
OPEN cGLs FOR SELECT * FROM generalledger WHERE coa# = rCOA.coa#;
LOOP
    FETCH cGLs INTO rGL;
    EXIT WHEN cGLs%NOTFOUND;
    DBMS_OUTPUT.PUT_LINE(
        rCOA.coa#||' '||
        TO_CHAR(rGL.dte)||' '||
        TO_CHAR(rGL.dr)||' '||
        TO_CHAR(rGL.cr));
    END LOOP;
    CLOSE cGLs;
END LOOP;
EXCEPTION WHEN OTHERS THEN CLOSE cGLs;
END;
/
```

In general, PL/SQL should only replace SQL when coding simply cannot be achieved in SQL (too complex and convoluted for SQL) or centralization on the database server is required.

7.6.3 Java or PL/SQL

Java can be used to construct stored procedures in much the same way that PL/SQL can. When should you use Java? That question has a very simple answer. Use Java when you are not accessing the database and writing code that is computationally heavy. What does this mean? When answering a question such as this, I always prefer to go back into the roots of a programming language or a database. In other words, what were PL/SQL and Java originally built for? What is their purpose?

Let's start by looking at PL/SQL. PL/SQL is effectively a primitive programming language and is purely an extension of SQL. SQL was originally built purely to access data in a relational database. Therefore, it follows that PL/SQL is of the same ilk as SQL. PL/SQL was originally devised to create stored procedures in Oracle Database. Stored procedures were devised for relational databases in general, not just Oracle Database, to allow for coding of self-contained blocks of transaction-based SQL code. Those blocks of code are executed on the database server, minimizing on-network traffic. PL/SQL is now much richer than stored procedure languages used in other relational databases. PL/SQL can be used to code complexity. This takes us to Java.

Why use Java? Java is an object-oriented programming language built for coding of highly complex front-end and back-end applications. If you know anything about objects, you will understand that objects in programming are superb at handling complexity. It is in the very nature of objects to handle complexity by breaking everything down into its most simplistic parts. Java can be used to handle highly complex coding sequences and to create Oracle Database stored procedures, much in the same way that PL/SQL can. Java is much more powerful than PL/SQL in doing lots of computations and number crunching. Java is better than PL/SQL at anything that does not involve accessing the database, especially complex code. Coding requirements when accessing a database are trivial in relation to the complex routines and functions required by applications-level coding.

There is one small but fairly common problem with using Java. Java is object oriented. Oracle Database is relational. Object and relational methodologies do not mix well. Many Java applications, because of their object nature, break things into very small, easily manageable pieces. Object-oriented design is all about easy management of complexity. In relational terms, management of complexity by severe breakdown and object black-boxing is an incredible level of normalization. Too much normalization leads to too much granularity and usually very slow performance. What commonly happens with Java applications is one or all of a number of things. These are some of the possibilities:

- Preloading of large data sets

- Separation of parts of SQL statements into separate commands sent to the database. For instance, a SELECT statement could be submitted and then filtering would be performed in the Java application. This leads to lots of full table scans and a plethora of other performance problems.

- Sometimes object design is imposed onto the database to such an extent as to continually connect to and disconnect from the database, for every SQL code execution. This is very heavy on database resource consumption.

So what's the answer to the nagging question of whether to use Java or PL/SQL? The answer is to use both, if your skills set permits it. *Java can be used to handle any kind of complex code not accessing the database. PL/SQL can be used to access the database*. If you cannot or do not wish to use a mix and prefer Java, then be aware that a relational database is not able to handle object-oriented design. Object orientation allows a complete and total *black box* breakdown into easily definable and understandable individual objects. A relational database model is completely opposite in its more efficient forms. Do not attempt to impose an object structure on a relational structure. Furthermore, even an object-relational database can sometimes be pushing the envelope a little too far. Object design is perfect for granularity. Relational models are not suited to granularity unless a fully normalized database model is the most efficient relational modeling approach for your application (this is rare).

7.7   Object and Relational Conflicts

Relational and object data model structures are completely different from each other. There is great potential for conflict when combining these two methodologies into what is called an object-relational database. These conflicts can hamper performance in a relational database such as Oracle Database.

7.7.1   Large Binary Objects in a Relational Database

The biggest benefit to the combination of objects and relations is that of including large binary objects into a relational structure, such as multimedia objects. However, there is a twist. In both relational and object databases, the most efficient storage method for multimedia objects is to use a BFILENAME pointer, which does not store the object in the database but contains a path and file name for the object. The object is stored externally to the database in the file system. Storing large binary objects in any database is inefficient because those binary objects can span multiple blocks, both Oracle Database blocks and operating system blocks. Even with Oracle Database 9*i*, multiple block sizes, and specific storage structures for LOB datatypes, large multimedia objects will span more than one block.

Storing data into a database that spans more than a single block is effectively row chaining, where a row is *chained* from one block to another. Chaining is not really an issue if the blocks are physically next to each other. Also, the DB_FILE_MULTIBLOCK_READ_COUNT parameter can help counteract this problem. The fact is that contiguous, defragmented block storage is extremely unlikely in any database environment. It is usually best to store large singular binary objects in the file system.

Note: (10*g*) BIGFILE tablespaces can possibly help alleviate these issues somewhat.

7.7.2   **Object-Relational Collections**

Including TABLE and VARRAY collections inside relational tables and within PL/SQL is generally a very bad idea. Collections are an object-methodological approach to object data abstraction and encapsulation. Object methodologies are completely opposed to those of relational databases. An object structure is spherical, allowing access from any point to any point within an entire database. A relational database is more two dimensional in nature and requires that access to data be passed through or down semi-hierarchical structures or into subset parts of a data model. Because PL/SQL is merely an extension of SQL, and SQL is a purely relational database access language, any type of object coding is best avoided using PL/SQL. If you want to write object code, use Java. Java is built for object structures.

The same approach applies to including object structures in tables. There are various instances in which collection substructures can be utilized in relational database tables. First normal form master detail and second normal form foreign key static table inclusion relationships are possibilities. However, storage structures remain applicable to a relational methodology and are still ultimately stored in rows (tuples). Tables and rows are two-dimensional. Object structures are multidimensional. The two do not fit together. If you must contain collections in tables in Oracle Database, various object collection types could be used. Associative arrays are the most efficient:

- *Nested table*. A nested table is a dynamic array. A dynamic array is a pointer. A pointer does not require a specific size limit, thus the use of the term *dynamic*. Dynamic implies that it can have any number of rows or entries in its array.

- *VARRAY*. A VARRAY is a fixed-length array. A fixed-length array is a reserved chunk of memory saved for multiple array rows. Unlike a dynamic array, a fixed-length array has space in memory reserved for the whole array structure.

- *Associative array.* An associative array is an indexed dynamic array and can potentially be accessed faster than a nested table because it can be accessed using an index.

Problems with objects in relational models are usually a misunderstanding of object modeling techniques. It is common knowledge that the approach required for object data modeling is completely different from that of relational modeling. The same is very likely to apply to object-relational modeling using object types such as nested table, VARRAY, or associative array collections in Oracle Database tables. Using these collection datatypes requires object and relational modeling skills, not only relational modeling skills.

7.8   Replacing DELETE with TRUNCATE

The DDL TRUNCATE command is faster than using the DELETE command when deleting all the rows from a table. The TRUNCATE command automatically commits and does not create any log entries or rollback. The obvious problem with TRUNCATE is that an error cannot be undone.

That ends this chapter on examining advanced concepts of how to create efficient SQL. In the next chapter, we will look at indexing and start to delve a little deeper into Oracle Database specifics.

7.9   Endnotes

1.   Oracle Data Warehouse Tuning for 10*g* (Gavin Powell, Digital Press, Aug 2005, ISBN: 1555583350)

8

Common-Sense Indexing

We have seen in the previous chapter how important it is to properly match various SQL code clauses with indexes. This chapter examines the internal structure of various different types of indexes, which apply in different circumstances and for different tasks. Where different index structures are applicable to different tasks, indexes will often perform very poorly when used inappropriately. Thus the title of this chapter being "Common-Sense Indexing" implies utilizing the appropriate index type under the correct circumstances. Let's start with looking at what should be indexed and how.

8.1   What and How to Index

When considering indexes, never be afraid of not indexing. On the contrary, do not always assume that an existing index should exist, simply because it does exist.

When considering use of unusual indexes such as clusters, bitmaps, and hashing, be aware of their applications. The only index type that is amenable to data changes is a BTree index. All other index types are effectively read-only type indexes and are preferably never used otherwise. This is not always the case in some other relational databases, but it is usually the case for Oracle Database. In most relational databases, clusters, bitmaps, and hash indexes do not manage overflow well, if at all. Overflow in an index, when searching for data, can result in *bouncing* from the index block to an area outside of the original index structure, often negating the point of using the index in the first place.

Database administrators should always keep a watchful eye on indexing in a database. There is never really available time, but when an application is released, it is always best to reexamine all indexing. Developers often create many indexes, sometimes each creating their own sets of indexes. The result can be overindexing. Too many indexes on a table will create a performance problem.

Note: (10*g*) The SQL Access Advisor interface in the Database Control can be used to assess index usefulness to a certain extent.

Note: Executing a DML command on a table will execute the same command on all of its indexes. For instance, inserting a single row into a table with four indexes comprises five changes to the database.

Be especially vigilant for the use of bitmap and function-based indexes. Bitmap indexes are usually only effective in read-only situations. Function-based indexes are nice, but I have never seen the optimizer use one effectively in a commercial environment. However, this is often because configuration parameters are inappropriately set. The parameters QUERY_REWRITE_ ENABLED and QUERY_REWRITE_INTEGRITY must be set to TRUE and TRUSTED respectively to allow use of function-based indexes. Developers and database administrators tend to like function-based indexes and bitmaps, especially when they have just read about them in the manual. Be alert for these unusual indexes because both bitmap and function-based indexes are often ineffective and can as a result be exceedingly detrimental to performance. I can remember one particular case where many bitmap indexes were used. The database was in excess of 200 Gb and had a fairly large combination, online and reporting, production database. When one of the bitmaps was changed to a BTree index—a process taking eight hours to run—it was completed in less than three minutes using the BTree indexes. This case involved heavy DML activity on the table on which the bitmap index was created.

8.1.1   When Not to Use Indexes

There are some circumstances where indexes can be detrimental to performance, and sometimes those indexes should not exist. The optimizer will occasionally ignore indexes and consider reading the entire table a faster option:

- *A table with a small number of columns may not benefit from an index if a large percentage of its rows are always retrieved from it.* The optimizer defaults to a full table scan if a large percentage of rows are read (usually over 5% to 10%, but this percentage can vary). In other words, the optimizer considers it more efficient to read just the table, rather than index and table, when many rows are read from the table.

- *Small static data tables may be so small that the optimizer will simply read those tables as a full table scan, ignoring indexes altogether.* In some cases, the optimizer may use an index on a small table where it should not, because a full table scan would be faster. An exception to this rule is in mutable joins where unique index hits are often used, even on small tables. If full table scans are faster than index reads in those mutable joins, you might want to remove indexes from the small tables altogether, or override with hints. Examine your small static data tables. Do they really need indexing?

Note: A hint is a comment added to a SQL command allowing overriding of the optimizer.

Note: Removing foreign key indexes, even from static data tables, can cause serious performance problems as a result of concurrent locking activities.

- *Sometimes tables created for reporting or data warehousing may already be in the correct physical order, commonly if those tables are only ever appended to use mass insertions.* Creating an index may be pointless in this type of situation, because the data may already be in the required physical order.

- *Indexes should usually be created on a small percentage of the columns in a table.* Large composite indexes may be relatively large (row length is equivalent to concatenated column width), compared with the table. The relative size between index and table is important. The larger the ratio of index to table physical size, the less helpful the index will be in terms of decreasing physical space to be read. Also, if the table's columns, which are not indexed, contain NULL values, it may be faster to read the entire table. Why create indexes?

- NULL values are not included in BTree indexes. Do not index columns containing NULL values in many rows, unless there is a specific use for it, such as filtering the column as NOT NULL (only scanning the index and the rows without NULL values).

8.1.2 Utilizing Referential Integrity Indexes

Referential integrity uses primary and foreign keys to validate relationships between rows in related tables. Oracle Database does not automatically create indexes on foreign keys, and it is advisable to do so manually.

Data models of different forms can have either single-column unique integer identifiers in one extreme or large composite column indexes at another extreme. It is often possible that application SQL code can generally make good use of referential integrity indexes when the data model matches the functionality of the application well. This is especially true in two cases:

- *Java object applications are often compatible with data model structure containing single-column unique integer identifiers (surrogate keys), where the integers match Java object identifiers.* This type of data model is often highly normalized and usually in great danger of being overnormalized. Alternate indexing is not common in Java top-down designed data models but can be used to validate nonidentifying unique values (not surrogate keys) such as unique names.

- *More traditional key structured data models containing multiple-column composite keys.* Indexes can also match application functionality well, but not as often as Java application object identifier structures. Typically, these types of data models have difficulty avoiding extensive alternate indexing. Composite indexes can contain multiple columns. As a result, alternate keys are not only additional in nature, but also used to apply different orders to primary and foreign keys, or even comprise additional, and perhaps reordered, subsets of those keys. Over time, the Oracle Database optimizer is becoming more capable of matching SQL code with dissimilar index orders, but there will always be limitations.

Any kind of reporting or data warehousing application requirements will cause a need for alternate indexing. Any online application with any type of reporting will generally be inclined in this direction as well.

If referential integrity indexing can be used for general SQL code tuning, then do so as much as possible. Ultimately, fewer indexes will be required, and thus applications will perform better in general.

8.1.2.1 Alternate and Secondary Indexing

Alternate indexing is also referred to as secondary indexing or tertiary indexing. Alternate indexing includes any indexes created against tables in a data model, which are not part of referential integrity rules (constraints). The need for alternate indexing is often a mismatch between the data model and functionality required by applications. Sometimes unique indexes are required on specific columns in data models, other than unique integer identifier columns (surrogate keys) in every table. The application could deal with this particular issue, but it may be best to place unique constraints in the database, for the same reasons that referential integrity should not be placed in the application or in triggers. Once again, excessive alternate indexing could indicate data model problems or simply a mismatch between data model and application requirements.

8.2 Types of Indexes

There are several general types of indexes:

- *No index*. A table without an index is known as being heap structured. It is quite literally in a heap. If this method of table access is efficient, which it can be, then do not create indexes for that table. Sometimes even referential integrity indexes can be detrimental to performance.

- *Static data index*. This is an index placed on a small static data table. Sometimes these tables do not require indexes for anything other than referential integrity because optimization may always choose a full table scan for better performance. In some cases, referential integrity indexes can be removed for better performance, especially where the static table contains no foreign key entries. Static implies no changes—ever! If data in a table never changes, why include added processing to verify referential integrity?

- *Dynamic data index*. These indexes expect changes to data and are thus subject to overflow. They may require frequent rebuilding. Rarely, if ever, should you use anything other than BTree-type indexing for dynamic data. Clustering, hashing, and bitmaps are usually only appropriate for read-only tables, with the exception of index-organized tables in rare circumstances. Index-organized tables effectively sort index and data values for an entire table into a BTree. Index-organized tables can perform well in OLTP-type databases but are more appropriate to data warehouses.

- *Read-only reporting index.* Read-only tables are much more flexible with respect to indexing. Oracle Database allows numerous types of indexes for read-only tables. Each index type has a specific application.

- *Unique and nonunique indexes.* A unique index allows only a single value in a table across all rows. Be careful creating unique indexes because every insertion or update to a uniquely indexed column or columns requires a scan of at least the entire index space (for that particular column).

- *Single-column and composite indexes.* Single-column indexes are more efficient than composite (multiple-column) indexes.

Indexes can be created on columns of all datatypes and any combination thereof. Just remember this one thing: by far the most efficient and easy to manage type of index is an index created on a unique integer identifier (often a surrogate key). In Oracle Database, these indexes are best incremented using Oracle Database sequence generators.

8.3   Types of Indexes in Oracle Database

These types of indexes are available in Oracle Database:

- Efficient as read-write indexes:
  - BTree (binary tree)
  - Function-based
  - Reverse key
- Efficient as read-only indexes:
  - Bitmap
  - Bitmap join
  - Index-organized table (sometimes useful in OLTP databases)
  - Cluster and hash cluster

- Domain indexes have a very specific application in an Oracle Database optional add-on and are out of the scope of this book.

There are also certain attributes of some index types relevant to tuning:

- Ascending or descending

- Uniqueness

- Composites

- Compression

- Reverse key indexes

- Unsorted indexes using the NOSORT option

- Null values

Let's look briefly at index syntax. Then we will proceed to describe each index structure, how they should be used, and how they can be tuned without delving too much into physical tuning. Physical and configuration tuning is covered in Part III of this book.

8.3.1 The Syntax of Oracle Database Indexes

Following is a syntax diagram for the CREATE INDEX and ALTER INDEX commands. This is Part II of this book, the SQL code tuning section. So once again, any physical attributes and configuration are reserved for possible discussion in Part III, covering physical and configuration tuning. Sections of the syntax diagram are highlighted to denote parts of Oracle Database index object maintenance, which are relevant to SQL code tuning. Specifically, grayed-out sections are physical tuning and are thus reserved for explanation in Part III.

```
CREATE [ UNIQUE | BITMAP ] INDEX [ schema.] index ON
{
    [ schema.]table [ alias ] ( column [, column … ] | expression )
    {
      [[ NO ] COMPRESS [ n ] ] [ NOSORT | REVERSE ]
      [ ONLINE ] [ COMPUTE STATISTICS ] [ TABLESPACE tablespace ]
      [[ NO ] LOGGING ]
      [ physical properties ]
[ partitioning properties ]
```

```
[ parallel properties ]
}
}
| CLUSTER [ schema.]cluster { cluster properties }
| Bitmap join index clause;


ALTER [ UNIQUE | BITMAP ] INDEX [ schema.]index
[
    [ ENABLE | DISABLE ] [ UNUSABLE ] [ COALESCE ]
    [ RENAME TO index ] [[ NO ] LOGGING ] [[ NO ] MONITORING USAGE ]
    [ REBUILD [[ NO ] COMPRESS [ n ]  ] [[ NO ] REVERSE ]
      [ ONLINE ] [ COMPUTE STATISTICS ] [ TABLESPACE tablespace ] [[
NO ] LOGGING ]
    ]
    [ physical properties ]
[ partitioning properties ]
[ parallel properties ]
    [ deallocate unused clause ]
[ allocate extent clause ]
]
| CLUSTER [ schema.]cluster { cluster properties };
```

8.3.2   Oracle Database BTree Indexes

Figure 8.1 shows the internal structure of a BTree index. Note that there are only three layers. Each separate boxed numbered block node in Figure 8.1 represents a block in an Oracle database. A block is the smallest physical unit in an Oracle database. Every read of a datafile will read one or more blocks. A unique index scan reading a single row will read the index datafile up to three times and the table once. A total of four blocks will be read: (1) the root node index block, (2) the second layer index branch block, (3) the index leaf block, and finally (4) the block in the table containing the row, using the ROWID pointer stored in the index. Indexes for very small tables may be contained in a single block and will thus consist of a root block only. All of these block references are accessed using ROWID pointers. ROWID pointers are very fast. *Unique index hits are the fastest way of accessing data in a database*.

A BTree index does not overflow like other types of indexes. If a block is filled, then a new block is created, and branch nodes are changed or added as required. The parent branch and root node contents could even be

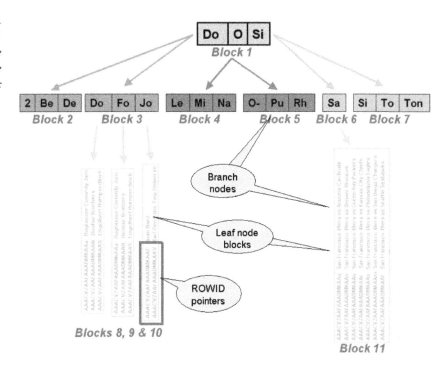

Figure 8.1
An Oracle Database BTree index

adjusted to prevent skewing. Only a change to an indexed table column will change a BTree index. BTree indexes are the best index for obtaining exact row *hits* (single row read, effectively a single block), range scans, and changes to the database. The only exception to the overflow rule for a BTree index is that duplicate index values, not fitting into a single block, can extend into new blocks. This type of overflow is not quite the same as overflow in other index types, because other index types do not update index structure *on the fly*, nearly as effectively as BTree indexes do, if at all.

The following query retrieves index statistics from the USER_INDEXES metadata view, sorted in branch level order for all the Accounts schema tables. The lower the branch depth level of the BTree, the better, because less searching through branches is required. In general, any nonunique index will become less efficient as it becomes larger and contains more duplicates:

- Branch level 0 indexes are all small static data tables.

- Branch level 1 indexes are either semi-static or semi-dynamic tables.

■ Branch level 2 indexes are very large tables including many nonunique foreign key indexes, which have low cardinality. A low cardinality index is a nonunique index with many duplicated values and few distinct values.

```
SELECT table_name,index_name,num_rows "Rows"
,blevel "Branch",leaf_blocks "LeafBlocks"
FROM user_indexes WHERE index_type = 'NORMAL' AND num_rows > 0
ORDER BY blevel, table_name, index_name;
```

TABLE_NAME	INDEX_NAME	Rows	Branch	LeafBlocks
CATEGORY	AK_CATEGORY_TEXT	13	0	1
CATEGORY	XPKCATEGORY	13	0	1
COA	XFK_COA_SUBTYPE	55	0	1
COA	XFK_COA_TYPE	55	0	1
COA	XPKCOA	55	0	1
POSTING	XFK_POSTING_CRCOA#	8	0	1
POSTING	XFK_POSTING_DRCOA#	8	0	1
POSTING	XPKPOSTING	8	0	1
STOCK	XFK_STOCK_CATEGORY	118	0	1
STOCK	XPKSTOCK	118	0	1
SUBTYPE	XPKSUBTYPE	4	0	1
TYPE	XPKTYPE	6	0	1
CASHBOOK	XPKCASHBOOK	188185	1	352
CASHBOOKLINE	XFK_CBL_CHEQUE	188185	1	418
CASHBOOKLINE	XFK_CBL_TRANS	188185	1	418
CASHBOOKLINE	XPKCASHBOOKLINE	188185	1	423
CUSTOMER	AK_CUSTOMER_NAME	2694	1	17
CUSTOMER	AK_CUSTOMER_TICKER	2694	1	12
CUSTOMER	XPKCUSTOMER	2694	1	5
ORDERS	XFK_ORDERS_CUSTOMER	31935	1	67
ORDERS	XFK_ORDERS_SUPPLIER	140369	1	293
ORDERS	XFK_ORDERS_TYPE	172304	1	313
ORDERS	XPKORDERS	172304	1	323
STOCK	AK_TEXT	118	1	2
STOCKSOURCE	XFK_STOCKSOURCE_STOCK	12083	1	24
STOCKSOURCE	XFK_STOCKSOURCE_SUPPLIER	12083	1	26
STOCKSOURCE	XPKSUPPLIER_STOCK	12083	1	46

SUPPLIER	AK_SUPPLIER_NAME	3874	1	27
SUPPLIER	AK_SUPPLIER_TICKER	3874	1	17
SUPPLIER	XPKSUPPLIER	3874	1	7
TRANSACTIONS	XFX_TRANS_CUSTOMER	33142	1	70
TRANSACTIONS	XFX_TRANS_ORDER	173511	1	386
TRANSACTIONS	XFX_TRANS_SUPPLIER	155043	1	324
TRANSACTIONS	XFX_TRANS_TYPE	188185	1	341
TRANSACTIONS	XPKTRANSACTIONS	188185	1	378
CASHBOOK	XFK_CB_CRCOA#	188185	2	446
CASHBOOK	XFK_CB_DRCOA#	188185	2	446
GENERALLEDGER	AK_GENERALLEDGER_1	752744	2	4014
GENERALLEDGER	AK_GL_DTE	752744	2	1992
GENERALLEDGER	XFK_GL_COA#	752744	2	1784
GENERALLEDGER	XPKGENERALLEDGER	752744	2	1425
ORDERSLINE	XFK_ORDERLINE_ORDER	540827	2	1201
ORDERSLINE	XFK_ORDERLINE_SM	540827	2	1204
ORDERSLINE	XPKORDERSLINE	540827	2	1215
STOCKMOVEMENT	XFK_SM_STOCK	570175	2	1124
STOCKMOVEMENT	XPKSTOCKMOVEMENT	570175	2	1069
TRANSACTIONS	XFX_TRANS_CRCOA#	188185	2	446
TRANSACTIONS	XFX_TRANS_DRCOA#	188185	2	446
TRANSACTIONSLINE	XFK_TRANSLINE_SM	570175	2	1270
TRANSACTIONSLINE	XFK_TRANSLINE_TRANS	570175	2	1267
TRANSACTIONSLINE	XPKTRANSACTIONSLINE	570175	2	1336

That's enough about BTree indexes for now. We will cover some non-physical tuning aspects shortly. Let's look at the other Oracle Database index types.

8.3.3 **Read-Only Indexing**

Read-only indexes are not always, but generally, applicable to reporting and data warehouse databases. This book is not intended as a data warehouse book.[1] However, these types of indexes can be used in online and client-server databases with one restriction: the more table changes are made, then the more often these types of indexes must be rebuilt. There are several important issues with respect to non-BTree indexes:

- They can be extremely fast in the proper circumstances. Read-only indexes are designed for exactly that and are built to perform well when reading data.

- Two issues are associated with read-only indexing when making changes to tables:

  - When changed, these indexes will generally overflow and rapidly become less efficient. Future read access requiring overflowed rows will search outside the original index structure, into physical overflow spaces. The point of an index is searching of preordered physical space.
  - The more changes made will make future changes even slower.

Before examining these index types in detail, it should be noted that these specialized index types are most often appropriate to read-only and data warehouse environments. There are always particular circumstances where indexes other than BTree indexes could be useful in OLTP environments. Let's look briefly at the different types of read-only indexes.

8.3.3.1 Bitmap Indexes

A bitmap index stores a value of 0 or 1 for a ROWID. The ROWID points to a row in a table. In Figure 8.2, a bitmap index is created on a column containing codes for states.

Figure 8.2
A bitmap index

ROWID	VENUE	CITY	STATE	COUNTRY
A,A,AHfV,A,A,JA,A,AK0KA,A,A	3com Park	San Francisco	CA	USA
A,A,AHfV,A,A,JA,A,AK0KA,A,B	Agenda Lounge	San Jose	CA	USA
A,A,AHfV,A,A,JA,A,AK0KA,A,C	Altamont Raceway Park	Tracy	CA	USA
A,A,AHfV,A,A,JA,A,AK0KA,A,D	Amador Theatre	Pleasanton	CA	USA
A,A,AHfV,A,A,JA,A,AK0KA,A,Q	Caesars	Lake Tahoe	NV	USA
A,A,AHfV,A,A,JA,A,AK0KA,A,R	Caesars Palace	Las Vegas	NV	USA
A,A,AHfV,A,A,JA,A,AK0LA,A,c	Madison Square Garden	New York	NY	USA
A,A,AHfV,A,A,JA,A,AK0LA,A,b	Yankee Stadium	New York	NY	USA

ROWID	STATE='CA'	STATE='NY'	STATE='NV'
A,A,AHfV,A,A,JA,A,AK0KA,A,A	1	0	0
A,A,AHfV,A,A,JA,A,AK0KA,A,B	1	0	0
A,A,AHfV,A,A,JA,A,AK0KA,A,C	1	0	0
A,A,AHfV,A,A,JA,A,AK0KA,A,D	1	0	0
A,A,AHfV,A,A,JA,A,AK0KA,A,Q	0	1	0
A,A,AHfV,A,A,JA,A,AK0KA,A,R	0	1	0
A,A,AHfV,A,A,JA,A,AK0LA,A,c	0	0	1
A,A,AHfV,A,A,JA,A,AK0LA,A,b	0	0	1

There are some things to be remembered when considering using bitmap indexes:

- *In general, bitmaps are effective for single-column indexes with low cardinality.* Low cardinality implies very few different values. However, bitmap indexes can perform relatively well with thousands of different values. The size of a bitmap index will be smaller than that of a BTree, and thus search speed is increased by searching through less physical space.

- *Bitmap indexes are much faster than BTree indexes* in read-only environments. Read-write environments such as in OLTP databases are also appropriate. However, extensive DML activity can drastically deteriorate bitmap index performance over time. Bitmap indexes must be rebuilt more frequently than BTree indexes.

- Probably the most significant performance issue with bitmap indexes is that *unlike BTree indexes, bitmaps will lock at the block level rather than at the row level*. With bitmap indexes, it becomes even more likely that locking will cause performance problems with UPDATE and DELETE commands. This is because a bitmap index will have more index entries per block as a result of less space used. UPDATE and DELETE commands require exclusive locks.

- *Bitmap indexes should not be used to create composite column indexes*. Composite values are likely to have too many different values (high cardinality). If composite column indexes are required, simply create multiple single-column bitmap indexes on each column. SQL WHERE clause filtering in Oracle Database can match multiple single-column bitmap indexes in the same query, in any order. Bitmap indexes can be used very effectively in this manner, as multiple individual column indexes, all of low cardinality, working together in a WHERE clause filter using all or some of those columns as the order of the WHERE clause is immaterial to the optimizer.

- *Bitmap indexes may be subject to overflow*. Bitmaps are often used in large data warehouse databases where changes are not made to tables other than complete reloads.

Note: Traditionally, any index type other than a BTree index involves overflow. Overflow implies links between blocks outside of the normal index structure, where values cannot fit into previously reserved index space. Overflow is detrimental to performance.

Like BTree indexes, bitmap indexes should probably be regularly rebuilt. However, for large databases, regular bitmap index rebuilds can consume more time than is acceptable. Therefore, bitmap indexes are most appropriate for large, low-cardinality, read-only, or static data tables.

Let's do some experimenting and show that bitmap indexes are faster than BTree indexes.

8.3.3.1.1   *Are Bitmap Indexes Faster Than BTree Indexes?*

The Transactions table contains a column called type having two possible values representing a customer- or a supplier-based transaction:

```
SQL> SELECT type "Type", COUNT(type) FROM transactions GROUP
BY type;


T COUNT(TYPE)
- -----------
P      175641
S       61994
```

I am going to create two temporary copies of the Transactions table. One will have a BTree index on the type column and the other a bitmap index:

```
CREATE TABLE btree_table AS SELECT * FROM transactions;
CREATE INDEX btree_index ON btree_table(type) COMPUTE
STATISTICS;
CREATE TABLE bitmap_table AS SELECT * FROM transactions;
CREATE BITMAP INDEX bitmap_index ON bitmap_table(type)
COMPUTE STATISTICS;
```

We need to generate statistics for the new objects, because the EXPLAIN PLAN command will be used to demonstrate:

```
ANALYZE TABLE btree_table COMPUTE STATISTICS;
ANALYZE TABLE bitmap_table COMPUTE STATISTICS;
```

Looking at the query plans, we can see that accessing the bitmap index is faster than using the BTree index. I used hints in order to force usage of the required indexes. The type = 'P' comparison accesses just shy of 75% of the table. The optimizer will do a full table scan without the hints. Using the BTree index:

```
EXPLAIN PLAN SET statement_id='TEST' FOR
SELECT /*+ INDEX(btree_table, btree_index) */ *
FROM btree_table WHERE type = 'P';
```

Query	Cost	Rows	Bytes
SELECT STATEMENT on	**1347**	94093	3387348
TABLE ACCESS BY INDEX ROWID on BTREE_TABLE	1347	94093	3387348
INDEX RANGE SCAN on **BTREE_INDEX**	171	94093	

And comparing with the bitmap index:

```
EXPLAIN PLAN SET statement_id='TEST' FOR
SELECT /*+ INDEX(bitmap_table, bitmap_index) */ *
FROM bitmap_table WHERE type = 'P';
```

Query	Cost	Rows	Bytes
SELECT STATEMENT on	**806**	94093	3387348
TABLE ACCESS BY INDEX ROWID on BITMAP_TABLE	806	94093	3387348
BITMAP CONVERSION TO ROWIDS on			
BITMAP INDEX SINGLE VALUE on **BITMAP_INDEX**			

Timing the SQL statements, we can see again that accessing the bitmap is much faster. A different-sized table with a different selection may have had a more significant difference. First, using the BTree index:

```
SQL> SELECT COUNT(*) FROM (
  2   SELECT /*+ INDEX(btree_table, btree_index) */ *
  3   FROM btree_table WHERE type = 'P');

  COUNT(*)
----------
     33142

Elapsed: 00:00:01.01
```

And again comparing with the bitmap index:

```
SQL> SELECT COUNT(*) FROM (
```

```
2   SELECT /*+ INDEX(bitmap_table, bitmap_index) */ *
3   FROM bitmap_table WHERE type = 'P');

COUNT(*)
----------
    33142


Elapsed: 00:00:00.00
```

Bitmap indexes can be significantly faster than BTree indexes. Costs in the two previous query plans decreased for the bitmap index from 1,347 to 806, a 40% decrease in cost.

Note: During the period in which these query plans were generated, no DML-type changes were made to the two new tables. In other words, there was no DML change activity that could have affected either index access or potential index overflow.

Let's clean up by dropping the tables, which will drop the attached indexes:

```
DROP TABLE btree_table;
DROP TABLE bitmap_table;
```

8.3.3.1.2 *Bitmap Index Locking*

As already stated, there is one particular case I remember where many bitmap indexes were used. The database was in excess of 200 Gb and had a fairly large combination online and reporting production database. When one of the bitmaps was changed to a BTree index, a process taking eight hours to run was completed in less than three minutes. Two possible causes would have been bitmap index block-level locks as a result of heavy DML activity or perhaps uncontrollable bitmap index overflow.

8.3.3.1.3 *Using Composite Bitmap Indexes*

Let's do query plans and some speed checking with composite column indexing:

```
CREATE TABLE btree_table AS SELECT * FROM stockmovement;
```

```
CREATE INDEX btree_index ON btree_table
(stock_id,qty,price,dte)
COMPUTE STATISTICS;
CREATE TABLE bitmap_table AS SELECT * FROM stockmovement;
CREATE BITMAP INDEX bitmap_index ON bitmap_table
(stock_id,qty,price,dte) COMPUTE STATISTICS;
```

Once again, we need to generate statistics for the new objects, because the EXPLAIN PLAN command will be used to demonstrate:

```
ANALYZE TABLE btree_table COMPUTE STATISTICS;
ANALYZE TABLE bitmap_table COMPUTE STATISTICS;
```

Begin with query plans using the EXPLAIN PLAN command. First, the BTree index:

```
EXPLAIN PLAN SET statement_id='TEST' FOR
SELECT /*+ INDEX(btree_table, btree_index) */ *
FROM btree_table
WHERE stock_id IN (SELECT stock_id FROM stock)
AND qty > 0
AND price > 0
AND dte < SYSDATE;
```

Query	Cost	Rows	Bytes
SELECT STATEMENT on	**10031**	16227	405675
TABLE ACCESS BY INDEX ROWID on BTREE_TABLE	85	138	3036
NESTED LOOPS on	10031	16227	405675
INDEX FULL SCAN on XPK_STOCK	1	118	354
INDEX RANGE SCAN on BTREE_INDEX	20	138	

And second, using the bitmap index:

```
EXPLAIN PLAN SET statement_id='TEST' FOR
SELECT /*+ INDEX_COMBINE(bitmap_table, bitmap_index) */ *
FROM bitmap_table
WHERE stock_id IN (SELECT stock_id FROM stock)
AND qty > 0
AND price > 0
```

```
AND dte < SYSDATE;

Query                                             Cost     Rows     Bytes
----------------------------------------------  ------  -------  ---------
SELECT STATEMENT   on                           7157     16227    405675
 NESTED LOOPS   on                              7157     16227    405675
  TABLE ACCESS BY INDEX ROWID on BITMAP_TABLE   7156     16227    356994
   BITMAP CONVERSION TO ROWIDS on
    BITMAP INDEX FULL SCAN on BITMAP_INDEX
  INDEX UNIQUE SCAN on XPK_STOCK                              1          3
```

Now some speed testing. First, the BTree index:

```
SQL> SELECT COUNT(*) FROM(
  2  SELECT /*+ INDEX(btree_table, btree_index) */ *
  3  FROM btree_table
  4  WHERE stock_id IN (SELECT stock_id FROM stock)
  5  AND qty > 0
  6  AND price > 0
  7  AND dte < SYSDATE);

  COUNT(*)
----------
    115590

Elapsed: 00:00:00.09
```

And the bitmap index:

```
SQL> SELECT COUNT(*) FROM(
  2  SELECT /*+ INDEX(bitmap_table, bitmap_index) */ *
  3  FROM bitmap_table
  4  WHERE stock_id IN (SELECT stock_id FROM stock)
  5  AND qty > 0
  6  AND price > 0
  7  AND dte < SYSDATE);

  COUNT(*)
----------
    115590

Elapsed: 00:00:00.02
```

We can see that even a composite bitmap index is faster than a composite BTree index. However, the cost increase is 10,031 to 7,157, only a 30% decrease in cost. It could probably be concluded that composite bitmap indexes do not perform as well as single-column bitmap indexes.

Note: Again, during the period in which these query plans were generated, no DML-type changes were made to the two new tables.

Now let's break the bitmap index into separate single-column indexes, run the query plan and timing tests again, and see if we get a performance improvement, as opposed to using the composite bitmap index. Drop the previous version of the bitmap index and create four separate bitmap indexes:

```
DROP INDEX bitmap_index;
CREATE BITMAP INDEX bitmap_index_stock_id ON
bitmap_table(stock_id);
CREATE BITMAP INDEX bitmap_index_qty ON bitmap_table(qty);
CREATE BITMAP INDEX bitmap_index_price ON
bitmap_table(price);
CREATE BITMAP INDEX bitmap_index_dte ON bitmap_table(dte);
```

Note that the hint has changed. The INDEX_COMBINE hint attempts to force usage of multiple bitmap indexes:

```
EXPLAIN PLAN SET statement_id='TEST' FOR
SELECT /*+ INDEX_COMBINE(bitmap_table) */ * FROM bitmap_table
WHERE stock_id IN (SELECT stock_id FROM stock)
AND qty > 0
AND price > 0
AND dte < SYSDATE;
```

Query	Cost	Rows	Bytes
SELECT STATEMENT on	**1004**	16226	405650
NESTED LOOPS on	1004	16226	405650
TABLE ACCESS BY INDEX ROWID on BITMAP_TABLE	1004	16226	356972
BITMAP CONVERSION TO ROWIDS on			
BITMAP AND on			
BITMAP MERGE on			
BITMAP INDEX RANGE SCAN on BITMAP_INDEX_DTE			

```
BITMAP MERGE   on
   BITMAP INDEX RANGE SCAN on BITMAP_INDEX_QTY
BITMAP MERGE   on
   BITMAP INDEX RANGE SCAN on BITMAP_INDEX_PRICE
INDEX UNIQUE SCAN on XPK_STOCK                                1        3
```

The cost difference between the composite bitmap index and the single-column bitmap indexes has increased significantly. Using single-column bitmap indexes is much faster than using composite bitmap indexes.

Now let's clean up:

```
DROP TABLE btree_table;
DROP TABLE bitmap_table;
```

8.3.3.1.4   *Do Bitmap Indexes Overflow?*

In the previous examples creating the indexes, after creating and populating the tables, built the indexes in the most efficient way. Now I am going to create a bitmap index in a slightly less appropriate place on a column with lower cardinality. The purpose here is to demonstrate the potential deterioration of bitmap indexes because of overflow. Following is a count of the rows of repeated values of the GeneralLedger.COA# column. The total row count is currently 1,045,681 rows:

```
SQL> SELECT coa#, COUNT(coa#) FROM generalledger GROUP BY
coa#;

COA#   COUNT(COA#)
-----  -----------
30001       377393
40003       145447
41000       246740
50001       203375
50028            1
60001        72725
```

First, we need to do a query plan for the current existing BTree index on the COA# column foreign key BTree index:

```
EXPLAIN PLAN SET statement_id='TEST' FOR
SELECT /*+ INDEX(generalledger, xfk_coa#) */ *
FROM generalledger WHERE coa# = '60001';
```

Query	Cost	Rows	Bytes
SELECT STATEMENT on	**3441**	177234	4076382
TABLE ACCESS BY INDEX ROWID on GENERALLEDGER	3441	177234	4076382
INDEX RANGE SCAN on XFK_COA#	422	177234	

Now I will change the foreign key index to a bitmap, generate statistics, and run the EXPLAIN PLAN command again. Clearly, the bitmap is faster than the BTree index. First, we create the bitmap index:

```
DROP INDEX xfk_coa#;
CREATE BITMAP INDEX xfk_coa#_bitmap ON generalledger(coa#)
COMPUTE STATISTICS;
ANALYZE TABLE generalledger COMPUTE STATISTICS;
```

And now the query plan (EXPLAIN PLAN) for the bitmap index:

```
EXPLAIN PLAN SET statement_id='TEST' FOR
SELECT /*+ INDEX(generalledger, xfk_coa#_bitmap) */ *
FROM generalledger WHERE coa# = '60001';
```

Query	Cost	Rows	Bytes
SELECT STATEMENT on	**1707**	177234	4076382
TABLE ACCESS BY INDEX ROWID on GENERALLEDGER	1707	177234	4076382
BITMAP CONVERSION TO ROWIDS on			
BITMAP INDEX SINGLE VALUE on XFK_COA#_BITMAP			

Notice how the cost of using the bitmap index is much lower than that of using the BTree index.

In the next step, I restart my database and begin processing to execute a large amount of concurrent activity, letting it run for a while. The objective is to find any deterioration in the bitmap index caused by excessive DML activity. The row count for the GeneralLedger table is now 10,000 rows more than previously. Statistics must be regenerated because rows have been added. Accurate and up-to-date statistics are always sensible:

```
ANALYZE TABLE generalledger COMPUTE STATISTICS;
ANALYZE INDEX xfk_coa#_bitmap COMPUTE STATISTICS;
```

And now for the query plan:

```
EXPLAIN PLAN SET statement_id='TEST' FOR
SELECT /*+ INDEX(generalledger, xfk_coa#_bitmap) */ *
FROM generalledger WHERE coa# = '60001';
```

```
Query                                           Cost    Rows      Bytes
---------------------------------------------   ------  -------   ---------
SELECT STATEMENT  on                            1729    178155    4097565
 TABLE ACCESS BY INDEX ROWID on GENERALLEDGER   1729    178155    4097565
  BITMAP CONVERSION TO ROWIDS on
   BITMAP INDEX SINGLE VALUE on XFK_COA#_BITMAP
```

We can see from the two previous query plans that the cost of using the bitmap index has decreased by about 1% after adding around 10,000 rows to the GeneralLedger table. Now I will run the same highly concurrent DML commands and add some more rows to the GeneralLedger table, only this time we will change the bitmap index back to a BTree index and compare the relative query cost deterioration. This is done by dropping the bitmap index and re-creating it as a BTree index:

```
DROP INDEX xfk_coa#_bitmap;
CREATE INDEX xfk_coa# ON generalledger(coa#);
```

Note: (10g) In Oracle Database 10g, a bitmap index can also be regenerated using the ALTER INDEX command. Unlike a BTree index, the ONLINE option cannot be used to rebuild a bitmap index (using the ALTER INDEX command), so concurrent activity could be affected. You could have rebuilt the bitmap index using the command ALTER INDEX xfk_coa#_bitmap REBUILD.

Once again, I have executed my concurrent processing and added another 10,000 rows to the GeneralLedger table. This time the BTree index is back in place. There is no longer a bitmap index. When processing is complete, we analyze statistics and run the EXPLAIN PLAN command again:

```
ANALYZE TABLE generalledger COMPUTE STATISTICS;
ANALYZE INDEX xfk_coa# COMPUTE STATISTICS;

EXPLAIN PLAN SET statement_id='TEST' FOR
SELECT /*+ INDEX(generalledger, xfk_coa#) */ *
FROM generalledger WHERE coa# = '60001';
```

Query	Cost	Rows	Bytes
SELECT STATEMENT on	**3466**	178155	4097565
TABLE ACCESS BY INDEX ROWID on GENERALLEDGER	3466	178155	4097565
INDEX RANGE SCAN on XFK_COA#	425	178155	

The increase in cost is slightly larger for the BTree index. This is unexpected. With respect to INSERT statements, bitmap indexes are not subject to overflow on this scale. There is a difference in that bitmap indexes appear to deteriorate at a slightly faster rate than BTree indexes deteriorate. On a much larger scale, and with a lot more data involved, and much larger tables, the situation might be very different.

8.3.3.1.5 *Bitmap Join Indexes*

A bitmap join index is simply a bitmap containing ROWID pointers of columns (or keys) used in the join from tables joined together. The index is created using a SQL join query statement.

Bitmap join indexes are appropriate for joining very large fact tables with smaller, static dimensional tables in data warehouses. This book focuses on OLTP database tuning and not data warehouse tuning. I have another book covering data warehouse tuning.[2] It makes sense to have two separate books on these two separate topics. Also, nobody wants to read a 1,500-page book, and no publisher really wants to print it.

8.3.3.2 **Clusters**

A cluster is literally a cluster or persistent *joining together* of data from one or more sources. These multiple sources are tables and indexes. In other words, a cluster places data and index space rows together into the same object. Obviously, clusters can be arranged such that they are very fast performers for read-only data. Any type of DML activity on a cluster will overflow. Rows read from overflow will be extremely heavy on performance. Clusters are intended for data warehouses.

A standard cluster stores index columns for multiple tables and some or all nonindexed columns. A cluster simply organizes parts of tables into a combination index and data space sorted structure. Datatypes must be consistent across tables.

Clusters are all about joins. Joins are queries that read data from a database, not DML database change activity. Thus clusters are unlikely to apply to OLTP databases but rather to data warehouses. Additionally, clusters are a somewhat dated method of dealing with prejoining data and have been superseded in both capability and flexibility by materialized views. Otherwise, the most effective clusters are those created in order to physically prejoin master-detail table relationships, joining some or all of the columns in both tables into a single physical object (a cluster).

8.3.3.2.1   *Hash Clusters*

A hash cluster is simply a cluster indexed using a hashing algorithm. Hash clusters are more efficient than standard clusters but are even more appropriate to read-only type data than are clusters. In older relational databases, hash indexes were often used against integer values for better data access speed. If data was changed, the hash index had to be rebuilt.

8.3.3.2.2   ⑩𝑔 **Sorted Hash Clusters**

A hash cluster essentially breaks up data into groups of hash values. Hash values are derived from a cluster key value, forcing common rows to be stored in the same physical location. A sorted hash cluster has an additional performance benefit for queries accessing rows in the order in which the hash cluster is ordered, thus the term sorted hash cluster.

8.3.3.2.3   *Index-Organized Tables*

A cluster is a join of more than one table. An index-organized table is a single table, physically organized in the order of a BTree index. In other words, the data space columns are added into the index structure leaf blocks of a binary tree. An index-organized table is effectively a BTree table where the entire table is the index. Block space is occupied by both data and index values. Much like clusters, the sorted structure of an index-organized table is not usually maintained efficiently by DML activity. However, index-organized tables have been known to be very effective performers, even in OLTP databases.

Any changes to any of the columns in the table affect the index directly because the table and the index are the same thing. It is possible that any DML activity could cause serious performance problems because of BTree index to overflow and skewing. After all, all of a table's columns are indexed, and there are effectively far fewer indexes per block than for a single-column index. However, search times using the BTree structure can be drastically improved. There are reports of good performance gains using index-organized tables in OLTP-type databases. I am currently unaware of exactly how these tables are used in relation to intensive DML activity.

Let's experiment a little with an index-organized table. We can begin by making a duplicate of the Transactions table, into a new table called TransIOT:

```
CREATE TABLE transIOT
(
        transaction_id        NUMBER NOT NULL,
        type                  CHAR(1) NOT NULL,
        customer_id           NUMBER NULL,
        supplier_id           NUMBER NULL,
        order_id              NUMBER NULL,
        amount                NUMBER(10,2) NOT NULL,
        dte                   DATE NOT NULL,
        drcoa#                CHAR(5) NOT NULL,
        crcoa#                CHAR(5) NOT NULL,
        CONSTRAINT        XPK_TRANSIOT PRIMARY KEY
(transaction_id)
)
ORGANIZATION INDEX TABLESPACE data NOLOGGING;
```

Copy the rows and commit changes:

```
INSERT INTO transIOT SELECT * FROM transactions;
COMMIT;
```

Add the same foreign key constraints:

```
ALTER TABLE transIOT ADD CONSTRAINT fk_transIOT_type
FOREIGN KEY(type) REFERENCES type;
ALTER TABLE transIOT ADD CONSTRAINT fk_transIOT_cust
FOREIGN KEY(customer_id) REFERENCES customer;
```

```
ALTER TABLE transIOT ADD CONSTRAINT fk_transIOT_supp
FOREIGN KEY(supplier_id) REFERENCES supplier;
ALTER TABLE transIOT ADD CONSTRAINT fk_transIOT_order
FOREIGN KEY(order_id) REFERENCES orders;
ALTER TABLE transIOT ADD CONSTRAINT FK_transIOT_drcoa
FOREIGN KEY(drcoa#) REFERENCES COA;
ALTER TABLE transIOT ADD CONSTRAINT fk_transIOT_crcoa
FOREIGN KEY(crcoa#) REFERENCES COA;
```

Now let's get a query plan for the Transaction table, utilizing the primary key. We should retrieve all of the columns because the index-organized table includes all columns in the index. So begin with a very small range of rows to ensure that the regular table's primary key is read:

```
EXPLAIN PLAN SET statement_id='TEST' FOR
SELECT * FROM transactions WHERE transaction_id < 10;
```

Query	Pos	Cost	Rows	Bytes
SELECT STATEMENT on	0	**3**	1	36
TABLE ACCESS BY INDEX ROWID on TRANSACTIONS	1	3	1	36
INDEX RANGE SCAN on XPK_TRANSACTIONS	1	2	1	

And now using the index-organized table, it is clear that reading the index-organized table is slower because so few rows are retrieved. More physical space is read for that few number of rows:

```
EXPLAIN PLAN SET statement_id='TEST' FOR
SELECT * FROM transiot WHERE transaction_id < 10;
```

Query	Pos	Cost	Rows	Bytes
SELECT STATEMENT on	0	**21**	24	2184
INDEX RANGE SCAN on XPK_TRANSIOT	1	21	24	2184

Now we go to the other extreme and read a lot of rows from both tables. Once again, we compare the cost values. Starting with the Transactions table:

```
EXPLAIN PLAN SET statement_id='TEST' FOR
SELECT * FROM transactions WHERE transaction_id < 5000;
```

```
Query                                    Pos    Cost     Rows     Bytes
-------------------------------------- ----  -------  --------  ---------
SELECT STATEMENT  on                      0    406      3510     126360
 TABLE ACCESS BY INDEX ROWID on TRANSACTIONS  1    406      3510     126360
  INDEX RANGE SCAN on XPK_TRANSACTIONS        1     11      3510
```

And for the index-organized table, even though a lot more byte space is covered, as more information is read from the database, the index-organized table begins to exceed the performance of the Transactions table (the heap-organized table):

```
EXPLAIN PLAN SET statement_id='TEST' FOR
SELECT * FROM transiot WHERE transaction_id < 5000;
```

```
Query                              Pos    Cost     Rows     Bytes
-------------------------------- ----  -------  --------  ---------
SELECT STATEMENT  on                0     21      3590     326690
 INDEX RANGE SCAN on XPK_TRANSIOT   1     21      3590     326690
```

It makes perfect sense to assume that as the amount of data retrieved is increased, the index-organized table will outperform the heap-organized table to a greater and greater degree. However, accessing the index-organized table not in the order of the primary key will cause even worse performance than the Transactions table. Additionally, intensive DML activity will very likely deteriorate the usefulness of the BTree index for the index-organized table, much faster than that for the BTree index on the heap-organized table.

Another interesting difference between index-organized tables and heap-organized tables is the performance of alternate indexing. From the previous script used to created the TransIOT index-organized table, you can see that foreign key indexes were created on the index-organized table, as for the heap-organized table (the two tables are identical apart from index organization). The following query plan uses the CUSTOMER_ID foreign key alternate index to access the Transactions table:

```
Query                                    Pos    Cost     Rows     Bytes
-------------------------------------- ----  -------  --------  ---------
SELECT STATEMENT  on                      0    196      220      7920
 TABLE ACCESS BY INDEX ROWID on TRANSACTIONS  1    196      220      7920
  INDEX RANGE SCAN on XFX_TRANS_CUSTOMER      1      2      220
```

This next query plan uses the same index on the CUSTOMER_ID column to access the TransIOT index-organized table, and the cost is higher:

Query	Pos	Cost	Rows	Bytes
SELECT STATEMENT on	0	**2210**	105	9555
INDEX FAST FULL SCAN on XPK_TRANSIOT	1	2210	105	9555

I then proceeded to perform the same operation on both tables, but this time using the 5,000 rows again. The index-organized table still insisted on a fast full index scan. The heap-organized table's full table scan was actually faster. For the heap-organized table:

Query	Pos	Cost	Rows	Bytes
SELECT STATEMENT on	0	**1623**	65881	2371716
TABLE ACCESS FULL on TRANSACTIONS	1	1623	65881	2371716

And for the index-organized table:

Query	Pos	Cost	Rows	Bytes
SELECT STATEMENT on	0	**2210**	70167	6385197
INDEX FAST FULL SCAN on XPK_TRANSIOT	1	2210	70167	6385197

Where and when to use index-organized tables in an OLTP database depends on the activity to which the table is usually subjected. Index-organized tables will be useful (or less useful) for performance in the following situations:

- Use an index-organized table with high read access, always in the order of the primary key.

- Alternate indexes can be created on index-organized tables, such as on foreign key columns, but a heap-organized table is likely to benefit more from alternate indexing.

- Any kind of DML change activity should decrease binary tree performance. This deterioration should occur more rapidly with an index-organized table because there are fewer indexes per block. The column length of the index includes all table columns, and thus the length of each index row value is that much longer. Binary trees deteriorate particularly rapidly when subjected to large amounts of deletion activity.

- Normal BTree indexes can be rebuilt, even online.

- Attempting to execute the following two commands in SQL*Plus, for my previously created TransIOT index-organized table, elicited errors:

```
ALTER TABLE transIOT REBUILD ONLINE;
ALTER TABLE transIOT REBUILD;
```

With respect to these two commands, index-organized tables cannot be rebuilt—certainly not online like regular BTree indexes. It is possible to use the MOVE TABLE clause within the ALTER TABLE command, in order to rebuild an index-organized table; there is even an ONLINE option. This syntax includes the term *relocate*, which in my mind implies recreation of the entire table (the index is the table). This could be cumbersome, but it is possible.

Note: (10*g*) Index-organized tables can now use global hash-partitioned indexes. Partitioning is covered in detail in Part III of this book.

And now let's clean up:

```
DROP TABLE TransIOT;
```

8.4   Tuning BTree Indexes

This is not a data warehouse tuning book. Tuning data warehouses is another subject. Any read-only indexes should generally not be used in OLTP or client-server databases. Therefore, this book will concentrate on potential tuning issues with BTree indexes. Some tuning issues have already been covered in this chapter. These issues have dealt with the philosophical side of how and what to index, some details about BTree indexing, and use of read-only indexes.

What can be done with BTree indexes to make them work faster?

8.4.1 **Overflow and Rebuilding**

Oracle Database BTree indexes do not overflow, but they can become skewed. Skewing can happen with a binary tree (e.g., when a large percentage of index values belong to a single branch). Look at the BTree representation in Figure 8.3, which shows a picture of what the Accounts schema GeneralLedger.COA# column foreign key index might look like physically. The set of leaf blocks for branch 1 has more than 300,000 rows. That's about 40% of the total rows. Branch 4 has more than 30,000 rows. That's about 5% of the total rows. That is not proportionate. In other words, when searching for COA# = '30001', then 40% of the total physical space is searched. When searching for COA# = '60001', only 5% is searched. This is a potentially skewed binary tree, because it is heavier in some parts.

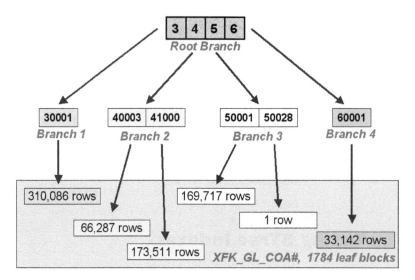

Figure 8.3
A skewed BTree index

The example in Figure 8.3 is a poor example and is presented more because of the nature of the GeneralLedger.COA# column data. The reason why is because most skewing of binary trees occurs when data is changed such that one particular area of a table is added to rather than another. The result is a binary tree that is heavily loaded in one or more specific places. The temptation in a case such as this is to use a bitmap index. Don't! The GeneralLedger table is a heavily DML active table. Over a long period of time, a bitmap index could deteriorate to the point of uselessness.

The answer to skewed binary indexes is the ALTER INDEX command using the REBUILD ONLINE options. Rebuilding an index will rebalance a BTree index and help spread everything out more evenly, particularly with respect to overflow. The ONLINE option will prevent disruption of current DML activity.

8.4.1.1 Lost Index Space

Let's dive just a little into some physical index tuning. When setting block storage management parameters for tables and indexes, there are numerous modifiable parameters. Two of these parameters are PCTUSED and PCTFREE. For tables there are two parameters, and for indexes there is one. PCTUSED allows reuse of a block when the occupied space in a block falls below the percentage specified, as a result of DML DELETE commands. The PCTFREE parameter allows allocation of free space to a block that is only usable by future DML UPDATE commands, including expanding column values. PCTFREE helps avoid row chaining. PCTUSED and PCTFREE will be covered in detail in physical tuning. The issue with indexing is that an index cannot have a PCTUSED parameter. What does this tell us about indexes? ***Deleted index space is not reclaimed unless an index is rebuilt*** using the ALTER INDEX index-name REBUILD command.

Note: PCTUSED and PCTFREE settings cannot be changed for already existing blocks.

Note: (10*g*) PCTUSED parameter values are ignored in locally managed tablespaces using automated segment space management. Automated segment space management will be covered in Part III. Automated segment space management is accepted practice in both Oracle Database 9*i* and recommended in Oracle Database 10*g*.

So large numbers of row insertions and deletions can over time denigrate the quality of BTree indexes. It is advisable to regularly rebuild Oracle Database BTree indexes for this reason if possible. The REBUILD ONLINE option will prevent interference with DML activity during an index rebuild.

It is possible to use the ALTER INDEX command with the COALESCE and DEALLOCATE UNUSED options. These options will not help very much and might make things worse. The COALESCE option attempts to amalgamate empty extents. The DEALLOCATE UNUSED option tries to reclaim space above the high water mark. Both of these are rare possibilities. On a previous consulting job, I executed a COALESCE command on some highly deteriorated BTree indexes, only to find the datafile containing those indexes about 25% larger after completion. Use index rebuilds. Once again, indexes can be rebuilt online as well without disrupting DML activity.

8.4.2 Reverse Key Indexes

Reverse key indexes are useful for high cardinality (unique values) in highly concurrent multiuser environments. Where index values are created in a sequential sequence, there can be problems with contention for index blocks, when multiple DML statements are accessing the same block. The sequential numbers will all be added into the same index block. This kind of problem often occurs with INSERT statements using incremental Oracle Database sequences as primary keys. All of the INSERT commands take a sequence number close to every other recently generated sequence. Thus all those sequences will be placed into the same block of the index, potentially locking the block and causing serious availability problems. This is known as *hot blocking*.

An answer to this problem is using reverse key indexes. What is a reverse key index? A reverse key index simply stores the bytes in the indexed column value, into the index, with the string of the bytes in reverse order as shown in Figure 8.4.

Figure 8.4
A reverse key index

ROWID	GENERALLEDGER_ID
AAAIF+AAJAAACuKAAA	344833
AAAIF+AAJAAACuKAAB	344834
AAAIF+AAJAAACuKAAC	344835
AAAIF+AAJAAACuKAAD	344836
AAAIF+AAJAAACuKAAE	344837
AAAIF+AAJAAACuKAAF	344838
AAAIF+AAJAAACuKAAG	344839
AAAIF+AAJAAACuKAAH	344840

Reverse Key Index

ROWID	GENERALLEDGER_ID
AAAIF+AAJAAACuKAAA	338443
AAAIF+AAJAAACuKAAB	438443
AAAIF+AAJAAACuKAAC	538443
AAAIF+AAJAAACuKAAD	638433
AAAIF+AAJAAACuKAAE	738443
AAAIF+AAJAAACuKAAF	838443
AAAIF+AAJAAACuKAAG	938443
AAAIF+AAJAAACuKAAH	48443

How do reverse key indexes resolve high-concurrency contention for index blocks on sequential key values? The act of reversing the bytes in the keys places those index values into separate blocks. This avoids contention for a single index block. The downside to use of reverse key indexes is that no efficient BTree traversals can be performed, and no index range scans can be executed. The index values are randomly scattered across the blocks of the index. The order of the index is maintained, and thus the index remains usable in the required order only.

In the Accounts schema, the GeneralLedger table is only ever inserted into, and the primary key is a sequence number. This primary key is a candidate for a reverse key index. It is probably unwise to make the GeneralLedger table's primary key index a reverse key index because it is very large and is accessed with DML commands other than INSERT.

Two things warrant mentioning: (1) attempting to detect index block contention is physical tuning and is not appropriate for this chapter, and (2) reverse index keys generally only apply in high-concurrency clustered Oracle Database RAC (parallel server) environments. Reverse key indexes allow for efficient heavy insertion activity but can be problematic for any sequentially ordered index matching or filtering activity unless searching for an exact row (no index range scans).

8.4.3 Compressed Composite Indexes

Compression of BTree indexes applies to composite column indexes only. A composite index sometimes represents a many-to-many join resolution entity or a master-detail relationship between a parent and child table; the composite index is placed on the child table. Compressing the index allows removal of repeating index column values from leaf blocks to a prefix. Figure 8.5 shows an example of what index compression does to an index; duplications are removed. A compressed index maintains a prefix key value pointing to ROWID pointers, which point to the table rows. A compressed index saves a little space. For really large indexes, it could potentially save a lot of space.

Index compression can have the following effects:

- Decrease the physical size of the index, allowing faster searching through less physical disk space.

- Searching composite indexes may be problematic when not ordering columns in indexes according to the exact order of the composite columns.

- DML activity may be a little slower for composite indexes because of the possible need to reconstruct the split structure between compressed and uncompressed columns.

- In general, searches using composite indexes cannot perform unique index hits and default to range scans. It is possible that exact hits could be obtained on the first prefix column of a compressed index because it is physically unique to the index.

Figure 8.5
*A compressed
composite column
index*

ROWID	Country	State	City	Venue
AAACVWAAFAAADGKABT	USA	CA	Modesto	Johanson High School
AAACVWAAFAAADGKABf	USA	CA	Modesto	Modesto Junior College Stadium
AAACVWAAFAAADGKABV	USA	CA	Monterey	Laguna Seca Recreation Area
AAACVWAAFAAADGKABh	USA	CA	Monterey	Monterey Fairgrounds
AAACVWAAFAAADGKABw	USA	CA	Monterey	Pebble Beach Golf Links
AAACVWAAFAAADGLAAH	USA	CA	Monterey	Steinbeck Forum Conference Center
AAACVWAAFAAADGKACU	USA	CA	Mountain View	Shoreline Amphitheatre
AAACVWAAFAAADGKABR	USA	CA	Murphys	Ironstone Winery
AAACVWAAFAAADGKAAS	USA	CA	Oakland	California Ball Room
AAACVWAAFAAADGKAAV	USA	CA	Oakland	Calvin Simmons Theatre

ROWID	Country	State	City	Venue
AAACVWAAFAAADGKABT	USA	CA	Modesto	Johanson High School
AAACVWAAFAAADGKABf				Modesto Junior College Stadium
AAACVWAAFAAADGKABV			Monterey	Laguna Seca Recreation Area
AAACVWAAFAAADGKABh				Monterey Fairgrounds
AAACVWAAFAAADGKABw				Pebble Beach Golf Links
AAACVWAAFAAADGLAAH				Steinbeck Forum Conference Center
AAACVWAAFAAADGKACU			Mountain View	Shoreline Amphitheatre
AAACVWAAFAAADGKABR			Murphys	Ironstone Winery
AAACVWAAFAAADGKAAS			Oakland	California Ball Room
AAACVWAAFAAADGKAAV				Calvin Simmons Theatre

- In highly concurrent environments, compressed composite indexes and the addition of prefix entries could potentially lock more blocks in indexes. Compressed indexes may perform less effectively under conditions of high concurrency.

Obviously, a single-column index cannot be compressed. There would not be any point since there is nothing to compress. When creating a compressed index, one can compress up to the number of columns in the composite index less one. Let's use the TransactionsLine table for our first example:

```
EXPLAIN PLAN SET statement_id='TEST' FOR
SELECT transaction_id, seq# FROM transactionsline;
```

Query	Cost	Rows	Bytes
SELECT STATEMENT on	**283**	739772	3698860
INDEX FAST FULL SCAN on XPK_TRANSACTIONSLINE	283	739772	3698860

The following ALTER INDEX DDL command will compress the two-column primary key index in the Accounts schema TransactionsLine table:

```
ALTER INDEX xpk_transactionsline REBUILD ONLINE COMPUTE
STATISTICS
COMPRESS 1;
```

Now let's run the same query once again:

```
EXPLAIN PLAN SET statement_id='TEST' FOR
SELECT transaction_id, seq# FROM transactionsline;
```

Query	Cost	Rows	Bytes
SELECT STATEMENT on	**254**	739772	3698860
INDEX FAST FULL SCAN on XPK_TRANSACTIONSLINE	254	739772	3698860

In the previous TransactionsLine table examples, there is a small decrease in cost as a result of compressing the index. The cost has been reduced from 283 down to 254, a 10% cost decrease.

Let's now use a different table that is much more applicable to composite indexing. The following query shows that there are in excess of thousands of rows for every COA# value. This is not the case with the TransactionsLine table master-detail relationship between the TRANSACTION_ID and SEQ# composite primary key columns:

```
SQL> SELECT coa#, COUNT(coa#) FROM generalledger GROUP BY
coa#;

COA#   COUNT(COA#)
-----  -----------
30001       377393
40003       145447
41000       246740
50001       203375
50028            1
60001        72725
```

Create a new index:

```
CREATE INDEX xak_composite ON
generalledger(coa#,generalledger_id)
ONLINE COMPUTE STATISTICS;
```

Find the cost of the use of the index uncompressed:

```
EXPLAIN PLAN SET statement_id='TEST' FOR
SELECT coa#, generalledger_id FROM generalledger;
```

Query	Cost	Rows	Bytes
SELECT STATEMENT on	**432**	912085	9120850
INDEX FAST FULL SCAN on XAK_COMPOSITE	432	912085	9120850

Now using the COMPRESS clause, we will remove duplicates of the COA# column from the index:

```
ALTER INDEX xak_composite REBUILD ONLINE COMPUTE STATISTICS
COMPRESS 1;
```

Now use the EXPLAIN PLAN command again:

```
EXPLAIN PLAN SET statement_id='TEST' FOR
    SELECT coa#, generalledger_id FROM generalledger;
```

Looking at the result following, the cost is lower. The difference is now 432 down to 316, a 25% decrease in cost.

Query	Cost	Rows	Bytes
SELECT STATEMENT on	**316**	912085	9120850
INDEX FAST FULL SCAN on XAK_COMPOSITE	316	912085	9120850

The TransactionsLine table examples showed a 10% decrease in cost, and the GeneralLedger table examples showed a decrease in cost of much more at 25%. The more duplicates removed by compression, the better the increase in performance.

On a more detailed level, we can conclude that the relationship between the TRANSACTION_ID and SEQ# columns should be in the range of thousands. This is not the case, however. The TransactionsLine table is probably inappropriate for a composite index. In a properly structured data model, composite indexes would probably be inappropriate for most many-to-many join resolution entities and master-detail relationships unless a traditional composite parent-child data model structure was used. Why? There are generally not enough repetitions of the prefix (the compressed columns) of the compressed index to warrant its use. The GeneralLedger.COA# column values repeat enough to show a marked performance increase.

8.4.3.1   Compressed Indexes and DML Activity

Do compressed indexes affect the performance of DML activity? A DML command executed using a compressed index may incur a small amount of overhead as opposed to an uncompressed index. Suffix index values are not stored directly with prefix values, and further interpretation is required. Here I am going to attempt to compare DML performance between compressed and uncompressed indexes.

The rows for GeneralLedger.COA# = '60001' table entries account for more than 5% of the table. The chances are the optimizer will often choose a full table scan rather than an index read. I am going to attempt to force the optimizer to use the composite index with a hint to avoid full table scans, because we are trying to compare indexes. We will start with the index uncompressed. I am using an UPDATE and a DELETE statement. INSERT is irrelevant in this case:

```
ALTER INDEX xak_composite REBUILD ONLINE COMPUTE STATISTICS
NOCOMPRESS;

EXPLAIN PLAN SET statement_id='TEST' FOR
   UPDATE /*+ INDEX(generalledger, xak_composite) */
generalledger SET dr=0, cr=0 WHERE coa# = '60001';
```

The cost of the UPDATE query is high. The optimizer probably would have selected a full table scan without the hint:

Query	Cost	Rows	Bytes
UPDATE STATEMENT on	**3016**	156159	1717749
UPDATE on GENERALLEDGER			
INDEX RANGE SCAN on XAK_COMPOSITE	488	156159	1717749

And for the DELETE:

```
EXPLAIN PLAN SET statement_id='TEST' FOR
DELETE FROM /*+ INDEX(generalledger, xak_composite) */
generalledger WHERE coa# = '60001';
```

Query	Cost	Rows	Bytes
DELETE STATEMENT on	**488**	156159	1561590
DELETE on GENERALLEDGER			
INDEX RANGE SCAN on XAK_COMPOSITE	488	156159	1561590

Now let's compress the index:

```
ALTER INDEX xak_composite REBUILD ONLINE COMPUTE STATISTICS
COMPRESS 1;
```

And examine the UPDATE command:

```
EXPLAIN PLAN SET statement_id='TEST' FOR
  UPDATE /*+ INDEX(generalledger, xak_composite) */
generalledger SET dr=0, cr=0 WHERE coa# = '60001';
```

Query	Cost	Rows	Bytes
UPDATE STATEMENT on	**2898**	156622	1722842
UPDATE on GENERALLEDGER			
INDEX RANGE SCAN on XAK_COMPOSITE	359	156622	1722842

And the DELETE command:

```
EXPLAIN PLAN SET statement_id='TEST' FOR
DELETE FROM /*+ INDEX(generalledger, xak_composite) */
Generalledger WHERE coa# = '60001';
```

Query	Cost	Rows	Bytes
DELETE STATEMENT on	**359**	156622	1566220
DELETE on GENERALLEDGER			
INDEX RANGE SCAN on XAK_COMPOSITE	359	156622	1566220

We can see from the four preceding query plans that DML activity is actually speeded up with the compressed index, even in an active database. Commercial databases with thousands of transactions per second may behave differently. Let's clean up by dropping extra indexes and uncompressing those still compressed for both the TransactionsLine and GeneralLedger tables. It is important to clean up after yourself:

```
ALTER INDEX xpk_transactionsline REBUILD ONLINE COMPUTE
STATISTICS
NOCOMPRESS;
DROP INDEX ak_composite;
```

8.4.4 Function-Based Indexes

A regular BTree index contains column values of indexed columns in index leaf blocks, which link to tables using ROWID pointers. A function-based index contains the result of an expression on a column (column values), placing the expression result into the index leaf blocks. How is this relevant

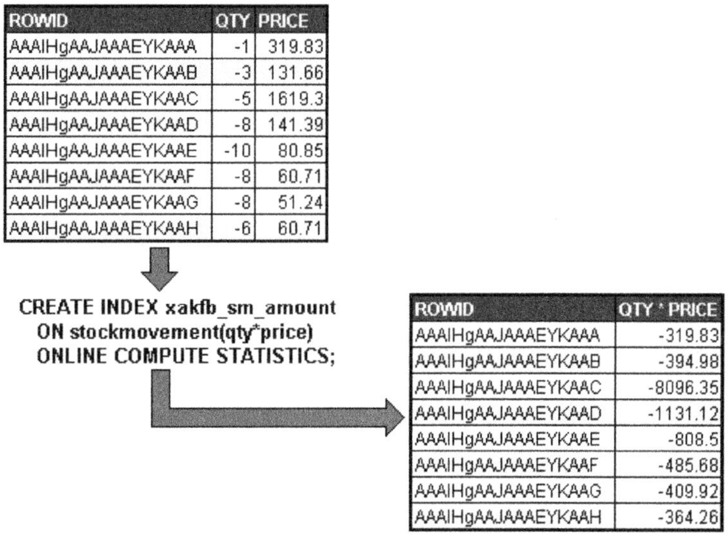

Figure 8.6
A function-based
index

ROWID	QTY	PRICE
AAAIHgAAJAAAEYKAAA	-1	319.83
AAAIHgAAJAAAEYKAAB	-3	131.66
AAAIHgAAJAAAEYKAAC	-5	1619.3
AAAIHgAAJAAAEYKAAD	-8	141.39
AAAIHgAAJAAAEYKAAE	-10	80.85
AAAIHgAAJAAAEYKAAF	-8	60.71
AAAIHgAAJAAAEYKAAG	-8	51.24
AAAIHgAAJAAAEYKAAH	-6	60.71

CREATE INDEX xakfb_sm_amount
ON stockmovement(qty*price)
ONLINE COMPUTE STATISTICS;

ROWID	QTY * PRICE
AAAIHgAAJAAAEYKAAA	-319.83
AAAIHgAAJAAAEYKAAB	-394.98
AAAIHgAAJAAAEYKAAC	-8096.35
AAAIHgAAJAAAEYKAAD	-1131.12
AAAIHgAAJAAAEYKAAE	-808.5
AAAIHgAAJAAAEYKAAF	-485.68
AAAIHgAAJAAAEYKAAG	-409.92
AAAIHgAAJAAAEYKAAH	-364.26

to tuning? A regular BTree index on a column will be completely ignored by the optimizer when a column is part of an expression in a SQL statement. Figure 8.6 shows an example of a function-based index.

Some specific settings are required in Oracle Database to allow use of function-based indexes:

- The cost-based optimizer is required.

Note: (10*g*) Rule-based optimization is desupported in Oracle 10*g*. The term desupported means rule-based optimization is still vaguely available but will eventually be removed from Oracle software altogether. It is strongly advised to phase out rule-based optimization.

- The user must:
  - Have the QUERY_REWRITE system privilege
  - Execute privileges on any user-defined functions
- Oracle Database configuration parameters must be set as follows:
  - QUERY_REWRITE_ENABLED = TRUE
  - QUERY REWRITE_INTEGRITY = TRUSTED

Let's go through some examples of the uses of function-based indexing. The following example simply shows a full table scan based on a WHERE clause filter on an expression of two columns. Individual indexes on the QTY and PRICE columns would make no difference to query plan cost. I am creating these indexes to prove the point:

```
CREATE INDEX xak_sm_qty ON stockmovement(qty)
ONLINE COMPUTE STATISTICS;
CREATE INDEX xak_sm_price ON stockmovement(price)
ONLINE COMPUTE STATISTICS;
```

And now for the query plan:

```
EXPLAIN PLAN SET statement_id='TEST' FOR
   SELECT * FROM stockmovement WHERE qty*price = 0;
Query                                  Cost    Rows     Bytes
------------------------------------ ------ -------- ---------
SELECT STATEMENT   on                  404    6456    135576
  TABLE ACCESS FULL on STOCKMOVEMENT   404    6456    135576
```

Now let's clean up and drop those two indexes:

```
DROP INDEX xak_sm_qty;
DROP INDEX xak_sm_price;
```

Now let's create a function-based index for the expression QTY*PRICE. My database is highly active. Once again, I use the ONLINE option of the CREATE INDEX command, allowing DML activity against the index during the index creation process. The ONLINE option creates the index elsewhere and copies it to the index file after creation, including any changes during the copying process. As always, the EXPLAIN PLAN command is useless without current statistics generation:

```
CREATE INDEX xakfb_sm_amount ON stockmovement(qty*price)
ONLINE COMPUTE STATISTICS;
```

And now for the EXPLAIN PLAN command:

```
EXPLAIN PLAN SET statement_id='TEST' FOR
    SELECT * FROM stockmovement WHERE qty*price = 0;
```

Notice in the query plan how the newly created function-based index is being range scanned. If the order of the columns in the expression was switched to PRICE*QTY, then the index would still be used, because the function-based index contains the result of the expression. The next example will reverse the order of the QTY and PRICE columns in the expression:

Query	Cost	Rows	Bytes
SELECT STATEMENT on	5	6456	135576
TABLE ACCESS BY INDEX ROWID on STOCKMOVEMENT	5	6456	135576
INDEX RANGE SCAN on XAKFB_SM_AMOUNT	3	2582	

In the following example, I have placed the expression into the SELECT statement alone, allowing a full index scan as opposed to a full table scan. Also, the order of the quantity and price columns is the reverse of the previous example:

```
EXPLAIN PLAN SET statement_id='TEST' FOR
    SELECT price*qty FROM stockmovement;
```

Query	Cost	Rows	Bytes
SELECT STATEMENT on	382	645604	4519228
INDEX FAST FULL SCAN on XAKFB_SM_AMOUNT	382	645604	4519228

We can also use user-defined functions to create function-based indexes:

```
CREATE OR REPLACE FUNCTION getAmount(
 pqty IN INTEGER DEFAULT 0
,pprice IN FLOAT DEFAULT 0) RETURN NUMBER DETERMINISTIC IS
BEGIN
     RETURN pqty*pprice;
END;
/
ALTER FUNCTION getAmount COMPILE;
```

Now let's drop and re-create the index again to use the user-defined function:

```
DROP INDEX xakfb_sm_amount;
CREATE INDEX xakfb_sm_amount ON stockmovement(getAmount(qty,
price))
ONLINE COMPUTE STATISTICS;
```

The query plan following should show a fast full index scan of the index created using the user-defined function:

```
EXPLAIN PLAN SET statement_id='TEST' FOR
SELECT getAmount(qty, price) FROM stockmovement;
```

Query	Cost	Rows	Bytes
SELECT STATEMENT on	561	570298	2851490
TABLE ACCESS FULL on STOCKMOVEMENT	561	570298	2851490

We are supposed to be able to use a function in a function-based index. The QTY*PRICE index and function will not be used again, so they will be dropped. Leaving unused indexes in the database is bad for performance. Whenever a table is updated, all its associated indexes are updated as well:

```
DROP INDEX xakfb_sm_amount;
DROP FUNCTION getAmount;
```

Function-based indexes can be useful. The biggest danger with function-based indexes is that developers could create a lot of them. It may be best to only create function-based indexes somewhere between the development and production release cycles, especially if database administrators are completely uninvolved in the development process, which is often the case.

8.4.5 NULLs and Indexes

What do we need to know about NULL values and indexes? NULL values are not included in indexes except for bitmap indexes. Therefore, when using an index against a table where NULL values exist, not only can the index be read, ignoring table columns, but also only non-NULL valued rows are read. Thus reading the index will not only read fewer columns but could potentially read fewer rows as well.

The Transactions table in the Accounts schema is a good example. A type = 'S' transaction will have a NULL SUPPLIER_ID, and a TYPE = 'P' transaction will have a NULL CUSTOMER_ID. These are the counts for different row types in the Transactions table:

```
SELECT t.counter "Transactions", s.counter "Sales"
 ,p.counter "Purchases", type_S.counter "Type=S"
 ,type_P.counter "Type=P"
FROM  (SELECT COUNT(*) as counter FROM transactions) t
 ,(SELECT COUNT(*) as counter FROM transactions
   WHERE customer_id IS NOT NULL) s
 ,(SELECT COUNT(*) as counter FROM transactions
   WHERE supplier_id IS NOT NULL) p
 ,(SELECT COUNT(*) as counter FROM transactions
   WHERE type = 'S') type_S
 ,(SELECT COUNT(*) as counter FROM transactions
   WHERE type = 'P') type_P;
```

```
Transactions     Sales  Purchases      Type=S     Type=P
------------ ---------- ---------- ---------- ----------
      188199      33158     155041      33158     155041
```

The CUSTOMER_ID and SUPPLIER_ID columns already have foreign key indexes. I do not have to create any new indexes. Let's use the CUSTOMER_ID column as an example. Note from the previous query result that the Transactions table has a total of 188,199 rows. Now we can force reading the index and demonstrate the resulting much lower number of rows accessed by reading only the non-NULL-valued index rows:

```
EXPLAIN PLAN SET statement_id='TEST' FOR
    SELECT customer_id FROM transactions
WHERE customer_id IS NOT NULL;
```

We now appear to have read 33,142 rows. The number of rows accessed is much fewer than the total number of rows in the table as expected. However, and quite confusingly so, there are 33,158 non-NULL-valued CUSTOMER_ID rows, and the fast full index scan reads slightly fewer rows. Why? I do not know.

Query	Cost	Rows	Bytes
SELECT STATEMENT on	**16**	**33142**	66284
INDEX FAST FULL SCAN on XFK_T_CUSTOMER	16	33142	66284

One point should be noted: If we wanted to read the NULL-valued CUSTOMER_ID rows from the Transactions table, we could change the CUSTOMER_ID column to NOT NULL and add a DEFAULT setting. We could subsequently search the index for the DEFAULT value and get the same result as searching for IS NULL on the table. This would ensure that we never get NULL values in the CUSTOMER_ID column and that a CUSTOMER_ID index can always be used instead of a full table scan. However, why would one ever want to read NULL values? In this case, one could simply SELECT using the SUPPLIER_ID column as NOT NULL and get the same result, again reading fewer index entries. If many SQL code statements are accessing tables with IS NULL comparisons, you might want to revisit your data model. IS NULL is a form of a negative comparison condition because you are attempting to find something that is not there. Think about why you are doing something like this. This type of SQL code is consistent with an approach to high usage of outer joins in SQL code. High numbers of outer joins are sometimes indicative of poor data referential integrity or perhaps even data model structure not providing for application requirements. The same potential indicators are apparent when searching using IS NULL conditions. Once again, why would you want to search for something that is simply not there?

That covers NULL values and indexing. So *how can BTree indexes be tuned* for better performance?

- *Use as few columns as possible.*

- *Only index integers if possible*, preferably unique integer identifier values.

- *Variations on BTree indexes* are *reversing index strings, compression,* and *function-based indexes.* Each of these variations will generally have very specific applications. They should be used sparingly and carefully.

- *NULL values are not indexed.*

8.5   Summarizing Indexes

This concludes the discussion of what could be termed *common-sense indexing.* Handling indexing in Oracle Database is somewhat based on indexing in any relational database. Indexing in a database should be as close as possible to indexing provided by the data model, particularly referential integrity indexing. If you have too much alternate and secondary indexing, you may want to consider revisiting your data model, if this is possible. If your data model does not provide the basic structural functionality for attached applications, then application requirements may require significant alteration to your data model.

There is much to be said for building the data model with application functionality in mind. On the other hand, if your applications require large numbers of joins and additions to the data model, it could be that performance may benefit substantially from creation of a separate reporting or data warehouse database. Highly active changeable concurrent environments, such as OLTP databases and applications, have very different requirements from those of any type of reporting or data warehouse functionality. The two simply do not mix very well when large-scale amounts of data or concurrent activity are involved. This is typical for OLTP databases that back Internet Web sites. Mixing large quantities of small transactions in an OLTP database with large I/O throughput quantities for reporting and data warehouse activity can cause severe performance issues.

In the next two chapters, we will revert back to the study of how to perform SQL code tuning. So far in this book we have not dug too far into the internal specifics of tuning SQL code in Oracle Database, more specifically Oracle SQL (Oracle's form of SQL). You should now have a basic knowledge of how to tune SQL code and build proper indexing in general. The next chapter will start to examine the explicit details of how to tune Oracle SQL code specifically in Oracle Database.

8.6 Endnotes

1. Oracle Data Warehouse Tuning for 10g (Gavin Powell, Digital Press, Aug 2005, ISBN: 1555583350) and Oracle 10g Data Warehousing (Lilian Hobbs, Digital Press, Nov 2004, ISBN: 1555583229)

2. Oracle Data Warehouse Tuning for 10g (Gavin Powell, Digital Press, Aug 2005, ISBN: 1555583350)

9

Oracle SQL Optimization and Statistics

So far in Part II, SQL Code Tuning, we have covered what SQL is, the basics of efficient SQL, and common-sense indexing. The first four chapters in Part II are not necessarily directly Oracle related. Their contents could apply to SQL in any relational database. Now we need to look at the specifics of Oracle Database with respect to SQL code tuning and the Oracle SQL code optimizer.

The last three chapters used the EXPLAIN PLAN command extensively for demonstration purposes. All of the types of data access shown in query plans are described in detail in this chapter and the next two chapters.

In this chapter and the next two chapters, we will try to understand how Oracle Database executes SQL code and how that SQL code can be tuned from a purely Oracle Database perspective. There will be some crossover in this chapter with configuration tuning. Numerous Oracle Database configuration parameters affect the way SQL code is executed. The essence of this chapter is to discover what exactly Oracle Database does when a SQL statement is submitted to the Oracle database engine. There are specific steps:

1. *Parsing*. Parsing is the verification of SQL code syntax and interpretive compilation into a form understandable by the Oracle database engine.

2. ***Optimization***. The optimizer attempts to automatically pick the fastest method of execution for a SQL code statement.

3. *Execution*. SQL code statements are executed in various forms and by various routes, decided on by the optimizer.

4. ***Return of results***. Results are passed back to the calling process.

Let's start with some brief descriptions.

9.1   What Is the Parser?

What happens when a SQL statement is sent to the database? A portion of memory is allocated to store the results of a SQL statement. This chunk of memory is called a cursor. Among other things, a cursor contains a pointer to the row in an index or table currently being fetched from the database. Unless a cursor is declared explicitly in a tool, such as PL/SQL, then a cursor is implicitly created for every SQL SELECT statement submitted to the Oracle database. When a SQL statement has finished executing, the cursor can either be left in memory as a reusable, already allocated chunk of memory, or it can be removed from memory all together.

The SQL statement is parsed. What is parsing? The meaning of the word *parsing* is that of syntactical and perhaps grammatical or semantic analysis of a sentence. In programming terms, parsing is a syntax check on a line of program code and between related lines. SQL statements are lines of program code, so the parser is effectively a compiler of SQL statements, much like a C compiler is a compiler or syntax analyzer of C programming language commands.

The Oracle SQL parser does a few other things. There is a portion of memory or a buffer in the Oracle Database configuration called the shared pool. The shared pool is used to store parsed execution plans for previously executed SQL statements. These previously parsed execution plans can be used to re-execute the SQL statement if an exact string, and I mean *exactly* the same string, is executed once again. Thus the optimizer does not have to do its work all over again. The result is that if the parser finds an existing SQL code statement in the shared pool, it does not have to call the optimizer and recalculate the execution plan for the SQL statement.

Parses can be split into two categories:

- *Hard parse*. No match is found in the shared pool for a SQL statement never before submitted to the database engine.
- *Soft parse*. A match is found for a SQL statement, perhaps submitted to the database engine by a different session.

Hard parses are more expensive in system resources than soft parses, but reparsing is best avoided altogether if possible.

9.2   What Is the Purpose of the Optimizer?

The purpose of the optimizer is to optimize the performance of SQL statements. The optimizer decides the best way to execute a SQL code statement in the fastest way possible, based on the information available to it. The optimizer can use various methods of assessing the best path of performance for a SQL code statement. These methods include:

- Rule-based approach:
  - Outlines
- Cost-based approach:
  - Statistics
  - Hints
  - Histograms

Note: (10*g*) Rule-based optimization is obsolete and scheduled for complete removal in a future version of Oracle Database.

Indexes against tables may or may not be used as the better option to execute a SQL statement. Sometimes the optimizer will decide that reading an entire table is more efficient than reading a small part of an index, to access a ROWID pointer accessing a small number of table rows.

Through the years and various versions of the Oracle SQL code, the optimizer has become more and more *intelligent*. In Oracle Database 10*g*, it can be relied on fairly heavily to produce the best performance for SQL code.

Note: (10*g*) Oracle Database 10*g* has optimizer improvements such as less of a need for SQL code statements to be case sensitive.

In general, the capabilities of the optimizer will deteriorate as the complexity of SQL code increases, and particularly the quality of SQL code decreases. The optimizer should not be affected by database size unless SQL code or the data model are poorly tuned and constructed. Database size merely exacerbates problems caused by poor design. Unfortunately, these circumstances happen often. In OLTP systems, SQL code can sometimes become so complex and convoluted that the optimizer simply cannot cope, executing full table scans on all tables. In data warehouses, tables are so large sometimes that special attention is needed because scale and poor coding are simply way beyond the capabilities of the optimizer.

9.2.1   **What Does the Optimizer Do?**

(9*i*) In Oracle Database 9*i*, the Oracle documentation states that the optimizer is cost based (for the cost-based optimizer). A cost for a query is a unit of work required to execute a query. Cost is an estimated value based on the amount of I/O, CPU, and memory to be used.

(10*g*) In Oracle Database 10*g*, the cost model is slightly altered. Cost is no longer a unit of work but now a unit of time, where costing estimation is based on CPU usage and I/O activity. In other words, memory usage estimation is no longer included.

The optimizer is documented as performing three separate stages when executing a query:

1. ***Transformation***. If it helps to change the query into something else, such as query rewrite to a materialized view, then the optimizer will rewrite a query to access the data from a materialized view.

2. ***Estimation***. The optimizer gathers more information by assessing how much data is retrieved from underlying tables, such as 10 rows from 1,000,000 rows; or is an entire table being read? This is called *selectivity*. Cardinality is also important, as in how many unique values exist and how many duplications of each of those unique values exist. Additionally, the estimation stage includes the costing estimation, which is based on the optimizer guessing at potential I/O activity and CPU usage. This is likely discovered based on statistics and answers to cardinality and how selective a query is.

3. ***Plan generation***. This is a plan that the optimizer creates, suggesting to the database how a query should be executed. For example, when 10 rows are read from a one-million-row table, it is likely (very likely) that the optimizer will select to not read the entire table. If there is an index, depending on the applicability of the index, the index will probably be read to find ROWIDs. ROWIDs will link directly to individual rows in the table.

There is one very important point to make about the optimizer. Under-standing all the stages that the optimizer goes through, and how it does it, will actually not really help you learn how to tune Oracle SQL code. You can read all about the optimizer and its internal machinations in the Oracle documentation. For the purposes of tuning queries and DML commands, you need to focus on query plans and statistics and the meaning of query plans. And make sure statistics are up to date.

The two most significant factors that allow effective tuning of Oracle SQL code are statistics and query plans:

1.   ***Statistics***. Statistics have to be present and they have to be up to date; otherwise, optimizer guesses based on statistical values will be inaccurate, making statistics useless. The optimizer will make bad guesses. Oracle Database 10*g* makes the statistics part easier by automating statistics gathering (to a certain extent).

2.   ***Query Plans***. Query plans are part and parcel of the plan genera-tion stage mentioned previously. The plan is the important thing, or at least the meaning of the plan. A query plan is the optimizer's best guess at how to execute a query. The optimizer has a multi-tude of options from which to choose to access data. These options are called access paths (the way rows in tables are retrieved by SQL statements). The previous two chapters included many query plans in examples. By now you should have a general idea of what some of those query plans were really doing. You didn't need that depth of understanding for the previ-ous two chapters because you were learning how to tune SQL coding, and not Oracle SQL for Oracle Database specifically. In the next three chapters, you get to cover the nitty-gritty detail of the meaning behind the different options (access paths) that pop up on the screen when you run an EXPLAIN PLAN command. What is the meaning of query plans?

9.2.2   **What Are Statistics?**

This book is all about trying to show how to solve problems. It is not about the details of how the internal parts and pieces of Oracle Database work. Describing the details of how the optimizer functions in terms of the steps it goes through, for every query, will not tell you how to tune queries, and these details can be found in Oracle documentation.

What are statistics? Statistics are very important to the optimizer and the cost-based approach. The more up-to-date those statistics are, then the more accurately the optimizer can predict the best way to execute a SQL statement. In very large or very active databases, continual update to statistics is impractical. This is likely to cause contention and is very time consuming. The more out of date statistics are, the less accurate the optimizer will be.

Statistics are a computation or estimation of the exact size and placement of data in tables and indexes. Statistics can be used by the optimizer to make a better assessment (a *guesstimate*) of actual data, producing a better query plan, potentially more accurately matching the data as it actually is in the database.

Note: Cost-based optimization uses statistics. Rule-based optimization did not use statistics.

9.2.3   **Query Plan Access Paths**

There are different ways of accessing data. Some are better than others depending on circumstances. Accessing a table through an index is usually, but not always, faster than accessing a table directly. Accessing a table directly will always result in a full table scan, which reads an entire table, reading all the blocks in the table. This is not a problem if the table is small. If a table is large, then reading the entire table can be a serious performance issue. There are four basic methods of accessing data:

1. *Full Table Scan*. Reading an entire table.

2. *Full Index Scan*. Reading an entire index and accessing table rows using ROWID pointers found in the index.

3. *Index Range Scan*. Traverses a subset of an index to search for a single value or a group of values across a range of index values. Table rows are accessed using ROWID pointers found in the index.

4. *Index Unique Scan or Hit*. An exact hit performs a minimal number of block reads on an index, usually three at the most, rapidly accessing a single row in the index. A ROWID pointer in the

index is used to access a single row in a table, reading a single block from the table.

Index unique scans are the fastest way to find data in an Oracle database. An index unique scan will likely be used when finding a single, uniquely identified row, using either the primary key or a unique alternate key. Range scans are a little slower because they potentially read more blocks in the index, passing more ROWID pointers to the table. A full index scan is faster than a full table scan because an index contains fewer columns than the table, occupying less physical space. Also, an index, being fewer columns in size, is often a compressed form of a table, and thus more index rows fit into a block than table blocks. Therefore, more indexes can be scanned in a single block read.

Different types of indexing methods also have specialized methods of accessing data, potentially speeding access to rows drastically from that of accessing rows directly from tables. Data access methods will be covered in detail in the next chapter. This chapter covers the groundwork, allowing you to understand what is coming next.

9.3   Rule-Based versus Cost-Based Optimization

Rule-based optimization used a set of predetermined rules to find the fastest access path to data in the database. Cost-based optimization uses statistical measurements of the data in the database and calculates the fastest access path. Cost-based optimization uses a realistic picture of data, and thus is potentially much more efficient than rule-based optimization, assuming statistics are maintained adequately.

9.3.1   Setting the Optimization Mode

Optimization can be set on a database-wide level in the Oracle database configuration parameter called OPTIMIZER_MODE. The default value is ALL_ROWS. In Oracle Database 9*i*, CHOOSE will allow use of cost-based optimization if statistics exist, but otherwise rule-based optimization will be used.

(10*g*) Settings of CHOOSE and RULE for the OPTMIZER_MODE parameter are obsolete because rule-based optimization is obsolete in Oracle Database 10*g*.

The OPTIMIZER_MODE parameter can be changed online using the ALTER SESSION command for the current session only. In Oracle Database 9*i*, if you wish to use rule-based optimization for a specific SQL statement, perhaps using the RULE hint is the better option.

(10*g*) The RULE hint is obsolete and no longer available.

Note: Setting OPTIMIZER_MODE = CHOOSE is by far the best all-around option for Oracle Database 9*i* and prior releases of Oracle Database.

All OPTIMIZER_MODE settings are covered (duplicated) by hints. A hint can be placed in an individual SQL statement. Hints will be covered later in this chapter. OPTIMIZER_MODE settings are as follows:

- OLTP small transactional databases:
    - *FIRST_ROWS_n*. Cost-based optimizing even without statistics for fastest performance of the first 1, 10, 100, or 1,000 rows retrieved. In other words, full index and table scans could suffer immensely, but short transactions retrieving small numbers of rows should perform better.
    - *FIRST_ROWS*. Fast delivery of the first few rows using a cost-based approach. FIRST_ROWS_n is more precise if your database needs this level of precision.

Note: FIRST_ROWS_1000 might always be the most prudent option. Any full index or table scanning over 1,000 rows could suffer using other options. There are hints applying behavior similar to FIRST_ROWS settings.

    - *CHOOSE*. Oracle Database 9*i* rule-based optimization is selected when no statistics are present, and cost-based optimization is used when some statistics are available, regardless of the reliability of those statistics. CHOOSE is optimized for full index and table scans but is the most common choice for all types of databases.

Note: (10*g*) CHOOSE is desupported.

- Data warehouse and reporting databases:

- *CHOOSE*. Oracle Database 9*i* rule-based optimization is selected when no statistics are present, and cost-based optimization is used when some statistics are available, regardless of the reliability of those statistics. CHOOSE is optimized for full index and table scans.

> **Note:** (10*g*) Dynamic sampling and automated statistics generation makes the possibility of no statistics for cost-based optimization to operate upon more or less impossible.

- *ALL_ROWS*. The opposite of FIRST_ROWS optimization using a cost-based approach even without statistics. ALL ROWS is optimized for full index and full table scans.

> **Note:** (10*g*) ALL_ROWS is the default value for the OPTIMIZER_MODE parameter.

- Preferably never (even in Oracle Database 9*i*):

  - *RULE*. Rule-based optimization ignores any existing statistics, presenting an unrealistic picture of data. Rule-based optimization can be used for backward compatibility with previous Oracle Database version tuned outlines, but otherwise avoid it!

> **Note:** (10*g*) CHOOSE and RULE are obsolete because rule-based optimization is desupported. Functionality still exists but will be completely removed from a future release of Oracle Database. That means very soon!

9.3.2 What Was Rule-Based Optimization?

Rule-based optimization used a set of rules allowing a best guess at how SQL code could be optimally executed. Many advanced SQL code tuning features and useful bells and whistles, introduced in recent Oracle Database versions, are only available when using cost-based optimization. Any SQL code statement could be persuaded to use a rule-based approach by inclusion of the RULE hint, regardless of the OPTIMIZER_MODE setting in the configuration parameter file.

> **Note:** (10*g*) Applications still using rule-based optimization should be updated if you ever plan to update Oracle Database software.

9.3.2.1 Outlines

Outlines can be used by a rule-based optimization approach in order to store previously tuned execution plans for SQL code. For cost-based optimization, an execution plan is the sequence of steps written to the PLAN_TABLE when the EXPLAIN PLAN command is used. We have seen extensive use of the EXPLAIN PLAN command in recent chapters. Outlines are stored in a specific schema in tables containing what effectively are previously tuned hint additions. These hint additions are used to override SQL code statements to tune performance of SQL code statements during execution. As for rule-based optimization, outlines will likely be removed in a future version of Oracle Database, possibly to be replaced with use of hints in SQL code.

9.3.2.2 (9*i*) Hints and Rule-Based Optimization

In the past, hints (or stored outlines) could be used in a rule-based optimized database to produce similar results to that of cost-based optimization. Perhaps you are unable to regularly generate accurate statistics, or statistics rapidly become out of date. Statistics can rapidly become out of date in large, active databases and can be expensive in resources to constantly maintain.

> **Note:** If statistics cannot be regularly maintained, improve SQL code performance using hints.

The OPTIMIZER_MODE in my Oracle Database 9*i* is set to CHOOSE, and I have statistics generated. In order to show hints functioning, I can temporarily use rule-based optimization or remove statistics, or both. I do both.

```
ALTER SESSION SET OPTIMIZER_MODE=RULE;


ANALYZE TABLE generalledger DELETE STATISTICS;
ANALYZE INDEX xpk_generalledger DELETE STATISTICS;
```

This first query plan uses a full table scan under rule-based optimization; note there are no cost, row, or bytes values shown.

```
EXPLAIN PLAN SET statement_id='TEST' FOR
   SELECT gl.generalledger_id FROM generalledger gl;
```

Query	Cost	Rows	Bytes
SELECT STATEMENT on			
TABLE ACCESS FULL on GENERALLEDGER			

The INDEX_FFS hint is used to override the rule-based optimizer, changing full access on the GeneralLedger table to an index fast full scan, on the primary key index of the GeneralLedger table.

```
EXPLAIN PLAN SET statement_id='TEST' FOR
   SELECT /*+ INDEX_FFS(gl XPK_GENERALLEDGER) */ gl.generalledger_id
FROM generalledger gl;
```

Query	Cost	Rows	Bytes
SELECT STATEMENT on	8	2000	26000
INDEX FAST FULL SCAN on XPK_GENERALLEDGER	8	2000	26000

I wanted to show you that hints can be used to override a query plan chosen by the optimizer, using rule-based optimization, regardless of the presence of statistics. Let's do some cleanup.

```
ALTER SESSION SET OPTIMIZER_MODE=CHOOSE;

ANALYZE TABLE generalledger COMPUTE STATISTICS;
ANALYZE INDEX xpk_generalledger COMPUTE STATISTICS;
```

The problem with using hints to override the optimizer in rule-based mode is as follows: If relative sizes of objects in a database change over time, any SQL code tuned with hints and executed under the rule-based optimizer could eventually become ugly with respect to performance.

9.3.3   What Is Cost-Based Optimization?

As already stated in the introduction to this section, cost-based optimization uses statistical measurements, as a measure of data existing in the database. These statistics are used to calculate the fastest access path to data. Cost-based optimization uses a realistic picture of data and is generally a lot more efficient than rule-based optimization. Statistics must exist on at least one object accessed in a SQL code statement for cost-based optimization to function. ***Keeping statistics up to date is absolutely critical.***

Note: (10*g*) Dynamic sampling and automated statistics generation makes the possibility of no statistics for cost-based optimization to operate upon more or less impossible.

Numerous Oracle Database configuration parameters can be used to influence the way the optimizer behaves with the cost-based approach.

9.3.3.1   Configuration Parameters and Cost-Based Optimization

Some configuration parameters will affect cost-based optimization. Most of these parameters should simply not normally be messed with and should be altered as a last resort. If you have a small database and are changing these parameters frequently, you may be avoiding essential SQL code tuning. SQL code tuning is a lot easier than altering configuration parameters. Altering configuration parameters appears simple but can sometimes have some unexpected results, in all sorts of interesting and often nasty places. These parameters are only listed in this chapter. More explicit explanations will be included in Part III:

- DB_FILE_MULTIBLOCK_READ_COUNT
- CURSOR_SHARING
- SORT_AREA_SIZE
- QUERY_REWRITE_ENABLED
- (9*i*) HASH_JOIN_ENABLED (removed from Oracle Database 10*g*)
- HASH_AREA_SIZE
- BITMAP_MERGE_AREA_SIZE
- OPTIMIZER_INDEX_CACHING

- OPTIMIZER_INDEX_COST_ADJ

- ⑨*i* OPTIMIZER_MAX_PERMUTATIONS (removed from Oracle Database 10*g*)

- OPTIMIZER_DYNAMIC SAMPLING

> **Note:** ⑩*g* Sort, bitmap, and hash configuration parameters are best substituted by the PGA_AGGREGATE_TARGET configuration parameter.

> **Note:** ⑩*g* Some parameters may have changed or been removed between Oracle Database 9*i* and Oracle Database 10*g*. Further discussion will be in Part III.

9.3.3.2 The Importance of Statistics and Realistic Statistics

The SQL code optimizer utilizes statistics to compile the most efficient methods of executing SQL statements. Statistics are measurements of the data, such as how large a table is and how useful an index is. When a SQL statement accesses a table, both the table and index states are important. States of database objects, such as tables and indexes, are contained within statistics. If statistics are out of date, then the optimizer is not functioning realistically. Out-of-date statistics would have the same effect on all types of databases. It is very important to duplicate statistics from production to tuning environments, either by copying onto a tuning database or by executing statistics gathering on a tuning database, consistent with the production database.

Making a copy of a production database to a tuning database is not an issue when the production database is small. When the production database is large, then continuous copying to a tuning database could be time consuming. Be aware that using the database import utility for even single-schema imports on even a small database can take a lot longer than the production database export. THE DBMS_STATS package can also be used to copy only statistics between databases, allowing for more realistic query plan testing.

9.3.3.2.1 Dynamic Sampling

For statistics to be realistic and effective, they must be frequently generated. In an OLTP database, data is changing all the time. Statistics can rapidly become redundant (out of date and useless). Cost-based optimization against redundant statistics can sometimes cause as big a performance problem as not having those statistics at all, depending on how relatively out of date statistics are. If statistics are out of date or not present, then dynamic sampling may be used. Dynamic sampling reads a small number of blocks in a table to make a best guess at statistics.

Note: (9*i*) The configuration parameter controlling dynamic sampling is OPTIMIZER_DYNAMIC_SAMPLING and is set on by default (1).

Note: (10*g*) OPTIMIZER_DYNAMIC_SAMPLING is defaulted to 2.

The default for Oracle Database 9*i* is 1 and for Oracle Database 10*g* is 2. Setting dynamic sampling to 0 will switch it off altogether. This is not recommended in Oracle Database 10*g*. The basic difference between a setting of 1 and 2 is that 1 causes dynamic sampling of tables in queries, if certain criteria are met. Setting dynamic sampling to 2 samples all tables that have not been analyzed, regardless of any rules. Dynamic sampling settings go all the way up to 10. In general, as levels approach 10, more data is analyzed. Leave the setting at its default level of 2, unless you have a pathological hatred for generating statistics. Also, Oracle Database 10*g* is very good at automated statistics gathering and management.

One of the most significant issues with respect to statistics is matching consistency of statistics between production, testing, and development databases. Most SQL code tuning is usually performed in development databases, but preferably in a test or dedicated tuning database—at least it should be! Test databases are more easily copied from production databases or parts of production databases. Test databases are often copied from production databases to get a realistic snapshot of a live production database. Development databases are often messy and convoluted. Tuning on a production database, particularly tuning involving SQL code changes, is extremely risky for the stability and current level of performance for a 24×7×365 OLTP Oracle installation.

The OPTIMIZER_DYNAMIC_SAMPLING parameter sets dynamic sampling of data, substituting for cost-based statistics, from between a setting of 0 and 10. Set to 0 dynamic sampling is disabled, and set to 10 the entire table is read. Settings in between simply change the number of blocks read for the sample.

9.3.3.3 Generating Statistics

Statistics can be generated using the ANALYZE command or the DBMS_STATS package. The ANALYZE command is potentially subject to deprecation in a future version of Oracle Database. In fact, Oracle Corporation discourages use of the ANALYZE command for statistics generation. Personally, I prefer the ANALYZE command as long as it is available because it is easy to use. However, the DBMS_STATS command is much more powerful, especially for large, complex databases.

9.3.3.3.1 What to Generate Statistics For

Statistics can be generated for tables and indexes, plus general system statistics. When using the ANALYZE command on a table, all indexes created on that table have statistics generated for them automatically at the same time as the table. System-level statistics will be covered in Part III. Schema-level statistics are generated for tables, indexes, and clusters for each schema. Schema statistics are accessible through the views USER_TABLES, USER_INDEXES, and USER_TAB_COLUMNS.

9.3.3.3.2 Tables

- *NUM_ROWS*. Rows in table
- *BLOCKS*. Blocks used by table
- *EMPTY_BLOCKS*. Blocks not used between highest appended block and high water mark. Reclaim these blocks by resizing the datafile.
- *AVG_SPACE*. Average empty space for all blocks in the table. Depends on PCT_FREE updates reserved space and PCT_USED after deletions.

> **Note:** (10g) PCT_USED and PCT_FREE are more or less redundant with locally managed tablespaces and the advent of automatic extent management and automatic segment space management.

- *CHAIN_CNT*. Rows spread across multiple blocks (row chaining) or having had their data moved (migrated), retaining the ROWID pointer in the original block as well
- *AVG_ROW_LEN*. Average byte length of a row
- *SAMPLE_SIZE*. Sample size of most recent statistics generation

- *LAST_ANALYZED.* Date of last statistics generation

9.3.3.3.3   Indexes

- *NUM_ROWS.* Rows in index

- *LEAF_BLOCKS.* Total leaf blocks containing actual ROWID and indexed column values

- *BLEVEL.* Depth of a BTree index from root to leaf blocks, usually 0 for small static tables ranging from 1 to 2 (three levels) for very large tables

- *DISTINCT_KEYS.* Unique values for a key

- *AVG_LEAF_BLOCKS_PER_KEY.* Ratio of DISTINCT_KEYS to leaf blocks. How many rows are pointed to by each key value.

- *AVG_DATA_BLOCKS_PER_KEY.* Ratio of DISTINCT_KEYS to table blocks. How many rows in a table are pointed to by each unique index value.

- *CLUSTERING_FACTOR.* Randomness between index and table blocks. A reverse key index will be more random. Thus the better sorted table and index blocks are in relation to each other, the better data is clustered, with respect to having closely related values clustered together. Closely related values are sequentially placed values with respect to how well sorting of rows and blocks in a table matches the sorting of rows and blocks within a related index.

- *SAMPLE_SIZE.* Sample size of most recent statistics generation

- *LAST_ANALYZED.* Date of last statistics generation

9.3.3.3.4   Columns

- *NUM_DISTINCT.* Unique column values

- *LOW_VALUE.* Lowest column value

- *HIGH_VALUE.* Highest column value

- *DENSITY.* Column density

- *NUM_NULLS.* Null values in column

- *NUM_BUCKETS.* Histogram buckets

- *SAMPLE_SIZE.* Sample size of most recent statistics generation

- *LAST_ANALYZED.* Date of last statistics generation

9.3.3.3.5 The ANALYZE Command

Let's look at syntax first. The highlighted parts in the following syntax diagram are the interesting parts because they deal with optimizer statistics:

```
ANALYZE { TABLE | INDEX | CLUSTER }
[ PARTITION ( partition ) | SUBPARTITION ( subpartition ) ]
COMPUTE [ SYSTEM ] STATISTICS [ FOR ... object specifics ... ]
ESTIMATE [ SYSTEM ] STATISTICS [ FOR ... object specifics ... ]
[ SAMPLE n { ROWS | PERCENT } ]
[ ... referential integrity | structural ... validation ]
LIST CHAINED ROWS INTO table
DELETE [ SYSTEM ] STATISTICS;
```

- **COMPUTE**. Calculates statistics for all rows and columns in an object (table, index, or cluster). Precise results are produced.

- **ESTIMATE**. Calculates statistics on a sample number or percentage of rows, defaulted to 1,064 rows.

- **DELETE**. Clears statistics.

- **SYSTEM**. Collects only system statistics, not user schema statistics.

COMPUTE can be time consuming and **must be executed in times of low activity**. Executing full statistics computations during highly active concurrent activity cycles could cause performance issues, perhaps even unpopular responses from end users. **ESTIMATE** is far less intrusive but less accurate and is also preferably executed **at times of low activity**.

A statistics generating script is included in Appendix B.

9.3.3.3.6 The DBMS_STATS Package

The DBMS_STATS package is more versatile and potentially faster than using the ANALYZE command to generate statistics. It is a little more complex to use. Some nonoptimizer statistics can only be gathered with the ANALYZE command. However, DBMS_STATS has parallel execution and Oracle partitioning benefits plus performance tuning capabilities that the ANALYZE command does not have.

The DBMS_STATS package can even be used to copy statistics between databases, thus allowing accurate simulated tuning between testing and production databases.

9.3.3.3.7 *Automated Statistics Gathering*

Some optimizer statistics generation can be performed automatically using the MONITORING clause of the CREATE TABLE or ALTER TABLE commands, and otherwise using the DBMS_STATS package.

9.3.3.3.8 (9*i*) Automatic Statistics Generation in Oracle Database 9*i*

The MONITORING clause may be a performance risk for very busy databases. Automated statistics gathering monitors table DML activity and automatically invokes statistics generation when a small percentage of table rows have been changed. Automatic statistics generation can cause performance problems for highly active concurrent databases. Automating generation of statistics is thus not recommended. Generation of statistics can be scheduled using scheduling software or the DBMS_JOBS package at times of known low activity.

9.3.3.3.9 (10*g*) Automatic Statistics Generation in Oracle Database 10*g*

Unlike Oracle Database 9*i*, automated statistics gathering in Oracle Database 10*g* is a big deal and a big step in the right direction. Rule-based optimization is obsolete in Oracle Database 10*g*, and thus for the purposes of efficiency there has to be some form of automation of statistical values. This topic is now a very large topic requiring dissimilation between automated and manual gathering of statistics. There is much new detail, perhaps being mostly enhancement on what is already there. There is a lot more emphasis on statistics and particularly automation thereof. Some further points are relevant:

- Dynamic sampling is now more significant.
- The sample table scanning SAMPLE clause is altered.
- CPU costing for the optimizer is now more significant.

Note: (10*g*) Probably most significantly, database objects with no statistics (missing or never generated) or stale statistics (out of date) are now automatically analyzed. So out-of-date statisitcs are now no longer a factor.

Automated statistics work by automatically (by default on database creation) using the GATHER_STATS_JOB job. The internal Oracle Database scheduler executes this job on a daily basis, by default. The term by default implies this can be changed. The GATHER_STATS_JOB job will find database objects with missing or stale statistics (more than 10% of rows have changed) and generate those statistics. The most sorely needed statistics are generated first because this procedure has a time limit on its execution. When the time limit is expired, the procedure stops execution regardless of whether all statistics have been executed or not. The GATHER STATS_JOB job calls a DBMS_STATS procedure to generate statistics. You can verify the GATHER_STATS_JOB using the query as shown in Figure 9.1.

Figure 9.1
Automated statistics gathering in Oracle Database 10g

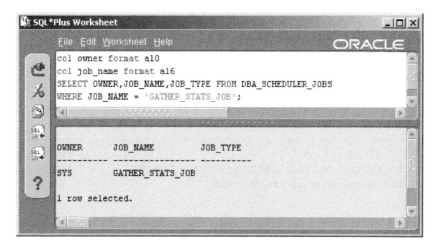

The easiest way to disable automated gathering of statistics is to disable the job altogether using the DBMS_JOBS package, logged in as the SYS user because SYS owns the DBMS_SCHEDULER package:

```
EXEC DBMS_SCHEDULER.DISABLE('GATHER_STATS_JOB');
```

Stale statistics will only be gathered when the STATISTICS_LEVEL is set to TYPICAL (the default) or ALL. Automated statistics gathering can be locked for individual objects using two procedures in the DBMS_STATS package. LOCK_TABLE_STATS locks tables and LOCK_SCHEMA_STATS locks an entire schema.

Individual database objects, such as highly DML active tables, can be reserved for manual statistics gathering. Sometimes database objects cannot have statistics gathered on them fast enough during the maintenance window. These objects can be removed from automated statistics gathering altogether to allow for manual statistics gathering using procedures, such as the DELETE_TABLE_STATS procedure in the DBMS_JOB package. In this situation, dynamic sampling can take over as well.

9.3.3.3.10   The SAMPLE Clause

The SAMPLE clause, or SAMPLE BLOCK clause, can be added to the FROM clause of a query as part of a SELECT statement. The SAMPLE clause causes the reading of a percentage of rows or blocks, in order to gather a statistical picture of data. That picture is passed to the optimizer, allowing a guess to be made at how data should be accessed. Here is a query plan using an index on the COA# foreign key column where the index is range scanned:

```
EXPLAIN PLAN SET statement_id='TEST' FOR
SELECT * FROM generalledger WHERE coa# = '50028';
```

Query	Pos	Cost	Rows	Bytes
SELECT STATEMENT on	0	**3512**	175325	4032475
TABLE ACCESS BY INDEX ROWID on GENERALLEDGER	1	3512	175325	4032475
INDEX RANGE SCAN on XFK_GL_COA#	1	448	175325	

Now we remove the statistics from the table and all indexes attached to the table:

```
ANALYZE TABLE generalledger DELETE STATISTICS;
```

And run the EXPLAIN PLAN command again and find we still have an index range scan but the cost is wildly underestimated, as compared with the previous statistically estimated values. The optimizer makes a wild guess:

```
EXPLAIN PLAN SET statement_id='TEST' FOR
SELECT * FROM generalledger WHERE coa# = '50028';
```

Query	Pos	Cost	Rows	Bytes
SELECT STATEMENT on	0	**2**	50	2750
TABLE ACCESS BY INDEX ROWID on GENERALLEDGER	1	2	50	2750
INDEX RANGE SCAN on XFK_GL_COA#	1	1	50	

Now let's use a SAMPLE clause to estimate a more realistic cost:

```
EXPLAIN PLAN SET statement_id='TEST' FOR
SELECT * FROM generalledger SAMPLE(1) WHERE coa# = '50028';
```

Query	Pos	Cost	Rows	Bytes
SELECT STATEMENT on	0	**2**	**1**	67
TABLE ACCESS BY INDEX ROWID on GENERALLEDGER	1	2	1	67
INDEX RANGE SCAN on XFK_GL_COA#	1	1	1	

The result in this query plan, sampled at 1% of the rows in the table, shows that the optimizer expects to read a single row using an index range scan. This is completely contradictory. A single row will be read from the table, but many rows could be read where a range of indexes will be scanned in the BTree index. Based on this result, I would regard the use of the SELECT statement SAMPLE clause with a fair amount of skepticism regarding its value. I see no reason to pursue further experimentation with the SAMPLE clause.

9.3.3.3.11 Timed Statistics

Timed statistics gathering is controlled by the TIMED_STATISTICS and TIMED_OS_STATISTICS configuration parameters. Setting this parameter has a negligible effect on performance and will be covered in Part III.

9.3.3.4 Histograms

A histogram is a mechanism used to provide an accurate mathematical picture to the optimizer of the distribution of values across a range of values. A traditional mathematical statistics histogram looks something like that shown in Figure 9.2.

Figure 9.2
An example histogram

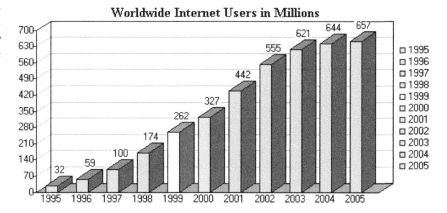

Oracle Database uses histograms to allow faster access to skewed distributions. The histogram shown in Figure 9.2 is a skewed or unbalanced distribution because most of the values are to the right of the diagram. A balanced distribution would have all the columns in the diagram being of exactly the same height. In that case, we would not need a histogram. It follows that histograms are completely pointless on unique indexes, because all of the columns would be the same height, and there would be a single value in each column. Additionally, use of bind variables in SQL statements will ignore histograms. Histograms are sometimes used where SQL code cannot or should not be altered to lower shared pool SQL code reparsing.

The Accounts schema GeneralLedger table has a nonunique foreign key index on the COA# column. Looking at Figure 9.3, we can see that the GeneralLedger.COA# foreign key index is potentially skewed or at least heavier in certain parts.

Figure 9.3
A skewed BTree index

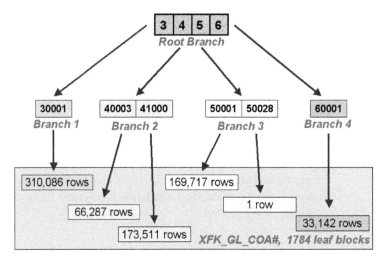

Following is the count of the rows in the GeneralLedger table. Notice how COA# = '30001' has almost 400,000 rows, and COA# = '60001' has only 75,000 rows. As a result of these varying row counts, it is likely that a lot more leaf index blocks are referenced by the branch containing '30001' than that of '60001'. This is a skewed or unbalanced distribution, leading to a potentially skewed BTree index:

```
SELECT coa#, COUNT(coa#) FROM generalledger GROUP BY coa#;
COA#   COUNT(COA#)

-----  -----------
30001       383357
```

```
          40003          151107
          41000          252552
          50001          206357
          50028               1
          60001           75555
```

Note: These counts are somewhat different from those in the previous chapter because the database is highly active and has grown.

Let's compare the costs of three queries reading rows, of three different COA# column values. Before doing this, I will refresh statistics for the GeneralLedger table, making sure we have no histograms to begin with:

```
ANALYZE TABLE generalledger DELETE STATISTICS;
ANALYZE INDEX xfk_gl_coa# DELETE STATISTICS;
ANALYZE INDEX xpk_generalledger DELETE STATISTICS;
ANALYZE TABLE generalledger COMPUTE STATISTICS;
ANALYZE INDEX xfk_gl_coa# COMPUTE STATISTICS;
ANALYZE INDEX xpk_generalledger COMPUTE STATISTICS;
```

Now let's compare the costs. Note that all cost, row, and byte values are identical:

```
EXPLAIN PLAN SET statement_id='TEST' FOR
SELECT coa# FROM generalledger WHERE coa# = '30001';
```

Query	Cost	Rows	Bytes
SELECT STATEMENT on	**425**	178155	890775
INDEX RANGE SCAN on XFK_COA#	425	178155	890775

```
EXPLAIN PLAN SET statement_id='TEST' FOR
SELECT coa# FROM generalledger WHERE coa# = '50028';
```

Query	Cost	Rows	Bytes
SELECT STATEMENT on	**425**	178155	890775
INDEX RANGE SCAN on XFK_COA#	425	178155	890775

```
EXPLAIN PLAN SET statement_id='TEST' FOR
SELECT coa# FROM generalledger WHERE coa# = '60001';
```

Query	Cost	Rows	Bytes
SELECT STATEMENT on	**425**	178155	890775
INDEX RANGE SCAN on XFK_COA#	425	178155	890775

Let's create a histogram on the GeneralLedger.COA# column. Histograms can be generated using the ANALYZE command or the DBMS_STATS package. I will stick with the ANALYZE command for now:

```
ANALYZE TABLE generalledger COMPUTE STATISTICS FOR COLUMNS coa#;
```

Note: Histograms require regeneration just like statistics do and can become stale and useless.

Created histograms can be examined using the USER_HISTOGRAMS view. Let's look at the query plans for each of the statements separately. In the next query plan, we can see a dramatic difference in the accuracy cost, row, and bytes value estimations. This is a direct result of creating a histogram. These query plan figures are now far more consistent, relative to each other, with the ratios of the numbers of rows for each COA# column value:

```
EXPLAIN PLAN SET statement_id='TEST' FOR
SELECT coa# FROM generalledger WHERE coa# = '30001';
```

Query	Cost	Rows	Bytes
SELECT STATEMENT on	**609**	383357	1916785
INDEX FAST FULL SCAN on XFK_COA#	609	383357	1916785

```
EXPLAIN PLAN SET statement_id='TEST' FOR
SELECT coa# FROM generalledger WHERE coa# = '50028';
```

```
Query                                       Cost      Rows     Bytes
------------------------------------------ -------- -------- ---------
SELECT STATEMENT   on                          3        1         5
  INDEX RANGE SCAN on XFK_COA#                  3        1         5


EXPLAIN PLAN SET statement_id='TEST' FOR
SELECT coa# FROM generalledger WHERE coa# = '60001';


Query                                       Cost      Rows     Bytes
------------------------------------------ -------- -------- ---------
SELECT STATEMENT   on                        182    75555    377775
  INDEX RANGE SCAN on XFK_COA#               182    75555    377775
```

Histograms can be very useful from a statistical and optimization estimation perspective.

This concludes this chapter on optimization and statistics. The next chapter will begin to dig into the interpretation of query plans and data access paths and why the optimizer selects a specific access path for any particular query.

10

How Oracle SQL Optimization Works

This chapter examines the details of how the optimizer accesses data in the database and also how the optimizer decides how data should be read. Typically, it is more efficient to read both a table and an index to find a row in a table. Sometimes, however, if a table is extremely small, the optimizer can choose to avoid indexes and read all the rows in a table.

This chapter consists of three distinct sections. The first and most important covers data access methods for tables, indexes, and joins between multiple tables. The term *data access method* describes the way in which tables are read. Tables can be read in part, or in whole, and in numerous different ways, especially with respect to joins. Each different method has its merits and disadvantages. The next section covers sorting, both inherent sorting and coded sorting using SQL clauses such as the ORDER BY and GROUP BY clause. The final section looks at some special cases. We begin with data access methods.

10.1   Data Access Methods

This section on data access methods will cover a lot of ground. It makes sense to describe briefly first. General areas covered are as follows:

- *Tables, Indexes, and Clusters*. There are numerous ways to access data objects. Materialized views could also be included under this section. Not only is query rewrite the default for new Oracle 10*g* databases, but materialized views can also be used in OLTP environments. However, materialized views are most commonly used in data warehouses.

- *Joins*. The optimizer has specific methods of joining tables, largely determined by table sizes.

- *Sorting*. The optimizer sorts SQL statement output in various ways.

- *Special Cases*. Concatenation, IN list operators, and UNION operators warrant special mention.

10.1.1 Accessing Tables and Indexes

In this section we examine the different ways in which the optimizer accesses tables and indexes. Tables can be full scanned, sampled, or scanned by a ROWID passed from an index. There are a multitude of ways in which indexes can be accessed and many ways in which index scanning can be affected. There are some important things to note about indexes:

- An index will occupy a small percentage of the physical space used by a table, thus searching through an index either precisely or fully is usually much faster than scanning a table.

- Reading an index to find a ROWID pointer to a table can speed up access to table rows phenomenally.

- Sometimes tables do not have to be read at all where an index contains all the retrieved column data.

10.1.1.1 Full Table Scans

A quick note about full table scans and fast full index scans is necessary before beginning this section. I have always been told that full scans read directly from disk, effectively bypassing the database buffer cache. This is why in a data warehouse, which is by nature always I/O intensive, the database buffer cache should be set to a minimum. In general, the database buffer cache is not utilized in a data warehouse in a useful manner. In an OLTP database, the database buffer cache is most effective when set to a conservative size. It is best utilized to share data that is shared by many users constantly.

So in the past my belief and instruction was that the database buffer cache is not read from when performing full table scans (and fast full index scans). A reader of the previous edition of this book provided evidence to the contrary. The reader repeated the same full table scan a few times. There was no competing database activity. Trace files indicated the full table scan read from disk the first time. Subsequent full table scans indicated database buffer cache loading activity.

This is unlikely to not imply that full scans do not read from disk, only that they load into the database buffer cache. In other words, full scans are likely to read directly from disk. They also load into the database buffer cache. The real issue with I/O activity and full table scans is that full scans are not supposed to read from the database buffer cache. Sometimes it is more efficient to read from disk than from the database buffer cache. So even though the database buffer cache is loaded by a full scan, it is reloaded as a result of a disk read. It is not read from. The full physical scan is responsible for the disk read.

This is how I understand this point at this juncture. Any evidence to the contrary is more than welcome and can be included in subsequent editions of this title.

Note: Full table scans and fast full index scans appear to always involve physical I/O activity. Data is read from disk into the database buffer cache. If the same data is read again, using a full scan, then the data will be read from disk again, into the database buffer cache. A full scan will not initiate a read from the database buffer cache. It follows that if the same data is read in a manner other than a full scan, it will more than likely be read from the database buffer cache, if it is still remaining in the database buffer cache.

10.1.1.1.1 Reading Many Blocks at Once

A full table scan can be speeded up by reading multiple blocks for each read. This can be done using the DB_FILE_MULTIBLOCK_READ_COUNT parameter, which is usually set between 4 and 16, typically 4, 8, or 16. The default value is 8. You might want to consider setting it to 4 or less for OLTP systems and 16 or higher for data warehouses.

Note: I set the value of DB_FILE_MULTIBLOCK_READ_COUNT on my Win2K server to various values between 1 and 128 and had no problems. This parameter is not restricted to specific values. Generally, it might be best to experiment with the parameter, setting it to as little as 1 for an OLTP database and as high as possible for a data warehouse.

A full table scan *may result* if the number of blocks occupied by a table is less than DB_FILE_MULTIBLOCK_READ_COUNT. Please note the emphasis on the term *may result*; it is not an absolute. The optimizer is getting more and more sophisticated with each new version of Oracle Database. The optimizer is unlikely to conclude that a full table scan is faster than an index, plus a ROWID pointer table read into an index, unless the table is very small or your query is extremely complex. Index reads are most likely where a unique index hit is involved on a large table.

10.1.1.1.2 Small Static Tables

For a small static table, a full table scan can often be the most efficient access method. A static table is obviously not changed, and there are never deletions. In many cases, a unique index hit will be preferred by the optimizer because the cost will be lower, particularly in mutable joins. Let's examine small static tables. Let's start by showing the row and block counts from the table statistics in the Accounts schema:

```
SELECT table_name, num_rows, blocks FROM user_tables ORDER BY 1;
```

TABLE_NAME	NUM_ROWS	BLOCKS
CASHBOOK	188185	1517
CASHBOOKLINE	188185	616
CATEGORY	13	1
COA	55	1
CUSTOMER	2694	60
GENERALLEDGER	752741	3244
ORDERS	172304	734
ORDERSLINE	540827	1713
PERIOD	72	1
PERIODSUM	221	1
POSTING	8	1
STOCK	118	4
STOCKMOVEMENT	570175	2333
STOCKSOURCE	12083	30
SUBTYPE	4	1
SUPPLIER	3874	85
TRANSACTIONS	188185	1231
TRANSACTIONSLINE	570175	1811
TYPE	6	1

Looking at the block space occupied by the Accounts schema tables, we can see that the COA and Type tables occupy a single block. First, let's show the relative costs between a unique index hit and a full table scan on the

Type table. The Type table is very small and occupies considerably less space than the single block it uses.

A full table scan on the Type table has a cost of 2:

```
EXPLAIN PLAN SET statement_id='TEST' FOR SELECT * FROM type;
```

Query	Cost	Rows	Bytes
SELECT STATEMENT on	**2**	6	**48**
TABLE ACCESS FULL on TYPE	2	6	48

The following query will access both the index and the table. Accessing a single row reads one-sixth of the bytes, and the cost is halved:

```
EXPLAIN PLAN SET statement_id='TEST' FOR
SELECT * FROM type WHERE type = 'A';
```

Query	Cost	Rows	Bytes
SELECT STATEMENT on	**1**	1	**8**
TABLE ACCESS BY INDEX ROWID on TYPE	1	1	8
INDEX UNIQUE SCAN on XPK_TYPE		6	

Even a full scan on just the index still has half the cost. The full scan of the index also reads fewer bytes than the unique index scan:

```
EXPLAIN PLAN SET statement_id='TEST' FOR SELECT type FROM
type;
```

Query	Cost	Rows	Bytes
SELECT STATEMENT on	1	6	**6**
INDEX FULL SCAN on XPK_TYPE	**1**	6	6

Now let's go completely nuts! Let's read the same table a multitude of times within the same query. We can see from the query plan following that even though the table is read many times, the optimizer will still assess the cost as 1. There are a multitude of unique index hits, even though the COA

table is read in its entirety. We could run timing tests. Results do not imply
that the optimizer is giving us the fastest option:

```
EXPLAIN PLAN SET statement_id='TEST' FOR
SELECT * FROM coa WHERE type IN
  (SELECT type FROM type WHERE type IN
   (SELECT type FROM type WHERE type IN
    (SELECT type FROM type WHERE type IN
     (SELECT type FROM type WHERE type IN
      (SELECT type FROM type WHERE type IN
       (SELECT type FROM type WHERE type IN
        (SELECT type FROM type WHERE type IN
         (SELECT type FROM type WHERE type IN
          (SELECT type FROM type WHERE type IN
           (SELECT type FROM type)))))))))));
```

Query	Cost	Rows	Bytes
SELECT STATEMENT on	**2**	55	1870
NESTED LOOPS on	2	55	1870
NESTED LOOPS on	2	55	1815
NESTED LOOPS on	2	55	1760
NESTED LOOPS on	2	55	1705
NESTED LOOPS on	2	55	1650
NESTED LOOPS on	2	55	1595
NESTED LOOPS on	2	55	1540
NESTED LOOPS on	2	55	1485
NESTED LOOPS on	2	55	1430
NESTED LOOPS on	2	55	1375
TABLE ACCESS FULL on COA	2	55	1320
INDEX UNIQUE SCAN on XPK_TYPE		1	1
INDEX UNIQUE SCAN on XPK_TYPE		1	1
INDEX UNIQUE SCAN on XPK_TYPE		1	1
INDEX UNIQUE SCAN on XPK_TYPE		1	1
INDEX UNIQUE SCAN on XPK_TYPE		1	1
INDEX UNIQUE SCAN on XPK_TYPE		1	1
INDEX UNIQUE SCAN on XPK_TYPE		1	1
INDEX UNIQUE SCAN on XPK_TYPE		1	1
INDEX UNIQUE SCAN on XPK_TYPE		1	1
INDEX UNIQUE SCAN on XPK_TYPE		1	1

Now we will attempt something a little more sensible by running the EXPLAIN PLAN command for a join, accessing the COA table four times and then time testing that query. There are four unique scans on the COA table:

```
EXPLAIN PLAN SET statement_id='TEST' FOR
   SELECT t.*, cb.*
   FROM transactions t JOIN cashbook cb
ON(t.transaction_id = cb.transaction_id)
   WHERE t.drcoa# IN (SELECT coa# FROM coa)
   AND t.crcoa# IN (SELECT coa# FROM coa)
   AND cb.drcoa# IN (SELECT coa# FROM coa)
   AND cb.crcoa# IN (SELECT coa# FROM coa);
```

Query	Cost	Rows	Bytes
SELECT STATEMENT on	**7036**	188185	22394015
NESTED LOOPS on	7036	188185	22394015
NESTED LOOPS on	7036	188185	21264905
NESTED LOOPS on	7036	188185	20135795
NESTED LOOPS on	7036	188185	19006685
MERGE JOIN on	7036	188185	17877575
TABLE ACCESS BY INDEX ROWID on CASHBOOK	826	188185	9973805
INDEX FULL SCAN on XFK_CB_TRANS	26	188185	
SORT JOIN on	6210	188185	7903770
TABLE ACCESS FULL on TRANSACTIONS	297	188185	7903770
INDEX UNIQUE SCAN on XPK_COA		1	6
INDEX UNIQUE SCAN on XPK_COA		1	6
INDEX UNIQUE SCAN on XPK_COA		1	6
INDEX UNIQUE SCAN on XPK_COA		1	6

In the next query plan, I have suggested a full table scan to the optimizer on the COA table, by incorporating overriding hints into the query.

Note: A hint can be used to suggest (some say force) the optimizer to change the way it generates a query plan.

The cost has a 20% increase:

```
EXPLAIN PLAN SET statement_id='TEST' FOR
      SELECT t.*, cb.*
      FROM transactions t JOIN cashbook cb
ON(t.transaction_id = cb.transaction_id)
      WHERE t.drcoa# IN (SELECT /*+ FULL(coa) */ coa# FROM coa)
      AND t.crcoa# IN (SELECT /*+ FULL(coa) */ coa# FROM coa)
      AND cb.drcoa# IN (SELECT /*+ FULL(coa) */ coa# FROM coa)
      AND cb.crcoa# IN (SELECT /*+ FULL(coa) */ coa# FROM coa);
```

Query	Cost	Rows	Bytes
SELECT STATEMENT on	**8240**	188185	22394015
HASH JOIN on	8240	188185	22394015
TABLE ACCESS FULL on COA	2	55	330
HASH JOIN on	7916	188185	21264905
TABLE ACCESS FULL on COA	2	55	330
HASH JOIN on	7607	188185	20135795
TABLE ACCESS FULL on COA	2	55	330
HASH JOIN on	7314	188185	19006685
TABLE ACCESS FULL on COA	2	55	330
MERGE JOIN on	7036	188185	17877575
TABLE ACCESS BY INDEX ROWID on CASHBOOK	826	188185	9973805
INDEX FULL SCAN on XFK_CB_TRANS	26	188185	
SORT JOIN on	6210	188185	7903770
TABLE ACCESS FULL on TRANSACTIONS	297	188185	7903770

Now let's do some timing tests. Even though query plan costs are higher for full table scans, the timing tests following show that the over-riding hint full table scans are actually almost twice as fast. Perhaps the optimizer should have been intelligent enough in the case of this query to force all of the COA tables to be read as full table scans. First, the query without the hints:

```
SQL> SELECT COUNT(*) FROM(SELECT t.*, cb.*
   2   FROM transactions t JOIN cashbook cb
   3   ON(t.transaction_id = cb.transaction_id)
   4   WHERE t.drcoa# IN (SELECT coa# FROM coa)
   5   AND t.crcoa# IN (SELECT coa# FROM coa)
   6   AND cb.drcoa# IN (SELECT coa# FROM coa)
   7   AND cb.crcoa# IN (SELECT coa# FROM coa));
```

```
      COUNT(*)
      ----------
         188185


Elapsed: 00:00:11.08
```

Next, the query including the hints:

```
SQL>    SELECT COUNT(*) FROM(SELECT t.*, cb.*
  2     FROM transactions t JOIN cashbook cb
  3     ON(t.transaction_id = cb.transaction_id)
  4     WHERE t.drcoa# IN (SELECT /*+ FULL(coa) */ coa# FROM
coa)
  5     AND t.crcoa# IN (SELECT /*+ FULL(coa) */ coa# FROM coa)
  6     AND cb.drcoa# IN (SELECT /*+ FULL(coa) */ coa# FROM
coa)
  7     AND cb.crcoa# IN (SELECT /*+ FULL(coa) */ coa# FROM
coa));

      COUNT(*)
      ----------
         188185


Elapsed: 00:00:07.07
```

The second query should be slower, but this is not the case in this situation. The simple explanation for this is because the COA table is small, and it is read four times. Therefore, it is faster to read the entire table four times, as opposed to reading the index and the table, four times each.

10.1.1.1.3 Reading Most of the Rows

Reading a large percentage of the rows in a table can cause the optimizer to perform a full table scan. This percentage is often stated as being anywhere between 5% and 25%. The following example, against the Stock table, switches from an index range scan to a full table scan at 95 rows out of 118 rows. That's about 80%. Note how the cost between the two queries is the same. The first query is less than 95 rows:

```
EXPLAIN PLAN SET statement_id='TEST' FOR
SELECT * FROM stock WHERE stock_id <= 94;
```

```
Query                               Pos    Cost     Rows      Bytes
----------------------------------  ----  -------  --------  ---------
SELECT STATEMENT   on                 0      5        94       21902
 TABLE ACCESS BY INDEX ROWID on STOCK  1     5        94       21902
  INDEX RANGE SCAN on XPK_STOCK        1      1        94
```

And this query is at 95 rows:

```
EXPLAIN PLAN SET statement_id='TEST' FOR
SELECT * FROM stock WHERE stock_id <= 95;
```

```
Query                          Pos    Cost     Rows      Bytes
-----------------------------  ----  -------  --------  ---------
SELECT STATEMENT   on            0      6        95       22135
 TABLE ACCESS FULL on STOCK      1      6        95       22135
```

Note: (10g) These two query plans are executed in Oracle Database 10g. So much for the optimizer switching to a full table scan at between 5% and 25% of all a table's rows read.

Note: (9i) Quite to the contrary, in Oracle Database 9i, the result was around 25%. The following query plans are produced in Oracle Database 9i, where the switch from index to full table scan occurred at 30 out of 118 rows. The first Oracle Database 9i query plan at 30 rows:

```
Query                                Cost     Rows      Bytes
-----------------------------------  ------  --------  ---------
SELECT STATEMENT   on                  2       29       6757
 TABLE ACCESS BY INDEX ROWID on STOCK  2      29        6757
  INDEX RANGE SCAN on XPK_STOCK         1      29
```

And the second Oracle Database 9i query plan at over 30 rows:

```
Query                          Cost     Rows      Bytes
-----------------------------  ------  --------  ---------
SELECT STATEMENT   on            2       30       6990
 TABLE ACCESS FULL on STOCK      2       30       6990
```

(10g) Now back to Oracle Database 10g, using a much larger table at just over one million rows, the change between index and full table scan occurs at somewhere between 50,000 and 60,000 rows, or around 5%. This first query plan reads just below 60,000 rows, using an index scan:

```
EXPLAIN PLAN SET statement_id='TEST' FOR
SELECT * FROM generalledger WHERE generalledger_id <= 402500;

Query                                          Pos    Cost    Rows     Bytes
---------------------------------------------- ----  ------- -------- ---------
SELECT STATEMENT    on                          0     4653    57641   1325743
 TABLE ACCESS BY INDEX ROWID on GENERALLEDGER   1     4653    57641   1325743
  INDEX RANGE SCAN on XPK_GENERALLEDGER         1      136    57641
```

The second query reads just over 60,000 rows and has switched to a full table scan:

```
EXPLAIN PLAN SET statement_id='TEST' FOR
SELECT * FROM generalledger WHERE generalledger_id <= 405000;

Query                                  Pos    Cost    Rows     Bytes
-------------------------------------- ----  ------- -------- ---------
SELECT STATEMENT    on                  0     4784    60140   1383220
 TABLE ACCESS FULL on GENERALLEDGER     1     4784    60140   1383220
```

Note: The WHERE clause filter on the GeneralLedger table queries above is filtering on the primary key. Primary key integer values are not consistent with table row counts as for the Stock table. A primary key value 400,000 represents about 55,000 rows in the GeneralLedger table.

10.1.1.1.4   *Reading Deleted Rows*

A full table scan simply reads the entire table. The biggest potential problem with a full table scan is that all blocks ever used by the table will be read, not just all the rows in the table. What does this mean? The high water mark bears mentioning. What is the high water mark? The high water mark for a table is the largest number of blocks ever allocated to a table. As rows are added to a table, the high water mark (number of blocks used) increases. When data is deleted from that table using the DELETE command, the high water mark does not decrease. Only the TRUNCATE command or recreating the table with the CREATE TABLE command will decrease the high water mark.

Assume a table had many rows added and then deleted completely using a DELETE command. Then the table is full table scanned. What will be the result? All the blocks deleted from the table will be read, even though the table has no rows at all. The following example proves this point. Full table scans on very large tables, which are subject to large amounts of deletion, can cause serious performance problems. Let's look at deleting from tables. The first query plan reads all data from the OrdersLine table. Note the cost, rows, and bytes read:

```
EXPLAIN PLAN SET statement_id='TEST' FOR SELECT * FROM
ordersline;
```

Query	Cost	Rows	Bytes
SELECT STATEMENT on	765	997903	15966448
TABLE ACCESS FULL on ORDERSLINE	**765**	**997903**	**15966448**

Now I delete all of the rows from the table and run the EXPLAIN PLAN command again. The rows and bytes values have decreased dramatically, but the cost is identical regardless of all rows being deleted. Additionally, I have updated statistics and am copying my OrdersLine table to a temporary table so that I can retrieve the OrdersLine table rows:

```
DROP TABLE tmp;
CREATE TABLE tmp AS SELECT * FROM ordersline;
DELETE FROM ordersline;
COMMIT;
ANALYZE TABLE ordersline COMPUTE STATISTICS;
EXPLAIN PLAN SET statement_id='TEST' FOR SELECT * FROM
ordersline;
```

Query	Cost	Rows	Bytes
SELECT STATEMENT on	765	1	52
TABLE ACCESS FULL on ORDERSLINE	**765**	**1**	**52**

Note: This query plan is reading an empty table.

Now I will TRUNCATE the table and run my EXPLAIN PLAN command again. I must not forget to compute the statistics again, otherwise the optimizer will use previously calculated statistics. That would be out-of-date statistics showing almost one million rows in the OrdersLine table, which is now an empty table. The query plan is drastically different now with the cost much reduced:

```
TRUNCATE TABLE ordersline;
ANALYZE TABLE ordersline COMPUTE STATISTICS;
EXPLAIN PLAN SET statement_id='TEST' FOR SELECT * FROM
ordersline;
```

Query	Cost	Rows	Bytes
SELECT STATEMENT on	2	1	52
TABLE ACCESS FULL on ORDERSLINE	**2**	**1**	**52**

Note: A serious potential problem with full table scans is scanning up to the high water mark. This includes blocks that once contained rows. Those rows are now deleted.

Now let's rebuild the OrdersLine table from the temporary table we created a few queries back:

```
INSERT INTO ordersline SELECT * FROM tmp;
COMMIT;
ANALYZE TABLE ordersline COMPUTE STATISTICS;
DROP TABLE tmp;
```

What can we conclude about full table scans? In short, full table scans are usually best avoided. In rare circumstances, a full table scan can be faster than an index scan, particularly for small static tables. A full table scan will result when no index is available, or when an index is missed accidentally by doing something like including a function on a column in a WHERE clause and no matching function-based index exists.

10.1.1.1.5   *Parallel Full Table Scans*

Let's try scanning a large table in parallel. Parallel scans can be induced on full table scans by using the PARALLEL hint or by setting the PARALLEL attribute when creating or altering a table. Let's look at changing a table. The GeneralLedger table is the largest table in the Accounts schema and is thus the most appropriate for parallel processing. Also, I have a dual-CPU machine. I do not, however, have Oracle partitioning installed at this point. Oracle partitioning is covered in Part III.

```
ALTER TABLE generalledger PARALLEL 2;
```

The degree of parallelism can be verified by using the following query:

```
SELECT table_name, degree FROM USER_TABLES ORDER BY 1;
```

Now let's look at a query plan. I am using an adjusted PLAN_TABLE query including the OTHER_TAG column (see Appendix B):

```
EXPLAIN PLAN SET statement_id='TEST' FOR SELECT * FROM generalledger;
```

Query		Cost	Rows
SELECT STATEMENT on		**195**	752740
TABLE ACCESS FULL on GENERALLEDGER	**PARALLEL_TO_SERIAL**	195	752740

Now let's remove the parallelism from the GeneralLedger table again:

```
ALTER TABLE generalledger NOPARALLEL;
```

Let's check the query plan again. There is no difference in cost:

```
EXPLAIN PLAN SET statement_id='TEST' FOR SELECT * FROM generalledger;
```

Query	Cost	Rows	Bytes
SELECT STATEMENT on	**195**	752740	19571240
TABLE ACCESS FULL on GENERALLEDGER	195	752740	19571240

Let's do some timing tests. Once again, we set the degree of parallelism on the GeneralLedger table to 2:

```
ALTER TABLE generalledger PARALLEL 2;

SQL> SELECT COUNT(*) FROM(SELECT /*+ FULL(gl) */ * FROM
generalledger gl);

  COUNT(*)
----------
   752741
```

Elapsed: 00:00:05.06

Now increase the degree of parallelism on the table:

```
ALTER TABLE generalledger PARALLEL 4;
```

The time taken is slightly less with the degree of parallelism increased:

```
SQL> SELECT COUNT(*) FROM(SELECT /*+ FULL(gl) */ * FROM
generalledger gl);

  COUNT(*)
----------
   752741
```

Elapsed: 00:00:05.02

Last, remove parallelism from the table altogether. The elapsed time is much faster without parallelism, as shown in the following query plan:

```
ALTER TABLE generalledger NOPARALLEL;

SQL> SELECT COUNT(*) FROM(SELECT /*+ FULL(gl) */ * FROM
generalledger gl);

  COUNT(*)
----------
   752741
```

Elapsed: 00:00:01.01

Parallel queries should only be used on very large row sets. OLTP databases should avoid large row sets, and therefore parallelism is most appropriate to large data warehouses, not to OLTP databases. Parallelism in general applies to full table scans, fast full index scans, and on-disk sorting. In other words, physical I/O activity benefits from parallelism, preferably using Oracle partitioning.

10.1.1.2 Sample Table Scans

A sample scan can be used to sample a percentage of a table either by rows or by blocks. This is useful if you want to examine a small part of a table. The row count is much lower in the second of the two sampled queries shown here, at 0.001%:

```
EXPLAIN PLAN SET statement_id='TEST' FOR SELECT * FROM generalledger;
```

Query	Cost	Rows	Bytes
SELECT STATEMENT on	715	**1068929**	24585367
TABLE ACCESS FULL on GENERALLEDGER	715	1068929	24585367

```
EXPLAIN PLAN SET statement_id='TEST' FOR
SELECT * FROM generalledger SAMPLE(0.001);
```

Query	Cost	Rows	Bytes
SELECT STATEMENT on	715	**11**	253
TABLE ACCESS SAMPLE on GENERALLEDGER	715	11	253

(10g) A seeding value option has been added to the sample clause to allow Oracle Database 10g to attempt to return the same sample of rows or blocks across different executions as shown in the following syntax:

```
SELECT … SAMPLE( % ) [ SEED n ];
```

Executing the same query with four different SEED values of 0, 1, 100,000, and 1,000,000 produced no difference in the query plan at all:

```
EXPLAIN PLAN SET statement_id='TEST' FOR
SELECT * FROM generalledger SAMPLE(0.001) SEED (100000);
```

Query	Pos	Cost	Rows	Bytes
SELECT STATEMENT on	0	4723	11	319
TABLE ACCESS SAMPLE on GENERALLEDGER	1	4723	11	319

10.1.1.3 ROWID Scans

A ROWID is an Oracle Database internal logical pointer to a row in a table. An index stores the indexed column values, plus a ROWID pointing to a row in a table. When an index is read, the ROWID found for an index value is used to retrieve that row from the table directly. For a unique index hit, at most three block reads are made in the index space, plus one block read in the table space. An index to table ROWID scan is shown in Figure 10.1.

Figure 10.1
Passing a ROWID pointer from an index to a table

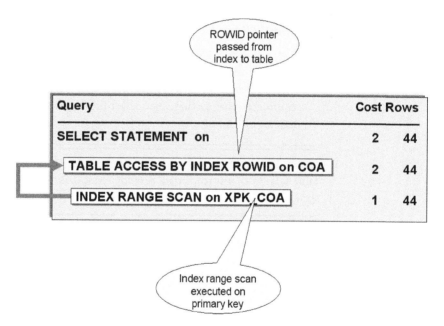

10.1.1.4 Index Scans

An index is a subset of a table containing a smaller number of columns. Each row in an index is linked to a table using a ROWID pointer. A ROWID pointer is an Oracle Database internal logical representation based on a datafile, a tablespace, a table, and a block. Effectively, a ROWID is an address pointer and is the fastest method of access for rows in an Oracle database.

There are numerous different types of index scans:

- *Index Unique Scan*. Uses a unique key to return a single ROWID. The ROWID then finds a single row in a table. A unique scan is an exact row hit on a table and the fastest access for both index and table.

- *Index Range Scan*. Scans a range of index values to find a range of ROWID pointers.

- *Reverse-Order Index Range Scan*. This is an index range scan in descending (reverse) order.

- *Index Skip Scan*. Allows skipping of the prefix of a composite index and searches the suffix index column values. In other words, if a composite index has three columns, the index can be searched using the second and third index columns only.

- *Index Full Scan*. Reads the entire index in the key order of the index.

- *Fast Full Index Scan*. Reads an entire index, as does an index full scan, but reads the index in physical block order, rather than key order. When reading a large percentage of a table and there is no requirement for sorting, then a fast full index scan can be much faster than an index full scan.

Note: A fast full index scan is executed in the same manner as that of a full table scan in that it reads data directly from disk. As a result, a fast full index scan will absolutely include I/O activity.

- *Index Join*. This is a join performed by selecting from multiple BTree indexes.

- *Bitmap Join*. Joins using bitmap key values, all read from indexes.

Let's demonstrate the use of each type of index scan.

10.1.1.4.1 *Index Unique Scan*

A unique scan (also called an exact index hit) reads a unique index and finds a single row. Unique scans usually occur with equality comparisons or IN and EXISTS subquery semi-join operators. This first query uses an equality comparison:

```
EXPLAIN PLAN SET statement_id= 'TEST' FOR
SELECT * FROM coa WHERE coa# = '60001';
```

```
Query                                     Cost      Rows     Bytes
------------------------------------   -------   --------  ---------
SELECT STATEMENT   on                      1         1        24
 TABLE ACCESS BY INDEX ROWID on COA        1         1        24
  INDEX UNIQUE SCAN on XPK_COA                      55
```

This query uses an IN semi-join operator:

```
EXPLAIN PLAN SET statement_id= 'TEST' FOR
   SELECT * FROM coa WHERE coa# = '60001'
AND type IN (SELECT type FROM type);
```

```
Query                                     Cost      Rows     Bytes
------------------------------------   -------   --------  ---------
SELECT STATEMENT   on                      1         1        25
 NESTED LOOPS   on                         1         1        25
  TABLE ACCESS BY INDEX ROWID on COA       1         1        24
   INDEX UNIQUE SCAN on XPK_COA            0         1
  INDEX UNIQUE SCAN on XPK_TYPE            0         6         6
```

And using the EXISTS semi-join operator:

```
EXPLAIN PLAN SET statement_id= 'TEST' FOR
   SELECT * FROM coa WHERE coa# = '60001'
AND EXISTS (SELECT type FROM type WHERE type = coa.type);
```

```
Query                                     Cost      Rows     Bytes
------------------------------------   -------   --------  ---------
SELECT STATEMENT   on                      1         1        25
 NESTED LOOPS   on                         1         1        25
  TABLE ACCESS BY INDEX ROWID on COA       1         1        24
   INDEX UNIQUE SCAN on XPK_COA            0         1
  INDEX UNIQUE SCAN on XPK_TYPE            0         6         6
```

10.1.1.4.2   *Index Range Scan*

Range scans typically occur with range comparisons <, >, <=, >=, and the BETWEEN operator. A range scan is less efficient than a unique scan because an index is traversed and read many times for a group of values, rather than up to the three reads required for a unique scan:

```
EXPLAIN PLAN SET statement_id= 'TEST' FOR
   SELECT * FROM generalledger WHERE generalledger_id < 10;
```

Query	Cost	Rows	Bytes
SELECT STATEMENT on	4	1	23
TABLE ACCESS BY INDEX ROWID on GENERALLEDGER	4	1	23
INDEX RANGE SCAN on XPK_GENERALLEDGER	3	1	

The next query reads the GeneralLedger table as opposed to the COA table. It reads a large percentage of a very large table. The optimizer switches from an index range scan to a full table scan because most of the table is read:

```
EXPLAIN PLAN SET statement_id='TEST' FOR
   SELECT * FROM generalledger WHERE generalledger_id > 10;
```

Query	Cost	Rows	Bytes
SELECT STATEMENT on	**715**	1068929	24585367
TABLE ACCESS FULL on GENERALLEDGER	715	1068929	24585367

Forcing index use also avoids a range scan, but the cost is very much higher than scanning the whole table, because an ordered full index scan is used. Suggesting a fast full index scan using the INDEX_FFS hint would probably be faster than a full table scan:

```
EXPLAIN PLAN SET statement_id='TEST' FOR
   SELECT /*+ INDEX(generalledger, XPK_GENERALLEDGER) */ *
FROM generalledger WHERE coa# < '60001';
```

Query	Cost	Rows	Bytes
SELECT STATEMENT on	**7052**	890774	20487802
TABLE ACCESS BY INDEX ROWID on GENERALLEDGER	7052	890774	20487802
INDEX FULL SCAN on XPK_GENERALLEDGER	2309	1068929	

10.1.1.4.3   Reverse-Order Index Range Scan

A reverse-order index range scan is used when rows are sorted in descending order:

```
EXPLAIN PLAN SET statement_id='TEST' FOR
    SELECT * FROM generalledger WHERE generalledger_id < 10
ORDER BY 1 DESC;
```

```
Query                                                Cost Rows    Bytes
---------------------------------------------------- ---- ----  ---------
SELECT STATEMENT   on                                 4    1        23
  TABLE ACCESS BY INDEX ROWID on GENERALLEDGER        4    1        23
    INDEX RANGE SCAN DESCENDING on XPK_GENERALLEDGER 3    1
```

10.1.1.4.4 *Index Skip Scan*

An index skip scan will allow skipping of a prefix column in a composite index and still utilize the index. This assumes that reading that index is faster than scanning the whole table. The Accounts schema does not have an appropriate index to demonstrate an index skip scan, so we can create one. The Orders table has a type column set to *S* for *Sales* or *P* for *Purchase*. An index skip scan is used when the prefix of a composite index has low cardinality (few unique values) and the suffix has high cardinality (many different values):

```
CREATE INDEX xak_o_type_customer ON orders(type, customer_id)
COMPUTE STATISTICS;
```

Now let's find some values:

```
SELECT * FROM(
SELECT type, customer_id, COUNT(customer_id) FROM orders
WHERE customer_id IS NOT NULL GROUP BY type, customer_id)
WHERE ROWNUM <= 10;
```

```
T CUSTOMER_ID COUNT(CUSTOMER_ID)
- ----------- ------------------
S           1                 22
S           2                  8
S           3                 47
S           4                  8
S           5                 41
S           6                 15
S           7                 15
S           8                 55
```

```
S           9               17
S          10               10
```

First, use the index as a composite:

```
EXPLAIN PLAN SET statement_id='TEST' FOR
SELECT type, customer_id FROM orders
WHERE type = 'S' AND customer_id = 8;
```

Query	Cost	Rows	Bytes
SELECT STATEMENT on	1	12	36
INDEX RANGE SCAN on XAK_O_TYPE_CUSTOMER	1	12	36

Now remove the type column index prefix from the WHERE clause. The same index is used with an index skip scan, skipping the prefix:

```
EXPLAIN PLAN SET statement_id='TEST' FOR
SELECT type, customer_id FROM orders WHERE customer_id = 8;
```

Query	Cost	Rows	Bytes
SELECT STATEMENT on	3	24	72
INDEX SKIP SCAN on XAK_O_TYPE_CUSTOMER	3	24	72

Selecting all columns uses a range scan on a different index because the CUSTOMER_ID column has an index. There is a foreign key index on the CUSTOMER_ID column:

```
EXPLAIN PLAN SET statement_id='TEST' FOR
SELECT * FROM orders WHERE customer_id = 8;
```

Query	Cost	Rows	Bytes
SELECT STATEMENT on	7	24	552
TABLE ACCESS BY INDEX ROWID on ORDERS	7	24	552
INDEX RANGE SCAN on XFK_O_CUSTOMER	1	24	

10.1.1.4.5   *Index Full Scan*

A full index scan reads the entire index in key order and not the physical block order of the index. Retrieved columns must be in the index with one non-NULL column, as can be seen in the following two examples. The first example shows a single-column primary key index and the second a multiple-column composite primary key index:

```
EXPLAIN PLAN SET statement_id='TEST' FOR SELECT stock_id FROM
stock;
```

```
Query                            Cost     Rows      Bytes

------------------------------ ------ -------- ---------

SELECT STATEMENT    on            1      118       354
   INDEX FULL SCAN on XPK_STOCK    1      118       354
```

```
EXPLAIN PLAN SET statement_id='TEST' FOR
SELECT year, period, coa# FROM periodsum;
```

```
Query                             Cost     Rows     Bytes

------------------------------- ------ -------- ---------

SELECT STATEMENT    on             1       45       450
   INDEX FULL SCAN on XPK_PERIODSUM 1      45       450
```

The benefit of a full index scan is a sorted result, because the index is scanned in sorted key order. Sometimes a full index scan is used by the optimizer to remove the need for sorting, when a SQL statement includes an ORDER BY or GROUP BY clause. Let's look into use of the ORDER BY clause first. This query, as shown in the query plan, executes a full index scan on the Stock table primary key index. Sorting for the ORDER BY clause is not shown in the query plan because the rows are read from the index using the index full scan, in the required STOCK_ID column sorted order:

```
EXPLAIN PLAN SET statement_id='TEST' FOR
SELECT stock_id FROM stock ORDER BY stock_id;
```

```
Query                            Cost     Rows      Bytes

------------------------------ ------ -------- ---------

SELECT STATEMENT    on            1      118       354
   INDEX FULL SCAN on XPK_STOCK    1      118       354
```

The inherent sorting of the full index scan can be proved again by the following example. The *INDEX FAST FULL SCAN* (fast full index scan) hint has been used to remove the ORDER BY clause index sorted order. We will cover the fast full index scan shortly. A fast full index scan reads the index in physical block order and not sorted key order. Thus the following query being read in physical order requires STOCK_ID column sorting to satisfy the ORDER BY clause. Notice the increase in cost from 2 to 4 to execute the *SORT ORDER BY on* step in the query plan:

```
EXPLAIN PLAN SET statement_id='TEST' FOR
SELECT /*+ INDEX_FFS(stock, xpk_stock) */ stock_id FROM stock
ORDER BY stock_id;
```

Query	Cost	Rows	Bytes
SELECT STATEMENT on	4	118	354
SORT ORDER BY on	4	118	354
INDEX FAST FULL SCAN on XPK_STOCK	2	118	354

Now let's look at the GROUP BY clause sorting catered for using a full index scan. The two following examples show no increase in cost for sorting and distinctly show that *NOSORT* is required. There is no extra sorting:

```
EXPLAIN PLAN SET statement_id='TEST' FOR
SELECT order_id, COUNT(order_id) FROM ordersline
GROUP BY order_id;
```

Query	Cost	Rows	Bytes
SELECT STATEMENT on	2784	226703	906812
SORT GROUP BY **NOSORT** on	2784	226703	906812
INDEX FULL SCAN on XFK_OL_ORDERS	2784	997903	3991612

And again the same thing:

```
EXPLAIN PLAN SET statement_id='TEST' FOR
SELECT order_id, seq#, COUNT(order_id) FROM ordersline
GROUP BY seq#, order_id;
```

Query	Cost	Rows	Bytes
SELECT STATEMENT on	3134	997903	5987418
SORT GROUP BY **NOSORT** on	**3134**	997903	5987418
INDEX FULL SCAN on XPK_ORDERSLINE	3134	997903	5987418

Sometimes a full index scan will be used, passing ROWID pointers to a table to retrieve rows in that table as opposed to only reading the index. Again there is no sorting required:

```
EXPLAIN PLAN SET statement_id='TEST' FOR
SELECT * FROM stock ORDER BY stock_id;
```

Query	Cost	Rows	Bytes
SELECT STATEMENT on	5	118	27612
TABLE ACCESS BY INDEX ROWID on STOCK	5	118	27612
INDEX FULL SCAN on XPK_STOCK	1	118	

The following example is interesting because the key-ordered index full scan is used to find both minimum and maximum values at either ends of the sorted key value range:

```
EXPLAIN PLAN SET statement_id='TEST' FOR
SELECT MIN(stock_id), MAX(stock_id) FROM stock;
```

Query	Cost	Rows	Bytes
SELECT STATEMENT on	1	1	3
SORT AGGREGATE on		1	3
INDEX FULL SCAN on XPK_STOCK	1	118	354

10.1.1.4.6   Fast Full Index Scan

A fast full index scan is a variation on, and in some respects an improvement to, a full index scan. Fast full index scans are only available for cost-based optimization. A full index scan reads an index in the sorted key index order. A fast full index scan is faster because it reads the index in physical order directly from the disk rather than in key order. A full index scan reading in key order will likely be a random physical search. When reading the entire index, the physical index may as well be read in physical sequential order unless the index order is required. The example following shows use of a fast full index scan where no ordering is specified. If the sequence of the columns were reversed, the fast full index scan would still be used:

```
EXPLAIN PLAN SET statement_id='TEST' FOR
SELECT stock_id, supplier_id FROM stocksource;
```

Query	Cost	Rows	Bytes
SELECT STATEMENT on	5	12083	72498
INDEX FAST FULL SCAN on XPK_STOCKSOURCE	5	12083	72498

Note: An additional benefit of a fast full index scan over a full index scan is that the DB_FILE_MULTIBLOCK_READ_COUNT can be utilized because the index is read in physical order directly from disk.

This second example is a modification of the first where an ORDER BY clause is added for the same columns retrieved, in the same sequence. The optimizer reverts back to an index full scan since the ORDER BY clause specifies that the index be read in sorted key order rather than unsorted physical order as the fast full index scan does:

```
EXPLAIN PLAN SET statement_id='TEST' FOR
SELECT stock_id, supplier_id FROM stocksource
ORDER BY stock_id, supplier_id;
```

Query	Cost	Rows	Bytes
SELECT STATEMENT on	25	12083	72498
INDEX FULL SCAN on XPK_STOCKSOURCE	25	12083	72498

Now let's force use of the unordered fast full index scan for the query shown previously with the ORDER BY clause added to show the difference in cost. Note the use of temporary sort space on disk to execute the sort plus the increase in cost for sorting denoted by *SORT ORDER BY on* in the query plan:

```
EXPLAIN PLAN SET statement_id='TEST' FOR
SELECT /*+ INDEX_FFS(stocksource, xpk_stocksource) */
```

```
stock_id, supplier_id FROM stocksource
ORDER BY stock_id, supplier_id;
```

```
Query                                   Cost   Rows   Bytes    Sort
--------------------------------------- ----  ------ ------- -------
SELECT STATEMENT  on                      53  12083   72498
 SORT ORDER BY on                         53  12083   72498  402000
  INDEX FAST FULL SCAN on XPK_STOCKSOURCE  5  12083   72498
```

Manual ORDER BY clause sorting is required, as shown in the previous example, because a fast full index scan does not read an index in key order.

> **Note:** Be careful utilizing inherent sorting, because it can be heavily dependent on the physical order of indexed values in tables.

Now let's look at some interesting effects of query variations on full and fast full index scans:

- The DISTINCT clause
- The COUNT function
- Retrieving from an index with NOT NULL
- Parallel execution with multiple CPUs

10.1.1.4.7   The DISTINCT Clause

DISTINCT always executes an inherent sort:

```
EXPLAIN PLAN SET statement_id='TEST' FOR
SELECT DISTINCT(stock_id) FROM stockmovement;
```

```
Query                                   Cost     Rows     Bytes
--------------------------------------- ------ -------- ---------
SELECT STATEMENT  on                     1506      118       354
 SORT UNIQUE on                          1506      118       354
  INDEX FAST FULL SCAN on XFK_SM_STOCK    312  1043460   3130380
```

Even when using the presorted full index scan, as in the next example, the DISTINCT clause still forces a sort. Thus the previous query using the

fast full index scan has a lower cost, even though the query plan specifies
SORT UNIQUE NOSORT on as opposed to *SORT UNIQUE on* in the
previous example:

```
EXPLAIN PLAN SET statement_id='TEST' FOR
SELECT /*+ ORDERED INDEX(stockmovement, xfk_sm_stock) */
DISTINCT(stock_id) FROM stockmovement ORDER BY 1;
```

Query	Cost	Rows	Bytes
SELECT STATEMENT on	3243	118	354
SORT UNIQUE NOSORT on	3243	118	354
INDEX FULL SCAN on XFK_SM_STOCK	2049	1043460	3130380

10.1.1.4.8   The COUNT Function

The COUNT function executes directly from the fast full index scan step
without sorting requirements. The step called *SORT AGGREGATE on* is
not a sort operation because no cost increase is associated with it:

```
EXPLAIN PLAN SET statement_id='TEST' FOR
  SELECT COUNT(*) FROM generalledger;
```

Query	Cost	Rows	Bytes
SELECT STATEMENT on	352	1	
SORT AGGREGATE on		1	
INDEX FAST FULL SCAN on XPK_GENERALLEDGER	352	1068929	

10.1.1.4.9   Retrieving with NOT NULL

The IS NOT NULL comparison allows use of the fast full index scan
option reading just non-null value rows from the index. If the query was
sorted with the ORDER BY clause, then the fast full index scan would
revert to a full index scan, taking advantage of the full index scan sorted
key traversal:

```
EXPLAIN PLAN SET statement_id='TEST' FOR
  SELECT customer_id FROM transactions
WHERE customer_id IS NOT NULL;
```

```
Query                                      Cost    Rows     Bytes
------------------------------------  ------ -------- ---------
SELECT STATEMENT   on                        29   64599    129198
  INDEX FAST FULL SCAN on XFK_T_CUSTOMER      29   64599    129198
```

10.1.1.4.10   Parallel Index Scan

Parallel scans can be executed on fast full index scans (block order index scans) but not on full index scans (key order) or index range scans. An index can have a degree of parallelism set for it using the CREATE INDEX or ALTER INDEX command (hints can also be used). Once again, queries in this section are executed on a dual-CPU machine, without Oracle partitioning. Oracle partitioning is covered in Part III. Let's do the same thing we did with parallel full table scans:

```
ALTER INDEX XFK_GL_COA# PARALLEL 2;

EXPLAIN PLAN SET statement_id='TEST' FOR
SELECT coa# FROM generalledger;
```

```
Query                                                    Cost    Rows
--------------------------------------------------  ---- -------
SELECT STATEMENT   on                                       4   752740
  INDEX FAST FULL SCAN on XFK_GL_COA# PARALLEL_TO_SERIAL    4   752740
```

Remove parallelism from the index:

```
ALTER INDEX XFK_GL_COA# NOPARALLEL;
```

Now let's check the query plan again. We have an increase in cost without parallelism:

```
EXPLAIN PLAN SET statement_id='TEST' FOR
SELECT coa# FROM generalledger;
```

```
Query                                 Cost    Rows     Bytes
------------------------------------  ------- -------- ---------
SELECT STATEMENT   on                      8   752740   4516440
  INDEX FAST FULL SCAN on XFK_GL_COA#      8   752740   4516440
```

Let's increase the degree of parallelism on the index. It seems that, unlike full table scans, fast full index scans are complemented by use of parallelism, even in a small database, with no Oracle partitioning:

```
ALTER INDEX XFK_GL_COA# PARALLEL 4;

EXPLAIN PLAN SET statement_id='TEST' FOR
SELECT coa# FROM generalledger;
```

The higher we set the degree of parallelism for the index, the lower the cost for the index fast full scan:

```
Query                                                   Cost   Rows
-------------------------------------------------- ---- -------
SELECT STATEMENT   on                                     2   752740
  INDEX FAST FULL SCAN on XFK_GL_COA# PARALLEL_TO_SERIAL   2   752740
```

Let's do some timing tests. The degree of parallelism is set first to NOPARALLEL, then to 2, and finally to 4. Starting with NOPARALLEL:

```
ALTER INDEX xfk_gl_coa# NOPARALLEL;

SQL> SELECT COUNT(*) FROM(SELECT coa# FROM generalledger);

  COUNT(*)
----------
    752741
```

Elapsed: 00:00:00.05

And now setting the degree of parallelism to 2:

```
ALTER INDEX xfk_gl_coa# PARALLEL 2;

SQL> SELECT COUNT(*) FROM(SELECT coa# FROM generalledger);

  COUNT(*)
----------
    752741
```

Elapsed: 00:00:03.01

Finally, setting the degree of parallelism to 4:

```
ALTER INDEX xfk_gl_coa# PARALLEL 4;

SQL> SELECT COUNT(*) FROM(SELECT coa# FROM generalledger);

  COUNT(*)
----------
    752741
```

Elapsed: 00:00:03.01

The timing tests show that using no parallelism (NO PARALLEL) on the fast full index scan is faster than when using degrees of parallelism of either 2 or 4. Therefore, in contradiction to the query plans, like fast full table scans, index fast full index scan parallelism is not helpful for performance in any database type, other than probably a data warehouse, unless Oracle partitioning is used.

10.1.1.4.11 *Index Join*

Index joins use a hashing function to join scans of multiple indexes together, if all columns can be retrieved from the indexes, no matter what type of index scans they are:

```
EXPLAIN PLAN SET statement_id='TEST' FOR
    SELECT
/*+ INDEX_JOIN(generalledger xpk_generalledger xfx_gl_coa#) */
generalledger_id, coa# FROM generalledger;
```

Query	Cost	Rows	Bytes
SELECT STATEMENT on	474818	1068929	10689290
VIEW on index$_join$_001	474818	1068929	10689290
HASH JOIN on		1068929	10689290
INDEX FAST FULL SCAN on XFK_COA#	2886	1068929	10689290
INDEX FAST FULL SCAN on XPK_GENERALLEDGER	2886	1068929	10689290

> **Note:** ⑨*i* Index joins are only available with cost-based optimization and statistics.

Following is the same query with a filtering restriction on the COA# column, changing one of the fast full index scans to an index range scan:

```
EXPLAIN PLAN SET statement_id='TEST' FOR
  SELECT
/*+ INDEX_JOIN(generalledger xpk_generalledger xfx_gl_coa#) */
generalledger_id, coa# FROM generalledger
WHERE coa# = '60001';
```

Query	Cost	Rows	Bytes
SELECT STATEMENT on	83648	178155	1781550
VIEW on index$_join$_001	83648	178155	1781550
HASH JOIN on		178155	1781550
INDEX RANGE SCAN on XFK_COA#	531	178155	1781550
INDEX FAST FULL SCAN on XPK_GENERALLEDGER	531	178155	1781550

10.1.1.4.12 *Bitmap Join*

The Accounts schema has no bitmap indexes, so I will create some bitmap indexes as a temporary measure on a copy of an existing table:

```
CREATE TABLE tmp AS SELECT * FROM periodsum;
ANALYZE TABLE tmp COMPUTE STATISTICS;
CREATE BITMAP INDEX xfk_tmp_year ON tmp(year) COMPUTE
STATISTICS;
CREATE BITMAP INDEX xfk_tmp_period ON tmp(period) COMPUTE
STATISTICS;
CREATE BITMAP INDEX xfk_tmp_coa# ON tmp(coa#) COMPUTE
STATISTICS;
```

> **Note:** ⑨*i* Bitmap joins are only available with cost-based optimization and statistics.

```
EXPLAIN PLAN SET statement_id='TEST' FOR
  SELECT /*+ INDEX_JOIN(tmp) */ year, period, coa# FROM tmp;
```

```
Query                                              Cost     Rows     Bytes
-------------------------------------------------  ------  --------  ---------
SELECT STATEMENT  on                                   6        45        405
 VIEW  on index$_join$_001                             6        45        405
   HASH JOIN  on                                                 45        405
   HASH JOIN  on                                                 45        405
    BITMAP CONVERSION TO ROWIDS on
      BITMAP INDEX FULL SCAN on XFK_TMP_COA#
    BITMAP CONVERSION TO ROWIDS on
      BITMAP INDEX FULL SCAN on XFK_TMP_PERIOD
   BITMAP CONVERSION TO ROWIDS on
     BITMAP INDEX FULL SCAN on XFK_TMP_YEAR
```

Now let's clean up and drop the temporary table. Dropping the table will destroy all of the indexes created on that table, at the same time:

```
DROP TABLE tmp;
```

10.1.1.5   Cluster and Hash Scans

Cluster and hash scans access cluster and hash clusters, respectively. Both work in a similar fashion to that of accessing a ROWID from one object and retrieving from another object using the ROWID pointer. Clusters are generally read-only object types and are usually used in data warehouses. This book is primarily about tuning OLTP databases.[1]

Let's cover clusters very briefly. A cluster is a read-only object. So, we will take advantage of the physical storage capabilities of Oracle Database, squashing as much data into each block as possible. Additionally, before creating the cluster, I have to log in as SYSTEM and explicitly grant the CREATE TABLE and CREATE CLUSTER privileges to my schema:

```
GRANT CREATE TABLE TO accounts;
GRANT CREATE CLUSTER TO accounts;
```

Now back to my Accounts schema and creating a cluster:

```
CREATE CLUSTER clu_tb (coa# CHAR(5))
PCTFREE 0 PCTUSED 99 SIZE 512 TABLESPACE DATA
STORAGE (INITIAL 1M NEXT 1M);
CREATE INDEX xclu_tb ON CLUSTER clu_tb TABLESPACE INDX
COMPUTE STATISTICS;
```

Now let's add a table to the cluster:

```
CREATE TABLE trialbalance CLUSTER clu_tb(coa#) AS SELECT * FROM coa;
ANALYZE TABLE trialbalance COMPUTE STATISTICS;

EXPLAIN PLAN SET statement_id='TEST' FOR
    SELECT /*+ CLUSTER(trialbalance) */ * FROM trialbalance
WHERE coa# = '50028';
```

Query	Cost	Rows	Bytes
SELECT STATEMENT on	1	1	24
TABLE ACCESS CLUSTER on TRIALBALANCE	1	1	24
INDEX UNIQUE SCAN on **XCLU_TB**		55	

And finally, let's clean up:

```
    DROP TABLE trialbalance;
    DROP CLUSTER clu_tb;
```

10.1.2   Joining Tables

Oracle Database takes specific steps internally when joining tables together in SQL statements. The optimizer decides on different types of join methods by using statistics on tables and indexes, when joining tables.

Note: Oracle Database calls a table or part of a table a row source. A row source is a chunk of memory, much like a cursor in PL/SQL, containing a pointer to a current position in a set of rows.

When multiple row sources are joined, the optimizer makes an assessment based on statistics and other factors to decide how two tables should be joined. These different join methods are listed and described in this section and have various different aspects and applications.

Note: I like to call what Oracle Corporation calls a row source a row set or set of rows, being a subset of a table.

10.1.2.1 Join Order Execution

In joins with more than two tables, one table is joined to the second, which is in turn joined to the third table, and so on. The optimizer will approach a join in this manner, adapting use of join methods accordingly. If the first join results in a small row set and the second join a large row set, then the result of the first join effectively joins to a large set of rows. Therefore, it is extremely important how tables are placed into the FROM clause both in the Oracle SQL proprietary and ANSI standard join format syntax, when constructing SQL join statements. A join statement, much like any SQL statement, is parsed from left to right and from top to bottom. This is not a hard-and-fast rule, as applied to joins and any SQL statement in general, but it is a good guide.

10.1.2.2 Types of Joins

Joins include the following types:

- *Nested Loop Join*. A nested loop is usually used between a sorted and an unsorted set of rows. Nested loops generally involve the joining of a small row set to a large row set. However, nested loop joins can also be the most efficient join for small row sets on both sides of the join.

- *Hash Join*. Hash joins are utilized between two large sets of rows where a smaller row set has a temporary hash table generated for it. Generation of the hash table creates extra overhead. A hash join is only faster than a nested loop when there are a large number of rows in the smaller row set and when both row sets have an equivalent numbers of rows (both row sets are not small). The optimizer will use a hash join rather than a nested loop join when the smaller row set is too large to warrant using a nested loop. When joining, the hash table is read, and each entry prompts a search into the larger table.

- *Sort Merge Join*. Sort merge joins are used between two large row sets where one or both row sets are unsorted. A sort merge join is chosen when row sets are too large for both nested loop and hash joins to be efficient. In a sort merge join, row sets are sorted first, separately, then merged together.

- *Other Join Types*. Joins classified as *other* are generally joins affecting or affected by the use of nested loop, hash, and sort merge joins. These types include semi-joins, bitmaps, star queries in data warehouses, multiple table (mutable) nested joins, and some types of joins that are often best avoided.

A hash join is the next worst option compared to that of a nested loop join. A sort-merge join is the least efficient option of all three. A nested loop join is preferable because it operates on small row sets, which lead to fast performance of joins. Any type of SQL code performs better when retrieving small row sets.

A nested loop join is typically used between an index and a full scan of some type, associating a value from the index to the full scan, or vice versa. A hash join is the same but often replaces a nested loop join when two full scans are involved, or when large row sets force the optimizer to decide that a hash join is faster than a nested loop. A hash join is the second best option because a hash join creates a hash table. The process of creating a hash table is an extra processing step as a replacement for the index used in a nested loop. A sort-merge join is used in favor of a nested loop or a hash join when two large row sets are involved or sorting is required.

The choice the optimizer makes between the three join types can depend on relative configuration parameter values. Configuration parameters affecting join type selection are as follows:

- *SORT_AREA_SIZE*. Increasing favors join types requiring sorting.
- *HASH_AREA_SIZE*. Increases the likelihood of hash joins.

Note: (9*i*) Set the HASH_JOIN_ENABLED configuration parameter to TRUE to enable the use of hash joins by the optimizer.

Note: (10*g*) HASH_JOIN_ENABLED is removed.

Note: The PGA_AGGREGATE_TARGET parameter is set to a nonzero value in Oracle Database 10*g* by default. This parameter causes the WORKAREA_SIZE_POLICY parameter to be set to AUTO. The result is that high memory usage activities including sorting, aggregates, hash joins, bitmap creations, and merges are handled automatically by the PGA_AGGREGATE_TARGET parameter. Setting the *_AREA_SIZE parameters, such as the SORT_AREA_SIZE and HASH_AREA_SIZE, is no longer necessary.

■ *DB_FILE_MULTIBLOCK_READ_COUNT.* Increases the likelihood of join types operating on large amounts of data such as a sort merge join.

Now let's examine and demonstrate each join method.

10.1.2.2.1 *Nested Loop Join*

A nested loop join is used between a sorted table and an unsorted table. The sorted table is scanned with a sorted index scan, and the unsorted table is accessed by a ROWID pointer, from the sorted table. A nested loop is literally a loop within a loop, thus the term *nested*, or one loop nested within another loop. The cursor for one SQL statement is executed within a driving SQL statement. A nested loop contains an outer and an inner loop, where the inner loop is driven by each row found by the outer loop. Obviously, the fewer rows in either loop, or the smaller one of the loops, the more efficient a nested loop is.

At this point in this book, you should notice that some changes have been made to the output of the query plan (contrary to query plans shown previously in this book):

■ The LEVEL pseudocolumn is shown on the left. The LEVEL pseudocolumn shows the branch layer in a hierarchical tree structured query result. In this case, LEVEL shows the layer in which the optimizer executes each function.

■ The position column (Pos) represents a sequence of execution in reverse. Thus in the first query plan shown following, the unique index scan is executed first on the COA table, for each row found by the fast full index scan in the GeneralLedger table. The nested loops join is driving the application of row selection from the GeneralLedger table accessing each match in the COA table. Thus the nested loop and index fast full scan are executed at the same time. The SELECT statement is obviously executed on the result of the nested loops join.

Note: Remember that a fast full index scan is a physically complete and sequential read of an index data space in block order. It is not sorted in index order.

Here's a query plan using a nested loop:

```
EXPLAIN PLAN SET statement_id='TEST' FOR
SELECT coa.coa#, gl.coa#
FROM coa JOIN generalledger gl ON(coa.coa# = gl.coa#);
```

Query	Cost	Rows	Bytes	Pos
1. SELECT STATEMENT on	609	1068929	10689290	0
2. **NESTED LOOPS** on	609	1068929	10689290	1
3. INDEX FAST FULL SCAN on XFK_COA#	609	1068929	5344645	1
3. INDEX UNIQUE SCAN on XPK_COA		1	5	2

This second query has the two tables swapped around in the FROM clause. The optimizer is intelligent enough to spot this:

```
EXPLAIN PLAN SET statement_id='TEST' FOR
SELECT coa.coa#, gl.coa#
FROM generalledger gl JOIN coa ON(gl.coa# = coa.coa#);
```

Query	Cost	Rows	Bytes	Pos
1. SELECT STATEMENT on	609	1068929	10689290	0
2. **NESTED LOOPS** on	609	1068929	10689290	1
3. INDEX FAST FULL SCAN on XFK_COA#	609	1068929	5344645	1
3. INDEX UNIQUE SCAN on XPK_COA		1	5	2

All rows in the inner loop row set will be accessed by each row in the outer loop row set. Notice I am not using the term *table* but rather the term *row set*. Once again, what is a row set? When filtering is included in a query, then the row set is a subset of the rows in a table or from a query result. Following is a modification to the previous example using filtering and retrieving nonindexed rows from the GeneralLedger table. This should provoke a full table scan on the GeneralLedger table. Note that the filtering is applied to the largest table, the GeneralLedger table:

```
EXPLAIN PLAN SET statement_id='TEST' FOR
SELECT coa.coa#, gl.dte, gl.dr, gl.dr FROM coa
JOIN generalledger gl ON(coa.coa# = gl.coa#)
WHERE gl.coa# = '60001';
```

This query plan is ugly! On the basis of an outer table driving an inner table, where all rows in the inner table are accessed by each row in the outer table, this join should be very inefficient. The unique scan on the COA table is accessing every row in the GeneralLedger table. It might make sense if the tables in the nested loop were reversed. The reason for the full table scan is because GL.COA# = '60001' accesses 7% of the GeneralLedger table:

Query	Cost	Rows	Bytes	Pos
1. SELECT STATEMENT on	1129	29692	593840	0
2. NESTED LOOPS on	1129	29692	593840	1
3. **INDEX UNIQUE SCAN on XPK_COA**		1	5	1
3. **TABLE ACCESS FULL on GENERALLEDGER**	1128	29693	445395	2

In the next example, the filter is placed on the smaller table, pushing the full table access into the outer loop. This is a very slightly better-performing join. The cost is the same, and timing tests following are the same as well. The row and byte values are much higher, which is significant. More data read is higher I/O, but that is physical tuning and will be covered in Part III:

```
EXPLAIN PLAN SET statement_id='TEST' FOR
SELECT coa.coa#, gl.dte, gl.dr, gl.dr
FROM coa JOIN generalledger gl ON(gl.coa# = coa.coa#)
WHERE coa.coa# = '60001';
```

Query	Cost	Rows	Bytes	Pos
1. SELECT STATEMENT on	1128	1068929	21378580	0
2. NESTED LOOPS on	1128	1068929	21378580	1
3. **TABLE ACCESS FULL on GENERALLEDGER**	1128	1068929	16033935	1
3. **INDEX UNIQUE SCAN on XPK_COA**		1	5	2

```
SQL> SELECT COUNT(*) FROM(SELECT coa.coa#, gl.dte, gl.dr, gl.dr FROM coa
  2   JOIN generalledger gl ON(coa.coa# = gl.coa#)
  3   WHERE gl.coa# = '60001');

  COUNT(*)
----------
     75555
```

Elapsed: 00:00:00.01

```
SQL> SELECT COUNT(*) FROM(SELECT coa.coa#, gl.dte, gl.dr, gl.dr
  2  FROM coa JOIN generalledger gl ON(gl.coa# = coa.coa#)
  3  WHERE coa.coa# = '60001');


  COUNT(*)
----------
     75555
```

Elapsed: 00:00:00.01

It should now be obvious that a nested loop join is used by the optimizer between a small, sorted row set, and a larger, unsorted row set. Let's abuse the optimizer a little further and partially contradict this point. The following example finds a single row in the GeneralLedger table and thus the COA table as well. Therefore, we are finding two small row sets. A nested loop in this situation is the most efficient option. A sort-merge would ignore the indexes, and a hash join would create a hash key table as a superfluous step:

```
EXPLAIN PLAN SET statement_id='TEST' FOR
SELECT coa.*, gl.*
FROM generalledger gl JOIN coa ON(gl.coa# = coa.coa#)
WHERE generalledger_id = 10;
```

Query	Cost	Rows	Bytes	Pos
1. SELECT STATEMENT on	4	1	47	0
2. NESTED LOOPS on	4	1	47	1
3. TABLE ACCESS BY INDEX ROWID on GENERALLEDGER	3	1	23	1
4. **INDEX UNIQUE SCAN** on XPK_GENERALLEDGER	2	1068929		1
3. TABLE ACCESS BY INDEX ROWID on CO	1	1	24	2
4. **INDEX UNIQUE SCAN** on XPK_COA		1		1

A nested loop join is used where a small and large row set are joined, and also where two very small row sets are joined. As you will see in the next section on hash joins, a hash join is often selected by the optimizer to replace a nested loop join when there are two large row sets. The following query uses a nested loop rather than a hash join because it reads a unique index, physically covering too few blocks to make a hash join more efficient than a nested loop. A hash join will be selected as being faster than a nested

loop join if the joined row sets get larger. This join is shown here because
there is a related example in the next section on hash joins:

```
EXPLAIN PLAN SET statement_id='TEST' FOR
    SELECT s.stock_id, sm.stockmovement_id
    FROM stock s JOIN stockmovement sm ON(s.stock_id = sm.stock_id)
WHERE s.stock_id < 10;
```

Query	Cost	Rows	Bytes	Pos
1. SELECT STATEMENT on	1032	6174	67914	0
2. NESTED LOOPS on	1032	6174	67914	1
3. TABLE ACCESS FULL on STOCKMOVEMENT	1032	80266	642128	1
3. **INDEX UNIQUE SCAN** on XPK_STOCK		1	3	2

10.1.2.2.2   Hash Join

Hash joins join large row sets together. A temporary hash table for the outer
or smaller table is used for matching rows in the inner table. The
HASH_AREA_SIZE configuration parameter determines the size of the
hash table to be placed into cache. When available cache space is exceeded,
hash tables are split apart and stored temporarily in temporary sort space.
This is detrimental to performance.

Note: $(10g)$ By default, the PGA_AGGREGATE_TARGET parameter
accounts for all *_AREA_SIZE parameters.

A hash key is mathematically most efficient for doing exact searches.
Consequently, equi-joins apply to hash joins. Range and anti-joins do not
apply to hash joins, although this is not always strictly true.

The second-to-last join in the previous section on nested loops used a
nested loop on a single row found in the larger table. Removing the filtering clause, as in the next join, makes the outer table too large for a nested
loop. The optimizer switches the nested loop to a hash join. In this case, it
is all about physical space covered. The optimizer considers it faster to
create and read a hash table, rather than use a nested loop, because a lot of
rows are accessed:

```
EXPLAIN PLAN SET statement_id='TEST' FOR
SELECT coa.*, gl.*
```

```
FROM generalledger gl JOIN coa ON(gl.coa# = coa.coa#);
```

Query	Cost	Rows	Bytes	Pos
1. SELECT STATEMENT on	1642	1068929	50239663	0
2. HASH JOIN on	1642	1068929	50239663	1
3. **TABLE ACCESS FULL** on COA	2	55	1320	1
3. **TABLE ACCESS FULL** on GENERALLEDGER	1128	1068929	24585367	2

The last join in the previous section on nested loop joins selected indexed column values only. The next query plan changes from a nested loop to a hash join because nonindexed table columns are selected. Reading too much physical space can make a nested loop less efficient:

```
EXPLAIN PLAN SET statement_id='TEST' FOR
    SELECT s.text, sm.qty, sm.price
    FROM stock s JOIN stockmovement sm ON(s.stock_id = sm.stock_id)
WHERE s.stock_id < 10;
```

Query	Cost	Rows	Bytes	Pos
1. SELECT STATEMENT on	1060	6174	345744	0
2. HASH JOIN on	1060	6174	345744	1
3. TABLE ACCESS BY INDEX ROWID on STOCK	2	9	405	1
4. **INDEX RANGE SCAN** on XPK_STOCK	1	9		1
3. TABLE ACCESS FULL on STOCKMOVEMENT	1032	80266	882926	2

10.1.2.2.3   Sort-Merge Join

A sort-merge join executes three separate steps. The first two steps sort both tables separately. The third step merges them together into a sorted result. Typically, a sort-merge join is used to join tables where no indexes are used on either table, or when sorting is imposed using ORDER BY or GROUP BY clauses. The first query following shows both the sorting and I/O columns. Notice the large values for sorting and I/O activity:

```
EXPLAIN PLAN SET statement_id='TEST' FOR
    SELECT * FROM transactionsline tl NATURAL JOIN stockmovement sm;
```

```
Query                                               Cost      Sort      IO
--------------------------------------------------  ------ ---------  --------
1. SELECT STATEMENT   on                            25616              25616
2.   MERGE JOIN   on                                25616              25616
3.     TABLE ACCESS BY INDEX ROWID on STOCKMOVEMENT  6619               6619
4.       INDEX FULL SCAN on XPK_STOCKMOVENT          2189               2189
3.     SORT JOIN on                                 18997  57869000    18997
4.       TABLE ACCESS FULL on TRANSACTIONS            800                800
```

A sort-merge join is likely to involve extensive I/O activity and use of temporary sort space on disk. Adjusting the SORT_AREA_SIZE configuration parameter can help, but increasing it will have adverse affects in other respects, to be discussed in Part III.

Note: (10g) By default, the PGA_AGGREGATE_TARGET parameter accounts for all *_AREA_SIZE parameters.

The next join is an alteration to the second-to-last hash join query shown in the previous section on hash joins, with the addition of an ORDER BY clause. The application of the ORDER BY clause persuades the optimizer to switch from a hash join to a sort-merge join. This avoids the sort required by the ORDER BY clause. The sort part of the sort-merge join takes care of the ORDER BY sorting required:

```
EXPLAIN PLAN SET statement_id='TEST' FOR
SELECT coa.*, gl.*
FROM generalledger gl JOIN coa ON(gl.coa# = coa.coa#)
ORDER BY coa.coa#;
```

Following is the query plan where there are two clearly distinct steps shown for sorting and merging (position column value 2 and position column value 1, respectively). The sort is executed on the COA table, and the merge joins the sorted result to the index full scan of the GeneralLedger table. Also note that the concept of an inner and an outer table do not apply as in hash and nested loop joins. As already stated, a sort-merge join has two separate steps: (1) sorting of two separate row sets, and (2) merging the sorted row sets together:

```
Query                                              Cost     Rows     Bytes    Pos
-------------------------------------------------  ------  --------  ---------  ------
1. SELECT STATEMENT   on                           20782  1068929  50239663     0
2.   MERGE JOIN   on                               20782  1068929  50239663     1
3.    TABLE ACCESS BY INDEX ROWID on GENERALLEDGER 20778  1068929  24585367     1
4.     INDEX FULL SCAN on XFK_COA#                   2536  1068929                1
3.    SORT JOIN on                                     4       55      1320      2
4.     TABLE ACCESS FULL on COA                        2       55      1320      1
```

A similar optimizer decision would apply for a GROUP BY clause, as shown in the following query:

```
EXPLAIN PLAN SET statement_id='TEST' FOR
SELECT o.order_id, SUM(ol.amount)
FROM ordersline ol JOIN orders o
ON(o.order_id = ol.order_id)
  GROUP BY o.order_id;
```

A sort is not required for the GROUP BY clause, as indicated by *SORT GROUP BY NOSORT on* in the query plan:

```
Query                                    Cost     Rows     Bytes     Pos
-------------------------------------  ------  --------  ---------  ------
1. SELECT STATEMENT   on               12243   226703   2947139      0
2.   SORT GROUP BY NOSORT on           12243   226703   2947139      1
3.    MERGE JOIN   on                  12243   997903  12972739      1
4.     INDEX FULL SCAN on XPK_ORDERS     479   226703    906812      1
4.     SORT JOIN on                    11764   997903   8981127      2
5.      TABLE ACCESS FULL on ORDERSLINE  765   997903   8981127      1
```

Sorting is also not required when a full index scan is used. Full index scans are read in index order and presorted. Fast full index scans are read in physical order and are not sorted in index order. A fast full index scan requires sorting:

```
EXPLAIN PLAN SET statement_id='TEST' FOR
  SELECT tl.transaction_id, sm.stockmovement_id
FROM transactionsline tl JOIN stockmovement sm
ON(tl.stockmovement_id = sm.stockmovement_id);
```

And here is the query plan. The sort part of the sort-merge join is applied to the fast full index scan in order to sort it into the required order:

Query	Cost	Rows	Bytes	Pos
1. SELECT STATEMENT on	10552	1027251	14381514	0
2. MERGE JOIN on	10552	1027251	14381514	1
3. TABLE ACCESS BY INDEX ROWID on TRANSACTIONS	826	1027251	9245259	1
4. **INDEX FULL SCAN** on XFK_TL_STOCKMOVEMENT	26	1027251		1
3. **SORT JOIN** on	9726	1043460	5217300	2
4. **INDEX FAST FULL SCAN** on XPK_STOCKMOVEMENT	526	1043460	5217300	1

In the next query is a sort-merge join, where a sort is executed on both row sets in the join. This join is completely ridiculous and overzealous but is demonstrative in getting a point across: both row sets are sorted first prior to being joined. The cost is noticeably monstrous!

```
EXPLAIN PLAN SET statement_id='TEST' FOR
    SELECT * FROM generalledger a, generalledger b WHERE a.dte=b.dte;
```

Query	Cost	Rows	Bytes	Pos
1. SELECT STATEMENT on	50949	#######	#########	0
2. MERGE JOIN on	50949	#######	#########	1
3. **SORT JOIN** on	25475	1068929	24585367	1
4. TABLE ACCESS FULL on GENERALLEDGER	1128	1068929	24585367	1
3. **SORT JOIN** on	25475	1068929	24585367	2
4. TABLE ACCESS FULL on GENERALLEDGER	1128	1068929	24585367	1

Sort-merge joins can be used as a better option to that of nested loops, or even hash joins, for larger data sets, or when range or anti-join comparisons and operators are involved.

Note: An anti-join is a negative join attempting to find something that is not in a row set. The result is always a full table scan.

10.1.2.3 Mutable Join Nesting

The three basic join types—nested loops, hash joins, and sort-merge joins—can be nested together and even mixed into mutable joins. Each join in a mutable join is processed sequentially, where the result of one join is joined to the next. Each separate join will be chosen by the optimizer based on the content, size, and sorted nature of the row sets, both retrieved from tables and produced by nested multilayered joins.

Note: A mutable join is a join of more than two tables. A complex mutable join is a mutable join with filtering.

Here is a very simple example joining three small tables:

```
EXPLAIN PLAN SET statement_id='TEST' FOR
SELECT t.text, coa.text
FROM type t JOIN coa USING(type)
     JOIN subtype st USING(subtype);
```

Full table access on the first two tables causes the hash join. The result is joined to the next table using a nested loop because of the use of the index:

Query	Cost	Rows	Bytes	Pos
1. SELECT STATEMENT on	5	55	1375	0
2. **NESTED LOOPS** on	5	55	1375	1
3. **HASH JOIN** on	5	55	1320	1
4. TABLE ACCESS FULL on TYPE	2	6	48	1
4. TABLE ACCESS FULL on COA	2	55	880	2
3. INDEX UNIQUE SCAN on XPK_SUBTYPE		1	1	2

This next example now includes a very large table. The index fast full scan and the size of the row set produced by the first two joins persuades the use of a hash join rather than a nested loop for the final join:

```
EXPLAIN PLAN SET statement_id='TEST' FOR
SELECT t.text, coa.text
FROM type t JOIN coa USING(type)
    JOIN subtype st USING(subtype)
    JOIN generalledger gl ON(gl.coa# = coa.coa#);
```

Query	Cost	Rows	Bytes	Pos
1. SELECT STATEMENT on	863	1068929	37412515	0
2. **HASH JOIN** on	863	1068929	37412515	1
3. **NESTED LOOPS** on	5	55	1650	1
4. **HASH JOIN** on	5	55	1595	1
5. TABLE ACCESS FULL on TYPE	2	6	48	1
5. TABLE ACCESS FULL on COA	2	55	1155	2
4. INDEX UNIQUE SCAN on XPK_SUBTYPE		1	1	2
3. INDEX FAST FULL SCAN on XFK_COA#	609	1068929	5344645	2

Here is a large join retrieving a small number of rows by using a WHERE clause filter. Nested loops are evident in abundance in the query plan because of the small row sets and all the indexes used:

```
EXPLAIN PLAN SET statement_id='TEST' FOR
SELECT t.text, coa.text
FROM type t JOIN coa USING(type)
   JOIN subtype st USING(subtype)
   JOIN generalledger gl ON(gl.coa# = coa.coa#)
WHERE gl.coa# = '40003';
```

Query	Cost	Rows	Bytes	Pos
1. SELECT STATEMENT on	425	29692	1039220	0
2. **NESTED LOOPS** on	425	29692	1039220	1
3. **NESTED LOOPS** on	2	1	30	1
4. **NESTED LOOPS** on	2	1	29	1
5. TABLE ACCESS BY INDEX ROWID on COA	1	1	21	1
6. INDEX UNIQUE SCAN on XPK_COA		55		1
5. TABLE ACCESS BY INDEX ROWID on TYPE	1	1	8	2
6. INDEX UNIQUE SCAN on XPK_TYPE		1		1
4. INDEX UNIQUE SCAN on XPK_SUBTYPE		1	1	2
3. INDEX RANGE SCAN on XFK_COA#	423	29693	148465	2

The next join is a really huge and nasty join. It is a poorly tuned query. The first filter is against the TransactionsLine table, which should be selected from first. However, this query shows all three join types in a single query plan:

```
EXPLAIN PLAN SET statement_id='TEST' FOR
SELECT c.name, tl.amount FROM customer c
 JOIN orders o USING(customer_id)
  JOIN ordersline ol USING(order_id)
   JOIN transactions t USING(customer_id)
    JOIN transactionsline tl USING(transaction_id)
     JOIN stockmovement sm
 ON(tl.stockmovement_id = sm.stockmovement_id)
      JOIN stock s USING(stock_id)
 WHERE tl.amount > 3170
 AND c.balance > 0;
```

Query	Cost	Rows	Bytes	Pos
1. SELECT STATEMENT on	16978	271539	17650035	0
2. **NESTED LOOPS** on	16978	271539	17650035	1
3. **MERGE JOIN** on	16978	271539	16835418	1
4. SORT JOIN on	8062	61688	3577904	1
5. HASH JOIN on	5917	61688	3577904	1
6. TABLE ACCESS FULL on CUSTOMER	16	2693	64632	1
6. HASH JOIN on	5427	61688	2097392	2
7. HASH JOIN on	4976	2621	73388	1
8. **HASH JOIN** on	4403	2621	57662	1
9. TABLE ACCESS FULL on TRANSACTIONSLINE	800	2621	36694	1
9. TABLE ACCESS FULL on STOCKMOVEMENT	1032	1043460	8347680	2
8. TABLE ACCESS FULL on TRANSACTIONS	390	64599	387594	2
7. TABLE ACCESS FULL on ORDERS	238	63392	380352	2
4. SORT JOIN on	8917	997903	3991612	2
5. INDEX FAST FULL SCAN on XFK_OL_OR	668	997903	3991612	1
3. INDEX UNIQUE SCAN on XPK_STOCK		1	3	2

Here is a somewhat tuned version of the previous query, removing tables from the join not having any selected columns. This query can be tuned further:

```
EXPLAIN PLAN SET statement_id='TEST' FOR
SELECT c.name, tl.amount
FROM customer c
 JOIN transactions t ON(t.customer_id = c.customer_id)
  JOIN transactionsline tl ON (tl.transaction_id = t.transaction_id)
WHERE c.balance > 0
AND tl.amount > 3170
AND EXISTS(
```

```
    SELECT o.customer_id FROM orders o
    WHERE o.customer_id = c.customer_id
    AND EXISTS(
        SELECT order_id FROM ordersline
        WHERE order_id = o.order_id))
AND EXISTS(
    SELECT sm.stockmovement_id FROM stockmovement sm
    WHERE sm.stockmovement_id = tl.stockmovement_id
    AND EXISTS(
        SELECT stock_id FROM stock
        WHERE stock_id = sm.stockmovement_id));
```

Query	Cost	Rows	Bytes
1. SELECT STATEMENT on	86	1	61
2. FILTER on			
3. TABLE ACCESS BY INDEX ROWID on TRANSACTIONSLINE	2	1	16
4. NESTED LOOPS on	19	1	61
5. NESTED LOOPS on	17	1	45
6. TABLE ACCESS FULL on CUSTOMER	15	1	38
6. TABLE ACCESS BY INDEX ROWID on TRANSACTIONS	2	12	84
7. INDEX RANGE SCAN on XFK_T_CUSTOMER	1	12	
5. INDEX RANGE SCAN on XFK_TL_TRANSACTION	1	3	
3. NESTED LOOPS on	66	201	2412
4. TABLE ACCESS BY INDEX ROWID on ORDERS	2	64	448
5. INDEX RANGE SCAN on XFK_O_CUSTOMER	1	12	
4. INDEX RANGE SCAN on XFK_OL_ORDERS	1	3	15
3. NESTED LOOPS on	1	1	9
4. INDEX UNIQUE SCAN on XPK_STOCKMOVEMENT	1	1	5
4. INDEX UNIQUE SCAN on XPK_STOCK		1	4

10.1.2.4 Semi-Join

In a previous chapter, we used what Oracle Corporation calls semi-joins to tune complex mutable joins. Semi-joins use the EXISTS and IN operators to join tables. It is called a semi-join because it is not really a join; columns cannot always be returned from the embedded subquery:

```
EXPLAIN PLAN SET statement_id='TEST' FOR
SELECT * FROM coa WHERE EXISTS
(SELECT type FROM type WHERE type = coa.type);
```

```
Query                              Cost    Rows    Bytes   Pos
---------------------------------- ------- ------- ------- ----
1. SELECT STATEMENT   on            2       55      1375    0
2.   NESTED LOOPS SEMI on           2       55      1375    1
3.     TABLE ACCESS FULL on COA     2       55      1320    1
3.     INDEX UNIQUE SCAN on XPK_TYPE        6       6       2
```

EXPLAIN PLAN SET statement_id='TEST' FOR
SELECT * FROM coa WHERE coa# **IN**
(SELECT coa# FROM generalledger);

```
Query                              Cost    Rows     Bytes    Pos
---------------------------------- ------- -------- -------- ----
1. SELECT STATEMENT   on            860     6        174      0
2.   HASH JOIN SEMI on              860     6        174      1
3.     TABLE ACCESS FULL on COA     2       55       1320     1
3.     INDEX FAST FULL SCAN on XFK_COA#  609  1068929  5344645  2
```

10.1.2.5   Joins to Avoid

Some joins are best avoided because they can perform very poorly. We have covered all the aspects of tuning SQL code in previous chapters. There are still some things that we need to watch out for that can be detected most easily at this level.

10.1.2.5.1   Cartesian Join

A Cartesian join is a Cartesian product. A Cartesian product joins two tables without a match condition. Every row in one table is matched with every row in the other table. The resulting row set is the multiplication of the rows in both tables, thus Cartesian product. In mathematics, a product of two numbers is a multiplication of those two numbers:

EXPLAIN PLAN SET statement_id='TEST' FOR
SELECT * **FROM coa, generalledger;**

```
Query                                 Cost    Rows      Bytes     Pos
------------------------------------- ------- --------- --------- ----
1. SELECT STATEMENT   on               62042  ######### #########  0
2.   MERGE JOIN CARTESIAN on           62042  ######### #########  1
3.     TABLE ACCESS FULL on COA        2       55        1320      1
3.     BUFFER SORT on                  62040   1068929   24585367  2
4.       TABLE ACCESS FULL on GENERALLEDGER  1128  1068929  24585367  1
```

10.1.2.5.2   Outer Join

Please accept my apologies for making a somewhat sweeping and opinionated statement, but I have often found outer joins to be a problem, or at least indicative of other possible problems. They have been discussed as such in previous chapters. The crux of the problem with outer join use is that they retrieve data from two tables, where some of the data is not matched. Outer join functionality is often applicable to reporting and data warehouses. In OLTP databases, their profligate use can sometimes be an indication of poor data model structure or even orphaned rows in tables. These types of problems can necessitate the use of outer joins. Performance can be seriously affected. Yes, outer joins can perform well. The issue is whether they should exist in your application SQL code. High occurrence of SQL code outer joins is sometimes indicative of data model or data problems, especially in an OLTP database.

Note: Nested loop and hash joins are completely contradictory to the objective of outer joins. Why? Nested loop and hash joins require an inner loop to be dependent on an outer loop. An outer join is completely contradictory to this because there is not a match between the inner and outer join tables for rows outside of the intersection. Additionally, an outer join generally retrieves large row sets to be useful because it usually has to retrieve a larger row set in order to cater for missing rows. Full table scans, full index reads, and range scans are more likely using outer joins in SQL code.

This is a left outer join between a small table and relatively much larger table:

```
EXPLAIN PLAN SET statement_id='TEST' FOR
SELECT c.name, COUNT(o.customer_id)
FROM customer c LEFT OUTER JOIN orders o
ON(c.customer_id = o.customer_id)
   WHERE c.lastdate = '24-MAY-02'
GROUP BY c.name;
```

Query	Cost	Rows	Bytes	Pos
1. SELECT STATEMENT on	25	7	217	0
2. SORT GROUP BY on	25	7	217	1
3. **NESTED LOOPS OUTER** on	23	156	4836	1
4. TABLE ACCESS FULL on CUSTOMER	16	7	203	1
4. INDEX RANGE SCAN on XFK_O_CUSTOMER	1	24	48	2

In this query, one of the tables is very much larger, and the optimizer reverts to an outer hash join:

```
EXPLAIN PLAN SET statement_id='TEST' FOR
    SELECT s.text, sm.qty, sm.price
    FROM stock s LEFT OUTER JOIN stockmovement sm
ON(s.stock_id = sm.stock_id)
WHERE s.stock_id < 10;
```

Query	Cost	Rows	Bytes	Pos
1. SELECT STATEMENT on	1060	6174	345744	0
2. **HASH JOIN OUTER** on	1060	6174	345744	1
3. TABLE ACCESS BY INDEX ROWID on STOCK	2	9	405	1
4. INDEX RANGE SCAN on XPK_STOCK	1	9		1
3. TABLE ACCESS FULL on STOCKMOVEMENT	1032	80266	882926	2

Two very large tables result in a sort-merge right outer join:

```
EXPLAIN PLAN SET statement_id='TEST' FOR
   SELECT tl.transaction_id, sm.stockmovement_id
FROM transactionsline tl RIGHT OUTER JOIN stockmovement sm
ON(tl.stockmovement_id = sm.stockmovement_id);
```

Query	Cost	Rows	Bytes	Pos
1. SELECT STATEMENT on	10552	1027251	14381514	0
2. MERGE JOIN OUTER on	10552	1027251	14381514	1
3. TABLE ACCESS BY INDEX ROWID on TRNSACTIONSLINE	826	1027251	9245259	1
4. INDEX FULL SCAN on XFK_TL_STOCKMOVEMENT	26	1027251		1
3. SORT JOIN on	9726	1043460	5217300	2
4. INDEX FAST FULL SCAN on XPK_STOCKMOVEMENT	526	1043460	5217300	1

The worst type of outer join is a full outer join. A full outer join is not a Cartesian product, but perhaps only just. It is actually a join, but it retrieves the intersection, plus all rows not in either table:

```
EXPLAIN PLAN SET statement_id='TEST' FOR
    SELECT tl.transaction_id, sm.stockmovement_id
FROM transactionsline tl FULL OUTER JOIN stockmovement sm
ON(tl.stockmovement_id = sm.stockmovement_id);
```

As can be seen from the following query plan, a full outer join creates a complete cost-excessive nightmarish mess! Avoid full outer joins altogether if possible:

```
Query                                            Cost      Rows     Bytes  Pos
-------------------------------------------   ------  --------  --------- ----
1. SELECT STATEMENT   on                       21808  1043460  27129960    0
2.   VIEW  on                                  21808  1043460  27129960    1
3.    UNION-ALL   on                                                       1
4.     MERGE JOIN OUTER on                     10552  1027251  14381514    1
5.       TABLE ACCESS BY INDEX ROWID on TRANSACTIONSLINE  826  1027251  9245259  1
6.         INDEX FULL SCAN on XFK_TL_STOCKMOVEMENT    26  1027251              1
5.       SORT JOIN on                           9726  1043460   5217300    2
6.         INDEX FAST FULL SCAN on XPK_STOCKMOVEMENT  526  1043460  5217300  1
4.     MERGE JOIN ANTI on                      11256    16209    162090    2
5.       INDEX FULL SCAN on XPK_STOCKMOVEMENT   2189  1043460   5217300    1
5.       SORT UNIQUE on                         9067  1027251   5136255    2
6.         INDEX FAST FULL SCAN on XFK_TL_STOCKMOVEMENT  8  1027251  5136255  1
```

Note: Full outer joins are occasionally used in data warehouses.

10.1.2.5.3 (10g) Grouped Outer Join

A grouped outer join allows joining of group aggregations of rows as outer joins, where a group can exist in one row set of a join, but not in another. You might be asking at this stage why the different join types were not explained in previous chapters. This is because this depth level was not really required to explain how to tune SQL code from the point of view of writing properly tuned SQL code, from a programming perspective. Most SQL code tuning is common sense and does not require the level of analytical complexity presented in this chapter. Query plans can be used for verification and perhaps even to make things like spotting of missing indexes more likely. The point to make at this stage is that previous chapters did not require an understanding of the different ways in which the optimizer joined tables, in order to completely understand all the best ways to tune SQL code from a purely SQL coding perspective.

10.2 Sorting

Different types of sorting operations are used by the optimizer. Numerous different types of operations trigger sorts, both implicitly and explicitly specified:

- **SORT UNIQUE**. Caused by the use of DISTINCT or a list of unique values.

- **SORT ORDER BY**. The ORDER BY clause forces a sort operation when indexes or other aspects in the query plan do not sort the rows, which is rare.

- **SORT GROUP BY**. The GROUP BY clause groups or aggregates rows into a summarized set of rows. Sorting is required to aggregate duplicate column values into their distinct groups.

- **SORT JOIN**. A sort on a column to be joined in a sort-merge join.

- **SORT AGGREGATE**. Aggregation across many rows.

10.2.1   Unique Sort

Here is a unique sort:

```
EXPLAIN PLAN SET statement_id='TEST' FOR
    SELECT DISTINCT(order_id) FROM ordersline;
```

Query	Cost	Rows	Bytes	Pos
1. SELECT STATEMENT on	8209	226703	906812	0
2. **SORT UNIQUE** on	8209	226703	906812	1
3. INDEX FAST FULL SCAN on XFK_OL_ORDER	668	997903	3991612	1

This query requires that QTY values in the subquery must be unique before being validated against QTY values in the calling query. There is no sense in checking the same value twice:

```
EXPLAIN PLAN SET statement_id='TEST' FOR
SELECT * FROM stockmovement WHERE qty IN
(SELECT qty FROM stockmovement);
```

Query	Cost	Rows	Bytes	Sort
SELECT STATEMENT on	16353	570175	15964900	
MERGE JOIN SEMI on	16353	570175	15964900	
SORT JOIN on	11979	570175	13684200	45802000
TABLE ACCESS FULL on STOCKMOVEMENT	355	570175	13684200	
SORT UNIQUE on	4374	570175	2280700	13755000
TABLE ACCESS FULL on STOCKMOVEMENT	355	570175	2280700	

10.2.2 ORDER BY Sort

In this first example, the entire table is read, and the ORDER BY clause forces a sort on one of the columns:

```
EXPLAIN PLAN SET statement_id='TEST' FOR
    SELECT * FROM customer ORDER BY name;
```

Query	Cost	Rows	Bytes	Pos	Sort
1. SELECT STATEMENT on	149	2694	360996	0	
2. **SORT ORDER BY** on	149	2694	360996	1	877000
3. TABLE ACCESS FULL on CUSTOMER	16	2694	360996	1	

This second example is different because the sort specified in the ORDER BY clause is catered for by the index full scan, a key value-ordered index scan. There is no *SORT ORDER BY on* step in the query plan because the index is already sorted:

```
EXPLAIN PLAN SET statement_id='TEST' FOR
    SELECT customer_id FROM customer ORDER BY customer_id;
```

Query	Cost	Rows	Bytes	Pos	Sort
1. SELECT STATEMENT on	7	2694	8082	0	
2. **INDEX FULL SCAN** on XPK_CUSTOMER	7	2694	8082	1	

Here is another example of the same thing. The GROUP BY clause causes a sort. The ORDER BY clause sorts the same thing and is thus superfluous, depending on the physical order of rows in the table:

```
EXPLAIN PLAN SET statement_id='TEST' FOR
SELECT amount, COUNT(amount) FROM ordersline
GROUP BY amount ORDER BY amount;
```

Query	Cost	Rows	Bytes	Pos	Sort
1. SELECT STATEMENT on	8682	97713	488565	0	
2. **SORT GROUP BY** on	8682	97713	488565	1	13214000
3. TABLE ACCESS FULL on ORDERSLINE	765	997903	4989515	1	

10.2.3   GROUP BY Sort

In this case, the GROUP BY clause sorts by the aggregated column:

```
EXPLAIN PLAN SET statement_id='TEST' FOR
SELECT amount, COUNT(amount) FROM ordersline GROUP BY amount;
```

Query	Cost	Rows	Bytes	Pos	Sort
1. SELECT STATEMENT on	8682	97713	488565	0	
2. **SORT GROUP BY** on	8682	97713	488565	1	13214000
3. TABLE ACCESS FULL on ORDERSLINE	765	997903	4989515	1	

Here is another example of a sort not required and indicated so by the optimizer as shown:

```
EXPLAIN PLAN SET statement_id='TEST' FOR
    SELECT customer_id, COUNT(customer_id) FROM customer
GROUP BY customer_id;
```

Query	Cost	Rows	Bytes	Pos	Sort
1. SELECT STATEMENT on	7	2694	8082	0	
2. SORT GROUP BY **NOSORT** on	7	2694	8082	1	
3. **INDEX FULL SCAN** on XPK_CUSTOMER	7	2694	8082	1	

10.2.4   Sort Merge Join Sort

In this example, the ORDER BY clause is executing the sort on the COA table as indicated by *SORT JOIN on* in the query plan, allowing *MERGE JOIN on* to occur on the COA# column between the two row sets:

```
EXPLAIN PLAN SET statement_id='TEST' FOR
SELECT coa.*, gl.*
FROM generalledger gl JOIN coa ON(gl.coa# = coa.coa#)
ORDER BY coa.coa#;
```

Query	Cost	Rows	Bytes	Pos	Sort
1. SELECT STATEMENT on	20782	1068929	50239663	0	
2. MERGE JOIN on	20782	1068929	50239663	1	

```
3.    TABLE ACCESS BY INDEX ROWID on GENERALLEDGER 20778 1068929 24585367   1
4.      INDEX FULL SCAN on XFK_COA#                   2536 1068929           1
3.    SORT JOIN on                                       4      55     1320  2
4.      TABLE ACCESS FULL on COA                         2      55     1320  1
```

10.2.5   Aggregate Sort

An aggregate sort is shown in the query plan for the following query:

```
EXPLAIN PLAN SET statement_id='TEST' FOR
    SELECT AVG(balance) FROM customer;
```

Query	Cost	Rows	Bytes	Pos
1. SELECT STATEMENT on	16	1	2	0
2. **SORT AGGREGATE** on		1	2	1
3. TABLE ACCESS FULL on CUSTOMER	16	2694	5388	1

10.3   Special Cases

There are some special cases. The ones of interest for discussion involve concatenation, IN list operators, and the UNION set operator.

10.3.1   Concatenation

Concatenation is used when OR separated conditions do not occur on the same column. The following query uses a hint to force concatenation, making the cost of the query slightly higher. The cost is higher using the hint because the PeriodSum table is small and a full table scan is quicker. Here is the hinted concatenation example:

```
EXPLAIN PLAN SET statement_id='TEST' FOR
    SELECT /*+ USE_CONCAT */ * FROM periodsum
WHERE year = 2001 OR period = 10 OR coa# = '60001';
```

Query	Cost	Rows	Bytes	Pos
1. SELECT STATEMENT on	**6**	11	165	0
2. **CONCATENATION** on				1
3. TABLE ACCESS BY INDEX ROWID on PERIODSUM	2	1	15	1
4. INDEX RANGE SCAN on XFK_PS_COA	1	1		1

```
3.    TABLE ACCESS FULL on PERIODSUM              2        1      15     2
3.    TABLE ACCESS BY INDEX ROWID on PERIODSUM    2        1      15     3
4.      INDEX RANGE SCAN on XPK_PERIODSUM         1        1             1
```

And here is the second example without the hint:

```
EXPLAIN PLAN SET statement_id='TEST' FOR
    SELECT * FROM periodsum
WHERE year = 2001 OR period = 10 OR coa# = '60001';
```

Query	Cost	Rows	Bytes	Pos
1. SELECT STATEMENT on	2	31	465	0
2. **TABLE ACCESS FULL** on PERIODSUM	2	31	465	1

Concatenation only becomes a performance advantage when row sets are extremely large. The next two examples use a very large query where the cost is decreased substantially by application of the USE_CONCAT hint. In this case, the optimizer fails to find the lowest cost option. However, timing tests executed on these two queries show that the query with the hint is slower, so the optimizer does not fail. Timing is shown after the queries. On the contrary, the query plan cost estimate fails because the cost values are spurious:

```
EXPLAIN PLAN SET statement_id='TEST' FOR
  SELECT * FROM transactions t
JOIN transactionsline tl USING(transaction_id)
  JOIN stockmovement sm USING(stockmovement_id)
    JOIN stock USING(stock_id)
WHERE t.type = 'S' OR tl.amount < 100 OR sm.qty = 0;
```

Query	Cost	Rows	Bytes	Pos
1. SELECT STATEMENT on	**71985**	1020650	########	0
2. HASH JOIN on	71985	1020650	########	1
3. TABLE ACCESS FULL on STOCK	2	118	27612	1
3. MERGE JOIN on	67130	1020650	76548750	2
4. SORT JOIN on	60057	1027251	40062789	1
5. MERGE JOIN on	25616	1027251	40062789	1
6. SORT JOIN on	6619	1043460	23999580	1

```
7.          TABLE ACCESS FULL on STOCKMOVEMENT      6619   1043460   23999580   1
6.        SORT JOIN on                             18997   1027251   16436016   2
7.          TABLE ACCESS FULL on TRANSACTIONSLINE    800   1027251   16436016   1
4.     FILTER   on                                                              2
5.       SORT JOIN on                                                           1
6.         TABLE ACCESS FULL on TRANSACTIONS         390    242584    8733024   1
```

And now using the USE_CONCAT hint:

```
EXPLAIN PLAN SET statement_id='TEST' FOR
    SELECT /*+ USE_CONCAT */ * FROM transactions t
JOIN transactionsline tl USING(transaction_id)
    JOIN stockmovement sm USING(stockmovement_id)
        JOIN stock USING(stock_id)
WHERE t.type = 'S' OR tl.amount < 100 OR sm.qty = 0;
```

```
Query                                                      Cost      Rows      Bytes  Pos
-----------------------------------------------------  -------  --------  ---------  ----
1. SELECT STATEMENT  on                                  20861    104406   32261454     0
2.   CONCATENATION   on                                                                 1
3.    NESTED LOOPS   on                                   6885     51363    3852225     1
4.     HASH JOIN  on                                      7134     51363   15871167     1
5.       TABLE ACCESS FULL on STOCK                          2       118      27612     1
5.       MERGE JOIN  on                                   2587     51363    2003157     2
6.         TABLE ACCESS BY INDEX ROWID on TRANSACTIONSLINE  826     51363     821808     1
7.           INDEX FULL SCAN on XFK_TL_STOCKMOVEMENT        26   1027251                1
6.         SORT JOIN on                                   1761     52173    1199979     2
7.           TABLE ACCESS FULL on STOCKMOVEMENT           1032     52173    1199979     1
4.     TABLE ACCESS BY INDEX ROWID on TRANSACTIONS         390    121292    4366512     2
5.       INDEX UNIQUE SCAN on XPK_TRANSACTIONS               2                          1
3.    HASH JOIN  on                                       7134     51363   15871167     2
4.     TABLE ACCESS FULL on STOCK                            2       118      27612     1
4.     MERGE JOIN   on                                    6885     51363    3852225     2
5.       SORT JOIN on                                     3646     51363    2003157     1
6.         MERGE JOIN  on                                 2587     51363    2003157     1
7.           SORT JOIN on                                  826     51363     821808     1
8.             TABLE ACCESS FULL on TRANSACTIONSLINE       826     51363     821808     1
7.           SORT JOIN on                                 1761     52173    1199979     2
8.             TABLE ACCESS FULL on STOCKMOVEMENT         1032     52173    1199979     1
5.       SORT JOIN on                                     3239    121292    4366512     2
6.         TABLE ACCESS FULL on TRANSACTIONS               390    121292    4366512     1
3.    HASH JOIN  on                                       7134     51363   15871167     3
4.     TABLE ACCESS FULL on STOCK                            2       118      27612     1
4.     MERGE JOIN   on                                    6885     51363    3852225     2
5.       SORT JOIN on                                     3646     51363    2003157     1
6.         MERGE JOIN  on                                 2587     51363    2003157     1
7.           SORT JOIN on                                  826     51363     821808     1
8.             TABLE ACCESS FULL on TRANSACTIONSLINE       826     51363     821808     1
```

7.	SORT JOIN on	1761	52173	1199979	2
8.	TABLE ACCESS FULL on STOCKMOVEMENT	1032	52173	1199979	1
5.	SORT JOIN on	3239	121292	4366512	2
6.	TABLE ACCESS FULL on TRANSACTIONS	390	121292	4366512	1

These are the timing tests:

```
SQL> SELECT COUNT(*) FROM(
  2  SELECT * FROM transactions t
  3  JOIN transactionsline tl USING(transaction_id)
  4   JOIN stockmovement sm USING(stockmovement_id)
  5    JOIN stock USING(stock_id)
  6  WHERE t.type = 'S' OR tl.amount < 100 OR sm.qty = 0);


  COUNT(*)
----------
   4989625


Elapsed: 00:22:08.08
SQL> SELECT COUNT(*) FROM(
  2  SELECT /*+ USE_CONCAT */ * FROM transactions t
  3  JOIN transactionsline tl USING(transaction_id)
  4   JOIN stockmovement sm USING(stockmovement_id)
  5    JOIN stock USING(stock_id)
  6  WHERE t.type = 'S' OR tl.amount < 100 OR sm.qty = 0);


  COUNT(*)
----------
   4989625


Elapsed: 00:28:23.09
```

10.3.2 The IN LIST Operator

Concatenation is used to merge OR conditions on different columns. The IN LIST operator is used to merge conditions on the same column as shown in the following query:

```
EXPLAIN PLAN SET statement_id='TEST' FOR
  SELECT * FROM coa NATURAL JOIN generalledger
   WHERE coa.type = 'A' OR coa.type = 'L'
OR coa.type = 'E' OR coa.type = 'I';
```

Query	Cost	Rows	Bytes	Pos
1. SELECT STATEMENT on	**1642**	1068929	50239663	0
2. HASH JOIN on	1642	1068929	50239663	1
3. **INLIST ITERATOR** on				1
4. TABLE ACCESS BY INDEX ROWID on COA	2	55	1320	1
5. INDEX RANGE SCAN on XFK_COA_TYPE	1	55		1
3. TABLE ACCESS FULL on GENERALLEDGER	1128	1068929	24585367	2

The following query is a variation on the previous query, forcing concatenation by using a hint. It is much higher in cost:

```
EXPLAIN PLAN SET statement_id='TEST' FOR
  SELECT /*+ USE_CONCAT */ * FROM coa NATURAL JOIN generalledger
  WHERE coa.type = 'A' OR coa.type = 'L'
OR coa.type = 'E' OR coa.type = 'I';
```

Each of four joins for COA.TYPE column values are concatenated together:

Query	Cost	Rows	Bytes	Pos
1. SELECT STATEMENT on	**6568**	4199364	########	0
2. **CONCATENATION** on				1
3. **HASH JOIN** on	1642	1049841	49342527	1
4. TABLE ACCESS BY INDEX ROWID on COA	2	14	336	1
5. INDEX RANGE SCAN on XFK_COA_TYPE	1	14		1
4. TABLE ACCESS FULL on GENERALLEDGER	1128	1068929	24585367	2
3. **HASH JOIN** on	1642	1049841	49342527	2
4. TABLE ACCESS BY INDEX ROWID on COA	2	14	336	1
5. INDEX RANGE SCAN on XFK_COA_TYPE	1	14		1
4. TABLE ACCESS FULL on GENERALLEDGER	1128	1068929	24585367	2
3. **HASH JOIN** on	1642	1049841	49342527	3
4. TABLE ACCESS BY INDEX ROWID on COA	2	14	336	1
5. INDEX RANGE SCAN on XFK_COA_TYPE	1	14		1
4. TABLE ACCESS FULL on GENERALLEDGER	1128	1068929	24585367	2
3. **HASH JOIN** on	1642	1049841	49342527	4
4. TABLE ACCESS BY INDEX ROWID on COA	2	14	336	1
5. INDEX RANGE SCAN on XFK_COA_TYPE	1	14		1
4. TABLE ACCESS FULL on GENERALLEDGER	1128	1068929	24585367	2

The previous query plan shows a concatenation of four separate joins. This leads us to the UNION set operator.

10.3.3 UNION, MINUS, and INTERSECT

The following UNION set operator concatenated query is effectively the same query as the previous query, which used the USE_CONCAT hint. Concatenation is faster than using UNION:

```
EXPLAIN PLAN SET statement_id='TEST' FOR
    SELECT * FROM coa NATURAL JOIN generalledger WHERE coa.type = 'A'
    UNION
    SELECT * FROM coa NATURAL JOIN generalledger WHERE coa.type = 'L'
    UNION
    SELECT * FROM coa NATURAL JOIN generalledger WHERE coa.type = 'E'
    UNION
    SELECT * FROM coa NATURAL JOIN generalledger WHERE coa.type = 'I';
```

Note the enormously higher cost as a result of using UNION rather than concatenation:

Query	Cost	Rows	Bytes	Pos
1. SELECT STATEMENT on	**171272**	4199364	########	0
2. SORT UNIQUE on	171272	4199364	########	1
3. **UNION-ALL** on				1
4. HASH JOIN on	1642	1049841	49342527	1
5. TABLE ACCESS BY INDEX ROWID on COA	2	14	336	1
6. INDEX RANGE SCAN on XFK_COA_TYPE	1	14		1
5. TABLE ACCESS FULL on GENERALLEDGER	1128	1068929	24585367	2
4. HASH JOIN on	1642	1049841	49342527	2
5. TABLE ACCESS BY INDEX ROWID on COA	2	14	336	1
6. INDEX RANGE SCAN on XFK_COA_TYPE	1	14		1
5. TABLE ACCESS FULL on GENERALLEDGER	1128	1068929	24585367	2
4. HASH JOIN on	1642	1049841	49342527	3
5. TABLE ACCESS BY INDEX ROWID on COA	2	14	336	1
6. INDEX RANGE SCAN on XFK_COA_TYPE	1	14		1
5. TABLE ACCESS FULL on GENERALLEDGER	1128	1068929	24585367	2
4. HASH JOIN on	1642	1049841	49342527	4
5. TABLE ACCESS BY INDEX ROWID on COA	2	14	336	1

```
6.      INDEX RANGE SCAN on XFK_COA_TYPE        1       14              1
5.      TABLE ACCESS FULL on GENERALLEDGER      1128    1068929  24585367    2
```

UNION is useful in a situation, such as in the following query, where ranges of values are split and displayed. Each has a different concatenated string. Using UNION generally creates very poorly performing SQL code:

```
SELECT 'OUT OF STOCK: '||text FROM stock WHERE qtyonhand <=0
UNION
SELECT 'UNDER STOCKED: ' ||text FROM stock WHERE qtyonhand BETWEEN 1
AND min-1
UNION
SELECT 'STOCKED: ' ||text FROM stock WHERE qtyonhand BETWEEN min AND
max
UNION
SELECT 'OVER STOCKED: ' ||text FROM stock WHERE qtyonhand > max;
```

```
'OUTOFSTOCK:'||TEXT
```

```
OUT OF STOCK: iRock MP3 Digital Audio Player by First International
OVER STOCKED: Compaq Presario 6016US Minitower
OVER STOCKED: Epson Perfection 2450 Photo Color Scanner
OVER STOCKED: Internet Design Shop XL by Boomerang Software
OVER STOCKED: Memorex 24X CD-R Media,700MB/80Min, Spindle, 30 Pack
OVER STOCKED: Palm m505 Handheld
OVER STOCKED: Sonnet Technologies HARMONi G3 Processor Upgrade/
FireWire
STOCKED: Corex CardScan Executive (600c/V6) Business Card Scanner
STOCKED: Epson Perfection 1250 Color Flatbed Scanner
STOCKED: Epson Perfection 1650 Color Flatbed Scanner
STOCKED: FrontPage 2002 by Microsoft
STOCKED: Hewlett-Packard Photo Scanner 1000 Color Scanner
STOCKED: Imation 32x Neon CD-R 700 MB/80 Min 50-pk Spindle
STOCKED: Logitech Cordless Freedom Optical Keyboard/Mouse
STOCKED: Logitech Internet Navigator Keyboard
STOCKED: Memorex 4.7GB DVD+R Media, 3-pack
STOCKED: TDK DVD-R Media, 4.7GB, 10 Pack
UNDER STOCKED: Apple Studio 17-inch TFT LCD Monitor
UNDER STOCKED: Envision Peripherals EN-5100 15-inch LCD Monitor
UNDER STOCKED: Hewlett-Packard ScanJet 7400c Flatbed Scanner
```

The MINUS and INTERSECT operators behave similarly to that of UNION, also both having very high cost. Avoid using UNION, UNION ALL, MINUS, and INTERSECT if possible. First, let's show the MINUS operator:

```
EXPLAIN PLAN SET statement_id='TEST' FOR
    SELECT * FROM coa NATURAL JOIN generalledger
    MINUS
    SELECT * FROM coa NATURAL JOIN generalledger
WHERE coa.type IN('E','I');
```

Query	Cost	Rows	Bytes
1. SELECT STATEMENT on	**143333**	1577577	########
2. **MINUS** on			
3. SORT UNIQUE on	72290	1577577	74146119
4. HASH JOIN on	2434	1577577	74146119
5. TABLE ACCESS FULL on COA	2	55	1320
5. TABLE ACCESS FULL on GENERALLEDGER	1677	1577577	36284271
3. SORT UNIQUE on	71043	1549406	72822082
4. HASH JOIN on	2434	1549406	72822082
5. INLIST ITERATOR on			
6. TABLE ACCESS BY INDEX ROWID on COA	2	28	672
7. INDEX RANGE SCAN on XFK_COA_TYPE	1	28	
5. TABLE ACCESS FULL on GENERALLEDGER	1677	1577577	36284271

Now the INTERSECT operator:

```
EXPLAIN PLAN SET statement_id='TEST' FOR
    SELECT * FROM coa NATURAL JOIN generalledger WHERE coa.type = 'A'
    INTERSECT
    SELECT * FROM coa NATURAL JOIN generalledger WHERE coa.type = 'L';
```

Query	Cost	Rows	Bytes
1. SELECT STATEMENT on	**142086**	1549406	########
2. **INTERSECTION** on			
3. SORT UNIQUE on	71043	1549406	72822082
4. HASH JOIN on	2434	1549406	72822082
5. TABLE ACCESS BY INDEX ROWID on COA	2	14	336

```
6.        INDEX RANGE SCAN on XFK_COA_TYPE          1        14
5.        TABLE ACCESS FULL on GENERALLEDGER     1677   1577577   36284271
3.   SORT UNIQUE on                             71043   1549406   72822082
4.   HASH JOIN   on                              2434   1549406   72822082
5.        TABLE ACCESS BY INDEX ROWID on COA        2        14        336
6.        INDEX RANGE SCAN on XFK_COA_TYPE          1        14
5.        TABLE ACCESS FULL on GENERALLEDGER     1677   1577577   36284271
```

This concludes this chapter on the Oracle Database internal specifics, covering data access methods, sorting, and some specialized cases. The next chapter examines using hints to suggest or force changes to how the optimizer accesses data.

10.4 **Endnotes**

1.   Oracle Data Warehouse Tuning for 10*g* (Gavin Powell, Digital Press, Aug 2005, ISBN: 1555583350)

11

Overriding Optimizer Behavior Using Hints

This chapter, and preceded by Chapters 9 and 10, attempts to show how Oracle Database executes SQL code and how that SQL code can be tuned from a purely Oracle Database perspective. This chapter is the final chapter in that process, describing hints and how hints can be utilized to change the way the optimizer assesses and how best to execute a query.

11.1　How to Use Hints

As we have seen in numerous places in this book so far, a hint can be used to suggest (some may say force) an alteration to the way the optimizer creates a query plan for a query. OLTP databases rarely require use of hints if statistics can be regularly maintained. In OracleDatabase 10*g,* statistics are automatically generated, so regular maintenance of statistics has become less of an issue.

Hints are more commonly used in large data warehouse or reporting databases, rule-based databases, or those lacking current or any statistics. Generating statistics can be time consuming. Using the DBMS_STATS package instead of the ANALYZE command may help alleviate some performance issues when generating statistics. Hints can be used to control the optimizer and to a certain extent freeze execution plans. This is much the same in function as outlines were used in older versions of Oracle Database. This book will not cover all available optimizer hints, only those relevant to OLTP databases, and those hints that are often the most useful.

The syntax of a hint is such that it is placed after a DML command between comments as shown, including the plus (+) sign:

```
SELECT /*+ CURSOR_SHARING_EXACT */ * FROM customer;
```

```
INSERT /*+ CURSOR_SHARING_EXACT */ INTO customer(customer_id, name, ticker)
VALUES(1000000, 'New Customer', 'TICK');

UPDATE /*+ CURSOR_SHARING_EXACT */ customer SET name = 'A New Customer'
WHERE customer_id = 1000000;

DELETE /*+ CURSOR_SHARING_EXACT */ FROM customer WHERE customer_id = 1000000;
```

> **Note:** ⑩*g* The CURSOR_SHARING_EXACT hint overrides the
> CURSOR_SHARING configuration parameter, for the specified query
> containing the hint. The FORCE setting for the CURSOR_SHARING is
> overridden. In general, this is not recommended for an OLTP database.

If an alias is used in a SQL statement, then any hints must refer to the alias and not the table or object selected from. The example shown following does not use any indexes on the customer table because the NO_INDEX hint is used:

```
EXPLAIN PLAN SET statement_id='TEST' FOR
SELECT /*+ NO_INDEX(c) */ customer_id FROM customer c
NATURAL JOIN transactions;
```

Query	Cost	Rows	Bytes
1. SELECT STATEMENT on	126	64599	322995
2. HASH JOIN on	126	64599	322995
3. **TABLE ACCESS FULL on CUSTOMER**	16	2694	8082
3. INDEX FAST FULL SCAN on XFK_T_CUSTOMER	44	64599	129198

This next example does use an index, and the hint forced it not to do as such. The hint in this query is incorrectly specified because it uses the table name and not the alias for the Customer table. The letter c (the alias) should be used and not customer (the name of the table):

```
EXPLAIN PLAN SET statement_id='TEST' FOR
SELECT /*+ NO_INDEX(customer) */ customer_id FROM customer c
NATURAL JOIN transactions;
```

```
Query                                           Cost    Rows     Bytes
--------------------------------------------   -------  -------  --------
1. SELECT STATEMENT  on                          44     64599    322995
2.   NESTED LOOPS  on                            44     64599    322995
3.     INDEX FAST FULL SCAN on XFK_T_CUSTOMER    44     64599    129198
3.     INDEX UNIQUE SCAN on XPK_CUSTOMER                    1         3
```

It is always a good idea to check query plans for SQL statements, if only to ensure that hints are coded in a syntactically correct manner. Incorrectly coded hints do not produce SQL code parser errors and may never be detected. This SQL statement will execute with no indication that a nonexistent is used:

```
SELECT /*+ STUPIDHINT */ * FROM customer;
```

This query will also execute with no indication that the CURSOR_SHARING_EXACT hint absolutely does not require any parameters:

```
SELECT /*+ CURSOR_SHARING_EXACT(HowUDuin?) */ * FROM
customer;
```

Note: Code hints carefully because they are commented. If they are incorrectly coded, an error will not be returned. The hint will be ignored.

Here is a query plan using an index fast full scan:

```
EXPLAIN PLAN SET statement_id='TEST' FOR
    SELECT customer_id FROM customer;
```

```
Query                                           Cost    Rows     Bytes
--------------------------------------------   -------  -------  --------
1. SELECT STATEMENT  on                           3      2694      8082
2.   INDEX FAST FULL SCAN on XPK_CUSTOMER         3      2694      8082
```

Note: (9i) Applying the RULE hint, as shown in the following query, forces the optimizer to ignore statistics, using rule-based optimization:

```
EXPLAIN PLAN SET statement_id='TEST' FOR
   SELECT /*+ RULE */ customer_id FROM customer;
```

In the following query plan, note that cost, row, and byte figures are not shown because rule-based optimization is used. That is because rule-based optimization does not require statistics as cost-based optimization does. In this situation, rule-based optimization considers that a full table scan is assumed to be the fastest option:

Query	Cost	Rows	Bytes
1. SELECT STATEMENT on			
2. **TABLE ACCESS FULL** on CUSTOMER			

Note: (10*g*) The RULE hint and rule-based optimization are obsolete.

We can influence rule-based optimization (the RULE hint) to use any index on the Customer table (the INDEX hint), as in the following query plan:

```
EXPLAIN PLAN SET statement_id='TEST' FOR
   SELECT /*+ RULE INDEX(customer) */ customer_id FROM
customer;
```

Once again, we get the index fast full scan. However, this time the cost is a little higher in order to both implement and then to override the rule-based optimizer:

Query	Cost	Rows	Bytes
1. SELECT STATEMENT on	7	2694	8082
2. **INDEX FULL SCAN** on XPK_CUSTOMER	7	2694	8082

11.2 Hints: Suggestion or Force?

My perception of hints is that they tend to suggest changes to the optimizer, rather than force those changes to occur. However, I have recently learned to the contrary that the optimizer will follow hints blindly without regard to the sensibility of those hints. The only requirement is that the conditions and requirements for executing queries using specified hints exist in the database. My opinion was always that the optimizer is intelligent enough to ignore a hint that will obviously cause a query to execute much slower. Let's make the point with examples. The following example shows a query plan selecting all rows from a large table:

```
EXPLAIN PLAN SET statement_id='TEST' FOR
SELECT * FROM Transactions;
```

The query plan shows the expected full table scan:

Query	Cost	Rows	Bytes
1. SELECT STATEMENT on	1567	223763	8055468
2. **TABLE ACCESS FULL** on TRANSACTIONS	1567	223763	8055468

This next example deliberately reads a single row from the same large table:

```
EXPLAIN PLAN SET statement_id='TEST' FOR
SELECT * FROM Transactions WHERE transaction_id=100000;
```

The result is a query plan using the primary key, with a much lower expected cost in execution:

Query	Cost	Rows	Bytes
1. SELECT STATEMENT on	2	1	36
2. TABLE ACCESS BY INDEX ROWID on TRANSACTIONS	2	1	36
3. **INDEX UNIQUE SCAN on XPK_TRANSACTIONS**	1	1	

This next example uses the previous query, but this time with an added hint. The FULL hint will suggest to the optimizer that the query should be executed using a full table scan, even when reading the single row required would be very much faster using the primary key index and the table:

```
EXPLAIN PLAN SET statement_id='TEST' FOR
SELECT /*+ FULL(Transactions) */ * FROM Transactions WHERE
transaction_id=100000;
```

This is the result:

```
Query                                   Cost    Rows    Bytes
--------------------------------------  ------- ------- ---------
1. SELECT STATEMENT  on                  1548       1      36
2. TABLE ACCESS FULL on TRANSACTIONS      1548       1      36
```

So it can be concluded from these examples that hints force the optimizer to select a specific path of execution.

Note: Hints DO NOT make suggestions to the optimizer!

A hint will change the query plan for a query, even if the hint is in extreme detriment to the performance of the query, so the optimizer is not that intelligent.

11.3 Classifying Hints

There are all sorts of hints for persuading the optimizer to do things differently. I like to categorize hints as follows:

- Influence the optimizer
- Alter table scans
- Alter index scans
- Alter joins
- Cause parallel SQL execution
- Alter queries and subqueries

This book will not cover all of the available hints in Oracle Database, only the interesting ones, and particularly those most appropriate to use in OLTP databases.[1] We will examine hints that are potentially useful within the scope of the subject matter presented in this book. Some hints have already been covered in this book, some even in prior chapters. Repetition is avoided where possible.

11.4 Influencing the Optimizer in General

Available hints:

- ***ALL_ROWS***. Suppresses indexes and favors full table scans to find all rows.

- ***FIRST_ROWS(n)***. More likely to use indexing since favoring a few rows.

- ***[NO_]CPU_COSTING.*** This hint was present in 10.1 (release 1 of Oracle Database 10*g*). It is not present in 10.2 (release 2 of Oracle Database 10*g*).

Note: (10*g*R2) By default, cost optimization is based on CPU and I/O estimations. Memory usage is no longer included as a factor in calculating costings. The CPU_COST column in the PLAN_TABLE (query plans) is by default filled. This leaves the CPU_COSTING hint with nothing to do. However, using the NO_CPU_COSTING hint in a query does leave the PLAN_TABLE.CPU_COST column empty, when executing a query plan.

- (9*i*) ***CHOOSE***. Choose cost-based optimization when statistics are present, but otherwise use rule-based optimization.

- (10*g*) The CHOOSE hint is obsolete.

- (9*i*) ***RULE***. Rule-based optimization

- (10*g*) The RULE hint and rule-based optimization are obsolete.

- ***CURSOR_SHARING_EXACT.*** Overrides behavior of configuration parameter CURSOR_SHARING=FORCE, changing literal values to bind variables.

- ***DYNAMIC_SAMPLING***. On-the-fly sampling that can be used if statistics are not present or out of date.

- ***REWRITE***. This hint can generally select materialized views to read from or a specific list of materialized views. The result is a partially automated query rewrite.

Let's experiment a little. My database is set to the default for Oracle Database 10*g* (ALL_ROWS) in the OPTIMIZER_MODE configuration parameters.

Note: ⑨*i* The default for the OPTIMIZER_MODE configuration parameter is CHOOSE. The CHOOSE option will favor cost-based optimization and use of statistics. However, CHOOSE will tend to favor full scans rather than more precise index scans.

Note: ⑩*g* The default for the OPTIMIZER_MODE configuration parameter is ALL_ROWS. The default for the OPTIMIZER_MODE parameter is now ALL_ROWS. The RULE and CHOOSE hints are obsolete.

Note: The OPTIMIZER_MODE parameter can be altered at the session level using a command such as ALTER SESSION SET OPTIMIZER_MODE=FIRST_ROWS(1000);

Note the difference in cost in the two following queries. The chances are the second query will be slower because it is reading all the rows from the table and the hint is stating otherwise. Once again, these two examples demonstrate the difference made by the hint:

```
EXPLAIN PLAN SET statement_id='TEST' FOR
SELECT * FROM generalledger;
```

Query	Cost	Rows	Bytes
1. SELECT STATEMENT on	**1128**	1068929	24585367
2. TABLE ACCESS FULL on GENERALLEDGER	1128	1068929	24585367

And now including the FIRST_ROWS(1) hint, forcing the optimizer to assume that a single row is being selected:

```
EXPLAIN PLAN SET statement_id='TEST' FOR
    SELECT /*+ FIRST_ROWS(1) */ * FROM generalledger;
```

Using the FIRST_ROWS(1) hint in this case, the cost is misleading because the query will still return all rows in the GeneralLedger table, which is very large. The cost is deceptively and most abnormally low in this case:

```
Query                                     Cost    Rows    Byte
-------------------------------------  -------  --------  --------
1. SELECT STATEMENT  on                    2        1        2
2.   TABLE ACCESS FULL on GENERALLEDGER     2        1        2
```

11.4.1   Altering Table Scans

Available hints:

- *FULL*. Force a full table scan. Typically, the FULL hint could be used on small static tables because it might sometimes be faster to read the entire table, rather than to read both the index and the table.

This first query uses an index range scan:

```
EXPLAIN PLAN SET statement_id='TEST' FOR
SELECT * FROM category WHERE category_id < 50;
```

```
Query                                     Cost    Rows    Bytes
-------------------------------------  -------  --------  ---------
1. SELECT STATEMENT  on                    2       13      143
2.   TABLE ACCESS BY INDEX ROWID on CATEGORY  2    13      143
3.     INDEX RANGE SCAN on XPK_CATEGORY    1       13
```

This second query forces a full table scan, has fewer steps, and lowers the number of bytes read:

```
EXPLAIN PLAN SET statement_id='TEST' FOR
SELECT /*+ FULL(category) */ category_id FROM category
WHERE category_id < 50;
```

```
Query                                     Cost    Rows    Bytes
-------------------------------------  -------  --------  ---------
1. SELECT STATEMENT  on                    2       13       26
2.   TABLE ACCESS FULL on CATEGORY         2       13       26
```

11.4.2　Altering Index Scans

Available hints:

- *INDEX[_ASC | _DESC].* Forces use of an index. If multiple indexes are specified, then the lowest-cost index is selected. The selected index is scanned as it is sorted, or as specified in ascending or descending order.

- *INDEX_FFS.* Forces a fast full index scan, reading the index in physical block order, and not in the order of the key, in which the index is constructed.

- *NO_INDEX.* Ignores the named indexes.

- *INDEX_COMBINE.* Typically used to combine use of multiple bitmap indexes, which are created in a single column each.

- *INDEX_JOIN.* Forces a join between indexes alone.

- ⑨*i* *AND_EQUAL.* Joins multiple index single-column scans.

- ⑩*g* The AND_EQUAL hint is deprecated.

- ⑩*g* *INDEX_SS[_ASC | DESC].* Forces an index skip scan.

- ⑩*g* *NO_INDEX_FFS and NO_INDEX_SS.* These hints force the optimizer to not use index fast full scans or index skip scans respectively.

- ⑩*g* *USE_NL_WITH_INDEX.* Forces a query to use a specific table as the inner loop of a nested loops join, with the option of using a particular index.

These are the indexes on the PeriodSum table:

PERIODSUM	BTree	XFK_PS_COA	COA#	1
PERIODSUM	BTree	XFK_PS_YEARPERIOD	YEAR	1
PERIODSUM	BTree	XFK_PS_YEARPERIOD	PERIOD	2
PERIODSUM	BTree	XPK_PERIODSUM	YEAR	1
PERIODSUM	BTree	XPK_PERIODSUM	PERIOD	2
PERIODSUM	BTree	XPK_PERIODSUM	COA#	3

The query plan for the following SQL statement uses a full table scan because all the columns in all the rows are being read:

```
EXPLAIN PLAN SET statement_id= 'TEST' FOR
SELECT * FROM periodsum;
```

Query	Cost	Rows	Bytes
1. SELECT STATEMENT on	**2**	45	675
2. **TABLE ACCESS FULL** on PERIODSUM	2	45	675

The next query forces use of the most efficient index available. The primary key index is unique and thus the most efficient. There is no change in cost. The optimizer was correct to choose the full table scan by default because reading index and table is probably slightly slower than reading just the table:

```
EXPLAIN PLAN SET statement_id= 'TEST' FOR
SELECT /*+ INDEX(periodsum) */ * FROM periodsum;
```

Query	Cost	Rows	Bytes
1. SELECT STATEMENT on	**2**	45	675
2. TABLE ACCESS BY INDEX ROWID on PERIODSUM	2	45	675
3. INDEX FULL SCAN on **XPK_PERIODSUM**	1	45	

The next query removes the primary key index from the equation by forcing the optimizer to choose between the more efficient of two other indexes (neither the primary key). The cost is slightly higher:

```
EXPLAIN PLAN SET statement_id= 'TEST' FOR
SELECT /*+ INDEX(periodsum, xfk_ps_coa xfk_ps_yearperiod) */
 * FROM periodsum;
```

Query	Cost	Rows	Bytes
1. SELECT STATEMENT on	**4**	45	675
2. TABLE ACCESS BY INDEX ROWID on PERIODSUM	4	45	675
3. INDEX FULL SCAN on **XFK_PS_COA**	3	45	

In the previous example, the optimizer selected the best key as being the foreign key pointing to the COA table. In the next example, we force the use of the foreign key pointing to the PeriodSum table, showing it is higher in cost than using the foreign key pointing to the COA table:

```
EXPLAIN PLAN SET statement_id= 'TEST' FOR
   SELECT /*+ INDEX(periodsum, xfk_ps_yearperiod) */ * FROM periodsum;
```

Query	Cost	Rows	Bytes
1. SELECT STATEMENT on	**5**	45	675
2. TABLE ACCESS BY INDEX ROWID on PERIODSUM	5	45	675
3. INDEX FULL SCAN on **XFK_PS_YEARPERIOD**	4	45	

We could also use the INDEX_DESC hint to scan an index in reverse order:

```
EXPLAIN PLAN SET statement_id= 'TEST' FOR
SELECT /*+ INDEX_DESC(customer) */ customer_id FROM customer;
```

Query	Cost	Rows	Bytes
1. SELECT STATEMENT on	7	2694	8082
2. INDEX FULL SCAN **DESCENDING** on XPK_CUSTOMER	7	2694	8082

Note: (9i) The AND_EQUAL hint has not been covered as of yet. This first example uses the foreign key index on the ORDER_ID column.

Note: (10g) The AND_EQUAL hint is deprecated.

```
EXPLAIN PLAN SET statement_id= 'TEST' FOR
   SELECT * FROM transactions WHERE type = 'S' AND order_id = 10;
```

Query	Cost	Rows	Bytes
1. SELECT STATEMENT on	2	1	36
2. TABLE ACCESS BY INDEX ROWID on TRANSACTIONS	2	1	36
3. INDEX RANGE SCAN on **XFK_T_ORDERS**	1	1	

The AND_EQUAL hint causes an alteration to the previous example by forcing use of both the TYPE and ORDER_ID foreign key indexes. It does not help the cost, but this is what the hint does.

Note: The cost-based optimizer is sophisticated in the latest versions of Oracle Database. Do not ever assume that by using hints your SQL code will execute faster. ALWAYS check the query plan with the EXPLAIN PLAN command when using hints.

```
EXPLAIN PLAN SET statement_id='TEST' FOR
   SELECT /*+ AND_EQUAL(transactions xfk_t_type xfk_t_orders)
*/ *
FROM transactions WHERE type = 'S' AND order_id = 10;
```

Note: ⑨*i* The following query plan will not show the AND EQUAL on step in Oracle Database 10*g*.

Query	Cost	Rows	Bytes
1. SELECT STATEMENT on	258	1	36
2. TABLE ACCESS BY INDEX ROWID on TRANSACTIONS	258	1	36
3. **AND–EQUAL** on			
4. INDEX RANGE SCAN on XFK_T_ORDERS			
4. INDEX RANGE SCAN on XFK_T_TYPE	256	121292	

Note: ⑩*g* Index hints include index names or table names with column lists. Table.COLUMN name settings can also be used, even with columns in separate tables for join indexes.

11.4.3 Altering Joins

Available hints:

- **ORDERED**. Makes the optimizer join tables in the sequence that those tables appear in the FROM clause of an SQL statement. There are other uses for this hint; refer to the section on DISTINCT in Chapter 10.

- **LEADING**. Makes the optimizer use a named table as the first table in the join, regardless of which table occurs first in the FROM clause.

- *USE_NL, USE_HASH, and USE_MERGE.* Force nested loops, hash join, or sort merge join respectively.

- (10*g*) *NO_USE_NL, NO_USE_HASH, and NO_USE_MERGE.* These hints force the optimizer to not use nested loops, hash joins, or sort merge joins respectively, in a particular query.

- (9*i*) *NL_AJ, HASH_AJ, MERGE_AJ, NL_SJ, HASH_SJ, and MERGE_SJ.* All of these hints change the join type for semi-join and anti-join subqueries.

Note: (10*g*) The hints NL_AJ, HASH_AJ, MERGE_AJ, NL_SJ, HASH_SJ, and MERGE_SJ are all deprecated.

We have already seen the ORDERED hint in this chapter, but I will reiterate with a different example because it is important. This first example does not use the ORDERED hint and accesses tables with the smaller of the COA and GeneralLedger tables in the outer loop:

```
EXPLAIN PLAN SET statement_id='TEST' FOR
    SELECT * FROM generalledger gl, coa WHERE coa.coa# = gl.coa#;
```

Query	Cost	Rows	Bytes
1. SELECT STATEMENT on	1642	1068929	50239663
2. HASH JOIN on	1642	1068929	50239663
3. TABLE ACCESS FULL on **COA**	2	55	1320
3. TABLE ACCESS FULL on GENERALLEDGER	1128	1068929	24585367

This second example applies the ORDERED hint and changes the order in which the optimizer accesses tables. This is based on the sequence of tables in the FROM clause:

```
EXPLAIN PLAN SET statement_id='TEST' FOR
    SELECT /*+ ORDERED */ * FROM generalledger gl, coa
    WHERE coa.coa# = gl.coa#;
```

Query	Cost	Rows	Bytes
1. SELECT STATEMENT on	4026	1068929	50239663
2. HASH JOIN on	4026	1068929	50239663

```
3.    TABLE ACCESS FULL on GENERALLEDGER      1128   1068929   24585367
3.    TABLE ACCESS FULL on COA                   2        55       1320
```

In the next example, not all tables are switched according to the FROM clause. The ORDERED hint manages to switch the Transactions and TransactionsLine tables. It does not change the sequence for the Customer table:

```
EXPLAIN PLAN SET statement_id='TEST' FOR
    SELECT /*+ ORDERED */ *
FROM transactionsline tl, transactions t, customer c
    WHERE t.transaction_id = tl.transaction_id
    AND c.customer_id = t.customer_id;
```

Query	Cost	Rows	Bytes
1. SELECT STATEMENT on	27327	273552	50880672
2. HASH JOIN on	27327	273552	50880672
3. TABLE ACCESS FULL on CUSTOMER	16	2694	360996
3. MERGE JOIN on	20905	273552	14224704
4. SORT JOIN on	18997	1027251	16436016
5. TABLE ACCESS FULL on **TRANSACTIONSLINE**	800	1027251	16436016
4. SORT JOIN on	1908	64599	2325564
5. TABLE ACCESS FULL on **TRANSACTIONS**	390	64599	2325564

The LEADING hint uses a named table as the first table in the join:

```
EXPLAIN PLAN SET statement_id='TEST' FOR
    SELECT /*+ LEADING(tl) */ *
FROM transactionsline tl, transactions t, customer c
    WHERE t.transaction_id = tl.transaction_id
    AND c.customer_id = t.customer_id;
```

Query	Cost	Rows	Bytes
1. SELECT STATEMENT on	26143	273552	50880672
2. HASH JOIN on	26143	273552	50880672
3. MERGE JOIN on	20905	273552	14224704
4. SORT JOIN on	18997	1027251	16436016
5. TABLE ACCESS FULL on **TRANSACTIONSLINE**	800	1027251	16436016
4. SORT JOIN on	1908	64599	2325564

5.	TABLE ACCESS FULL on TRANSACTIONS	390	64599	2325564
3.	TABLE ACCESS FULL on CUSTOMER	16	2694	360996

11.4.4 Cause Parallel SQL Execution

Available hints:

- *[NO]_PARALLEL*. Parallel execution, preferably on multiple CPUs, or servers, or a computer capable of parallel processing.

- *PQ_DISTRIBUTE*. Improves a parallel join.

- *[NO]_PARALLEL_INDEX*. Process index scans for partitions in parallel.

Note: (10*g*) The NOPARALLEL and NOPARALLEL_INDEX hints are renamed to NO_PARALLEL and NO_PARALLEL_INDEX respectively.

In Chapter 10 we examined performance using parallel settings on both full table scans and fast full index scans. Parallelism was detrimental to performance. Parallel SQL statements are usually only beneficial in very large data warehouse databases, with very high I/O throughput activity. Some DDL commands can be executed in parallel, such as index creation, which can be highly beneficial in OLTP databases. Using parallelism with Oracle partitioning and multiple disks is significant in all types of databases and will be examined in Part III.

11.4.5 Altering Queries and Subqueries

Available hints:

- *[NO]CACHE*. CACHE can be used to force data into a Most Recently Used (MRU) list. NOCACHE pushes data to a Least Recently Used (LRU) list.

- (9*i*) *ORDERED_PREDICATES*. Preserves SQL statement precedence of evaluation, such as the sequence of comparisons in a WHERE clause.

Note: (10*g*) The ORDERED_PREDICATES hint is deprecated.

- *[NO_]UNNEST*. Undoes subquery layers by allowing the optimizer to attempt to merge subqueries into a calling query. Use of this hint might actually be detrimental to performance tuning of multilayered SQL statements.

- *[NO_]PUSH_SUBQ.* Resolves subqueries first (PUSH_SUBQ) or last (NO_PUSH_SUBQ).

Note: Contrary to what was stated in the previous edition of this book, a hint is more of an instruction than a suggestion to the optimizer.

11.5 (10g) Naming Query Blocks for Hints

The QB_NAME hint allows you to name a query block and its syntax as follows:

```
/*+ QB_NAME(<name>) */
```

The name of that query block can be used in a hint, referring back to the query block. That named query block can then be accessed in a hint that is placed in an outer query or an inline view (FROM clause subquery). The result is that tables in the query block that is named can be affected by results of an outer query or an inline view. Here is an example:

```
SELECT /*+ QB_NAME(block) FULL(@block GeneralLedger) */ *
FROM GeneralLedger;
```

As shown in the previous query, the query block is accessed by name from within the hint using the @ sign (@block).

11.5.1 (10g) Global Table Hints

A global table hint allows insertion of hints into embedded queries, such as an inline view in a view object, and you do not have to query in the view, and no change to the view is required. Let's say you have a view that includes an inline view as in the following example:

```
CREATE VIEW Entries AS
SELECT coa.coa#, coa.text, types.typename, types.subtypename
FROM COA coa,
(
```

```
SELECT Type.type, Type.text AS TypeName
    ,SubType.subtype, SubType.text AS SubTypeName
    FROM Type CROSS JOIN SubType
) types
WHERE types.type = COA.type AND types.subtype = COA.subtype;
```

Let's get a query plan for this query (inside the view, not the view):

```
EXPLAIN PLAN SET statement_id='TEST' FOR
SELECT * FROM Entries;
```

And here's the query plan:

Query	Cost	Rows	Bytes
1. SELECT STATEMENT on	8	55	2090
2. NESTED LOOPS on	8	55	2090
3. NESTED LOOPS on	7	55	1650
4. TABLE ACCESS FULL on SUBTYPE	6	4	36
4. TABLE ACCESS BY INDEX ROWID on COA	1	14	294
5. INDEX RANGE SCAN on XFK_COA_SUBTYPE	0	14	
3. TABLE ACCESS BY INDEX ROWID on TYPE	1	1	8
4. INDEX UNIQUE SCAN on XPK_TYPE	0	1	

Now we want to apply a hint inside the subquery of the inline view, without changing the view. This query against the view will change the index scan on the Type table, inside the view, to a full table scan:

```
EXPLAIN PLAN SET statement_id='TEST' FOR
SELECT /*+ FULL(Entries.types.Type) */ * FROM Entries;
```

This is the query plan:

Query	Cost	Rows	Bytes
1. SELECT STATEMENT on	8	55	2090
2. NESTED LOOPS on	8	55	2090
3. NESTED LOOPS on	7	55	1650
4. TABLE ACCESS FULL on SUBTYPE	6	4	36

4.	TABLE ACCESS BY INDEX ROWID on COA	1	14	294
5.	INDEX RANGE SCAN on XFK_COA_SUBTYPE	0	14	
3.	**TABLE ACCESS BY INDEX ROWID on TYPE**	**1**	**1**	**8**
4.	**INDEX UNIQUE SCAN on XPK_TYPE**	**0**	**1**	

The FULL hint specifies a full table scan on the Type table, based on the view name (Entries) and the name of the inline view within the view (types). This process does not appear to function using a FULL hint (attempted to) induced full table scan.

There is also something called a (10*g*) complex index hint. The failure of getting it to work with the global table hint makes me reluctant to repeat the same process when creating a complex index hint. A complex index hint allows specification of an index hint to use a list of column names, as opposed to an explicitly named index.

The last three chapters have attempted to show how Oracle Database executes SQL code and how that SQL code can be tuned from a purely Oracle Database perspective. This chapter concludes that demonstration. The next chapter digs into the tools that can be used to find queries, which can or may be causing performance problems.

11.6 Endnotes

1.   Oracle Data Warehouse Tuning for 10*g* (Gavin Powell, Digital Press, Aug 2005, ISBN: 1555583350)

12

How to Find Problem Queries

Problem queries are queries taking too long to run or hoarding too many resources or both. Problem queries are common in ad hoc user SQL environments and sometimes a result of poor SQL coding, or even impossible-to-build SQL queries because the underlying database model is inadequate or inappropriate.

Database administrators often have the responsibility of ensuring that performance-impacting queries are located and tuned. Also, if end users or application developers are responsible for submitting poorly performing queries to a database, then tactful advice and even some training might be beneficial to all in an organization. This chapter discusses some of the various tools that can be used to find problem queries.

12.1 Tools to Detect Problems

This book is intended as a step-by-step learning guide teaching tuning of Oracle installations. You should now have an understanding of SQL code tuning from the most important perspective. What is that perspective? You should have an understanding of how to tune SQL code without having to use all sorts of fancy and complicated SQL code tuning tools. In other words, when a specific tool suggests a specific approach, you are likely to understand any reasoning behind that suggestion and decide whether you should implement it or not.

Why is this approach better? Because it should always be viewed as a last resort to fall back on detailed analysis with specific tools. On the other hand, some Oracle tools are getting easier to use, with each newly introduced version of Oracle Database software.

Overall, it is better to know how to properly build tuned SQL code in the first place without having to take drastic measures, such as use of the

EXPLAIN PLAN command, and more significantly, hours and hours poring over trace files. For one thing, trace files are highly complex and time consuming to digest, and production of trace files at a useful level for SQL coding performance can produce a significant performance drain on a database, perhaps providing far more information than is ever necessary.

Various Oracle Corporation and non–Oracle Corporation tools can be used to find and tune problematic and poorly performing SQL code. What are these tools?

- EXPLAIN PLAN
- SQL Trace with TKPROF
- (10*g*) TRCSESS
- Autotracing in SQL*Plus
- (9*i*) Oracle Trace

Note: (10*g*) Oracle Trace has been deprecated, including all ORACLE_TRACE_% configuration parameters.

- Oracle Performance views
- Oracle Enterprise Manager, the Database Control, and (10*g*) automated SQL tuning will be covered in the next chapter explicitly, being topics in themselves.

Note: (9*i*) The Oracle Enterprise Manager Console and the (10*g*) Database Control are more tuning tools that encompass both SQL tuning and physical tuning. Therefore, these tools tend to merge the tuning approach covered in both Parts II and III of this book.

Now let's examine the use of some Oracle Database tuning tools in detail.

12.2 EXPLAIN PLAN

We have seen extensive use of the EXPLAIN PLAN command in this book so far, but it has not really been essential to describe the nitty-gritty of what precisely the EXPLAIN PLAN command does. From my perspective, this type of information falls under the guise of reference material. I find that initially bombarding the reader with too much reference material can cause a lot of confusion and an even larger amount of boredom.

Once again, so far in this book you have learned about data model tuning and SQL code tuning. SQL code tuning has been covered from the perspective of writing usable SQL code rather than an in-depth analysis of the tools used to find problems. Therefore, writing SQL code properly in the first place might help avoid having to use in-depth and overbearing SQL code tuning tools. It is by far better to build properly tuned SQL code without having to immediately resort to masses of interpretive output, such as that produced by trace files or STATSPACK.

12.2.1 What Does EXPLAIN PLAN Produce?

The optimizer creates a query plan for every SQL statement, be it a DML command or a SELECT statement. DML commands are INSERT, UPDATE, DELETE, and MERGE commands. A query plan is selected by the optimizer as a method of best performance for the execution of a SQL statement. The EXPLAIN PLAN command simply creates readable descriptions of the steps in the query plan and inserts those steps as entries into a table called the PLAN_TABLE.

A SQL statement query plan contains several general items. These items describe how a SQL statement should be executed:

- The sequence in which tables are accessed

- Probably most importantly, an estimated or guesstimated cost of the query plan as a whole, and a cost for each step

- Less importantly, details such as I/O estimates, temporary sort space usage, rows accessed and bytes read, among others

- A method of access for each table

- Join methods for any joins

- Filtering and sorting operations

- Other specialized factors such as parallel processing or concatenation

Note that these operations are not necessarily executed on a table itself, but rather what is effectively a row set. A row set is either a filtered or indexed subset of a table or a resulting set of rows produced by a join. A join is a join between two tables, a table and a row set, or even two row sets.

Several things are important to note: (1) the optimizer is not always right; (2) the query plan can be changed or at least influenced using hints; and (3) the EXPLAIN PLAN command makes a best guess of how the optimizer should execute a query. This best guess is not the actual query execution plan. Actual query execution plans can be found in the V$SQL_PLAN performance view.

Note: Query plan costs are estimates only. They are not sacrosanct. A query plan produced by the EXPLAIN PLAN command is a guess at how a piece of SQL code is most efficiently executed. The query plan may most necessarily be used on execution, and if executed to the letter, it may not even be the most efficient option.

12.2.2 What to Look for in Query Plans

What should one be searching for in query plans with respect to creating high-performance SQL code statements? Bad things! Well, what are *bad things*? This phrase is colloquial, but it is descriptive. We need to search for anything that may be potentially problematic, slowing down the execution of a SQL statement. We have already seen a lot of potential problems in previous chapters. What are some common *red flags* to watch out for?

- Full table scans and poor use of indexing, or lack of use of indexing:
    - Inappropriate use of indexing where full table scans can sometimes be faster
    - Overindexing on individual tables or too many indexes in a database in general
    - Large selections from large tables sometimes caused by filtering too late
    - Unnecessary sorting
- Joins:
    - Sort-merge joins where nested loops or hash joins can be used
    - Cartesian joins, some outer joins, and anti-joins
    - Highly complex mutable (multiple-table) joins
    - Noncorrelated subquery semi-joins

- Using views, especially multiple layers of views calling subviews
- Inherently poorly performing steps like UNION and concatenation operations

12.2.3 Problems Producing Query Plans

Cost-based optimization is far more efficient than rule-based optimization. Statistics must exist for cost-based optimization to be used. If statistics are out of date, then statistics may be inconsistent with data in the database. This can lead to incorrect assessment of the best-performing query plan for SQL code by the optimizer.

Note: (10*g*) Rule-based optimization is obsolete.

Note: (10*g*) More automated statistics gathering tends to alleviate statistics management in previous versions of Oracle Database.

Statistics can be copied between different databases using the export (exp) and import (imp) utilities or even using the DBMS_STATS package. Several things are of paramount importance to tuning SQL code with respect to statistics:

- The existence of statistics in all tables and indexes

- Realistic statistics perhaps matching production database environments. Development, testing, tuning, and production databases can often be vastly different physically. Statistics may vary wildly.

- Different databases can be placed on different hardware platforms, where those different hardware platforms have differing configurations. Those differing configurations can affect how the optimizer creates query plans. Different configurations can be differences in numbers of CPUs, storage media such as the presence of RAID arrays or not, and perhaps most importantly, different Oracle installation configuration parameters. For instance, differences between the SORT_AREA_SIZE and HASH_AREA_SIZE parameters on different database servers can affect optimizer choices between nested loops and hash joins.

Note: (10*g*) The PGA_AGGREGATE_TARGET parameter contains and
automates management of all the *_AREA_SIZE parameters.

12.2.4   EXPLAIN PLAN Command Syntax

```
EXPLAIN PLAN
[ SET STATEMENT_ID = 'string' ]
[ INTO [schema.]table[@dblink] ]
FOR sql_statement;
```

This simplest version of the EXPLAIN PLAN command generates
entries directly into the PLAN_TABLE:

```
EXPLAIN PLAN FOR SELECT * FROM generalledger;
```

Using a query like the following one, we can examine the
PLAN_TABLE entries:

```
COL Cost FORMAT 9990;
COL Rows FORMAT 999990;
COL Bytes FORMAT 99999990;
COL Query FORMAT a40;
SELECT operation||' '||options||' on '||object_name "Query"
   ,cost "Cost"
   ,cardinality "Rows"
   ,bytes "Bytes"
FROM plan_table ORDER BY id;
```

This is the result of the previous query:

Query	Cost	Rows	Bytes
SELECT STATEMENT on	778	752741	17313043
TABLE ACCESS FULL on GENERALLEDGER	778	752741	17313043

The EXPLAIN PLAN command does not delete any previous entries
from the PLAN_TABLE. Execution of the previous EXPLAIN PLAN
command will add the same two rows again. Delete previously added rows

before executing the EXPLAIN PLAN command again. In this case, we can simply issue the DELETE or TRUNCATE commands to clear the PLAN_TABLE completely. In a multiuser development database, this would be a problem. Multiple coders could be generating PLAN_TABLE entries. It would probably irritate other developers to continuously be removing all entries from the PLAN_TABLE. We can use specific identifying values to remove only the PLAN_TABLE rows generated. The SET_STATEMENT_ID = 'string' option can be used to generate session-specific PLAN_TABLE entries and isolate specific output, assuming no other coders are using the same string value:

```
EXPLAIN PLAN SET STATEMENT_ID = 'TEST'
FOR SELECT * FROM generalledger;
```

Change the PLAN_TABLE query accordingly:

```
COL Cost FORMAT 9990;
COL Rows FORMAT 999990;
COL Bytes FORMAT 99999990;
COL Query FORMAT a40;
SELECT operation||' '||options||' on '||object_name "Query"
    ,cost "Cost"
    ,cardinality "Rows"
    ,bytes "Bytes"
FROM plan_table WHERE statement_id = 'TEST' ORDER BY id;
```

Note: The optional INTO table clause can be used to place PLAN_TABLE output into a table other than the PLAN_TABLE.

The FOR clause part of the EXPLAIN PLAN command is passed a SQL statement. That SQL statement can be any SQL statement type for which the optimizer generates a query plan:

- SELECT
- INSERT, UPDATE, DELETE, MERGE
- CREATE TABLE AS SELECT …
- CREATE INDEX
- ALTER INDEX … REBUILD …

Following are some examples. At this stage, we will use a more sophisticated version of the PLAN_TABLE query already used in previous chapters (see Appendix B):

```
EXPLAIN PLAN SET STATEMENT_ID = 'TEST' FOR
INSERT INTO coa(coa#, type, subtype, text) VALUES( '60007', 'I', 'S',
'Consulting Fees');
```

Query	Cost	Rows	Bytes
1. INSERT STATEMENT on	2	55	1320

```
EXPLAIN PLAN SET STATEMENT_ID = 'TEST' FOR
UPDATE coa SET text =  'Consulting Fees' WHERE coa# =  '60007';
```

Query	Cost	Rows	Bytes
1. UPDATE STATEMENT on	1	1	19
2. UPDATE on COA			
3. INDEX UNIQUE SCAN on XPK_COA		1	19

```
EXPLAIN PLAN SET STATEMENT_ID = 'TEST' FOR
DELETE FROM coa WHERE coa# =  '60007';
```

Query	Cost	Rows	Bytes
1. DELETE STATEMENT on	1	1	7
2. DELETE on COA			
3. TABLE ACCESS BY INDEX ROWID on COA	1	1	7
4. INDEX UNIQUE SCAN on XPK_COA		55	

```
CREATE TABLE tmp AS
SELECT coa#, type, subtype, text FROM coa WHERE ROWNUM < 1;
INSERT INTO tmp VALUES( '60008', 'I', 'S', 'Other Income');
INSERT INTO tmp VALUES( '60001', 'I', 'S', 'Primary Sales');
EXPLAIN PLAN SET STATEMENT_ID = 'TEST' FOR
MERGE INTO coa USING tmp ON(coa.coa# = tmp.coa#)
WHEN MATCHED THEN UPDATE SET coa.text = tmp.text
WHEN NOT MATCHED THEN
INSERT VALUES(tmp.coa#, tmp.type, tmp.subtype, tmp.text,
NULL, NULL, NULL);
```

Query	Cost	Rows	Bytes
1. MERGE STATEMENT on	9189	369820	26996860
2. MERGE on COA			
3. VIEW on			
4. HASH JOIN OUTER on	5	82	4920
5. TABLE ACCESS FULL on TMP	2	82	2542
5. TABLE ACCESS FULL on COA	2	55	1595

```
EXPLAIN PLAN SET STATEMENT_ID = 'TEST' FOR
CREATE TABLE tmp AS SELECT * FROM generalledger;
```

Query	Cost	Rows	Bytes
1. CREATE TABLE STATEMENT on	778	752741	17313043
2. LOAD AS SELECT on			
3. TABLE ACCESS FULL on GENERALLEDGER	778	752741	17313043

```
EXPLAIN PLAN SET STATEMENT_ID = 'TEST' FOR
CREATE INDEX xak_gl_coa#_dte ON generalledger(coa#, dte);
```

Query	Cost	Rows	Bytes
1. CREATE INDEX STATEMENT on	778	752741	9032892
2. INDEX BUILD NON UNIQUE on XAK_GL_COA#_DTE			
3. SORT CREATE INDEX on		752741	9032892
4. TABLE ACCESS FULL on GENERALLEDGER	778	752741	9032892

```
EXPLAIN PLAN SET STATEMENT_ID = 'TEST' FOR
ALTER INDEX xfk_gl_coa# REBUILD ONLINE;
```

Query	Cost	Rows	Bytes
1. ALTER INDEX STATEMENT on	101	752741	9032892
2. INDEX BUILD NON UNIQUE on XAK_GL_COA#_DT			
3. SORT CREATE INDEX on		752741	9032892
4. TABLE ACCESS FULL on GENERALLEDGER	101	752741	9032892

As you can see, all sundry of SQL statements can be passed through the EXPLAIN PLAN command. This produces a query plan estimate of how a SQL statement will be executed and how much it might cost in resources.

12.2.5 How to Create the PLAN_TABLE

Use the script called UTLXPLAN.SQL to create the PLAN_TABLE. This script is located on the database server in the $ORACLE_HOME/rdbms/admin directory on a UNIX box and in the ORACLE_HOME\rdbms\admin directory on a Windows machine. The UTLXPLAN.SQL script contains a simple table creation command.

Also in that directory are two other scripts called UTLXPLS.SQL and UTLXPLP.SQL. The latter version involves a reference to a column called OTHER_TAG containing details of parallel execution. Use UTLXPLS.SQL for serial execution and UTLXPLP.SQL for parallel execution. These two scripts can be used to display PLAN_TABLE query plans using the DBMS_XPLAN package. I prefer to use a hierarchical query as seen in this chapter already and used extensively in previous chapters (see Appendix B).

Note: (10*g*) Two new columns in the PLAN_TABLE are ACCESS_PREDICATES and FILTER_PREDICATES.

12.2.6 What Is Not Provided in Query Plans?

A query plan will not necessarily tell you everything about a SQL code statement. There are things not included in query plans that can potentially affect performance drastically. It is always best to attempt to tune SQL code from the perspective of the SQL code, as described in the first few chapters of Part II. Use query plans for verification and fine tuning. In the extreme, tracing can be used. Timing tests can be used to assess the speed of execution of SQL statements. However, be careful of executing large SQL code statements and killing database performance, particularly on a production database. Small portions of tables can be used for testing and counts using the COUNT function as a wrapper function to minimize performance impact, as in the following example:

```
SQL> SELECT COUNT(*) FROM(SELECT * FROM generalledger);


  COUNT(*)
----------
    752741


Elapsed: 00:00:00.03
```

Using the COUNT function as a wrapper is a simplistic and effective timing mechanism. It avoids having to include the display of data into a tool such as SQL*Plus. In the previous example, the data content of the very large GeneralLedger table is not being transferred over the network, only a counter of its total number of rows.

Displaying thousands or even millions of rows in SQL*Plus will take forever to display and could slow down your database and flood your network. Every SQL statement tested as a timing test should probably be executed at least twice. This allows loading into buffer caches, perhaps accounting for differences in retrieval from buffers and disk. The aim is to test SQL code efficiency, not the behavior of the database buffer cache. That comes in Part II of this book.

A method of running timing tests using the COUNT function may be relatively ineffective running against a highly active concurrent database, especially if concurrent activity fluctuates within the space of time of executing such timing SQL code statements. This type of testing might be a little misleading on computers running anything other than Oracle software. A squeaky-clean environment would be the most informative option.

Query plans do not tell you everything. Tracing and TKPROF is the next step up in complexity from using EXPLAIN PLAN. Additionally, SQL Trace and TKPROF can be used to determine SQL statement performance at a deeper level by allowing analysis of resource consumption.

12.3 SQL Trace and TKPROF

SQL Trace causes trace files to be produced by Oracle Database. Various items of interest are generated into trace files. This information comprises details of CPU and I/O needs. Also included are parsing and execution information, processed rows, commit, and rollback activity. The output in trace files is time consuming to interpret by hand. TKPROF is a formatting utility used to format trace file output into an easily readable form. TKPROF can be used to produce EXPLAIN PLAN query plans, as well as store past output from statistics collections previously written to trace files, into a file called TKPROF_TABLE.

12.3.1 Setting up SQL Trace

SQL Trace can be configured for instance-level use or for a session, for a session either within a current open session, or from one session to another. Setting instance-wide tracing can cause serious performance problems. It is better for performance to enable tracing only from a current session or for a specific session. However, not using instance-wide tracing can miss a lot of useful information. I am using instance-level tracing because I am not working on a production server database. Start by setting the TIMED_STATISTICS, TIMED_OS_STATISTICS, and MAX_DUMP_FILE_SIZE configuration parameters in your parameter file:

```
TIMED_STATISTICS = TRUE
TIMED_OS_STATISTICS = 5
MAX_DUMP_FILE_SIZE = 1M
```

Note: These parameters can be changed in either the text or binary parameter files or both. Using the binary parameter file allows use of the ALTER SYSTEM command, and obviously tools such as the Database Control.

Note: (10gR2) Setting MAX_DUMP_FILE_SIZE using the ALTER SYSTEM command seems to work only when set to an integer. For example, 1024000 works fine. This is probably a bug in my version of OracleDatabase 10g (10.2.0.1). My guess is that this is a byte value setting. Setting it to 1M returns an error.

The effect on performance of setting the TIMED_STATISTICS parameter is negligible. The parameters previously shown enable collection of statistics, including CPU and I/O statistics. TIMED_STATISTICS writes information to both trace files plus the V$SYSSTATS and V$SESSSTATS performance views. TIMED_OS_STATISTICS is a timing mechanism for statistics collection, triggering system statistics collection periodically.

The MAX_DUMP_FILE_SIZE parameter will truncate each trace file in the USER_DUMP_DEST directory, the default target directory for trace files, usually the $ORACLE_BASE/admin/$ORACLE_SID/udump directory.

Next set the SQL_TRACE parameter to switch on SQL Trace. The TRACE_ENABLED parameter could also be set to TRUE, but we will avoid that. Setting TRACE_ENABLED tends to produce copious amounts of detail, which is more relevant to Oracle support personnel than anything else:

```
SQL_TRACE = TRUE
```

> **Note:** Using SQL_TRACE can have a severe performance impact on production systems.

Trace files contain generated statistics. In past versions of Oracle, trace levels could be set. Oracle Database 9*i* introduced the parameter called STATISTICS_LEVEL, which can be set to BASIC, TYPICAL, or ALL. The default is TYPICAL. Setting ALL would incur significant overhead and have a noticeable effect on performance. In my database, I set the STATISTICS_LEVEL parameter to ALL to gather as much information as possible. Note that setting this parameter to ALL automatically sets the TIMED_OS_STATISTICS parameter to 5:

```
STATISTICS_LEVEL = ALL
```

12.3.1.1 Session-Level Tracing

Specific sessions can be traced. Tracing at the session level can help remove tracing overhead from the database in general and focus on a specific session. Personally, I have never seen the value in using session-level tracing. Far too much information is produced. There are easier ways to track down problems than by using session-level tracing. The following command traces the current session. Tracing a specific session may be most applicable to tracking down some really nasty SQL code, such as in a prerelease application, or one that should not have been released, or perhaps in an ad hoc SQL environment:

```
ALTER SESSION SET SQL_TRACE = TRUE;
```

This command will trace a session other than the current session (someone else's session):

```
DBMS_SYSTEM_SET_SQL_TRACE_IN SESSION(SID, SERIAL#, TRUE);
```

12.3.1.2 Finding Trace Files

One of the biggest problems with trace files is finding them. Many files can be generated. You could find the files applicable to specific processes by including tags in your SQL code, such as SELECT 'my trace file' FROM DUAL, or by checking datestamps in the operating system. Typically, a trace file is named in the following format:

```
$ORACLE_SID_ora_<pid>.trc
```

The descriptor *pid* represents the process ID, which generated the trace file. The process ID can be found with the following query, which finds the process identifier using the process and session addresses, plus the session auditing identifier as the session identifier:

```
SELECT spid FROM v$process
WHERE addr = (SELECT paddr FROM v$session
WHERE audsid = USERENV('sessionid'));
```

12.3.2 Using SQL Trace

The next logical step is to use SQL Trace. I have now set up my Oracle Database binary configuration parameter file (spfile<SID>.ora) with various parameter changes, using the ALTER SYSTEM command:

```
ALTER SYSTEM SET TIMED_STATISTICS = TRUE;
ALTER SYSTEM SET TIMED_OS_STATISTICS=5;
ALTER SYSTEM SET MAX_DUMP_FILE_SIZE = 1024000;
ALTER SYSTEM SET SQL_TRACE = TRUE;
ALTER SYSTEM SET STATISTICS_LEVEL = ALL;
```

I can also set up these parameters in the text file. If any of these parameters had a V$PARAMETER.ISSYS_MODIFIABLE not equal to IMMEDIATE, then I would have to bounce my database to instantiate the change into the database instance. I can find the appropriate settings for these parameters easily using the following query:

```
COL NAME FORMAT A32
COL SESSION FORMAT A10
COL SYSTEM FORMAT A10
SELECT ISSES_MODIFIABLE "Session", ISSYS_MODIFIABLE "System",
NAME
FROM V$PARAMETER
WHERE NAME IN ('timed_statistics','timed_os_statistics',
'max_dump_file_size','sql_trace','statistics_level');
```

This is the result of the previous query on my database after executing the ALTER SYSTEM commands of all five parameters:

```
Session     System      NAME
----------  ----------  --------------------
TRUE        IMMEDIATE   timed_statistics
TRUE        IMMEDIATE   timed_os_statistics
TRUE        IMMEDIATE   max_dump_file_size
TRUE        IMMEDIATE   sql_trace
TRUE        IMMEDIATE   statistics_level
```

Note: (9i) In the previous edition, using Oracle Database 9i, I changed the text parameter file and bounced my database to instantiate these configuration parameter changes.

The next step is starting up my highly active concurrent database scripting (see Appendix B). These scripts use the DBMS_JOBS package to repetitively execute a slew of database changes to my Accounts schema, from multiple concurrently executed database jobs using the DBMS_JOBS package. I have to be able to find trace files for each session because I am running sessions using the DBMS_JOBS package.

Now that my database jobs are running, I need to change the process identifier query to access multiple sessions and find a trace file that way. So how do I find the appropriate sessions? Log into a database administrator user such as SYSTEM and execute a query something like this:

```
COL USERNAME FORMAT A16
SELECT username, saddr, paddr, sid, serial#
FROM v$session WHERE username = 'ACCOUNTS';
```

This query finds the following sessions:

USERNAME	SADDR	PADDR	SID	SERIAL#
ACCOUNTS	703E7D1C	702D2D50	178	110
ACCOUNTS	703EDB04	702D2760	183	45
ACCOUNTS	703F0094	702D2170	185	41
ACCOUNTS	6FC365A0	702CC270	190	939
ACCOUNTS	6FC37868	702D0FA0	191	1043
ACCOUNTS	6FC44700	702D1590	202	55
ACCOUNTS	6FC502D0	702D09B0	212	245

Now we can link sessions and processes to find trace file names:

```
SELECT 'c:\oracle\product\10.2.0\admin\oltp\udump\
oltp_ora_'||spid||'.trc'
"Trace File"
FROM v$process
WHERE addr IN (SELECT paddr FROM V$SESSION WHERE username =
'ACCOUNTS');
```

These are the trace files we find:

```
Trace File
------------------------------------------------------------
c:\oracle\product\10.2.0\admin\oltp\udump\oltp_ora_1188.trc
c:\oracle\product\10.2.0\admin\oltp\udump\oltp_ora_964.trc
c:\oracle\product\10.2.0\admin\oltp\udump\oltp_ora_1208.trc
c:\oracle\product\10.2.0\admin\oltp\udump\oltp_ora_1052.trc
c:\oracle\product\10.2.0\admin\oltp\udump\oltp_ora_1068.trc
c:\oracle\product\10.2.0\admin\oltp\udump\oltp_ora_1088.trc
c:\oracle\product\10.2.0\admin\oltp\udump\oltp_ora_804.trc
```

Trace files can look like the gibberish shown following. They are really very easily interpreted:

```
=====================
PARSING IN CURSOR #3 len=56 dep=1 uid=0 oct=3 lid=0 tim=13822711723
hv=4049165760 ad='67f67898'
select order#,columns,types from access$ where d_obj#=:1
END OF STMT
PARSE #3:c=0,e=145,p=0,cr=0,cu=0,mis=0,r=0,dep=1,og=4,tim=13822711703
EXEC #3:c=0,e=136,p=0,cr=0,cu=0,mis=0,r=0,dep=1,og=4,tim=13822714183
FETCH #3:c=0,e=114,p=0,cr=3,cu=0,mis=0,r=1,dep=1,og=4,tim=13822714826
FETCH #3:c=0,e=78,p=0,cr=2,cu=0,mis=0,r=1,dep=1,og=4,tim=13822715459
FETCH #3:c=0,e=67,p=0,cr=2,cu=0,mis=0,r=1,dep=1,og=4,tim=13822716065
FETCH #3:c=0,e=64,p=0,cr=2,cu=0,mis=0,r=1,dep=1,og=4,tim=13822716662
FETCH #3:c=0,e=65,p=0,cr=2,cu=0,mis=0,r=1,dep=1,og=4,tim=13822717260
FETCH #3:c=0,e=42,p=0,cr=1,cu=0,mis=0,r=0,dep=1,og=4,tim=13822717850
STAT #3 id=1 cnt=5 pid=0 pos=1 obj=97 op='TABLE ACCESS BY INDEX ROWID
ACCESS$ '
STAT #3 id=2 cnt=5 pid=1 pos=1 obj=129 op='INDEX RANGE SCAN I_ACCESS1 '
```

Making trace files more easily readable is where TKPROF comes into play.

12.3.3 **TKPROF**

TKPROF is essentially a text-formatting or text-parsing utility used to massage trace files into a readable format.

12.3.3.1 **Syntax of TKPROF**

TKPROF is available on the database server in the $ORACLE_HOME\ rdbms\admin directory. To examine TKPROF utility syntax, type TKPROF or TKPROF HELP=Y at the command line and hit the return key, as with many other Oracle Database utilities. TKPROF accepts an input trace file and outputs a formatted file. Execution plans can also be generated using TKPROF from trace files for all SQL code in the trace input file. Additionally, TKPROF can generate a historical record of both all recursive and nonrecursive SQL code executed by a session. This is the TKPROF command syntax:

```
TKPROF tracefile formatted
    [ SORT = { option | ( option list ) } ]
    [ PRINT = n ]
    [ AGGREGATE = { YES | NO } ]
    [ INSERT = scriptfile ]
    [ SYS = { YES | NO } ]
    [ [ TABLE = [schema.]table ] EXPLAIN = username/password ]
    [ RECORD = scriptfile ]
```

These commands are explained as follows:

- *SORT.* Sorts by specified options; there are a multitude of them.

- *PRINT.* Prints the first *n* SQL statements in the trace file.

- *AGGREGATE.* Groups multiple users using the same SQL text.

- *INSERT.* Writes out a SQL script to generate statistics into the database.

- *TABLE.* The name of the table to which query plans are written. Optionally, the *EXPLAIN* clause can be used to create SQL statement query plans.

- **RECORD**. Writes out a SQL script usable to replay all nonrecursive SQL events.

- **SYS**. SYS user SQL statements and recursive SQL. A recursive SQL statement occurs when, for instance, a SQL statement requires a new extent and an extent must be created before completion of the SQL statement.

12.3.3.2   Using TKPROF

Now I am simply executing TKPROF on the trace file I found earlier using all useful options. On Windows, a script like this could go into a batch called RTK.BAT, for instance:

```
TKPROF c:\oracle\product\10.2.0\admin\oltp\udump\
oltp_ora_%1.trc c:\tmp\%1.out
 INSERT=c:\tmp\%1.ins
 TABLE=PLAN_TABLE EXPLAIN=accounts/accounts
 RECORD=c:\tmp\%1.rec
 SYS=YES
```

The batch file would be executed like this, where 1188 is the first trace file process ID picked from the list shown previously:

```
RTK 1188
```

TKPROF will produce files called 1188.OUT, 1188.INS, and 1188.REC. The .OUT file contains the formatted output. The .INS file contains a statistics generation script. The .REC file contains a record of nonrecursive SQL commands executed.

12.3.3.3   Interpretation of TKPROF Output

Following are sections of sample TKPROF output. Some commentary is required. The first section of the TKPROF output shown is a SQL code SELECT statement contained in the trace file:

```
********************************************************************

SELECT a.supplier_id, a.price from (
      select supplier_id, min(price) as price
      from stocksource
```

```
    where stock_id = :b1
    group by supplier_id
    order by price
) a where rownum = 1
```

The next section from the TKPROF output shows statistics generated by the execution of this SELECT statement expressed in three separate steps:

call	count	cpu	elapsed	disk	query	current	rows
Parse	1	0.07	0.08	0	56	0	0
Execute	10	0.02	0.01	0	0	0	0
Fetch	10	0.10	0.17	36	256	0	10
total	21	0.19	0.27	36	312	0	10

Let's examine the three steps shown in the previous output:

1. *Parse*. Checks validity of syntax, objects, and security, and generation of the query plan by the optimizer.

2. *Execute*. Step for execution of SQL code. DML changes rows and SELECT builds appropriate cursor in memory.

3. *Fetch*. A cursor created by a SELECT statement is used to fetch the rows.

Repeating the second part of the TKPROF output for clarity, let's follow it by examining the separate columns:

call	count	cpu	elapsed	disk	query	current	rows
Parse	1	0.07	0.08	0	56	0	0
Execute	10	0.02	0.01	0	0	0	0
Fetch	10	0.10	0.17	36	256	0	10
total	21	0.19	0.27	36	312	0	10

The columns in the output above mean the following:

- **Count**. Parse, execute, and fetch calls or executions of each type
- **CPU**. Processor time
- **Elapsed**. Total time elapsed
- **Disk**. Physical disk reads
- **Query**. Read-only query block retrievals
- **Current**. Read-write block retrievals or changes
- **Rows**. Rows processed

The importance of the preceding TKPROF output is the ratios between the columns. What are these ratios and why are they significant?

- **Physical Disk Reads vs. Logical Reads**. This is disk / (query + current). The lower this ratio is, the better, but not always. An extremely low ratio could indicate poorly tuned SQL code, or an extremely high ratio could be normal depending on the application type. There is current thought in the Oracle community that logical reads in the extreme are not as efficient as once thought. Use of huge amounts of RAM and loading entire databases into the database buffer cache is often nowhere near as efficient as we are led to believe. On the contrary, LRU and MRU lists are significant because, for instance, reading a large table can push everything useful out of memory. This subject is discussed further in Part III.

- **Block Reads vs. Rows**. Blocks reads are often stated as being logical reads only: (query + current). I like to lump together the logical and the physical block reads: (query + current + disk), because they are all reads. The more blocks required to be read for each row, the worse performance could possibly be.

- **Parse vs. Execute**. We have a ratio of 1:10, which is good. If there were more parses than executions, it would imply that SQL code is being reparsed unnecessarily and the shared pool is not being shared enough, for a multitude of reasons but most likely because of poorly tuned SQL code.

The rest of the output shows a general analysis plus a query plan:

```
Misses in library cache during parse: 1
Optimizer goal: CHOOSE
Parsing user id: 88  (ACCOUNTS)   (recursive depth: 1)


Rows    Execution Plan
------- ----------------------------------------------------
    0   SELECT STATEMENT    GOAL: CHOOSE
    0    COUNT (STOPKEY)
    0     VIEW
    0      SORT (ORDER BY STOPKEY)
    0       SORT (GROUP BY)
    0        TABLE ACCESS    GOAL: ANALYZED (BY INDEX ROWID) OF
                 'STOCKSOURCE'
    0         INDEX (RANGE SCAN) OF 'XFK_SS_STOCK' (NON-UNIQUE)
```

Personally, I look at using tracing of any form and TKPROF as a very last resort. The amount of extra tuning information gained from TKPROF output is minimal if SQL code is written properly in the first place. Using TKPROF can be useful in situations where you cannot get at the SQL code. For instance, (1) in situations where all SQL code is embedded in applications code or stored procedures, or (2) where an Oracle database administrator is brought in on a temporary basis, or (3) simply because the database administrator cannot get access to SQL code or there is lack of communication with application developers. Tuning SQL code without any knowledge of the application can be very difficult. I have used TKPROF in the past to examine all trace files available on database servers and produce TKPROF EXPLAIN option-generated query plans for all SQL code. I then passed recommendations on to developers for potential embedded SQL code changes. Before resorting to TKPROF, I found and tuned the worst-performing SQL code statements using other tools and Oracle performance views. Example scripting for performing TKPROF EXPLAIN option query plan analysis for all SQL code executed and recorded in trace files can be found in Appendix B.

Let's go through an example showing tuning using SQL Trace and TKPROF. This is a very nasty join query from a previous chapter:

```
EXPLAIN PLAN SET statement_id='TEST' FOR
SELECT c.name
```

```
FROM customer c JOIN orders o USING(customer_id)
JOIN ordersline ol USING(order_id)
JOIN transactions t USING(customer_id)
JOIN transactionsline tl USING(transaction_id)
WHERE c.balance > 0;
```

This is its query plan. Note the high cost:

Query	Cost	Rows	Bytes
1. SELECT STATEMENT on	**1345027**	#######	########
2. HASH JOIN on	1345027	#######	########
3. TABLE ACCESS FULL on CUSTOMER	16	1795	44875
3. MERGE JOIN on	37726	#######	########
4. SORT JOIN on	18298	#######	########
5. MERGE JOIN on	18298	#######	########
6. SORT JOIN on	16864	934659	9346590
7. MERGE JOIN on	6044	934659	9346590
8. SORT JOIN on	4388	1916444	7665776
9. INDEX FAST FULL SCAN on XFK_TL_TRANSACTION	4388	1916444	7665776
8. SORT JOIN on	1656	166323	997938
9. TABLE ACCESS FULL on TRANSACTIONS	556	166323	997938
6. SORT JOIN on	1434	165116	990696
7. TABLE ACCESS FULL on ORDERS	344	165116	990696
4. SORT JOIN on	19428	1887096	7548384
5. TABLE ACCESS FULL on ORDERSLINE	1518	1887096	7548384

Here is a tuned version of the same query:

```
EXPLAIN PLAN SET statement_id='TEST' FOR
SELECT c.name FROM customer c
WHERE c.balance > 0
AND EXISTS(
        SELECT o.order_id FROM orders o
        WHERE o.customer_id = c.customer_id
        AND EXISTS(
            SELECT order_id FROM ordersline
            WHERE order_id = o.order_id
        )
)
AND EXISTS(
SELECT t.transaction_id FROM transactions t
WHERE t.customer_id = c.customer_id
AND EXISTS(
```

```
              SELECT transaction_id FROM transactionsline
      WHERE transaction_id = t.transaction_id
      )
      );
```

Here is the query plan for the tuned version of the query. This tuned version is more than 500 times less in cost. That is quite a difference:

```
Query                                                  Cost      Rows     Bytes
---------------------------------------------------  --------- -------- ---------
1. SELECT STATEMENT  on                                2228         4       100
2.  FILTER  on
3.   TABLE ACCESS FULL on CUSTOMER                       16         4       100
3.   NESTED LOOPS  on                                   271       700      7000
4.    TABLE ACCESS BY INDEX ROWID on ORDERS              29       121       726
5.     INDEX RANGE SCAN on XFK_O_CUSTOMER                 1        61
4.    INDEX RANGE SCAN on XFK_OL_ORDERS                   2         6        24
3.   NESTED LOOPS  on                                   282       711      7110
4.    TABLE ACCESS BY INDEX ROWID on TRANSACTIONS        28       127       762
5.     INDEX RANGE SCAN on XFK_T_CUSTOMER                 1        62
4.    INDEX RANGE SCAN on XFK_TL_TRANSACTION              2         6        24
```

Now let's use SQL Trace and TKPROF to show what changed when tuning this query. Here is the query not tuned:

```
EXPLAIN PLAN SET statement_id='TEST' FOR
SELECT c.name
FROM customer c JOIN orders o USING(customer_id)
JOIN ordersline ol USING(order_id)
JOIN transactions t USING(customer_id)
JOIN transactionsline tl USING(transaction_id)
WHERE c.balance > 0
```

```
call     count   cpu    elapsed      disk   query   current      rows
-------  ------  ----  ----------  -------- -------- --------  ----------
Parse        1  0.52       1.20          0      818        0           0
Execute      1  0.09       0.09          0       24        0           0
Fetch        0  0.00       0.00          0        0        0           0
-------  ------  ----  ----------  -------- -------- --------  ----------
total        2  0.61       1.30          0      842        0           0
```

Misses in library cache during parse: 1

```
Optimizer goal: CHOOSE
Parsing user id: 84  (ACCOUNTS)

Rows    Row Source Operation
----    --------------------------------------------------
   0  HASH JOIN
   0   TABLE ACCESS FULL CUSTOMER
   0   MERGE JOIN
   0    SORT JOIN
   0     MERGE JOIN
   0      SORT JOIN
   0       MERGE JOIN
   0        SORT JOIN
   0         INDEX FAST FULL SCAN XFK_TL_TRANSACTION (object id 34989)
   0        SORT JOIN
   0         TABLE ACCESS FULL TRANSACTIONS
   0       SORT JOIN
   0        TABLE ACCESS FULL ORDERS
   0      SORT JOIN
   0       TABLE ACCESS FULL ORDERSLINE
```

Here is the tuned version of the query:

```
EXPLAIN PLAN SET statement_id='TEST' FOR
SELECT c.name FROM customer c
WHERE c.balance > 0
AND EXISTS(
  SELECT o.order_id FROM orders o
  WHERE o.customer_id = c.customer_id
  AND EXISTS(
   SELECT order_id FROM ordersline
   WHERE order_id = o.order_id
  )
)
AND EXISTS(
SELECT t.transaction_id FROM transactions t
WHERE t.customer_id = c.customer_id
AND EXISTS(
   SELECT transaction_id FROM transactionsline
WHERE transaction_id = t.transaction_id
 )
```

)

call	count	cpu	elapsed	disk	query	current	rows
Parse	1	0.02	0.01	0	0	0	0
Execute	1	0.03	0.02	0	0	0	0
Fetch	0	0.00	0.00	0	0	0	0
total	2	**0.05**	**0.04**	0	**0**	0	0

Misses in library cache during parse: 1
Optimizer goal: CHOOSE
Parsing user id: 84 (ACCOUNTS)

Rows	Row Source Operation
0	FILTER
0	TABLE ACCESS FULL CUSTOMER
0	NESTED LOOPS
0	TABLE ACCESS BY INDEX ROWID ORDERS
0	INDEX RANGE SCAN XFK_O_CUSTOMER (object id 32584)
0	INDEX RANGE SCAN XFK_OL_ORDERS (object id 32588)
0	NESTED LOOPS
0	TABLE ACCESS BY INDEX ROWID TRANSACTIONS
0	INDEX RANGE SCAN XFK_T_CUSTOMER (object id 32633)
0	INDEX RANGE SCAN XFK_TL_TRANSACTION (object id 34989)

All that is a lot of information. What I want to do is focus on the statistics section produced by SQL Trace and TKPROF. This is the statistics section for the query not tuned:

call	count	cpu	elapsed	disk	query	current	rows
Parse	1	**0.52**	1.20	0	818	0	0
Execute	1	**0.09**	0.09	0	24	0	0
Fetch	0	0.00	0.00	0	0	0	0
total	2	**0.61**	**1.30**	0	**842**	0	0

Shown next is the statistics section for the query tuned:

call	count	cpu	elapsed	disk	query	current	rows
Parse	1	**0.02**	0.01	0	0	0	0
Execute	1	**0.03**	0.02	0	0	0	0
Fetch	0	0.00	0.00	0	0	0	0
total	2	**0.05**	**0.04**	0	**0**	0	0

Obviously, we can see that both CPU usage and elapsed times have decreased substantially. Parse time is substantially decreased, and execute time is decreased to a lesser degree. The different ratios are less distinct than the cost differences for the query plans. This probably implies that the query plan is not accurate. This could be something related to statistics. Parse time is reduced because fewer rows are accessed, and probably less SQL code library cache is being used. The execution time is decreased because fewer rows are retrieved, and thus the query is reading less physical space. In short, the tuned query is a lot faster.

The only point to note in the case of tuning this query with SQL Trace and TKPROF is that the query was tuned in a previous chapter just by recoding the SQL statement more efficiently. The extreme of utilizing SQL Trace and TKPROF was not required to tune this SQL code statement. Additionally, in examining this TKPROF output, there is much detailed information provided, but there is no information about how to tune the SQL code. It does not tell you how to make the query better, only that there might be a problem. You still have to manually change the coding by hand.

Leaving SQL Trace on for extended periods of time can allow gathering of large amounts of analyzable trace files. However, tracing will affect performance drastically, so it is better switched off when not being used. Trace files can also use a lot of disk space over time.

12.4 ⑩ TRCSESS

The TRCSESS utility is new to Oracle Database 10*g* and can be used to amalgamate information from multiple trace files, all into a single output file. This is based on grouping criteria such as a session or a database, among other factors. This utility is useful in several ways, especially in a shared-server environment, merging information about one specific session from multiple trace files. In a shared-server environment, a single trace file can be shared by multiple sessions, or a single session can have tracing information written to multiple trace files. The TRCSESS utility can be used to merge tracing entries from a single session into a single trace file.

All the TRCSESS utility does essentially is to find multiple trace files and merge them into a single file. That file can then be passed through a formatting utility such as TKPROF to make that output more easily readable. Using the TRCSESS utility is self-explanatory. Examine all options by retrieving the help screen in a shell as follows:

```
trcsess help=y
```

12.4.1 (10g) **End-to-End Tracing**

End-to-end tracing is simply the use of the TRCSESS utility to track a user activity, across a multiple-tiered environment, from the client application, through to the database server. An Oracle database can use a shared-server configuration, or if some type of middle tier (application or Web server) is in use, sharing of database processes between multiple user sessions. The result in this situation is that a single session can have tracing activity recorded in multiple trace files. As already discussed, the TRCSESS utility can be used to extract the chunks of tracing activity from multiple trace files into individual files based on several criteria, as follows:

- *Client ID*. The login name
- *Session ID*. A session identifier exists for the life of a database connection
- *Instance*. Multiple instance environments
- *Service*. A grouping of applications
- *Module*. A subset of an application
- *Action*. Some type of database event

End-to-end tracing can be accomplished very easily using the Database Control. Select the Performance tab, and find the Top Consumers at the bottom left of the page. Then you can select to merge tracing information based on any of the links across the top of the page. This tool is very useful, as shown in Figure 12.1.

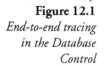

Figure 12.1
*End-to-end tracing
in the Database
Control*

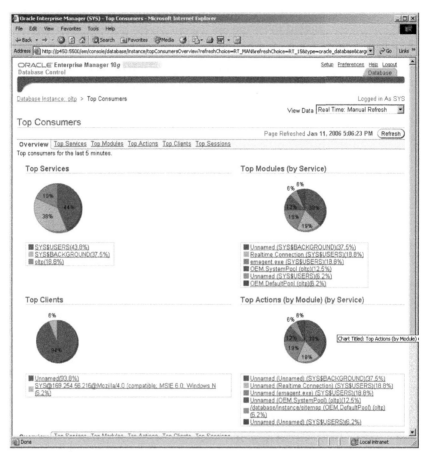

12.5 Autotrace

The AUTOTRACE command is a SET command option in SQL*Plus. Every SQL statement issued in SQL*Plus can get some of the information that can be found using SQL Trace, TKPROF, and the EXPLAIN PLAN command. The syntax for AUTOTRACE is as follows:

```
SET AUTOTRACE { OFF | ON EXPLAIN | ON STATISTICS | ON |
TRACEONLY }
```

I find that if I am using AUTOTRACE, I should probably be using the TRACEONLY option, which suppresses a display of returned rows. Also,

AUTOTRACE will not function without the PLAN_TABLE in place. Here is an example of what AUTOTRACE produces in SQL*Plus:

```
SET AUTOTRACE TRACEONLY;
SELECT coa.coa#, coa.text, SUM(gl.dr + gl.cr)
FROM coa JOIN generalledger gl ON(coa.coa# = gl.coa#)
WHERE coa.type = 'A'
GROUP BY coa.coa#, coa.text;


Execution Plan
-----------------------------------------------------------
    0       SELECT STATEMENT Optimizer=CHOOSE (Cost=420 Card=139 Bytes=7
    1    0    SORT (GROUP BY) (Cost=420 Card=139 Bytes=7784)
    2    1      TABLE ACCESS (BY INDEX ROWID) OF 'GENERALLEDGER' (Cost=2
    3    2        NESTED LOOPS (Cost=30 Card=66243 Bytes=3709608)
    4    3          TABLE ACCESS (FULL) OF 'COA' (Cost=2 Card=14 Bytes=3
    5    3          INDEX (RANGE SCAN) OF 'XFK_COA#' (NON-UNIQUE) (Cost=


Statistics
-----------------------------------------------------------
        0  recursive calls
        0  db block gets
     4876  consistent gets
        0  physical reads
        0  redo size
      565  bytes sent via SQL*Net to client
      499  bytes received via SQL*Net from client
        2  SQL*Net roundtrips to/from client
        1  sorts (memory)
0  sorts (disk)
rows processed
```

Autotrace can be useful, but its formatting is not my personal preference. It's a side issue, but using Oracle Database 10.2.0.1.0, I got an error when attempting to execute the command SET AUTOTRACE ON; in SQL*Plus. The STATISTICS_LEVEL parameter was set to ALL. I got a role enable error:

```
SQL> set autotrace on;
SP2-0618: Cannot find the Session Identifier.  Check
PLUSTRACE role is enabled
```

```
SP2-0611: Error enabling STATISTICS report
SQL> show parameters
ORA-00942: table or view does not exist
```

- The error disappeared when setting the STATISTICS_LEVEL parameter to TYPICAL:

```
ALTER SYSTEM SET statistics_level = TYPICAL;
```

12.6 Oracle Database Performance Views for Tuning SQL

Most performance views are applicable to physical and configuration tuning and are covered in Part III. Additionally, the Oracle Database Wait Event Interface , which utilizes the SQL code views described here, is covered in Part III.

Note: A thorough analysis and demonstration of the Wait Event Interface is included at the end of this book, because the Wait Event Interface uses details covered in both the second and third parts.

Four views are examined in this section: V$SQLAREA, V$SQL, V$SQLTEXT, and V$SQL_PLAN. These performance views can be used to find poorly performing queries. Once again, most of the problems that can be highlighted with these performance views should not exist if SQL code is properly built in the first place. This is as described in previous chapters and reiterated in this chapter. The first three of these performance views access SQL statements parsed and resident in the SGA library cache. V$SQL_PLAN contains currently cached query execution plans or actual execution plans.

12.6.1 Finding Cached SQL Code

- *V$SQLAREA*. Contains part of the text of each SQL query up to 1,000 characters, plus a lot of statistics. Interesting columns in this performance view are the following:

  - SQL_TEXT
  - SORTS
  - FETCHES

- EXECUTIONS
- LOADS
- PARSE_CALLS
- DISK_READS
- BUFFER_GETS
- ROWS_PROCESSED

- *V$SQL*. This view is similar to V$SQLAREA except with more statistics and without aggregation on rows as in V$SQLAREA. Interesting columns in this performance view in addition to that in V$SQLAREA are as follows:

  - OPTIMIZER_COST
  - CPU_TIME
  - ELAPSED_TIME

- *V$SQLTEXT*. Contains the entire SQL query text divided up into separate rows of 64 characters each.

Note: Much of the statistical information in these previous three performance views is part of physical and configuration tuning and is covered in Part III, if appropriate. Additionally, a lot of the information that can be gathered from these performance views can be retrieved using SQL Trace and TKPROF, among various other tools, especially Oracle Enterprise Manager and the Database Control.

- *V$SQL_PLAN*. Cached execution plans of recently executed SQL statements can be viewed using the V$SQL_PLAN performance view. The EXPLAIN PLAN command generates potential query plans into the PLAN_TABLE. On the contrary, the V$SQL_PLAN view contains actual query execution plans for recently executed SQL statements. Three other related performance views are V$SQL_PLAN_STATISTICS, V$SQL_PLAN_STATISTICS_ALL, and the V$SQL_WORKAREA queries.

12.6.1.1 Examining SQL Code

Let's start with V$SQLAREA. I could hook from V$SQLAREA into currently active Accounts schema sessions, but I am not doing that because the queries become horrendously complicated. This information is reserved for an examination of the Oracle Database Wait Event Interface in Part III. At this stage, we will focus on SQL code issues exclusively. Find SQL text for a particular user as follows:

```
SELECT * FROM v$sqlarea WHERE parsing_user_id =
(SELECT user_id FROM dba_users WHERE username = 'ACCOUNTS');
```

Now we could retrieve specific columns and sort in descending order to get the hardest-hitting SQL code statements listed first. Quite often the number of executions is the most significant factor:

```
SELECT executions, disk_reads, buffer_gets, rows_processed,
sorts,
sql_text
FROM v$sqlarea WHERE parsing_user_id =
(SELECT user_id FROM dba_users WHERE username = 'ACCOUNTS')
ORDER BY executions DESC;
```

The V$SQL performance view gives us some slightly different information. The following query is sorted in decreasing optimizer cost order:

```
SELECT sa.rows_processed, s.optimizer_cost, s.cpu_time,
s.elapsed_time,
sa.sql_text
FROM v$sqlarea sa, v$sql s
WHERE sa.parsing_user_id =
(SELECT user_id FROM dba_users WHERE username = 'ACCOUNTS')
AND s.sql_text = sa.sql_text
ORDER BY s.optimizer_cost DESC;
```

Now let's join the V$SQLAREA and V$SQLTEXT views to retrieve the entire SQL code text string for each SQL code statement in V$SQLAREA. We will also include some data, the first five rows:

```
SELECT * FROM(
SELECT st.sql_text
FROM v$sqlarea sa, v$sqltext st
WHERE sa.hash_value = st.hash_value AND sa.address = st.address
AND sa.parsing_user_id =
(SELECT user_id FROM dba_users WHERE username = 'ACCOUNTS')
ORDER BY st.hash_value, st.address, st.piece)
WHERE ROWNUM <= 5;
```

```
SQL_TEXT
-----------------------------------------------------------------
INSERT into stockmovement values(stockmovement_seq.nextval,:b4,(
:b3*-1),:b2,:b1)    returning stockmovement_id  INTO :b0
INSERT into generalledger values (generalledger_seq.nextval,:b1
      ,ABS(:b2       -:b3         ),0,:b4    )
SELECT transaction_id from transactions where order_id = :b1
```

I can also use the V$SQLTEXT_WITH_NEWLINES view to make the output a little more readable. Again, the first five rows have been included:

```
SELECT * FROM(
SELECT st.sql_text
FROM v$sqlarea sa, v$sqltext_with_newlines st
WHERE sa.hash_value = st.hash_value AND sa.address = st.address
AND sa.parsing_user_id =
   (SELECT user_id FROM dba_users WHERE username = 'ACCOUNTS')
ORDER BY st.hash_value, st.address, st.piece)
WHERE ROWNUM <= 5;
```

```
SQL_TEXT
-----------------------------------------------------------------
INSERT into stockmovement values(stockmovement_seq.nextval,:b4,(
:b3*-1),:b2,:b1)
SELECT * FROM(
ith_newlines st
ss = st.address
```

12.6.1.2 Hard-Hitting SQL Code

Significant factors for finding poorly performing SQL code include measurements such as rows processed, disk and buffer reads per row, sorts per row, parses per execution, and others. So let's find some simple ratios using the various performance views to find the worst-performing SQL code. Let's start with V$SQLAREA.

12.6.1.2.1 *Using V$SQLAREA*

V$SQLAREA gives us a window into parsing and execution statistics.

12.6.1.2.2 **Executions**

The following query finds the ten queries that are executed the most often:

```
SELECT * FROM (
SELECT executions "Execs", rows_processed "Rows", sql_text
FROM v$sqlarea WHERE parsing_user_id =
(SELECT user_id FROM dba_users WHERE username = 'ACCOUNTS')
ORDER BY executions DESC
) WHERE ROWNUM <= 10;


    Execs     Rows SQL_TEXT
---------- -------- ---------------------------------------------------
    107785   107785 INSERT into cashbookline values(:b3,:b2,:b1)
    107785   107785 INSERT into ordersline values(:b4,:b3,:b2,:b1)
    107785   107782 INSERT into transactionsline values(:b4,:b3,:b2,:b
    107785   107785 INSERT into stockmovement values(stockmovement_seq
     81823    81823 SELECT to_number(to_char(SYSTIMESTAMP,'FF3'))+1 fr
     53909    53909 SELECT systimestamp FROM sys.dual
     34208        0 COMMIT
     32391    32391 INSERT into generalledger values (generalledger_se
     32391    32391 INSERT into generalledger values (generalledger_se
     22438    22438 INSERT into cashbookline values(:b3,:b2,(:b1*-1))
```

12.6.1.2.3   Disk + Buffer Reads per Row

This query looks at highest data access queries:

```
SELECT * FROM(
SELECT ROUND((disk_reads + buffer_gets)/rows_processed) "Reads/Row"
,disk_reads + buffer_gets "Reads"
,rows_processed "Rows", sql_text
FROM v$sqlarea WHERE parsing_user_id =
(SELECT user_id FROM dba_users WHERE username = 'ACCOUNTS')
AND rows_processed > 0 AND (disk_reads + buffer_gets) > 0
ORDER BY ROUND((disk_reads + buffer_gets)/rows_processed) DESC
) WHERE ROWNUM <= 10;


 Reads/Row      Reads     Rows SQL_TEXT
---------- ---------- -------- ---------------------------------------------------
      9971      29912        3 select count(*) from generalledger
      5562       5562        1 select min(id),min(parent_id) from v$sq
      5265       5265        1 select count(*) from v$sql_plan
      1330       3991        3 SELECT TRIM(LEVEL)||'. '||LPAD (' ', LE
      1325       3974        3 SELECT TRIM(LEVEL)||'. '||LPAD (' ', LE
      1310       3929        3  select p.operation, p.options, p.objec
```

```
1308      3925        3 SELECT TRIM(LEVEL)||'. '||LPAD (' ', LE
1303      3909        3  select s.sql_text, p.operation, p.opti
 897   3719117      4148 SELECT min(order_id),max(order_id) from
 841  14626647     17386 DECLARE job BINARY_INTEGER := :job; nex
```

12.6.1.2.4 Rows per Sort

Fewer rows per sort may indicate a lack of indexing, lack of use of indexes, or superfluously ordered SQL code statements. That's too much sorting!

```
SELECT * FROM(
SELECT ROUND(rows_processed/sorts) "Rows/Sort"
    ,rows_processed "Rows"
    ,Sorts "Sorts", sql_text
FROM v$sqlarea WHERE parsing_user_id =
    (SELECT user_id FROM dba_users WHERE username = 'ACCOUNTS')
AND rows_processed > 0 AND sorts > 0
ORDER BY ROUND(rows_processed/sorts) ASC
) WHERE ROWNUM <= 10;
```

Rows/Sort	Rows	Sorts	SQL_TEXT
1	15616	31232	SELECT a.supplier_id, a.price from (
1	3	3	SELECT (disk_reads + buffer_gets)/row
2	3	2	select p.operation, p.options, p.objec
2	3	2	select s.sql_text, p.operation, p.opti
2	27	12	SELECT * FROM (SELECT executions, rows
3	10	4	SELECT * FROM(SELECT ROUND((sorts)/r
3	10	4	SELECT * FROM (SELECT ROUND(parse_cal
3	10	4	SELECT * FROM (SELECT ROUND(fetches/r
3	20	8	SELECT * FROM (SELECT ROUND(buffer_ge
3	10	4	SELECT * FROM (SELECT ROUND((buffer_g

12.6.1.2.5 Rows per Fetch

The fewer rows fetched for each fetch, the worse the performance. We are looking for problems, not successes:

```
SELECT * FROM (
SELECT ROUND(rows_processed/fetches) "Rows/Fetch"
    ,rows_processed "Rows", fetches "Fetches", sql_text
FROM v$sqlarea WHERE parsing_user_id =
```

```
      (SELECT user_id FROM dba_users WHERE username = 'ACCOUNTS')
AND rows_processed > 0 AND fetches > 0
ORDER BY ROUND(rows_processed/fetches) ASC
) WHERE ROWNUM <= 10;
```

```
Rows/Fetch     Rows     Fetches SQL_TEXT
---------- --------- ----------- ------------------------------------
         1         2           2 select user from dual
         1         4           4 SELECT USER FROM DUAL
         1     14532       14532 SELECT max(stock_id) from stock
         1         1           1 select count(*) from v$sql_plan
         1        10          16 SELECT job from user_jobs
         1     19060       19060 select SYSDATE+1/86400 from dual
         1         4           4 SELECT DECODE('A','A','1','2') FROM DUA
         1     14532       14532 SELECT max(customer_id) from customer
         1         3           3 select count(*) from generalledger
         1     59213       59213 SELECT systimestamp FROM sys.dual
```

12.6.1.2.6   Parses per Execution

More parsing means that previously parsed SQL code in the shared pool is not being reused efficiently. This can indicate lack of SQL code bind variables. The CURSOR_SHARING parameter SIMILAR or FORCE settings can help:

```
SELECT * FROM (
SELECT ROUND(parse_calls/executions) "Parses/Exec"
,parse_calls "Parses", executions "Execs", sql_text
FROM v$sqlarea WHERE parsing_user_id =
(SELECT user_id FROM dba_users WHERE username = 'ACCOUNTS')
AND parse_calls > 0 AND executions > 0
ORDER BY ROUND(parse_calls/executions) ASC
) WHERE ROWNUM <= 10;
```

```
Parses/Exec     Parses      Execs SQL_TEXT
----------- ---------- ---------- ------------------------------------
          0      17490      54306 SELECT systimestamp FROM sys.dual
          0      13315     108638 INSERT into cashbookline values(:b3,
          0      13315     108638 INSERT into ordersline values(:b4,:b
          0      13315     108638 INSERT into transactionsline values(
          0       2364      22646 INSERT into ordersline values(:b4,:b
          0       2364      22646 INSERT into cashbookline values(:b3,
```

```
0        2364    22646 INSERT into stockmovement values(sto
0         685     3757 INSERT into stockmovement values
0       17490    82425 SELECT to_number(to_char(SYSTIMESTAM
0        2364    22646 INSERT into transactionsline values(
```

12.6.1.2.7 Disk versus Logical Reads

Traditionally, disk I/O is slower than reading data from memory. However, logical memory reads involve CPU and potential cache latch contention overhead, to maintain consistency between multiple sessions accessing the same buffer blocks. Logical versus physical disk reads are known as the Buffer Cache Hit Ratio. Changing this ratio is quite often not a performance solution but more likely a symptom or indication of other potential problems. Try not to take this ratio as seriously as most Oracle Database and Oracle-oriented documentation has described in the past. In the extreme, a greater than 95% Buffer Cache Hit ratio is an unreliable measure of database performance health. More on this topic is discussed in Part III. In general, use any type of ratio as a symptom or an indicator of a possible problem. Do not attempt to tune the ratio, but rather find the problem.

Note: Current research indicates that logical reads are perhaps as little as only 30 times faster than physical reads, not thousands or hundreds of times faster as previously thought.

```
COLUMN bchr HEADING "Buffer Cache Hit Ratio" FORMAT a24;
SELECT * FROM (
SELECT ROUND((buffer_gets/(buffer_gets+disk_reads))*100)||'%' AS bchr
    ,sql_text
FROM v$sqlarea WHERE parsing_user_id =
    (SELECT user_id FROM dba_users WHERE username = 'ACCOUNTS')
AND buffer_gets > 0 AND disk_reads > 0
ORDER BY ROUND((buffer_gets / (buffer_gets + disk_reads))*100) ASC
) WHERE ROWNUM <= 10;


Buffer Cache Hit Ratio   SQL_TEXT
-----------------------   ---------------------------------------------
29%                       SELECT * FROM ( SELECT  ROUND(buffer_gets / (
30%                       SELECT * FROM ( SELECT  ROUND((buffer_gets /
31%                       SELECT * FROM ( SELECT  ROUND(fetches/rows_pr
31%                       SELECT * FROM ( SELECT  ROUND(parse_calls/exe
32%                       SELECT sa.rows_processed, s.optimizer_cost, s
```

```
32%                           SELECT * FROM ( SELECT executions "Execs", ro
33%                           SELECT * FROM ( SELECT  ROUND((buffer_gets /
33%                           SELECT * FROM ( SELECT executions, rows_proce
33%                           SELECT * FROM ( SELECT executions, rows_proce
33%                           SELECT * FROM ( SELECT  ROUND((disk_reads + b
```

12.6.1.2.8 *Using V$SQL*

Now let's use V$SQL to look at optimizer cost, CPU, and elapsed time.

12.6.1.2.9 Optimizer Cost

```
SELECT * FROM(
SELECT s.optimizer_cost "Cost", sa.rows_processed "Rows", sa.sql_text
FROM v$sqlarea sa, v$sql s
WHERE sa.parsing_user_id =
    (SELECT user_id FROM dba_users WHERE username = 'ACCOUNTS')
AND s.sql_text = sa.sql_text
ORDER BY s.optimizer_cost DESC
) WHERE ROWNUM <= 10;


    Cost     Rows SQL_TEXT
--------- -------- -------------------------------------------------
    2019     4160 INSERT into stockmovement values      (:b5,:b4,:b3,:
    2019   122208 INSERT into stockmovement values(stockmovement_seq.
    2019    25474 INSERT into stockmovement values(stockmovement_seq.
    1677    36755 INSERT into generalledger values (generalledger_seq
    1677     7394 INSERT into generalledger values (generalledger_seq
    1677    36755 INSERT into generalledger values (generalledger_seq
    1677     7394 INSERT into generalledger values (generalledger_seq
    1540    25474 INSERT into transactionsline values(:b4,:b3,(:b2*-1
    1540   122205 INSERT into transactionsline values(:b4,:b3,:b2,:b1
    1518    25474 INSERT into ordersline values(:b4,:b3,(:b2*-1),:b1)
```

12.6.1.2.10 CPU Time

```
SELECT * FROM(
SELECT s.cpu_time "CPU", sa.rows_processed "Rows", sa.sql_text
FROM v$sqlarea sa, v$sql s
WHERE sa.parsing_user_id =
    (SELECT user_id FROM dba_users WHERE username = 'ACCOUNTS')
AND s.sql_text = sa.sql_text
ORDER BY s.cpu_time DESC
) WHERE ROWNUM <= 10;
```

```
       CPU     Rows SQL_TEXT
---------- -------- --------------------------------------------------
5216000189    19747 DECLARE job BINARY_INTEGER := :job; next_date DATE
2578878295     4689 SELECT min(order_id),max(order_id) from orders
 310826983   122566 INSERT into transactionsline values(:b4,:b3,:b2,:b
 302695184   122573 INSERT into ordersline values(:b4,:b3,:b2,:b1)
 297647959    17735 SELECT a.supplier_id, a.price from (   select supp
 260374370   122588 INSERT into stockmovement values(stockmovement_seq
 244912201   122569 INSERT into cashbookline values(:b3,:b2,:b1)
 155974301    15062 INSERT into transactions values(transactions_seq.n
 147301740    15062 INSERT into cashbook values(cheque_seq.nextval,:b3
 100884998    36889 INSERT into generalledger values (generalledger_se
```

12.6.1.2.11   Elapsed Time

```
SELECT * FROM(
SELECT s.elapsed_time "Time", sa.rows_processed "Rows", sa.sql_text
FROM v$sqlarea sa, v$sql s
WHERE sa.parsing_user_id =
   (SELECT user_id FROM dba_users WHERE username = 'ACCOUNTS')
AND s.sql_text = sa.sql_text
ORDER BY s.elapsed_time DESC
) WHERE ROWNUM <= 10;
```

```
      Time     Rows SQL_TEXT
---------- -------- --------------------------------------------------
4.4771E+10    19792 DECLARE job BINARY_INTEGER := :job; next_date DATE
1.7155E+10     4707 SELECT min(order_id),max(order_id) from orders
2809286653    15091 INSERT into transactions values(transactions_seq.n
2739120692   122853 INSERT into transactionsline values(:b4,:b3,:b2,:b
2649237617   122857 INSERT into ordersline values(:b4,:b3,:b2,:b1)
2061587320   122854 INSERT into cashbookline values(:b3,:b2,:b1)
1974169102    15091 INSERT into orders values(orders_seq.nextval,:b3,n
1885794542    17769 SELECT a.supplier_id, a.price from (   select supp
1731725989    36965 INSERT into generalledger values (generalledger_se
1601419096   122865 INSERT into stockmovement values(stockmovement_seq
```

So what was the point of showing all of these different sorted versions of the same query? If you look closely, you might see some patterns. A number of the sections have a lot of INSERT statements. My high-concurrency DBMS_JOBS executed OLTP activity performs copious amounts of INSERT activity. There is also a fair amount of UPDATE and DELETE activity as well. Also, notice some versions of this query have a lot of SELECT activity. DML and particularly INSERT DML activity is obvious in queries dealing with a high number of executions and CPU time. Most of all, the other measurements involve amounts of data found and thus include SELECT statements.

The high INSERT· statement activity begs the following question: Why is INSERT activity using up so many resources? Probably because I am inserting multiple rows into the same blocks in the buffer cache and the database files. This probably involves both index and data spaces. I am probably getting locking problems with contention for buffer and disk blocks. These are called hot blocks. I could resolve these issues by perhaps changing some primary key integer identifier indexes to reverse key indexes. However, this would probably result in my database growing so fast that I would eventually run out of disk space. So for the purposes of maintaining my simulation, I will leave my current configuration the way it is.

12.6.1.3   Examining Cached Query Plans with V$SQL_PLAN

Now let's examine cached query execution plans in V$SQL_PLAN. This performance view is best queried by matching SQL statements from V$SQLAREA or V$SQL views, using the common ADDRESS and HASH_VALUE columns. Using V$SQL_PLAN can be something like this:

```
SELECT TRIM(depth)||'. '||LPAD (' ', depth - 1)||operation
    ||' '||options||' on '||object_name "Query"
   ,cost "Cost"
   ,cardinality "Rows"
   ,bytes "Bytes"
FROMv$sql_plan
ORDER BY address, hash_value, parent_id, id;

Query
---------------------------------------------
0. SELECT STATEMENT   on
1. COUNT STOPKEY on
2.   VIEW  on
3.    SORT ORDER BY STOPKEY on
4.     NESTED LOOPS OUTER on
5.      NESTED LOOPS OUTER on
5.      TABLE ACCESS CLUSTER on USER$
6.       FIXED TABLE FULL on X$KQLFXPL
```

```
6.        TABLE ACCESS BY INDEX ROWID on OBJ$
7.          INDEX UNIQUE SCAN on I_OBJ1
6.          INDEX UNIQUE SCAN on I_USER#
0. SELECT STATEMENT    on
1. NESTED LOOPS OUTER on
2.  NESTED LOOPS OUTER on
2.  TABLE ACCESS CLUSTER on USER$
3.   FIXED TABLE FULL on X$KQLFXPL
3.   TABLE ACCESS BY INDEX ROWID on OBJ$
4.     INDEX UNIQUE SCAN on I_OBJ1
3.    INDEX UNIQUE SCAN on I_USER#
```

That concludes this discussion of how to find problem queries and the tools used to accomplish this task. In the next chapter, we look at how to tune SQL code in Oracle Database using the far more intuitive tools, the Oracle Enterprise Manager and Database Control.

Automated SQL Tuning

In the previous edition of this book, covering Oracle 9i Database (9.2) and Oracle 10*g* Database (10.1), this chapter consisted of a graphical presentation including the Index Tuning Wizard, SQL Analyze, and Oracle Expert. These tools no longer exist in name in Oracle 10*g* Database, version 2 (10.2); today they exist in the form of the SQL Access Advisor. The SQL Access Advisor can be very useful.

Note: The previous version of this chapter has been moved to the appendices for backward compatibility with Oracle 9*i*.

In Oracle 10*g* Database, the front-end tuning tools (all written in Java), except the most basic version of the Oracle Enterprise Manager Console, have been completely removed. This functionality is now placed into the Database Control. This chapter begins with automated SQL tuning. The Database Control is recommended as the interface best suited for managing automated SQL tuning. And therefore this chapter begins the process of examination of the Database Control but focuses on tuning SQL code from within the Database Control.

What is automatic SQL tuning? Automatic SQL tuning, new to Oracle 10*g* Database, enables the optimizer to be switched from normal mode into a tuning mode. That tuning mode can consume large amounts of resources and because of that is largely intended for use only with complicated and long-running queries. Automated SQL tuning can be performed manually using commands executed from within SQL*Plus, but it is recommended to use only the Database Control. Using the Database Control is so much easier.

In general automated SQL tuning involves the following parts:

- Automatic collection of statistics using the Automatic Workload Repository (AWR).

- Automatic performance diagnostics using the Automatic Database Diagnostic Monitor (ADDM).

- Automatic SQL tuning using the SQL tuning advisor, SQL tuning sets, and SQL profiles.

- Data warehouses and materialized view analysis using SQL Access Advisor. [1] Also included in the SQL Access Advisor is the capability to make recommendations on what to change with indexing and materialized views.

13.1   Automatic Gathering of Statistics

Statistics gathering is automated by default in Oracle 10*g* Database using a scheduled job. Find that scheduled job using this query and you should see a GATHER_STATS_JOB listed in the output:

```
SELECT * FROM DBA_SCHEDULER_JOBS;
```

There is nothing complex about this automation process. All you need to do is ensure that the STATISTICS_LEVEL parameter is set to at least TYPICAL, and automated statistics gathering will be performed for you between certain time periods. Some obvious problems could arise:

- If your database is very large, then the default windows of time that Oracle 10*g* has set for statistics gathering may not be sufficient to gather statistics on all of your data.

- Automated statistics is performed between 22h00 and 06h00 on weekdays, as well as over weekends. This can cause two possible problems:

    - If your business is global, your database might need to function equally at all times; thus, gathering of statistics at any time could be a problem.

    - If data in your database changes more frequently than on a daily basis, gathering statistics once a day may not be often enough.

If any of these scenarios occur, you might have to gather statistics manually or disable automated gathering of statistics and implement your own plans. One of the most frequent performance issues occurring with Oracle databases in the past has been the issue of stale or nonexistent statistics. It is surprising how the performance of many Oracle installations are compromised by a lack of statistics, or a lack of frequent enough gathering of statistics. Automated gathering of statistics is intended to tackle this issue.

13.2 The AWR and the ADDM

Essentially the Automatic Workload Repository (AWR) executes statistical snapshots of the database. A snapshot takes a mathematical picture of the state of a database at a specific point in time.

Note: STATSPACK does the same kind of thing.

13.2.1 The AWR

Snapshots are then used by the Automatic Database Diagnostic Monitor (ADDM) to analyze and make assessments.

The AWR can be found in the Database Control, under the Administration tab, under Statistics Management, as shown in Figure 13.1.

Configuring the AWR is really very simple, as shown in Figure 13.2.

The following statistics are gathered by the AWR:

- Objects such as tables and indexes
- (10*g*) Active Session History (ASH) statistics (activity of recent sessions)
- SQL statements causing high impact on resources
- System level statistics in V$SYSSTAT and V$SESSTAT performance views
- (10*g*) V$SYS_TIME_MODEL and V$SESS_TIME_MODEL performance views

Figure 13.1
Finding the AWR

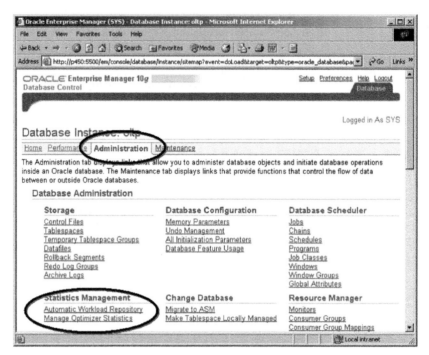

Figure 13.2
Configuring the AWR

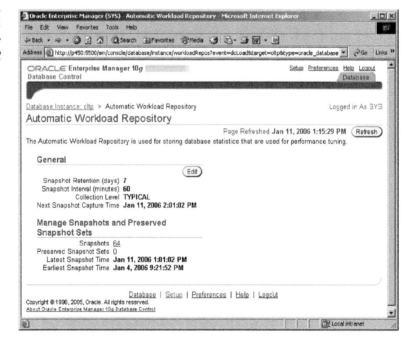

Basically, everything! And it's not difficult to implement—or even that big a deal.

13.2.2 The ADDM

Just like STATSPACK, the ADDM uses multiple snapshots taken by the AWR and then performs an analysis between two snapshots. These are the types of common issues that the ADDM looks for:

The ADDM considers the following types of problems:

- Overextended use of CPU time. This can be for all sorts of reasons.

- Sizing of memory structures. It is rarely sensible to continue increasing buffers, such as the SGA and the database buffer cache. This tends to hide problems temporarily.

- Heavy I/O usage, which in a data warehouse, for instance, is normal.

- High-consumption SQL statements are either those causing problems or those doing a lot of work. Also included here would be PL/SQL and Java code chewing up excessive resources.

- Configuration issues involving file sizing, archives, inappropriate parameter settings, concurrency issues, hot blocking, and locking contention.

- Generally anything that is just very busy.

The ADDM can be found under the Performance tag of the Database Control, as shown in Figure 13.3.

The next step to take is to start up my simulation of high OLTP database activity and let the AWR collect snapshots over a period of time. When I execute the ADDM, it compares a newly generated snapshot with the most recently executed snapshot and produces the result shown in Figure 13.4.

The ADDM report, as shown in Figure 13.4, tells me that there are a few interesting things going on in my database, as is to be expected, which are probably not good:

- SQL statements consuming significant database time were found.

Figure 13.3
Executing the ADDM

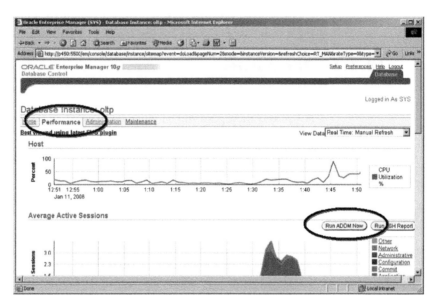

- The throughput of the I/O subsystem was significantly lower than expected.

- The buffer cache was undersized, causing significant additional read I/O.

The report allows me to click on each of the issues, as a link, looking for more detail. Let's take a quick look at the second and third items in the previous list. Figure 13.5 shows the details of the I/O subsystem. My I/O subsystem is an issue because I am running on a geriatric computer with old disks, and there are only two disks. I have no RAID array, I have a single CPU, and I am not using any kind of striping. The only physical separation is a split of the Oracle binaries with my datafiles. I fully expect the ADDM to point this out. Unfortunately, writing books for a living does not bring home very much money, so I have not as yet been able to update my server hardware. However, expensive hardware can also serve a negative purpose by concealing other problems, such as inefficient SQL coding.

Figure 13.6 shows me that my database buffer cache is much too small. I have set my database buffer cache to 32Mb because I am running two other databases on this computer at the same time, in addition to the Database Control. The Database Control consumes tremendous resources.

Figure 13.4
The result of executing the ADDM

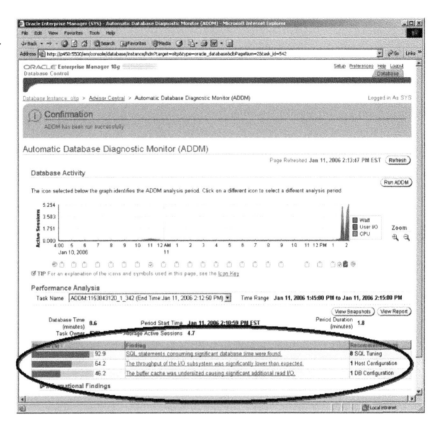

Figure 13.7 shows me that the ADDM is finding significant issues with poorly performing SQL coding in my database. This is interesting.

What I have now done in Figure 13.8 is to click the Hide link for all the SQL statements shown in the ADDM report.

As shown in Figure 13.8, I can run the advisor on each SQL statement and get a recommendation. Figure 13.9 shows the content behind the hardest hitting SQL code in my database at this point in time. This item happens to be the main procedure that executes all my simulation code. I expect this!

Figure 13.10 shows the bottom half of the screen from Figure 13.9. Perhaps the most obvious thing is the pie chart showing sessions waiting to read and write to disk. This goes hand in hand with the I/O subsystem issue shown in Figure 13.5 and the memory issue shown in Figure 13.6. Additionally, my OLTP simulation coding executes multiple jobs every second;

Figure 13.5
ADDM and the
I/O subsystem

Figure 13.6
ADDM and use of
memory

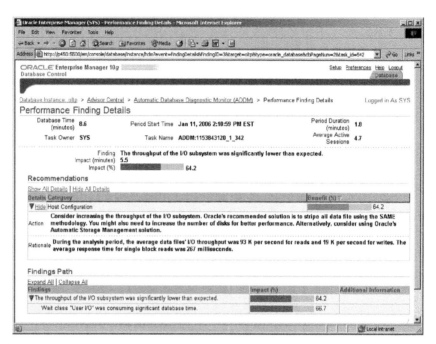

Figure 13.7
ADDM and SQL coding

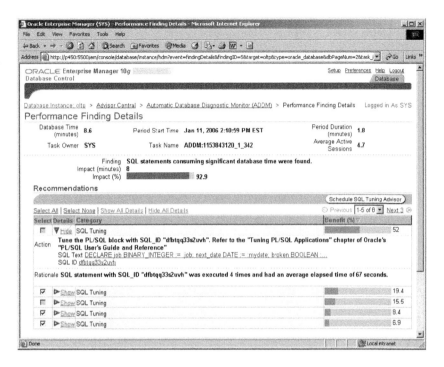

Figure 13.8
ADDM and SQL coding in detail

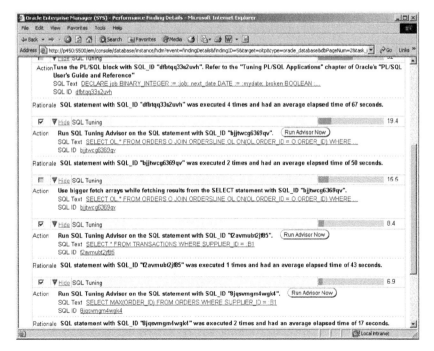

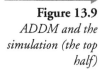

Figure 13.9
*ADDM and the
simulation (the top
half)*

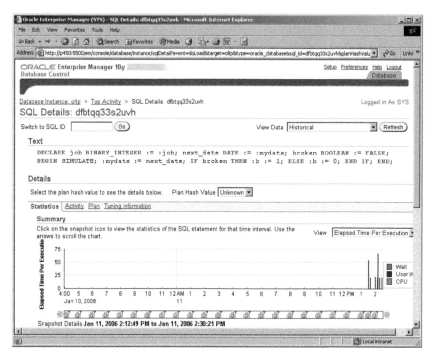

each job runs a slew of both query and DML activity, keeping all resources on my database server very busy indeed.

The next logical step to take is to click each of the links for each of the queries shown in Figure 13.8. Every single query shows me the same problem shown in Figure 13.10, with user session waits for the I/O subsystem at close to 100%.

Before messing with the database buffer cache, I will click the Run Advisor Now button, shown in Figure 13.8, for the second query on the list, just to see what it throws at me. Figure 13.11 shows the result—unfortunately, it does not tell me anything at all.

The next thing to do is to change the database buffer cache by resizing it up to 80Mb. Then I will restart the database and execute my simulation code, while waiting for two more AWR snapshots to be taken—automatically, of course.

So I resized the database buffer cache from 32Mb to 80Mb. I also changed the DB_FILE_MULTIBLOCK_READ_COUNT parameter from 1 to 8. The result of a new ADDM report, with two new snapshots, and my simulation code running again is shown in Figure 13.12.

Figure 13.10
*ADDM and the
simulation (the
bottom half)*

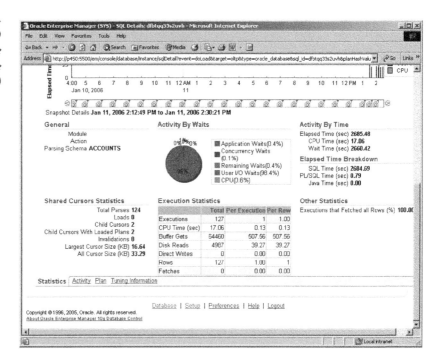

As shown in Figure 13.12, blindly following the recommendations of the ADDM makes the situation worse, which is very interesting. Additionally hard parsing has cropped up with a larger database buffer cache, which is simply irritating because that tells me that the SGA is not big enough as well, or may even be too big. The shared pool is now the same as the database buffer cache, at 80Mb.

Note: Sizing the database buffer cache and shared pool to sizes over 100Mb is common. However, there is much to be said for not sizing these buffers above minimal amounts. Doing so tends to temporarily alleviate problems by hiding them. And the larger a buffer is, the more complex it becomes for Oracle Database to manage. Bigger is not better. You'll find out more about these concepts in Part III of this book.

Essentially my database is overstressed, and it's deliberate. The picture in Figure 13.2 shows me that the performance issues are perhaps now a little more evenly spread among various different things. One very important point to note is that over 70% of the performance issues indicated are caused by SQL statements. Additionally, most of the SQL statements are the same as they were before in Figure 13.8, finding exactly the same prob-

Figure 13.11
ADDM and the simulation (the bottom half)

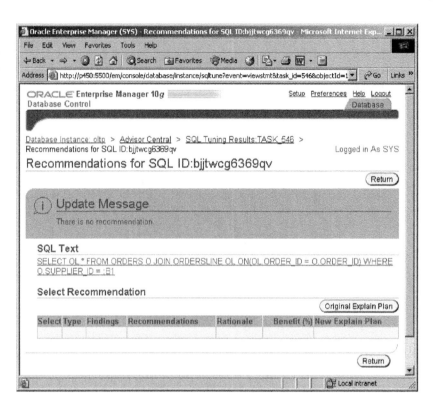

Figure 13.12
Following ADDM recommendations

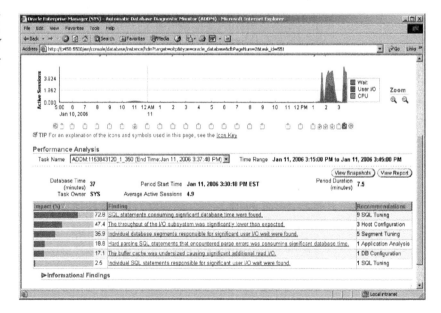

lems. This database is very, very busy. There is a lot of hot blocking activity because too many sessions are trying to share too little data. When I drill down into the segment issues (the third problem area shown in Figure 13.12), I find that indexing is indicated as a problem. Some of this is shown in Figure 13.13. One interesting point shown in Figure 13.13 is that the Rationale commentary shows no full object scans—just a lot of reading. These items show both index and table issues. The Rationale commentary shows everything as 0 full object scans. This means that indexes are being used, and there is no full table scanning or even full index scanning occurring. Perhaps the only thing that could be done would be to rebuild BTree indexes. That might help. It might not. All I am really discovering using this tool is, once again, that my database is really, really busy. That's the idea. It's telling me that my hardware is not capable of handling this level of activity. I already know that.

Figure 13.13
ADDM and indexing

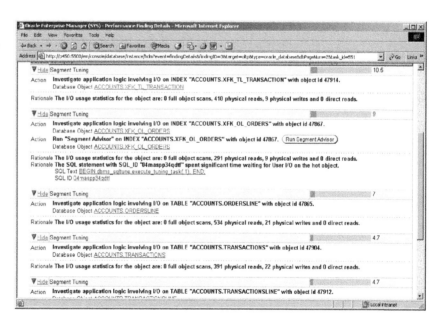

13.3 Automating SQL Tuning

Having dug around in this new stuff for a while, I am so far not seeing anything automated about it. I am seeing automated statistics gathering and automated snapshots (much like STATSPACK did in the past), plus diagnostics. All this is very good and very useful. Where's the automated SQL tuning part?

Essentially the optimizer can be placed into tuning, preferably for really nasty SQL statements, such as those shown by the ADDM. And then it is probably best to examine those statements manually first, just to make sure there is nothing really obviously wrong with them, or right with them.

Automatic SQL tuning uses the SQL tuning advisor, SQL tuning sets, and SQL profiles. More appropriate to a data warehouse and materialized view analysis is the SQLAccess Advisor. It works a little like this:

- **SQL Profiler**. Profiles for SQL statements can be built and stored in the database for specific SQL statements. A profile is little like a Unix profile, in that when a Unix user logs into the operating system, that user gets a slew of settings specific to themselves (similar to all your desktop settings in Windows). Profiles are then reused whenever an SQL statement is executed. So SQL profiles are a little bit like outlines where a query is stored. However, the profiles go one better by allowing changes to the query plan and changes to the profile, based on more up-to-date statistics.

- **SQL Tuning set**. Tuning sets contain groups of SQL statements, where each tuning set has its own statistical context. It's a little like grouping queries for specific applications. You can then use those SQL tuning sets to help with performance tuning by comparison.

- **SQL Tuning Advisor**. This part of the puzzle takes input from the other two and spits out advice.

The act of automated profiling of SQL statements, along with up-to-date statistics, is like applying hints to SQL code. The overall effect is one of some automation of tuning without actually changing SQL code itself, which would probably scare most database administrators completely silly. SQL profiling would function something akin to adding automated hints into SQL code. Obviously SQL profiles can become outdated, and the furtther displaced the profiles become from that of current statistics, the more likely those profiles should be updated.

The next step is to use the Database Control to go into the Tuning Advisor. The Tuning Advisor can be found under the Home tab, under the Advisor Central link, shown at the bottom of the page on the left. It looks like the picture shown in Figure 13.14.

As you can see there are various links for advice related to segments, undo space, memory usage, and SQL code, among other things. One thing

Figure 13.14
The Tuning
Advisor

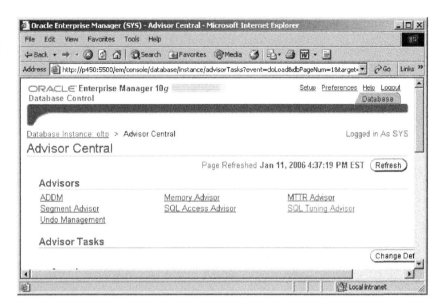

Figure 13.14
The Tuning Advisor

I find very interesting is the two graphs that appear under the Memory Advisor. Both are shown in Figure 13.15.

Figure 13.15 shows that according to both the curves, both buffers are at, if not very close to, their optimal values for the existing architecture and activity on my database server.

The curves on the graphs show that for the shared pool, changing its size upward would enable relatively very little savings in parse times. So the shared pool is set to an almost optimal value. Looking at the curve for the database buffer cache, sizing the database memory segment upward would also make little difference relative to the rest of the curve. This is somewhat contrary to the previous recommendation of sizing the database buffer cache upward even more.

The SQL Tuning Advisor shows a number of links, the most interesting of which is the Top Activity link. This screen, as shown in Figure 13.6, gives me access to the TopSQL and the TopSessions tools.

The top SQL statements shown in the TopSQL tool on the left side of Figure 3.16 are actually queries used by the snapshots executed previously with the AWR and ADDM tools. The TopSQL and TopSessions tools will be examined later in this book in Part IV. It is not really appropriate at this point in this book to describe how these tools are used and what they can be used for. These tools encompass all forms of tuning, including all that is described in Part III.

Figure 13.15
*The Memory
Advisor*

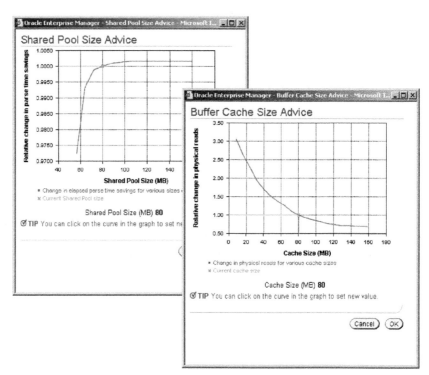

Figure 13.16
*The SQL Tuning
Advisor*

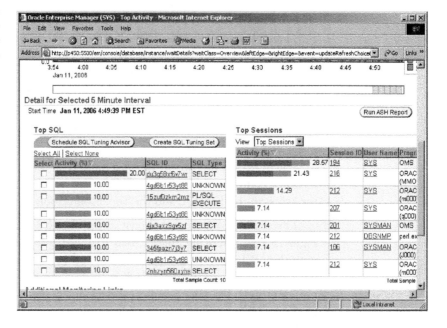

That is about all we can cover on the subject of tuning SQL code using the Database Control without beginning to transgress on physical and configuration tuning—the subject matter of Part III of this book.

Note: Far more detailed discussion about the use of the Database Control will be covered in Part IV. There are a number of reasons for this approach: (1) In Part IV all the parts of tuning a database are put together in one section, (2) I am trying to avoid repetition of the same topics, and (3) I am trying not write a book that has only one single chapter—the idea is to divide everything up into progressively more complex steps, as you read through the book. In other words, I prefer not to throw too much at you all at once.

The next chapter, on physical and configuration tuning, is the first chapter in Part III of this book.

13.4 Endnotes

1.   Oracle Data Warehouse Tuning for 10*g* (Gavin Powell, Digital Press, Aug 2005, ISBN: 1555583350)

Part III
Physical and Configuration Tuning

14

Tuning Oracle Database File Structures

We begin the examination of physical and configuration tuning by looking at a logical architecture of an Oracle database. This chapter will examine the file structure layers of Oracle Database and the logical structures within the Oracle database controlling and utilizing the file structures. An Oracle database in its simplest form is made up of files stored in the file system of an operating system such as Unix, Linux, or Windows. The management, control, and linkage of all those files together are what is called the Oracle Instance. The Oracle Instance is effectively an instantiation on a server of the shared global area (the memory structures) plus a number of processes.

14.1 Oracle Database Architecture and the Physical Layer

The architecture of an Oracle installation could be called the physical layer of an Oracle database. Architecturally speaking, as we already know, Oracle Database is made up of the Oracle Instance and Oracle database files. The Instance contains the running Oracle binary software, and the database files contain the data for the Oracle Instance to access. Database files reside in the file system of the operating system.

14.1.1 The Oracle Instance

The Oracle Instance is the part of Oracle Database sitting resident in memory when an Oracle database is active and available for use. That instantiation of Oracle Database is made up of processes or programs and reserved memory buffer cache areas.

14.1.1.1   **Buffers**

Most of the aspects of tuning memory buffer cache areas are discussed in Chapter 17. The different buffers are shown in Figure 14.1.

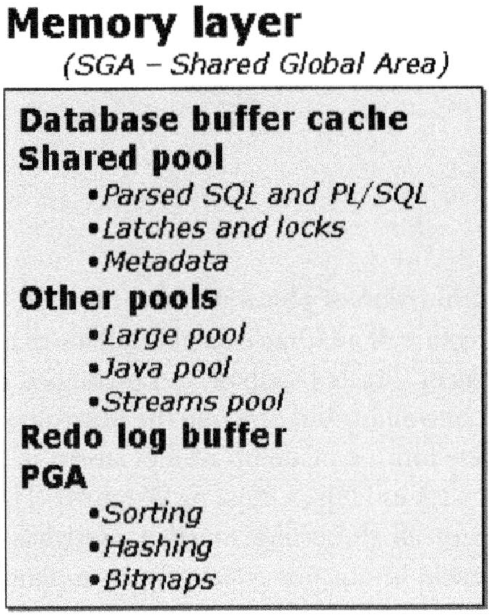

Figure 14.1
*Oracle Instance
memory cache
buffers*

Memory layer
(SGA – Shared Global Area)

Database buffer cache
Shared pool
  • *Parsed SQL and PL/SQL*
  • *Latches and locks*
  • *Metadata*
Other pools
  • *Large pool*
  • *Java pool*
  • *Streams pool*
Redo log buffer
PGA
  • *Sorting*
  • *Hashing*
  • *Bitmaps*

14.1.1.2   **Processes**

Nothing can be done to speed up a process itself by changing anything in Oracle Database. However, Oracle processes can be examined at the operating system level to perhaps help determine the source of other problems. For instance, enormous amounts of I/O or CPU time could show various potential bottlenecks. In other words, a process itself is not tunable—only factors the process is affecting, or being affected by, are tunable. Building on Figure 14.1 the diagram in Figure 14.2 shows some of the Oracle processes plus the previous picture of the Oracle Instance.

There are a multitude of utilities in operating systems such as Unix and Linux that can be used to detect problems with processes. Some of those utilities available on a Solaris flavor Unix box are as follows:

■ *top*. This utility shows a real-time picture of processes, CPU, and memory usage:

```
last pid: 15713; load averages: 0.01, 0.01, 0.01
```

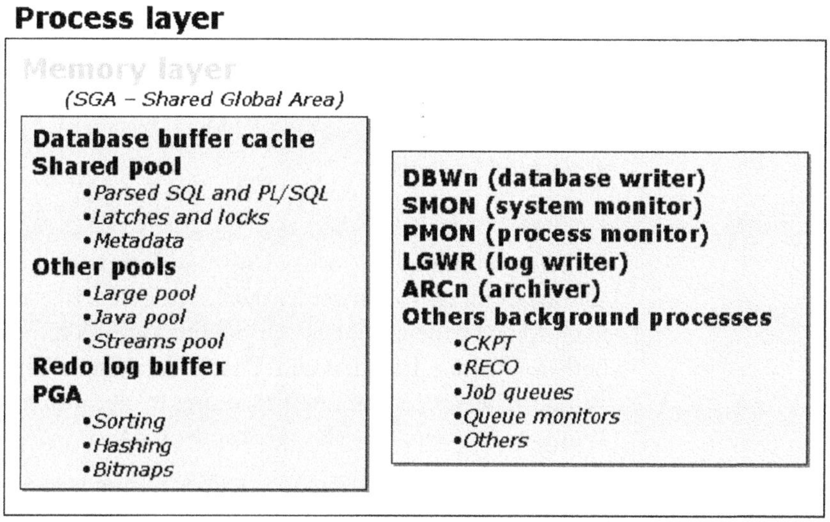

Figure 14.2
*Oracle Instance
process and
memory layers*

Process layer

Memory layer

(SGA – Shared Global Area)

Database buffer cache
Shared pool
  •*Parsed SQL and PL/SQL*
  •*Latches and locks*
  •*Metadata*
Other pools
  •*Large pool*
  •*Java pool*
  •*Streams pool*
Redo log buffer
PGA
  •*Sorting*
  •*Hashing*
  •*Bitmaps*

DBWn (database writer)
SMON (system monitor)
PMON (process monitor)
LGWR (log writer)
ARCn (archiver)
Others background processes
  •*CKPT*
  •*RECO*
  •*Job queues*
  •*Queue monitors*
  •*Others*

```
58 processes:  57 sleeping, 1 on cpu
CPU states: 99.7% idle,0.0% user,0.3% kernel,0.0% iowait,0.0% swap
Memory: 1024M real, 34M free, 598M swap in use, 2263M swap free
```

PID	USERNAME	THR	PRI	NICE	SIZE	RES	STATE	TIME	CPU	COMMAND
15713	oracle	1	58	0	2136K	1664K	cpu0	0:00	0.08%	top
1732	build	26	58	0	195M	60M	sleep	5:45	0.05%	java
14478	user1	25	58	0	182M	40M	sleep	1:08	0.01%	java
15711	root	1	58	0	2152K	1728K	sleep	0:00	0.00%	sendmail
127	root	1	58	0	3208K	2672K	sleep	0:38	0.00%	in.named
235	root	1	58	0	1752K	1056K	sleep	0:20	0.00%	sshd1
9259	oracle	1	58	0	9144K	4544K	sleep	0:18	0.00%	tnslsnr
14829	user2	22	58	0	50M	25M	sleep	0:03	0.00%	java
14950	user2	21	0	0	46M	19M	sleep	0:01	0.00%	java
1609	build	20	0	0	167M	18M	sleep	0:01	0.00%	java
179	root	8	52	0	2376K	1944K	sleep	0:01	0.00%	nscd
143	daemon	4	44	0	2184K	1568K	sleep	0:00	0.00%	statd
138	root	1	48	0	2008K	1584K	sleep	0:00	0.00%	inetd
231	root	1	48	0	2096K	1552K	sleep	0:00	0.00%	sendmail

■ *sar.* The System Activity Reporter examines CPU, swapping, paging, memory, and buffer usage for specified time periods.

- *sadc*. Server activity statistics collection examines CPU, buffers, I/O, switching, system calls, file access, queues, and IPCs, among other things.

- *vmstat*. Virtual memory statistics.

- *iostat*. I/O statistics.

There are numerous other Unix and Linux utilities and tools for doing all sorts of things to inspect hardware resource usage at the operating system level. Most of these utilities can provide clues as to performance problems, both for Oracle Instance and Oracle databases. What can be done on a Windows server to examine processing in the way that Unix utilities can? Windows Performance Manager can be used.

Within the Oracle database itself, operating system level statistics can be found in the V$SYSSTAT and V$SESSSTAT views. The V$SYSTEM_ EVENT and numerous other related views can be used to track bottlenecks through analysis of wait events, the Oracle Database Wait Event Interface, and the (10g) Database Control. These subjects are covered in some detail in later chapters.

14.1.2   The Oracle Database or File System Layer

An Oracle database is effectively the file system layer in the operating system plus the Oracle Instance. The Instance is an instantiation or execution of Oracle binaries running in memory, comprised of processes and memory buffers. An active and accessible Oracle database is an Oracle database using the Oracle Instance to access Oracle database files, as shown in Figure 14.3.

Figure 14.3 also shows different types of Oracle database files. These types of files are as follows:

- *Datafiles*. These contain all physical data, such as tables, indexes, database metadata, procedural code, and anything stored in the database as accessible or usable by an Oracle database user.

- *Redo logs*. These are transaction records of all database changes.

- *Archive logs*. These are historical copies of recycled redo logs maintaining a complete history of all database change activity.

- *Controlfiles*. These contain pointers to all datafiles and log files used for synchronization between all of those files.

Figure 14.3
The Oracle database and the Oracle Instance

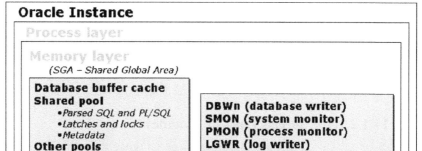

Oracle Database

Oracle Instance

Process layer

Memory layer

(SGA – Shared Global Area)

Database buffer cache
Shared pool
  •*Parsed SQL and PL/SQL*
  •*Latches and locks*
  •*Metadata*
Other pools
  •*Large pool*
  •*Java pool*
  •*Streams pool*
Redo log buffer
PGA
  •*Sorting*
  •*Hashing*
  •*Bitmaps*

DBWn (database writer)
SMON (system monitor)
PMON (process monitor)
LGWR (log writer)
ARCn (archiver)
Others background processes
  •*CKPT*
  •*RECO*
  •*Job queues*
  •*Queue monitors*
  •*Others*

Datafiles   Redo Logs   Archive Logs   Control Files   Config Files

- *Parameter file*. The configuration parameter file provides a Unix-like profile for an Oracle database every time it is started up. A Unix profile is a configuration file used to set parameters for a user every time that user logs onto a Unix computer. This is similar to all the things you see on your desktop when you log into a Windows operating system computer. The parameter file is discussed throughout this book.

14.1.2.1   How Oracle Database Files Fit Together

As already discussed, there are a number of different types of files at the file system level that a running Oracle Instance use to control and gain access to data in the database. Datafiles contain all table and index data. Redo log files contain a record of all transactions or metadata database changes to the database. Redo logs are cyclic such that they are reused. When a redo log file is full, it can be copied to an archive log file. An archive log file is a historical redo log file. The copied redo log file is once again ready for reuse to contain new database activity records.

The most important file in the file system structure of Oracle database files is the controlfile. The controlfile contains pointers to all the datafiles, redo logs, and archived redo logs. The controlfile stores the current time state of a particular datafile by matching up what are called system change numbers (SCNs) between datafiles and log files. An SCN is a sequential number used to synchronize changes between datafiles and redo logs. If SCN values are higher in redo logs than datafiles, then the controlfile knows that datafiles are older versions than they should be. This may happen because the datafiles are recovered backups or because redo log entries, which are always written before datafiles, are updated and the datafiles have not yet been synchronized with the latest changes.

14.1.2.1.1   Special Types of Datafiles

There are a number of special types of datafiles in an Oracle database. These files are the SYSTEM datafile, the ⑩g SYSAUX (metadata auxiliary datafile), undo datafiles, and temporary datafiles. The SYSTEM datafile stores all the metadata or the data about the data.

Note: ⑩g The SYSAUX tablespace is created automatically along with the SYSTEM tablespace when a database is created. The SYSAUX tablespace contains options, Oracle tools, repositories, and even some types of metadata previously stored in the SYSTEM tablespace.

Note: ⑨i Undo datafiles used to be called rollback datafiles. Rollback was manually managed rollback space. Undo is automatically managed by Oracle Database.

Undo datafiles allow for the undoing of certain types of previously processed but uncommitted transactions. Undo entries also cater to the multiuser ability of sessions to *snapshot* data at a specific point in time regardless of changes made by other sessions.

Note: Automatic undo, a much more easily manageable and sophisticated type of rollback, was released in Oracle Database 9*i*. Automated undo allows for the retention of uncommitted as well as already committed data, permitting queries that can flashback, thus providing a snapshot of data at a previous point in time.

Temporary datafiles allow for large sorts to be sorted using disk space when memory resident sort space is used up. Figure 14.4 shows a general map of Oracle database file system structure plus pointer links and flow of data between them.

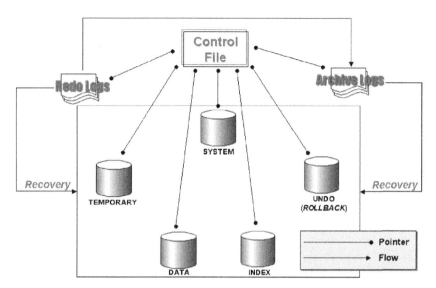

Figure 14.4
*Relationships
between Oracle
database files*

14.1.2.2   Tuning Datafiles

Little can be done to tune datafiles themselves. Most Oracle Database physical tuning with datafiles is performed from the tablespaces overlaying those datafiles. A datafile can have its extent growth parameter changed using the ALTER DATABASE command, and Oracle Partitioning can be implemented.

Note: Any changes to datafiles such as an extent size change using the ALTER DATABASE command will affect only new extents, not existing extent sizes. The same applies to any block changes. Block level tuning will be covered in Chapter 16.

Datafiles can be tuned much more effectively at the file system level in the operating system. Factors such as striping and RAID arrays can help tune datafile I/O access rates enormously. Oracle Partitioning allows the separation of large sets of data into separate datafiles, perhaps placing different partition datafiles onto different disks. Automated Storage Management (ASM) and Oracle Managed Files (OMF) can help and hinder performance. ASM and OMF will be discussed later in this chapter.

Manual striping is a primitive implementation of the functionality of RAID arrays. Striping refers to various methods of splitting datafiles into parts and spreading them across separate storage areas, or even within the same storage area, for rapid random concurrent access.

Note: Separation of table and index tablespaces onto separate disks or even the same disk is a form of striping since the two datafiles underlying the tablespaces are likely to be accessed concurrently due to the nature of their content.

Modern RAID arrays have all sorts of bells and whistles allowing striping, mirroring, Oracle Partitioning, and other aids to speed up I/O, such as dissimilation between sequential and random access. Indexes and log files should be accessed and written sequentially. Tables should be accessed and written randomly, since index scans help to pinpoint table access. This is especially true of OLTP databases.

As already mentioned, Oracle Partitioning allows the splitting of datafile content into separate datafiles. What this means is that a very large table and its associated indexes could be separated into separate datafiles. As far as reading data from the datafile on a heavily striped RAID array, partitioning of datafiles might be irrelevant. Oracle Partitioning certainly is partially irrelevant as far as striping of datafiles onto an already striped RAID array is concerned. However, partitioning of datafiles still has two uses, both of which can have a distinct effect on I/O and processing of datafiles—even on a striped RAID array. First, separate partitions using separate datafiles can be unplugged and plugged into a set of datafiles in a partition set with the speed of a rename command. What this means is that a datafile partition within a large table can be added or removed without accessing any other datafiles in the partition. This leads us to the second datafile I/O benefit of using Oracle Partitioning: SQL code can be executed within the range of a partition datafile, requiring only physical access to the datafile required to satisfy the SQL code. So SQL code reading partitioned datafiles can read single partitions in a set of partitions, reducing I/O rates drastically. This is called partition pruning. Partition pruning can have substantial benefits to performance in very large databases.

14.1.2.3   Controlfiles

The only thing to mention with respect to tuning of controlfiles is that creation of multiple controlfiles is a very sensible practice.

Note: Using multiple controlfiles is known as multiplexing of controlfiles.

Multiple controlfiles stored on separate disks assures that a copy of the controlfile can be recovered should one be lost or become corrupted. The performance effect of multiple controlfiles is negligible. However, utilizing modern RAID arrays makes the chances of corruption very remote.

14.1.2.4   Tuning Redo Logs and Archive Logs

Tuning of redo logs and archived logs is important to Oracle database efficiency. The size of redo logs must be specified when created by a database administrator. Both the number and sizes of redo logs are important.

The more redo logs created for a database there are, the less likely that writing of the redo logs is going to catch up with the archiving process. Let's say, for example, your database has three small redo logs. Heavy transactional activity will rapidly switch the redo logs but the archive process which copies redo logs to the archived log files may not be fast enough to keep up. What happens then is that all database transactional change activity halts until a redo log can be archived and recycled. A redo log will not be recycled if it has not as yet been archived. A halt will occur and effectively stop all database activity until all necessary archiving has completed and a redo log is cleared for reuse.

The same problem can occur if redo logs are too small. With high DML activity, small redo logs can result in excessive switching. A redo log file is switched from CURRENT to ACTIVE (or INACTIVE) when it has filled. If redo log files are too small and a lot of switching is occurring, with high transactional activity, the same situation can occur. Once again the archive process may not be able to keep up, potentially temporarily halting the database.

A similar problem can occur with redo log and archiving performance when redo log files are too large. The archive process copies redo log files to archived log files. Sometimes, especially on Windows systems, very large redo log files can take so long to copy that transactional activity will once again catch up with the archive process. Yet again, the result could be a temporary availability halt. I have seen this large file copying problem occurring on a large Unix-based system, but only once. The redo log files were sized at 500Mb. Yes, they were half a gigabyte. That is much too large for redo log files. The system was highly active and highly concurrent. It had a mixture of OLTP and data warehouse activity (Yoiks!). It also had enormous amounts of CPU time and space wastage as a result of terrible SQL code. Additionally, there were bitmap indexes on transactional tables. This particular system had all sorts of problems. I managed to resolve some of these problems. Unfortunately, this particular startup company then decided to look like it was running out of money. Much to my relief, I was fortunate enough to be able to accept a better job offer elsewhere. This particular company also had a history of database administrators dropping entire production databases by mistake, among other scary things. There was not really much that could be done in this situation. The fact is this: someone had resized the redo logs up to a ridiculous amount in a vague trial-and-error approach while attempting to solve other problems. The result of this kind of experimentation is often further problems. Be warned! Be careful and do not change things (line configuration parameters) without understanding the potential effects first. Additionally, it is also wise to record the state of a database before making changes. Simply writing down changes and making frequent backups can often help to recover from critical situations rapidly, minimizing possible down time.

Let's get back to logging. So what is the best remedy for efficient log writing and archiving of redo logs, to prevent a database from halting or perhaps worse? There is no hard and fast solution. Every database is different. Additionally the size of the redo log buffer can have a profound effect on redo log file writes and archiving performance. There is one important thing to remember: the redo log buffer should not be the same size as the redo log files and should generally be a very small percentage of redo log file size. Redo log buffer tuning is discussed in Chapter 17.

A number of things are important to remember about a redo log buffer flush. The redo log buffer is flushed (or written to the current redo log file) whenever

- A COMMIT or ROLLBACK is issued
- The redo log buffer is partially to one-third full
- Every 3 seconds
- If the redo log reaches 1Mb

Note: There is conflicting information as to what specific circumstances flush the redo log buffer. The points listed here may not be agreed upon by all and even by Oracle documentation. This list covers what I find to be a general consensus of opinion among DBAs.

Note: On the subject of redo log buffer flushing and checkpoints, the following is agreed upon by many DBAs. A checkpoint is a process of flushing dirty buffers from database buffer cache to disk storage. The redo log buffer is not flushed to disk when a checkpoint occurs. This is the consensus of opinion from a number of DBAs and contrary to many Oracle software texts.

So how does the size of the log buffer affect the redo log files? The most common and most successful sizes for the redo log buffer range from 32K to 512K, with occasional sizes as much as 1M. I have seen many databases with problems when the redo log buffer is larger than 512K. Multiple archive processes can help to speed up archiving and alleviate pressure from elsewhere within highly active databases.

Note: Using multiple controlfiles is known as multiplexing of controlfiles.

So what do we do with redo log files? How large should they be, and how many should be created? Should redo logs be duplexed?

Note: Using multiple redo log files within each redo log group is known as duplexing redo log files. Duplexed redo log files are copies of redo log files that are written to simultaneously and in parallel.

Duplexed redo logs are used for the sake of recoverability. Redo log duplexing is not really necessary with the more sophisticated types of RAID arrays; rather, it is extra insurance. Generally, flushing the redo log buffer to duplexed redo logs on servers with more than a single CPU has a negligible impact on performance.

How large should redo log files be and how many should be created? The more transactional activity there is, the more redo logs you should have. If redo logs are continually switching, then make the redo log files a little larger. However, do not make redo log files so large that you get a performance bottleneck when redo logs are switched and copied to archive logs. If redo logs are getting too large, then either add more redo logs or perhaps try to tune other factors, such as the log buffer. In short, tuning of logging is a juggling process between multiple factors. If you must change things, make small changes and observe.

Another potential problem with using very large redo log files can occur when using standby databases. A standby database requires passing of redo log files over SQL*Net. A slow connection between two machines can cause a bottleneck. Perhaps the answer in this case would be to improve your network connection. Changing the SQL*Net packet size can help your standby database log file transfers but may slow network performance for small transactions. If you are operating a fast-response OLTP database through to your customers, changing packet size might not be a prudent solution.

This leads us to the networking layer.

14.1.3   The Networking Layer

Another part of the architecture of Oracle software is the networking layer. Oracle Database has a proprietary networking software layer. This layer of software has multiple names in different versions of Oracle Database. All are the same thing. SQL*Net sits on top of a protocol such as TCP/IP. It allows for easy formatting and access for connections between client machines and an Oracle database server.

Network tuning will be covered in Chapter 18. There is much more to Oracle networking software than just SQL*Net. And contrary to popular opinion, in some circumstances, there is much that can be done to tune Oracle networking software.

14.2 Tuning and the Logical Layer

I like to call anything in an Oracle database above the datafiles the logical layer. This layer is logical in nature because it overlays the underlying physical datafile structure in the operating system (in the file system). The mapping between the physical and logical layers is not necessarily direct or one to one in nature. Figure 14.5 shows a quick picture of the overall structure of both physical and logical Oracle database architecture.

Figure 14.5 shows the various structural layers in an Oracle database.

- *Physical layers*. Segments, extents, and blocks are all contained within a datafile:
  - *Datafiles*. Datafiles contain data, metadata, undo (formerly rollback), sorting space, and clusters, among other things.
  - *Extent*. An extent is a new chunk added to a datafile when the datafile is increased in size in order to accommodate new data.
  - *Block*. A block is the smallest physical structure in an Oracle datafile.

Figure 14.5
Oracle Database physical and logical structure

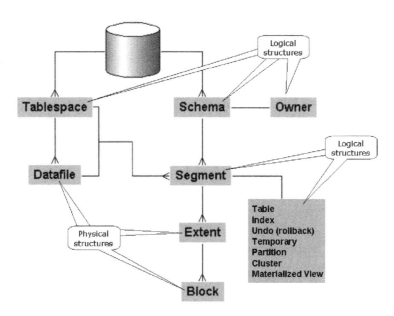

- *Logical layers*. All logical layers, such as tables and indexes, are contained within tablespaces. In addition, all physical layers (the datafiles) are accessible through tablespaces. Thus, datafiles, extents, and blocks are all accessible and tunable through tablespaces and their contained schema objects:

  - *Tablespace*. A tablespace can have many datafiles.
  - *Schema*. A schema is the same thing as an owner or username.
  - *Segment*. A segment can be a part of a tablespace, a datafile, and a schema. Table, index, undo (formerly rollback), temporary, partitions, clusters, and materialized views are all different types of segments.

Now let's examine how we can tune tablespaces.

14.2.1 Tablespaces

A tablespace has a referencing map similar to the map on the boot sector of a hard disk drive. When opening a file on a hard disk drive, the map is accessed in order to find the address at which the file physically begins on the disk. An Oracle tablespace contains a map in the headers of datafiles that describes all extents within underlying datafiles, allowing rapid access to specific addresses in those datafiles. This map of extents can either be stored in database metadata (a dictionary-managed tablespace) or in a bitmap attached to the header of a datafile (a locally managed tablespace). Thus, two different general datafile structures can be created from a tablespace:

- **_Dictionary-managed tablespace_**. Extent and block locations are stored in database metadata. Accessing data from a dictionary-managed tablespace is less efficient because database metadata must be searched internally in Oracle Database, using SQL-type functionality to find addresses of data in datafiles.

Note: Dictionary-managed tablespaces will be deprecated in a future version of Oracle Database.

- **_Locally managed tablespace_**. Extent and block locations are managed by and stored in a bitmap contained within header portions of datafiles, not elsewhere in SYSTEM tablespace metadata. Accessing the extent map of a locally managed tablespace using the file header contained bitmap is much faster than searching through database metadata to find physical addresses of data within a datafile.

Note: (10*g*) Locally managed tablespaces with automatically allocated extents are the default.

Conversion to locally managed tablespaces has been a gradual process in recent versions of Oracle Database. In the latest version of Oracle Database, all tablespaces are created as locally managed tablespaces. As a result, it is probably now safe to assume that locally managed tablespaces have been industry-standard tested and should always be used.

Note: All physical and storage parameters are inherited from datafile to tablespace, and ultimately to all objects created in a tablespace. Many of these structural parameters can be overridden. A tablespace can override datafile parameters. In turn, database objects, such as tables and indexes, can override tablespace parameters.

14.2.1.1 ⑨*i* Dictionary-Managed Tablespaces

PCTINCREASE should be always be explicitly set to zero (0) for any type of tablespace. PCTINCREASE makes each new extent a percentage larger than the previous extent created. The problem with PCTINCREASE is that because each new extent is larger than the previous extent, any extent that has all of its contents completely deleted will probably never be reused. The result is a lot of empty space in a datafile and fragmentation. Fragmentation can be partially resolved by using the COALESCE option of the ALTER TABLESPACE command. Coalescence attempts to take smaller empty extents and merge them into a smaller number of larger extents. On a previous consulting job, I coalesced a number of fragmented tablespaces in order to conserve and defragment space. The result was worse performance and larger datafiles. If you have to use dictionary managed tablespaces, never set PCTINCREASE to anything but zero. The NEXT parameter is used to specify the size of each subsequently created extent. Setting small extent sizes can be used for tablespaces containing only very small tables. It might be better to override the NEXT parameter at the table and index object level. I usually set the size of NEXT in the order of megabytes, such as 1M, depending on potential growth rate.

Do not use dictionary-managed tablespaces, as they will eventually be deprecated from Oracle Database. Locally managed tablespaces have all the useful and well-performing attributes of dictionary tablespaces, with the parameters that are most likely to cause problems disallowed or having no effect. Both the PCTINCREASE and NEXT parameters are ignored for locally managed tablespaces.

Note: Dictionary-managed tablespaces will be deprecated in a future version of Oracle Database. Converting a dictionary-managed tablespace to a locally managed tablespace requires the use of the DBMS_SPACE_ ADMIN package.

14.2.1.2 ⑩*g* Locally Managed Tablespaces

Locally managed tablespaces are better than dictionary-managed tablespace. Two reasons are as follows:

- **No extent map recursion**. A dictionary-managed tablespace stores the locational map of all its extents (physical chunks) inside the SYSTEM tablespace. When searching for a new extent to increase the size of the datafile, a search is done through the SYSTEM table. These searches can become recursive, which can be heavy time and resource consumers. A locally managed tablespace stores its extent map in a bitmap in the header of each datafile in the locally managed tablespace, and there is therefore no recursion into the SYSTEM tablespace. There can, however, be some contention for datafile header bitmaps if concurrent DML activity is extremely heavy. The solution then is to create many datafiles for each locally managed tablespace, dividing up the bitmaps into many small bitmaps, reducing contention.

■ **Automatic coalescence**. Use automatic extent allocation and automatic segment space management when creating locally managed tablespaces. Previously in this chapter, we discussed how the PCTIN-CREASE parameter caused problems with lost space in dictionary-managed tablespaces. Automatic extent allocation and automatic segment space management force the following: (1) active monitoring of free space (2) different extent sizes, (3) automated coalescence of freed up space, even when the extents are of different sizes. Larger extents are more likely to be reused. Wasted extents, as a result of deletion of all data from an entire extent, can cause serious performance problems. As you know from previous chapters, any type of full scan will read all physical parts of a table or index, including extents where all content is deleted.

What are the factors that help in tuning locally managed tablespaces? Let's start with a syntax diagram for the CREATE TABLESPACE command. Certain parts are highlighted:

```
CREATE [ UNDO ] TABLESPACE tablespace
    [ DATAFILE 'file' SIZE n[K|M] [ REUSE ]
        [ AUTOEXTEND { OFF
            | ON [ NEXT n[K|M]
                [ MAXSIZE { UNLIMITED | n[K|M] } ]
]
        } ]
    ]
[ MINIMUM EXTENT n[K|M] ]
    [ BLOCKSIZE n[K] ]
    [ [NO]LOGGING ]
    [ EXTENT MANAGEMENT { DICTIONARY
```

```
      |  LOCAL  [  {  AUTOALLOCATE  |  UNIFORM  [  SIZE  n[K|M]  ]  }  ]
}  ]
[  SEGMENT  SPACE  MANAGEMENT  {  AUTO  |  MANUAL  }  ]
[
    DEFAULT  [  [NO]COMPRESS  ]  STORAGE(
        [  INITIAL  n[K|M]  ]  [  NEXT  n[K|M]  ]  [  PCTINCREASE  n  ]
        [  MINEXTENTS  n  ]  [  MAXEXTENTS  {  n  |  UNLIMITED  }  ])
];
```

Note: If a database is created with a locally managed SYSTEM tablespace, then dictionary-managed tablespaces cannot be created in that database. Additionally, the SYSTEM tablespace cannot be changed from local to dictionary managed.

The most up-to-date form of CREATE TABLESPACE syntax is a locally managed tablespace, using automatic extent allocation and automatic segment space management. Let Oracle Database do it for you; it seems to work better this way. ASM will be discussed later in this chapter:

```
CREATE SMALLFILE
    TABLESPACE "TEST"
    LOGGING
    DATAFILE '$ORACLE_HOME/ORADATA/&ORACLE_SID/<filename>'
   SIZE nnnM EXTENT MANAGEMENT LOCAL SEGMENT SPACE MANAGEMENT

    AUTO;
```

This script is a direct copy of a CREATE TABLESPACE statement, using all the defaults, when creating a tablespace in the Oracle Enterprise Manager Console. As stated in many places in this book, default settings are usually the best way in Oracle software, indicating all the best options in relation to established commercial use.

Now let's go through the highlighted parts of the CREATE TABLESPACE syntax.

14.2.1.2.1 Auto Extend

This option automatically extends the datafile. So, a tablespace creation should always be automatically extended with a specified size for the NEXT parameter. Specifying the NEXT parameter assures that datafiles grow with consistent, reusable extent sizes. If extent sizes are too small, then a large table could have so many extents to search through that performance will seriously degrade. The NEXT parameter is defaulted to the block size. Do not leave NEXT undeclared and defaulted. The default for the block size is usually too small. Only small static tables and indexes could have sizes for NEXT of below 1M. For some tables, well over 1M is prudent.

Setting MAXSIZE UNLIMITED is also sensible because if a maximum datafile size is specified, the database will cease to function if datafiles ever reach a maximum size. It is better to extend Oracle tablespace datafiles automatically and monitor disk space usage using scripting in the operating system.

14.2.1.2.2   Minimum Extent Sizes

This option specifies that every extent in a datafile is at least the specified size, minimizing on fragmentation.

14.2.1.2.3   Block Size

Permanent tablespaces can be created with block sizes different than the DB_BLOCK_SIZE database block size parameter. Appropriate DB_nK_ CACHE_SIZE parameters must be created in the configuration parameter file to cater to such tablespaces. Obviously, a tablespace with a smaller block size is useful to contain smaller tables. A tablespace with a larger block size is good for large tables when reading large amounts of data at once. I have personally never experimented with this aspect of Oracle Database in a highly active production environment. However, I would certainly suggest using varying block-sized tablespaces for storage of large objects such as LOBs. LOBs contained within tables can be stored in a tablespace separate from the tablespace in which the table resides.

14.2.1.2.4   Logging

Switching off logging as the default for a tablespace will increase perfor-mance in your database. However, no logging will result in minimal redo log entries and an unrecoverable database. Do not switch off logging for the sake of performance. The only type of tablespace for which it is sensible to have no logging for is data that is never changed. You can also make a tablespace read only using the ALTER TABLESPACE command. There is no logging for read only tablespaces because read only does not allow any DML changes. Do not use NOLOGGING on read-write tablespaces unless you are prepared to lose your entire database in the event of a disas-ter. Individual objects in tablespaces can be forced into logging mode when other tables are not, even if the tablespace is set to NOLOGGING. Once again, any type of no logging setting is risky.

14.2.1.2.5 Extent Management

The EXTENT MANAGEMENT clause allows specification of a locally managed or dictionary-managed tablespace. Stick to locally managed tablespaces unless you have a very good reason.

Note: When a database SYSTEM tablespace is created as locally managed, all tablespaces in that database must be locally managed.

Note: (9*i*) When using dictionary-managed tablespaces, once again, the most efficient datafile structure for growth is consistent extent sizes. Differing extent sizes in datafiles will result in fragmentation and associated slow access times due to bouncing around a disk when searching for data. Coalescence is generally useless when trying to reclaim deleted space where extent sizes differ.

Note: (10*g*) In past versions of Oracle Database, automatic extent allocation was not recommended as varying. Oracle Documentation stated that very small variable extent sizes were created. In Oracle Database 9*i* Release 2 (9.2) and beyond, automatic extent allocation is recommended, as default extent sizes are uniformly set at 1M.

If using manual extent allocation, always use the UNIFORM SIZE clause for extent management to ensure consistency of extent sizes across a datafile. The more growth you have, the larger the extent size should be. I generally use 1M and very much larger values for very large databases or databases with high growth rates. Small objects can have smaller extent sizes as long as the database administrator is absolutely sure that large tables, or high growth rate tables, will never be placed in that tablespace. Database administrators are rarely involved in the development process, and thus a database administrator is unlikely to have enough knowledge of applications to make these types of decisions.

Keep extent sizes consistent and never below 1M.

14.2.1.2.6   Segment Space Management

A segment space management specification is allowed for locally managed nontemporary tablespaces. Automatic segment space management, as specified by the SEGMENT SPACE MANAGEMENT AUTO clause, eliminates the need to declare PCTUSED, FREELIST, and FREELIST GROUPS values for objects created in a tablespace. These settings are now bitmap managed automatically by Oracle Database.

Note: Setting values for PCTUSED, FREELIST, and FREELIST_ GROUPS in database objects such as tables will be ignored if the containing tablespace is set to automatic segment space management.

In past versions of Oracle Database, manual free list management was usually only required for very highly concurrent active OLTP databases or Oracle RAC (Parallel Server) installations. For dictionary-managed tablespaces, access to the PCTUSED parameter sometimes helped immensely with tuning for performance in the following respect. The default value for PCTUSED is very low at 40%. Any database with heavy deletion activity could have a lot of wasted space with PCTUSED set to 40%. Deleted rows are still read by full scans and can ultimately result in serious performance problems. One of the biggest problems with manually setting the PCTUSED value for a table was that it was often set based on subjective guesswork due to a lack of understanding. Otherwise it was simply left at the default value. Automatic management of free space resolves these issues.

Note: One of the reviewers for this book commented that automatic segment space management realizes up to 35% performance improvement, specifically in Oracle RAC environments.

Note: (10*g*) Locally managed tablespaces with automatic extent management and automatic segment space management have been the default since Oracle Database 9*i* Release 2 (9.2). This indicates that tablespaces should be created as such.

14.2.1.2.7 ⑩g BIGFILE Tablespaces

Oracle Database 10g allows division of tablespace types for locally managed tablespaces into two categories: (1) SMALLFILE tablespaces, and (2) BIG-FILE tablespaces. A SMALLFILE tablespace is the default.

Note: SMALLFILE or BIGFILE can be set as the default for a database as a whole, using the CREATE DATABASE or ALTER DATABASE commands.

A BIGFILE tablespace contains a single datafile, which can be up to 128 Tb for a block size of 32K. The general trend for database technology at the file structure level is fewer, larger files. Many years ago relational databases had a single datafile for every table or index. Some database engines still do. The most bleeding-edge database engines are object databases. The most recently developed object databases generally have a single large datafile. The performance benefit of maintaining a single large file is significant. I would suggest that it is likely that Oracle Database will continue on this path of development. In a future version of Oracle Database, BIGFILE tablespaces may be the default, and perhaps eventually the only option, where all physical storage structure within that BIGFILE tablespace is automatically managed, transparent, and inaccessible to database administrators. For example, splitting files up physically using striping on a RAID array is managed at the operating system level and is not a requirement from within the database. Oracle Database 10g introduced Automated Storage Management (ASM). ASM can implement striping managed from within an Oracle database. This *may* once again hint at less emphasis on explicit management of physical storage structures.

14.2.1.2.8 Avoiding Datafile Header Contention

Datafile header contention can be avoided when using locally managed tablespaces in busy Oracle installations by creating a large number of small datafiles for each tablespace. Datafile header contention is avoided because extent bitmaps attached to each datafile are not overstressed in highly concurrent environments. This is a new fangled way of doing things and is not to be confused with manual striping. It is not striping! Locally managed tablespaces have bitmaps in datafile headers in much the same way that dictionary-managed tablespaces use metadata storage to store extent maps. Datafile header contention under highly concurrent conditions is more likely because bitmaps compress far more than metadata storage.

Now let's take a look at the different types of functions of tablespaces.

14.2.1.3   Temporary Sort Space

Temporary sort space is catered for in two ways: (1) sort buffers declared by the SORT_AREA_SIZE parameter, and (2) a temporary sort space tablespace and datafile on disk. It might make sense to size temporary sort space to a multiple of the SORT_AREA_SIZE parameter.

Note: (10*g*) All *_AREA_SIZE parameters, including the SORT_AREA_SIZE parameter, are now superseded by automated connection memory management using the PGA_AGGREGATE_TARGET parameter.

14.2.1.3.1   (9*i*) Temporary Tablespaces in Oracle Database 9*i* Database

In Oracle Database 9*i*, the story for temporary tablespaces is a little different. A temporary tablespace is specially structured for sorting and is best implemented as a locally managed tablespace. This is the syntax for creating a temporary tablespace:

```
CREATE TEMPORARY TABLESPACE tablespace
    [ TEMPFILE 'file' [ SIZE n[K|M] ] ]
    [ EXTENT MANAGEMENT LOCAL ]
    [ UNIFORM [ SIZE n[K|M] ] ];
```

Here is an example temporary tablespace creation command. This is how I create temporary tablespaces with Oracle Database 9*i* Database Release 2 (9.2), which has changed in Oracle 10*g* Database. This is the type of temporary tablespace structure that I trust completely for performance and stability in Oracle Database 9*i* Database Release 2 (9.2):

```
CREATE TEMPORARY TABLESPACE TEMP TEMPFILE
'$ORACLE_HOME/oradata/$ORACLE_SID/temp01.dbf' SIZE 100M
AUTOEXTEND ON NEXT 1M MAXSIZE UNLIMITED EXTENT MANAGEMENT
LOCAL UNIFORM SIZE 1M;
```

It is important to allocate the use of a temporary tablespace automatically to a user either by using the CREATE DATABASE command or when creating the user with the CREATE USER command. The ALTER USER command can be used later on.

A temporary tablespace is used by an Oracle database for various operations, such as index creation and large sorts in SQL code. Temporary sort space is used to shift sorting operations from the sort buffer to disk when a sort operation does not fit into the maximum sort buffer size allocated for each session. Note that every session obtains a buffer area equal to the SORT_AREA_SIZE parameter for sorting purposes. Every session should have access to a temporary tablespace for sorting on disk when the sort buffer is too small for a particular sort operation. Sorting will be covered more later on.

One common mistake with respect to sorting can have severe implications on performance. As already stated, if a user does not have a temporary tablespace allocated for on-disk sorting overflow from the sort buffer, there will be a problem. Prior to Oracle Database 9i, the CREATE DATABASE command did not allow the setting of a default sorting temporary tablespace for automatic allocation to a newly created user. Quite often, database administrators forgot about allocating a temporary tablespace to a user altogether. The result was that the SYSTEM tablespace contained overflow sorting onto disk from the sort buffer. The SYSTEM tablespace contains the database metadata and is probably the most critical tablespace in an Oracle database with respect to performance. Whenever a database administrator is confronted with a new database, perhaps in a new job, temporary sort space on disk is one of the first things to check.

14.2.1.3.2 ⑩*g* **Temporary Tablespaces in Oracle Database 10*g***

An Oracle Database 10*g* temporary tablespace must be created, locally managed, and with automatic extent allocation switched off, with a default uniform extent size of 1Mb, as in the following command (again this is a direct copy from the Oracle Enterprise Manager Console):

```
CREATE SMALLFILE
    TEMPORARY TABLESPACE "" TEMPFILE
    '$ORACLE_HOME/ORADATA/$ORACLE_SID/temp01.dbf' SIZE 5M
EXTENT
    MANAGEMENT LOCAL UNIFORM SIZE 1M;
```

Also in Oracle Database 10*g*, a CREATE DATABASE command can allocate and create a temporary tablespace, alleviating the need to assign each user the appropriate temporary tablespace. If a temporary tablespace is not assigned in the CREATE DATABASE command or when creating a user, SYSTEM tablespace is still used for on-disk sorting.

Now let's look at temporary sort space usage. The following queries check that users are using appropriate default and temporary tablespaces.

The TEMP tablespace is my temporary sorting tablespace, and the DATA tablespace contains application tables. The SYSTEM tablespace is used for Oracle Database metadata. (10*g*) The SYSAUX tablespace is created automatically, along with the SYSTEM tablespace when a database is created. The SYSAUX tablespace contains options, Oracle tools, repositories, and even some types of metadata previously stored for the Oracle Database 9*i* in the SYSTEM tablespace. The structure for Oracle Database 10*g* is shown in the following script output:

```
COL username FORMAT a20;
COL default_tablespace FORMAT a20;
COL temporary_tablespace FORMAT a20;
SELECT username, default_tablespace, temporary_tablespace
FROM dba_users ORDER BY 1;
```

```
USERNAME              DEFAULT_TABLESPACE    TEMPORARY_TABLESPACE
--------------------  --------------------  --------------------
ACCOUNTS              DATA                  TEMP
ACCSTEST              DATA                  TEMP
ANONYMOUS             SYSAUX                TEMP
BOOKS                 DATA                  TEMP
CONCERTS              DATA                  TEMP
DBSNMP                SYSAUX                TEMP
DEMOGRAPHICS          DATA                  TEMP
DIP                   USERS                 TEMP
EMPLOYEES             DATA                  TEMP
EXFSYS                SYSAUX                TEMP
MDSYS                 SYSAUX                TEMP
MGMT_VIEW             SYSTEM                TEMP
MUSIC                 DATA                  TEMP
ORDPLUGINS            SYSAUX                TEMP
ORDSYS                SYSAUX                TEMP
OUTLN                 SYSTEM                TEMP
SI_INFORMTN_SCHEMA    SYSAUX                TEMP
SYS                   SYSTEM                TEMP
SYSMAN                SYSAUX                TEMP
SYSTEM                SYSTEM                TEMP
TRACKING              DATA                  TEMP
TSMSYS                USERS                 TEMP
WMSYS                 SYSAUX                TEMP
XDB                   SYSAUX                TEMP
```

> **Note:** (10*g*) The SYSAUX tablespace contains options mentioned earlier, including the OEM repository, RMAN, and outlines. These options were stored in separate tablespaces in Oracle Database 9*i*.

One other thing that should be checked is that the temporary tablespace TEMP really is a temporary tablespace and not a permanent tablespace. This is a common error as well:

```
COL tablespace_name FORMAT a20;
SELECT tablespace_name, contents FROM dba_tablespaces ORDER
BY 1;


TABLESPACE_NAME        CONTENTS
--------------------   ---------
DATA                   PERMANENT
INDX                   PERMANENT
OBJECTS                PERMANENT
SYSAUX                 PERMANENT
SYSTEM                 PERMANENT
TEMP                   TEMPORARY
UNDOTBS1               UNDO
USERS                  PERMANENT
```

14.2.1.3.3 (10*g*) Tablespace Groups

Tablespace groups can only be used for temporary sort space in an ASM instance. On disk, temporary space can be allocated as tablespace groups where a tablespace group can contain multiple locally managed temporary tablespaces. A tablespace group will allow spreading of SQL execution sorting across multiple temporary tablespaces, thereby potentially speeding up sorting operations. Processing is distributed. A user can be allocated a tablespace group as a temporary sort space as opposed to just a single temporary tablespace. Temporary tablespace groups allow increased access to on-disk sort space by effectively allowing a split of sorts into multiple tablespaces, which can help performance.

14.2.1.4 Manual Rollback and Automatic Undo

Manual rollback and automatic undo both do the same thing, except that automated undo is the more recent and more sophisticated innovation.

Note: ⑩ Manual rollback segments do still function in Oracle Database 10*g* but they are obsolete and replaced by automatic undo (automatic rollback).

Rollback has two functions: (1) allowing the undoing of noncommitted transactions, and (2) allowing for a consistent point-in-time snapshot of data. This snapshot capability allows different sessions to find data as it was at a specific time, regardless of any other uncommitted transactions, which have already changed the database. Let's examine automatic undo first.

14.2.1.4.1   ⑩ **Automated Undo**

The automated undo tablespace was introduced in Oracle Database 9*i*. An undo tablespace automates rollback (undo) segment management. Rollback segments no longer have to be manually created and manually tuned. Many database administrators had problems tuning rollback segments. There are a number of undo configuration parameters for controlling automated undo:

- *UNDO_MANAGEMENT.* This switches automated undo on and off. It is set to AUTO by default. Set it to MANUAL to use manual rollback segments.

- *UNDO_TABLESPACE.* The name of an undo tablespace must be specified.

- *UNDO_RETENTION.* Places a time period for how much committed undo data is kept. When using the Database Configuration Assistant, default parameters for this value appear to be set to over 10,000 for a data warehouse and under 1,000 for OLTP databases. Documentation on this parameter is vague, and it is unclear whether setting this parameter to too short a time period will result in uncommitted information being overwritten.

An undo tablespace can be created with the tablespace retention clause. The tablespace retention clause can be set in two different ways: RETENTION_GUARANTEE or RETENTION_NOGUARANTEE. The latter is the default, where undo information not yet expired can be consumed by active transactions. Nonexpired undo data could be required for a rollback on a transaction. The RETENTION_GUARANTEE setting guarantees that this will never happen.

Let's look at rollback segments.

14.2.1.4.2 Manual Rollback Segments

(9*i*) In previous versions of Oracle Database (before Oracle Database 9*i*), rollback involved creation and tuning of rollback segments. Some database installations still use manual rollback segments, although it is probably rare. So for this edition, I will still include this section.

Rollback segments are placed into a permanent tablespace. Rollback segments are separate physical areas that have individual or multiple transactions allocated to them at the same time. In an OLTP system, it is best to create a large number of small rollback segments, even up to the maximum of 50 rollback segments. This helps to divide up different transactions into different rollback segments, minimizing contention between rollback segments. A database with large transactional throughput could be better served with fewer, much larger rollback segments. If a rollback segment expands up to a specified limited number of extents, a transaction will fail and rollback. Sometimes in ad hoc SQL code and development environments, it is best to limit rollback segment maximum extents in order to avoid runaway transactions. A runaway transaction can completely destroy database performance.

This command creates a rollback segment in a rollback tablespace called RBS:

```
create public rollback segment rb00 tablespace rbs storage
(initial 16K next 16K optimal 64K minextents 2 maxextents 64);
```

The OPTIMAL parameter retains space in a rollback segment after completion of a transaction. The setting of OPTIMAL is a debatable issue and depends on database activity and transaction size. When a transaction is committed and rollback cleared, then the rollback segment will be cleared physically back to its optimal size. In the case of the rollback segment creation command shown earlier, the OPTIMAL value is set to 64K, and the initial size to 16K. This will assure that transactions larger than 16K will always have 64K of space available before having to extend. Also, rollback segments will be of consistent sizes. On the other hand, continual resizing of rollback segments could also affect performance. Check for rollback resizing using this query:

```
SELECT n.name, s.shrinks, s.gets FROM v$rollname n,
v$rollstat s
WHERE n.usn = s.usn AND s.status = 'ONLINE';
```

Note: (10*g*) This command will return a list of automated undo segments.

So we set rollback sizing parameters according to the size of transactions in the database. For an OLTP database, with very small transactions, these values could be as small as the values shown of 16K extent size with an optimal value of 64K.

Do not forget to place rollback segments online. The same can be achieved by placing all rollback segments into the ROLLBACK_SEGMENTS configuration parameter, placing all listed rollback segments online at database startup.

```
alter rollback segment rb00 online;
```

14.3 Automating Database File Structures

The two topics of interest here are Oracle Managed Files (OMF) and Automated Storage Management (ASM). In general, it is strongly suspected that OMF hurts performance and that ASM may help performance in some situations. OMF makes database administration activities easier.

Let's begin with OMF.

14.3.1 Oracle Managed Files

OMF offers a higher level of automation in terms of management of datafiles. For example, when dropping tablespace, OMF will automatically delete datafiles from the operating system.

Three configuration parameters can be set with varying levels of datafile management automation:

- **DB_CREATE_FILE_DEST**. This stores all datafiles, redo log files, and controlfiles. Redo log files and controlfiles will be contained in the directory determined by this parameter; no definitions for the DB_CREATE_ONLINE_LOG_DEST_n directories are created.

- **DB_CREATE_ONLINE_LOG_DEST_*n*.** This stores redo log files and controlfiles in a specified directory. N implies that there can be up to 5 copies, duplexing redo log files, and multiplexing controlfiles.

- **DB_RECOVERY_FILE_DEST.** This directory contains archive log files (if not otherwise specified), RMAN backup copies, and flash log files. This directory will also contain a single copy of redo log files and controlfiles if defined, but DB_CREATE_ONLINE_LOG_DEST_n parameters are not defined.

Note: Setting any one of these parameters will automatically implement OMF, depending on which parameters are set.

You can even mix OMF architecture with manually managed files.

So how can an OMF database be tuned? The answer is, it can't—not from the perspective of the datafiles and their placement. The only thing that can be done is to reshape the file system using striping, preferably with a tool that implements architectural structures at the operating system and hardware, such as striping and mirroring.

Does OMF help Oracle Database performance in general? This is an unknown, but I have heard that OMF can hurt performance substantially for OLTP databases. OMF is intended to ease database administration activities. OMF is not intended to help general database performance.

And now for a brief description of ASM, which utilizes OMF as part of ASM.

14.3.2 (10g) Automatic Storage Management

ASM effectively extends OMF aspects of easy file management by managing Oracle Database files within groups of disk locations. Oracle Database files include datafiles, redo log files, archive log files, and controlfiles. In other words, everything! ASM has the following architectural aspects:

- **Disk groups**. ASM allows you to set up groups of separate disks. You can then mirror as a two-way mirror, a three-way mirror, or no mirror at all. A two-way mirror will duplicate each datafile across two disks, a three-way mirror onto three disks, and no mirroring assumes there is mirroring at a level beneath the Oracle database, such as in the operating system or using special software intended for that purpose.

■ **Automated tuning rebalancing**. You can add and remove disks to and from a group. If this occurs, ASM will automatically rebalance Oracle Database files between the remaining disk groups. No manual intervention is required. Consequently, automated rebalancing allows for disk replacement on disk failure, assuming, of course, that two-way or three-way mirroring is used with ASM. The performance tuning aspect of ASM is that the rebalancing process is automated, with no database administrator intervention required.

When it comes to tuning ASM Oracle databases, it comes down to making sure that all disks in a group have equal size and performance. Also Oracle database files should be distributed onto separate groups according to the function of those files, if different disk groups have differing performance. Therefore, it makes more sense to place datafiles on faster disks than those of archive log files.

Additionally, there appears to be a general consensus that ASM makes sense for Oracle Real Application Clusters (RAC) environments simply because it makes file management that much easier. With respect to general performance, using ASM with a single Oracle Instance database does not appear to compete well with operating system level striping and mirroring or with overlay striping and mirroring software such as Veritas. A piece of software like Veritas is purposely built for this type of architectural structure. How could Oracle Database compete? It is unlikely. It makes sense to use ASM for Oracle RAC environments because clustered databases are just complicated!

The next chapter will delve a little deeper into the logical layers of the Oracle database and examine physical tuning of database objects, such as tables and indexes.

15

Object Tuning

There are two layers to object physical tuning. The first layer allows for special behavior applied to objects, such as tables and indexes. These special behaviors will be covered in this chapter. The second layer is explicit block and extent level tuning within objects. Explicit block and extent level tuning are what I like to call low-level architecture and will be covered in Chapter 17.

This chapter looks at object level physical tuning. What is object level physical tuning? This subject encompasses changes to an object, such as a table. This involves modifying the underlying physical structure, without necessarily affecting the block structure. This chapter is split into the different objects: tables, indexes, sequences, and synonyms. Much of the detail for many object types is covered in the first section on tables. Each subsequent section is expanded to cover details specific to the different object types.

Note: This book covers only OLTP database type tuning, and not data warehouse tuning. Data warehouse [1]–specific objects such as materialized views are not included in this book, although much of what is discussed applies to data warehouse–type objects as well.

15.1 Tables

So what can be done with table objects?

15.1.1   Caching

This option, which is much like the keep and recycle buffer pools from a previous version of Oracle Database, applies to full table scans only. Caching will allow the forcing of small, static tables into a most recently used (MRU) cache and large, seldom-used tables into a least recently used (LRU) cache.

For my Accounts schema I could do something similar to that shown following. The GeneralLedger and StockMovement tables are large, and I would like to force any full table scans on very large tables out of cache as soon as possible. Small static lookup tables in my Accounts schema are Type, Subtype, COA, Stock, and Category. I would want to force these lookup tables to remain in cache for as long as possible:

```
ALTER TABLE generalledger NOCACHE;
ALTER TABLE stockmovement NOCACHE;
ALTER TABLE type CACHE;
ALTER TABLE subtype CACHE;
ALTER TABLE coa CACHE;
ALTER TABLE stock CACHE;
ALTER TABLE category CACHE;
```

The Customer and Supplier tables are semistatic and not cached. This is because they are large and not generally full table scanned. Other static tables, such as Period and PeriodSum, are not cached because they are rarely used. Changes will be made to these pools with further discussion on caching tables and indexes in Chapter 18.

Note: There are numerous methods of caching objects in Oracle Database. Caching is not necessarily particularly useful, at times actually causing more problems than it resolves.

15.1.2   Logging

Logging can be switched off where redo log entries are minimized. Switching off logging for an object, such as a table, will help performance. However, setting forced logging for an entire database, or switching logging off when running a standby with Data Guard, is pointless. It is not recommended because recoverability can be seriously affected. Logging applies to indexes as well as tables. Indexes are recoverable without logging because they can be rebuilt. Rebuilding indexes is not a problem as long as applications can account for slow access speeds. No indexes are available when they are being rebuilt as a result of recovery.

15.1.3 Table Parallelism

A table can be set to be accessible either in parallel or not in parallel for the purposes of DML and SELECT activity. Parallel execution applies to database servers with more than one CPU. My examples were executed on a rather geriatric dual 300MHz PII CPU database server.

Some points to note about parallelism:

- *Full table scan*. A query must contain a full table scan to be executed in parallel.
- *Oracle partitioning*. It is most appropriate to use parallelism with Oracle Partitioning, or a powerful machine with plenty of RAM, and at least two CPUs.
- *CREATE TABLE AS SELECT*. This is often believed to be executable in parallel. It is, but only from a remote database.
- *Bitmaps*. Using bitmap indexes in an OLTP database is unwise. Parallel operations on tables using bitmap indexes in data warehouses are the common use.

So what does use parallelism? Let's use a large table in the Accounts schema. First of all, make sure that the table has no parallelism:

```
ALTER TABLE generalledger NOPARALLEL;
```

Now create a temporary table and compute statistics:

```
CREATE TABLE tmp1 AS SELECT * FROM generalledger;
ANALYZE TABLE tmp1 COMPUTE STATISTICS;
```

Now count the rows with parallelism switched off. The time elapsed is less than one second:

```
SQL> SELECT COUNT(*) FROM (SELECT * FROM tmp1);

  COUNT(*)
----------
    752741
```

Elapsed: 00:00:00.07

Here is the query plan:

```
EXPLAIN PLAN SET STATEMENT_ID = 'TEST' FOR
SELECT COUNT(*) FROM (SELECT * FROM tmp1);
```

```
Query                            Cost
------------------------------ ---------
1. SELECT STATEMENT  on          495
2.   SORT AGGREGATE on
3.     TABLE ACCESS FULL on TMP1  495
```

Now set the temporary table to PARALLEL 2:

```
ALTER TABLE tmp1 PARALLEL 2;
```

Count the rows again. Note that the time elapsed has more than qua-
drupled using parallelism. This same result was found in Chapter 10. Figure 15.1 shows a picture of CPU usage for both processors. Notice that the
query executed in parallel is using both processors, even though the elapsed
time is slower. It is quite possible that my somewhat geriatric dual CPU
machine is simply not powerful enough:

```
SQL> SELECT COUNT(*) FROM (SELECT * FROM tmp1);

  COUNT(*)
----------
    752741
```

Elapsed: 00:00:03.04

Here is the query plan again:

```
EXPLAIN PLAN SET STATEMENT_ID = 'TEST' FOR
SELECT COUNT(*) FROM (SELECT * FROM tmp1);
```

The cost for the parallel executed query is about half that of the serially executed query. Even though the query plan looks better, the execution time is worse. My database server machine is probably simply just too old:

```
Query                                                              Cost
------------------------------------------------------------------ ----
1. SELECT STATEMENT   on                                            248
2.   SORT AGGREGATE on
3.     SORT AGGREGATE on   PARALLEL_TO_SERIAL
4.       TABLE ACCESS FULL on TMP1 PARALLEL_COMBINED_WITH_PARENT   248
```

Figure 15.1
*Parallel versus
serial (nonparallel)
processing*

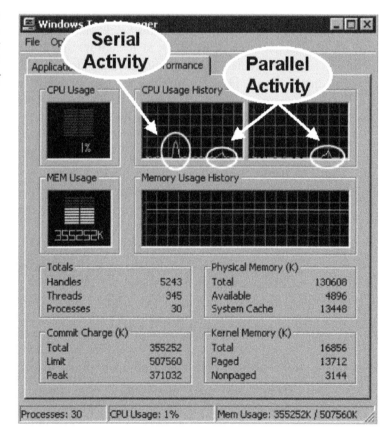

It is sensible to conclude that parallel processing works best with Oracle Partitioning, and probably with very large partitioned tables as well. My Accounts schema tables, at two million rows, are possibly not large enough to show any effect. My hardware platform is also inadequate. Oracle Partitioning will be covered in detail in Chapter 19.

15.1.4 Storing LOBs Separately

LOB objects such as images are usually physically very large in relation to normal textual data. Storing a large chunk of space into a table row block is very likely to result in large numbers of rows being occupied by multiple blocks. In other words, substantial row chaining and row migration could result. Row chaining and row migration are inefficient. Oracle Database allows LOB objects to be stored in a tablespace that is physically separated from the tablespace in which the relational table row (the text-type columns in the table) is stored.

I have two LOB objects in the Stock table of my Accounts schema. The first object is called Stock.DESCRIPTION and is a text CLOB column. The second object is called Stock.IMAGE and is a BLOB column containing an image. How do I change my Stock table to store the contents of these columns in a specialized objects tablespace? One method of moving the image column to a specialized objects tablespace called OBJECTS is shown here. There is no problem dropping and recreating the column because I have not as yet stored any images in the table:

```
ALTER TABLE stock DROP COLUMN image;
ALTER TABLE stock ADD (image BLOB) LOB (image)
STORE AS image (TABLESPACE objects);
```

There are various special LOB parameters. These parameters can sometimes affect performance adversely:

- **STORAGE IN ROW.** Set at DISABLE, it will store only a pointer in the relational section of the table row. It is much more efficient to store only the pointer to a contiguous binary object in a table.

- **CHUNK.** Disk space reserved for LOB manipulation.

- **PCTVERSION.** This refers to multiple versions of storage of the same LOB object.

■ *RETENTION*. This refers to how many old versions can be stored.

■ *FREEPOOLS*. These are LOB freelists for high concurrency access.

The most important instruction for LOB objects with respect to tuning is to store them out of line. Out of line implies separated from the relational data in table rows.

The most efficient method of storing multimedia-type objects is to use a BFILE pointer. A BFILE pointer contains the full path and file name of an object file. The object file is located somewhere on disk, external of the Oracle database. In other words, BFILE objects are stored as a part of the underlying operating system file system, rather than the Oracle Database file system. BFILE pointers are the most efficient LOB type object storage for both relational and object databases.

15.1.5 Dropping Columns

Dropping columns from very large tables can cause a problem. Simply dropping a column using the DROP COLUMN clause, from a very large table, could cause an exclusive table lock. During the process of dropping a column, both the column definition is removed from the metadata and data values are physically removed from data blocks. In very high availability systems, dropping a column from a table can cause serious performance problems.

There are two options for column removal from a table in addition to the DROP COLUMN option, shown in the second and third bullets in the following list:

■ *DROP COLUMN*. This removes the column both physically and from metadata (logically):

```
ALTER TABLE table DROP { COLUMN column | ( column [, column … ] ) };
```

■ *SET UNUSED COLUMN*. This removes access to the column by removing visible and end-user accessible metadata.{**AU: Please check edit.**} This avoids slowing or interrupting service. Use this option for high usage, very large tables in highly available databases. Perhaps even small lookup tables could experience such problems when a column is dropped from them. It all depends on how much the table is accessed concurrently:

```
ALTER TABLE table SET UNUSED
{ COLUMN column | ( column [, column … ] ) };
```

■ ***DROP UNUSED COLUMNS***. This destroys any remaining metadata and physical column values for any unused columns. Use this option in low-activity times to remove the column entirely, subsequent to having used the SET UNUSED COLUMN option previously. Use the DROP UNUSED option to reclaim physical space:

```
ALTER TABLE table DROP { UNUSED COLUMNS | COLUMNS CONTINUE };
```

Note: You can also use the DBMS_REDEFINITION package, which allows object changes with the database online. How performance is affected for a large and busy OLTP database is unknown to me at present.

15.1.6   Deallocating Unused Space

Unused space above the high-water mark can be cleared for reuse. Deallocation can help to make a table smaller, particularly if extensive deletion has occurred:

```
ALTER TABLE table DEALLOCATE UNUSED [KEEP integer [ K | M ]];
```

Reclaiming any unused space can also be performed using the SHRINK clause. The SHRINK clause allows us to compact a segment, which is a database object such as a table, by adjusting the high-water mark:

```
ALTER TABLE table SHRINK [ COMPACT | CACADE ];
```

You can only use the SHRINK clause for locally managed tablespaces, using automated segment management. The SHRINK clause is allowed for various database object types, including tables, index-organized tables, indexes, partitions, and materialized views.

The COMPACT option does not adjust the high-water mark and releasing space. The CASCADE option will include dependent objects.

15.2 Indexes

Many factors affecting indexes and types of indexes were discussed in detail in Chapter 8, including index compression. Even though there is some crossover with the previous section on tables, there are a few other factors to consider.

15.2.1 Monitoring

The simplest use for monitoring is to tell whether or not an index is used. When an index is monitored as being used, the V$OBJECT_USAGE.USED column will contain a YES value. An index not used after monitoring over a period of time could possibly be dropped.

Note: Never drop foreign key indexes. You could get some serious concurrency locking problems as a result. Oracle Database may also not report on foreign key index use when referential integrity uses those indexes.

Note: Monitoring applies to both tables and indexes. However, when testing on my database, I got absolutely no sensible response for monitoring of tables for DML activity.

Let's experiment. This query creates a script allowing monitoring of indexes for all the tables in the Accounts schema. The EXECUTE IMMEDIATE command executes each ALTER INDEX command as it is generated:

```
DECLARE
    CURSOR cIndexes IS
    SELECT index_name FROM user_indexes
WHERE index_type != 'LOB';
BEGIN
    FOR rIndex IN cIndexes LOOP
EXECUTE IMMEDIATE 'ALTER INDEX '||rIndex.index_name
||' MONITORING USAGE';
```

```
        END LOOP;
END;
/
```

The result will be something like this:

```
ALTER INDEX XFK_COA# MONITORING USAGE;
ALTER INDEX XFK_SM_STOCK MONITORING USAGE;
ALTER INDEX XPK_GENERALLEDGER MONITORING USAGE;
ALTER INDEX XPK_STOCKMOVEMENT MONITORING USAGE;
...
```

Now I change all these tables with the previous script. Then I execute my DBMS_JOBS package scripting to start up my highly active concurrent OLTP database. After that, I query the V$OBJECT_USAGE performance view and see if I can find any unused indexes:

```
SQL> SELECT COUNT(*) FROM v$object_usage WHERE used = 'NO';
  COUNT(*)
----------
        42
```

Many of the indexes I have in my Accounts schema are not used.

Note: Foreign key indexes will not be flagged as used when utilized for validation of referential integrity. Once again, be careful not to remove foreign key indexes. You will get a lot of performance problems if you do. When foreign keys are not indexed, table exclusive locks are extremely likely. Most of the unused indexes in my Accounts schema are foreign key indexes.

I could use a query such as this to find exact details of monitoring:

```
SELECT start_monitoring "Start", end_monitoring "End", used
,index_name "Index" FROM v$object_usage WHERE used = 'NO';
```

It is important for performance tuning to drop unused indexes. This is because a DML operation executed on a table results in a DML operation on the table, plus all indexes created against that table. The fewer objects requiring changes there are, the faster the DML activity will be. Indexing usually speeds up data retrieval. When deciding on the necessity for an index, it is sensible to weigh your approach among DML activity, query SELECT activity, and the need for foreign key indexes.

15.2.2   Index Parallelism

Index creations and rebuilds can be executed in parallel. There are three indexes on the Accounts.GeneralLedger table. Let's rebuild one of them:

```
SQL> ALTER INDEX xfk_coa# REBUILD;

Index altered.
```

Elapsed: 00:00:30.00

Now let's rebuild the same index in parallel:

```
SQL> ALTER INDEX xfk_coa# REBUILD PARALLEL 2;

Index altered.
```

Elapsed: 00:02:56.04

It appears that the parallel rebuild is quite a bit slower. Again, this is probably related to my dual CPU server being out of date. Then again, perhaps not.

Let's try creating the index from scratch, both serially and in parallel. First serially:

```
SQL> DROP INDEX xfk_coa#;

Index dropped.

Elapsed: 00:00:00.04

SQL> CREATE INDEX xfk_coa# ON generalledger(coa#);

Index created.
```

Elapsed: 00:05:24.01

Second, let's create the index in parallel:

```
SQL> DROP INDEX xfk_coa#;

Index dropped.

Elapsed: 00:00:00.01

SQL> CREATE INDEX xfk_coa# ON generalledger(coa#) PARALLEL 2;

Index created.

Elapsed: 00:06:02.06
```

Once again, parallel processing on my dual CPU machine is slower. And once again, my dual CPU database server has limited RAM, limited disk capacity, and limited I/O performance. It is possible that a combination of these factors causes parallel processing to be abnormally slow on this particular database server. Then again, parallel processing requires extra processing and coordination between different processes. In my experience, parallelism is often only effective in very large databases, often only on high-end Unix machines with at least four CPUs. Utilizing Oracle Partitioning will help performance substantially as well.

15.2.3 Fragmentation and Coalescing

Indexes can become defragmented by large amounts of deletion. Space in index leaf blocks is not reclaimed for reuse when rows are deleted. Coalescence of indexes can help to alleviate loss of space by attempting to merge neighboring blocks together, where those blocks are empty:

```
ALTER INDEX <indexname> COALESCE;
```

Be aware that it is more effective to reclaim index space by rebuilding the index. Accessing data using an index is likely to be slower during the rebuilding process but much more effective for the index when rebuilt. Also indexes can be rebuilt with the ONLINE option. The ONLINE option does not disrupt DML activity using that index:

```
ALTER INDEX <indexname> REBUILD ONLINE;
```

15.3 **Index-Organized Tables and Clusters**

Some of what applies to tables and indexes applies to index-organized tables and clusters as well. These objects will not be examined in any particular detail because they are most often used in data warehouses. However index-organized tables can be successful in OLTP databases in specific circumstances.

Many commercial OLTP databases are a combination of online small transactional DML activity, in addition to some DSS reporting or listing activity mixed in. Even though index-organized tables may be useful in OLTP databases, they are likely to become unbalanced indexes, faster than a simple index would. An unbalanced index is a skewed index where the underlying binary has far more values in one part of the tree. This makes index scanning slower for some queries. Then again, binary trees do rearrange themselves automatically to a certain extent, somewhat limiting binary tree skewing.

Skewing is not as much of a problem as overflow. Degradation in index-organized tables is possible over time under heavy DML activity. Any changes to data can slot into current index structure, rearrange the structure, or overflow into nonoptimally physically located segments. Any of these three situations can degrade performance for any type of index. However, index-organized tables can be more adversely affected, especially with excessive DML activity that changes existing table rows. An index-organized table includes data within the structure of the index because all the columns of a table are effectively indexed. An index-organized table is potentially much larger and complex than a normal BTree index on one or two columns. There is much higher risk of UPDATE and DELETE DML activity degrading index structure substantially and fairly quickly. Rapidly degrading indexes have to be more frequently rebuilt to maintain their efficiency. Regularly rebuilding indexes can be executed with the index remaining available during the rebuild process. And rebuilding indexes constantly takes time and resources away from applications.

Index-organized tables are possibly most appropriate for OLTP databases servicing object built applications, Java written perhaps, where sequence numbers are used to generate primary keys. Using reverse key indexes on the primary keys could help alleviate hot block issues if the index-organized table is subject to high concurrent insertion rates, especially in Oracle RAC and clustered environments.

Chapter 8 contains some experimentation using a relatively large index-organized table.

15.4 Sequences

Sequences can be cached. Twenty sequences are cached by default. If a system failure occurs then all cached sequences are lost.

Note: Only sequence numbers are lost if a database server crashes—not log file recoverable rows in tables. Sequences can also be lost if some kind of a rollback occurs.

If local law requires that all things like invoices must have sequence numbers added, then always create sequences with the NOCACHE option. Generally, extensive sequence caching is useful for highly active concurrent OLTP or Oracle RAC installations. I have never seen extensive caching of sequences adversely affect performance except in circumstances where sequences were abused.

15.5 Synonyms and Views

Synonyms could potentially be used to help replace nested layers of views to enhance performance. Synonyms are also often used to allow the creation of multiple users where access to data is pointed to a central schema. Profligate use of public synonyms can cause a security issue, depending on what is granted to them; more importantly, perhaps, is potential contention in highly concurrent environments. On the other hand, there is little that does not result in contention in highly concurrent environments.

Using synonyms can have a similar effect to that of using views. Synonyms can help to organize, but they can ultimately cause metadata performance issues as a result of the extra layers of metadata. Using views can sometimes create performance problems, perhaps if there are multiple layers of views in use. Large amounts of metadata could possibly cause problems in the shared pool and might even degrade the performance of the optimizer, simply by adding too much complexity, especially with multiple layers of views and synonyms.

Synonyms and views are often used for similar reasons. Views and synonyms are sometimes used when a database is designed and built from the top down, namely from the perspective of an application. A relational database has simplistic structure. Applications can handle complexity for which relational database structure is not intended.

Note: Object databases can handle complexity.

Extensive use of views and synonyms is common of applications tending to attempt to overuse relational database structure, imposing complex structure onto that relational database. In other words, it might be prudent to not overuse views and synonyms in order to simplify application coding. Performance of your application could suffer immensely in the long run if too many layers of complexity are imposed on the database layer. A relational database is intended to organize, store, allow changes to data, and retrieve data. A relational database does not have the processing power of an application tool. Keep complex application functionality out of the database if you want good performance. A similar approach should apply to PL/SQL. Use PL/SQL to access data, rather than to perform non–data accessing calculations and processing. The Oracle Java JVM can be utilized for complex processing.

Views can be used to implement security. The biggest issue with views is that any filtering executed on a query of a view is applied to the result of the view. The query executed within a view will always be executed in its entirety, regardless of filtering on the query executed against the view.

Be careful when using synonyms and views. The fact is really that using database objects like views and synonyms is not a problem in itself. The performance issue, especially with respect to views, is that the views are commonly misused. Views are often used to hide complexity from applications. Then developers may create WHERE clause filters against those views, expecting the views to behave like tables. Filtering a view will filter the results of the view, not the results of the underlying table. So if you want to find 10 rows from a view, which retrieves all 1,000,000 rows from an underlying table, you will read all 1,000,000 rows—just to find 10 rows.

15.6 ⑩ₘ The Recycle Bin

Oracle Database 10*g* introduces a recycle bin, much like the recycle bin in the Windows operating system. This feature is certainly very useful from the perspective of database administration, but it could cause problems with space and perhaps even performance if the recycle bin is not regularly monitored and cleared.

Check the contents of the recycle bin by selecting from the RECY-CLEBIN or USER_RECYCLEBIN views.

This chapter covered some rather vague aspects of Oracle Database logical object tuning, even containing some necessary repetition from previous chapters. The next chapter will look into block level tuning regardless of the object type.

15.7 Endnotes

1.   Oracle Data Warehouse Tuning for 10*g* (Gavin Powell, Digital Press, Aug 2005, ISBN: 1555583350)

16

Low-Level Physical Tuning

This chapter will cover the second layer of object physical tuning, dealing with explicit block and extent level tuning within objects. I like to call block and extent level tuning low-level physical tuning.

There are a few things we need to reiterate and freshly discover before going too deeply into low-level Oracle Database tuning.

Note: There are many pre-Oracle 10*g* Database installations still in existence. This chapter is retained for backward compatibility with Oracle 9*i* Database as well as prior versions of Oracle Database.

Note: ⑨*i* The large majority of the detail in this chapter is about dictionary-managed tablespaces.

Note: ⑩*g* Most of the detail in this chapter is irrelevant to locally managed tablespaces when using the recommended automated extent management and the automated segment space management features. Locally managed tablespaces are the norm.

16.1 What Is the High-Water Mark?

Often a table, index, or database object is referred to as a segment. The high-water mark of a segment is the maximum number of blocks ever used in that segment. Space can be removed from segments by deletions, fully or partially freeing up blocks. Therefore, the high-water mark of a table is the highest block number ever used by that table for data. This is not the same thing as not allocated extent space. The high-water mark is not reset when data is deleted. When a full table scan is performed, each block is read up to the table's high-water mark. If a new table with 100 free blocks has inserts filling 70 blocks, followed by deletes freeing 20 blocks, then that table's high-water mark is 70 blocks and not 50 blocks (70–20). A full table scan on this table will physically read 70 blocks, even though 20 of those 70 blocks have been deleted. This is yet another reason that it is good for performance to avoid full table scans and use indexes. This is especially true of large tables with extensive DML deletion activity.

It is true that full table scans will be faster than index plus table reads, particularly for index range scans, if enough rows are read. However, the point about the high-water mark is that the more deletions that occur, without reuse of fully or partially freed up blocks, the more likely a full table scan will read deleted blocks. Small transactional OLTP databases do not benefit generally from full scans of any kind unless tables are very small and static.

16.2   Space Used in a Database

There can be a lot of wasted space in datafiles because of various-sized extents, as new extents cannot fit into smaller, older empty extents. This type of behavior was common in older versions of Oracle Database, where the default value for PCTINCREASE, in dictionary-managed tablespaces, was set to 50%. Extents can be coalesced and possibly reused by joining adjacent extents together. In my experience, coalescence and deallocation are not very effective.

The following query result shows the full database size of my testing database as 4,489Mb. About 75% of that space is used. This means that 25% of currently allocated extent space is wasted or not as yet used. This space could simply be allocated space, but it could also be deleted space that has not as of yet been reused:

*****	%Free	%Used	Mb Free	Mb Used	Size
Database Size	22	78	998	3491	4489

Here is the same output expanded for all tablespaces in the database. All tablespaces are locally managed:

Tablespace	%Free	%Used	Mb Free	Mb Used
SYSTEM	2	98	7	403
OEM	0	100	0	749
CWMLITE	53	47	11	9
DRSYS	52	48	10	10
RBS	95	5	690	33
USERS	48	52	30	32
ODM	53	47	11	9
TOOLS	39	61	4	6
DATA	17	83	165	812
XDB	0	100	0	38
INDX	5	95	66	1381
OBJECTS	31	69	4	9
SMALLDATA	75	25	0	0

The scripts to produce these queries, along with scripts displaying sizes for all table and index segments and extents, are included in Appendix B.

16.3 What Are Row Chaining and Row Migration?

Row chaining and migration refer to the overflow of blocks to other blocks when data cannot fit into a single block. Additionally, chained blocks might be spread across disk storage haphazardly, somewhat like overflow to a separate part of a disk storage area. A lot of row chaining and row migration can make for very poor performance.

More specifically, row chaining occurs when a row is too large for a single block and thus the row is *chained*, or spread across multiple blocks. Row migration occurs when updating. Updating increases the row size, prohibiting the whole row from fitting into a single block. The row is migrated or moved elsewhere, leaving only a pointer in the original block. It is possible that a row migration can lead to a row chain as well, if the row is large enough. Row chains can be removed by table reconstruction, such as recreating the table or using export and reimport utilities.

Row migration can be minimized by allocating more empty (free) space in each block when the block is first used for insertion. The down side to increasing free space on initial block insertion is that rows will be less compacted. The result will be fewer rows per block on average. High row-to-block ratios (high row density) lead to faster access time because there are more rows read per block when blocks are scanned.

Row chaining is obviously more likely to occur when using smaller block sizes, either at the database level or in smaller tablespaces when using variable block-sized tablespaces.

16.4　Different Types of Objects

The size and usage of tables affect the way that physical structure should be organized. What are the different types of objects from this perspective?

- ■ ***Transactional data***. Tables with high DML activity can have a profound effect on physical requirements. Updates on large datatypes making column values larger should have more free space available for future updates. High deletion activity dictates that blocks will become available for insertions again when a threshold is reached. Less space is wasted when blocks are more likely to be reused. Tables with high insertion activity and little update or deletion activity do not have to reserve free space.

- ■ ***Read-only and static data***. Read-only or static tables such as data warehouse dimension tables or OLTP database lookup tables do not require any reserved space for later changes. In these cases, all block space can be used when initially filling the tables.

- ■ ***Large tables***. Regardless of volatility, both large and small tables should be treated differently. Very large tables should use as much space as possible in each block in order to minimize disk space used. The more physical space that is read when data is retrieved, the more I/O and CPU time is used, and thus the worse the performance is.

- ■ ***Small tables***. Very small tables with high concurrency rates can present problems all their own. Small static tables that are never changed are generally not a problem as long as any foreign keys are indexed. Some small semistatic tables can present serious concurrency issues when they are subject to high amounts of DML activity. The Accounts schema has a number of tables of this nature, particularly the Customer, Supplier, and COA tables. Each of these tables has summarized values. Originally, I used triggers in my DBMS_JOBS-initiated highly active database code. I had serious problems with deadlocks updating the summary columns. I disabled the triggers and updated these columns in batch mode when my activity code was no longer running. High concurrency changes can be made to small tables at the block level to resolve this problem. Years ago when working in the Ingres relational database, the only method of resolving this type of problem was by filling each row with an empty column (a filler column), padding each row up to the block size. Thus, each row occupied a single block, and there was little concurrency competition between different records that were stored in the same block. Of course, in those days Ingres block locked rather than row locked. Oracle Database locks rows and does not lock at the block level. Using filler columns is an extreme solution but always a possibility even with Oracle Database.

16.5 How Much Block and Extent Tuning?

The simple answer to this question is not too much. Look for extremes and adjust block-sizing parameters for specific tables and indexes. Also remember that as of Oracle 9*i* Database, it is possible to separate out problematic tables into discrete block-size tablespaces, achieving separation both physically and in memory.

16.6 Choosing Database Block Size

In general, larger block sizes are appropriate to read-only data warehouse–type databases. Smaller block sizes are appropriate to highly concurrent, highly active OLTP databases with small transactions. Block size can be 2K, 4K, 8K, 16K, and 32K. OLTP databases can benefit from smaller block sizes because I/O activity is frequent but usually occurs in very small chunks. An OLTP database could have serious problems reading a few bytes of data from 32K blocks. Data warehouses can benefit from larger block sizes because large amounts of I/O activity are performed all at once. A data warehouse would suffer immense performance problems reading huge volumes of data from a block size of 2K because of the huge number of blocks it would have to read.

Note: Available block sizes and DB_nK_CACHE_SIZE parameters may vary for different operating systems. A 32K block size is not available for Win2K SP3 running Oracle 9*i* or Oracle 10*g*.

A block size of 8K is the Oracle Database default. I have never seen an OLTP Oracle database with a block size of less than 8K, other than older versions of Oracle Database. Definitely beware of an OLTP Oracle database with 16K or 32K block size.

One other important factor is the DB_FILE_MULTIBLOCK_READ_COUNT parameter.

Note: (9*i*) The SORT_MULTIBLOCK_READ_COUNT was deprecated in Oracle 9*i* Database and is not even in the manuals for Oracle 10*g* Database.

The DB_FILE_MULTIBLOCK_READ_COUNT parameter allows the reading of multiple blocks at once. The default value for this parameter is operating system–dependent and is usually 8 for OLTP databases. I generally set this value to 8, but it can be set to 4 or even 2 for OLTP databases, depending on reporting and the nastiness of application SQL code. It can be higher for a data warehouse. Any reporting or poorly written SQL code tends to warrant a possible higher setting for the DB_FILE_MULTIBLOCK_READ_COUNT parameter. Bad SQL code tends to execute more full scanning anyway. Setting the DB_FILE_MULTIBLOCK_READ_COUNT parameter higher will encourage more full physical scanning.

So beware of OLTP databases with block size larger than 8K and a high DB_FILE_MULTIBLOCK_READ_COUNT. Large blocks and large block read counts do not fit well with small transactions and high DML activity. The result could be wasted I/O and probably extensive locking and latch wait problems. Bigger reads keep more blocks busy at once. Do not set high values for anything to do with block size for OLTP databases. Do the opposite for data warehouse databases. Let's look further at different types of databases briefly:

- *OLTP/DSS database*. A smaller block size of perhaps 8K is preferable. If some reporting is required, then multiple block reads can be taken advantage of. Also poorly written SQL code is common, which may execute a lot of full scans. Locking and latch wait problems could result, but it is best to keep to commonly used standards. A block size of 8K is a commonly used standard. *A balance between low block contention and the ability to read large amounts of data is important*. With larger block sizes, lock levels can become incremental, in that locks on rows can degenerate into block locks and sometimes even exclusive table locks. The reason is that there are more rows contained in each block.

■ *High DML concurrency OLTP database with small transactions.* Use a small block size, perhaps even 4K or 2K. These block sizes are generally not used, but very good performance would be gained for small transactions. Additionally, table row lengths must be short. *Getting less block contention is important.* A small block size is better for index searches. As a side issue, very high concurrency databases can have concurrency parameters adjusted to help with multiple session access and updates. However, high concurrency settings reserve more block header space and reduce block space available for data.

■ *Data warehouse or read only.* Use the largest block size possible (32K), assuming there is low concurrency. Higher concurrency should probably have the block size changed to 16K. *Reading large amounts of data at once is important for heavy I/O activity access.* Larger block size is better for full table scans, as they tend to encourage them.

Note: There is no reason that different tables in any type of database could not be placed into different block-sized tablespaces. Many issues can be resolved by using multiple block sizes, effectively providing multiple, non-conflicting pools of data at both the physical I/O and memory buffer levels. Multiple block-sized tablespaces can replace the KEEP and RECYCLE database buffer pools introduced in Oracle 8*i* Database.

16.7 Physical Block Structure

I like to make a distinction between physical block attributes and extent attributes. A block is a subset of an extent. Blocks contain data values. Extents are added to datafiles when a database object, such as a table, requires more physical datafile space, and none can be allocated from existing unused extents. Extents can be sized, and blocks can have specific allocation behaviors.

In this section, we will discuss what is known as either the segments clause or the physical attributes clause. We will cover the storage clause later in this chapter. Physical attributes affect the physical structure of blocks and apply to objects such as tables, indexes, or clusters. Some factors apply to all object types and some apply to specific object types.

16.7.1   What Is in a Block?

A data block is the smallest unit of storage in a database. The block format is the same, regardless of the type of object contained in the data block. In general, an Oracle Database block is divided into specific parts. These parts can be described vaguely as follows:

- *Fixed header.* The fixed header space contains general block information, such as block address and segment type. The fixed block header is as shown in Figure 16.1, and size may vary by segment type.

Figure 16.1
Block fixed header

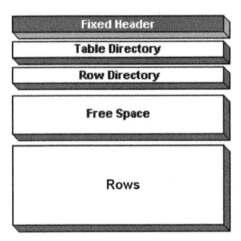

- *Table directory.* The table directory space stores information about the tables and rows stored in the block, as shown in Figure 16.2. Only clusters allow two or more tables to share a block.

- *Row directory.* The row directory area contains information about all rows in the block, as shown in Figure 16.3. Each row requires a few bytes of overhead. The row directory grows as rows are added to the block.

- *Free space.* The free space area is the amount of space available for either insertion of new rows into the block or updates to existing rows, as shown in Figure 16.4.

- *Row data.* The row data space contains table or index data, as shown in Figure 16.5.

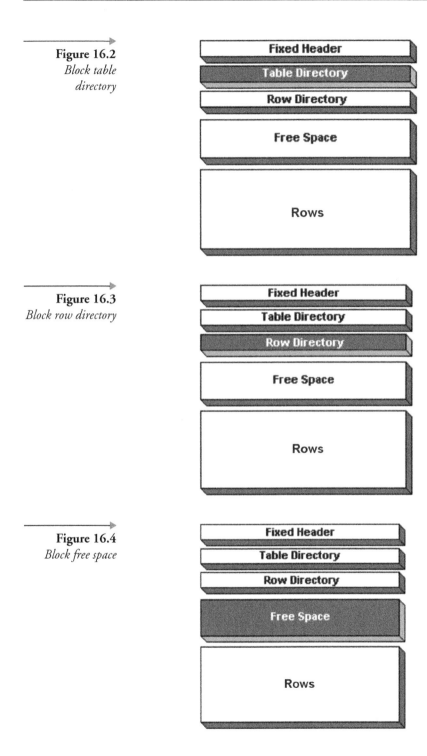

Figure 16.2
Block table directory

Figure 16.3
Block row directory

Figure 16.4
Block free space

Figure 16.5
Block row data

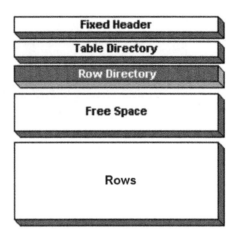

16.7.2 Block Space Management

Two parameters or settings are used to control how physical space is used in a block. PCTUSED determines how much space is required before rows can be inserted into a block. PCTFREE determines how much space is left free in a block when that block is first added to.

Default values for PCTUSED and PCTFREE are 40% and 10%, respectively:

- **PCTUSED.** When a block has rows deleted such that its capacity falls below 40%, it is placed onto a list of blocks available for insertion of new rows.

Note: Indexes do not reclaim space at the leaf block level where the index column values are stored. PCTUSED does not apply to indexes and index-organized tables. This makes it essential to occasionally rebuild BTree indexes if their tables are subject to heavy deletion activity.

- **PCTFREE.** In every block, 10% of space is reserved as empty. When a row is updated and a row's length is increased, that free space is used by the extra bytes required.

By no means do the Oracle Database default values have to be used. In fact, it is advisable to change these values for certain types of combinations of DML activity on tables and indexes.

Let's go through the process of tuning the block structure in the Accounts schema. My Accounts schema is a heavily concurrent DML-intensive database. I will also adjust the approach, assuming that an application would be running against this schema, including some reporting based on content in tables. First of all, take a look at Figure 16.6. Figure 16.6 shows all tables with rows and blocks occupied after statistics generation.

The number of rows in a table and the number of blocks occupied are both important with respect to both DML and query SELECT activity. Searching fewer rows is faster. Searching less physical space is also better. On the contrary, a few rows being accessed by many sessions using DML statements all at once can cause performance problems as well. Accessing a lot of rows in a single block is good for data retrieval—but not necessarily for concurrent changes.

Possible changes for PCTUSED and PCTFREE parameters are shown in Figure 16.7. Index block structures must be changed in the same way that their respective tables are changed. This is because indexes undergo the same DML and query SELECT activity as their respective tables do.

What exactly have I done in Figure 16.7? That is the question that should be asked. I have done various things for various reasons. Let's work through a list to break it up into easily understandable pieces.

What are influential factors for altering PCTUSED and PCTFREE?

- *Type of table*. A static table either does not change or changes very little, and it is usually very small, though not necessarily too small. Static tables are usually lookup tables in an OLTP database (dimensions in a data warehouse), but they can be subject to small amounts of DML activity.

- *Number of rows*. Distinguish between extremely small, average, and very large tables. Extremely small tables generally fit into a single block. Average-sized tables are often static but occupy less than 100 blocks. Extremely large tables can have millions of rows and can potentially occupy millions of blocks.

- *Insert activity*. Raise PCTUSED for high insert activity to allow for reuse of blocks more easily.

Figure 16.6

*Accounts schema
current row and
block numbers*

Table	Type	Rows	Blocks	MBytes
CASHBOOK	T	450957	4067	32
CASHBOOKLINE	T	2529733	6557	51
CATEGORY	SL	13	1	
COA	S	55	1	
CUSTOMER	SS	2694	60	
GENERALLEDGER	TL	2158809	9654	75
ORDERS	T	435076	1924	15
ORDERSLINE	T	2866927	9757	76
PERIOD	S	72	1	
PERIODSUM	S	221	1	
POSTING	S	8	1	
STOCK	S	118	4	
STOCKMOVEMENT	TL	3032315	12937	101
STOCKSOURCE	SS	12083	30	
SUBTYPE	SL	4	1	
SUPPLIER	SS	3874	85	1
TRANSACTIONS	T	450957	3091	24
TRANSACTIONSLINE	T	2896275	9847	77
TYPE	SL	6	1	
		14840197	58020	452

Static Lookup	SL
Static (subject to DML)	S
Semi Static (Large)	SS
Transactional	T
Transaction Large	TL

Figure 16.6

Accounts schema current row and block numbers

- **Update activity.** Raise PCTFREE for high update activity involving possible row length changes.

- **Delete activity.** Raise PCTUSED to allow for future reuse of blocks.

- **Select activity.** Lower PCTFREE and raise PCTUSED to squash more rows into each block, increasing data retrieval performance.

- **Potential concurrency.** This is very important. The more rows in a single block that have DML activity on them at once (concurrently), then the more likely hot blocking and locking will occur. Locking can cause the biggest potential performance problems due to lock and latch waits, especially in highly active OLTP databases like my Accounts schema.

Figure 16.7

Changes to block structure space usage

Table	Type	Rows	Insert	Update	Delete	Select	%Free	%Used
CASHBOOK	T	450957	H				1	80
CASHBOOKLINE	T	2529733	H				1	80
CATEGORY	SL	13	EL	EL	EL		0	99
COA	S	55	EL	EH	EL	EH	50	10
CUSTOMER	SS	2694	L	VH	VL	VH	20	70
GENERALLEDGER	TL	2158809	EH		H	H	0	99
ORDERS	T	435076	H				1	80
ORDERSLINE	T	2866927	H				1	80
PERIOD	S	72	EL		EL	EL	0	99
PERIODSUM	S	221	EL	EH	EL		30	20
POSTING	S	8	EL		EL	EH	0	99
STOCK	S	118	EL	VH	EL	VH	30	20
STOCKMOVEMENT	TL	3032315	EH		H	H	0	99
STOCKSOURCE	SS	12083	EL	H	EL	VH	5	60
SUBTYPE	SL	4	EL		EL	EH	0	99
SUPPLIER	SS	3874	L	VH	VL	VH	20	70
TRANSACTIONS	T	450957	H				1	80
TRANSACTIONSLINE	T	2896275	H				1	80
TYPE	SL	6	EL		EL	EH	0	99
		14840197					**8**	**75**

Static Lookup	SL			
Static (subject to DML)	S	Extreme	EH / EL	
Semi Static (Large)	SS	Very	VH / VL	
Transactional	T	Low/High	L / H	
Transaction Large	TL			

Note: The biggest danger of setting low PCTFREE values is chained and migrated rows. Check the CHAIN_CNT statistic column in the USER_TABLES view.

Now I will group the tables and examine why I changed values for each table grouping:

- *Static lookup*. Category, Period, Subtype, and Type. These tables have PCTFREE = 0 and PCTUSED = 99. There is no point reserving free space for tables not subject to any DML activity. Lookup tables are only ever read and may as well be squashed up as much as possible. This helps to ensure a single block read every time.

- *Static (subject to DML)*. The Period and Posting tables are subject to very occasional DML activity, and so settings other than 0 and 99 would probably be pointless. Additionally, the Posting table is subject to intense query SELECT activity. This is better served by ensuring fewer blocks are occupied. The PeriodSum, Stock, and COA tables have high PCTFREE and low PCTUSED values for two reasons:

1. All three tables are subject to a lot of updates. The COA table is higher than the Period and Posting tables because those updates involve higher row length growth. PCTFREE and PCTUSED can only be applied to new blocks. Thus, existing data cannot be affected. It makes sense to change these values on empty tables and then fill the tables with rows. Columns will be null valued to start with. Three columns on the COA table are updated constantly. The Stock table has more rows updated but not as often. The same occurs with the PeriodSum table because it is an aggregation of the COA table.

2. The second reason for high PCTFREE and low PCTUSED is to attempt to alleviate potential DML activity concurrency issues. Oracle Database locks rows, and, unlike other relational databases, does not escalate row locking to block locks, even if there is high concurrent DML activity. Concurrent capacity in a block can be increased using the INITRANS and MAXTRANS parameters. High concurrent block activity can, however, lead to hot blocks and contention. Therefore, it makes sense to attempt to distribute rows over more blocks. These tables are small, and multiple blocks read counts will probably cover a single read, even though there are potentially more blocks. The chances are, if all the block and row size values were calculated precisely, PCTFREE would probably have to be a lot higher. It is best to utilize a combination of multiple parameters including PCTUSED, PCTFREE, and INITRANS.

Note: (10*g*) MAXTRANS is deprecated.

- *Semistatic (large)*. The Customer and Supplier tables are updated frequently but are much larger than the other static tables. The Customer and Supplier tables are subject to a lot of lookup activity and warrant relatively high PCTUSED values. PCTFREE is low at 20% but allows for some updating row length growth. The StockSource table does not grow nearly as much as Customer and Supplier tables, in terms of updates, because only a single column is changed, rather than three columns. Also, queries executing against the StockSource table tend to read large numbers of rows.

- *Transactional*. All standard transaction tables involve three master detail relationships for orders, transactions, and cashbook entries. These tables are generally largely subject to insertion activity due to the nature of their purpose. That is what transactional tables quite often do. They add new data to a database. It is very unlikely that an accounting system would have frequent changes to invoices. Accounting practices are strictly controlled. Changes to transactions involve new transactions executing the opposite effect. In other words, a sale transaction is documented using an invoice. A return of sale does not change the invoice, but rather creates a new transaction called a credit note. The invoice and credit note are separate transactions. As a result, all six of these tables have minimal PCTFREE and fairly high PCTUSED values. PCTUSED is not set to an extreme of 80%. This is because transactional files in accounting systems are typically purged or transferred to archives at the end of distinct periods, such as every quarter.

- *Transactional large*. The GeneralLedger and StockMovement tables are very similar to logs or audit trails. A log file is filled over a period of time and then purged. Purging processing may involve aggregation into other tables, archiving, or even complete destruction of data. These types of tables are usually subject to heavy insertion and full table scan query SELECT activity. So, PCTFREE is 0 and PCTUSED is high, but not too high. Therefore PCTUSED is 80% and not 99% because these tables are large and space must be conserved. On the contrary, INSERT commands are better executed into clean blocks if possible, where appending of data would be faster than searching for usable blocks. When a table like this is purged, it is probably best to TRUNCATE the entire table, rather than delete, or perhaps even drop and recreate the table. If that is the case, then PCTUSED can be set to 99%.

16.7.2.1 Assessing PCTFREE Settings

A vague attempt can be made at assessing PCTFREE settings using a query like the following one:

```
COL Table FORMAT a16;
COL Rows FORMAT 9999999;
COL Blocks FORMAT 9999999;
```

```
COL RPB FORMAT 9999999 HEADING "Rows/Block";
COL SU FORMAT 9999999 HEADING "Space Used %";

SELECT table_name "Table", num_rows "Rows", blocks "Blocks"
     ,num_rows/blocks AS RPB, ROUND(avg_space/8192*100) AS SU
     ,chain_cnt "Chaining"
FROM user_tables ORDER BY table_name;
```

The results of this query are shown next. Bear in mind that no changes have been made to PCTUSED and PCTFREE values in the Accounts schema at the time of execution of this query. All tables over 1,000 rows have over 10% of free space. This is a particularly obvious problem for the GeneralLedger and StockMovement tables because they never have any update activity:

Table	Rows	Blocks	Rows/Block	Space Used %	Chaining
CASHBOOK	450957	4067	111	13	0
CASHBOOKLINE	2529733	6557	386	11	0
CATEGORY	13	1	13	96	0
COA	55	1	55	77	0
CUSTOMER	2694	60	45	17	0
GENERALLEDGER	**2158809**	**9654**	**224**	**10**	**0**
ORDERS	435076	1924	226	13	0
ORDERSLINE	2866927	9757	294	12	0
PERIOD	72	1	72	68	0
PERIODSUM	221	1	221	35	0
POSTING	8	1	8	94	0
STOCK	118	4	30	27	0
STOCKMOVEMENT	**3032315**	**12937**	**234**	**10**	**0**
STOCKSOURCE	12083	30	403	15	0
SUBTYPE	4	1	4	98	0
SUPPLIER	3874	85	46	16	0
TRANSACTIONS	450957	3091	146	13	0
TRANSACTIONSLINE	2896275	9847	294	12	0
TYPE	6	1	6	98	0

16.7.3 Block Concurrency

Block level concurrency determines the number of locks that can be placed on a block. Concurrency capacity is the ability of rows in the same block to be accessed by multiple sessions at the same time, for both DML and query SELECT activity. At the block level, the parameters INITRANS and MAXTRANS help to control block concurrency. The INITRANS parameter can be increased for higher levels of concurrency:

- **INITRANS**. This parameter determines the initial concurrency allowance for a block. Increasing INITRANS increases block concurrency (active transactions per block) but decreases available row data block space. This is because more space is reserved in each block to allow for higher transactional concurrency rates.

Note: INITRANS must always be at least twice as much for an index as it is for its parent table. The default for a table is 1 and an index is 2. Set INITRANS more than twice for indexes, when indexes are nonunique. The more duplicated values that there are in an index (the lower its cardinality), the higher INITRANS should be, because searches on those values will be more likely to be in the same block.

- **MAXTRANS**. This parameter determines the maximum number of active transactions per block. The more active transactions there are, the more space is required in block header areas and the less space is allowed for row data.

Note: (10*g*) MAXTRANS is obsolete and no longer available.

Let's look once again at the Accounts schema and determine appropriate changes to INITRANS parameters.

Note: (9*i*) I did alter MAXTRANS parameter values, even in the first edition of this book.

Possible changes to INITRANS are shown in Figure 16.8.

In Figure 16.8 INITRANS values have been adjusted to account for potential DML activity concurrency; multiple transactions are changing rows in the same block at once.

Most drastically changed are the COA and PeriodSum tables, based on the high amount of their DML activity. The Stock table INITRANS value

Figure 16.8
Changes to block
structure
concurrency

Table	Type	Rows	Concurrent	DML	Select	%Free	%Used	Initrans
CASHBOOK	T	450957		H		1	80	1
CASHBOOKLINE	T	2529733		H		1	80	1
CATEGORY	SL	13				0	99	1
COA	S	55	EH	EH	EH	50	10	16
CUSTOMER	SS	2694	H	VH	VH	20	70	2
GENERALLEDGER	TL	2158809	H	EH	H	0	99	2
ORDERS	T	435076		H		1	80	1
ORDERSLINE	T	2866927		H		1	80	1
PERIOD	S	72			EL	0	99	1
PERIODSUM	S	221	VH	EH		30	20	8
POSTING	S	8	EH		EH	0	99	2
STOCK	S	118	VH	VH	VH	30	20	4
STOCKMOVEMENT	TL	3032315	H	EH	H	0	99	2
STOCKSOURCE	SS	12083		H	VH	5	60	1
SUBTYPE	SL	4	EH		EH	0	99	2
SUPPLIER	SS	3874	H	VH	VH	20	70	2
TRANSACTIONS	T	450957		H		1	80	1
TRANSACTIONSLINE	T	2896275		H		1	80	1
TYPE	SL	6	EH		EH	0	99	2
		14840197				8	75	3

Static Lookup	SL			
Static (subject to DML)	S	Extreme	EH / EL	
Semi Static (Large)	SS	Very	VH / VL	
Transactional	T	Low/High	L / H	
Transaction Large	TL			

is lower because it occupies more physical blocks than the other two tables (see Figure 16.6). The large static tables have INITRANS set to 2 because they are subject to concurrent UPDATE command activity. Setting INI-TRANS to 2 for the GeneralLedger and StockMovement tables is probably an unwise choice. These tables are subject to intense INSERT command activity. A reduction in concurrency problems could probably be resolved by changing their sequence number–generated primary keys into reverse key indexes. Reverse key indexes would prevent concurrent sequential inser-tions of similar key values into the same block for the primary key index.

Note: Blocks already created cannot have their PCTUSED, PCTFREE, INITRANS, and MAXTTRANS parameters changed. Changes only apply to new blocks.

16.8   Extent Level Storage Parameters

> **Note:** (10g) Automated extent management in locally managed tablespaces avoids the complexity and potential inefficiencies when using the STORAGE clause for dictionary-managed tablespaces.

Extent level storage parameters apply to groups of blocks created in an extent, when a segment in a tablespace is increased in size. A segment is increased in size when more space is required by new data. There are a number of parameters using the following syntax. Also, some parameters apply to specific object types:

```
STORAGE({
    [ INITIAL n[K|M] ] [ NEXT n[K|M] ]
    [ MINEXTENTS n ] [ MAXEXTENTS { n | UNLIMITED } ]
    [ PCTINCREASE n ]
    [ FREELISTS n ] [ FREELIST GROUPS n ]
    [ OPTIMAL [ n[K|M] | NULL ] ]
    [ BUFFER_POOL { KEEP | RECYCLE | DEFAULT } ]});
```

Let's look at the details.

16.8.1   Setting Extent Sizes

Initial and next extent sizes can be set using the INITIAL and NEXT parameters. As far as physical tuning is concerned, here are a number of pointers:

- Use a minimal number of extent sizes between different tablespaces and database objects, such as tables and indexes. For some databases, all extent sizes can be consistent throughout.

- If using different extent sizes, then standardize different objects according to a rule, such as functionality or growth rates.

- Do not use Oracle Database defaults. They are small and will ultimately give you a lot of problems if your database grows at even a reasonable rate.

INITIAL sets the size of the first extent. NEXT sets the size for all but the first extent, unless PCTINCREASE is used. PCTINCREASE is best avoided. Generally you can use kilobyte (K) ranges for small tables, but use nothing less than 1M for anything larger than that. If you do want to use sizes matching each table, then do not use too many different sizes, especially in the same tablespace. Deleted extents are not reused unless new extent requirements can fit into the old extent. Defragmentation on large tables is a much more serious problem than fitting a one-block static table into a 1M extent; space is wasted physically but access time is not increased. Oracle Database reads in blocks and not in extents. It reads one block multiplied by the multiblock read count parameter value. 1M will not be read. If you must use multiple extent sizes, perhaps separate different objects into different tablespaces based on differing extent sizes. Perhaps even use multiple block-size-tablespaces. These things will help to alleviate fragmentation in the future.

16.8.2 Minimum and Maximum Extents

The MINEXTENTS value specifies that any new extent added to a datafile must be created at a minimum value, helping to alleviate fragmentation.

MAXEXTENTS should be set to UNLIMITED for everything but objects you know are uncontrollable and when you are not concerned about causing a problem if MAXEXTENTS is reached. Do not set MAXEXTENTS UNLIMITED for rollback segments if there is any development or ad hoc SQL activity. Runaway transactions do occur sometimes and can cause rollback, which resizes a datafile upward so far as to fill all disk space and potentially crash your database.

Note: (10gR2) Manual rollback is still available for backward compatibility, and will eventually be removed from Oracle Database altogether. However, manual rollback is obsolete and replaced by automatic undo (automatic rollback).

16.8.3 Variable Extent Sizes

PCTINCREASE can be used to gradually increase the size of extents. Do not use it. In a past version of Oracle Database, PCTINCREASE had to be set to at least 1. This was required to help automate tablespace level coalescence. The default for PCTINCREASE was 50% in past versions of Oracle

Database. Manual coalescence never really worked very well, so I do not see why automated coalescence should either. Also the defragmentation problem will crop up once again.

PCTINCREASE increases each new extent as a percentage increase of the previous extent. Any deleted extents will likely never be used again because they will all be different sizes. When a new extent is added to a datafile, an existing empty extent can be reused if it is smaller or equal in size to the newly created extent. The PCTINCREASE parameter was the culprit of many Oracle databases in the past being much larger and much slower than they should have been. Fortunately, locally managed tablespaces ignore the PCTINCREASE parameter.

16.8.4   **Managing Concurrency**

The FREELIST GROUPS and FREELIST parameters are generally only meaningful in very highly concurrent environments, such as Oracle RAC (parallel server/clustered) environments. These parameters are beyond the scope of this book.

16.8.5   **Minimizing Rollback Resizing**

The OPTIMAL parameter determines the number of extents to which a rollback segment will shrink after having extended and completed a transaction. If OPTIMAL is not set, then no rollback segment shrinkage will occur. Shrinking rollback segments will result in those rollback segments potentially extending once again when reused. Continuous extending and shrinking are a waste of time and hardware resources. Increase OPTIMAL until it matches the size of most transactions. This can be assessed by minimizing the SHRINKS column in the V$ROLLSTAT dynamic performance view.

Note: (10gR2) Manual rollback is still available for backward compatibility but will eventually be removed from Oracle Database altogether. Manual rollback is obsolete and replaced by automatic undo (automatic rollback).

Setting this parameter is not required for automatic undo.

16.8.6 **Different Cache Recently Used Lists**

The BUFFER_POOL storage setting allows for objects such as tables to be placed into different parts of the database buffer cache, or more specifically have them placed into either the MRU or LRU lists. The MRU list allows faster access by retaining blocks in the database buffer cache. The LRU list forces blocks out of the database buffer cache faster.

Various other options exist in Oracle Database for the purpose of caching specific tables in the database buffer cache. One is the CACHE option in the CREATE TABLE and ALTER TABLE commands. Another is using multiple block sizes for tablespaces and their related multiple-sized database buffer caches. The DB_KEEP_CACHE_SIZE and DB_RECYCLE_CACHE_SIZE parameters are to be used in favor of the BUFFER_POOL storage setting.

Note: (9*i*) BUFFER_POOL settings of KEEP and RECYCLE are Oracle 9*i* Database technology.

Note: (10*g*) The DB_KEEP_CACHE_SIZE and DB_RECYCLE_CACHE_SIZE parameters are Oracle 10*g* technology.

This chapter covered the low-level aspects of physical tuning encompassing block and extent structures.

Note: There are many pre-Oracle 10*g* Database installations still in existence. This chapter is retained for backward compatibility with Oracle 9*i* Database as well as prior versions of Oracle Database.

(9*i*) A large majority of the detail in this chapter are about dictionary-managed tablespaces.

(10*g*) Most of the detail in this chapter is irrelevant to locally managed tablespaces when using the recommended automated extent management and the automated segment space management features.

The next chapter will cover hardware resource usage tuning in the areas of CPU, memory, and I/O usage.

17

Hardware Resource Usage Tuning

This chapter will briefly introduce hardware resource usage tuning, specifically dealing with CPU usage, memory usage, and I/O usage. More of the details on how to tune these various areas of an Oracle installation will be covered in later chapters. Let's start with tuning CPU usage.

17.1 Tuning Oracle CPU Usage

Central processing unit (CPU) usage can be best assessed at peak times and thus peak CPU workload times. What are peak workloads? This depends entirely on your application. An online transaction processing (OLTP), or Internet application, is generally active and available 24 hours a day, 365 days a year. There may be peak times and quiet times for OLTP databases. Any very large and highly active OLTP database generally passes batch operation work onto a data warehouse database wherever possible. Decision support systems (DSS)–type databases tend to be a mixture of OLTP, client server, and data warehouse–type functionality. Therefore, some databases may have peak workloads for different types of activity at different times of the day. It is quite possible that client server or OLTP-type service is provided during the day and batch operations are processed at night. The point to be made is this: do not waste your time looking for something wrong with CPU usage when the CPU is idle. Wait until the CPU is very busy and then try to figure out what is overloading it, if anything. The CPU could simply be busy because that is what it is meant to be doing—being busy!

So what do we do about tuning CPU usage? Well, we cannot actually tune CPU usage itself, we can only determine what is being processed at any particular time and try to figure out what is causing heavy load or spiking. From there, perhaps we can tune what is being processed and perhaps better distribute processing if there is conflict, as a result of different types of processing executing concurrently. Obviously, processors can be upgraded and multiple CPU hardware platforms can be purchased. The crux of tuning CPU usage is to find out what is causing the problem and then tune the cause rather than attempt to *do something about the CPU*.

17.1.1   Busy I/O and Intense CPU Activity

Is I/O activity intense, and are CPUs very busy? If this is the case then it means that I/O is performing at a speed that is relatively too close to that of CPU processing time. I/O activity should be much slower than the CPU. The CPU is very much a faster piece of hardware than disk storage, without question. Excessive CPU activity can be due to a number of causes. We will concentrate on things that are directly Oracle Database–related, rather than dig into the operating system too much.

17.1.1.1   Swapping and Paging

Swapping and paging are not precisely the same thing, but the two terms are often used together in a confusing manner. A swap or a page fault occurs when a chunk of data is required but that chunk is not in memory. The chunk of data is then retrieved from swap space on disk and exchanged with something else if there is not enough space in RAM. Thus the information is swapped between RAM and a swap file on disk.

Note: A swap file in Windows is called a paging file. The Windows paging file is added to RAM and constitutes virtual memory. The Windows paging file can be found in the System icon of the Control Panel.

Swapping or paging between disk and RAM physical memory is not a problem unless it occurs frequently, generating large amounts of I/O. Sometimes a process can cause a lot of swapping over and over again.

Swapping and paging can cause unnecessary use of the CPU, with respect to Oracle Database, often as a result of something caused within an Oracle Database configuration or a specific application activity. The easy, short-term solution to swapping and paging is purchasing more RAM. However, as a system is scaled upward in size and activity, if other problems are continuously placated and hidden by making hardware upgrades, those hardware upgrades may eventually become very expensive.

17.1.2 Possible Causes of High CPU Activity

Unnecessary CPU use can often be the result of Oracle Database activity and related applications behavior.

17.1.2.1 Poorly Tuned SQL Code

Poorly tuned SQL code can cause a lot of reparsing, which can cause intense CPU activity. Following are parsing and execution statistics:

```
COL name FORMAT a20;
SELECT name, value FROM v$sysstat
WHERE name LIKE '%parse%' OR name LIKE '%execute count%';
```

This is the result:

```
NAME                       VALUE
---------------------- --------
parse time cpu              1618
parse time elapsed        15096
parse count (total)       82683
parse count (hard)          293
parse count (failure)         8
execute count            184523
```

In the next query, currently executing SQL code is interrogated. Note that the Product column is a product (a multiplication) of both parses and executions. The frequency of parses is more important than just the parses or executions:

```
COL sql_text FORMAT A38;
SELECT * FROM(
SELECT  parse_calls*executions "Product", parse_calls
"Parses"
 ,executions "Execs", sql_text FROM v$sqlarea ORDER BY 1 DESC)
WHERE ROWNUM <= 10;
```

This is the result:

```
  Product      Parses       Execs SQL_TEXT
---------- ----------- ----------- ----------------------------------------
  53740146       2454       21899 INSERT into cashbookline values(:b3,:b
  53740146       2454       21899 INSERT into ordersline values(:b4,:b3,
  53740146       2454       21899 INSERT into transactionsline values(:b
  53740146       2454       21899 INSERT into stockmovement values(stock
  49695750       3250       15291 SELECT to_number(to_char(SYSTIMESTAMP,
  40742689       6383        6383 COMMIT
  37466641       6121        6121 INSERT into generalledger values (gene
  37466641       6121        6121 INSERT into generalledger values (gene
  32890000       3250       10120 SELECT systimestamp FROM sys.dual
  10575504       3252        3252 select privilege#,level from sysauth$
```

Increasing the SESSION_CACHED_CURSORS parameter allows caching of more SQL statements per session. This potentially helps to reduce parsing. However, the use of bind variables in SQL code will reduce parsing much more significantly, especially for highly concurrent OLTP databases, where SQL code is highly shareable and when SQL code is poorly tuned.

17.1.2.2 Poor Index Usage

Missing indexes or too many large composite indexes can cause a lot of full table scans, leading to high I/O, swapping, and probably high CPU usage times. Lack of use of indexes is most likely indicated by too many full table scans, particularly those on large tables, as indicated in the following query by full table scans on long tables (*table scans (long tables)*):

```
COL name FORMAT a32;
SELECT name, value FROM v$sysstat
WHERE name IN ('table scans (short tables)'
 ,'table scans (long tables)','table fetch by rowid');
```

This is the result:

```
NAME                                 VALUE
--------------------------------- ----------
table scans (short tables)           40420
table scans (long tables)              111
table fetch by rowid                 85673
```

17.1.2.3 (10*g*) **Automated Undo and** (9*i*) **Manual Rollback**

Problems with high undo (or rollback) activity can possibly be resolved by increasing the COMMIT command frequency in SQL code. This can have the effect of reducing the number of SQL statements in single transactions. The overall result is a reduction in transaction size. However, higher commit rates will lead to higher CPU usage and more frequent I/O activity.

Automated undo tends to feel like it is a little less controllable with respect to disk space usage for an administrator who is used to using manual rollback. On the other hand, automated undo removes much of the tuning requirements for manual rollback. And automated undo does appear to perform better in both Oracle 10*g* Database and Oracle Database 9*i*. However, it does not hurt to understand how rollback works because manual rollback and automated undo are essentially performing the same function. You will read about manual rollback shortly. The benefits of using automated undo over manual rollback are numerous. For example, automated undo can be used for high-speed flashback recovery where undo space, in addition to redo log entries, can be used to maintain point-in-time database recovery efforts and examine database data as snapshots in the recent past (a flashback), should the needs ever arise.

Note: (10*g*) Manual rollback is obsolete.

The following query shows a picture of automated undo segment statistics when executing highly active concurrency processing in my Accounts schema:

```
COL undob FORMAT 99990;
COL trans FORMAT 99990;
COL snapshot2old FORMAT 9999999990;
SELECT  undoblks "UndoB", txncount "Trans"
 ,maxquerylen "LongestQuery", maxconcurrency "MaxConcurrency"

 ,ssolderrcnt "Snapshot2Old", nospaceerrcnt "FreeSpaceWait"
FROM v$undostat;
```

This is a partial result of this query, which in my Oracle 10*g* Database returns 145 rows:

UndoB	Trans	LongestQuery	MaxConcurrency	Snapshot2Old	FreeSpaceWait
186	24596	30	66	0	0
4152	24339	71	67	0	0
3703	18835	58	62	0	0
2991	13644	143	74	0	0
2734	9175	13	1	0	0
2696	5372	12	3	0	0
975	1383	12	2	0	0

Serious problems with undo space can sometimes cause *snapshot too old* errors. Snapshot too old errors occur when undo space runs out of space, such uncommitted transactions being overwritten.

Adjust the UNDO_RETENTION parameter to remove snapshot too old errors when using automated undo segments for rollback.

Now let's take a look at manual rollback segments in an Oracle Database 9*i*. **The previous version of this book was written with an Oracle Database 9*i* and used manual rollback segments.**

Note: All the queries shown following can be executed against both manual rollback and automated undo space, depending on what is configured, regardless of the version of Oracle Database.

The query shown next can be used to check rollback segment usage in relation to extension and shrinkage:

Note: (10*g*) Manual rollback is obsolete, but demonstrating its use can help to explain how undo space functions.

```
COL RBS FORMAT a4;
SELECT  n.name "RBS", s.extends "Extends", s.shrinks
"Shrinks"
 ,s.wraps "Wraps", s.aveshrink "AveShrink"
 ,s.aveactive "AveActive"
FROM v$rollname n JOIN v$rollstat s USING(usn)
WHERE n.name != 'SYSTEM';
```

The query result shows wrapping on all manual rollback segments. Rollback segment wraps are not a serious problem. It is a commonly held misconception that wrapping is reuse of the first extent of the currently used rollback segment, causing a snapshot too old error. On the contrary, wrapping is merely expansion of a transaction into a new extent inside the same rollback segment. Excessive wrapping could imply that storage parameters within a rollback segment might be adjusted upward to prevent wrapping:

RBS	Extends	Shrinks	Wraps	AveShrink	AveActive
RB00	0	0	13	0	779254
RB01	0	0	12	0	749639
RB02	0	0	12	0	749639
RB03	0	0	12	0	749330
RB04	0	0	13	0	779254
RB05	0	0	12	0	749330
RB06	0	0	12	0	749330
RB07	0	0	12	0	749330
RB08	0	0	13	0	779254
RB09	0	0	11	0	716991
RB10	0	0	13	0	778713
RB11	0	0	13	0	779254
RB12	0	0	12	0	749330
RB13	0	0	12	0	749330
RB14	0	0	12	0	749639
RB15	0	0	12	0	749639

Note: Do not confuse snapshot too old errors with wrapping in manual rollback segments. A snapshot too old error is cause by not retaining enough undo space or by not creating large enough rollback segments.

Now let's take a different perspective and examine the amount and spread of activity within rollback segments:

```
COL RBS FORMAT a4;
SELECT  n.name "RBS", s.status, s.waits, s.gets, s.writes
,s.xacts "Active Trans"
FROM v$rollname n JOIN v$rollstat s USING(usn)
WHERE n.name != 'SYSTEM';
```

The following query result shows a few interesting points. Transactions are fairly well spread across all the rollback segments, which is good. However, it might be that there are too many transactions per rollback segment. The impact of transactions per rollback segment depends somewhat on transaction size, which is extremely small in my database. There appears to be a fair amount of waiting for space in rollback segments; this is not so good, as something cannot continue to process until something else is out of the way:

RBS	STATUS	WAITS	GETS	WRITES	Active Trans
RB00	ONLINE	9	6452	10669902	5
RB01	ONLINE	15	6375	10485074	4
RB02	ONLINE	14	6614	10670958	5
RB03	ONLINE	14	6800	10670618	5
RB04	ONLINE	19	6872	10759932	4
RB05	ONLINE	7	6431	10527624	5
RB06	ONLINE	13	6478	10707842	4
RB07	ONLINE	13	6345	10324652	4
RB08	ONLINE	10	6662	11237024	4
RB09	ONLINE	16	6270	9979316	4
RB10	ONLINE	14	6668	11021116	5
RB11	ONLINE	11	6412	10775736	3
RB12	ONLINE	13	6762	10702146	4
RB13	ONLINE	6	6476	10279358	5
RB14	ONLINE	12	6497	10475656	5
RB15	ONLINE	9	6341	10398742	4

Transaction waits on rollback segments appear to occur. So let's dig further in that direction. The next query will give an impression of rollback segment contention (competition) for use of rollback segments. At just over 3%, it might be warranted to create more rollback segments. It certainly would not do any harm:

```
SELECT ROUND(SUM(waits/gets)*100,2)||'%' "Contention" FROM
v$rollstat;
```

This is the result:

```
Contention
---------------
3.34%
```

I originally had 16 consistently sized rollback segments, which are then increased to 50 rollback segments. And now for some further querying to see if there is any improvement after having increased the number of rollback segments:

```
COL RBS FORMAT a4;
SELECT  n.name "RBS", s.status, s.waits, s.gets, s.writes
,s.xacts "Active Trans"
FROM v$rollname n JOIN v$rollstat s USING(usn)
WHERE n.name != 'SYSTEM' ORDER BY 1;
```

The query looks only at the first 10 out of 50 rollback segments. Transactions are now better spread across rollback segments. There are fewer active transactions in each rollback segment. Additionally there are much fewer waits:

RBS	STATUS	WAITS	GETS	WRITES	Active Trans
RB00	ONLINE	0	149	158860	1
RB01	ONLINE	0	134	167698	1
RB02	ONLINE	0	145	203588	1
RB03	ONLINE	0	155	186144	2
RB04	ONLINE	0	149	147222	1
RB05	ONLINE	2	276	166638	2
RB06	ONLINE	0	150	151052	1
RB07	ONLINE	0	116	171126	1
RB08	ONLINE	0	145	215020	1
RB09	ONLINE	3	133	202338	1

Looking at contention again, much to my surprise, it has actually increased. This is a classic example of a ratio giving a false impression. I also restarted my database so all rollback statistics are cleared. As time passes, this ratio slowly decreased. When I first started up my database after adding new rollback segments, the ratio was over 12%. It dropped off to around 7%. Over time, it decreased further. Additionally, I was running more than 100 concurrent simulation jobs. Prior to bouncing the database, I was only running 10 jobs per second. The contention percentage shown previously was misleading, as is the following one:

```
COL contention FORMAT 9999999990;
SELECT   AVG(xacts) "Trans per RBS"
         ,ROUND(SUM(waits/gets)*100,2)||'%' "Contention"
FROM v$rollstat;
```

The previous percentage for contention was based on a much smaller load on the database. This current contention value shown here is misleading because it requires a period of time to settle down and build up statistics:

```
Trans per RBS Contention
------------- ------------
   1.35294118 6.92%
```

17.1.2.4 Temporary Sort Space

Temporary sort space can be interrogated using a query such as the following one. Increasing the SORT_AREA_SIZE parameter decreases requirements for temporary sort space on disk but potentially increases memory requirements for database connections:

```
COL username FORMAT a10;
COL segtype FORMAT a10;
SELECT  username, segtype, extents "Extents Allocated"
  ,blocks "Blocks Allocated"
FROM v$tempseg_usage;
```

This is the result:

```
USERNAME    SEGTYPE     Extents Allocated Blocks Allocated
----------  ----------  ----------------- ----------------
ACCSTEST    SORT                       47             6016
```

Note: (10*g*) Automated session connection memory is now the recommended configuration. All _AREA_SIZE configuration parameters are contained within and maintained automatically by the PGA_AGGREGATE_ TARGET configuration parameter.

17.1.2.5   Row Locks and Latch Waits

Table (or row) locking and latch waits can cause waiting, sleeping, and spinning of processes. Locks in the database are possibly indicative of poor data model design or perhaps use of trigger code for event detection. Latch waits can be caused by poor buffer configuration parameters and, yet once again, poor SQL coding.

It is important to note that buffer cache areas can be inappropriately sized in one of four ways: (1) buffers can be too small, (2) buffers can be the wrong sizes in relation to other buffers, (3) buffers can be sized incorrectly according to application requirements, and (4) buffers can even be too large. Making buffers too small can cause latch contention issues. Very large buffers may require intense management by Oracle Database software. There can become a point where the database buffer cache or the shared pool can become so large as to somewhat negate their usefulness. Additionally, large buffers increase the temptation to create sloppy SQL code. Many database administrators simply increase buffer sizes when there is a problem without ever solving the root cause of that problem. Then again, those root causes can often be too expensive to solve anyway, as they may involve expensive application rewrites. Quite often a problem is determined as a result of a low ratio, such as the database buffer cache hit ratio. Ratios will be examined in a later chapter.

Note: Ratios provide possible symptoms of problem but are not problems themselves.

Oracle Database tuning documentation, and many other publications, often stress the importance of ratios far too much. Ratios are symptomatic of problems and should not be used as a measurement of performance. Ratios should be used as indicators of possible performance problems. And those problems may not necessarily be directly related to those ratios.

Various performance views can be used to track locks and latch wait events. Wait events, latches, and the Oracle Database Wait Event Interface will be covered in some detail in later chapters. The V$SYSTEM_EVENT performance view can be used to determine wait events for free latches:

```
COL event FORMAT a20;
COL waits FORMAT 9999990;
COL timeouts FORMAT 99999990;
COL average FORMAT 99999990;
```

```
SELECT  event "Event", time_waited "Total Time", total_waits
"Waits"
 ,average_wait "Average", total_timeouts "Timeouts"
FROM V$SYSTEM_EVENT
WHERE event = 'latch free'
ORDER BY EVENT;
```

This is the result showing latch-free events:

Event	Total Time	Waits	Average	Timeouts
latch free	77421	23645	3	3304

There are many more events than this, and they will be covered in later chapters.

17.1.2.6 High Network Activity

High network activity with many small queries can cause unnecessarily high CPU activity. It is often the case that breaking SQL code into object-like, independent chunks is a cause of excessive network activity. Be aware that breaking SQL code into small constituent parts is more natural to object designs than relational design. On the contrary, reduction of complexity into smaller parts leads to simplicity in tuning, especially when it comes to SQL code. There is a fine balance between making transactions small enough and using large complex SQL code join statements. Do not be concerned about network activity with SQL*Net too much. If you are sure that your network is the bottleneck, take a look at your network—never overcomplicate SQL code to compensate for other problems.

The next query shows idle SQL*Net events. These values can help to describe Oracle network usage activity. However, for an OLTP database server, high network activity is normal, so there is no performance issue in this case:

```
SELECT name FROM v$EVENT_NAME
WHERE name LIKE '%SQL*Net%' OR name LIKE '%ispatcher%'
OR name LIKE '%virtual circuit%';
```

This is the result:

```
NAME
----------------------------------
alter system set dispatcher
virtual circuit status
dispatcher timer
dispatcher listen timer
SQL*Net message to client
SQL*Net message to dblink
SQL*Net more data to client
SQL*Net more data to dblink
SQL*Net message from client
SQL*Net more data from client
SQL*Net message from dblink
SQL*Net more data from dblink
SQL*Net break/reset to client
SQL*Net break/reset to dblink
dispatcher shutdown
latch: virtual circuit queues
```

17.2 How Oracle Database Uses Memory

Tuning the way that Oracle Database uses memory is a highly complex subject. This section will serve as an introduction to how Oracle Database uses memory, along with a brief description of tuning Oracle Database memory usage.

Oracle Database uses memory as a number of buffers to cache both instructions and data. These buffers are placed into both RAM and virtual memory. The purpose of the buffers is to help speed up performance. It is usually best to contain all buffers in RAM and not spread them into virtual memory. Also, do not neglect memory requirements for the operating system and anything else running on your database server. If something can be accessed from a memory buffer, rather than from disk storage, then I/O activity will be reduced because accessing memory is much faster than accessing something from disk storage.

Note: There is a limit to how large memory buffers can be. Managing the multiuser aspects of obtaining information from buffers is much more complex than managing locking of table data stored on disk. There is a point where buffers can become too big and complicated for Oracle Database software to manage, and size can become detrimental to performance.

The different buffers have to be tuned not only in relation to CPU usage and I/O activity, but also in relation to each other. Some buffers depend on the proper sizes of other buffers to perform at optimal pace. Here we will briefly introduce tuning the buffer cache areas from a generalized perspective. What are the separate buffers areas?

- *The database buffer cache*. This contains database object data, such as table and index rows for fast access in RAM, reducing I/O.

Note: (10*g*) The ALTER SYSTEM command allows flushing of the database buffer cache. This option should only be used for testing purposes.

- *The shared pool*. This contains highly shareable information, such as database metadata and parsed SQL code.

Note: Do not flush the shared pool on a production server. The apparent need to frequently flush the shared pool could be a symptom of oversizing of the shared pool. A large shared pool is sometimes a result of application issues. Flushing the shared pool will not resolve application issues, and it absolutely will hurt performance because anything shareable must be reloaded.

- *The large pool*. This is a cache area less structured than the shared pool. The large pool is similar in function to the shared pool, except that is usually used to contain shared pool overflow requirements, such as some very large batch operations.

- *The java pool*. This is used for the Oracle JVM and some Oracle 10*g* front-end tools, which are written in Java.

- *The streams pool*. This is used for the Oracle Streams (a pipeline between two nodes).

- *PGA memory*. PGA is essentially session connection buffering. Every database connection creates a session. Shared memory areas are allocated to each session, within both the shared pool and the large pool, depending on configuration. Some applications continually connect and disconnect from the database for every SQL code command executed. This type of activity is common in Java object applications.

Objects tend to oversimplify complexity, whereas a relational database can thrive on complexity.

- *The redo log buffer.* Redo log entries record all database change activity, where the redo log buffer acts as a step down between CPU and I/O.

All of the buffers mentioned here—the database buffer cache, the shared pool, the large pool, the Java pool, and the streams pool—are collectively known as the system global area (SGA).

Note: PGA memory and the redo log buffer are not included in the SGA.

The SGA can be examined using the SHOW SGA command in SQL*Plus, or you can query the V$SGA performance view:

```
SHOW SGA;

Total System Global Area   122755896 bytes
Fixed Size                    453432 bytes
Variable Size               88080384 bytes
Database Buffers            33554432 bytes
Redo Buffers                  667648 bytes
```

The V$SGASTAT performance view will provide memory allocations to all parts of the system global area:

```
COL name FORMAT a32;
SELECT pool, name, bytes FROM v$sgastat
WHERE pool IS NULL
OR pool != 'shared pool' OR (pool = 'shared pool'
   AND (name IN('dictionary cache','enqueue','library
cache','parameters',
                'processes','sessions','free memory')))
ORDER BY pool DESC NULLS FIRST, name;
```

The result shows the buffer cache, fixed SGA, and database buffer cache as not being part of any pool. Also shown are the streams pool, large pool, Java pool, and various sections of the shared pool:

```
POOL          NAME                                  BYTES
------------  --------------------------------  ----------
              buffer_cache                      16777216
              fixed_sga                          1247660
              log_buffer                         2945024
streams pool  free memory                        4194304
shared pool   enqueue                             210664
shared pool   free memory                       25655032
shared pool   library cache                      4808888
shared pool   processes                              600
shared pool   sessions                            818044
large pool    PX msg pool                         206208
large pool    free memory                        3988096
java pool     free memory                        4194304
```

It is best to make sure that the entire SGA fits into RAM and does not overflow onto temporary disk space or virtual memory. As already stated, space should be reserved in RAM for other operations on a database server computer, such as applications and the operating system.

Note: The LOCK_SGA parameter forces the entire SGA to remain in RAM, excluding the use of virtual memory disk space. Only some platforms support this parameter.

Note: (10*g*) A new performance view called V$SGAINFO gives a better picture of the SGA, using a query like this:

```
SELECT * FROM V$SGAINFO;
```

This is the result:

```
NAME                                   BYTES RES
--------------------------------  ---------- ---
Fixed SGA Size                       1247660 No
Redo Buffers                         2945024 No
Buffer Cache Size                   16777216 Yes
Shared Pool Size                    83886080 Yes
```

```
Large Pool Size                        4194304 Yes
Java Pool Size                         4194304 Yes
Streams Pool Size                      4194304 Yes
Granule Size                           4194304 No
Maximum SGA Size                     121634816 No
Startup overhead in Shared Pool       37748736 No
Free SGA Memory Available              4194304
```

Figure 17.1 shows the equivalent SGA and PGA memory buffers as displayed and maintainable from in the Database Control.

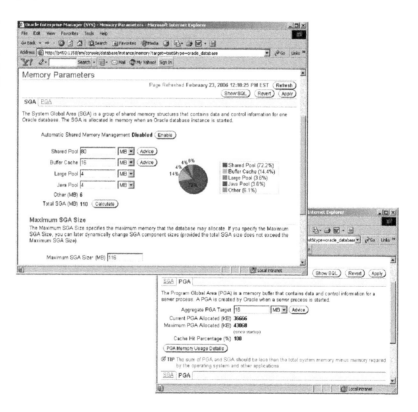

Figure 17.1
SGA and PGA parameters in the Database Control

The Database Control screens shown in Figure 17.1 can be found under the *Administration* link, under the *Database Configuration* header, and under the *Memory Parameters* link. Also, the SGA_MAX_SIZE parameter (shown in Figure 17.1 by the Maximum SGA Size entry field) is present to ensure that any automated allocation of SGA does not exceed an unmanageable upper limit.

17.2.1   The System Global Area

The SGA is the set of buffers used to contain much of the memory activity applicable to the database server. As stated earlier, the SGA consists of the database buffer cache, the shared pool, the large pool, the Java pool, and the streams pool.

17.2.1.1   (10g) Automated SGA Memory Management

Automatic shared memory management allows the database to automatically manage and tune all of the buffers contained within the SGA. These buffers are (1) the database buffer cache (DB_CACHE_SZIE), (2) the shared pool (SHARED_POOL_SIZE), (3) the large pool (LARGE_POOL_SIZE), (4) the Java pool (JAVA_POOL_SIZE), and (4) the streams pool (STREAMS_POOL_SIZE).

In order to configure automated shared memory management the SGA_TARGET parameter must be set to a value that is not 0. Additionally, the STATISTICS_LEVEL parameter cannot be set to BASIC.

Note: Setting any of the buffers contained with SGA_TARGET to nonzero values, when SGA_TARGET is set, designates minimum sizes for those buffers within SGA_TARGET.

Buffer areas excluded from the SGA_TARGET parameter, and thus excluded from automatic SGA memory management, are the log buffer and database buffer caches other than DB_CACHE_SIZE, including all nondefault block size database buffer caches and the keep and recycle database buffer caches (i.e., DB_nK_CACHE_SIZE, DB_KEEP_CACHE_SIZE, and DB_RECYCLE_CACHE_SIZE parameters).

Handling automated SGA memory in the Database Control is very easy. Examine the SGA memory parameters in Figure 17.1 for the Database Control. Above all the memory settings is an item called *Automatic Shared Memory Management*. Figure 17.1 shows that automatic SGA is disabled. Click the *Enable* button to enable automated SGA. The result is shown in Figure 17.2.

17.2.1.1.1   Automated SGA Performance and Monitoring

Tuning the automated SGA in Oracle 10g Database involves using the SGA advisor in the Database Control. Figure 17.2 shows an *Advice* button, next

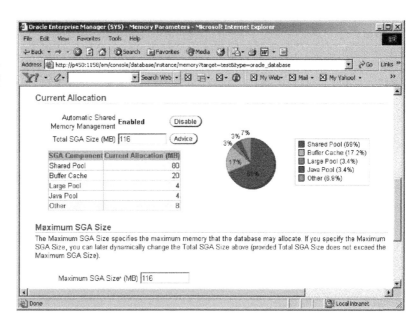

Figure 17.2
*SGA and PGA
parameters in the
Database Control*

to the Total SGA Size entry. If you click the Advice button, you get the screen shown in Figure 17.3.

Note: The V$SGA_TARGET_ADVICE view does the same thing but in SQL*Plus.

Looking at Figure 17.3, you can see that the advisor estimates an increase in overall performance of 5% by doubling the size of the SGA_TARGET parameter. However, 5% is not much, so this really isn't very impressive.

The problem with increasing the SGA_TARGET parameter is that you cannot control the relative sizes of the shared pool and the database buffer cache within the SGA_TARGET value. Well, actually you can, but from my experience the influence over the SGA_TARGET value might be the wrong way around. You can set each of the buffers contained within the SGA_TARGET value, but these settings will assume minimum values for those specific pools within the automated SGA. Some of the biggest issues with OLTP databases are high concurrency and the need to share, as much as possible, any preparsed SQL and metadata contained within the shared pool. Thus, logically it would seem that settings might want to be maximums rather than minimums in some cases. However, if you want to, for

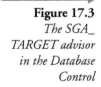

Figure 17.3
*The SGA_*
TARGET advisor
in the Database
Control

instance, ensure that the database buffer cache is much bigger than the shared pool, then it makes sense that setting a high minimum for the database buffer cache will have the desired effect. Additionally, many database installations do not actually use the Java pool, large pool, and streams pool—perhaps allowing those three pools to be set to zero or very close to zero.

Ultimately there is not really all that much you can do to tune automated SGA memory, apart from resizing the SGA_TARGET parameter. And, remember, it is just as likely that you should make buffers smaller as you should make them larger.

17.2.1.2 (9*i*) Manual SGA Memory Management

Manual SGA management essentially allows more flexibility in controlling the individual buffers. Manual SGA memory is still permitted in Oracle 10*g* Database within the Database Control. Manual PGA memory is not available in the Oracle 10*g* Database Control. This could indicate that automated SGA is not as yet industry tested. I have not so far had any problems with it, although I don't see any overall difference in performance. So it is appropriate to include a discussion of management and tuning of manual SGA management of each of the buffers within the SGA.

17.2.1.2.1 The Database Buffer Cache

The database buffer cache is available in Oracle Database 9*i* in two forms. The first form is the original form using the DB_BLOCK_BUFFERS parameter and various other parameters. The second is using the DB_CACHE_SIZE parameter, along with its associated parameters. In general, the same rules and methods govern the way in which the two database buffer caches are tuned. The DB_BLOCK_BUFFERS parameter will not be covered in this book.

Note: (10*g*) The DB_BLOCK_BUFFERS parameter was deprecated in Oracle Database 9*i* but still usable. This parameter is also still available in Oracle Database 10*g*.

Some Oracle texts and documentation may state that the database buffer cache can be bypassed when executing full scans. There is some evidence to the contrary that can be found in trace files. Even a full scan will still pass through the database buffer cache mechanism. This is why it is common for a data warehouse to have the database buffer cache set to a miniscule value (forcing minimal use of the database buffer cache because a data warehouse is I/O heavy, generally with negligible concurrency). Therefore, for high I/O activity, one can possibly assume that the amount of hits in the cache there is very low in relation to disk reads. Two further factors warrant discussion at this stage:

- ***Multiple block-sized buffer pool.*** Oracle Database 9*i* and beyond (including Oracle 10*g*) allow for tablespaces with different block sizes. Large transactions can benefit from larger block-sized tablespaces, and small transactions from smaller block sizes. The database buffer cache is thus split into separate caches involving all but the default (DB_CACHE_SIZE), using parameters named DB_[2 | 4 | 8 | 16 | 32]K_CACHE_SIZE.

Note: Available block sizes and thus DB_nK_CACHE_SIZE parameters may vary for different operating systems. A 32K block size is not available for Win2K SP3 running Oracle Database 9*i* through Oracle 10*g* Database Release 2 (10.2).

- *Multiple buffer pools.* Oracle Database 9*i* and beyond manage keep and recycle pools using the DB_KEEP_CACHE_SIZE and DB_RECYCLE_CACHE_SIZE parameters, respectively. The keep pool should be used to attempt to keep small static or frequently used tables and indexes in memory. The recycle pool should be used to remove large, infrequently accessed row sets from memory as quickly as possible. The keep and recycle pools can only contain blocks contained in default block–sized tablespaces, determined by the DB_CACHE_SIZE parameter. DB*n*K_CACHE_SIZE buffers are not allowed. This makes sense because the two types of buffers can both be divided up between frequent static data (keep and small blocks) and infrequent transactional data (recycle and large blocks).

Note: Individual tables and indexes can be copied to keep and recycle pools using the BUFFER POOL KEEP and BUFFER POOL RECYCLE options in the ALTER TABLE and ALTER INDEX statement STORAGE clauses.

17.2.1.2.2 Database Buffer Cache Advice

Now I start up my simulation database with a small number of jobs. The database buffer cache advisor performance view is called V$DB_CACHE_ ADVICE. The following query should describe the potential database buffer cache hit ratio decreasing, as the cache size increases:

```
COL pool FORMAT a10;
SELECT (SELECT ROUND(value/1024/1024,0) FROM v$parameter
    WHERE name = 'db_cache_size') "Current Cache(Mb)"
,name "Pool", size_for_estimate "Projected Cache(Mb)"
,ROUND(100-estd_physical_read_factor,0) "Cache Hit Ratio%"
FROM v$db_cache_advice
WHERE block_size = (SELECT value FROM v$parameter
    WHERE name = 'db_block_size')
ORDER BY 3;
```

The following result shows that the current DB_CACHE_SIZE is set to 28Mb. This is quite small. Notice that the estimate of resizing the database buffer cache between 12Mb and 56Mb indicates there will be no difference in the cache hit ratio whatsoever:

Current Cache(Mb)	Pool	Projected Cache(Mb)	Cache Hit Ratio%
28	DEFAULT	4	98
28	DEFAULT	8	98
28	DEFAULT	12	99
28	DEFAULT	16	99
28	DEFAULT	20	99
28	DEFAULT	24	99
28	DEFAULT	28	99
28	DEFAULT	32	99
28	DEFAULT	36	99
28	DEFAULT	40	99
28	DEFAULT	44	99
28	DEFAULT	48	99
28	DEFAULT	52	99
28	DEFAULT	56	99

The Database Control equivalent database buffer cache advisor is shown in Figure 17.4. The curve is at a nice angle for increasing the database buffer cache size. However, compared with the previous results using the V$DB_CACHE_ADVICE performance view, I would leave the DB_CACHE_SIZE parameter as it is. Any change is likely to make little difference at all.

For my Accounts schema, I could decide to move some static and some very large tables into the keep and recycle buffer pools, respectively. So I change the keep and recycle pool buffers as follows, setting the keep pool to approximately 5% of the recycle pool:

```
ALTER SYSTEM SET DB_KEEP_CACHE_SIZE=56K;
ALTER SYSTEM SET DB_RECYCLE_CACHE_SIZE=1M;
```

The changes can be verified using a SHOW PARAMETERS command or a simple query on the V$PARAMETER view.

Note: (10*g*) Many more parameters can be changed online in Oracle 10*g* Database. In Oracle Database 9*i*, it might be necessary to restart the database to change the keep and recycle pool parameters.

Figure 17.4
*The database
buffer cache
advisor in the
Database Control*

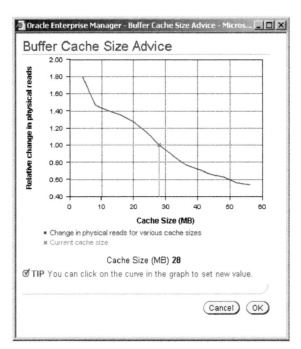

In my Accounts schema, I could distribute tables to different pools as shown in the following examples, placing the smallest tables in the keep pool and the largest tables in the recycle pool. There are many other factors to consider. Assuming that static data sizes are known, the keep pool could be sized more precisely to actual data sizes. The Customer and Supplier tables are semistatic and relatively large; thus, depending on current activity, they could possibly benefit from being part of the keep pool:

```
ALTER TABLE type STORAGE(BUFFER_POOL KEEP);
ALTER TABLE subtype STORAGE(BUFFER_POOL KEEP);
ALTER TABLE period STORAGE(BUFFER_POOL KEEP);
ALTER TABLE posting STORAGE(BUFFER_POOL KEEP);
ALTER TABLE category STORAGE(BUFFER_POOL KEEP);
ALTER TABLE coa STORAGE(BUFFER_POOL KEEP);
ALTER TABLE generalledger STORAGE(BUFFER_POOL RECYCLE);
ALTER TABLE stockmovement STORAGE(BUFFER_POOL RECYCLE);
```

The tables shown here are pushed into keep and recycle pools. It would make sense to examine their respective indexes. Indexes can be shifted to different pools, regardless of where their parent tables are placed. I have placed small static tables into the keep pool to account for optimizer full table scans. Full table scans do not read indexes. Therefore, there is no point in placing static table indexes into the keep pool. It would, however, be sensible to place Customer and Supplier indexes into the keep pool based on the same reasoning, as those tables are semistatic and much larger, making full table scans less likely:

```
ALTER INDEX xak_cust_name STORAGE(BUFFER_POOL KEEP);
ALTER INDEX xak_cust_ticker STORAGE(BUFFER_POOL KEEP);
ALTER INDEX xak_supp_name STORAGE(BUFFER_POOL KEEP);
ALTER INDEX xak_supp_ticker STORAGE(BUFFER_POOL KEEP);
ALTER INDEX xpk_customer STORAGE(BUFFER_POOL KEEP);
ALTER INDEX xpk_supplier STORAGE(BUFFER_POOL KEEP);
```

Contrary to this, large joins including these static tables are likely to require fast access to static tables and their indexes. So perhaps static table indexes, and not the tables, should be placed in the keep pool. A decision like this depends on applications and the ways the tables are used.

Let's look at the V$DB_CACHE_ADVICE performance view again, restricting the output somewhat:

```
COL pool FORMAT a10;
SELECT (SELECT ROUND(value/1024/1024,0) FROM v$parameter
    WHERE name = 'db_cache_size') "Current Cache(Mb)"
,name "Pool", size_for_estimate "Projected Cache(Mb)"
,ROUND(100-estd_physical_read_factor,0) "Cache Hit Ratio%"
FROM v$db_cache_advice
WHERE block_size = (
    SELECT value FROM v$parameter
    WHERE name = 'db_block_size')
AND size_for_estimate IN (4,8,32)
ORDER BY 2, 3;
```

The keep pool is set at 5% of the default pool, which is 56Kb. The V$DB_CACHE_ADVICE view does not offer an estimate less than 4M; thus, there is no useful response for the keep pool:

Current Cache(Mb)	Pool	Projected Cache(Mb)	Cache Hit Ratio%
28	DEFAULT	4	98
28	DEFAULT	8	99
28	DEFAULT	32	99
28	KEEP	4	
28	KEEP	8	
28	RECYCLE	4	99
28	RECYCLE	8	99

The level of detail shown here for the keep and recycle pools is not available in the Database Control.

17.2.1.2.3   The Shared Pool

The shared pool allows for sharing and reuse of information. The shared pool retains highly shareable data in memory used simultaneously by many database users. Things stored in the shared pool include such items as previously parsed and executed SQL code, latches protecting buffer areas, and data dictionary metadata. All of these items are heavily used by all sessions connected to the database. The shared pool is set using the SHARED_POOL_SIZE parameter. Setting the SHARED_POOL_RESERVED_SIZE parameter to a small percentage of the shared pool, normally less than 10%, will reserve a small portion of the shared pool for contiguous large transactions. This can help to avoid large amounts of defragmentation in the shared pool when large transactions are executed. Defragmentation in the shared pool can cause serious wait event and latch contention problems.

> **Note:** Wait events and latches will be explained in later chapters. In general, a wait event is when one operation is forced to wait for another operation to complete. A latch is a special type of very-high-speed lock used in one of the buffers.

The reserved section of the shared pool can be examined with the following query:

```
SELECT request_misses, request_failures, free_space
FROM v$shared_pool_reserved;
```

Even when running large queries on my database, free space remains constant at around 3Mb, which is the setting for the SHARED_POOL_RESERVED_SIZE parameter. My reserved shared pool is never used because the rest of the shared pool is large enough and not suffering from fragmentation as a result of poorly tuned SQL code. Request misses implies that flushing occurred because the shared pool reserved portion is not large enough for large transactions, or it is being used. Request failures are worse. If either of the misses or failures columns has a value greater than zero, try increasing the value of the parameter SHARED_POOL_RESERVED_SIZE. I have seen some success setting this parameter to values of 10% and more of the shared pool for databases executing large amounts of poorly tuned SQL code. The default setting is 5%. The better solution is to tune the SQL code, but that is often not possible. If you are going to tell a customer to rewrite an application, you might as well be telling them to reinvent the wheel. Using bind variables in SQL code or forcing their use with the CURSOR_SHARING parameter can alleviate these issues substantially, but be cautious using cursor sharing in a data warehouse. As always, there is no better solution than tuning SQL code. Using bind variables as a quick fix to avoid tuning poorly built SQL code is relative to how scalable the database needs to be in the long term. Additionally, data warehouse databases perform best without bind variable use due to matching of statistics over vast quantities of data and the use of histograms. Using bind variables in SQL code will offset the accuracy of statistics in large data warehouses:

```
REQUEST_MISSES REQUEST_FAILURES FREE_SPACE
-------------- ---------------- ----------
             0                0    2014320
```

The shared pool is quite literally a shared area of memory containing various types of information in various caches used to help Oracle Database perform better. What are these different memory caches?

- *The library cache*. This is parsed SQL and PL/SQL code plus optimized query execution plans for SQL code.

- *The metadata cache*. This is information about the data stored in memory for rapid access.

Tuning and sizing the shared pool correctly is critical to performance. Proper *sharing* of high-usage information between many users is more critical than proper tuning of other buffers, aside from perhaps a completely inappropriately sized redo log buffer. The database buffer cache is not as important as the shared pool because data in the shared pool is more likely to be shared by more users.

17.2.1.2.4 The Library Cache

The library cache contains parsed SQL code and latches. It is important to note that efficiently tuned SQL code will not affect library cache performance directly. Properly tuned SQL code will help database performance in general. Bind variables used in SQL code will help to allow the library cache to share previously parsed SQL code. An issue with sharing using bind variables is that in very large or widely variant data sets, bind variables can generalize statistics. This need to use statistics precisely is more important in data warehouses, where exact value searches with statistics can potentially perform much faster.

SQL code tuning is covered in Part II of this book. Most of the aspects of SQL code tuning that affect performance of the library cache are based on the way in which SQL code is written and the ways in which applications manage connections to the database. Latches and locks will be covered later in this book. Management of latches can become difficult if shared pool space allocated to latch management is too low, or if the shared pool is either too small or filled with too many different things.

Examine library cache statistics using the V$LIBRARYCACHE performance view. The GETS column applies to locking requests, the PINS column applies to pins in the shared pool, RELOADS indicates I/O activity, and INVALIDATIONS denotes SQL code reparsing:

```
SELECT namespace, gets, pins, reloads, invalidations
FROM v$librarycache;
```

This is the result:

NAMESPACE	GETS	PINS	RELOADS	INVALIDATIONS
SQL AREA	97385	1577407	16	0
TABLE/PROCEDURE	50741	494446	0	0
BODY	24624	24623	0	0

TRIGGER	52336	52336	0	0
INDEX	66	35	0	0
CLUSTER	167	221	0	0
OBJECT	0	0	0	0
PIPE	0	0	0	0
JAVA SOURCE	0	0	0	0
JAVA RESOURCE	0	0	0	0
JAVA DATA	0	0	0	0

Here are a few pointers:

- *Maintain connections*. Do not continuously connect and disconnect from the database for every SQL code operation. Establishing and breaking a database connection involves starting up and stopping of processes, plus allocation and release of chunks of memory. It is better to share connections, especially with large numbers of users, preferably using a middle-tier server utilizing some type of connection pooling. An Oracle shared servers configuration is not as effective as a middle tier because connection pool management takes processing power away from the database server.

- *Generated SQL*. Generated SQL is SQL that is generated on the fly from within an application. This type of application-based SQL code is always unpredictable and largely dependent on the coding skills of multiple programmers. Additionally, programmers always have their own distinctive styles, and enforcing standards can be difficult.

- *Copying schemas to different users*. There is some weight to be granted for creating separate schemas for each user. However, this type of application-based database design tends to be top-down and not built from the perspective of database efficiency. See the next section on the metadata (dictionary) cache.

- *PL/SQL and DDL*. PL/SQL can help because packages can be pinned into contiguous areas of memory at database startup. However, many developers will balk at the idea of placing too much business logic and application-type processing into a database. Executing DDL commands on highly active objects is detrimental to performance because many DDL commands will invoke table locks, among other unpleasant things.

- *SESSION_CACHED_CURSORS*. The library cache effectively caches cursors at the database level. The SESSION_CACHED_

CURSORS parameter can be used to cache cursors for each session. A cached cursor is a reusable cursor. Reusing a cursor removes the need for reprocessing:

```
SELECT name, value FROM v$sysstat WHERE name
IN('session cursor cache count','session cursor cache hits');
```

This is the result:

```
NAME                              VALUE
--------------------------------- ----------
session cursor cache hits         39577
session cursor cache count         3489
```

Search for unnecessary parse calls using the V$SQLAREA view:

```
COL execs FORMAT 9999990
COL parses FORMAT 99990
COL fetches FORMAT 999990
COL loads FORMAT 9990
COL invalids FORMAT 9999990
COL i/o FORMAT 99990
COL hits FORMAT 9999990
COL rows FORMAT 999990
COL sorts FORMAT 9990
COL sql FORMAT a32
SELECT * FROM(
SELECT executions "Execs"--Executions
        ,parse_calls "Parses"--Parses
        ,fetches "Fetches"--Fetches
        ,loads"Loads"--Loads and reloads
        ,invalidations "Invalids"--Invalidations
        ,disk_reads "I/O"--I/O
        ,buffer_gets "Hits"--Buffer hits
        ,rows_processed "Rows"--Rows
        ,sorts"Sorts"--Sorts
        ,sql_text "SQL"
FROM v$sqlarea
ORDER BY executions DESC
) WHERE ROWNUM <= 10;
```

This is the result of the query:

Execs	Parses	Fetches	Loads	I/O	Hits	Rows	Sorts	SQL
210140	24788	0	1	1477	2315765	210139	0	INSERT in
210140	24788	0	1	2205	3666266	210140	0	INSERT in
210140	24788	0	1	2081	3664461	210131	0	INSERT in
210137	24789	0	1	3022	1875467	210142	0	INSERT in
154342	32775	154342	1	164	463030	154342	0	SELECT to
101918	32773	101918	1	180	305762	101918	0	SELECT sy
64544	64544	0	1	0	32273	0	0	COMMIT
61054	61056	0	1	19950	824522	61054	0	INSERT in
61050	61050	0	1	14588	786704	61050	0	INSERT in
45193	4603	0	1	330	499322	45193	0	INSERT in

- ■ **CURSOR_SPACE_FOR_TIME**. This parameter can be set to TRUE to remove cursors from the shared pool only when they are closed, rather than aging them out according to MRU and LRU lists. A parameter like this can cause problems if, for instance, cursors are left open by applications, or ad hoc SQL code power users leave SQL code running or uncommitted. What happens if someone goes to lunch?

17.2.1.2.5   The Metadata or Dictionary Cache

The metadata cache contains all of the database definitional data, such as table and index structural definitions, as part of the shared pool. Metadata is generally accessed much more frequently than anything else in the database and is absolutely critical for efficiency.

Too much metadata in the database can cause serious performance problems. Let's once again examine a top-down database design built from the perspective of an application. Sometimes these types of database designs are characterized by profligate use of schema copies, views, and synonyms, increasing memory requirements for metadata even further. It is often best from a performance perspective to access objects directly. Be aware of creating too many logical object layers. Views and synonyms can often be used to enhance security or make application coding easier. Be forewarned of the hidden costs of building your database structure from the point of view of making application coding easier. If your database gets large, you will very likely have performance issues.

The metadata cache can be examined in great detail using the V$ROW-CACHE performance view. My Accounts schema high-activity code, using DBMS_JOBS scheduled mass DML activity, is apparent in the results of the next query. The Accounts schema uses sequences as primary keys so there is high sequence activity:

```
SELECT COUNT "Entries", GETS "Requests", GETMISSES "Misses"
,MODIFICATIONS "DML Activity", parameter "Area"
FROM v$rowcache;
```

This is the result:

Entries	Requests	Misses	DML Activity	Area
0	0	0	0	dc_free_extents
0	0	0	0	dc_used_extents
168	9462	1826	5	dc_segments
8	33537	24	0	dc_tablespaces
0	1	1	0	dc_tablespace_quotas
0	60	30	0	dc_files
16	48823	52	0	dc_users
12	**611**	**11**	**31**	**dc_rollback_segments**
346	**12340**	**2573**	**66**	**dc_objects**
21	10085	125	0	dc_global_oids
0	0	0	0	dc_constraints
296	**38197**	**1884**	**55**	**dc_object_ids**
5	**495**	**21**	**495**	**dc_sequences**
4	3484	17	0	dc_usernames
0	0	0	0	dc_database_links
822	31920	8403	0	dc_histogram_defs
0	0	0	0	kqlsubheap_object
0	0	0	0	dc_table_scns
0	0	0	0	dc_outlines
1	1356	1	0	dc_profiles
0	0	0	0	global database name
0	0	0	0	rule_info
0	0	0	0	rule_or_piece
0	0	0	0	dc_qmc_cache_entries
0	0	0	0	dc_qmc_ldap_cache_entries
0	0	0	0	qmtmrcin_cache_entries

0	0	0	0	qmtmrctn_cache_entries
0	0	0	0	qmtmrcip_cache_entries
0	0	0	0	qmtmrctp_cache_entries
0	0	0	0	qmtmrciq_cache_entries
0	0	0	0	qmtmrctq_cache_entries
16	**185**	**80**	**6**	**outstanding_alerts**
1	**105**	**1**	**4**	**dc_awr_control**
0	0	0	0	dc_hintsets
0	0	0	0	dc_users
42	885	239	0	dc_object_grants
492	9655	2132	0	dc_histogram_data
100	5341	319	0	dc_histogram_data
0	0	0	0	dc_partition_scns
24	1894	44	0	dc_users
0	0	0	0	dc_users
0	0	0	0	rule_fast_operators

17.2.1.2.6 Pinning Objects in the Shared Pool

PL/SQL packages can be pinned in memory to place them into a contiguous area, preventing further parsing processing.

> **Note:** Contiguous means that something is physically located in just one place in memory, making access to the package read from a single chunk of memory, as opposed to many fragmented chunks of memory space.

Packages should be pinned at database startup to ensure that contiguous areas of memory are used and parts of packages are not spread out (fragmented) all over the shared pool. Packages can be pinned into memory using the KEEP procedure in the DBMS_SHARED_POOL package:

```
DBMS_SHARED_POOL.[UN]KEEP (object, type);
```

The type parameter is set as P, C, R, or Q for a package, a cursor, a trigger, or a sequence.

17.2.1.2.7 Shared Pool Advice

The V$SHARED_POOL_ADVICE performance view provides potential information for varying shared pool sizes. Unfortunately, as can be seen in the following query result, there are no differences between estimates in the various columns:

```
SELECT (SELECT ROUND(value/1024/1024,0) FROM v$parameter
    WHERE name = 'shared_pool_size') "Current Mb"
, shared_pool_size_for_estimate "Projected Mb"
, ROUND(shared_pool_size_factor*100) "%"
, ESTD_LC_SIZE "Library Mb"
, ESTD_LC_TIME_SAVED "Parse Savings"
,ESTD_LC_MEMORY_OBJECT_HITS "Hits"
FROM v$shared_pool_advice
ORDER BY 1;
```

This is the result:

Current Mb	Projected Mb	%	Library Mb	Parse Savings	Hits
64	32	50	7	121352	2824153
64	40	63	7	121352	2824153
64	48	75	7	121352	2824153
64	56	88	7	121352	2824153
64	64	100	7	121352	2824153
64	72	113	7	121352	2824153
64	80	125	7	121352	2824153
64	88	138	7	121352	2824153
64	96	150	7	121352	2824153
64	104	163	7	121352	2824153
64	112	175	7	121352	2824153
64	120	188	7	121352	2824153
64	128	200	7	121352	2824153

The V$LIBRARY_CACHE_MEMORY performance view provides a window into the Library cache part of the shared pool:

```
SELECT  lc_namespace "Library"
 ,LC_INUSE_MEMORY_OBJECTS "Objects"
 ,LC_INUSE_MEMORY_SIZE "Objects Mb"
 ,LC_FREEABLE_MEMORY_OBJECTS "Freeable Objects"
 ,LC_FREEABLE_MEMORY_SIZE "Freeable Mb"
FROM v$library_cache_memory;
```

This is the result:

Library	Objects	Objects Mb	Freeable Objects	Freeable Mb
BODY	0	0	18	0
CLUSTER	13	0	4	0
INDEX	8	0	31	0
JAVA DATA	0	0	0	0
JAVA RESOURCE	0	0	0	0
JAVA SOURCE	0	0	0	0
OBJECT	0	0	0	0
OTHER/SYSTEM	0	0	6	0
PIPE	0	0	0	0
SQL AREA	75	0	757	5
TABLE/PROCEDURE	61	0	521	1
TRIGGER	6	0	27	0

The Database Control equivalent shared pool advisor is shown in Figure 17.5. The curve levels out substantially at shared pool sizes larger than the current shared pool size. Again, as indicated for the database buffer cache in Figure 17.4, little difference in performance is likely to be gained by increasing the size of the shared pool.

Figure 17.5
The shared pool advisor in the Database Control

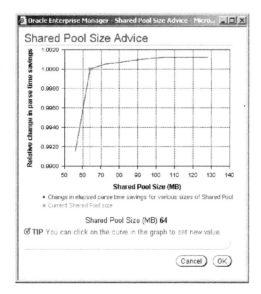

17.2.1.2.8   The Large Pool

The large pool is not a subset of the shared pool buffer but is used as an area of memory to contain what could possibly be termed shared pool buffer overflow, under certain circumstances:

- Some shared server session connection memory
- Backup processing
- Parallel execution

17.2.1.2.9   Shared Servers and Virtual Circuits in the Large Pool

When using shared servers (connection pooling on the database server) and no dedicated servers, a virtual circuit is a chunk of memory reserved for a shared database connection through a dispatcher process. A dispatcher process can support multiple concurrent client processes, where each client connection is communicated with using a virtual circuit; the virtual circuit is used to pass requests and responses from and to the client.

17.2.1.2.10   The Streams Pool

The streams pool is used as a buffering mechanism for Oracle Streams. Oracle Streams is a little like a pipeline between two nodes and can be used to implement backup, distribution, or standby database architectures. The configuration parameter STREAMS_POOL_SIZE can be set to 0 to save memory space. There is a view called V$STREAMS_POOL_ADVICE that provides estimates for resizing the streams pool.

17.2.1.2.11   The Java Pool

The Java pool is set using the JAVA_POOL_SIZE parameter. This parameter is used by some Java-written tools and the Oracle Java Virtual Machine (JVM). The JVM is used to write stored procedures in the Java programming language, as opposed to writing stored procedures in PL/SQL. The configuration parameter JAVA_POOL_SIZE can be set to 0 to save memory space. There is a view called V$JAVA_POOL_ADVICE, providing estimates for resizing of the Java pool. Another view called V$JAVA_LIBRARY_CACHE_MEMORY shows a library cache of Java objects.

17.2.2   The Program Global Area

The Program Global Area (PGA) memory is essentially allocated for each session connected to a database. Oracle Database 9*i* introduced automated

PGA memory management where the PGA_TARGET configuration replaced all the AREA_SIZE parameters.

There is some difference between Oracle shared server and dedicated server connections. In a dedicated server connection, all session connection memory is placed into PGA memory.

Note: Dedicated server connection configurations can perform well even at 1,000 concurrent connections.

Note: (9*i*) Automated memory management can only be used with dedicated server database connections.

In a shared server environment, some session connection memory is pushed into other buffers such as the large pool.

Note: (10*g*) Using the two parameters WORKAREA_SIZE_POLICY = AUTO and PGA_AGGREGATE_TARGET for automated session connection memory management has been both defaulted and recommended by Oracle Corporation since Oracle Database 9*i* as better performing.

Various parameters are involved in controlling session-level PGA connection memory.

17.2.2.1   (10*g*) Automated PGA Memory Management

If the PGA_AGGREGATE_TARGET parameter is defined, then the database will utilize automated PGA memory management. Automated memory management is far easier to maintain and monitor, in comparison to the manual PGA management of all the AREA_SIZE parameters. Setting the PGA_AGGREGATE_TARGET parameter to a value of nonzero automatically sets the WORKAREA_SIZE_POLICY parameter to AUTO.

Note: (9*i*) In Oracle Database 9*i*, the WORKAREA_SIZE_POLICY parameter had to be explicitly set to AUTO.

All the underlying AREA_SIZE parameters will be sized automatically, as shown by the following SQL*Plus SHOW PARAMETERS commands:

```
SQL> show parameters pga

NAME                                  TYPE        VALUE
------------------------------------- ----------- -----------
pga_aggregate_target                  big integer 16M
```

What automated PGA management does is to divide the value in the PGA_AGGREGATE_TARGET parameter into all the underlying AREA_SIZE parameters:

```
SQL> show parameters area_size

NAME                                  TYPE        VALUE
------------------------------------- ----------- -----------
bitmap_merge_area_size                integer     1048576
create_bitmap_area_size               integer     8388608
hash_area_size                        integer     131072
sort_area_size                        integer     65536
workarea_size_policy                  string      AUTO
```

Statistics can be obtained from the V$PGASTAT performance view:

```
SELECT * FROM v$pgastat;
```

This is the result:

```
NAME                                  VALUE UNIT
------------------------------------- ---------- ------------
aggregate PGA target parameter        16777216 bytes
aggregate PGA auto target             4194304 bytes
global memory bound                   3354624 bytes
total PGA inuse                       17583104 bytes
total PGA allocated                   42642432 bytes
maximum PGA allocated                 56039424 bytes
total freeable PGA memory             0 bytes
process count                         28
max processes count                   35
PGA memory freed back to OS           0 bytes
total PGA used for auto workareas     0 bytes
maximum PGA used for auto workareas   3159040 bytes
total PGA used for manual workareas   0 bytes
```

```
maximum PGA used for manual workareas          4096 bytes
over allocation count                         11857
bytes processed                          3922759680 bytes
extra bytes read/written                          0 bytes
cache hit percentage                            100 percent
recompute count (total)                       11968
```

17.2.2.1.1 Automated PGA Performance and Monitoring

The V$PGA_TARGET_ADVICE and V$PGA_TARGET_ADVICE_ HISTOGRAM performance views are predictive, advisory views, useful for automated PGA memory. The following query projects the percentage hit rate of finding something in PGA memory, based on projected sizes for the PGA_AGGREGATE_TARGET parameter size:

```
SELECT (SELECT ROUND(value/1024/1024,0) FROM v$parameter
    WHERE name = 'pga_aggregate_target') "Current Mb"
, ROUND(pga_target_for_estimate/1024/1024,0) "Projected Mb"
, ROUND(estd_pga_cache_hit_percentage) "%"
FROM v$pga_target_advice
ORDER BY 2;
```

This is the result, showing that the only change that would make a difference would be a reduction in the size of the PGA_ AGGREGATE_TARGET parameter and the hit rate would become worse. Thus, there is no point in changing the value:

```
Current Mb Projected Mb          %
---------- ------------ ----------
        16           12         96
        16           16        100
        16           19        100
        16           22        100
        16           26        100
        16           29        100
        16           32        100
        16           48        100
        16           64        100
        16           96        100
        16          128        100
```

Figure 17.6 shows the same information in the Database Control. Click the Performance link, the Advisor Central link, and the Memory Advisor link, followed by the PGA link.

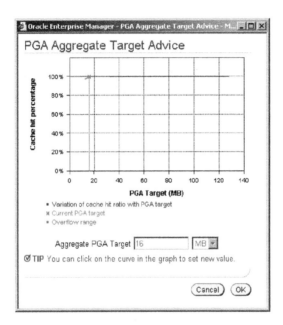

Figure 17.6
PGA advisor in the Database Control

Various other dynamic performance views can be used to give advice and make predictions on how the PGA_AGGREGATE_TARGET value should be set. Running through did not show that the size I currently have set in my database should be changed, even with the simulation code running.

The only point to make is that the size of the PGA is relative to the number of concurrent connections to a database, as well as other factors, such as the frequency and size of sorting, bitmaps, and hash tables. In OLTP environments, where there are extreme concurrency requirements, it is quite common for PGA memory requirements to far exceed requirements for the database buffer cache or even the shared pool. Quite often, an Internet OLTP application has a very small number of tables and uses bind variables in application code (or sets the CURSOR_SHARING parameter to FORCE). The result is a very small shared pool and database buffer cache, in relation to a very large PGA memory segment. Obviously, specific settings are dependent on many factors, which are quite often explicit even to specific application and database architecture.

17.2.2.2 ⑨*i* **Manual PGA Memory Management**

Manual management of PGA memory goes all the way back to Oracle8*i* Database, but manual PGA is still heavily utilized in Oracle Database 9*i* installations. Manual PGA management is not even available in the Database Control in Oracle 10*g* Database but is still available by changing the parameter files specifically. Configuring for manual PGA memory management in Oracle Database 9*i* requires setting the PGA_AGGREGATE_ TARGET parameter to 0 or the WORKAREA_SIZE_POLICY parameter equal to MANUAL.

Note: ⑩*g* Configuring manual PGA memory management in Oracle 10*g* is not recommended and could result in poor utilization of PGA memory.

- ***WORKAREA_SIZE_POLICY = MANUAL.*** This option switches off the use of the PGA_AGGREGATE_TARGET parameter.

- ***SORT_AREA_SIZE = n.*** This determines the size of the sort buffer. When the buffer is exceeded for a connection, a sort will be passed to temporary sort space on disk. Serious performance problems can occur in some situations:

  - If the sort buffer is too small and too many sorts are moved to disk, heavy I/O will result.
  - Too large a sort buffer could potentially use up too much memory because every database connection is allocated the amount of memory specified in the sort buffer, as a maximum for sorting. For example, if the SORT_AREA_SIZE parameter is set to 1Mb, then 2,000 users could require up to 2Gb of RAM, assuming there are enough connections executing concurrent sorting.
  - Make sure a temporary sorting tablespace is created in the database and that each user is allocated that temporary tablespace. The default temporary sorting tablespace can be set in the CREATE DATABASE or ALTER DATABASE commands. If not set, the SYSTEM metadata tablespace will be used for sorting.

Note: ⑩*g* On disk temporary space can be allocated as tablespace groups. A tablespace group can contain multiple locally managed temporary tablespaces. A tablespace group will allow spreading of SQL execution sorting across multiple temporary tablespaces, potentially speeding up sorting operations. Processing is distributed. A user can be allocated a tablespace group as a temporary sort space, as opposed to just a single temporary tablespace.

- *SORT_AREA_RETAINED_SIZE* = *less than 10% of SORT_ AREA_SIZE*. This parameter helps to retain memory space for multiple sorts in the same query.

Note: It is possible that the value of the SORT_AREA_RETAINED_SIZE parameter should be set equal to the SORT_AREA_SIZE parameter, especially where large sorts are very common. This may often apply because many OLTP databases are in reality OLTP/DSS databases.

- *CREATE_BITMAP_AREA_SIZE* = *n*. This is used to create bitmap indexes in memory.
- *BITMAP_MERGE_AREA_SIZE* = *n*. This is used in memory bitmap merge operations.
- *HASH_AREA_SIZE* = *n*. This is used for hash joins in SQL join statements.

17.2.3 Other Memory Buffers

The following pools are manually sized components and are not affected by either automated SGA or automated PGA memory management configuration:

- The redo log buffer
- Nondefault database buffer cache areas (not DB_CACHE_SIZE), including the DB_nK_CACHE_SIZE, DB_KEEP_CACHE_SIZE and DB_RECYCLE_CACHE_SIZE parameters
- Various fixed SGA memory sections, allocated and managed internally by Oracle Database software

17.2.3.1 The Redo Log Buffer

The redo log buffer is a cyclical buffer, which when under certain circumstances is either fully or partially flushed to the currently active redo log file. The redo log buffer cache will be written to redo log files when it is one-third full, a COMMIT or ROLLBACK command is issued, every 3 seconds, or if it reaches 1Mb.

Note: A checkpoint is a process of flushing dirty buffers from database buffer cache to disk storage. The redo log buffer is not flushed to disk when a checkpoint occurs. This is the consensus of opinion from a number of DBAs and contrary to many Oracle software texts.

During a checkpoint, the database writer (DBWR) will post the log writer (LGWR) to write redo entries. Redo is written from the log buffer to redo log files on disk. This will occur if the DBWR process has to write dirty blocks for which redo entries have not yet been written. This is essential for recoverability. Nothing will be written to datafiles without first being written to redo log files. The DBWR process will actually stop and wait for the LGWR process to complete writing redo log entries. As already stated, redo log entries are always written to disk before database changes to ensure recoverability. Redo log files are best placed onto the fastest disk storage available.

What can cause problems with respect to the redo log buffer?

■ The size of the redo log buffer must be appropriate for database activity.

Note: It is unlikely that the size of the redo log buffer will ever need to be changed from the default value created by the Database Configuration Assistant. Quite often, the log buffer is inappropriately sized because it has been tampered with.

■ The number and size of redo log files can cause problems.
■ The frequency of log switching can affect the availability of redo log files for buffer flushing.

How can we tell if the redo log buffer is too small? Contrary to popular belief, the ***redo log space requests*** entry in the V$SYSSTAT view records requests for the buffer to write out to a redo log file, rather than requests for space in the buffer. The ***redo entries*** statistic tells us how often redo entries are copied into the buffer. The ***redo writes*** statistic tells us how often buffer entries were written to redo log files. The ***redo buffer allocation retries*** event tells us about retries required (when a process has attempted to allocate free space in the log buffer). If the LGWR falls behind, ***redo buffer allocation retries*** will occur. However, this event can also occur when a log switch occurs. Therefore the occurrence of this event can have more than one meaning. If this event occurs because log buffer space is unavailable, then the log buffer may be too small. On the contrary, if it occurs because of a log switch, then perhaps the log files are too small. Speeding up log writing by using faster disks should always be considered first.

17.3 Tuning Oracle I/O Usage

Different types of applications require different approaches to tuning. OLTP databases need quick response times for small transactions. Data warehouses or batch processing requires high throughput of large transactions. A number of factors are important with respect to tuning of I/O with Oracle Database. The two most important factors with respect to I/O are efficiency and recoverability. Do not necessarily sacrifice recoverability to gain a little extra efficiency, unless down time and partial data loss can be tolerated. For an OLTP database, down time is usually not acceptable. In fact, for most databases, data loss is not acceptable. There are various methods for performance tuning I/O activity:

- ***Striping***. Evenly distribute I/O by physically distributing files.

- ***Seek time***. Choose an adequate number of disks with adequate seek times. Seek time is a measure of how long it takes to find a piece of data on a hard drive.

- ***Contention***. High levels of contention due to high I/O request waits can be relieved using striping. Striping spreads files across multiple disks.

- ***Mirroring***. Mirroring is a process of real-time maintenance of multiple copies of data. Mirroring can be expensive in I/O time writes, but some mirroring facilities allow for parallel reads of multiple mirrors.

- ***Block size and multiple block reads***. Block size can have a drastic effect on I/O, but with Oracle Database 9*i* and beyond, multiple-sized block tablespaces are allowed, so this issue can become more manageable. The DB_FILE_MULTIBLOCK_READ_COUNT parameter can have a profound effect on access speed, depending on application and database type, allowing many blocks to be read at once. Larger transactions benefit from larger block sizes because multiple blocks can be accessed with a single read. On the contrary, a large number of blocks read at once can be detrimental to small transactions. This is because full table scans are more likely, and too much data is read. The DB_FILE_MULTIBLOCK_READ_COUNT parameter is discussed in other chapters, but in general a larger value will encourage more full table scans.

Note: (10g) The DB_FILE_MULTIBLOCK_READ_COUNT parameter is automatically tuned when not explicitly set.

The V$FILESTAT dynamic performance view can be somewhat useful in assessing I/O for a database, as shown in the next query. Notice how busy all of the SYSTEM, UNDO (rollback), DATA, and INDX datafiles are. These activity levels and ratios are consistent with a DML-intensive OLTP database:

```
SELECT fs.phyrds "Reads", fs.phywrts "Writes"
,fs.avgiotim "Average I/O Time", df.name "Datafile"
FROM v$datafile df, v$filestat fs WHERE df.file# = fs.file#;
```

This is the result:

```
    Reads     Writes Avg I/O Time Datafile
---------- ---------- ------------ ------------------------------------------------------
     12676        325            0 C:\ORACLE\PRODUCT\10.2.0\ORADATA\TEST\SYSTEM01.DBF
        75        167            0 C:\ORACLE\PRODUCT\10.2.0\ORADATA\TEST\UNDOTBS01.DBF
      2366        722            0 C:\ORACLE\PRODUCT\10.2.0\ORADATA\TEST\SYSAUX01.DBF
       771         18            0 D:\ORACLE\PRODUCT\10.2.0\ORADATA\TEST\DATA01.DBF
       496         57            0 D:\ORACLE\PRODUCT\10.2.0\ORADATA\TEST\INDX01.DBF
       817         21            0 D:\ORACLE\PRODUCT\10.2.0\ORADATA\TEST\DATA02.DBF
       855         15            0 D:\ORACLE\PRODUCT\10.2.0\ORADATA\TEST\DATA03.DBF
       853         22            0 D:\ORACLE\PRODUCT\10.2.0\ORADATA\TEST\DATA04.DBF
       806         29            0 D:\ORACLE\PRODUCT\10.2.0\ORADATA\TEST\DATA05.DBF
       381         53            0 D:\ORACLE\PRODUCT\10.2.0\ORADATA\TEST\INDX02.DBF
       395         41            0 D:\ORACLE\PRODUCT\10.2.0\ORADATA\TEST\INDX03.DBF
       326         28            0 D:\ORACLE\PRODUCT\10.2.0\ORADATA\TEST\INDX04.DBF
       252          4            0 D:\ORACLE\PRODUCT\10.2.0\ORADATA\TEST\INDX05.DBF
         6          2           21 D:\ORACLE\PRODUCT\10.2.0\ORADATA\TEST\OBJ01.DBF
```

The next query looks at I/O activity for all datafiles in all tablespaces, including the temporary sort tablespace called TEMP:

```
COL ts FORMAT a10 HEADING "Tablespace";
COL reads FORMAT 999990;
COL writes FORMAT 999990;
COL br FORMAT 999990 HEADING "BlksRead";
COL bw FORMAT 999990 HEADING "BlksWrite";
COL rtime FORMAT 999990;
COL wtime FORMAT 999990;
SELECT ts.name AS ts, fs.phyrds "Reads", fs.phywrts "Writes"
     ,fs.phyblkrd AS br, fs.phyblkwrt AS bw
     ,fs.readtim "RTime", fs.writetim "WTime"
FROM v$tablespace ts, v$datafile df, v$filestat fs
WHERE ts.ts# = df.ts# AND df.file# = fs.file#
UNION
SELECT ts.name AS ts, ts.phyrds "Reads", ts.phywrts "Writes"
     ,ts.phyblkrd AS br, ts.phyblkwrt AS bw
     ,ts.readtim "RTime", ts.writetim "WTime"
FROM v$tablespace ts, v$tempfile tf, v$tempstat ts
WHERE ts.ts# = tf.ts# AND tf.file# = ts.file# ORDER BY 1;
```

This query does not tell us much. In general, reads appear much more numerous than writes, except for undo segments and temporary sort space. In this situation, for my busy database, this is normal for temporary sort space. Read values in undo segments are indicative of transactions read from rollback to maintain data consistency, because what is being read has already changed. This type of activity needs to be minimized at the application level if possible, if other performance factors are not compromised. For an OLTP database block, to I/O rates should be as close as possible. Also read times should be much faster than write times, probably faster than in this case. This disparity could be application related and a result of read consistency, reading data from already changed data in rollback:

Tablespace	Reads	Writes	BlksRead	BlksWrite	RTime	WTime
DATA	1124	47	1374	47	4100	179
DATA	1154	48	1422	49	4287	164
DATA	1205	34	1468	35	4701	67
DATA	1221	52	1405	53	5179	217
DATA	1282	51	1506	51	5467	335
INDX	378	20	378	21	1222	115
INDX	461	68	487	70	1730	843
INDX	555	88	775	91	2131	400

INDX	649	113	869	116	2887	1076
INDX	831	143	991	174	3159	1138
OBJECTS	6	2	6	2	75	16
SYSAUX	3076	1047	5189	1506	41342	12028
SYSTEM	17220	534	60829	1027	279588	5439
TEMP	1940	1896	1980	1896	18423	15373
UNDOTBS1	106	259	106	1300	4049	3468

Let's get a slightly different picture and use the same query but produce relative rates:

```
COL ts FORMAT a10 HEADING "Tablespace";
SELECT ts.name AS ts
     ,ROUND(fs.phyrds/(fs.phywrts+1),1) "Read/Write"
     ,ROUND(fs.phyblkrd/(fs.phyrds+1),1) "Blocks/Read"
     ,ROUND(fs.phyblkwrt/(fs.phywrts+1),1) "Blocks/Write"
     ,ROUND(fs.readtim/(fs.writetim+1),1) "Read/Write Time"
FROM v$tablespace ts, v$datafile df, v$filestat fs
WHERE ts.ts# = df.ts# AND df.file# = fs.file#
UNION
SELECT ts.name AS ts
     ,ROUND(ts.phyrds/(ts.phywrts+1),1) "Read/Write"
     ,ROUND(ts.phyblkrd/(ts.phyrds+1),1) "Blocks/Read"
     ,ROUND(ts.phyblkwrt/(ts.phywrts+1),1) "Blocks/Write"
     ,ROUND(ts.readtim/(ts.writetim+1),1) "Read/Write Time"
FROM v$tablespace ts, v$tempfile tf, v$tempstat ts
WHERE ts.ts# = tf.ts# AND tf.file# = ts.file# ORDER BY 1;
```

In this query output we can see relative ratios. Note that these numbers are not necessarily meaningful because they are application dependent. In an OLTP database, there should be more write activity than read activity and preferably fewer blocks per read and definitely fewer blocks per write. A data warehouse would be exactly the opposite. More blocks per read imply full scans of one type or another. Full table scans in particular are not generally good for OLTP databases unless there is a mix of OLTP and DSS activity. Otherwise, data model complexity causes full scans to occur frequently as a result of SQL code using large convoluted joins, among other possibilities:

Tablespace	Read/Write	Blocks/Read	Blocks/Write	Read/Write Time
DATA	17.7	1.2	1	9
DATA	18.2	1.2	1	7.4
DATA	18.4	1.2	1.2	25.1
DATA	23.5	1.2	1	36
DATA	24	1.2	1	14
INDX	5.5	1.3	1	2.2
INDX	6.2	1.2	1.2	2.9
INDX	7	1.3	1	4.6
INDX	7.1	1.2	1.1	3.3
INDX	11.4	1.2	1.2	8.5
OBJECTS	2	.9	.7	4.4
SYSAUX	2.8	1.8	1.4	3.3
SYSTEM	36.1	4	1.8	49.8
TEMP	1	1.1	1.1	1.1
UNDOTBS1	.3	1	4.8	1

The result might be a little clearer with 0 rounding, as in the following query:

```
COL ts FORMAT a10 HEADING "Tablespace";
SELECT ts.name AS ts
      ,ROUND(fs.phyrds/(fs.phywrts+1),0) "Read/Write"
      ,ROUND(fs.phyblkrd/(fs.phyrds+1),0) "Blocks/Read"
      ,ROUND(fs.phyblkwrt/(fs.phywrts+1),0) "Blocks/Write"
      ,ROUND(fs.readtim/(fs.writetim+1),0) "Read/Write Time"
FROM v$tablespace ts, v$datafile df, v$filestat fs
WHERE ts.ts# = df.ts# AND df.file# = fs.file#
UNION
SELECT ts.name AS ts
      ,ROUND(ts.phyrds/(ts.phywrts+1),0) "Read/Write"
      ,ROUND(ts.phyblkrd/(ts.phyrds+1),0) "Blocks/Read"
      ,ROUND(ts.phyblkwrt/(ts.phywrts+1),0) "Blocks/Write"
      ,ROUND(ts.readtim/(ts.writetim+1),0) "Read/Write Time"
FROM v$tablespace ts, v$tempfile tf, v$tempstat ts
WHERE ts.ts# = tf.ts# AND tf.file# = ts.file# ORDER BY 1;
```

This is the result:

Tablespace	Read/Write	Blocks/Read	Blocks/Write	Read/Write Time
DATA	20	1	1	7
DATA	20	1	1	10
DATA	21	1	1	26
DATA	25	1	1	15
DATA	26	1	1	40
INDX	5	1	1	2
INDX	6	1	1	2
INDX	7	1	1	4
INDX	8	1	1	4
INDX	14	1	1	11
OBJECTS	2	1	1	4
SYSAUX	3	2	1	3
SYSTEM	35	4	2	47
TEMP	1	1	1	1
UNDOTBS1	0	1	5	1

17.3.1   RAID Arrays

The RAID acronym stands for redundant array of inexpensive disks. In other words, a RAID array is lots of small cheap disks. RAID arrays, in numerous levels of sophistication and vast differences in cost (some exorbitant), can provide enormous increases in performance, loss recoverability, and reliability. There are different types of RAID architectures. The basic RAID types used with Oracle databases are generally RAID 0, RAID 1, RAID 0+1, and RAID 5:

- **RAID 0**. RAID 0 is striping. Striping is a process of splitting files into little pieces and spreading those pieces over multiple disks. RAID 0 can provide fast random read and write access performance but nothing in the way of rapid recoverability and redundancy. RAID 0 is the most efficient method for OLTP databases because of the rapid random access factor on small amounts of data. However, RAID 0 is a little risky because recoverability is unsure. RAID 0 could possibly be insured for recoverability and availability using clustered failovers or even failover standby databases for automated, instant, up-to-the-moment replacement of service loss.

- **RAID 1**. RAID 1 is mirroring. Mirroring allows the creation of multiple copies of files, making duplicate entries into multiple files every time a change is made to a file. RAID 1 can cause I/O bottleneck problems with respect to high-usage areas of disk storage, namely high-usage database objects such as frequently written tables. On the contrary, read access can be extremely fast because some highly sophisticated RAID arrays can read more than one mirror copy of a file at the same time, allowing for parallel reads. RAID 1 is potentially appropriate for sequential access of redo logs and index spaces in OLTP databases, and in data warehouses for any types of read. RAID 1 is not appropriate for random access of table rows from indexes that use ROWID pointers.

- *RAID 0+1*. This option combines the best aspects of RAID 0 and RAID 1, providing both striping for read and write access performance plus mirroring recoverability and parallel read access. RAID 0+1 is not as fast as RAID 0, but it's faster than RAID 1 and also a little less recoverable than RAID 1.

- *RAID 5*. RAID 5 provides a more simplistic version of mirroring, where only parity is duplicated, rather than a complete duplicate as provided by mirroring under RAID 1. RAID 5 can be particularly effective in very expensive RAID array architectures, containing specialized buffering RAM, built onboard within the architecture of the RAID array itself. RAID 5 is best used for sequential reading and not random write access. RAID 5 is not appropriate for OLTP databases other than to contain log files and perhaps indexes.

17.3.2 (10g) **Oracle Automatic Storage Management**

Oracle Automatic Storage Management (ASM) is a volume manager specifically built for Oracle Database and Oracle Database files. It is fully integrated into Oracle Database software. The extra administration associated with file system and volume manager software is taken care of automatically by ASM. The result is easier management of Oracle Database as a file system, plus the performance of asynchronous I/O and raw partitions, without the complexity of raw disk management.

Note: Asynchronous I/O is potentially much more efficient that synchronous I/O because there is less dependence between different processes. Thus, a process may begin executing before the completion of another partially related process. More specifically, an application issuing an I/O request to a disk can continue processing as data is transferred, thereby increasing the performance of I/O activities in general.

Note: Raw partitions do not have to overhead of an operating system–based file system and format imposed onto a disk.

Essentially ASM is an extension of Oracle Managed Files (OMF), where all files are automatically created, deleted, and managed by the ASM volume manager software. Additionally, the recoverability and performance of striping and mirroring are also built in to ASM.

ASM can be of benefit when using Oracle Real Application Clusters (RAC). A shared Oracle home decreases administrative work when dealing with more than one node in an Oracle RAC cluster.

17.3.2.1 ASM Performance

By incorporating automated striping and mirroring, ASM removes the necessity for manual I/O and storage tuning of Oracle Database files. However, similar I/O attributes for disks within a disk group are advisable. For example, place redo log files on a disk group with high sequential I/O performance. Use disk groups with slower hard drives for lower write activity files. It follows that mixing hard drives of varying read-write speeds, within the same group, is inadvisable.

Automated load balancing is a factor allowing ASM to distribute data across each disk group for maximum performance. ASM splits files at the extent level, dividing files into 1Mb extent sizes. Those 1Mb extents are then spread uniformly across all the disks in a disk group. I/O performance is effectively taken care of automatically. As already stated, ASM mirrors at the extent level, rather than the file level. What this means is that some files can be mirrored, and others do not have to be. For example, a frequently read file can be mirrored to enhance parallel read performance. And another file that is changed frequently can have no mirroring configured, helping to increase DML activity performance.

17.3.2.2 Administrative Pros and Cons of ASM

Administration is simplified, grouping files into disk groups, thus removing the need to have to administer what could be thousands of Oracle Database files in a very large environment. The result is management of a much smaller set of disk groups, divided up by functionality and purpose, rather than simply as a multitude of many files. And as for use of OMF—ASM being an extension of OMF—naming of files and deletion of files is automatic. Also, load balancing of files is completely automated. Load balancing also includes automated redistribution of files when a disk fails, is removed, or is added into a disk group. And the database can remain online. Oracle RAC benefits from the provision of volume management, raw partitioning, and a file system.

One of the potential disadvantages of using ASM is, for example, that apparently a single disk failure can corrupt an entire database. That can be quite a disadvantage.

17.3.2.3   ASM High-Availability Features

ASM comes built in with the high-availability features of two-way mirroring, three-way mirroring, and striping. Additionally, mirroring can be switched off altogether. Multiple mirrored copies help recoverability simply because multiple copies of the same data are retained. It can also speed up read performance by allowing for parallel read of the same data. However, mirroring can slow write performance because multiple copies must be maintained. Striping allows for better random access read and write performance, with small transaction sizes, which is often more beneficial for OLTP databases. However, striping, without using mirroring at all, reduces recoverability.

Once again, further details on problem detection and tuning of I/O are discussed in later chapters, particularly when covering wait events and latches. The next chapter will deal with tuning network usage.

18

Tuning Network Usage

This chapter will cover Oracle network tuning. Oracle networking software is sometimes known as Oracle net services, or just net services. Many times I have heard that the only way to tune Net Services is to change the session data unit (SDU) buffer size. This is not correct. There are many ways in which Net Services configuration can be adjusted, improving performance under varying circumstances. The easiest method of describing how is to describe each facet of Net Services tuning and to display by example. Let's begin with the listener process and its various possible configurations.

Note: (10g) Managing network configuration files is simplified, as manual configuration is no longer required. Additionally, performance enhancements have been made, including support for high-speed networks and better network bandwidth use between database servers and application servers.

18.1 The Listener

The listener is a process residing on a database server or other machine that *listens* for database connection requests. When a request is received, the listener hands off (or passes) on the connection to a database server process. The following is a very simple listener configuration file. This file is called listener.ora by default and is placed in the $ORACLE_HOME/network/admin directory:

```
LISTENER =
  (DESCRIPTION_LIST =
    (DESCRIPTION =
```

```
        (ADDRESS = (PROTOCOL = TCP) (HOST = <hostname>) (PORT =
1521))
    )
  )


SID_LIST_LISTENER =
  (SID_LIST =
    (SID_DESC =
      (GLOBAL_DBNAME = <SID>.<xyz.com>)
      (SID_NAME = <SID>)
      (ORACLE_HOME = /oracle/product/10.2.0/db_1)
    )
  )
```

What can be done to tune or at least improve the listener under certain circumstances?

- *Listener queue size*. This allows a larger number of listener requests to be serviced by allowing requests to wait in a queue.
- *Listener logging and tracing*. Logging is defaulted on. Tracing is defaulted off.
- *Multiple listeners and load balancing*. Randomized load balancing can be created between multiple listeners pointing at the same database.

18.1.1   Listener Queue Size

Very large quantities of network requests and traffic to the listener can cause the listener to use a queue in order to allow the listener to keep up with requests. If there are too many requests, then waiting requests to the listener will be queued. The default length of the listener queue is operating system-specific and can be increased by setting the QUEUESIZE parameter in the listener configuration file:

```
LISTENER =
  (DESCRIPTION_LIST =
    (DESCRIPTION =
      (ADDRESS =
        (PROTOCOL = TCP)
        (HOST = <hostname>)
```

```
          (PORT = 1521)
          (QUEUESIZE = 50)
        )
      )
    )

SID_LIST_LISTENER =
  (SID_LIST =
    (SID_DESC =
      (GLOBAL_DBNAME = <SID>.<xyz.com>)
      (SID_NAME = <SID>)
      (ORACLE_HOME = /oracle/product/10.2.0/db_1)
    )
  )
```

18.1.2 Switching Off Listener Logging and Tracing

By default, a file called $ORACLE_HOME/network/log/listener.log is created and constantly appended to. Tracing can also be switched on but is off by default. Logging and tracing of the listener process can be switched off by setting the appropriate configuration parameters in the listener.ora file. Switch off listener logging and tracing, if tracing is switched on. Log and trace files can become extremely large and will affect performance. Unless truly needed, do not log or trace the listener process:

```
LISTENER =
  (DESCRIPTION_LIST =
    (DESCRIPTION =
      (ADDRESS = (PROTOCOL = TCP) (HOST = <hostname>) (PORT =
1521))
    )
  )

SID_LIST_LISTENER =
  (SID_LIST =
    (SID_DESC =
      (GLOBAL_DBNAME = <SID>.<xyz.com>)
      (SID_NAME = <SID>)
      (ORACLE_HOME = /oracle/product/10.2.0/db_1)
    )
  )
```

```
      LOGGING_LISTENER = OFF
      TRACE_LEVEL_LISTENER = OFF
```

18.1.3 Multiple Listeners and Load Balancing

Load balancing can help performance by providing multiple listener connection points to a database server. If one listener is busy, then another listener process can be deferred to. This reduces load on the first listener. So,
let's add a listener. The listener.ora configuration might now look something like that shown following. Note that the listener called LISTENER2
uses a different port number from that of the listener called LISTENER.
Both of the two listeners, LISTENER and LISTENER2, allow connections
to the same database:

```
LISTENER =
  (DESCRIPTION_LIST =
    (DESCRIPTION =
      (ADDRESS = (PROTOCOL = TCP) (HOST = <hostname>) (PORT =
1521))
    )
  )

LISTENER2 =
  (DESCRIPTION_LIST =
    (DESCRIPTION =
      (ADDRESS = (PROTOCOL = TCP) (HOST = <hostname>) (PORT =
1522))
    )
  )

SID_LIST_LISTENER =
  (SID_LIST =
    (SID_DESC =
      (GLOBAL_DBNAME = <SID>.<xyz.com>)
      (SID_NAME = <SID>)
      (ORACLE_HOME = /oracle/product/10.2.0/db_1)
    )
  )

SID_LIST_LISTENER2 =
  (SID_LIST =
    (SID_DESC =
```

```
        (GLOBAL_DBNAME = <SID>.<xyz.com>)
        (SID_NAME = <SID>)
        (ORACLE_HOME = /oracle/product/10.2.0/db_1)
    )
  )
```

So how do we implement load balancing between multiple listener processes? The configuration file shown following is the client configuration file called the Transparent Network Substrate (TNS). This file is placed in the $ORACLE_HOME/network/admin directory and is called tnsnames.ora. The tnsnames.ora file is a local naming client connection configuration file. The tnsnames.ora file can be placed on both Oracle server and client installations, specifying how a client process such as SQL*Plus communicates with a listener process (from a database server or a client computer). Note that there are two connection strings with ports 1521 and 1522, matching the different listener address in the previously shown listener.ora file:

```
<TNSname> =
  (DESCRIPTION =
    (ADDRESS_LIST =
      (LOAD_BALANCE = YES)
      (ADDRESS = (PROTOCOL = TCP) (HOST = <hostname>) (PORT =
1521))
      (ADDRESS = (PROTOCOL = TCP) (HOST = <hostname>) (PORT =
1522))
    )
    (CONNECT_DATA = (SID = <SID>) (ORACLE_HOME = /oracle/
product/10.2.0/db_1))
  )
```

18.2 Network Naming Methods

Oracle Database can use a number of different network naming methods. What is a naming method? A naming method is a way in which a node name on a network will be translated into a form understandable and routable by hardware and network software on that network. The only fact that can really be stated about tuning naming methods, with respect to Oracle Database, is as follows: The smaller the number of steps required to pass messages across a network using net services software there are, the faster database communication will be. It should be noted, however, that not much can be done to speed up net services in this respect. There are five different configurations available. Applying different configuration parameters within the different naming methods can help to increase Oracle net services performance processing in certain situations:

- ■ *Local naming*. This uses a configuration file called tnsnames.ora (TNS). This method is the default method and the most commonly used. Using an IP address instead of a hostname will be noticeably faster. However, if network IP addresses change frequently, which they are want to do, this could cause a maintenance problem.

- ■ *Directory naming*. Net service names and their mappings are stored in a lightweight directory access protocol (LDAP) server, much like a DNS server.

- ■ ⑨ *Oracle names*. This is typically used for globally distributed networks involving the use of an Oracle names server. The Oracle names server is used to store service addresses and net service names. An Oracle names server can reside on a machine separate from that of the database server, thus distributing processing.

Note: ⑩ Oracle names is desupported. Migration to directory naming is advised.

- ■ *Host naming*. This is the simplest method of database communication, using operating system–based IP address-to-hostname mapping host files. Host files on Solaris Unix are placed in the /etc/system directory. In Windows, the c:\windows\system32\drivers\etc directory is used.

- ■ *External naming*. This refers to third-party naming services.

- ■ ⑩ *Easy connect*. This allows a direct connection to a database server using a connection string, as shown in this syntax diagram and the following example:

```
CONNECT <user>/<password>@<host>:<port>/<service>
```

This example connects to a database server on a computer called 2000server host, through port 1521, connecting to the database called TEST:

```
CONNECT system/<password>@2000server:1521/TEST
```

18.2.1   Local Naming

As far as tuning is concerned, local naming using the tnsnames.ora file is the naming method that will suffice for explanatory purposes.

18.2.1.1   Dedicated Versus Shared Servers

When a user connects to a database, a server process is used to service the connection. The server process can be either a dedicated or a shared server process. For the dedicated option, a dedicated server process is started up and retained for the duration of the connection. A shared server process, on the other hand, is shared indirectly between different connections through dispatcher processes. Shared server processes and dispatchers comprise what used to be called Oracle Shared Services.

Note: Shared servers was called MTS or multithreaded server prior to Oracle Database 9*i*. In Oracle Database 10*g*, it is called shared servers.

Shared server processes and dispatchers will be covered later on in this chapter. Both dedicated and shared server connections are shown in Figure 18.1.

Figure 18.1
Dedicated versus shared server configuration

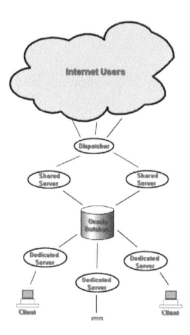

A dedicated server process can be used to allocate a dedicated connection to a local name. A dedicated server process connection can be forced to occur, even in a shared server process configuration, and is necessary for certain types of functionality, such as using Recovery Manager (RMAN).

The following is an example tnsnames.ora file containing TNS name connections for an OLTP database and an RMAN backup connection. RMAN requires a dedicated server connection:

```
<TNSname> =
  (DESCRIPTION =
    (ADDRESS_LIST =
      (ADDRESS = (PROTOCOL = TCP) (HOST = <hostname>) (PORT =
1521))
    )
    (CONNECT_DATA =
      (SID = <SID>)
      (ORACLE_HOME = /oracle/product/10.2.0/db_1)
      (SERVER = SHARED)
    )
  )


RMAN =
  (DESCRIPTION =
    (ADDRESS_LIST =
      (ADDRESS = (PROTOCOL = TCP) (HOST = <hostname>) (PORT =
1521))
    )
    (CONNECT_DATA = (SERVICE_NAME = RMAN) (SERVER =
DEDICATED))
  )
```

18.2.1.2   The Session Data Unit Buffer (SDU)

Net services uses a buffer to contain information ready for sending over a network. The buffer is flushed to the network and sent either on request or when it is full. The larger the buffer is, the more information is sent over the network at once. SDU buffer size can range from 512 bytes to 32Kb. The default setting is operating system dependent. The following example shows a tnsnames.ora configuration file with its SDU buffer size altered. Sessions containing large transactions may benefit from a larger SDU buffer size:

```
<TNSname> =
  (DESCRIPTION =
    (ADDRESS_LIST =
      (ADDRESS = (PROTOCOL = TCP) (HOST = <hostname>) (PORT =
1521))
    )
    (SDU=1024)
    (CONNECT_DATA = (SID = <SID>) (ORACLE_HOME = /oracle/
product/10.2.0/db_1)
    )
  )
```

18.3 Connection Profiles

A profile is a definitional configuration placed onto a client or server machine, such that parameters within the profile definition determine how a connection to that server machine will behave. For instance, on a Unix machine, each Unix user has a profile. Essentially this profile declares variables global to the user (local variables), along with default behavior required. Unix user profiles would contain such variables as path names. The following is a stripped down example Unix profile for a Unix Oracle database administrator user on an Oracle Database 8*i* Release 2 (8.1.7) database server. This file is out of date but good for explaining what a profile is:

```
#This .cshrc file is executed in tcsh (/usr/local/bin/tcsh)
on Solaris
setenv ORACLE_BASE /<mp1>/oracle
setenv ORACLE_HOME /<mp1>/oracle/product/8.1.7
setenv ORACLE_DOC /<mp1>/oracle/doc
setenv LD_LIBRARY_PATH /<mp1>/oracle/product/8.1.7/lib:/usr/
openwin/lib
setenv JAVA_HOME /<mp1>/oracle/product/jre/1.1.8
setenv TNS_ADMIN /<mp1>/oracle/product/8.1.7/network/admin
setenv ORACLE_SID <SID>
setenv ORACLE_DBF1 /<mp1>/oracle/oradata/$ORACLE_SID
setenv ORACLE_DBF2 /<mp2>/oracle/oradata/$ORACLE_SID
setenv ORACLE_BACKUPS /<mp2>/backups
setenv ORACLE_SBIN /<mp1>/oracle/product/8.1.7/sbin
setenv ORACLE_ALERT /<mp1>/oracle/admin/$ORACLE_SID/bdump
setenv EDITOR vi
```

```
setenv PATH /bin:/usr/bin:/etc:/usr/ccs/bin:/usr/openwin/
bin:/usr/ucb
setenv PATH ${PATH}:/usr/local/bin:/usr/sbin:/usr/X/
bin:$JAVA_HOME
setenv PATH ${PATH}:/<mp1>/oracle/product/8.1.7/bin
setenv PATH ${PATH}:/<mp1>/oracle/product/8.1.7/sbin

set host='hostname'
alias sp 'set prompt="$user@$host:r":"$cwd> "'
alias cd 'cd \!*;sp'
alias rm 'rm -i'
alias ll 'ls -la'
cd

alias dbs  'cd $ORACLE_HOME/dbs'
alias bin  'cd $ORACLE_HOME'
alias net8 'cd $TNS_ADMIN'
alias pfile 'cd $ORACLE_BASE/admin/$ORACLE_SID/pfile'
alias alert 'cd $ORACLE_ALERT'
alias sbin 'cd $ORACLE_HOME/sbin'
alias dbf1 'cd $ORACLE_BASE/oradata/$ORACLE_SID'
alias dbf2 'cd /<mp2>/oracle/oradata/$ORACLE_SID'

set filec
set history=100
umask 077
```

The $ORACLE_HOME/network/admin/sqlnet.ora file can be used to contain profile information for connections to an Oracle database server. In the same way that a Unix profile is instantiated when a Unix user logs into Unix, the sqlnet.ora file instantiates a profile into a session through net services. Net Services profile parameters are numerous and generally cover client logging, net services security authentication, net services tracing (switch all this off), Connection Manager configuration, and even network outage detection and I/O buffer space configuration parameters.

Note: (10*g*) Network outage detection and I/O buffer space configuration parameters are new to Oracle Database 10*g*.

It appears that recent versions of Oracle Database are increasingly using Net Services profile parameters on client machines. Expect more usage of Net Services profile parameters in the future.

As far as tuning Net Services profile parameters is concerned, a number of parameters are of immediate interest to tuning:

- *TCP.NODELAY=YES*. Large amounts of data passed through Net Services can have the buffer flushed to the network immediately. Otherwise, there may be a delay before information is passed over the network.

- *USE_DEDICATED_SERVER=YES*. Force all connections to the database server from the current client machine to connect to dedicated server connections, adding (SERVER = DEDICATED) to name connection descriptions.

- *SQLNET.EXPIRE_TIME=5*. Timeout on client Net Services connections allows automatic termination of idle Net Services connections to the database server in order to help free up needed resources.

- (10*g*) *SQLNET timeout parameters*. These parameters can help to prevent a database server from being blocked by time-consuming network request operations (defined as an integer in seconds):
  - *SQLNET.SEND_TIMEOUT*. Place an allowed time limit on send operations over a network.
  - *SQLNET.RECV_TIMEOUT*. Place an allowed time limit on receive operations over a network.
  - *SQLNET.INBOUND_CONNECT_TIMEOUT*. Place an allowed time limit on client database connection requests.

- (10*g*) *SQLNET I/O buffer space parameters*. These parameters can help utilize improved network bandwidth by promoting continuous flow of data over a network (defined as an integer in bytes):
  - *SQLNET.RECV_BUFFER_SIZE*. This is generally defined on the receiving side of a network connection (the client side). The client side requires configuration in the sqlnet.ora or tnsnames.ora files.
  - *SQLNET.SEND_BUF_SIZE*. This is generally defined on the sending side of a network connection (the server side). The server side requires configuration in the listener.ora and sqlnet.ora files.

Using these profile parameters will not really make that much difference to the overall performance, unless they are targeted at resolving a specific performance problem. What happens when ad hoc SQL code users go to lunch? Connections not executing COMMIT or ROLLBACK commands, if they are required, could possibly use timeout-capable connections.

18.4   Shared Servers

When using a dedicated server configuration, connections are granted exclusively to a specific user request. Therefore, one dedicated server process, plus a chunk of connection cache in memory, is allocated to each connection. As a result, dedicated servers are not scalable up to a large number of users. A solution to high resource usage is to share those resources using shared servers and dispatchers. A shared server process can be shared between multiple user connections, where dispatcher processes dispatch requests and results between a shared server process and a client connection. In effect, shared processes are rarely idle because they are shared (frequently switched) between different user connections.

Some functions, mostly database administration functions, are best served, and sometimes only served, by dedicated server connections. When using a dedicated server configuration, connection requests are routed by the listener process. The listener passes the client process an address for an available dedicated server process, which may have to be spawned. In the case of a shared server configuration, the listener will pass the client process the address of an available dispatcher process (spawned if none are available). The dispatcher process in turn sends the client process the address of a shared server process. The client process then communicates with the database server using a shared server process.

18.4.1   Shared Server Configuration Parameters

Shared server configuration parameters are set in the database server configuration parameters file. Simple example parameter settings for using shared servers and dispatchers are as follows:

```
DISPATCHERS = "(PROTOCOL=TCP) (DISPATCHERS=1) (PORT=1522)"
SHARED_SERVERS = 2
CIRCUITS = 10
SHARED_SERVER_SESSIONS = 10
MAX_DISPATCHERS = 3
MAX_SHARED_SERVERS = 5
```

Note: (10*g*) Many parameters have been greatly simplified, particularly the shared server parameters. The SHARED_SERVERS parameter is the only required parameter to instantiate a shared server configuration. The DISPATCHERS parameter is now automated and no longer always required to be explicitly defined.

18.4.1.1 (9*i*) Oracle Database 9*i* Shared Server Configuration

SHARED_SERVERS and DISPATCHERS parameters are created at database startup. CIRCUITS are virtual circuits for both inbound and outbound network traffic. A virtual circuit is a chunk of memory that passes requests and responses between dispatcher and shared server processes. SHARED_SERVER_SESSIONS denotes user sessions per shared server. MAX_DISPATCHERS limits the number of dispatchers and connections per dispatcher. MAX_SHARED_SERVERS specifies the maximum number of shared servers allowed.

The DISPATCHERS parameter can get a lot more complicated. The DISPATCHERS parameter in the configuration parameter file is very much like a TNS name connection string. Effectively, a dispatcher is a connection string because it performs a routing function between client processes and shared server processes:

```
DISPATCHERS = "(PROTOCOL=TCP) (DISPATCHERS=1) (PORT=1521)"
```

Now we can add further specifications to the DISPATCHERS parameter:

```
DISPATCHERS = "(DESCRIPTION=(ADDRESS=
   (PROTOCOL=TCP) (DISPATCHERS=1) (PORT=1521)
(QUEUESIZE=50)))
   (SESSIONS=500) (CONNECTIONS=500) (MULTIPLEX=ON) (POOL=ON)
(TICK=2)"
```

- **POOL=ON**. This option enables connection pooling. When using connection pooling, not only are shared servers shared, but dispatchers are shared as well. This increases scalability in terms of network connections and the number of concurrent users.

■ *TICK*. This sets a timeout on a connection request and response, making an idle connection available for use by another client request or a shared server response when the timeout is exceeded.

■ *MULTIPLEX=ON*. Oracle Connection Manager provides scalability by providing network node addresses plus routing directions to those network nodes. Oracle Connection Manager is more of a listening router rather than a simple network names storage facility. Additionally, Oracle Connection Manager can provide what is called multiplexing (or funneling), in addition to other features, such as protocol transparency. Funneling is relevant to tuning. Connection concentration or funneling permits multiple connections between two processes. This can allow a shared server process to service more connection requests than using connection pooling alone. The result is multiple client connection requests serviced by a single dispatcher process. Multiple Connection Managers can increase the number of concurrent client connections serviced astronomically.

Note: (10g) Oracle Connection Manager is improved, now including dynamic configuration, enhanced access control, and better scalability.

There can also be multiple dispatchers using different ports:

```
DISPATCHERS = "(PROTOCOL=TCP) (DISPATCHERS=1) (PORT=1521)"
DISPATCHERS = "(PROTOCOL=TCP) (DISPATCHERS=1) (PORT=1522)"
```

More dispatchers will decrease user resource usage but can decrease performance for each user because of all the switching. However, if connection numbers are high, then shared server processes are scalable if a middle tier is not utilized. On a Windows server, set a single dispatcher for between every 200 to 1,000 connections, depending on application type and database server type.

18.4.2 Network Performance Views

Network performance views involve views for shared servers, dispatchers, and virtual circuits, in addition to the usual event and wait event statistics views. These are the shared server parameter settings I used in my Oracle Database 9*i* version:

```
SHARED_SERVERS = 2
CIRCUITS = 5
SHARED_SERVER_SESSIONS = 5
MAX_SHARED_SERVERS = 5
MAX_DISPATCHERS = 3
```

Note: (10*g*) The SHARED_SERVERS parameter is the only required configuration parameter.

When executing queries within this section, I had between 10 and 100 concurrent jobs running in my Accounts schema on my database.

18.4.2.1 Shared Servers

Three views that can be used to inspect shared server usage are the V$SHARED_SERVER, V$QUEUE, and V$SHARED_SERVER_ MONITOR performance views. This query reads the V$SHARED_ SERVER performance view:

```
COL name FORMAT a4;
SELECT name, messages, bytes, breaks, idle, busy, requests
FROM v$shared_server;
```

The result shows two shared server processes are running and only one is in use:

NAME	MESSAGES	BYTES	BREAKS	IDLE	BUSY	REQUESTS
S000	284	49131	0	810433	4385	141
S001	0	0	0	814722	0	0

The next query shows possible shared server process contention. The COMMON type examines shared server processes only, in one-hundredths of a second. The average wait per activity shown is less than 3 one-hundredths of a second. This is not a problem because only one shared server process is used:

```
SELECT wait/totalq FROM v$QUEUE WHERE type = 'COMMON';
```

This is the result:

```
WAIT/TOTALQ
-----------
 .269503546
```

The V$SHARED_SERVER_MONITOR view holds the highest reached values since database startup. My parameter values could be substantially reduced:

```
SELECT MAXIMUM_CONNECTIONS "Circuits"
,MAXIMUM_SESSIONS "Shared_Server_Sessions"
,SERVERS_STARTED "Started"
,SERVERS_TERMINATED "Terminated"
,SERVERS_HIGHWATER "Max_Shared_Servers"
FROM v$shared_server_monitor;
```

This is the result:

```
Circuits Shared_Server_Sessions Started Terminated Max_Shared_Servers
-------- ---------------------- ------- ---------- ------------------
       3                      3       0          0                  2
```

18.4.2.2 Dispatchers

Use the V$DISPATCHER, V$QUEUE, and V$DISPATCHER_RATE performance views to monitor dispatcher activity. The first query shows dispatcher activity. There is little competition for this single dispatcher. Therefore, examining V$DISPATCHER_RATE output is pointless in this case:

```
COL name FORMAT a4;
COL status FORMAT a10;
SELECT name, status, messages, bytes, busy, idle, busy/idle
FROM v$dispatcher;
```

This is the result:

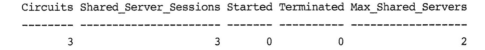

```
NAME STATUS       MESSAGES       BYTES       BUSY       IDLE  BUSY/IDLE
---- ---------- ---------- ---------- ---------- ---------- ----------
D000 WAIT              284      49131         25     852372  .00002933
```

As with shared servers, the next query on the V$QUEUE performance view shows possible dispatcher process contention. The DISPATCHER value examines dispatcher processes only, in one-hundredths of a second. The average wait per activity is nonexistent:

```
SELECT wait/totalq FROM v$QUEUE WHERE type = 'DISPATCHER';
```

This is the result:

```
WAIT/TOTALQ
-----------
          0
```

18.4.2.3 Virtual Circuits

The V$CIRCUIT performance view provides a picture of shared server to dispatcher database connections. This query indicates no problems:

```
SELECT status, queue, bytes, breaks FROM v$circuit;
```

This is the result:

STATUS	QUEUE	BYTES	BREAKS
NORMAL	NONE	9033	0
NORMAL	NONE	8675	0
NORMAL	SERVER	11484	0

18.4.2.4 Using Events

Events such as *virtual circuit status* and *dispatcher timer* can be used to detect potential problems with shared servers and dispatchers. Events of interest are as follows:

```
SELECT name "Event" FROM v$EVENT_NAME
WHERE name LIKE '%dispatcher%' OR name LIKE '%circuit%' OR
name LIKE '%SQL*Net%';
```

This is the result:

```
Event
-------------------------------
alter system set dispatcher
virtual circuit status
dispatcher timer
dispatcher listen timer
SQL*Net message to client
SQL*Net message to dblink
SQL*Net more data to client
SQL*Net more data to dblink
SQL*Net message from client
SQL*Net more data from client
SQL*Net message from dblink
SQL*Net more data from dblink
SQL*Net break/reset to client
SQL*Net break/reset to dblink
dispatcher shutdown
latch: virtual circuit queues
```

Some simple event statistics can be gathered with this query:

```
COL event FORMAT a30;
COL waits FORMAT 9999990;
COL timeouts FORMAT 99999990;
COL average FORMAT 99999990;
SELECT event "Event", time_waited "Total Time", total_waits
"Waits"
    ,average_wait "Average", total_timeouts "Timeouts"
FROM V$SYSTEM_EVENT
WHERE event IN (
    SELECT name FROM v$EVENT_NAME
WHERE name LIKE '%dispatcher%' OR name LIKE '%circuit%' OR
name LIKE '%SQL*Net%'
) ORDER BY EVENT;
```

This is the result:

```
Event                          Total Time    Waits   Average  Timeouts
------------------------------ ----------  --------  --------- ----------
SQL*Net break/reset to client           3         8          0          0
```

```
SQL*Net message from client        605113      340      1780         0
SQL*Net message to client               0      344         0         0
SQL*Net more data to client             0        8         0         0
dispatcher timer                   958324      630      1521       483
virtual circuit status            1871562      765      2446       618
```

That is all there is to know about basic Oracle network software tuning. The next chapter will look into Oracle Partitioning and parallelism.

19

Oracle Partitioning and Parallelism

This chapter will cover Oracle Partitioning and some parallel processing within those partitions. There are also various unique actions that can be performed with partitioning, such as moving and exchanging of entire chunks of data at the speed of a Unix move (mv) command. Obviously the storage subsystem determines the speed of any kind of move command. However, separate partitions can be plugged in and out of a partitioned object. We will start with a brief introduction as to what exactly can be done with partitioning, following with some experimentation showing the performance benefits of Oracle Partitioning.

One more brief point before beginning with this chapter: I have another book published called *Oracle Data Warehouse Tuning for 10*g.[1] Much as I would like to include the content from that book into this one, I cannot, as this book would wind up being more than 1,000 pages. At 1,000 pages, we might need a truck to carry it around in. For parallel processing other than that related to Oracle Partitioning, please refer to the following sections of my data warehouse tuning book: Chapters 6, 7, 10, and 12.

19.1 What Is Oracle Partitioning?

Oracle Partitioning is the splitting of data sets into separate physical files using separate partition tablespaces. Partitions can actually coexist in the same physical file, but the same effect might not be achieved. Then again, separating partitions into separate datafiles is not essential with certain types of RAID array architectures.

Separate partitions are accessible in parallel, individually, or in groups. Why is partitioning relevant to tuning? Partitioning can be used to break large tables into smaller subsets. Processing of smaller subsets of data both separately and in parallel with each other is potentially very much faster than executing serial processing on very large data sets. Partitioning and parallelism generally only apply to very large databases on high-end multiple CPU server platforms. This is not always the case, though. Figure 19.1 shows a picture of how partitioning can be used to split a physical datafile containing a table into multiple physical datafiles mapped individually to separate partitions within that table.

Figure 19.1
Physical partitioning

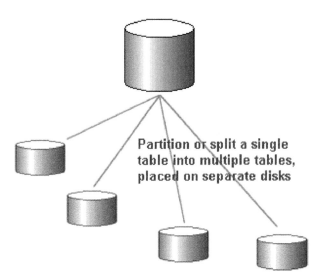

Partition or split a single table into multiple tables, placed on separate disks

19.1.1   Why Is Oracle Partitioning Beneficial?

Oracle Partitioning is beneficial usually in very large database environments and less frequently in smaller databases. This depends on application requirements for the following reasons:

■ Parallel processing is a way of splitting data into separately located physical files. Separating table and index datafiles onto separate disks in a nonpartitioned database is a form of simple partitioning. It is often highly beneficial to read index and data spaces from separate locations because table and index physical spaces are often read almost in parallel. Partitioning can enhance the benefits of splitting datafiles.

■ Different partitions within the same table can have different physical storage structures. Different partitions within a table can even be both read-write and read only, perhaps allowing separation of archived and current data.

- Backup, recovery, and utility usage (SQL*Loader, Export, and Import) can utilize parallel processing and activities on individual partitions.

The Optimizer can access individual partitions when processing SQL code. This process is termed *partition pruning* because partitions can potentially be removed from the database read required by a query. Additionally, the Optimizer can execute against multiple partitions using parallel processing, generally on high-end multiple CPU server platforms, with datafiles spread across multiple disks.

Note: Rows can also be accessed by partition name, effectively allowing manual partition pruning.

- Parallel processing on a multiple CPU platform, in tandem with Oracle Partitioning, applies all these performance-enhancement aspects to both DML and DDL commands.

19.1.2   How Are Tables and Indexes Partitioned?

Partitions can be created on single or multiple columns of a table. A table can be divided into separate partitions based on three methods: (1) ranges of values, (2) values in lists, and (3) hashing algorithms in columns. Additionally, partitions can be one of two composites of the already mentioned three partitioning methods.

A partition is divided based on what is called a *partition key*. This key is internal to Oracle Database. The partition key is the data definition splitting table rows into separate partitions. For example, a range partition on a table could have rows separated into different partitions based on a date for each row, perhaps dividing financial data into quarters. The partition key is that date column, as defined by the range partition.

What are the specifics of the different partitioning methods?

- *Range partition*. This splits rows in a table based on ranges of values (e.g., splitting a table of transactions into periods, such as the four quarters in a year, where the four quarters would be derived from a transaction date).

- *List partition*. This splits rows based on lists of values, dividing rows into separate partitions based on matches between list entries and row column values. For example, a table containing state codes such as NY (New York) and CA (California) could be split up into separate partitions for each state.

- *Hash partition*. A hashing algorithm separates rows based on a column specification into a specified number of separate partitions. The hash value is calculated internally from the partition key. This partitioning method splits the number of rows in a table evenly across all partitions.

- *Composite partition*. Partitions can contain subpartitions of two types: (1) a range partition can contain multiple hash subpartitions, and (2) a range partition can contain multiple list subpartitions.

Partitions can have indexes. How are indexes built for partitions? There are two types of partitioning indexes:

- *Local index*. These indexes have the same structure as their relative table partitions and are based on the partition key. Local indexes are preferred due to more automated maintenance.

- *Global index*. These indexes are BTree indexes and are created on partitioned tables but are not the same structure as the partitioning key.

- (10g) *Hash-partitioned global index*. A hash index allows for a more even spread of index values, allowing an improvement in index performance. BTree indexes with a large number of similar values can result in unbalanced BTree structures, where a small number of leaf blocks in the index contain most of the values, which is inefficient. A hash index can alleviate this problem by spreading indexes evenly. However, hash indexes typically do not lend themselves to constant changes to indexes. Thus, hash-partitioned global indexes might be best suited to tables that are somewhat static in nature, specifically in relation to the partition key values.

Let's now examine and experiment with different partitioning methods in my Accounts schema database. The machine used is once again my rather geriatric dual 300MHz PII CPU box. Additionally, this machine has different drives for separating different physical partition datafiles.

19.1.3 Oracle Partitioning Methods

I will use the Accounts schema to examine the usefulness of the different partitioning methods.

19.1.3.1 Partitioning by Range

The GeneralLedger table is most appropriately partitioned by date range. Partitioning by date may not make any difference to this table with respect to row inserts because rows are only added in the current period, or the most recent partition. However, it could help performance for creating financial statements, such as balance sheets. Accounting reports of this nature are usually reported by date range periods. So it is more than appropriate to divide such a table based on a date range. The following shows the division of data in the GeneralLedger table. These numbers are not exactly correct because the financial year in the Accounts data starts on March 1; for the purposes of this example, this reduced level of accuracy is good enough:

```
SELECT TO_CHAR(dte,'YYYY') "Year"
,COUNT(TO_CHAR(dte,'YYYY')) "Entries"
FROM generalledger GROUP BY TO_CHAR(dte,'YYYY') ORDER BY 1;
```

This is the result of the query, showing the total number of entries contained within each year:

```
Year    Entries
----    ----------
1999     195888
2000     208624
2001     213660
2002     134568
```

New partitions can have separate tablespaces. How big is the GeneralLedger table?

```
COL Object FORMAT a24;
COL Type FORMAT a5;
```

```
SELECT segment_name "Object", segment_type "Type"
, ROUND(SUM(bytes)/1024/1024) "Mb"
, SUM(blocks) "Blocks"
FROM dba_extents
WHERE owner = 'ACCOUNTS'
AND segment_name = 'GENERALLEDGER'
GROUP BY segment_name, segment_type;
```

The following query result shows that the GeneralLedger table is sized at approximately 26Mb:

```
Object                      Type         Mb     Blocks
----------------------      -----  ----------  ----------
GENERALLEDGER               TABLE        26       3328
```

Data in the GeneralLedger table covers four years, from 1999 through 2002. There are about 200,000 rows for each of the four years stored in the table. I create four partitions of 6Mb each. That should be enough space to contain the rows in each partition.

Note: The script to create these four data tablespaces is included in Appendix A.

Note: In my database, the 6Mb partition datafiles extended when rows were added because appropriate physical storage structure was not set for each separate partition. Partitions can have independent physical storage parameters. Physical storage tuning is covered in other chapters; this chapter focuses solely on partitioning.

I also create four index partition tablespaces and grant unlimited quotas on all the tablespaces to the Accounts schema. As with the data files, the indexes are spread across the four available disk drives.

Note: The script to create these four index tablespaces is included in Appendix A.

Range partitions are created like this:

```
CREATE TABLE GLP
(
    generalledger_id      NUMBER NOT NULL
   ,coa#                  CHAR(5) NOT NULL
   ,dr                    NUMBER(10,2) NOT NULL
   ,cr                    NUMBER(10,2) NOT NULL
   ,dte                   DATE NOT NULL
   ,CONSTRAINT XPK_GLP PRIMARY KEY (generalledger_id)
   ,CONSTRAINT FK_GLP_COA# FOREIGN KEY (coa#) REFERENCES COA
) TABLESPACE indx
PARTITION BY RANGE(dte)(
 PARTITION DATAGLP1999 VALUES LESS THAN
(TO_DATE('2000-03-01','YYYY-MM-DD')) TABLESPACE DATAGLP1999
,PARTITION DATAGLP2000 VALUES LESS THAN
(TO_DATE('2001-03-01','YYYY-MM-DD')) TABLESPACE DATAGLP2000
,PARTITION DATAGLP2001 VALUES LESS THAN
(TO_DATE('2002-03-01','YYYY-MM-DD')) TABLESPACE DATAGLP2001
,PARTITION DATAGLP2002 VALUES LESS THAN
(MAXVALUE) TABLESPACE DATAGLP2002);
```

No indexes are created as of yet.

Now I add the data from the GeneralLedger table into the partitioned table called GLP:

```
INSERT INTO glp SELECT * FROM generalledger;
COMMIT;
ANALYZE TABLE glp COMPUTE STATISTICS;
```

Note: Executing the ANALYZE statement against a table should automatically generate statistics for all indexes attached to that table. I am being overzealous for the sake of clarity.

Now let's try some queries. This first query retrieves all rows from the nonpartitioned GeneralLedger table as a query to measure against:

```
EXPLAIN PLAN SET statement_id='TEST' FOR SELECT * FROM
generalledger;
```

This is the result:

```
Query                                         Cost      Rows       Bytes
-----------------------------------------  --------  --------  ----------
1. SELECT STATEMENT    on                      835    739469    19226194
2.   TABLE ACCESS FULL on GENERALLEDGER        835    739469    19226194
```

The next query reads only the 1999 financial year partition, using partition pruning, indicated by the drastic decrease in the number of rows read. The cost is therefore much lower. The pruning of unwanted partitions allows only the 1999 partition to be read, based on the date in the WHERE clause:

```
EXPLAIN PLAN SET statement_id='TEST' FOR
SELECT * FROM glp WHERE dte < TO_DATE('2000-01-01','YYYY-MM-
DD');
```

(10g) The Oracle Database 10g version of this query is shown next, indicating that the table is partition pruned, and a single partition is read. Note the values 1 and 1 at the tail of the *Query* column for the second line of the query plan in the following result. These columns are the PARTITION_START and PARTITION_STOP columns in the PLAN_TABLE, denoting the first and the last partitions read. In this case, only the first partition was read:

```
Query                                      Cost    Rows      Bytes
-----------------------------------------  ----  -------  ---------
1. SELECT STATEMENT    on                    48      602      13244
2.   PARTITION RANGE SINGLE on    1 1        48      602      13244
3.     TABLE ACCESS FULL on GLP   1 1        48      602      13244
```

(9i) The Oracle Database 9i version of the previous query contains a slightly different query plan, but the meaning is still the same:

```
Query                                      Cost    Rows      Bytes
-----------------------------------------  ----  -------  ---------
1. SELECT STATEMENT    on                   203   195888    4505424
2.   TABLE ACCESS FULL on GLP   1 1         203   195888    4505424
```

This next query reads a different partition:

```
EXPLAIN PLAN SET statement_id='TEST' FOR
SELECT * FROM glp
WHERE dte BETWEEN TO_DATE('2002-03-01','YYYY-MM-DD')
AND TO_DATE('2003-02-28','YYYY-MM-DD');
```

Again, note the two numbers tailing the second line of the query plan *Query* column—only the fourth partition is read to satisfy the query:

```
Query                               Cost   Rows     Bytes
---------------------------------- ----  -------  ---------
1. SELECT STATEMENT    on            348   104977   2414471
2.   PARTITION RANGE SINGLE on    4 4  348   104977   2414471
3.     TABLE ACCESS FULL on GLP  4 4  348   104977   2414471
```

Now I create a foreign key BTree global index on the COA# column and four local indexes on each of the partitions (on the partition key, which is the composite of the DTE and COA# columns):

```
CREATE INDEX FKX_GLP_1 ON GLP(coa#) TABLESPACE indx;
CREATE INDEX LK_GLP_1 ON GLP (dte, coa#) LOCAL(
     PARTITION INDXGLP1999 TABLESPACE INDXGLP1999
    ,PARTITION INDXGLP2000 TABLESPACE INDXGLP2000
    ,PARTITION INDXGLP2001 TABLESPACE INDXGLP2001
    ,PARTITION INDXGLP2002 TABLESPACE INDXGLP2002);
ANALYZE INDEX fkx_glp_1 COMPUTE STATISTICS;
ANALYZE INDEX lk_glp_1 COMPUTE STATISTICS
```

Here we have created a global index on the composite of the DTE and COA# columns, as well as a global index on just the COA# column. We can demonstrate the use of the local index by repeating the following query:

```
EXPLAIN PLAN SET statement_id='TEST' FOR
SELECT * FROM glp WHERE dte < TO_DATE('2000-01-01','YYYY-MM-DD');
```

This is the result, clearly showing the use of the local index with the first partition:

```
Query                                                   Cost    Rows      Bytes
------------------------------------------------    ----  -------   ---------
1. SELECT STATEMENT  on                                  25     602      13244
2.   PARTITION RANGE SINGLE on    1 1                     25     602      13244
3.     TABLE ACCESS BY LOCAL INDEX ROWID on GLP  1 1      25     602      13244
4.       INDEX RANGE SCAN on LK_GLP_1  1 1                 4      32
```

Now let's use the BTree global index. Before we do that, let's count General-Ledger rows by COA# field value, as opposed to by the year the entry falls in:

```
SELECT coa#, COUNT(coa#) FROM generalledger GROUP BY
TO_CHAR(coa#) ORDER BY 1;
```

The result shows a somewhat skewed (unbalanced) distribution, where some COA# entries contain hundreds of thousands of entries, some contain tens of thousands, and 50028 contains only a single row:

```
COA#   COUNT(COA#)
-----  -----------
30001      310086
50001      169717
41000      173511
40003       66284
50028           1
60001       33142
```

Now use a hint to force the use of the BTree global partition index. The hint has to be used because without it, the optimizer would opt for a full table scan, which is faster than the index range scan on the global index called FKX_GLP_1:

```
EXPLAIN PLAN SET statement_id='TEST' FOR
SELECT /*+ INDEX(GLP) */ * FROM glp WHERE coa# = '50028';
```

This is the result demonstrating the use of the global index:

Query	Cost	Rows	Bytes
1. SELECT STATEMENT on	2353	125457	2885511
2. TABLE ACCESS BY **GLOBAL INDEX** ROWID on GLP ROW LOCATION	2353	125457	2885511
3. **INDEX RANGE SCAN on FKX_GLP_1**	386	125457	

(10*g*) Now let's change the BTree into a hash key index instead, simply by dropping and recreating the global partition index:

```
DROP INDEX FKX_GLP_1;
CREATE INDEX FKX_GLP_1 ON GLP(coa#) GLOBAL PARTITION BY HASH
(coa#)
PARTITIONS 4 TABLESPACE indx;
ANALYZE INDEX fkx_glp_1 COMPUTE STATISTICS;
```

And we can reexecute the query containing the hint:

```
EXPLAIN PLAN SET statement_id='TEST' FOR
SELECT /*+ INDEX(GLP) */ * FROM glp WHERE coa# = '50028';
```

Although the numerical indicators have not decreased, you can clearly see the use of the global hash-partitioned index:

Query	Cost	Rows	Bytes
1. SELECT STATEMENT on	2353	125457	2885511
2. PARTITION HASH SINGLE on 1 1	2353	125457	2885511
3. TABLE ACCESS BY GLOBAL INDEX ROWID on GLP ROW LOCATION	2353	125457	2885511
4. INDEX RANGE SCAN on FKX_GLP_1 1 1	386	125457	

There is no apparent difference between performance using a BTree or a hash key global partitioned in this case, whether retrieving one row or thousands of rows. However, when running timing tests, using the two different indexes, the queries against the GLP table with the hash key global index were just a little faster. A very much larger database may see a noticeable performance improvement by using global hash key indexes.

This proves a few facts about pruning partitions and partition-based indexing, where SQL code accesses partitions containing only required data.

Note: Rows can also be accessed by partition name, effectively allowing manual partition pruning.

19.1.3.2 Partitioning by List

In the Accounts schema, the Transactions table could be split into two partitions based on the type column. The Transactions table contains both sales invoices sent to customers and purchase invoices sent from suppliers. The type column contains the value *S* for a sale and *P* for a purchase. The size of the Transactions table is about 10Mb. The ratio of purchases to sales is 80%. This dictates the size of the tablespaces for the two partitions. Let's create the partitioned version of the Transactions table. This time, I will ignore referential integrity and indexes, simply creating the partitioned table. We are not trying to prove anything about indexing. We are merely trying to show that partitioning by itself can increase performance dramatically, especially for full table scans, if used appropriately:

Note: Scripting to create tablespaces is included in Appendix A.

```
CREATE TABLE tsp(
    transaction_id      NUMBER NOT NULL
    ,type               CHAR(1) NOT NULL
    ,customer_id        NUMBER NULL
    ,supplier_id        NUMBER NULL
    ,order_id           NUMBER NULL
    ,amount             NUMBER(10,2) NOT NULL
    ,dte                DATE NOT NULL
    ,drcoa#             CHAR(5) NOT NULL
    ,crcoa#             CHAR(5) NOT NULL)
PARTITION BY LIST (type)(
    PARTITION purchases VALUES ('P') TABLESPACE DATATSP
    ,PARTITION sales VALUES ('S') TABLESPACE DATATSS);
```

Add the rows to the new partition table:

```
INSERT INTO tsp SELECT * FROM transactions;
COMMIT;
ANALYZE TABLE tsp COMPUTE STATISTICS;
```

Once again, retrieve data from the nonpartitioned table as a measure of performance:

```
EXPLAIN PLAN SET statement_id='TEST' FOR SELECT * FROM
transactions;
```

This is the result:

Query	Cost	Rows	Bytes
1. SELECT STATEMENT on	**317**	188185	7903770
2. **TABLE ACCESS FULL on TRANSACTIONS**	317	188185	7903770

Now get all rows from the partitioned table:

```
EXPLAIN PLAN SET statement_id='TEST' FOR SELECT * FROM tsp;
```

Fewer bytes are read with the same number of rows, but the cost is very slightly higher, perhaps due to the second step in the query plan. The entire table with all partitions is being read anyway, so there is no reason that reading a partitioned version of the table should be faster:

Query	Cost	Rows	Bytes
1. SELECT STATEMENT on	**328**	188185	6774660
2. PARTITION LIST ALL on 1 2	328	188185	6774660
3. TABLE ACCESS FULL on TSP 1 2	328	**188185**	**6774660**

Now let's go one step further and read all the rows from the partition, reading both partitions in parallel. The parallel read is suggested to the optimizer by using the PARALLEL hint. The two separate partitions are stored in two separate tablespaces, and the two datafiles mapped by the tablespace are stored on two separate disk drives. Both processors and both separate disks are assisting the performance of parallel execution:

```
EXPLAIN PLAN SET statement_id='TEST' FOR
SELECT /*+ PARALLEL(tsp, 2) */ * FROM tsp;
```

The cost is lower, even though the number of rows is the same. There are only two partitions for this partitioned by list table; the PARTITION_START and PARTITION_STOP values tailing the *Query* column show both partitions read:

```
Query                                                            Cost    Rows     Bytes
---------------------------------------------------------------  ----  -------  ---------
1. SELECT STATEMENT  on                                          179   188185   6774660
2.  PX COORDINATOR  on
3.   PX SEND QC (RANDOM) on :TQ10000 PARALLEL_TO_SERIAL           179   188185   6774660
4.    PX BLOCK ITERATOR on  PARALLEL_COMBINED_WITH_CHILD 1 2      179   188185   6774660
5.     TABLE ACCESS FULL on TSP PARALLEL_COMBINED_WITH_PARENT 1 2 179   188185   6774660
```

Now read only the sales transactions:

```
EXPLAIN PLAN SET statement_id='TEST' FOR
SELECT * FROM tsp WHERE type = 'S';
```

In this case, only the second partition is read because sales transactions occupy the second partition. Consequently, the cost is much lower and fewer rows are read:

```
Query                             Cost    Rows     Bytes
--------------------------------- ----  -------  ---------
1. SELECT STATEMENT  on            67    33142   1159970
2.  PARTITION LIST SINGLE  on  2 2 67    33142   1159970
3.   TABLE ACCESS FULL on TSP  2 2 67    33142   1159970
```

And now we read the sales transactions, suggesting parallel execution to utilize both processors by using the PARALLEL hint once again:

```
EXPLAIN PLAN SET statement_id='TEST' FOR
SELECT /*+ PARALLEL(tsp, 2) */ * FROM tsp WHERE type = 'S';
```

The cost is again lower, and the same number of rows is accessed:

```
Query                                                   Cost    Rows     Bytes
------------------------------------------------------  ----  -------  ---------
1. SELECT STATEMENT  on                                  37    33142   1159970
2.  PX COORDINATOR  on
3.   PX SEND QC (RANDOM) on :TQ10000 PARALLEL_TO_SERIAL   37    33142   1159970
```

```
4.    PX BLOCK ITERATOR on  PARALLEL_COMBINED_WITH_CHILD 2 2     37   33142   1159970
5.    TABLE ACCESS FULL on TSP PARALLEL_COMBINED_WITH_PARENT 2 2  37   33142   1159970
```

19.1.3.3 Hash Partitions

A hash partition can be used when range or list partitioning is inappropriate. Most of the large tables in the Accounts schema have a potential range or list partition column in the form of a date or some kind of type column. Two tables not delimited in this fashion are the OrdersLine and TransactionsLine tables. Let's demonstrate using the OrdersLine table. First, create a partitioned table.

Note: Scripting to create tablespaces is included in Appendix A.

```
CREATE TABLE olp(
        order_id             NUMBER NOT NULL
       ,seq#                 NUMBER NOT NULL
       ,amount               NUMBER(10,2) NOT NULL
       ,stockmovement_id     NUMBER NOT NULL)
PARTITION BY HASH(order_id) PARTITIONS 3
STORE IN(dataol1,dataol2,dataol3);
```

Now add the rows to the partitioned table:

```
INSERT INTO olp SELECT * FROM ordersline;
COMMIT;
ANALYZE TABLE olp COMPUTE STATISTICS;
```

Now query the nonpartitioned table:

```
EXPLAIN PLAN SET statement_id='TEST' FOR SELECT * FROM
ordersline;
```

This is the result:

Query	Cost	Rows	Bytes
1. SELECT STATEMENT on	**463**	540827	8112405
2. TABLE ACCESS FULL on ORDERSLINE	463	**540827**	**8112405**

And now query the partitioned table in parallel:

```
EXPLAIN PLAN SET statement_id='TEST' FOR
SELECT /*+ PARALLEL(olp, 2) */ * FROM olp;
```

The cost is more or less halved, indicating fewer rows and fewer bytes read:

Query	Cost	Rows	Bytes
1. SELECT STATEMENT on	**258**	540827	8112405
2. PX COORDINATOR on			
3. PX SEND QC (RANDOM) on :TQ10000 PARALLEL_TO_SERIAL	258	540827	8112405
4. PX BLOCK ITERATOR on PARALLEL_COMBINED_WITH_CHILD 1 3	258	540827	8112405
5. TABLE ACCESS FULL on OLP PARALLEL_COMBINED_WITH_PARENT 1 3	258	**540827**	8112405

19.1.3.4   Composite Partitions

Composite partitions can be of two forms: (1) a range partition containing hash subpartitions, or (2) a range partition containing list subpartitions. Various tables in the Accounts schema could be partitioned using a range-hash partition. The Orders, Transactions, GeneralLedger, and StockMovement tables could be range-hash partitioned on the DTE column for the range partition, and the primary key identifier column could be partitioned{**AU: Please check edit.**} for the contained hash subpartitions:

```
CREATE TABLE glprh(
    generalledger_id NUMBER NOT NULL
   ,coa# CHAR(5) NOT NULL
   ,dr NUMBER(10,2) NOT NULL
   ,cr NUMBER(10,2) NOT NULL
   ,dte DATE NOT NULL)
PARTITION BY RANGE(dte) SUBPARTITION BY
HASH(generalledger_id)
   SUBPARTITIONS 3 STORE IN (dataol1,dataol2,dataol3)
(PARTITION DATAGLP1999 VALUES LESS THAN
(TO_DATE('2000-01-01','YYYY-MM-DD')) TABLESPACE DATAGLP1999
,PARTITION DATAGLP2000 VALUES LESS THAN
(TO_DATE('2001-01-01','YYYY-MM-DD')) TABLESPACE DATAGLP2000
,PARTITION DATAGLP2001 VALUES LESS THAN
(TO_DATE('2002-01-01','YYYY-MM-DD')) TABLESPACE DATAGLP2001
,PARTITION DATAGLP2002 VALUES LESS THAN
(MAXVALUE) TABLESPACE DATAGLP2002);
```

The GeneralLedger table in the Accounts schema could be range-list partitioned on the DTE column for the range, and the COA# column, for the list subpartition. The Orders and Transactions tables are not functionally appropriate for range-list partitioning on their respective DTE and TYPE columns:

Note: There is no scripting to create tablespaces in this table creation statement because this table was not created.

```
CREATE TABLE glprl(
    generalledger_id NUMBER NOT NULL
   ,coa# CHAR(5) NOT NULL
   ,dr NUMBER(10,2) NOT NULL
   ,cr NUMBER(10,2) NOT NULL
   ,dte DATE NOT NULL)
PARTITION BY RANGE(dte) SUBPARTITION BY LIST(coa#)
(PARTITION DATAGLP1999 VALUES LESS THAN
 (TO_DATE('2000-01-01','YYYY-MM-DD')) TABLESPACE DATAGLP1999
    (SUBPARTITION assets1999 VALUES('20001','20002')
    ,SUBPARTITION liabilities1999 VALUES('10001','10002')
    ,SUBPARTITION expenses1999 VALUES('50001','50002')
    ,SUBPARTITION incomes1999 VALUES('60001','60002'))
,PARTITION DATAGLP2000 VALUES LESS THAN
 (TO_DATE('2001-01-01','YYYY-MM-DD')) TABLESPACE DATAGLP2000
    (SUBPARTITION assets2000 VALUES('20001','20002')
    ,SUBPARTITION liabilities2000 VALUES('10001','10002')
    ,SUBPARTITION expenses2000 VALUES('50001','50002')
    ,SUBPARTITION incomes2000 VALUES('60001','60002'))
,PARTITION DATAGLP2001 VALUES LESS THAN
 (TO_DATE('2002-01-01','YYYY-MM-DD')) TABLESPACE DATAGLP2001
    (SUBPARTITION assets2001 VALUES('20001','20002')
    ,SUBPARTITION liabilities2001 VALUES('10001','10002')
    ,SUBPARTITION expenses2001 VALUES('50001','50002')
    ,SUBPARTITION incomes2001 VALUES('60001','60002'))
,PARTITION DATAGLP2002 VALUES LESS THAN
 (MAXVALUE) TABLESPACE DATAGLP2002
    (SUBPARTITION assets2002 VALUES('20001','20002')
    ,SUBPARTITION liabilities2002 VALUES('10001','10002')
    ,SUBPARTITION expenses2002 VALUES('50001','50002')
    ,SUBPARTITION incomes2002 VALUES('60001','60002')));
```

19.2   **Tricks with Partitions**

Why is this section entitled Tricks with Partitions? Partitions can have things done to them on an individual basis. For example, without partitioning, if one wanted to remove all of the rows for the year 1999 from the GeneralLedger table, then the entire GeneralLedger table would be have to be full table scanned, as for the following DELETE statement:

```
DELETE FROM GeneralLedger WHERE TO_CHAR(dte,'YYYY') = 1999;
```

Using the partition table GLP, created as a date range partition on the GeneralLedger table, one would not even have to full table scan one-fifth of the rows. Simply drop the partition. Dropping a single partition one-fifth the size of the table is much faster than removing 20% of the rows from the nonpartitioned table.

What are some other actions beneficial to general database performance that can be performed specifically with partitions?

- *Add, drop, and truncate*. Individual partitions can be added, dropped, or even truncated without affecting the rest of the partitions in a table.

- *Split and merge*. A partition can be split into two partitions or two partitions can be merged into a single partition. Once again, there is no effect on rows outside of the partitions being split or merged.

- *Rename*. Individual partitions can be renamed.

- *Move*. A partition can be moved into a separate tablespace with the speed of a Unix mv command. This is akin to renaming the file pointer for the datafile. Changing a file pointer is a simple tablespace header change. No costly SQL code is involved in transferring data between tablespaces.

- *Exchange*. Partitions and subpartitions can be converted into tables and vice versa. Again there is no costly SQL code involved in transferring data.

To reiterate, all of these listed actions will not affect the rest of the data in a partitioned table because they operate on specific partitions. Only specified partitions are read or accessed.

The important point to note about partitioning is that it is a tuning method in itself. There are obviously ways to tune partitions individually. For example, different partitions and their related indexes can have individual partition physical storage attributes. Storage tuning is covered in other chapters of this book. Additionally, actions can be taken on individual partitions, such as moving and exchanging. Equivalent actions on nonpartitioned tables would either be impossible or involve intense SQL activity. These special partition actions cannot be done nearly as efficiently with large nonpartitioned tables. Partitioning has been presented in this chapter as a tuning technique in itself.

This is all that needs to be discussed with respect to partitioning and tuning. This chapter completes the analysis of physical and configuration tuning for Oracle Database. The next chapter, the first chapter in Part IV of this book, is on tuning everything at once, including both physical and configuration tuning, as well as SQL code tuning.

19.3 Endnotes

1. Oracle Data Warehouse Tuning for 10*g* (Gavin Powell, Digital Press, Aug 2005, ISBN: 1555583350)

Part IV
Tuning Everything at Once

20

Ratios: Possible Symptoms of Problems

There is much to be said for not using various ratios as tuning indicators—in fact, for not using any of them. Many of these ratios can conceal some very large and ugly numbers because they divide one number by another. The denominator (the number used to divide by) simply disappears. Ratios can be useful to indicate a possible problem or problems. A low or high ratio could indicate a possible problem. It could also conceal a possible problem. Additionally, a ratio can also indicate no problem at all. A ratio is best viewed as a possible symptom of a problem, rather than as a problem by itself.

Ratios have received a lot of bad press recently. Much of this is founded in truth. However, ratios should not be completely ignored. I find even the database buffer cache hit ratio useful. However, it is not necessarily a bad thing if it is low or high. An unexpected ratio could be a result of application behavior. A common misinterpretation of ratios made in the past was that an unacceptable value was assumed to be tunable. A ratio is not tunable. However, it might indicate that something else could be tunable, such as an ugly SQL statement in an application full of very-well-tuned SQL code. If the database buffer cache is *doing something weird*, like going up and down like a yoyo, say between 60% and 90% every 5 seconds, then something odd may be going on. Increasing the size of the database buffer cache will not help you to find that ugly SQL code statement. Nasty things might be even further concealed. The whole point of tuning is finding things and solving them, not attempting to conceal and bury them behind meaningless percentages.

The database buffer cache and the shared pool can suffer from tuning of their respective ratios, not only because problems causing unpalatable ratios are not being solved, but also because extremely large buffers are much more difficult for Oracle Database to manage.

Note: Use ratios as symptoms or indicators of potential problems. Tuning the ratios themselves by changing buffer sizes is often a complete waste of time! It also might make things worse.

So ratios are not completely useless—they can provide clues as to where to look for a problem when attempting to solve a performance problem. The solution is perhaps to use both ratios and other tools to resolve performance issues.

The V$SYSSTAT performance view is the source of many ratios. What are some of these ratios?

- *Database buffer cache hit ratios*. These are cached database table and index blocks versus those read from disk.
- *Table access ratios*. Full table scanning small static tables can help performance. Full table scanning large tables can completely devastate database performance. The best performance method for accessing tables is by index ROWID pointers and full scans on small tables.
- *Index use ratio*. Compare index key reads to table reads.
- *Dictionary cache hit ratio*. This refers to database metadata in the shared pool.
- *Library cache hit ratios*. This refers to library cache parsing activity in the shared pool.
- *Disk sort ratio*. How much temporary disk sort space is used?
- *Chained rows ratio*. This is the proportion of rows fetched involving row chaining. Row chaining is overflow of blocks to other blocks because information cannot fit into a single block. This can make data retrieval inefficient. It is extremely likely that chained blocks may be spread across disk storage haphazardly.
- *Parse ratios*. Parsing is expensive. The less parsing, the better.
- *Latch hit ratio*. Latches protect memory buffers from concurrent use.

20.1   Database Buffer Cache Hit Ratio

This measures a ratio between blocks found in the buffer and those found on disk. It is a ratio of logical I/O blocks (LIOs) to disk or physical I/O blocks (PIOs).

This ratio should not be used as an indicator of database performance health. In the past, Oracle software documentation touted the database buffer cache hit ratio as being one of the most important tuning metrics. It is the opinion of many that this statement is often a complete and absolute falsity. LIOs are not *free*. LIOs are generally faster than PIOs, but not nearly as much faster as most Oracle software documentation would lead us to believe. Buffers in memory are much more complex to manage than simple disk I/O because of latch contention, ordered free lists, high concurrency, and fragmentation, and the list of items goes on. Reading from a buffer can sometimes be much more complex than performing I/O.

If the database buffer cache hit ratio is high, then data is being found in memory. If the ratio is low, then queries are executing a fair amount of I/O. It is very difficult to state with impunity what causes this ratio to be high or low. The problem is that most existing documentation assumes that a high hit ratio is good. On the contrary, sometimes a not-so-high hit ratio is also an indicator of good performance health. For example, many full table scans are sometimes necessary, both on large and small tables, depending on application and database type. Full table scans perform I/O and partially bypass the database buffer cache. This can artificially lower the ratio. Very poorly tuned SQL code, particularly joins, can cause unwanted full table scans. This also lowers the ratio. In the opposite direction, lack of use of SQL code bind variables can cause a very high hit ratio if the database buffer is sized much too large.

In general, do not simply attempt to tune the database buffer cache hit ratio. Do not jump to the conclusion that the database buffer cache must always be made larger. Consider even reducing the database buffer cache if the hit ratio is high, potentially freeing up memory for other requirements. Attempt to isolate the cause of the problem, then decide if there is a problem, finally tuning a real problem rather than a ratio.

Note: To reiterate—a ratio is a possible symptom of a problem and may point the way to the problem itself. In many situations, resizing the database buffer cache may conceal rather than resolve a problem and may even hinder performance even more.

Calculating the database buffer cache hit ratio is the same for both the Oracle Database 8*i* DB_BLOCK_BUFFERS and the Oracle Database 9*i* DB_CACHE_SIZE parameters. Oracle Database 10*g* follows suit with Oracle Database 10*g*, as shown in this expression:

```
Database read buffer cache hit ratio =
1 — (physical reads / (db block gets + consistent gets))
```

These are the values I am interested in to calculate the read hit ratio:

```
SELECT value, name FROM V$SYSSTAT WHERE name IN
   ('physical reads', 'db block gets', 'consistent gets');

    VALUE NAME
---------- --------------------------------------------------------
     2031 physical reads
     3861 db block gets
    85832 consistent gets
```

```
Database buffer cache hit ratio =
1 — (physical reads / (db block changes + consistent changes))
```

Here is a query to calculate the database buffer cache hit ratio:

```
SELECT 'Database Buffer Cache Hit Ratio ' "Ratio"
, ROUND((1 —
    ((SELECT SUM(value) FROM V$SYSSTAT WHERE name = 'physical reads')
   / ((SELECT SUM(value) FROM V$SYSSTAT WHERE name = 'db block gets')
   + (SELECT SUM(value) FROM V$SYSSTAT WHERE name = 'consistent gets')
))) * 100)||'%' "Percentage"
FROM DUAL;
```

Note: All of the ratio queries in this chapter can be executed using joins, but we would not be able to see an immediate visual comparison of different ratios. There is a meaning to my madness in this respect. Please keep reading.

This is the result of the previous query. This ratio is possibly healthy because it is not too high, but not necessarily. This value does not really tell me anything at all:

```
Ratio                                      Percentage
------------------------------------------ ----------
Database Buffer Cache Hit Ratio            95%
```

20.1.0.1 Multiple Database Buffer Cache Pools

Secondary database buffer cache pools can be set up in two ways: (1) (9*i*) the keep and recycle pools, and (2) (10*g*) multiple block–sized caches (with respectively sized tablespaces).

20.1.0.1.1 (9*i*) The Default, Keep, and Recycle Pools

In Oracle 9*i* Database, the DB_KEEP_CACHE_SIZE and DB_RECYCLE_CACHE_SIZE parameters would be used. These parameters allow the forcing of MRU data to be retained and LRU data to be discarded. This can help create less interference from other data in the main database buffer cache. Depending on the size and function of the database, these parameters could be set at 5% and 25% of the DB_CACHE_SIZE parameter, respectively. These parameters must be a multiple of the standard block size, as defined by the DB_BLOCK_SIZE parameter:

```
ALTER SYSTEM SET db_keep_cache_size = 5M;
ALTER SYSTEM SET db_recycle_cache_size = 20M;
```

Inspecting database buffer cache hit ratios for other database buffer cache pools can be done, as shown in the next query. In Chapter 15, we pushed certain tables into the keep cache (MRU list) and other tables into the recycle cache (LRU list), using the following commands:

```
ALTER TABLE generalledger NOCACHE;
ALTER TABLE stockmovement NOCACHE;
ALTER TABLE type CACHE;
ALTER TABLE subtype CACHE;
ALTER TABLE coa CACHE;
ALTER TABLE stock CACHE;
ALTER TABLE category CACHE;
```

The subquery is used for the ratio calculation to avoid divisions by zero. This is because a division by zero is mathematically undefined and if executed returns an error:

```
COL pool FORMAT a10;
SELECT a.name "Pool", a.physical_reads, a.db_block_gets
, a.consistent_gets
,(SELECT ROUND(
```

```
(1-(physical_reads / (db_block_gets + consistent_gets)))*100)
    FROM v$buffer_pool_statistics
    WHERE db_block_gets+consistent_gets != 0
    AND name = a.name) "Ratio"
FROM v$buffer_pool_statistics a;
```

The keep pool should be high; the recycle pool should probably be low:

Pool	PHYSICAL_READS	DB_BLOCK_GETS	CONSISTENT_GETS	Ratio
KEEP	40	246570	12816	100
RECYCLE	75755	2874944	120748	97
DEFAULT	822495	17304843	10330119	97

In Chapter 15, small static tables were pushed into the keep pool, excluding their indexes. This assumes that the optimizer would usually full table scan the small static tables. Large dynamic tables were pushed into the recycle pool.

So let's be a little more specific about allocating objects to the different pools. The Customer and Supplier tables are large semistatic tables, and nothing was done with them. It might makes more sense to place only their indexes into the keep pool. The two largest tables, the GeneralLedger and StockMovement tables, could be placed into the recycle pool. The results—100%, 97%, and 97% on the keep, recycle, and default pools, respectively—could tell us a number of things. However, these ratios could also hide a lot of information. Let's cover a few things to drive home the point about potentially misleading information, obtainable from taking database buffer ratios at face value. Most importantly, even though ratios are high for the keep and recycle pools, the physical and logical read numbers are low enough to be negligible.

So, small static tables may often be full table scanned by the optimizer. So contrary to what has already been shown, pushing full scanned small tables into a keep cache might actually be pointless. Why? Because full table scans are read physically from disk (even though they are passed through the database buffer cache mechanism). So, there may very well be no point in putting them into the keep pool. Should their indexes be placed in the keep pool? Yes, if those small tables are used in large joins. The optimizer may often use index reads, even for small static tables, in very-well-tuned SQL code joins. So, I will push small static tables back into the default pool and place their indexes in the keep pool. This time I'll use the STORAGE clause because the ALTER INDEX does not allow CACHE and NOCACHE clauses, and I don't see them in the latest Oracle documentation. Additionally, the NOCACHE option is the default. This seems a little confusing:

```
ALTER TABLE category STORAGE(BUFFER_POOL DEFAULT);
ALTER TABLE coa STORAGE(BUFFER_POOL DEFAULT);
ALTER TABLE customer STORAGE(BUFFER_POOL DEFAULT);
ALTER TABLE period STORAGE(BUFFER_POOL DEFAULT);
ALTER TABLE posting STORAGE(BUFFER_POOL DEFAULT);
ALTER TABLE subtype STORAGE(BUFFER_POOL DEFAULT);
ALTER TABLE supplier STORAGE(BUFFER_POOL DEFAULT);
ALTER TABLE type STORAGE(BUFFER_POOL DEFAULT);


ALTER INDEX xak_categ_text STORAGE(BUFFER_POOL KEEP);
ALTER INDEX xfk_coa_subtype STORAGE(BUFFER_POOL KEEP);
ALTER INDEX xfk_coa_type STORAGE(BUFFER_POOL KEEP);
ALTER INDEX xfk_post_crcoa STORAGE(BUFFER_POOL KEEP);
ALTER INDEX xfk_post_drcoa STORAGE(BUFFER_POOL KEEP);
ALTER INDEX xpk_category STORAGE(BUFFER_POOL KEEP);
ALTER INDEX xpk_coa STORAGE(BUFFER_POOL KEEP);
ALTER INDEX xpk_period STORAGE(BUFFER_POOL KEEP);
ALTER INDEX xpk_posting STORAGE(BUFFER_POOL KEEP);
ALTER INDEX xpk_subtype STORAGE(BUFFER_POOL KEEP);
ALTER INDEX xpk_type STORAGE(BUFFER_POOL KEEP);
```

Note: As you already know, there are various methods of allocating objects into different cache pools. The STORAGE clause is from Oracle 9*i* Database and even Oracle8*i* Database vintage. The CACHE and NOCACHE clauses are applicable to Oracle 10*g* Database.

Essentially, the keep pool could be used to avoid removal of static data from cache, as a result of reading of larger tables and indexes. The recycle has the opposite function, by pushing large, preferably infrequent objects out of memory as quickly as possible.

In my highly active Accounts schema, the two largest tables, the GeneralLedger and StockMovement tables, are only ever inserted into. Referential integrity activity checks on primary and foreign keys might make it useful to place the referential integrity indexes into the keep pool and simply ignore the tables, pushing them back into the default pool:

```
ALTER TABLE generalledger STORAGE(BUFFER_POOL DEFAULT);
ALTER TABLE stockmovement STORAGE(BUFFER_POOL DEFAULT);

ALTER INDEX xfk_coa# STORAGE(BUFFER_POOL KEEP);
ALTER INDEX xfk_sm_stock STORAGE(BUFFER_POOL KEEP);
ALTER INDEX xpk_generalledger STORAGE(BUFFER_POOL KEEP);
ALTER INDEX xpk_stockmovement STORAGE(BUFFER_POOL KEEP);
```

After a period of time, the V$BUFFER_POOL_STATISTICS view contains values shown in the following query result (using the same query as before). We can see that use of all pools is the same as before. Use of the keep pool remains negligible. My active Accounts schema, by the very nature of its activity, would not make much use of the keep or recycle pools anyway:

Pool	PHYSICAL_READS	DB_BLOCK_GETS	CONSISTENT_GETS	Ratio
KEEP	233	274857	13305	100
RECYCLE	77446	2958975	124690	97
DEFAULT	869020	18045781	10803769	97

Note: Using the keep and recycle pools is subjective and unpredictable unless knowledge of application activity is well known. Some applications behave differently during the day (e.g., OLTP activity) than they do at night (e.g., batch activity). Different buffer pool settings would be advisable for different activity cycles. Is it really worth using the keep and recycle pools? Perhaps not! Experiment first!

In conclusion, perhaps it is advisable to only use specific database buffer pools when applications involve a mixture of OLTP and reporting activity. This may be particularly true where large, properly tuned SQL code joins are concerned. And remember that full table scans bypass the database buffer cache to a certain extent. There is little point in pushing tables into the keep pool unless they are commonly read using index ROWID pointers.

20.1.0.1.2 (10g) Multiple Block-Sized Caches

In Oracle 10g Database you can use multiple database buffer caches. This option was available in Oracle 9i Database, but it was less commonly used than the ALTER TABLE and ALTER INDEX command options.

Multiple block-sized caches are separated into different block sizes, where each cache has its own tablespace. With a default block size of 8K, the DB_2K_CACHE_SIZE, DB_4K_CACHE_SIZE, DB_16K_CACHE_SIZE, and DB_32K_CACHE_SIZE parameters can be set using related tablespaces.

Small, static data tables can go into a small tablespace. My database has a default block size of 8K. This prohibits the setting of the DB_8K_CACHE_SIZE parameter. It already exists in the form of the DB_CACHE_SIZE parameter. If the DB_2K_CACHE_SIZE parameter was not set, the database may have to be bounced prior to the creation of this tablespace. The tablespace cannot be created without the existence of a value in the correct cache parameter. So let's begin by setting appropriate cache parameters.

Before we set anything, we should clean up what we did in the previous section and push all tables and indexes back into the default database buffer cache pool. You can use a query like this to inspect your objects:

```
COL table_name FORMAT A16
COL index_name FORMAT A16
SELECT table_name AS "Table", NULL, buffer_pool, cache FROM
user_tables
WHERE buffer_pool != 'DEFAULT' OR TRIM(cache)='Y'
UNION
SELECT table_name, index_name, NULL, buffer_pool FROM
user_indexes
WHERE buffer_pool != 'DEFAULT'
ORDER BY 1, 2 NULLS FIRST;
```

This is the result in my database at this point:

Table	Index	BUFFER_CACHE	
CATEGORY		DEFAULT	Y
CATEGORY	XAK_CATEG_TEXT		KEEP
CATEGORY	XPK_CATEGORY		KEEP

COA		DEFAULT	Y
COA	XFK_COA_SUBTYPE		KEEP
COA	XFK_COA_TYPE		KEEP
COA	XPK_COA		KEEP
GENERALLEDGER	XFK_COA#		KEEP
GENERALLEDGER	XPK_GENERALLEDGER		KEEP
PERIOD	XPK_PERIOD		KEEP
POSTING	XFK_POST_CRCOA		KEEP
POSTING	XFK_POST_DRCOA		KEEP
POSTING	XPK_POSTING		KEEP
STOCK		DEFAULT	Y
STOCKMOVEMENT	XFK_SM_STOCK		KEEP
STOCKMOVEMENT	XPK_STOCKMOVEMENT		KEEP
SUBTYPE		DEFAULT	Y
SUBTYPE	XPK_SUBTYPE		KEEP
TYPE		DEFAULT	Y
TYPE	XPK_TYPE		KEEP

Now I can use the following commands to undo the various CACHE clause and buffer STORAGE clause settings. This query finds all CACHE set tables and resets them to the default setting:

```
SELECT 'ALTER TABLE '||table_name||' NOCACHE;'
FROM USER_TABLES WHERE TRIM(cache)='Y';
```

This is the result of the query that can be executed:

```
ALTER TABLE TYPE NOCACHE;
ALTER TABLE SUBTYPE NOCACHE;
ALTER TABLE STOCK NOCACHE;
ALTER TABLE COA NOCACHE;
ALTER TABLE CATEGORY NOCACHE;
```

And for the indexes:

```
SELECT 'ALTER INDEX '||index_name||' STORAGE(BUFFER_POOL
DEFAULT);'
FROM USER_INDEXES WHERE BUFFER_POOL!='DEFAULT';
```

The result of that can be executed:

```
ALTER INDEX XPK_TYPE STORAGE(BUFFER_POOL DEFAULT);
ALTER INDEX XPK_SUBTYPE STORAGE(BUFFER_POOL DEFAULT);
ALTER INDEX XPK_STOCKMOVEMENT STORAGE(BUFFER_POOL DEFAULT);
ALTER INDEX XFK_SM_STOCK STORAGE(BUFFER_POOL DEFAULT);
ALTER INDEX XPK_POSTING STORAGE(BUFFER_POOL DEFAULT);
ALTER INDEX XFK_POST_DRCOA STORAGE(BUFFER_POOL DEFAULT);
ALTER INDEX XFK_POST_CRCOA STORAGE(BUFFER_POOL DEFAULT);
ALTER INDEX XPK_PERIOD STORAGE(BUFFER_POOL DEFAULT);
ALTER INDEX XPK_GENERALLEDGER STORAGE(BUFFER_POOL DEFAULT);
ALTER INDEX XFK_COA# STORAGE(BUFFER_POOL DEFAULT);
ALTER INDEX XPK_COA STORAGE(BUFFER_POOL DEFAULT);
ALTER INDEX XFK_COA_TYPE STORAGE(BUFFER_POOL DEFAULT);
ALTER INDEX XFK_COA_SUBTYPE STORAGE(BUFFER_POOL DEFAULT);
ALTER INDEX XPK_CATEGORY STORAGE(BUFFER_POOL DEFAULT);
ALTER INDEX XAK_CATEG_TEXT STORAGE(BUFFER_POOL DEFAULT);
```

Now let's go ahead and create separate block-sized database buffer cache pools (execute as a DBA user):

```
ALTER SYSTEM SET db_2K_cache_size = 2M;
ALTER SYSTEM SET db_4K_cache_size = 4M;
ALTER SYSTEM SET db_16K_cache_size = 16M;
```

Note: Available block sizes and DB_nK_CACHE_SIZE parameters may vary for different operating systems. A 32K block size is not available for Win2K SP4 running Oracle 9*i* Database or Oracle 10*g* Database.

Now let's create a number of tablespaces for each of the three previously created database buffer cache pools, splitting data and index spaces:

```
CREATE TABLESPACE DATA2K
    DATAFILE 'C:\ORACLE\PRODUCT\10.2.0\ORADATA\TEST\
DATA2K.dbf'
    SIZE 2M AUTOEXTEND ON BLOCKSIZE 2048
    EXTENT MANAGEMENT LOCAL SEGMENT SPACE MANAGEMENT AUTO;

CREATE TABLESPACE INDX2K
    DATAFILE 'D:\ORACLE\PRODUCT\10.2.0\ORADATA\TEST\
INDX2K.dbf'
    SIZE 2M AUTOEXTEND ON BLOCKSIZE 2048
```

```
      EXTENT MANAGEMENT LOCAL SEGMENT SPACE MANAGEMENT AUTO;

CREATE TABLESPACE DATA4K
    DATAFILE 'C:\ORACLE\PRODUCT\10.2.0\ORADATA\TEST\
DATA4K.dbf'
    SIZE 4M AUTOEXTEND ON BLOCKSIZE 4096
    EXTENT MANAGEMENT LOCAL SEGMENT SPACE MANAGEMENT AUTO;

CREATE TABLESPACE INDX4K
    DATAFILE 'D:\ORACLE\PRODUCT\10.2.0\ORADATA\TEST\
INDX4K.dbf'
    SIZE 4M AUTOEXTEND ON BLOCKSIZE 4096
    EXTENT MANAGEMENT LOCAL SEGMENT SPACE MANAGEMENT AUTO;

CREATE TABLESPACE DATA16K
    DATAFILE 'C:\ORACLE\PRODUCT\10.2.0\ORADATA\TEST\
DATA16K.dbf'
    SIZE 16M AUTOEXTEND ON BLOCKSIZE 16384
    EXTENT MANAGEMENT LOCAL SEGMENT SPACE MANAGEMENT AUTO;

CREATE TABLESPACE INDX16K
    DATAFILE 'D:\ORACLE\PRODUCT\10.2.0\ORADATA\TEST\
INDX16K.dbf'
    SIZE 16M AUTOEXTEND ON BLOCKSIZE 16384
    EXTENT MANAGEMENT LOCAL SEGMENT SPACE MANAGEMENT AUTO;
```

Tables and indexes should usually be separated into different tablespaces. Even when RAID arrays are used, index datafiles should be accessed sequentially, and table datafiles should be accessed mostly in a random fashion from the index datafile. Some applications and database types require full scans of indexes. Potentially full scanned indexes could be placed into randomly accessed storage media structures, as long as you are sure those indexes are always accessed with physical fast full index scans.

The ratio between sizes of table and index tablespaces depends on how you index your data model with respect to referential integrity, your use of sequence identifiers, and how much alternate indexing there is. A properly designed OLTP data model will have a minimum of indexing and will likely use much less space for indexing than for tables. A data warehouse, more traditional, or perhaps a poorly designed OLTP database could need a lot more index space than table space. Some data models have many indexes for each table, and most of those indexes are often composite column indexes. These types of data models will usually have much bigger index tablespaces than table tablespaces. This structure tends to partially negate the performance benefits of indexing. As a side issue, physical space problems are often common in OLTP databases using bitmap rather than BTree indexes.

Multiple block-sized tablespaces will be experimented with in the next chapter. General experimentation with multiple tablespace and cache block sizes does not reveal any performance benefits. My database is busy and also relatively small and simple compared with database installations out in the big wide world. Experimenting is encouraged but preferably not on a production server.

20.2 Table Access Ratios

Full scanning small static tables can sometimes be more efficient than reading both index and table. Full scans on large tables are often executed in data warehouses and for reporting. Full table scans are not necessarily a bad thing. However, poorly tuned SQL code can cause unwanted full table scans. Many applications inadvertently retrieve all table rows using views and subsequently filter view results. Querying a view will always execute the SQL code underlying the view in its fullest form, applying data retrieval SQL code filtering requirements only to the result of the view. So full table scans can be a very bad thing as well.

There are five ratios that might be useful. They are as follows:

- short scan / (short scan + long scan)
- short scan / (short scan + long scan + by rowid)
- long scan / (short scan + long scan + by rowid)
- by rowid / (short scan + long scan + by rowid)
- (short_scan + by rowid) / (short scan + long scan + by rowid)
  - *short scan*. This implies full table scan of a small table. *Good*.
  - *long scan*. This implies full table scan of a large table. *Bad!*
  - *by rowid*. This implies access to a table row via an index-unique hit, a range scan, or a full index scan. *Good and bad*, depending on table size and usage.

The statistics we are interested in are as follows:

```
SELECT value, name FROM V$SYSSTAT WHERE name IN
('table fetch by rowid', 'table scans (short tables)'
, 'table scans (long tables)');
```

Here is the result of this query:

```
    VALUE NAME
--------- -----------------------------
     8554 table scans (short tables)
       22 table scans (long tables)
   467976 table fetch by rowid
```

Note: For the statistic table scans (short tables), the table must have the CACHE option set for the table (ALTER TABLE table CACHE;).

```
SELECT 'Short to Long Full Table Scans' "Ratio"
, ROUND(
(SELECT SUM(value) FROM V$SYSSTAT
 WHERE name = 'table scans (short tables)')
/ (SELECT SUM(value) FROM V$SYSSTAT WHERE name IN
  ('table scans (short tables)', 'table scans (long tables)'))
* 100, 2)||'%' "Percentage"
FROM DUAL
UNION
SELECT 'Short Table Scans ' "Ratio"
, ROUND(
(SELECT SUM(value) FROM V$SYSSTAT
 WHERE name = 'table scans (short tables)')
/ (SELECT SUM(value) FROM V$SYSSTAT WHERE name IN
  ('table scans (short tables)', 'table scans (long tables)'
  , 'table fetch by rowid'))
* 100, 2)||'%' "Percentage"
FROM DUAL
UNION
SELECT 'Long Table Scans ' "Ratio"
, ROUND(
(SELECT SUM(value) FROM V$SYSSTAT
 WHERE name = 'table scans (long tables)')
/ (SELECT SUM(value) FROM V$SYSSTAT WHERE name
   IN ('table scans (short tables)', 'table scans (long
tables)'
```

```
        , 'table fetch by rowid'))
* 100, 2)||'%' "Percentage"
FROM DUAL
UNION
SELECT 'Table by Index ' "Ratio"
, ROUND(
(SELECT SUM(value) FROM V$SYSSTAT WHERE name = 'table fetch by
rowid')
/ (SELECT SUM(value) FROM V$SYSSTAT WHERE name
    IN ('table scans (short tables)', 'table scans (long
tables)'
    , 'table fetch by rowid'))
* 100, 2)||'%' "Percentage"
FROM DUAL
UNION
SELECT 'Efficient Table Access ' "Ratio"
, ROUND(
(SELECT SUM(value) FROM V$SYSSTAT WHERE name
  IN ('table scans (short tables)','table fetch by rowid'))
/ (SELECT SUM(value) FROM V$SYSSTAT WHERE name
  IN ('table scans (short tables)', 'table scans (long
tables)'
  , 'table fetch by rowid'))
* 100, 2)||'%' "Percentage"
FROM DUAL;
```

As you can see from the following results, table and index access in my Accounts schema could be fairly well tuned. Most of the full table scans on large tables are probably a result of ad hoc counting of all the rows in those tables. There is a lot of short table scanning offsetting the table by index access. Overall, using short full table scans, as opposed to index access by ROWID pointers, can give better efficiency.

```
Ratio                         Percentage
----------------------------- ----------
Efficient Table Access        99.97%
Long Table Scans              .03%
Short Table Scans             31.16%
Short to Long Full Table Scans 99.92%
Table by Index                68.81%
```

20.3   **Index Use Ratio**

These are simple ratios trying to assess the percentage of index usage as compared to table scans. This value is not precise. These are the statistics I am interested in:

```
SELECT value, name FROM V$SYSSTAT WHERE name IN
('table fetch by rowid', 'table scans (short tables)'
, 'table scans (long tables)')
OR name LIKE 'index fast full%' OR name = 'index fetch by
key';
```

This is the result:

```
    VALUE NAME
---------- ------------------------------------
       75 table scans (short tables)
      116 table scans (long tables)
     3983 table fetch by rowid
        0 index fast full scans (full)
        0 index fast full scans (rowid ranges)
        0 index fast full scans (direct read)
     2770 index fetch by key
```

This next query gives an idea of index usage percentages:

```
SELECT 'Index to Table Ratio ' "Ratio" , ROUND(
(SELECT SUM(value) FROM V$SYSSTAT
    WHERE name LIKE 'index fast full%'
    OR name = 'index fetch by key'
    OR name = 'table fetch by rowid')
/ (SELECT SUM(value) FROM V$SYSSTAT WHERE name IN
('table scans (short tables)', 'table scans (long tables)')
),0)||':1' "Result"
FROM DUAL;
```

The result is shown next. This number may or may not be good, depending on applications. However, my highly active processing generally uses only referential integrity indexing, whose index hits may not necessarily be recorded. As a result, this ratio could be very misleading. This is another example of a ratio that is not necessarily very useful:

```
Ratio                    Result
--------------------     -------------
Index to Table Ratio     30:1
```

20.4 ⑨*i* **Dictionary Cache Hit Ratio**

This ratio looks at buffer activity versus disk activity for database metadata. How well is metadata accessed in memory from the shared pool without having to resort to physical disk activity?

```
SELECT 'Dictionary Cache Hit Ratio ' "Ratio"
,ROUND((1 - (SUM(GETMISSES) / SUM(GETS))) * 100,2)||'%'
"Percentage"
FROM V$ROWCACHE;
```

```
Ratio                        Percentage
--------------------------   ----------
Dictionary Cache Hit Ratio   99.86%
```

20.5 ⑨*i* **Library Cache Hit Ratios**

These ratios show library cache preparsing and reloading activity:

```
SELECT 'Library Lock Requests' "Ratio"
 , ROUND(AVG(gethitratio) * 100, 2)
||'%' "Percentage" FROM V$LIBRARYCACHE
UNION
SELECT 'Library Pin Requests' "Ratio", ROUND(AVG(pinhitratio)
* 100, 2)
||'%' "Percentage" FROM V$LIBRARYCACHE
UNION
SELECT 'Library I/O Reloads' "Ratio"
, ROUND((SUM(reloads) / SUM(pins)) * 100, 2)
||'%' "Percentage" FROM V$LIBRARYCACHE
UNION
SELECT 'Library Reparses' "Ratio"
, ROUND((SUM(reloads) / SUM(pins)) * 100, 2)
||'%' "Percentage" FROM V$LIBRARYCACHE;
```

```
Ratio                    Percentage
--------------------     ----------
Library I/O Reloads      0%
Library Lock Requests    96.31%
```

```
Library Pin Requests   96.1%
Library Reparses       0%
```

20.6 ⑨ᵢ **Disk Sort Ratio**

Increase the size of the SORT_AREA_SIZE parameter to prevent sorting to disk. When using shared servers, a smaller sort buffer may ultimately preserve memory resources for other essential processing. Retain a chunk of sort space memory for idle connections by setting the SORT_AREA_RETAINED_SIZE parameter to a small percentage of the SORT_AREA_SIZE parameter (usually 10%). Do not set SORT_AREA_RETAINED_SIZE in an OLTP database equal to SORT_AREA_SIZE. Do so for a data warehouse. This query checks in memory sort space usage:

```
SELECT 'Sorts in Memory ' "Ratio"
, ROUND(
 (SELECT SUM(value) FROM V$SYSSTAT WHERE name = 'sorts
(memory)')
 / (SELECT SUM(value) FROM V$SYSSTAT
   WHERE name IN ('sorts (memory)', 'sorts (disk)')) * 100, 2)
||'%' "Percentage"
FROM DUAL;
```

A ratio of memory to disk sorts of less than 100% is not necessarily a problem:

```
Ratio             Percentage
----------------- ------------------
Sorts in Memory   98.89%
```

Note: ⑩g Using the two parameters WORKAREA_SIZE_POLICY = AUTO and PGA_AGGREGATE_TARGET for automated session connection memory management has been recommended as better performing by Oracle Corporation since Oracle 9*i* Database. Dedicated server connection configurations can perform well even at 1,000 concurrent connections. Automated session connection memory management only functions for a dedicated server configuration.

> **Note:** (10*g*) Oracle recommends automated memory management for both PGA and SGA memory.

20.7 (9*i*) **Chained Rows Ratio**

Chained rows in Oracle Database are a result of row migration or row chaining. Row chaining occurs when a row is too large for a single block, so the row is *chained* or spread across multiple blocks. Row migration can occur when updating a row that increases the size of the row beyond the capacity of free space in the block. This prohibits the whole row from fitting into a single block. The result is that the row is migrated (or moved) elsewhere, leaving only a pointer in the original block. It is possible that a row migration can lead to a row chain as well if the row becomes large enough. A lot of row chaining in a database is a big problem. Row chains can only be removed by recreating the table or by using an export dump and then reimporting.

Row chaining and migration can be minimized by leaving more empty space in each block when first inserting rows. This is accomplished by setting PCTFREE to a higher value. PCTFREE leaves empty space in a block for subsequent updates by reserving more space for future updates. The down side to increasing PCTFREE is that rows will be less compacted, and there will be fewer rows per block on average. High row-to-block density leads to faster access time because there are more rows read per block. The approach is dependent on requirements and behavior required by applications.

> **Note:** (10*g*) With the advent of locally managed tablespaces and automated segment space management, free space is managed automatically.

```
SELECT 'Chained Rows ' "Ratio"
, ROUND(
(SELECT SUM(value) FROM V$SYSSTAT
 WHERE name = 'table fetch continued row')
/ (SELECT SUM(value) FROM V$SYSSTAT
    WHERE name IN ('table scan rows gotten', 'table fetch by
rowid'))
* 100, 3)||'%' "Percentage"
FROM DUAL;
```

This is the result, which is low enough to be completely negligible in my database:

```
Ratio           Percentage
-------------   ----------
Chained Rows    0%
```

20.8 ⑨*i* **Parse Ratios**

Parsing involves syntax checking and building of an execution query plan for SQL code. Every time SQL code is parsed, its cursor and query plan are stored in the shared pool. The stored shared cursors can be reused by matching SQL code statements. That match must be an exact text string match. Parsing is expensive, so always pay attention to parse-related ratios. The less reparsing in the shared pool, the better.

The most obvious solution is increasing the size of the shared pool. However, increasing the shared pool to a ridiculous amount can cause its own problems. One of the most common causes of heavy reparsing is a lack of bind variables in SQL code. Setting the CURSOR_SHARING configuration parameter to SIMILAR or FORCE can help alleviate this problem without recoding SQL code. Also, increasing the SESSION_CACHED_CURSORS can help reduce reparsing by caching more session-specific cursors per session:

```
SELECT 'Soft Parses ' "Ratio"
, ROUND(
((SELECT SUM(value) FROM V$SYSSTAT WHERE name = 'parse count
(total)')
- (SELECT SUM(value) FROM V$SYSSTAT WHERE name = 'parse count
(hard)'))
/ (SELECT SUM(value) FROM V$SYSSTAT WHERE name = 'execute
count')
* 100, 2)||'%' "Percentage"
FROM DUAL
UNION
SELECT 'Hard Parses ' "Ratio"
, ROUND(
(SELECT SUM(value) FROM V$SYSSTAT WHERE name = 'parse count
(hard)')
/ (SELECT SUM(value) FROM V$SYSSTAT WHERE name = 'execute
count')
```

```
* 100, 2)||'%' "Percentage"
FROM DUAL
UNION
SELECT 'Parse Failures ' "Ratio"
, ROUND(
(SELECT SUM(value) FROM V$SYSSTAT
 WHERE name = 'parse count (failures)')
/ (SELECT SUM(value) FROM V$SYSSTAT WHERE name = 'parse count
(total)')
* 100, 2)||'%' "Percentage"
FROM DUAL;
```

This is the result of the previous query:

```
Ratio            Percentage
---------------  ----------
Hard Parses      .04%
Parse Failures   0%
Soft Parses      44.98%
```

20.9 (9i) **Latch Hit Ratio**

As already stated, latches protect memory buffers from concurrent usage. We have a healthy ratio for the Accounts schema active database at well over 99%. However, this ratio does not necessarily show much because not only are the numbers hidden, individual hit rates for specific latches are not shown:

```
SELECT 'Latch Hit Ratio ' "Ratio"
, ROUND(
(SELECT SUM(gets) - SUM(misses) FROM V$LATCH)
/ (SELECT SUM(gets) FROM V$LATCH)
* 100, 2)||'%' "Percentage"
FROM DUAL;
```

This is the result:

```
Ratio            Percentage
---------------  ---------------------------------------
Latch Hit Ratio  99.96%
```

That's enough ratios for now. There are many others. Obviously all the examples here would be best written into a stored procedure. Executing all the ratios together gives the following result:

```
Ratio                                 Percentage
------------------------------------- ----------
Chained Rows                              0%
Database Buffer Cache Hit Ratio          95%
Dictionary Cache Hit Ratio            99.86%
Efficient Table Access                99.97%
Hard Parses                            0.04%
Index to Table Ratio                   30:1
Latch Hit Ratio                       99.96%
Library I/O Reloads                       0%
Library Lock Requests                 96.31%
Library Pin Requests                   96.1%
Library Reparses                          0%
Long Table Scans                       0.03%
Parse Failures                            0%
Short Table Scans                     31.16%
Short to Long Full Table Scans        99.92%
Soft Parses                           44.98%
Sorts in Memory                       98.89%
Table by Index                        68.81%
```

20.10 (10*g*) Ratios in the Database Control

Two important facts about ratios and Oracle 10*g* Database are as follows:

- PGA memory is automatically managed.
- SGA memory is recommended as automatically managed in Release 2.

Both of these points make many of the ratios demonstrated in this chapter more or less irrelevant.

The Database Control is the recommended tuning tool for Oracle 10*g* Databases. Within the Database Control are something known as metrics. A metrics is a measure that can have a threshold set against it. When a metrics threshold is exceeded, then a warning is sent to the user because a potential problem exists. Included in the metrics are a number of ratios. By default, these ratios do not have threshold settings. In other words, the default setup for metrics, used to measure things such as database performance, do not have thresholds for any of the ratios included into the default metrics settings. Thus, it might be safe to assume that those thresholds are assumed to be irrelevant.

Is it therefore also possible to assume that ratios might be completely irrelevant to tuning an Oracle 10*g* Database? This point I am not quite so sure of. Even though ratios hide the denominator within a calculation, they are still possibly useful in critical performance environments.

I also find it an extremely unlikely scenario that database administrators will do away with their favorite tools, such as ratios, in favor of an unknown, such as the Database Control and its metrics baselines. It may be that tuning using only the Database Control and its metrics is targeted at the smaller database installations, making performance tuning an easier task to accomplish. The cost of not getting the best-performance tuning results might perhaps be more cost effective than hiring expensive consultants to resolve what could often be very simple problems.

Additionally, automated SGA is not a strict requirement, indicating perhaps that the intelligence of the Database Control is not yet commercially tested. Thus, ratios are left in this book for now.

Note: The Database Control will be examined in further detail in later chapters.

Numerous potential ratios can be used to attempt to assess symptoms of database health. Once again, be aware that a ratio divides one number by another. This division of two numbers can hide the values in those numerator and denominator values, which can be independently significant. The next chapter will look at wait events. Many things can happen in the database, potentially causing one task to wait for another to complete.

21

Wait Events

A wait event is a database event indicating that something is waiting for something else. In other words, a process could be waiting for another process to release a resource that the first process requires. In more technical terms, a wait event occurs because something is being processed where other processes that are waiting for its completion are dependent on the result of the event causing the wait. When one process waits for another to complete, a wait event is recorded in Oracle database statistics.

Note: The TIMED_STATISTICS configuration parameter must be set to TRUE.

Note: (10*g*) The default for the TIMED_STATISTICS parameter is true.

Much like ratio calculations, wait events are sometimes best analyzed as symptoms of problems, such as contention (competition for a resource). The frequency of a wait event may point to a symptom of a problem, rather than a problem itself. Resolving a wait event is not necessarily a direct solution to a performance problem. Therefore, tune the problem causing the wait event. Do not necessarily simply attempt to reduce wait events without being sure that the real cause of the problem is addressed, although sometimes this will be the case. Understand the problem first. Also note that frequent occurrences of some wait events are normal, depending on database type and the type of applications accessing the database.

There are numerous performance views involved in recording wait event details. These are some of them:

- **V$EVENT_NAME.** This refers to all possible events.

- **V$SYSTEM_EVENT.** This refers to total waits for all occurring database events, aggregated for all sessions.

- **V$SESSION_EVENT.** This is the same information as V$SYSTEM_EVENT, but details events per session rather than aggregates for all sessions.

- **V$SESSION_WAIT.** This view is session level and shows a real time picture, where wait events are listed as they are happening. This view contains hooks to physical objects and sessions, through sessions ultimately leading to SQL code, among many other things.

- **V$WAITSTAT.** This shows contention or competition for access to different types of blocks, such as datafile blocks, undo, and sort space.

There is much more to wait events than what is presented in this chapter. This chapter and the next chapter present wait events and latches. The Oracle Database Wait Event Interface will be covered briefly, later in this book. The Oracle Database Wait Event Interface can be used to drill down through a multitude of performance views in an attempt to isolate events causing performance bottlenecks. Before going into the Oracle Database Wait Event Interface, we need to examine the things we are looking for in that interface: wait events in this chapter and latches in the next chapter.

Note: (10g) Numerous wait model changes, including changes to various V$ performance views, and a number of additional V$ performance views, will be covered later in this book.

Wait events can be divided into significant and idle events. A significant event is an event potentially indicating a problem, such as physical or logical resource contention. An idle event describes an activity, such as process polling, and is usually not an indication of a problem. First of all, let's get idle events out of the way so that we know what can be ignored.

21.1 Idle Events

An idle event is an event that is idle because nothing is happening. It is a result of a process that is waiting for something else to respond. Idle events are insignificant as far as performance is concerned. However, idle events can sometimes show a distinct lack of activity, a lack of use of resources, or simply overconfiguration. High idle times in specific areas, such as for Oracle Net Services (SQL*Net) network usage is quite normal. Then again, high idle times on Net Services configuration could indicate overconfiguration of shared servers, where perhaps a client process is waiting for submission of a command to the database. Overconfiguration is not really a problem except that hardware resources may be wasted. Those resources might be better utilized elsewhere.

All possible database events are listed in the V$EVENT_NAME view. This view contains a lot of entries. Events in this view are applicable to all Oracle software options, such as Oracle Replication. This book covers only Oracle Database tuning and does not delve into Oracle optional applications and architectures, other than Oracle Partitioning.

Note: (10*g*) There is now a CLASS column in the V$SYSTEM_EVENT view, allowing classification of events, including idle events.

21.1.1   (9*i*) **Idle Events in Oracle 9***i* **Database**

My concurrently active OLTP database has specific events in its simulation. These following events using the displayed query are generally idle and irrelevant for anything but information. I can isolate idle events with a query such as this:

```
SELECT name FROM v$event_name
WHERE name LIKE '%null%' OR name LIKE '%timer%'
OR name LIKE '%SQL*Net%' OR name LIKE '%rdbms ipc%'
OR name LIKE '%ispatcher%' OR name LIKE '%virtual circuit%'
OR name LIKE '%PX%' OR name LIKE '%pipe%' OR name LIKE
'%message%'
OR name LIKE 'jobq%';
```

There are a lot of rows returned as idle events, so I will not display the results here. The query is placed into a function, as shown following, for ease of use in queries in the rest of this book against the V$SYSTEM_EVENT performance view. This is the function, which I store into my database for later use, under the SYS user:

```
CREATE OR REPLACE FUNCTION IdleEvent(pEvent IN VARCHAR2
DEFAULT NULL)
```

```
    RETURN VARCHAR2 IS
        CURSOR cIdleEvents IS
            SELECT name FROM v$event_name
            WHERE name LIKE '%null%' OR name LIKE '%timer%'
            OR name LIKE '%SQL*Net%' OR name LIKE '%rdbms ipc%'
            OR name LIKE '%ispatcher%' OR name LIKE '%virtual
circuit%'
            OR name LIKE '%PX%' OR name LIKE '%pipe%'
            OR name LIKE '%message%' OR name LIKE 'jobq%';
    BEGIN
        FOR rIdleEvent in cIdleEvents LOOP
            IF pEvent = rIdleEvent.name THEN
              RETURN NULL;
            END IF;
        END LOOP;
        RETURN pEvent;
    EXCEPTION WHEN OTHERS THEN
        DBMS_OUTPUT.PUT_LINE(SQLERRM(SQLCODE));
    END;
    /
    ALTER FUNCTION IdleEvent COMPILE;
    /
```

Note: ⑨*i* If using STATSPACK, the STATS$IDLE_EVENTS table can be used.

The only idle events that warrant examination are those having to do with Oracle networking software. On rare occasions, excessive occurrence of SQL*Net idle events could possibly indicate bottleneck issues with the network.

Note: Idle events indicate potential bottleneck issues with something external to Oracle Database software.

However, as already stated, excessive network activity is often normal. Other chapters in this book cover Oracle network usage tuning.

Another idle event occurring often in my database is the ***jobq slave wait*** event. This wait event does not indicate a problem. It occurs because I am executing multiple jobs simultaneously on the same data to simulate a highly active concurrent OLTP database. The intention is to produce tunable problems, which it most certainly does. When the background processes that are used to service jobs find that there are no queued jobs to be processed, they will enter into this wait state.

21.1.2 (10*g*) **Idle Events in Oracle 10*g* Database**

The V$SYSTEM_EVENT view now has a WAIT_CLASS column added, as shown by the following query:

```
SELECT wait_class, COUNT(wait_class) FROM v$system_event
GROUP BY wait_class ORDER BY 1;
```

This is the result, and as we can see, events are classified, including a classification for idle events:

```
WAIT_CLASS        COUNT(WAIT_CLASS)
----------------  -----------------
Application                       4
Commit                            1
Concurrency                      14
Configuration                     2
Idle                             13
Network                           3
Other                            18
System I/O                        8
User I/O                         10
```

However, some events would still remain idle events in my database because of its particular architecture. So I will thus continue to use the IdleEvents procedure, in addition to the WAIT_CLASS column in the V$SYSTEM_EVENT view:

```
CREATE OR REPLACE FUNCTION IdleEvent(pEvent IN VARCHAR2
DEFAULT NULL)
RETURN VARCHAR2 IS
    CURSOR cIdleEvents IS
        SELECT name FROM v$event_name
        WHERE wait_class = 'Idle'
                OR name LIKE '%null%' OR name LIKE '%timer%'
```

```
          OR name LIKE '%SQL*Net%' OR name LIKE '%rdbms ipc%'
          OR name LIKE '%ispatcher%' OR name LIKE '%virtual
circuit%'
          OR name LIKE '%PX%' OR name LIKE '%pipe%'
          OR name LIKE '%message%' OR name LIKE 'jobq%'
                 OR name LIKE 'Streams%';
BEGIN
    FOR rIdleEvent in cIdleEvents LOOP
        IF pEvent = rIdleEvent.name THEN
            RETURN NULL;
        END IF;
    END LOOP;
    RETURN pEvent;
EXCEPTION WHEN OTHERS THEN
    DBMS_OUTPUT.PUT_LINE(SQLERRM(SQLCODE));
END;
/
ALTER FUNCTION IdleEvent COMPILE;
/
```

Note: (10*g*) The number of idle events is expanded. Streams events are added as being irrelevant to my database because I have a zero-sized streams buffer.

Now let's proceed to examine significant database and wait events.

21.2 **Significant Events**

First, let's simply pick out significant events from the database I have running:

```
COL event FORMAT a30;
COL waits FORMAT 9999990;
COL timeouts FORMAT 99999990;
COL average FORMAT 99999990;
SELECT event "Event", time_waited "Total Time", total_waits
"Waits"
,average_wait "Average", total_timeouts "Timeouts"
FROM v$system_event
WHERE IdleEvent(event) IS NOT NULL
ORDER BY event;
```

Following is the list of significant performance-affecting events from my Oracle 9*i* Database, containing the highly concurrent active Accounts schema:

Event	Total Time	Waits	Average	Timeouts
LGWR wait for redo copy	29257	14557	2	5854
async disk IO	0	54	0	0
buffer busy waits	426039	131236	3	61
buffer deadlock	**50977**	**8944**	**6**	**8944**
control file heartbeat	411	1	411	1
control file parallel write	7349	8888	1	0
control file sequential read	6335	3632	2	0
db file parallel write	30626	5694	5	2815
db file scattered read	74492	28648	3	0
db file sequential read	467185	80872	6	0
db file single write	27	54	0	0
direct path read	58	108	1	0
direct path write	14	78	0	0
enqueue	93255	9865	9	63
instance state change	0	2	0	0
latch free	110683	29690	4	3254
library cache load lock	303	39	8	0
library cache pin	1894	186	10	0
log file parallel write	34751	21291	2	19359
log file sequential read	42	58	1	0
log file single write	22	58	0	0
log file switch completion	1189	79	15	0
log file sync	150289	15409	10	140
process startup	348	7	50	2
refresh controlfile command	24	1	24	0
row cache lock	19	14	1	0

And this is the same result using the Oracle 10*g* Database. The result is mostly the same, except for many new types of wait events, covering more specific aspects of latch and enqueue activities:

Event	Total Time	Waits	Average	Timeouts
Data file init write	104	39	3	0

LGWR wait for redo copy	6	79	0	1
Log archive I/O	0	1	0	0
buffer busy waits	811	451	2	0
buffer deadlock	**0**	**1**	**0**	**1**
control file heartbeat	401	1	401	1
control file parallel write	3376	2944	1	0
control file sequential read	12523	4737	3	0
db file parallel read	2591	159	16	0
db file parallel write	16709	21311	1	0
db file scattered read	148227	40538	4	0
db file sequential read	639500	242289	3	0
db file single write	23	28	1	0
direct path read	25	75	0	0
direct path read temp	1029	965	1	0
direct path write	7	165	0	0
direct path write temp	393	274	1	0
enq: HW - contention	**3**	**6**	**1**	**0**
enq: RO - fast object reuse	**1**	**19**	**0**	**0**
enq: SQ - contention	**130**	**87**	**2**	**0**
enq: TM - contention	**6242**	**41**	**152**	**13**
enq: TX - contention	**6**	**1**	**6**	**0**
enq: TX - index contention	**2414**	**511**	**5**	**0**
enq: TX - row lock contention	**23163**	**679**	**34**	**14**
free buffer waits	92	63	1	13
latch free	**12**	**221**	**0**	**0**
latch: In memory undo latch	**3**	**49**	**0**	**0**
latch: cache buffers chains	**32**	**275**	**0**	**0**
latch: cache buffers lru chain	**2**	**26**	**0**	**0**
latch: enqueue hash chains	**256**	**10**	**26**	**0**
latch: library cache	**11**	**58**	**0**	**0**
latch: library cache lock	**0**	**6**	**0**	**0**
latch: library cache pin	**2**	**9**	**0**	**0**
latch: object queue header ope	**0**	**1**	**0**	**0**
latch: redo allocation	**0**	**4**	**0**	**0**
latch: redo writing	**0**	**1**	**0**	**0**
latch: row cache objects	**0**	**7**	**0**	**0**
latch: session allocation	**2**	**16**	**0**	**0**
latch: shared pool	**1**	**6**	**0**	**0**
library cache load lock	1355	19	71	3
library cache pin	1299	42	31	1
log file parallel write	10734	12919	1	0

log file sequential read	192	16	12	0
log file single write	10	11	1	0
log file switch completion	463	10	46	0
log file sync	7163	7382	1	1
os thread startup	1557	141	11	11
read by other session	122889	96473	1	15
recovery read	0	3	0	0
row cache lock	90	5	18	0
write complete waits	7	1	7	0

Note: The most important factor is the total time spent waiting (Total Time), not the number of waits (Waits).

Note: (10*g*) The new latch and enqueue (enq) events help to divide up both latch and enqueue wait events.

It makes perfectly logical sense that when assessing the impact of a wait event, it should be weighed against all other wait events. It is, of course, true that some wait events are completely debilitating to the database, no matter what their percentage of occurrence. One example of this is the occurrence of *buffer deadlock* events in my previous V$SYSTEM_EVENT query listing. Deadlocks are always a serious problem but are fortunately very unusual. Additionally, Oracle can resolve some of them automatically. Deadlocks occur in my highly active database because I am deliberately trying to stress out my database. In particular, I am using triggers and hot block table updates on summary columns. I get deadlocks. That is not really too surprising.

Note: Deadlocks are rare and are usually a result of coding design issues and not high load! Database performance is often highly dependent on the way in which applications are built.

There are two main approaches when examining events:

- *Total wait time*. Some types of events may not occur frequently, but their wait times could be significant in that those total wait times exceed the total wait times of more frequently occurring events. Obviously, this approach is relative between different events and their possible performance impact.

- *Polling over a period of time*. In this chapter, I have used temporary tables and some very simple stored procedures to poll real-time views over a period of time. This type of statistics collection can be executed easily using STATSPACK. The reason for including this level of detail in this book is to promote understanding. Once a reasonable level of understanding is gained, then using a tool like STATSPACK will be a matter of reading the manual for correct syntax because you will understand clearly what STATSPACK is trying to achieve. This book is intended as a performance tuning teaching guide, not a database administration reference manual.

Before we examine significant wait events in detail, we need another query. I want to know what the total wait time for each event is as a percentage measured against every other event. A query like the one shown next can give me a better idea, not a solution. Remember, we are looking for symptoms of problems not solutions. Here is the query:

```
COL percentage FORMAT 9999999990;
SELECT event "Event", total_waits "Waits", time_waited "Total
Time"
   ,TO_CHAR(
      (time_waited /
         (SELECT SUM(time_waited) FROM v$system_event
         WHERE IdleEvent(event) IS NOT NULL)
   )*100, 990.99) "Percentage"
FROM v$system_event WHERE IdleEvent(event) IS NOT NULL ORDER
BY event;
```

Here is the result. I would probably want to examine anything in detail greater than 1%. More potentially catastrophic wait events such as deadlocks I would examine if they were greater than zero. Some of the more interesting events are highlighted first for my Oracle 9*i* Database:

Event	Waits	Total Time	Percent
LGWR wait for redo copy	14591	29377	0.37
async disk IO	54	0	0.00

buffer busy waits	131301	426285	**5.40**
buffer deadlock	8948	51000	0.65
control file heartbeat	1	411	0.01
control file parallel write	8892	7360	0.09
control file sequential read	3635	6374	0.08
db file parallel write	5702	30652	0.39
db file scattered read	28648	74492	0.94
db file sequential read	81015	468348	**5.93**
db file single write	54	27	0.00
direct path read	108	58	0.00
direct path write	78	14	0.00
enqueue	9872	93266	**1.18**
instance state change	2	0	0.00
latch free	29734	110921	**1.41**
library cache load lock	39	303	0.00
library cache pin	186	1894	0.02
log file parallel write	21323	34836	0.44
log file sequential read	58	42	0.00
log file single write	58	22	0.00
log file switch completion	79	1189	0.02
log file sync	15437	150731	**1.91**
process startup	7	348	0.00
refresh controlfile command	1	24	0.00
row cache lock	14	19	**0.00**

And second for my Oracle 10*g* Database:

Event	Waits	Total Time	Percent
Data file init write	39	104	0.01
LGWR wait for redo copy	79	6	0.00
Log archive I/O	1	0	0.00
buffer busy waits	452	812	**0.08**
buffer deadlock	1	0	0.00
control file heartbeat	1	401	0.04
control file parallel write	2978	3398	0.33
control file sequential read	4737	12523	1.22
db file parallel read	159	2591	0.25
db file parallel write	21505	16960	1.65
db file scattered read	42525	156875	15.28

db file sequential read	**245020**	**649920**	**63.30**
db file single write	28	23	0.00
direct path read	75	25	0.00
direct path read temp	965	1029	0.10
direct path write	165	7	0.00
direct path write temp	274	393	0.04
enq: HW - contention	**6**	**3**	**0.00**
enq: RO - fast object reuse	**19**	**1**	**0.00**
enq: SQ - contention	**87**	**130**	**0.01**
enq: TM - contention	**47**	**7383**	**0.72**
enq: TX - contention	**1**	**6**	**0.00**
enq: TX - index contention	**511**	**2414**	**0.24**
enq: TX - row lock contention	**687**	**25087**	**2.44**
free buffer waits	63	92	0.01
latch free	**224**	**12**	**0.00**
latch: In memory undo latch	49	3	0.00
latch: cache buffers chains	276	32	0.00
latch: cache buffers lru chain	26	2	0.00
latch: enqueue hash chains	10	256	0.02
latch: library cache	59	11	0.00
latch: library cache lock	6	0	0.00
latch: library cache pin	9	2	0.00
latch: object queue header ope	1	0	0.00
latch: redo allocation	4	0	0.00
latch: redo writing	1	0	0.00
latch: row cache objects	7	0	0.00
latch: session allocation	16	2	0.00
latch: shared pool	6	1	0.00
library cache load lock	19	1355	0.13
library cache pin	42	1299	0.13
log file parallel write	13040	10797	1.05
log file sequential read	16	192	0.02
log file single write	11	10	0.00
log file switch completion	10	463	0.05
log file sync	**7439**	**7197**	**0.70**
os thread startup	141	1557	0.15
read by other session	96957	123579	12.04
recovery read	3	0	0.00
row cache lock	**5**	**90**	**0.01**
write complete waits	1	7	0.00

What are some significant database events (not necessarily highlighted here)?

- ***Buffer busy waits***. While waiting for a database buffer cache block to be available, the block is being read in or changed.

- ***Datafile scattered and sequential reads***. These are reads of the datafile's physical blocks on disk. A scattered read is potentially random reading into scattered noncontiguous parts of the buffer (full physical scans). A sequential read is more focused (index reads).

- ***Direct path read and writes***. This refers to the passing of sorting and hash joins to temporary sort space on disk.

- ***Free buffer waits***. This occurs when no free or clean blocks are available in the database buffer cache, and database buffer cache dirty blocks are waiting to be written out to disk.

- ***Row cache lock waits***. This occurs when metadata cache waits on schema object definitions (e.g., when something like a table definition is being waited on).

- ***Library cache waits***. The library cache contains parsed SQL code, PL/SQL blocks, and optimized query plans.

- ***Redo log waits***. This refers to redo log wait events.

- ***Automated undo waits***. This occurs when automatic undo space is being waited on, perhaps due to high-frequency of DML activity.

Note: (9*i*) Wait events can help determine sizes and numbers of rollback segments, when using manual rollback segments.

- ***Enqueue waits***. This refers to various locking events on data files (table rows), or latches waiting for busy buffers.

- ***Latch free waits***. This occurs when a latch is required to access an area of a buffer that is busy.

Now let's examine these significant events in turn.

21.2.1   **Buffer Busy Waits**

A buffer busy wait occurs when more than one process is attempting to access a single database buffer cache block at once. In other words, the block is not in memory. Another process could already be reading the block into memory, or the block is already in memory and currently being changed by another process.

Obviously, it is a major problem if many DML statements are attempting to alter something in a block at the same time. Let's query the V$WAITSTAT view to see exactly which types of buffers are causing a problem and examine a few others as well:

```
SELECT * FROM v$waitstat:
```

$9i$ This result of the V$WAITSTAT query is using an Oracle $9i$ Database:

CLASS	COUNT	TIME
data block	141860	474325
sort block	0	0
save undo block	0	0
segment header	157	195
save undo header	0	0
free list	0	0
extent map	0	0
1st level bmb	0	0
2nd level bmb	0	0
3rd level bmb	0	0
bitmap block	0	0
bitmap index block	0	0
file header block	2	34
unused	0	0
system undo header	0	0
system undo block	0	0
undo header	614	1487
undo block	27	103

And the following result is using an Oracle $10g$ Database. Data block and segment header issues are still apparent. Some undo space waiting is occurring. The difference between the two database versions are the *bmb* entries. I cannot find anything on the Internet or in the Oracle documentation describing what these rows mean. However, my best guess is datafile header bitmaps on locally managed tablespaces, which should be expected:

CLASS	COUNT	TIME
data block	4343	4781
sort block	0	0
save undo block	0	0
segment header	19	40
save undo header	0	0
free list	0	0
extent map	0	0
1st level bmb	31	34
2nd level bmb	26	15
3rd level bmb	0	0
bitmap block	0	0
bitmap index block	0	0
file header block	0	0
unused	0	0
system undo header	0	0
system undo block	0	0
undo header	4	2
undo block	0	0

Note: The V$WAITSTAT performance view shows a breakdown of buffer busy wait events by class of buffer.

These are the different V$WAITSTAT categories:

- *Data block*. This indicates database buffer cache dirty writes, or an inability to read from the disk due to contention with other competing requests.

- *Sort block*. This indicates that there is not enough sort space, or that temporary sort is either nonexistent on disk or is not defaulted for the current user.

- *Segment header.* This refers to contention for the first block of a table or index. A segment can be a table or index, as well as other database objects.

- *Free list*. This occurs when there is too much free space maintained for each block.

- (9i) *Extent map*. Extents may be poorly sized if there is too much recursion. Perhaps extent sizes are all different or they are too small. This is likely to be less common using locally managed tablespaces than dictionary-managed tablespaces.

Note: (10g) Dictionary-managed tablespaces will be deprecated in a future version of Oracle Database.

- *Bitmap block*. This is bitmap contention (first-, second-, and third-level bmb events). There appears to be some significant activity with wait events on tablespace bitmap directories, as shown earlier in the Oracle 10g Database query. This type of contention can sometimes be alleviated in an OLTP database by creating multiple datafiles for each tablespace. The beneficial effect splits datafile header bitmap activity in locally managed tablespaces.

- *File header block*. This is datafile contention.

- *Undo header and block*. (10g) If automated undo is used, then it may be a good idea to change the UNDO_RETENTION parameter. In the unlikely event you are still using (9i) manual rollback, this might indicate insufficient rollback segments, that rollback segments are too small, or inconsistent sizes across all rollback segments.

It appears that we have problems with data blocks (tables and indexes), segment headers, and undo space. This is consistent for both versions of the database. My Oracle 9i Database uses both manual rollback and automated undo at different points in time in order to demonstrate both. My Oracle 10g Database uses automated undo only. We can use the DBA_EXTENTS, V$SESSION_WAIT, and V$SESSION views to find objects causing problems. This query might help in this respect:

```
SELECT de.segment_name, sw.event
FROM dba_extents de, (
    SELECT sw.event, sw.p1 AS file_id, sw.p2 AS block_id
```

```
    FROM v$session_wait sw
WHERE IdleEvent(event) IS NOT NULL
AND sw.sid IN
      (SELECT sid FROM v$session WHERE username = 'ACCOUNTS')
   AND sw.event != 'null event'
) sw
WHERE de.owner = 'ACCOUNTS'
AND de.file_id = sw.file_id AND de.block_id = sw.block_id;
```

This previous query could be extremely slow. Any queries on the DBA_EXTENTS view in my Oracle 9*i* Database are incredibly slow. My physical storage structure is poorly organized, and my database is extremely busy. As a result, I decided to do some manual statistics collection. What I did was to create a temporary table and insert the results of the subquery semijoin between the V$SESSION and V$SESSION_WAIT views. I also know the username I am looking at, namely the Accounts schema. The result looks something like this:

```
DROP TABLE tmp;
CREATE TABLE tmp (event VARCHAR2(64), file_id NUMBER,
block_id NUMBER);
BEGIN
  FOR counter IN 1..1000 LOOP
     INSERT INTO tmp
       SELECT sw.event AS event
  ,sw.p1 AS file_id, sw.p2 AS block_id
       FROM v$session_wait sw
 WHERE IdleEvent(event) IS NOT NULL
       AND sw.sid IN
         (SELECT sid FROM v$session WHERE username =
'ACCOUNTS')
 AND sw.event != 'null event';
     COMMIT;
  END LOOP;
END;
/
```

Note: This type of analysis is easy with STATSPACK and even easier using the Database Control or the Oracle Database Wait Event Interface. All of these tools will be covered later in this book in chapters specifically dedicated to using these tools.

The execution of this anonymous procedure generated over a thousand rows into my temporary table. I then did this:

```
SELECT COUNT(event), event FROM tmp GROUP BY event;
```

This is the result from my Oracle 9*i* Database:

```
COUNT(EVENT) EVENT
------------ -----------------------
          90 buffer busy waits
          12 buffer deadlock
         688 db file sequential read
          97 enqueue
          48 latch free
          91 log file sync
```

There is a problem because we have 90 buffer busy waits. Use a query like this to find out which tables and indexes are affected:

```
SELECT DISTINCT(segment_name) FROM dba_extents
WHERE (file_id, block_id) IN
 (SELECT file_id, block_id FROM tmp WHERE event = 'buffer busy
waits')
AND owner = 'ACCOUNTS';
```

Then I joined the temporary table and the DBA_EXTENTS view and got some interesting results. The query returned over 3,000 rows. Ouch! Well I know there are problems in my database—serious problems. That is the way I intended it to be. In fact I know which tables are probably causing the problems with sequence number–generated primary keys and locking of index blocks. The GeneralLedger and StockMovement tables are prime culprits for this type of activity because they are most heavily added to using triggers. *Yukkity-yuk!* The triggers do what I want them to do. They make my coding easier but can cause performance problems. I am deliberately trying to create performance problems that I can analyze.

Executing the same query again but this time in my Oracle 10*g* Database, I got a very different result:

```
SELECT COUNT(event), event FROM tmp GROUP BY event;
```

This is the result from my Oracle 10*g* Database:

```
COUNT(EVENT) EVENT
------------ ---------------------------------
          31 enq: TX - row lock contention
           5 log file sync
           1 latch: enqueue hash chains
          49 read by other session
         600 db file sequential read
          31 enq: TM - contention
         261 db file scattered read
           1 enq: TX - index contention
```

As shown by the query result here, there are no buffer busy waits in the Oracle 10*g* Database. However, there are some specific row locking issues (enqueue wait events), plus a very large proportion of scattered and sequential read wait events. So the Oracle 9*i* Database has segment issues, and the Oracle 10*g* Database has I/O issues. Why is an unknown at this point, but my best guess is that Oracle database memory management has improved dramatically and that the I/O issues have now taken precedence as being the biggest cause of performance problems.

I decided to take a leap forward in this case and investigated these segment I/O issues from within the Database Control. Figure 21.1 shows the Transactions table in my Accounts schema causing most of the I/O contention. Essentially, this table is central to the simulation processing in my Accounts schema database. This issue is an expected bottleneck.

Figure 21.2 shows the drilldown into the ACCOUNTS.TRANSACTIONS table shown in Figure 21.1.

As shown in Figure 21.2, both the table and all the indexes on this table are having problems. Believe it or not, this is actually normal for this table. However, in a real-world environment, it would be necessary to remove some of these issues, particularly as the table is very busy. I have deliberately created a simulated application that would produce errors such as this. There are, of course, possible options, such as creating reverse key indexes. However, it is more likely that my simulation is the primary culprit.

Figure 21.3 shows two Database Control, Segment Advisor jobs. The first is listed as CREATED (incomplete) and the second as COMPLETED.

Figure 21.4 is essentially the same information as given in Figure 21.1, Figure 21.2, and Figure 21.3. Figure 21.4 shows a higher level picture,

Figure 21.1
*Looking for I/O
bottlenecks using
the Database
Control*

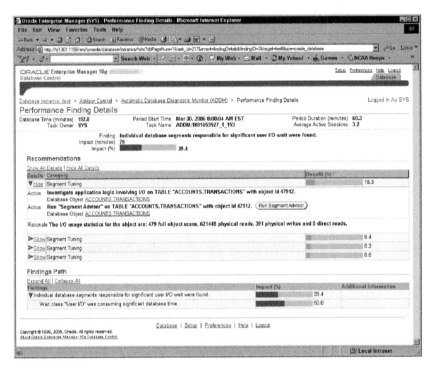

including errors on both segments and SQL statements. Essentially, the SQL statements in my application are causing the segment wait event errors.

21.2.1.1 Causes of Buffer Busy Waits

Looking back at the query on V$WAITSTAT, my Accounts database is having problems with data blocks, segment headers, undo headers, undo blocks, and file header blocks; just one or two problems. My database is highly active and requires a very high degree of concurrency on the server computer I am using:

- **Data block.** These errors usually occur when there are index problems resulting in too many full table scans or mass data insertions adding multiple rows to the same block. My database uses sequence number primary keys and is doing a lot of insertion activity. The larger, more active insertion tables could utilize reverse key indexes on the primary keys to avoid index hot block contention.

- **Segment header.** This generally occurs with lack of block concurrency. Better settings for FREELISTS and INITRANS might help. Once again, tablespaces are all locally managed, allowing for better automated management of physical space than for tablespaces in my

Figure 21.2
I/O bottlenecks on a specific table in the Database Control

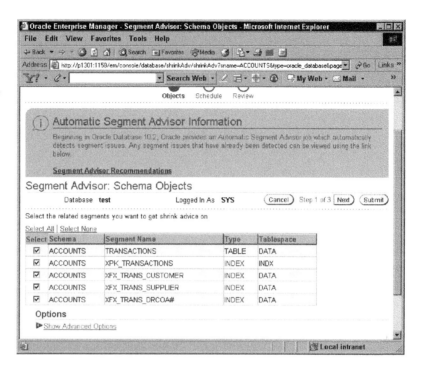

Figure 21.3
Segment Advisor jobs in the Database Control

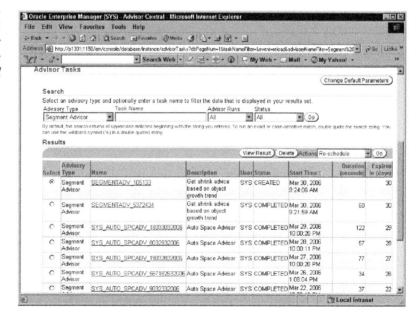

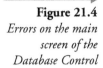

Figure 21.4
*Errors on the main
screen of the
Database Control*

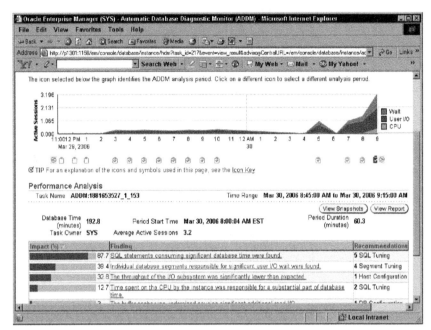

Accounts schema database. This database is simply very busy. Also having tablespaces set to automatic segment space management would help to better manage freespace and concurrency.

Note: Setting values for PCTUSED, FREELIST, and FREELIST_ GROUPS in database objects, such as tables, will be ignored if the containing tablespace is set to automatic segment space management. Automated segment space management is reputed to realize up to 35% performance improvement, specifically in Oracle RAC environments.

- **Undo header.** Undo space header problems hint at creating more rollback segments if using manual rollback. If using locally managed tablespace, perhaps use striping of one form or another.

- **Undo block.** In Oracle 9*i* Database, using manual rollback, this error is touted as indicating a need to make existing rollback segments larger. I do not agree with this approach. An OLTP database requires as many rollback segments as possible, small and sized the same. Perhaps extent size increments could even be substantially decreased, assuming all transactions are small. When using automated undo, again striping might be a prospective option.

21.2.1.2   Decreasing Buffer Busy Waits

Let's take another look at all events:

```
COL percentage FORMAT 9999999990
COL event FORMAT A32
SELECT event "Event", total_waits "Waits", time_waited
"Total"
 ,TO_CHAR(
  (time_waited /
   (SELECT SUM(time_waited) FROM v$system_event
    WHERE IdleEvent(event) IS NOT NULL)
 )*100, 990.99) "Percentage"
FROM v$system_event WHERE IdleEvent(event) IS NOT NULL ORDER
BY event;
```

This is the result using an Oracle 9*i* Database:

Event	Waits	Total Time	Percent
LGWR wait for redo copy	100	84	0.00
buffer busy waits	114429	1721602	8.68
buffer deadlock	31	116	0.00
control file heartbeat	1	410	0.00
control file parallel write	2568	40352	0.20
control file sequential read	1163	11180	0.06
db file parallel write	3618	42457	0.21
db file scattered read	114041	3148406	15.87
db file sequential read	718549	14837478	74.78
direct path read	31	3	0.00
direct path write	9	0	0.00
enqueue	343	24617	0.12
latch free	632	6341	0.03
library cache load lock	8	76	0.00
library cache pin	86	1508	0.01
log file parallel write	5314	4155	0.02
log file sequential read	24	41	0.00
log file single write	24	17	0.00
log file sync	1651	1810	0.01
process startup	1	82	0.00
refresh controlfile command	1	6	0.00
row cache lock	9	106	0.00

And this is the result using and Oracle 10g Database:

Event	Waits	Total	Percent
Data file init write	39	104	0.01
LGWR wait for redo copy	79	6	0.00
Log archive I/O	1	0	0.00
buffer busy waits	454	814	0.08
buffer deadlock	1	0	0.00
control file heartbeat	1	401	0.04
control file parallel write	3027	3443	0.33
control file sequential read	4798	12626	1.22
db file parallel read	159	2591	0.25
db file parallel write	21661	17072	1.64
db file scattered read	42544	156891	15.11
db file sequential read	249742	658705	63.44
db file single write	28	23	0.00
direct path read	90	25	0.00
direct path read temp	965	1029	0.10
direct path write	180	8	0.00
direct path write temp	274	393	0.04
enq: HW - contention	6	3	0.00
enq: RO - fast object reuse	19	1	0.00
enq: SQ - contention	87	130	0.01
enq: TM - contention	47	7383	0.71
enq: TX - contention	1	6	0.00
enq: TX - index contention	513	2432	0.23
enq: TX - row lock contention	687	25087	2.42
free buffer waits	63	92	0.01
latch free	226	12	0.00
latch: In memory undo latch	49	3	0.00
latch: cache buffers chains	277	32	0.00
latch: cache buffers lru chain	26	2	0.00
latch: enqueue hash chains	10	256	0.02
latch: library cache	62	12	0.00
latch: library cache lock	6	0	0.00
latch: library cache pin	9	2	0.00
latch: object queue header opera	1	0	0.00
latch: redo allocation	5	0	0.00
latch: redo writing	1	0	0.00
latch: row cache objects	7	0	0.00

```
latch: session allocation          16          2      0.00
latch: shared pool                  6          1      0.00
library cache load lock            19       1355      0.13
library cache pin                  42       1299      0.13
log file parallel write         13225      10885      1.05
log file sequential read           16        192      0.02
log file single write              11         10      0.00
log file switch completion         10        463      0.04
log file sync                    7539       7246      0.70
os thread startup                 143       1561      0.15
read by other session           99424     125967     12.13
recovery read                       3          0      0.00
row cache lock                      5         90      0.01
write complete waits                1          7      0.00
```

And now let's examine ***buffer busy waits*** specifically:

```
COL event FORMAT a30;
COL percentage FORMAT 9999999990;
SELECT event "Event" ,ROUND((time_waited /
    (SELECT SUM(time_waited) FROM v$system_event
     WHERE IdleEvent(event) IS NOT NULL))*100, 0) "%"
FROM v$system_event WHERE event = 'buffer busy waits';
```

My current percentage of buffer busy waits is 9%:

```
Event                               %
------------------------------- ----------
buffer busy waits                   9
```

Now let's make a few changes to try to reduce those ***buffer busy wait*** events. Increase the database buffer cache size to reduce buffer contention:

```
ALTER SYSTEM SET db_cache_size = 64M;
```

Reduce multiple block read counts into the database buffer cache to reduce the amount read at the same time:

```
ALTER SYSTEM SET db_file_multiblock_read_count = 1;
```

Some of the larger tables are subject to heavy sequential primary key sequence insertion activity and potential concurrency problems. I do get segment header contention but no freelist contention. Using reverse key indexes on these primary keys may reduce segment header contention:

```
ALTER INDEX XPK_GENERALLEDGER REBUILD REVERSE;
ALTER INDEX XPK_STOCKMOVEMENT REBUILD REVERSE;
```

Using automated segment space management, even in Oracle 9*i* Database, may help with percentage used space and freelist space management. In the previous chapter, both data and index data space tablespaces were created for nondefault block sizes of 2K, 4K, and 16K. Also, the different block-sized database buffer cache areas were created. All tablespaces were created as locally managed, including automated extent management and automated segment space management (these settings could help with concurrency). Additionally, the data and index data space are separated onto two different drives. Let's begin by moving some of the tables in the Accounts schema into the different block-sized tablespaces. Begin by moving static tables into the 2K tablespace:

```
ALTER TABLE type MOVE TABLESPACE DATA2K;
ALTER TABLE subtype MOVE TABLESPACE DATA2K;
ALTER TABLE coa MOVE TABLESPACE DATA2K;
ALTER TABLE category MOVE TABLESPACE DATA2K;
ALTER TABLE stock MOVE TABLESPACE DATA2K;
```

And now move all the static table indexes into the 2K tablespace:

```
ALTER INDEX XAK_CATEG_TEXT REBUILD ONLINE TABLESPACE INDX2K;
ALTER INDEX XPK_CATEGORY REBUILD ONLINE TABLESPACE INDX2K;
ALTER INDEX XFK_COA_SUBTYPE REBUILD ONLINE TABLESPACE INDX2K;
ALTER INDEX XFK_COA_TYPE REBUILD ONLINE TABLESPACE INDX2K;
ALTER INDEX XPK_COA REBUILD ONLINE TABLESPACE INDX2K;
ALTER INDEX XAK_STOCK_TEXT REBUILD ONLINE TABLESPACE INDX2K;
ALTER INDEX XFK_S_CATEGORY REBUILD ONLINE TABLESPACE INDX2K;
ALTER INDEX XPK_STOCK REBUILD ONLINE TABLESPACE INDX2K;
ALTER INDEX XPK_SUBTYPE REBUILD ONLINE TABLESPACE INDX2K;
ALTER INDEX XPK_TYPE REBUILD ONLINE TABLESPACE INDX2K;
```

Now let's take another look at ***buffer busy waits*** after allowing the database to execute my high-concurrency processing for over an hour with the new tablespaces and parameter settings:

```
COL event FORMAT a30;
COL percentage FORMAT 9999999990;
SELECT event "Event" ,ROUND((time_waited /
    (SELECT SUM(time_waited) FROM v$system_event
    WHERE IdleEvent(event) IS NOT NULL))*100, 0) "%"
FROM v$system_event WHERE event = 'buffer busy waits';
```

My Oracle 9*i* Database gave me a result that is totally opposite to that expected. My ***buffer busy waits*** are now 45%. I expected less than 9%. Additionally, the percentage of buffer busy wait events is climbing over time. Drilling down into the Oracle Database Wait Event Interface might help to resolve this issue more easily or perhaps even show that there is no problem:

```
SELECT event "Event", total_waits "Waits", time_waited "Total

 ,TO_CHAR(
  (time_waited /
   (SELECT SUM(time_waited) FROM v$system_event
   WHERE IdleEvent(event) IS NOT NULL)
 )*100, 990.99) "Percentage"
FROM v$system_event WHERE IdleEvent(event) IS NOT NULL ORDER
BY event;
```

The Oracle 9*i* Database result is

```
Event                                    %
------------------------------ ----------
buffer busy waits                        45
```

The Oracle 10*g* Database result is quite different, much improved, and what I would expect, with buffer busy waits becoming less frequent (falling down to zero):

```
Event                               %
----------------------------  ----------
buffer busy waits                   0
```

Let's take a look at all events again:

```
COL event FORMAT a32
COL percentage FORMAT 9999999990;
SELECT event "Event", total_waits "Waits", time_waited
"Total"
 ,TO_CHAR(
  (time_waited /
   (SELECT SUM(time_waited) FROM v$system_event
   WHERE IdleEvent(event) IS NOT NULL)
 )*100, 990.99) "Percentage"
FROM v$system_event WHERE IdleEvent(event) IS NOT NULL ORDER
BY event;
```

This is the Oracle 9*i* Database version:

```
Event                          Waits Total Time Percent
----------------------------  ----------  ----------  -------
LGWR wait for redo copy           38          24     0.00
buffer busy waits             456308     4672151    45.07
buffer deadlock                   13          12     0.00
control file heartbeat             1         410     0.00
control file parallel write     1429       14323     0.14
control file sequential read     712        4260     0.04
db file parallel write          1610       16889     0.16
db file sequential read       409662     5630885    54.32
direct path read                  37           0     0.00
direct path write                 11           1     0.00
enqueue                          360       21290     0.21
instance state change              1           0     0.00
latch free                      1295         827     0.01
library cache load lock           26         270     0.00
library cache pin                 68         919     0.01
log file parallel write         2944        2187     0.02
log file sequential read          24          47     0.00
log file single write             24          17     0.00
```

log file sync	1000	1553	0.01
process startup	1	23	0.00
refresh controlfile command	1	4	0.00
row cache lock	16	11	0.00

And this is the same thing again for the Oracle 10*g* Database:

Event	Waits	Total	Percent
Data file init write	12	31	0.02
LGWR wait for redo copy	25	0	0.00
Log archive I/O	1	0	0.00
buffer busy waits	**81**	**186**	**0.12**
checkpoint completed	1	196	0.12
class slave wait	1	500	0.32
control file heartbeat	1	400	0.25
control file parallel write	626	1595	1.01
control file sequential read	1707	4837	3.06
db file parallel read	11	118	0.07
db file parallel write	3213	2395	1.52
db file scattered read	**487**	**1248**	**0.79**
db file sequential read	**30546**	**114598**	**72.58**
db file single write	25	19	0.01
direct path read	84	9	0.01
direct path read temp	4	0	0.00
direct path write	42	5	0.00
enq: CF - contention	2	64	0.04
enq: HW - contention	27	506	0.32
enq: SQ - contention	2	5	0.00
enq: TL - contention	1	33	0.02
enq: TM - contention	1	83	0.05
enq: TX - contention	5	140	0.09
enq: TX - index contention	127	570	0.36
enq: TX - row lock contention	5	82	0.05
job scheduler coordinator slave	3	3012	1.91
latch free	46	11	0.01
latch: In memory undo latch	5	1	0.00
latch: cache buffers chains	41	30	0.02
latch: cache buffers lru chain	3	0	0.00
latch: library cache	14	7	0.00
latch: library cache pin	8	4	0.00

```
latch: redo allocation              4        1     0.00
latch: row cache objects            1        2     0.00
latch: session allocation           8        2     0.00
latch: shared pool                  1        0     0.00
latch: undo global data             1        0     0.00
library cache load lock            49     2122     1.34
library cache pin                  54     2197     1.39
log file parallel write          3170     6396     4.05
log file sequential read           14      230     0.15
log file single write               7       13     0.01
log file sync                    1926     6527     4.13
os thread startup                  55      558     0.35
rdbms ipc reply                    19      955     0.60
read by other session            6237     7939     5.03
recovery read                       3      175     0.11
reliable message                   99       46     0.03
```

In the previous query result, the *db file sequential read* event is higher and *db file scattered read* events are non-existent or relatively negligible (for Oracle 10*g* Database). It is possible that higher *buffer busy wait* events are caused by hot blocks on static tables, within the new 2K-sized tablespaces, although this should be less likely because the block size is smaller.

Obviously all these changes did not appear to help too much, so I will change them all back. Be careful with any of these types of changes. It is possible that placing the much larger Customer and Supplier tables into the 2K block-sized tablespaces may help performance. The static data I did place into the 2K block-sized tablespaces are small enough tables as to probably be negligible. Additionally, there is so much small transactional activity in my database that management of the extra tablespaces and the extra database buffer cache area perhaps caused more problems than were solved.

Note: Increasing the size of the database buffer cache, and even splitting that cache into two, had no useful effect whatsoever. Quite often, a high database buffer cache hit ratio is a result of a very much oversized database buffer cache. This is usually done in an attempt to tune the database buffer cache hit ratio. There is no sense in tuning the untunable.

```
ALTER SYSTEM SET db_cache_size = 64M;
ALTER SYSTEM SET db_file_multiblock_read_count = 8;
```

```
ALTER INDEX XPK_GENERALLEDGER REBUILD NOREVERSE;
ALTER INDEX XPK_STOCKMOVEMENT REBUILD NOREVERSE;

ALTER TABLE type MOVE TABLESPACE DATA;
ALTER TABLE subtype MOVE TABLESPACE DATA;
ALTER TABLE coa MOVE TABLESPACE DATA;
ALTER TABLE category MOVE TABLESPACE DATA;
ALTER TABLE stock MOVE TABLESPACE DATA;

ALTER INDEX XAK_CATEG_TEXT REBUILD ONLINE TABLESPACE INDX;
ALTER INDEX XPK_CATEGORY REBUILD ONLINE TABLESPACE INDX;
ALTER INDEX XFK_COA_SUBTYPE REBUILD ONLINE TABLESPACE INDX;
ALTER INDEX XFK_COA_TYPE REBUILD ONLINE TABLESPACE INDX;
ALTER INDEX XPK_COA REBUILD ONLINE TABLESPACE INDX;
ALTER INDEX XAK_STOCK_TEXT REBUILD ONLINE TABLESPACE INDX;
ALTER INDEX XFK_S_CATEGORY REBUILD ONLINE TABLESPACE INDX;
ALTER INDEX XPK_STOCK REBUILD ONLINE TABLESPACE INDX;
ALTER INDEX XPK_SUBTYPE REBUILD ONLINE TABLESPACE INDX;
ALTER INDEX XPK_TYPE REBUILD ONLINE TABLESPACE INDX;

DROP TABLESPACE data2k INCLUDING CONTENTS;
DROP TABLESPACE indx2k INCLUDING CONTENTS;
DROP TABLESPACE data4k INCLUDING CONTENTS;
DROP TABLESPACE indx4k INCLUDING CONTENTS;
DROP TABLESPACE data16k INCLUDING CONTENTS;
DROP TABLESPACE indx16k INCLUDING CONTENTS;

ALTER SYSTEM SET db_2k_cache_size = 0;
ALTER SYSTEM SET db_4k_cache_size = 0;
ALTER SYSTEM SET db_16k_cache_size = 0;
```

21.2.2   **Datafile Scattered and Sequential Reads**

These are disk reading events:

- *db file scattered read*. The simplest explanation for this event is that it occurs during full physical scans, full table, or fast full index scans. There are large amounts of I/O, which read more than one block at once. This can have the effect of scattering blocks all over the database buffer cache, leading to fragmentation of the buffer.

- *db file sequential read*. This event usually, but not always, occurs during a single block read of data from disk. The event is either an index to table ROWID pointer access or perhaps a very small, single block table read.

Note: Other activities causing these events are usually negligible with respect to performance, especially in a highly active database.

Unfortunately, there is a lot of conflicting documentation and opinion as to exactly what can be done to reduce the occurrence of these events—and even whether their frequency *should* be reduced. Requirements between full and precise scanning are mainly application dependent. In other words, OLTP databases with small transactions should have mostly sequential reads. Data warehouses should most often use scattered reads. This is not an absolute for every application and every database. Excessive scattered reads are not necessarily a sign of poor performance in an OLTP database.

Additionally, high amounts of full physical scanning can indicate possible fragmentation or perhaps a multiple block scanning setting inappropriate for the application (for example, the DB_FILE_MULTIBLOCK_READ_ COUNT parameter), among other possible causes.

Once again, full physical scans are not necessarily a bad thing. Fast and very costly disk RAID arrays may sometimes read multiple blocks faster than single blocks, and more full scans will result. This may of course be relative to how much data is read and how much is required. So, full physical scans are still likely to be healthier in data warehouses and reporting than OLTP databases. The threshold when full physical scans become less efficient may simply be higher with more expensive equipment.

Isolate specific culprit objects by joining V$SESSION, V$SESSION_ WAIT, and DBA_EXTENTS views. In general, use of random and sequential access is often application dependent. Properly tuned OLTP database SQL code will often execute more sequential access on indexes. Significant scattered read access is often due to full table scans on smaller tables and index fast full scans, both of which can and do have a positive impact on performance. My Accounts schema is executing heavy sequential index access appropriate to many small-sized transactions. This is normal for a highly active OLTP database. My Accounts schema database is more or less properly tuned with respect to sequential and scattered reads. Current values are as shown.

```
COL event FORMAT a32;
COL percentage FORMAT 9999999990;
```

```
SELECT event "Event"
    ,ROUND(
        (time_waited /
            (SELECT SUM(time_waited) FROM v$system_event
            WHERE IdleEvent(event) IS NOT NULL)
    )*100, 0) "%"
FROM v$system_event WHERE event IN
    ('db file sequential read','db file scattered read');
```

Multiple configuration changes have altered the statistics in my database somewhat, as can been seen. These values are fairly good and consistent with my application requirements. This is the result for my Oracle 9*i* Database:

```
Event                               %
------------------------------- ----------
db file sequential read             76
db file scattered read              11
```

A similar result appears for my Oracle 10*g* Database:

```
Event                               %
------------------------------- ----------
db file sequential read             68
db file scattered read              1
```

Let's make a very simple change, encouraging the optimizer to perform more full physical scans. Physical scans are beneficial to larger transactions, such as when batch processing or in a data warehouse:

```
ALTER SYSTEM SET db_file_multiblock_read_count = 128;
```

My Oracle 9*i* Database showed that sequential reads increased and scattered reads decreased. This is not as expected. Perhaps I could temporarily disable some key indexes and have the desired effect. However, it is interesting that full physical scan rates have actually been reduced and not increased:

```
Event                                  %
------------------------------  ----------
db file sequential read                84
db file scattered read                  8
```

I let my Oracle 10*g* Database run for about 10 minutes and got little difference at all. Then again, we began with a very small percentage of scattered reads and getting that number down to zero would be a 100%
decrease, rather than a 25% decrease, as is the case for the Oracle 9*i* Database. However, the sequential reads increased for the Oracle 10*g* Database,
so it could be surmised that scattered reads have relatively decreased:

```
Event                                  %
------------------------------  ----------
db file sequential read                71
db file scattered read                  1
```

Both I/O read and full physical scan activity in my database is minimal
due to the nature of my high-concurrency coding. Decreasing the database
buffer cache size at the same time might have the desired ill effect, increasing the likelihood of full table scans. Let's make the database buffer cache
seriously small:

```
ALTER SYSTEM SET db_cache_size=4M;
```

And let's check the same events after a few minutes of execution. Once
again, there is little response, and it is the opposite of what is expected. If by
now I have not pointed out the danger of randomly changing parameters
according to published documentation, then I am wasting my time. Most
of the reason that I am not getting the expected results is because my application code simply does not benefit from any of the configuration changes
made in this chapter so far. My data model design is efficient, and my application concurrency code has an absolute minimal footprint on hardware
resources. The value of data model and SQL code tuning cannot be stressed
more vehemently! This result is from my Oracle 9*i* Database:

```
Event                                  %
------------------------------  ----------
db file sequential read                85
db file scattered read                  6
```

My Oracle 10*g* Database showed no difference, apart from vacillating a little around the previously shown values of 71% for sequential reads and 1% for scattered reads.

21.2.3 Direct Path Reads and Writes

These are disk sorting events:

- *Direct path read*
- *Direct path write*

Note: Both these events involve asynchronous I/O, available in Windows but not always on Unix.

These two events occur when sorting passes to disk or hash joins are not executed entirely in memory. SORT_AREA_SIZE and HASH_AREA_SIZE parameters could be increased. Increasing these parameters may use up too much memory in a large concurrent shared server environment. Increasing these parameters could also cause more problems than are resolved. In short, it is better to tune the root cause of a problem, in this case likely to be SQL code, rather than allow poorly tuned SQL code statements to coexist with oversized buffer configuration values.

Note: (10*g*) Sorting parameters are automated and included in PGA automated memory management, as of Oracle 9*i* Database. Automated PGA is the only choice in Oracle 10*g* Database, when accessed from within the Database Control.

21.2.4 Free Buffer Waits

The *free buffer waits* event occurs when there are no free clean blocks available in the database buffer cache. In other words, there are too many dirty (changed) blocks in the database buffer cache, waiting to be written to disk. The reason that this event happens is simple to explain. There is too much going on. You could get a bigger machine, faster disks, or even create more database writer processes. The truth is that free buffer wait events often occur when dirty buffers are not written out to disk fast enough due to one or a combination of the previously mentioned factors.

Free buffer wait events can also occur when the database buffer cache is too small, where the percentage of dirty blocks waiting to be written to disk is continuously high. If the database buffer cache is too small, high DML activity and latch wait problems could cause the database writer processes to be unable to keep up.

Once again, to reiterate a previously mentioned premise, do not simply resize buffers to enormous amounts of memory. The general purpose of buffer caches is to behave as fast temporary transfer mechanisms and to enhance high sharing and concurrency capability. The database buffer cache is a fast temporary transfer mechanism catering to vast differences in speed between CPU processing and disk I/O performance. The shared pool allows for very high concurrency or sharing of previously obtained objects and executed code. Sizing the database buffer cache and the shared pool to fill all available RAM based on high buffer cache hit ratios is not a solution; it does not solve the underlying problems. Low and high cache hit ratios generally indicate problems on a deeper level, not able to be resolved by simply bumping up those caches to ridiculous sizes.

Note: (10*g*) Automated SGA memory management will manage the main database buffer cache and the shared pool for you. It is advisable to ensure that the SGA_MAX_SIZE parameter is set to avoid runaway resizing. There is no such thing as a PGA_MAX_SIZE parameter, and this has been known to cause problems. It is also possible that PGA memory should be much larger than SGA memory in very large OLTP database environments.

21.2.5 Row Cache Lock Waits

Row cache lock waits are usually SYSTEM tablespace metadata update locks or latch waits. The Accounts schema does have a small number of row cache lock waits. The number is below 1% and probably negligible.

21.2.6 Library Cache Waits

The library cache contains parsed SQL code, PL/SQL blocks, and optimized query plans. Three types of wait events occur in the library cache:

- *Library cache lock*. This refers to loading and locking an object into memory.

- *Library cache load lock*. In this case, the system cannot obtain a lock to load an object into memory.

- *Library cache pin*. An object is pinned into memory.

Both row cache lock and library cache wait events occur in the shared pool. In trying to create a problem, I will make the following changes in the configuration parameter file and bounce my database.

Note: (9*i*) This procedure was performed in my Oracle 9*i* Database ONLY! Oracle 10*g* Database will not allow me to do this—it's nonsensical anyway but demonstrative. I tried changing these parameters online using the ALTER SYSTEM command in Oracle 9*i* Database. It crashed the database.

Setting the SHARED_POOL_RESERVED_SIZE parameter to 0 will force the database to automatically to set that parameter to 5% of the SHARED_POOL_SIZE parameter:

```
shared_pool_reserved_size = 0
shared_pool_size = 4M
COL event FORMAT a30;
COL percentage FORMAT 9999999990;
SELECT event "Event"
   ,ROUND(
      (time_waited /
         (SELECT SUM(time_waited) FROM v$system_event
         WHERE IdleEvent(event) IS NOT NULL)
   )*100, 2) "%"
FROM v$system_event
WHERE event LIKE 'library cache%' OR event LIKE 'row cache%';
```

This time I get an expected result. Since my shared pool is too small, I found a marked increase in both row cache and library cache areas. I also got a few very nasty ORA-00600 internal error codes in my alert log due to a serious shortage of shared pool space. Don't try this one at home! The point is made though. The smaller the shared pool is, the more shared pool–type wait events will occur. On the contrary, do not size the shared pool up and up simply to cope with application SQL code and data model design issues, as you will eventually encounter scalability issues—probably at a point where you have enough paying customers to cause you a serious business problem, when you can least afford lack of scalability:

```
Event                                      %
------------------------------------ ----------
row cache lock                           .38
library cache pin                      16.72
library cache load lock                 1.59
```

21.2.7 Redo Log Waits

Redo log waits are affected by the redo log buffer, redo log files, and archive log files. Many things affect the efficiency of logging in an Oracle database. Performance is more likely to be adversely affected by a log buffer that is too small rather than too large. The most profound effect on log performance is usually disk I/O speed and physical architecture during log buffer flushing to disk and copying of redo log files to archive log files.

When examining redo log waits and problems, look for the redo log buffer running out of space, too much time taken to write redo logs or copy archives, and perhaps even too much redo log file switching:

- *Redo entries*. How often are redo entries copied into the buffer?

- *Redo writes*. How often are buffer entries written to redo log files?

- *Redo buffer allocation retries*. This event indicates failure to allocate space in the redo log buffer, due to either slow log writer processing speed or a log switch. The log buffer or redo log files could be too small. This event can also indicate poorly performing disk I/O where log files are stored.

- *Redo log space requests*. Requests for the buffer to write out to a redo log file are recorded. This typically occurs during a log switch.

Note: The redo log space requests event has been misinterpreted in the past and does not indicate requests for space in the log buffer.

- *Redo sync writes*. A COMMIT command will require the database writer process to write dirty blocks to disk. Any required redo log entries must be flushed from the log buffer to redo log files prior to database writer activity, for the sake of recoverability. High frequency of this event could indicate high COMMIT rates, which may or may not be a problem, but can often be caused by application requirements or poor SQL coding.

A *redo buffer allocation retries* event occurs if the log buffer is too small. However, I have never found it useful, even on the largest databases, to make a log buffer larger than 1Mb—and rarely above 512K. Log buffer size is entirely dependent on transaction size. I have seen log buffers in excess of 500Mb because of a misunderstanding of its purpose, causing other problems, prior to tuning of course. The redo log buffer does not have to be equivalent to redo log file sizes. Additionally, writing a large redo log file to disk can take a lot of time. Redo log buffer and file events are found by querying the V$SYSSTAT view:

```
COL name FORMAT a32;
SELECT value, name FROM v$sysstat WHERE name LIKE '%redo%'
ORDER BY 1 DESC;
```

Results are as follows, and were very similar for both Oracle 9*i* and Oracle 10*g* Database:

```
     VALUE NAME
---------- --------------------------------
  86290896 redo size
    927748 redo wastage
    293852 redo entries
    175867 redo blocks written
     25776 redo write time
     23132 redo synch time
      3920 redo writer latching time
      3569 redo writes
      1870 redo synch writes
        50 redo buffer allocation retries
         0 redo log space requests
         0 redo log space wait time
         0 redo log switch interrupts
         0 redo ordering marks
```

There is no sense in having a huge redo log buffer. The redo log buffer is cyclic in nature. This means that redo log entries can be written to one part of the buffer, at the same time that other entries in another part of the buffer are flushed to disk. Contention can occur sometimes when the redo log buffer is too small. However, depending on database activity, configuration, and application behavior, a large redo log buffer could possibly cause problems by having to flush large chunks of data to disk. Once again, a memory cache buffer is a high-speed bridge between CPU and disk storage, not a temporary storage area. The purpose of buffers is twofold: (1) to manage speed differences between CPU and disk storage, and (2) to take advantage of CPU speed over that of disk storage.

Note: Most redo log waits are as a direct result of poor I/O response time or contention, rarely log buffer size, unless the LOG_BUFFER parameter has been tampered with.

Do not assume that the redo log buffer is always the source of redo log and archive problems. One very easy method of assessing redo log problems is to check time stamps for both redo logs and archive logs on disk. If the dates are the same, then there could be excessive log switching, and redo log files might be too small. Obviously this task can be accomplished using various Oracle database views. Personally, I prefer to simply examine file timestamps in the operating system. Automated scripting for this type of functionality is also faster built at the operating system level. Checking timestamps on archive logs can be found with the following query:

```
SELECT * FROM (
  SELECT TO_CHAR(completion_time,'MM/DD/YYYY HH24:MI:SS')
"Timestamp"
  ,name "Archive Log" FROM v$archived_log ORDER BY 1 DESC)
WHERE ROWNUM < 10;
```

My timestamps are very close together, and thus redo log file sizes in my database are probably too small. However, my database is not archived, and no archive logs are being written. As far as my database is concerned, there is nothing to tune in this case:

```
Timestamp             Archive Log
-------------------   ---------------------------------------------
04/02/2003 20:12:55   F:\ORACLE\ORADATA\TEST\ARCHIVE\ARC_1350.ARC
04/02/2003 20:12:54   F:\ORACLE\ORADATA\TEST\ARCHIVE\ARC_1349.ARC
04/02/2003 20:12:53   F:\ORACLE\ORADATA\TEST\ARCHIVE\ARC_1347.ARC
04/02/2003 20:12:53   F:\ORACLE\ORADATA\TEST\ARCHIVE\ARC_1348.ARC
04/02/2003 20:12:52   F:\ORACLE\ORADATA\TEST\ARCHIVE\ARC_1346.ARC
04/02/2003 20:12:51   F:\ORACLE\ORADATA\TEST\ARCHIVE\ARC_1345.ARC
04/02/2003 20:12:50   F:\ORACLE\ORADATA\TEST\ARCHIVE\ARC_1343.ARC
```

```
04/02/2003 20:12:50 F:\ORACLE\ORADATA\TEST\ARCHIVE\ARC_1344.ARC
04/02/2003 20:12:49 F:\ORACLE\ORADATA\TEST\ARCHIVE\ARC_1342.ARC
```

If the database is periodically halting, then archiving could be temporarily halting the database, waiting for redo log files to be copied to archive log files. This situation is possible where all redo files contain nonarchived redo log entries. The redo log files are cyclic, just like the redo log buffer. If all redo log files are waiting to be copied to archive log files, then no logging activity can occur until at least one redo log file is archived. The database will wait for archiving to catch up to ensure recoverability. In this case, perhaps create more redo log files or another archive process. The speed of disk storage and network communication to the disks containing redo log and archive log files could also be an issue. For example, standby database log file transfers should have a good network connection.

There are a number of other interesting facts about redo log files:

- **Duplexed redo logs**. Multiple redo log file copies or duplexed redo log files are not an issue for performance. This is especially the case on a multiple CPU platform. Redo log files will be written in parallel. Redo log files are I/O bound and not CPU bound. This means that the I/O disk structure is much more important to redo logs. CPU use is more or less negligible in this respect.

- **Log appending**. Redo and archive log files are written to sequentially by appending. They are best placed onto sequential access disk storage RAID array structures.

- **Alternating log files**. In extreme circumstances, alternate redo log files can be split onto separate disk storage areas because they may be open at the same time. In other words, the first redo log file is being archived, while the second is flushed to from the redo log buffer. Splitting alternate redo log files to separate disks allows for two different disks, which in turn allows for less I/O conflict.

Tuning redo and archive details is not all about the redo log buffer. "Guesstimate" changes to the redo log buffer will probably not solve performance problems and could make things worse.

21.2.8 Undo and Rollback Waits

Rollback segment and automated undo wait statistics can be obtained from the V$WAITSTAT performance view as shown next. At this point, my Accounts schema database uses manual rollback segments in my Oracle 9*i* Database and automated undo in my Oracle 10*g* Database:

```
SELECT class "Event", count, time FROM v$waitstat
WHERE class LIKE '%undo%' ORDER BY class;
```

This is the result for my Oracle 9*i* Database:

Event	COUNT	TIME
save undo block	0	0
save undo header	0	0
system undo block	0	0
system undo header	0	0
undo block	**16**	**63**
undo header	**128**	**355**

The result in my Oracle 10*g* Database is much better, showing far few wait events using automated undo:

Event	COUNT	TIME
save undo block	0	0
save undo header	0	0
system undo block	0	0
system undo header	0	0
undo block	**3**	**5**
undo header	0	0

Comparing rollback wait events and database buffer cache activity is a little vague at best. Large quantities of undo wait events, in relation to general database activity, could be indicative of a performance problem. But it could also be normal for the database and applications involved. Let's say that an application is performing a lot of undo activity. A high incidence of ROLLBACK command–instigated rollback activity could be abnormal.

Application rollback activity is much more likely to be caused by heavy DML activity. This could also result in high undo space usage to obtain consistent point-in-time snapshot views of data. This is also normal. Increasing commit frequency at the application level can help to alleviate rollback use but can cause other problems as well.

Comparing rollback wait events to database buffer cache events should produce a very low ratio. Perhaps a high ratio implies that rollback space is being waited for. If the percentage of rollback space wait events to database buffer cache is high, then it may indicate that rollback space is not large enough. For the equivalent when using manual rollback, perhaps there are either not enough rollback segments or those rollback segments are not large enough. This query shows a negligible ratio of well below 1% using automated undo:

```
SELECT (
    (SELECT SUM(count) FROM v$waitstat
        WHERE class IN ('undo header', 'undo block'))
  /(SELECT SUM(value) FROM v$sysstat
        WHERE name IN ('db block gets', 'consistent gets')))
  *100 "Rollback vs DBCache"
FROM DUAL;


Rollback vs DBCache
-------------------
        .000192354
```

High undo activity may not necessarily indicate a problem. High rollback rates could be an application requirement. However, transaction failures would be an issue. Investigate applications.

Automated undo has a parameter called UNDO_RETENTION. This parameter allows retention of committed rollback database changes for a period of time. The more potentially unnecessary data retained, then perhaps the more out of control automated undo could become. Default values for the UNDO_RETENTION parameter, using the Oracle Database Configuration Assistant, appears to be 900 for an OLTP database creation and 10,800 for a data warehouse database creation. It might be best not to oversize this parameter. The V$UNDOSTAT and V$ROLLSTAT performance views provide useful information about undo and rollback space.

A highly concurrent small transaction load OLTP database will require as many small manual rollback segments as possible. In the case of automated undo, a lower value for the UNDO_RETENTION parameter is appropriate to smaller transactions. The opposite is true for large transactions when executing batch processing or in a data warehouse.

21.2.9 Enqueue Waits

This type of wait event is caused by a lock on a row or a buffer latch wait. This wait event occurs when another request is waiting for a lock held by another session process. To find locks, we use the V$SESSION_WAIT and V$LOCK views. My database has an enqueue locking value of over 1%, so it is possibly an issue. Additionally, there are deadlocks, exemplifying this point further.

Note: Deadlocks are usually caused by poor application coding, such as the use of triggers. This is most certainly the case in my database.

Oracle Database has many different types of enqueue events. These are some of the more significant and common ones:

- *TM*. This is DML enqueue, sometimes due to lack of indexing on foreign keys or just lack of indexing in general.
- *TX*. This is transactional enqueue, or exclusive lock on a row or a table (hopefully on a row and not a table).
- *SQ*. These are sequence numbers.

This query is executed against the V$LOCK performance view on my database in the Accounts schema, monitored over about 30 seconds. These numbers can be written off as normal:

```
SELECT type "Lock", COUNT(type) "Locks" FROM v$lock GROUP BY
type;
```

This is the Oracle 9*i* Database result:

```
Lo        Locks
--   ----------
SQ            10
TX            80
```

And this is the Oracle 10*g* Database result:

```
Lo        Locks
--   ----------
RS             1
RT             1
CF             1
XR             1
MR            16
TS             1
```

Many older relational databases implemented what was called incremental locking. Incremental locking successively locked larger objects (or amounts of data), as the amount of resources to maintain current locking grew. Oracle Database does not escalate locking, even if contention can appear to cause this type of behavior. Block-level contention can occur in Oracle Database when enough concurrent DML row locking activity occurs in a single block, which can be counteracted by changing block-level concurrency storage parameter settings. Certain types of DML activity can cause different types of locking. In general, Oracle Database locking will occur in different ways as follows:

- *Row share*. This is read share lock on a single row.

- *Row exclusive*. This is write lock on a row, excluding write access to other sessions.

- *Table share*. This is as with rows, but for an entire table.

- *Table exclusive*. This is as with rows, but for an entire table.

Removing locks from a database instance can be an administration issue when serious. Resolving locking issues in terms of tuning out the locks is more of an SQL code and data model issue, possibly the result of poor application coding and design.

> **Note:** ⑨*i* Enqueue numbers can be altered using the ENQUEUE_
> RESOURCES parameter.

Resource limitations can be monitored using the V$RESOURCE_
LIMIT performance view:

```
COL resource FORMAT a24;
SELECT RESOURCE_NAME "Resource", INITIAL_ALLOCATION "Initial"
,CURRENT_UTILIZATION "Current", MAX_UTILIZATION "Max"
,LIMIT_VALUE "Limit"
FROM v$resource_limit WHERE resource_name NOT LIKE('g%')
ORDER BY 1;
```

This is the result from my Oracle 9*i* Database:

Resource	Initial	Current	Max	Limit
branches	247	0	0	UNLIMITED
cmtcallbk	247	0	0	UNLIMITED
dml_locks	988	71	134	UNLIMITED
enqueue_locks	2890	29	31	2890
enqueue_resources	1208	43	43	UNLIMITED
max_rollback_segments	50	17	17	50
max_shared_servers	5	2	2	5
parallel_max_servers	11	0	0	11
processes	200	26	29	200
sessions	225	32	36	225
sort_segment_locks	UNLIMITED	0	1	UNLIMITED
temporary_table_locks	UNLIMITED	0	0	UNLIMITED
transactions	247	10	14	UNLIMITED

And this is the Oracle 10*g* Database result, showing a few more options as UNLIMITED:

Resource	Initial	Current	Max	Limit
branches	187	0	0	UNLIMITED
cmtcallbk	187	0	1	UNLIMITED

dml_locks	748	0	47 UNLIMITED
enqueue_locks	2260	22	35 2260
enqueue_resources	968	22	48 UNLIMITED
max_rollback_segments	187	11	11 65535
max_shared_servers	UNLIMITED	1	1 UNLIMITED
parallel_max_servers	20	0	0 3600
processes	150	28	34 150
sessions	170	32	43 170
sort_segment_locks	UNLIMITED	0	1 UNLIMITED
temporary_table_locks	UNLIMITED	0	0 UNLIMITED
transactions	187	1	7 UNLIMITED

In my database, enqueue wait events occur at a steady rate of around 1%. This first query is executed against my Oracle 9*i* Database, using *enqueue* in the WHERE clause:

```
COL event FORMAT a30;
COL percentage FORMAT 9999999990;
SELECT event "Event"
    ,ROUND(
        (time_waited /
            (SELECT SUM(time_waited) FROM v$system_event
            WHERE IdleEvent(event) IS NOT NULL)
    )*100, 2) "%"
FROM v$system_event WHERE event = 'enqueue';
```

This is the result for Oracle 9*i* Database:

```
Event                                    %
------------------------------ ----------
enqueue                               1.02
```

Now we do the same with Oracle 10*g* Database, but as seen previously in this chapter latch and enqueue wait events have become a lot more specific. So the query is altered to contain a LIKE clause match against the string *enq:* in the WHERE clause:

```
COL event FORMAT a30;
COL percentage FORMAT 9999999990;
SELECT event "Event"
```

```
    ,ROUND(
        (time_waited /
            (SELECT SUM(time_waited) FROM v$system_event
            WHERE IdleEvent(event) IS NOT NULL)
    )*100, 2) "%"
FROM v$system_event WHERE event LIKE 'enq:%';
```

You even get a very brief explanation as to the nature of each type of enqueue wait event:

```
Event                               %
--------------------------- ----------
enq: TM - contention              .24
enq: HW - contention                0
enq: TX - row lock contention    2.39
enq: TX - index contention        .37
enq: SQ - contention              .02
enq: TX - contention                0
```

Let's try to produce some *enqueue* wait events. First, I drop all my Accounts schema foreign key indexes using a command like the following, which generates DDL commands. I have scripts to regenerate all my foreign key indexes:

```
SELECT 'DROP INDEX '||index_name|| ';'
FROM user_indexes WHERE index_name LIKE 'XFK_%';
```

Now let's check the types of locks occurring:

```
SELECT type "Lock", COUNT(type) "Locks" FROM v$lock GROUP BY
type;
```

In my Oracle 9*i* Database, there is an increase in TM and TX enqueue lock events. This is because I have removed all my foreign key indexes:

```
Lo    Locks
--  ----------
CF         1
JQ        24
```

```
MR          10
RT           1
TM          52
TS           1
TX           9
XR           1
```

In Oracle 10*g* Database, the following result was obtained immediately after dropping the foreign key indexes:

```
Lo      Locks

--   ----------

RS          1
RT          1
CF          1
XR          1
MR         16
TS          1
```

After a few minutes of the simulation running, with no foreign key indexes in place, more enqueue locks had been recorded in system statistics:

```
Lo      Locks

--   ----------

RS          1
RT          1
CF          1
XR          1
MR         16
JQ          4
WF          1
TM         33
TX          1
TS          1
```

Now I am checking all wait events again:

```
COL percentage FORMAT 9999999990;
SELECT event "Event", total_waits "Waits", time_waited
"Total"
 ,TO_CHAR(
  (time_waited /
   (SELECT SUM(time_waited) FROM v$system_event
    WHERE IdleEvent(event) IS NOT NULL)
 )*100, 990.99) "Percentage"
FROM v$system_event WHERE IdleEvent(event) IS NOT NULL ORDER
BY event;
```

As to be expected, enqueue wait events have increased slightly. Notice how *db file scattered read* events are dramatically increased, most likely due to full physical table scanning of tables during referential integrity checks on foreign keys with no indexes or where the optimizer utilizes foreign key indexes in SQL code.

This is the result for my Oracle 9*i* Database:

Event	Waits	Total	Percent
LGWR wait for redo copy	16	28	0.00
buffer busy waits	58396	238368	9.40
buffer deadlock	7	38	0.00
control file heartbeat	1	410	0.02
control file parallel write	369	3467	0.14
control file sequential read	283	1104	0.04
db file parallel write	86	755	0.03
db file scattered read	**102816**	**1774183**	**69.94**
db file sequential read	32830	426158	16.80
direct path read	31	2	0.00
direct path write	9	0	0.00
enqueue	**304**	**80489**	**3.17**
latch free	683	9212	0.36
library cache load lock	5	23	0.00
library cache pin	118	1748	0.07
log file parallel write	376	257	0.01
log file sequential read	24	40	0.00
log file single write	24	17	0.00
log file sync	74	284	0.01
refresh controlfile command	1	6	0.00
row cache lock	3	46	0.00

This is the result for my Oracle 10*g* Database:

Event	Waits	Total	Percent
Data file init write	18	43	0.01
LGWR wait for redo copy	76	5	0.00
Log archive I/O	1	0	0.00
buffer busy waits	415	729	0.09
buffer deadlock	1	0	0.00
class slave wait	1	501	0.06
control file heartbeat	1	401	0.05
control file parallel write	2575	2940	0.37
control file sequential read	4337	11561	1.47
db file parallel read	156	2530	0.32
db file parallel write	19572	14968	1.91
db file scattered read	**24399**	**77736**	**9.91**
db file sequential read	212344	525199	66.94
db file single write	21	21	0.00
direct path read	75	25	0.00
direct path read temp	4	0	0.00
direct path write	53	7	0.00
enq: HW - contention	**6**	**3**	**0.00**
enq: RO - fast object reuse	**19**	**1**	**0.00**
enq: SQ - contention	**80**	**126**	**0.02**
enq: TM - contention	**18**	**2431**	**0.31**
enq: TX - contention	**1**	**6**	**0.00**
enq: TX - index contention	**491**	**2338**	**0.30**
enq: TX - row lock contention	**654**	**17963**	**2.29**
free buffer waits	61	91	0.01
latch free	193	11	0.00
latch: In memory undo latch	48	3	0.00
latch: cache buffers chains	230	28	0.00
latch: cache buffers lru chain	18	2	0.00
latch: enqueue hash chains	8	199	0.03
latch: library cache	50	10	0.00
latch: library cache lock	6	0	0.00
latch: library cache pin	9	2	0.00
latch: object queue header ope	1	0	0.00
latch: redo allocation	4	0	0.00
latch: redo writing	1	0	0.00
latch: row cache objects	6	0	0.00

```
latch: session allocation         16          2     0.00
latch: shared pool                 5          1     0.00
library cache load lock           19       1355     0.17
library cache pin                 38       1299     0.17
log file parallel write        11744       9410     1.20
log file sequential read          14        186     0.02
log file single write              9         10     0.00
log file switch completion         7        307     0.04
log file sync                   6788       6677     0.85
os thread startup                136       1525     0.19
rdbms ipc reply                  259       1084     0.14
read by other session          85000     102847    13.11
recovery read                      3          0     0.00
reliable message                 103         22     0.00
row cache lock                     5         90     0.01
write complete waits               1          7     0.00
```

21.2.10 Latch Free Waits

Latches are a special type of locking mechanism that protect buffers in memory. Latches are used to lock blocks in buffers to ensure that multiple sessions or processes do not alter the same space in memory at the same time. Unlike a lock waiting for lock release, a latch can spin or sleep and then retry to access the same buffer area repeatedly. Latches protect buffers from corruption by changes from different processes at the same time.

My database shows a *latch free* wait value of less than 2%. This is insignificant due to the nature of the wait event. It is normal for a database to have to wait for access to parts of Oracle Database buffer caches. The buffer caches should be a great deal smaller than physical areas in the datafiles. Sizing buffers too small can cause buffer contention or competition for memory access due to not enough available space in memory for cache buffers. On the contrary, sizing buffers too large can possibly cause the same problems. Managing data in buffers is much more complex than managing data in disk storage.

In Oracle 10*g* Database, the latch events in the V$SYSTEM_EVENT view are now much more detailed:

```
COL event FORMAT a30;
COL percentage FORMAT 9999999990;
SELECT event "Event"
```

```
,ROUND(
    (time_waited /
        (SELECT SUM(time_waited) FROM v$system_event
        WHERE IdleEvent(event) IS NOT NULL)
    )*100, 2) "%"
FROM v$system_event WHERE event LIKE 'latch:%';
```

This is the result of the previous query. Latch enqueue events are prevalent because I dropped all my foreign key indexes:

```
Event                                %
------------------------------ ----------
latch: cache buffers chains           0
latch: redo writing                   0
latch: In memory undo latch           0
latch: row cache objects              0
latch: shared pool                    0
latch: library cache                  0
latch: library cache lock             0
latch: library cache pin              0
latch: session allocation             0
latch: enqueue hash chains          .03
latch: cache buffers lru chain        0
latch: object queue header ope        0
latch: redo allocation                0
```

21.3 ⑩g **Wait Events in the Database Control**

Wait events are essentially buried within the metrics structure of the Database Control. You can get at specific wait event categories through the use of the *Top???* tools, such as TopSessions and TopConsumers.

A not-so-simple method of getting directly at some wait event details is to go into a tool, such as the Instance Locks monitor. Select a process and click the Session Details button at the top right of the Database Control window. You will then be able to click a link called Wait Event.

History is at the top left of the window. You can then click on the various wait events or wait event classes, and get graphical displays and more information, depending on what options you select and click.

The Database Control functions by attempting to make monitoring and performance somewhat artificially intelligent. So, the more traditional methods of gathering and analyzing statistics from a tool like SQL*Plus are a very different approach than that of using the Database Control. SQL statements against V$ performance views and metadata views give you access to all statistics at the same time, including things not appropriate to a specific bottleneck. The Database Control tends to divide information, such as wait events, into more easily understandable categories. The Database Control gives a better bird's-eye picture of a database, allowing for rapid localization of any particular problem—sometimes even before a problem has occurred.

It makes perfect sense to analyze the Database Control within a specific chapter dedicated to using the Database Control as a tuning tool from the perspective of the entire database (as opposed to just examining wait events). Wait events are used internally by the Database Control to intelligently analyze potential issues. The Database Control will then present a DBA with an analysis. That analysis will very likely not include wait event information in any specific detail at all, but rather contains pointers to a solution to an actual problem. In other words, the Database Control is attempting to perform the interpretation that a performance tuning expert would do. Does it work? Will it replace the expertise of performance tuners en masse? That is highly unlikely but remains to be seen.

As a result, the Database Control will be examined in its entirety, in order to do it justice as a performance tuning and monitoring tool, in a subsequent chapter. It simply does not make sense to mix it up between the Database Control and more traditional, and perhaps far more detailed, performance tuning methods.

A latch wait event is a specific type of wait event. Latch wait events can be found by querying the V$SESSION_WAIT performance view, drilling down using the various latch V$ performance views. Latches are a major topic all by themselves. Therefore, this is a good point to end this general discussion of events and wait events and pass the examination of latches onto the next chapter. The next chapter will look into latches in detail, along with some special wait events applicable to latches and how to handle those events.

22

Latches

Wait events were introduced in the previous chapter. A wait event is recorded when one thing is waiting for another. There are many different types of wait events. High latch free wait event rates indicate latch misses showing possible problems with SGA memory buffers. High quantities of latch misses can seriously affect overall database performance. What is required is not being acquired.

22.1   What Is a Latch?

Latches protect memory buffers much like locks protect table rows. When a latch is already held on an area of a buffer, a latch free wait event occurs if another process attempts to access the same area of data and the process fails to do so. There are numerous types of latches for all the different types of memory buffer areas. Latches apply to items, such as data in the database buffer cache, preventing multiple simultaneous changes to the same data.

Note: A latch cannot be tuned. Latch problems are indicative of other problems and can help to focus where significant performance problems may be occurring.

Note: (10*g*) Oracle 9*i* Database Release 2 (9.2) has 239 latches. Oracle Database 10*g* Release 2 has 382 latches.

22.1.1 **Latch Misses, Spins, and Sleeps**

In the previous chapter, we saw that a latch free wait event is generated when a latch is missed.

Note: (10*g*) There are many more latch wait events, where there are only two in Oracle 9*i* Database.

What is a missed latch? When a latch is requested and the section of a buffer requested is *latched* (or held by another process), then a latch free wait event is generated. Therefore, the second request for a latch, which is already retained by another process, will wait for the required latch to be freed up for use. A lock on a table row simply waits for release of that table row by constantly retrying for a lock. On the contrary, a latch miss will generate one of two types of action: (1) place the latch in immediate mode, where immediate mode will cause the process requesting the latch to take an alternative action, or (2) place the latch request into a willing-to-wait mode. Willing-to-wait mode causes the latch to repeatedly retry and spin. When the latch has spun a number of times, it will sleep for a period of time, reawakening to retry and potentially spin, and perhaps even sleep again. The number of times a latch will retry to acquire the latch depends on an internal parameter that used to be called SPIN_COUNT in Oracle8*i* Database.

Spinning latches can consume enormous amounts of CPU time. When a latch spins, it repeatedly requests a latch. This can affect performance drastically if many latches are spinning at the same time. The following query shows gets, misses, and a miss rate for all latches in my database. The redo copy latch is not an issue, as it is a potentially immediate mode latch. Other miss rates are not too significant, but there is still potential for problems:

```
COL latch FORMAT a28;
COL gets FORMAT 99999990 HEADING "Gets";
COL misses FORMAT 99990 HEADING "Misses";
COL sleeps FORMAT 99990 HEADING "Sleep";
COL immediate_gets FORMAT 99999990 HEADING "IGet";
COL immediate_misses FORMAT 9990 HEADING "IMiss";
SELECT name "Latch", gets, misses
  ,TO_CHAR(ROUND((misses/gets)*100,2),'99990.00') "Miss Rate"
  ,immediate_gets, immediate_misses
FROM v$latch WHERE gets!=0 AND misses!=0 ORDER BY 4 DESC;
```

This is the result for my Oracle 9*i* Database:

Latch	Gets	Misses	Miss Rate	IGet	IMiss
redo copy	1620	243	15.00	240928	2138
cache buffers lru chain	**8022562**	**6651**	**0.08**	**2119**	**0**
multiblock read objects	6253965	2356	0.04	42	0
cache buffers chains	**34445102**	**9074**	**0.03**	**4957516**	**847**
sequence cache	55793	7	0.01	0	0
library cache	**2019837**	**177**	**0.01**	**0**	**0**
session allocation	**500846**	**15**	**0.00**	**0**	**0**
library cache pin	**1451385**	**15**	**0.00**	**0**	**0**
library cache pin allocation	**332613**	**6**	**0.00**	**0**	**0**
shared pool	**757897**	**6**	**0.00**	**0**	**0**
undo global data	80337	1	0.00	0	0
dml lock allocation	441665	5	0.00	0	0
enqueues	286118	1	0.00	0	0
redo allocation	267146	8	0.00	0	0
simulator lru latch	564509	19	0.00	48	0

This is the result for my Oracle 10*g* Database. The result between the two database versions is similar:

Latch	Gets	Misses	Miss Rate	IGet	IMiss
qmn task queue latch	2666	340	12.75	0	0
slave class create	62	5	8.06	0	0
Memory Management Latch	354	6	1.69	6247	0
KWQMN job cache list latch	499	3	0.60	0	0
redo allocation	49385	3	0.01	90492	0
library cache	**955082**	**14**	**0.00**	**270**	**1**
In memory undo latch	77747	1	0.00	17135	0
library cache pin	**632270**	**1**	**0.00**	**19**	**0**
enqueue hash chains	418966	6	0.00	42	5
cache buffers chains	**2695243**	**14**	**0.00**	**418897**	**2**
simulator lru latch	95696	3	0.00	6774	0
cache buffers lru chain	**152277**	**1**	**0.00**	**561861**	**64**
session allocation	**578992**	**2**	**0.00**	**0**	**0**
shared pool	**277415**	**5**	**0.00**	**0**	**0**
simulator hash latch	148916	1	0.00	0	0
row cache objects	658652	2	0.00	624	0

Note: Latches shown in the previous example containing the letters qmn or QMN are relevant to Advanced Queuing and thus Oracle Streams. My Oracle 10*g* has a zero-size streams pool, so the latches are irrelevant.

Let's take a slightly different perspective in my Accounts schema database, once again using the V$LATCH performance view. This time, we focus on the total waiting time for each latch, which is more important than the number of misses (I am also ignoring any latches containing qmn or QMN):

```
COL latch FORMAT a28;
COL misses FORMAT 99990 HEADING "Miss";
COL sleeps FORMAT 99990 HEADING "Sleep";
SELECT name "Latch", ROUND(wait_time/1000) "WaitTime"
 ,ROUND((wait_time
   /(SELECT SUM(wait_time) FROM v$latch))*100,0) "Percent"
 ,misses, sleeps
FROM v$latch WHERE wait_time!=0 AND UPPER(name) NOT LIKE
'%QMN%'
ORDER BY 3 DESC;
```

The picture is somewhat different. Library cache events have become more significant, the shared pool latch has become the least significant, and the cache buffers chains latch has disappeared due to zero waiting time. The session allocation latch is interesting. This latch tells us about database connection activity. Continual connection and disconnection from the database can cause problems. There are many other latches used in Oracle Database, not shown here. This query shows significant latch activity in my Oracle 9*i* Database:

Latch	WaitTime	Percent	Miss	Sleep
cache buffers lru chain	**10068**	**49**	**6653**	**7113**
redo copy	3693	18	243	297
library cache	**3520**	**17**	**177**	**207**
multiblock read objects	2434	12	2357	2390
session allocation	**569**	**3**	**15**	**16**
library cache pin	**108**	**1**	**15**	**18**
enqueues	**10**	**0**	**1**	**1**

library cache pin allocation	**21**	**0**	**6**	**7**
simulator lru latch	14	0	19	20
redo allocation	35	0	8	9
dml lock allocation	50	0	5	7
undo global data	0	0	1	1
sequence cache	41	0	7	7
shared pool	**31**	**0**	**6**	**6**

The Oracle 10*g* Database result looks a little different, showing that table row locks (enqueue latches) are more significant than memory buffer latches. This probably indicates that Oracle 10*g* Database is much more proficient at managing its memory buffers:

Latch	WaitTime	Percent	Miss	Sleep
enqueue hash chains	**7372**	**94**	**15**	**15**
library cache	**170**	**2**	**18**	**21**
slave class create	75	1	6	6
shared pool	**54**	**1**	**7**	**7**
simulator lru latch	6	0	7	14
Memory Management Latch	5	0	6	6
In memory undo latch	1	0	3	4
library cache pin	**0**	**0**	**1**	**1**
cache buffers chains	**32**	**0**	**50**	**76**
cache buffers lru chain	**0**	**0**	**1**	**1**
session allocation	**1**	**0**	**2**	**2**
redo allocation	0	0	4	4
simulator hash latch	0	0	2	3
row cache objects	0	0	2	2

All in all, you have been introduced to potential latch issues in the Accounts schema. Let's a take a small step sideways and briefly examine latch performance views.

22.1.2 Latch Performance Views

There are a number of Oracle Database performance views for examining latches and latch statistics. The most important of those views are the V$LATCH and the V$LATCHHOLDER performance views:

- **V$LATCH**. This is an aggregation of all latch statistics.

- **V$LATCHNAME**. This refers to all possible latches in an Oracle database.

- **V$LATCHHOLDER**. This contains real-time current latch information about sessions and processes holding latches. This view can be used in conjunction with other views, such as V$SESSION, V$SESSION_WAIT, and V$PROCESS. These views allow examination of latch problems as they occur.

- **V$LATCH_MISSES**. This provides details about latch misses.

- **V$LATCH_PARENT and V$LATCH_CHILDREN**. These refer to child and parent details of latches.

22.1.3   Latches in Real Time

Now let's take a look at my database containing the active Accounts schema in real time. I use an anonymous PL/SQL procedure to poll latches in the database many times at the session level as those latches occur. The objective is to get a useful result over a period of time:

```
DROP TABLE statistics_latches;
CREATE TABLE statistics_latches(event varchar2(64)
,latch varchar2(64), address NUMBER, latch# NUMBER
,sleeps NUMBER);
BEGIN
 FOR counter IN 1..100000 LOOP
  INSERT INTO statistics_latches
  --
  --P1 is the latch address, P2 is the latch number, P3 is the
number
  -- of sleeps
  --
  SELECT sw.event AS event, l.name AS latch, sw.p1 AS address,
   sw.p2 AS latch#, sw.p3 AS sleep
  FROM v$session_wait sw, v$latchname l
  WHERE sw.event = 'latch free' AND sw.p2 = l.latch#;
  COMMIT;
 END LOOP;
END;
/
```

> **Note:** This type of processing can be done easily with STATSPACK, the Oracle Database Wait Event Interface, or using the Database Control. The purpose here is to explain the details so that you understand how things work.

As shown next, by running a query against the table created we can see that the database buffer cache and the library cache have potential latch free wait problems, among other potential latch performance possibilities:

```
SELECT latch "Latch", COUNT(latch) "Latch Waits", SUM(sleeps)
"Sleeps"
FROM statistics_latches GROUP BY latch;
```

This is the result for Oracle 9*i* Database:

Latch	Latch Waits	Sleep
cache buffers chains	**63**	**0**
cache buffers lru chain	**26**	**7**
dml lock allocation	1	0
enqueue hash chains	11	0
library cache	**1**	**0**
multiblock read objects	2	0
redo allocation	1	0
redo copy	6	0

Next is the result for Oracle 10*g* Database. Once again, ignore any indicators of qmn (Advanced Queuing or Oracle Streams). The result remains consistent in that we are seeing better management of memory buffers, or perhaps just making table row lock issues come to light more significantly:

Latch	Latch Waits	Sleep
dml lock allocation	59	0
qmn task queue latch	6	0
SGA IO buffer pool latch	7	0
simulator lru latch	7	0
SQL memory manager latch	131	0

Now we know a little about latches and potential latch problems in the Accounts schema. Let's examine what the most significant latches are for an Oracle installation, indicating potential latch problems and resulting performance issues.

I could make similar changes to configuration and otherwise, in common with changes made in the previous chapter, attempting to both increase and decrease the occurrence of particular latches. At this point, these actions are not necessary. I am still getting the same information, when examining both wait events in the previous chapter and latches in the current chapter. Latches simply provide better focused details.

22.2 The Most Significant Latches

The most significant latches occur with respect to use of the most highly used memory buffer structures in the System Global Area (SGA). The SGA includes the database buffers, the shared pool, and a few other bits and pieces. The shared pool contains various subset buffer cache structures, including the library cache, the metadata cache, and parsed SQL code.

Note: Concurrency requirements for the shared pool are much higher than for the database buffer cache.

The database buffer cache is simply a speed bridge between datafiles and data access. The shared pool attempts to minimize processing repetition, which can be substantial. Missing a latch in the shared pool is a much more significant event than missing a latch in the database buffer cache. The concept of sharing is much more important with respect to the shared pool.

As already stated, a latch is similar to a lock on a row in a table. The difference is that a latch is used to allocate a hold on a section of a buffer in memory.

What are the different types of latches and to which buffers do they apply?

- *Database buffer cache latches*: cache buffers lru chain, cache buffers chains, cache buffer handles, multiblock read objects, cache protection latch

- *Shared pool, library, and metadata cache latches*: shared pool, sequence cache, library cache, library cache pin, library cache pin allocation, library cache load lock, row cache objects
- *Redo log buffer latches*: redo allocation, redo copy, redo writing
- *Network and database connection latches*: virtual circuit buffers, virtual circuit queues, virtual circuits, session allocation, session switching, session idle bit, session queue latch

22.2.1 The Database Buffer Cache

Two latches are significant in the database buffer cache:

- *Cache buffers lru chain*. This latch is acquired for one of two reasons: (1) when copying a new block into the cache, the block must be locked in cache to prevent any changes to it during the I/O process from disk to buffer, and (2) when writing a dirty block to disk, the block cannot be changed or read into the cache again until I/O from buffer to disk is complete. Excessive waits on this latch could be a result of swapping between cache and disk in order to cope with constant requirements for different blocks.

  Potential culprits:

  - There is excessive I/O activity from full scans or lots of I/O throughput activity, such as in a data warehouse. Thus, this could be normal for a data warehouse.
  - The database buffer cache could be too small.
  - Index structures are inappropriate, superfluous, missing, or highly degraded.
  - The SQL code is poorly tuned.
  - Too few database writer (DBWR) processes are unable to keep up with the load.

  Potential solutions:

  - Reduce full scanning by tuning SQL code properly.
  - Reduce the DB_FILE_MULTIBLOCK_READ_COUNT parameter to discourage full scans.

Note: (10*g*) The DB_FILE_MULTIBLOCK_READ_COUNT parameter is automatically controlled if not set. It defaults to a large value but will decrease in size if the number of concurrent sessions becomes excessive.

- Create multiple cache sizes and tablespaces or create separate buffer pools. This allows separation in two ways:
  - It separates highly active and less used data.
  - It separates full scans from single block reads. In other words, separate SQL code that deals with lots of rows from SQL code that deals with small numbers of rows.
- Increase database buffer cache size. This is always the easy option but rarely the correct one, often pushing performance issues aside without dealing with a problem.
- Use more database writer processes. In OLTP databases high I/O is usually caused by poorly tuned SQL code, often causing excessive full physical scans. Full table scans and overuse of fast full index scans will cause heavy I/O activity. Both of these activities can tend to read information directly from disk, partially bypassing the usefulness of the database buffer cache altogether.

Note: When a full scan occurs, the most likely scenario is that data is read from disk and passing through the database buffer. The phrase most likely is used because I can't find documentation and DBAs to agree on how this stuff really works. The database buffer cache is not bypassed, but it is not read from if blocks are already in memory. This is likely the most efficient method for a full scan.

Any required blocks already in the buffer exacerbate the problem because they are read from disk and copied into the buffer, even though they already exist in the buffer; latches are required anyway, increasing block contention because the same data block is read. Poorly tuned SQL code often results in repeated full table scanning of the same table, continuously read from disk, copied into the database buffer cache, but never read from the database buffer cache itself. Just imagine! The database buffer cache entries exist but are effectively never reused. In an extreme situation, performing the same full table scans over and over again can make the database buffer cache more or less useless if all query plans only use full table scans. This is a very unlikely extreme, but the database buffer cache might as well be set to zero in this case.

Note: Data warehouses commonly have a minimally sized database buffer cache because the database buffer cache is not used.

- *Caches buffer chains*. This latch is acquired when a block is accessed and pinned. A block is pinned because something is changing it. This latch prevents another process from changing the block at the same time, which is essential to data integrity. A lot of DML activity with very high I/O rates in SQL code can cause waits on this latch to occur too often. Tune the SQL code. Otherwise, this latch is commonly caused by what are called *hot blocks*. A hot block is a block in the buffer cache subject to change by too many sessions simultaneously. Hot block issues are often a consequence of data model design flaws. Some types of data model culprits are as follows:

  - Static or semistatic lookup data tables that are subject to change. These types of updates should be done in batch mode and avoided during times of peak activity. Summary column updates in parent tables are common causes.
  - System reference tables, perhaps similar in function to Oracle Database sequences but that store centrally located information for all data. The Oracle Database configuration parameter file is a perfect example of a system reference file, except in its case it is stored in memory and not in a database table. Many applications use tables of this nature. Updates by applications to tables of this type can cause serious hot block issues. These types of tables were common in single user databases in the last century and are completely incompatible with any type of multiuser database engine.
  - Primary keys using sequence generators as index values, where index leaf blocks are accessed at high concurrency rates. Reverse primary key indexes can help on tables with very high insertion rates, attempting to store consecutive sequence values into the same index leaf block. Appended log or audit trail tables with sequence number–generated primary key indexes are typical culprits.

  What can be done about hot blocks?

- Proper data model and database object design are the best approach but can be expensive to rectify after the design stage.

- Block concurrency levels can be raised using the INITRANS parameter, among other methods. Block structural changes are covered in a previous chapter.

Note: (10g) Fully automated, locally managed tablespaces remove the need to have to fiddle with parameters like INITRANS.

- Use reverse key indexes on sequential primary keys that use sequences for tables with extremely high concurrent insertion rates.
- Changing block structure will affect only new blocks, not already created blocks. Changing existing block storage structure requires table, tablespace, or even database recreation. Using automated segment space management can help with block-level concurrency issues. Setting values for PCTUSED, FREELIST, and FREELIST_GROUPS in database objects such as tables will be ignored if the containing tablespace is set to automatic segment space management.

Hot blocks can be caused by excessively high I/O but are more likely the result of data model design flaws or indexing issues.

22.2.2 **The Shared Pool**

Shared pool latches can be divided into three areas: (1) the shared pool, (2) the library cache, and (3) the metadata or dictionary cache.

The shared pool latch covers the shared pool as a whole, including library and metadata caches, and usually occurs when the shared pool buffer is sized too large. A very large shared pool requires excessive maintenance using long freelists. It can also occur when the shared pool is too small. Waits on the sequence latch imply that cached sequence values are experiencing a lack of buffer space. There is very high sequence usage.

22.2.2.1 **Library Cache Latches**

Library cache latches generally involve SQL code problems.

Note: Tune SQL code properly. Properly tuned SQL code will alleviate and resolve many other problems. Proper SQL code tuning simply cannot be ignored or avoided.

- *Library cache*. This latch is acquired to add and parse a new SQL code statement into the library cache for future sharing. If an application requires frequent reparsing, then it is possible that SQL code is not matching existing SQL code statements already in the library cache. This can be as a result of lack of bind variable use or lack of consistency in SQL coding. SQL code must match exactly for reuse, down to the case of characters and even the number of spaces between an equals sign and column values in a where clause join. Formatting should be standardized because it has to be precise.

Note: Setting the CURSOR_SHARING parameter to FORCE or SIMILAR can help decrease reparsing. However, the accuracy of the optimizer in relation to statistics might be decreased in large databases.

Note: (10g) Case sensitivity of SQL code is less important to performance due to optimizer improvements.

- *Library cache load lock*. This latch is a library cache or database object lock catering for concurrency.
- *Library cache pin*. A pin is acquired after a library cache load lock latch is acquired. A wait on this latch occurs when an SQL code statement already in the library cache is executed again. A reexecuted SQL statement implies that an SQL statement is reparsed because it is not matched. Once again, the cause is probably no bind variable use and inconsistent SQL coding standards.

Once again, to reiterate, the biggest cause of latch problems with the library cache, and perhaps the shared pool and even an entire Oracle installation in general, is often the result of poorly coded and tuned SQL code. There are various methods of resolving SQL code issues:

- Increasing shared pool size can help to reduce reparsing of SQL code. On the contrary, excessive shared pool size can cause other problems.
- Bind variables, bind variables, bind variables, and then bind variables again! The CURSOR_SHARING parameter can be set to SIMILAR or FORCE. There are possible side effects using the CURSOR_

SHARING parameter as well. Let's make sure we understand exactly what bind variable use is. This SQL statement uses a bind variable:

```
SELECT * FROM customer WHERE name = :name;
```

This SQL statement uses not a bind variable but a literal value:

```
SELECT * FROM customer WHERE name = 'Joe';
```

This SQL statement will be reparsed because the string "Joe" is not the same as the string "Jim":

```
SELECT * FROM customer WHERE name = 'Jim';
```

If both of the SQL code statements finding Joe and Jim were submitted to the database using a bind variable, as in the first example, then the SQL code SELECT statement would have been parsed once. Does this seem trivial? To get an idea of scale, imagine a scenario exemplifying sharing and the shared use of the shared pool library cache, from a realistic perspective.

Let's say you have 10,000 users who are all executing a statement like this, at exactly the same time:

```
SELECT * FROM customer where name = :name;
```

All 10,000 executions will not be reparsed because a bind variable is used. Now imagine replacing the bind variable with every one of the different 10,000 customers' names. You now have 10,000 reparse operations, and thus the shared pool might need to be 10,000 times bigger. Now, if you had a full application with many tables, indexes, and a multitude of SQL statements using complex joins, the list goes on. You can imagine what happens to the shared pool.

Note: Data warehouse databases are different, as queries and amounts of data are very large. It is sometimes prudent not to use bind variables. Why? Because using bind variables tends to lower optimizer accuracy in relation to statistics. Statistics are very important when querying very large data sets. Once again, setting the CURSOR_SHARING parameter to SIMILAR or FORCE will cause the optimizer to lose query plan accuracy due to less precise use of statistics.

It is so very important to create properly tuned SQL code from the start.

22.2.2.2 Metadata Cache Latches

Latch waits on the row cache objects latch implies that there is contention for cache loaded data dictionary metadata definitions. In other words, logical objects such as table or index definitions are not fitting into cache. This type of situation is usually a result of design issues, caused perhaps by applications where each end user has a separate schema or perhaps applications with multiple layers of views. Both of these factors are often utilized for ease of applications programming but can be most unfortunate for performance if scalability becomes an important requirement. Most successful businesses require scalability if growth is the intention.

22.2.3 The Redo Log Buffer

The redo log buffer uses three latches:

- *Redo allocation*. This is acquired to allow for space in the buffer prior to writing to the buffer.

- *Redo copy*. This is acquired to make actual buffer entries. Latch free waits on the redo copy latch are usually high because multiple latches are checked before spinning. Additionally, parallel CPU platforms allow for multiple redo copy latches and as a result parallel copies into the redo log buffer.

- *Redo writing*. Writing from the log buffer to a redo log file verifies that the log writer process is inactive before allowing the write to occur.

22.2.4 Network and Database Connection Latches

Most of these types of latches are trivial. Sometimes virtual circuit latch problems can indicate issues with shared server and dispatcher configuration parameters, and perhaps even shared or large pool configuration issues.

That is enough information about latches. In a specific environment such as an OLTP or data warehouse database, different functionality and behavior is likely to make different latch occurrences more prevalent. The next chapter will briefly examine various tools used for physical and configuration tuning of Oracle installations.

23

Tools and Utilities

There are a multitude of tools available to both monitor and tune Oracle installations. This chapter will introduce some of those tools in detail and categorize what each tool can do. It is best to explain some of the various tools graphically. Let's begin with (9*i*) Oracle Enterprise Manager and the (10*g*) Database Control.

The emphasis in the first edition of this book is on grass-roots tuning, without utilizing the tools too much. This helps to promote understanding by teaching the basics, as opposed to teaching how to use the tools without having to understand what they are actually doing. Far greater emphasis is placed on automation of tuning using tools in Oracle Database 10*g*, particularly Release 2. The Database Control has a few issues in Release 1, which appear to have been ironed out in Release 2 of Oracle 10*g* Database. This second edition has served to demonstrate these tools, including that they work or do not work, how well they work, and how useful they are. However, this second edition also includes all the grass-roots tuning without tools. The objective of this book remains to promote understanding, by teaching basics, followed by use of tools. That way, when you get to use the tools, you might have a better idea of how to solve problems. The GUI tools such as the Database Control don't really solve problems for you. However, they are easier to use and might help to indicate what is causing a performance problem much faster than something like STATSPACK would.

23.1 (9*i*) **Oracle Enterprise Manager**

Oracle Enterprise Manager, in relation to physical tuning, can be divided into two parts: (1) diagnostic, and (2) tuning tools. Diagnosis usually implies monitoring for potential problems, sometimes repairing them. Tuning and analysis can automatically repair possible performance problems.

23.1.1   Diagnostics Pack

With respect to physical tuning, the interesting parts of the diagnostics pack are as follows:

- *Event monitoring.* This allows definition, automated detection of, and potential automated *FixIt* jobs. *Fixit* jobs can automatically correct problems.

- *Lock monitoring.* This allows monitoring and resolution of locks in a database.

- *TopSessions.* This detects and displays the top best or worst performing sessions, ordered by a large number of different possible sorting parameters.

- *TopSQL.* This detects and displays the top best and worst performing SQL statements, again ordered by a large number of different possible sorting parameters.

- *Performance Manager.* Performance Manager wraps everything together, such as the details contained in the TopSessions and TopSQL tools but with extra functionality and GUI usability.

Note: The ultimate in Oracle Enterprise Manager performance monitoring is the bottleneck drilldown GUI window interface, which searches into the Oracle Database Wait Event Interface.

23.1.1.1   Event Monitoring

Event monitoring covers areas such as performance, resource usage, and how space is used, among many other topics. There is an absolute plethora of events that can be included for automated detection and potential *FixIt* action to resolve problems. Figure 23.1 shows a very small subsection of the fully user definable event detection tool. The event detection construction tool is accessible from the Event menu in the Oracle Enterprise Manager Console.

23.1.1.2   Lock Monitoring

Figure 23.2 shows lists of locks on a very busy database. The drilldown menu in Figure 23.2 shows various options, including the option to kill off

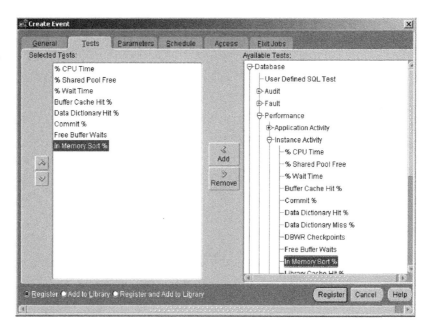

a session. Sometimes it is necessary to kill a session that causes potentially damaging problems.

23.1.1.3 TopSessions

The TopSessions tool allows ordered visualization of statistical performance information. The best or worst sessions can be displayed first. Figure 23.3 shows the first ten sessions executing the most physical reads.

23.1.1.4 TopSQL

TopSQL is similar to the TopSessions tool, where the TopSQL tool detects and displays the best or worst performing SQL statements. As with the previously mentioned tools, results can also be displayed in a large number of different possible orders. An example of TopSQL is shown in Figure 23.4.

23.1.1.5 Performance Manager

The Performance Manager is a very comprehensive tool. It allows an intensive GUI picture of an environment with every possible monitoring and performance metric imaginable. The Performance Manager appears complex, but it is very comprehensive and very easy to use.

Figure 23.5 shows the Performance Overview screen. This screen is accessible from the Oracle Enterprise Manager Console on the Tools menu.

Figure 23.2
*Monitoring and
managing locking*

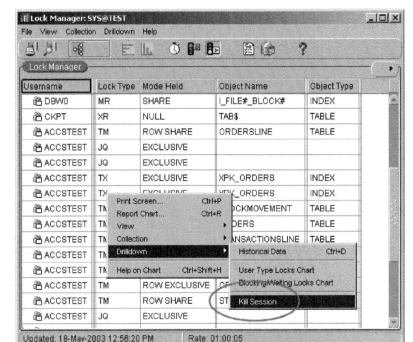

Select the Diagnostic Pack submenu. The Performance Overview interface gives an overall picture of database performance and is highly adaptable, depending on requirements and what you want to monitor.

The Performance Manager allows simple drilldown further into the separate subset areas of those shown in the Performance Overview interface. You can drilldown into the Oracle Database Wait Event Interface. The Oracle Database Wait Event Interface is a specialized section of Oracle Enterprise Manager software and will be covered in a later chapter. Figure 23.6 shows a small part of the possible types of information that can be monitored with the Performance Manager.

Figure 23.7 shows a drilldown into a screen showing latch get rates and latch miss rates.

Finally Figure 23.8 shows a detailed analysis of latches.

23.1.2 Tuning Pack

As far as physical tuning is concerned, only the Tablespace Map and Reorg Wizard tools are of interest. Other parts of the Oracle Enterprise Manager tuning pack are covered in a previous chapter.

Figure 23.3
*TopSessions
monitoring in a
specified order*

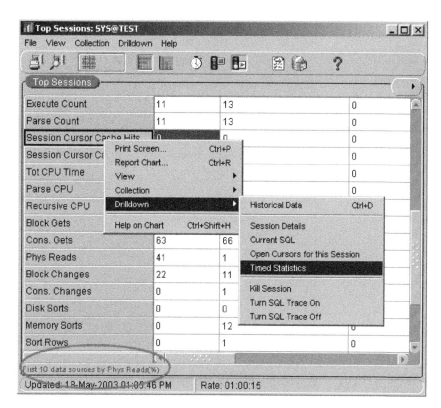

23.1.2.1   Tablespace Map and the Reorg Wizard

The Tablespace Map presents a graphical representation of physical data distribution within tablespaces. After executing a Tablespace Analysis in the INDX tablespace of my database, two indexes are recommended for reorganization, as shown in Figure 23.9.

As can be seen in the drop-down menu in Figure 23.9, various options are available:

- *Tablespace Analysis*. Analyze a tablespace for problems, such as fragmentation.

- *Reorganize Tablespace*. Execute the Reorg Wizard.

- *Reorganize Selected Segments*. Execute reorganization on selected indexes (segments) only.

Figure 23.4
TopSQL statements

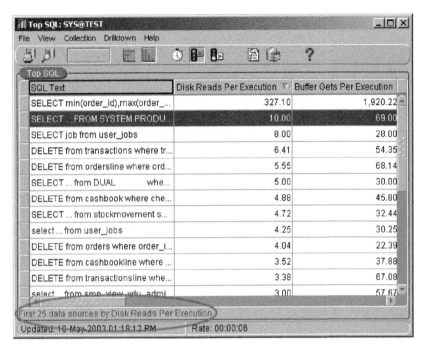

Figure 23.5
The Performance Overview tool

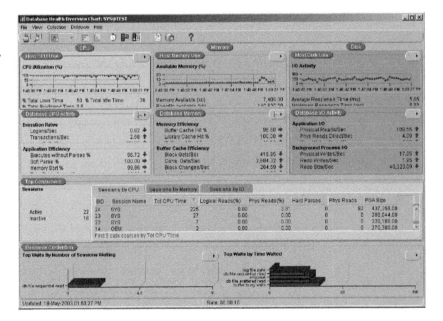

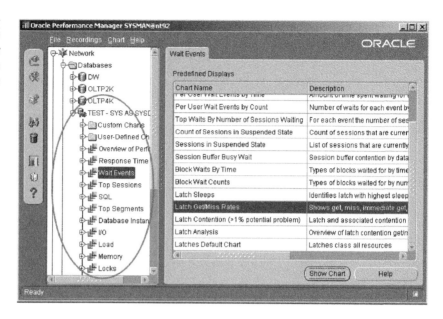

Figure 23.6
The Performance Manager main screen

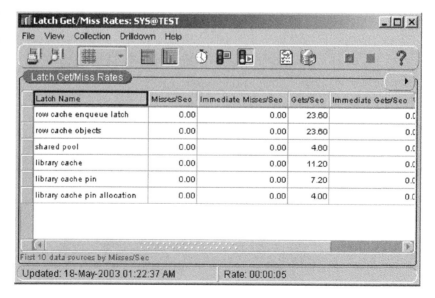

Figure 23.7
Latch get and miss rates drilldown

- ***Coalesce Free Extents***. Coalescence attempts to merge empty adjacent physical areas into single reusable chunks of disk storage space. In the past, I have not found coalescence to be particularly useful.

Figure 23.8
Latch analysis

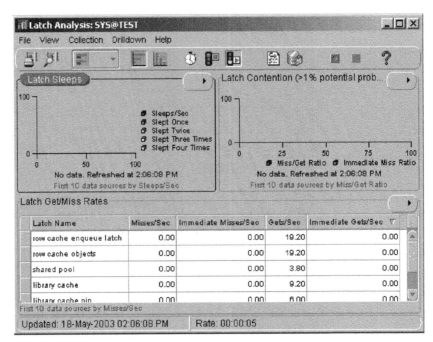

Figure 23.9
*After execution of
Tablespace Analysis*

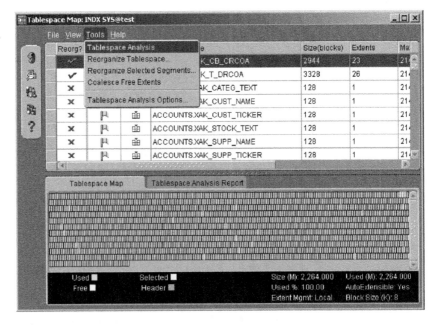

Figure 23.10 simply shows the same screen as in Figure 23.9 except with the Tablespace Analysis Report tab selected. The tablespace analysis report describes exactly why the table analysis process considers these indexes due for reorganization: fragmentation.

Figure 23.10
What should be reorganized and why

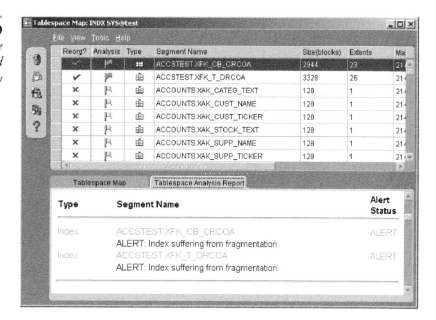

The result of execution of the Reorg Wizard and tablespace coalescence on the INDX tablespace is shown in Figure 23.11. The actual reorganization process is created as a scheduled job (instantly executed or scheduled to run in the future). The job is executed by the job control scheduling system, visible in the Oracle Enterprise Manager Console job scheduling screen.

23.1.2.2   Tools Useful for Tuning SQL Code

Oracle Enterprise Manager is a large suite of software tools used to manage and tune Oracle databases across an enterprise. The Tuning Pack contains several applications for both preemptive and reactive tuning of SQL coding in an Oracle installation:

- *Index Tuning Wizard*. This searches for inefficient indexes and makes suggestions for new indexes, removal of superfluous indexing, and changes to existing indexes.

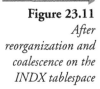

Figure 23.11
*After
reorganization and
coalescence on the
INDX tablespace*

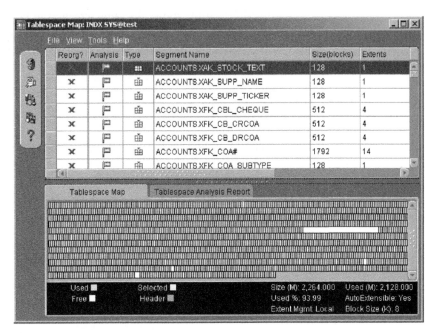

- **SQL Analyze**. This allows SQL code analysis, potential optimization, SQL statement editing, and even some capability for automated tuning.

- **Oracle Expert**. This allows recommendations and implementation of possible tuning approaches.

- **Outlines**. Outline performance assessment and management are also included in the Tuning Pack. Outlines will eventually be deprecated from a future version of Oracle Database; thus, they are not covered in this book.

Let's start by taking a look at the Index Tuning Wizard.

23.1.2.2.1   Index Tuning Wizard

The Index Tuning Wizard attempts to find inefficient indexes from a cost-based optimization perspective. Inefficient indexing was covered in a previous chapter on common sense indexing. The Index Tuning Wizard makes recommendations. These recommendations include adding new indexes, rebuilding current indexes, and index type changes such as changing from a Bitmap to a BTree.

Any changes with the database can warrant running the Index Tuning Wizard. If your database consistently changes over time, this tool could be executed periodically.

On a more practical note, using a tool such as this to automatically regenerate indexes can be detrimental to performance in itself. Interrogation of database statistics should suffice to interrogate indexing capabilities. Also, when I have used this tool in the past, recommendations to create new and rebuild existing indexes have been somewhat *wild* to say the least. I would propose extreme caution when taking heed of recommendations reported by this tool. In general, OLTP systems are highly active, and any index rebuilds should be executed with the ONLINE option in order to avoid application errors. The mere act of rebuilding an index can cause a severe performance hit. For an OLTP database, any recommendation to change an index type from a BTree to any other index type should probably be completely ignored. Bitmap indexes are not really useful for anything but read-only environments. I have even heard complaints about Bitmap index use in data warehouses. Additionally, BTree indexing will only become inefficient when skewed. Skewing is generally a result of data content, and not much can be done about that unless the data model can be altered. The only case where BTree indexes should occasionally be rebuilt is when a table undergoes a lot of deletion. Deleted leaf blocks are not reclaimed in BTree indexes.

I executed the Index Tuning Wizard on my highly active database. It appears from the following example that the Index Tuning Wizard searches through past SQL code statements, attempting to match WHERE, ORDER BY, and GROUP BY clauses against indexes. If an index does not exist, it suggests creating one. The composite index suggested for creation in the following example is not strictly necessary. Let's examine this example. Figure 23.12 shows the initial screen for the Index Tuning Wizard.

The next screen shown in Figure 23.13 allows an option of selecting different database types. Index requirements between the two extremes of OLTP and data warehousing are totally different. OLTP databases require exact hits on single rows. Data warehouses require retrieval of large numbers of rows at once.

Then either a single schema or multiple schemas can be selected for index analysis, as shown in Figure 23.14.

Figure 23.15 shows a recommendation to modify an index on the Transactions table.

Figure 23.12
*The Index Tuning
Wizard*

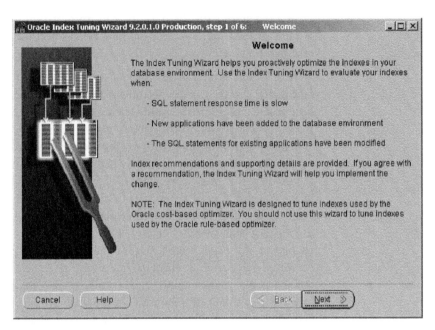

Figure 23.13
*Select the
application type*

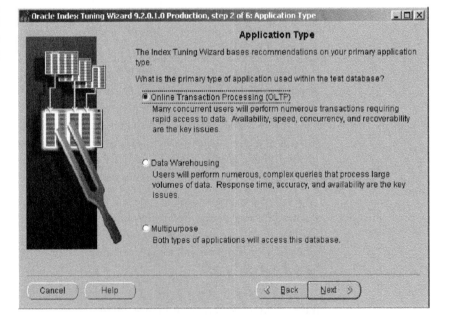

The change recommended in Figure 23.15 is suggested as being altered from a single column to a multiple column index. The suggestion is sensible because, as shown in Index Tuning Wizard output, included later in

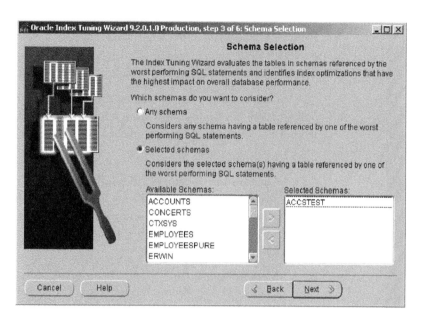

Figure 23.14
Select schemas to analyze

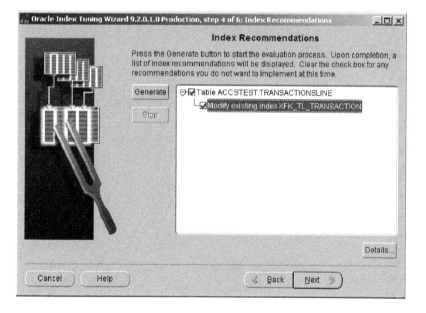

Figure 23.15
The Index Tuning Wizard makes suggestions

this chapter, this index is accessed by a SQL statement using the two columns suggested for the composite index. However, this index is a foreign key index on the TransactionsLine table pointing to the primary key on the Transactions table. This index can absolutely not be altered in my Accounts schema.

Note: Oracle Database does not create indexes on foreign key constraints automatically.

Oracle Database is not aware that this index is actually a single column–only foreign key index. Or, more succinctly, the Index Tuning Wizard ignores foreign keys. This recommendation is poor for two further reasons:

1.   The number of values in the suffix (second column) of the composite index is minimal. As a result, indexing the composite would have little effect on any SQL accessing both columns at once. The single column index would suffice for good performance.

2.   My application code simply does not require a composite index in this case; a composite index is totally inappropriate.

The following script shows the Index Tuning Wizard output, suggesting why the index should be changed. Note the composite column access in the WHERE clause:

```
A change to an existing B*-tree index is recommended for the
table ACCSTEST.TRANSACTIONSLINE.


Index before recommendations
----------------------------


TRANSACTION_ID

Recommended columns
-------------------


TRANSACTION_ID
     There was at least one reference by an equality operator.

STOCKMOVEMENT_ID
     There was at least one reference by an equality operator.
     There was at least one reference by SELECT, ORDER-BY or
GROUP-BY
     clauses.
     Number of rows in the table: 1551030
```

```
Distinct values in the index: 1551030

******************* SQL Statement Information
*******************

The recommendation above is based on the following SQL:
```

SQL: **SELECT stockmovement_seq.NEXTVAL, sm.stock_id,**
      sm.qty * -1 qty, sm.price, :b1
   FROM stockmovement sm
   WHERE EXISTS (SELECT stockmovement_id
                  FROM transactionsline
                  WHERE stockmovement_id =
                      sm.stockmovement_id
                  AND transaction_id = :b2)

The Index Tuning Wizard also produces the code necessary to regenerate the index. Performing these DDL statements in a highly available OLTP database is a very bad idea because the ONLINE option is excluded. If this table is large, which it is, and there is access to the table between dropping and completion of the CREATE INDEX statement, and SQL code accesses the index—then any rows not yet built in the index will simply not be found by the SQL statements:

```
--CREATE Index Recommendations
DROP INDEX ACCSTEST.XFK_TL_TRANSACTION;
CREATE INDEX ACCSTEST.XFK_TL_TRANSACTION
    ON ACCSTEST.TRANSACTIONSLINE
        (TRANSACTION_ID,
         STOCKMOVEMENT_ID)
    LOGGING
    INITRANS 2
    MAXTRANS 255
    TABLESPACE INDX
    PCTFREE 10
    STORAGE (
        INITIAL 1024K
        NEXT 1024K
        PCTINCREASE 0
        MINEXTENTS 1
        MAXEXTENTS 2147483645) ONLINE;
```

I have grave doubts about the usefulness of the Index Tuning Wizard in any highly active OLTP database. Most OLTP databases are required to be available permanently. Perhaps this tool would be more useful for data warehouses? For the CREATE INDEX statement shown previously, at least the ONLINE option should be used. To reiterate, the ONLINE option was not generated for the statement created by the Index Tuning Wizard; I added it. Additionally, better availability would be gained by using the ALTER INDEX statement with the REBUILD and ONLINE options. ALTER INDEX REBUILD ONLINE would never create a situation of the index not existing. In the preceding script, the index does not exist between the DROP and CREATE statements.

Over the years, the parts and pieces in Oracle Enterprise Manager have become much better as tuning tools. The problem with making index recommendations in this context is that indexing is abstracted from applications and data model to a database engine. The database engine is not an expert on what the applications are attempting to achieve. And it should not be expected to be an expert either.

23.1.2.2.2   SQL Analyze

Tuning SQL code is one of the most effective methods of tuning an Oracle installation and its attached applications. However, tuning of SQL code can sometimes be difficult and very time consuming. SQL code embedded in applications can involve application code changes, which may not be too difficult, but may involve resistance from developers and quite understandably so.

Developers are, of course, correct to resist any code changes. Code changes can cause a stable application to rapidly become very unstable. In a production environment, the cliché *if it works, don't fix it* holds true in many cases. Additionally, tuning of SQL code can require that the personnel tuning that code have extensive knowledge of all aspects of the database and any applications. This is often a difficult, if not impossible, scenario.

SQL Analyze is a tool that can be used to assist in tuning SQL code by allowing SQL code analysis, potential optimization, SQL statement editing, and even some capability for automated tuning. Allowing SQL Analyze to automatically tune SQL code could be risky. In the past, when using automated tuning features in Oracle Enterprise Manager, I have found the more automated aspects to be somewhat dubious at best. Making automated changes in production environments is contrary to the approach of most database administrators. The unpredictability of automated changes is relatively unknown. Database administrators are generally exceedingly cautious and for good reason. Production databases are often required to be running constantly, and any potential changes could cause loss of service. For most OLTP database installations, down time is absolutely not acceptable. Customers can get very upset. When customers are upset, they go to the competition.

SQL Analyze can be used to do a large number of things. SQL Analyze allows access to initialization parameters, current cache TopSQL (hardest hitting SQL statements), plus stored historical SQL statements. In general, SQL Analyze can be divided into two main sections. The first as shown in Figure 23.16 shows the analysis stage.

Figure 23.16
*SQL Analyze and
the analysis stage*

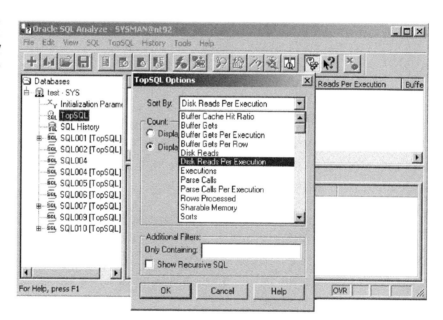

As can be seen in Figure 23.16, the analysis stage allows retrieval of the worst-performing SQL statements. Take note of all the different sort ordering options. The sort orders are consistent with SQL Trace and TKPROF output sort orders, as described in a previous chapter. Disk reads per execution is the default because it shows disk access for the execution of an SQL statement.

Figure 23.17 shows a selection of TopSQL selected SQL statements in the top right box, sorted in order of disk reads per execution. Note access to configuration parameters in the bottom right box.

The second main section of SQL Analyze has rich capabilities and is very useful indeed, as seen in Figures 23.18 through 23.23. SQL Analyze

Figure 23.17
*SQL Analyze single
SQL statement
assessment and
testing*

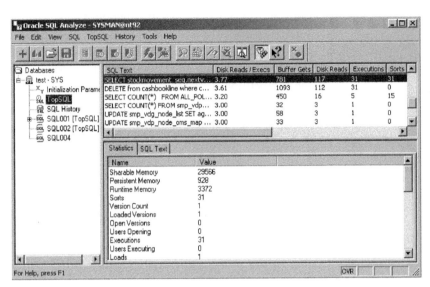

Figure 23.17
*SQL Analyze single
SQL statement
assessment and
testing*

allows for numerous actions and assessments on individual SQL code statements, providing a GUI into both query plans and execution statistics.

Figure 23.18 shows the SQL code text in the bottom right box for a highlighted SQL statement.

Figure 23.18
*SQL Analyze SQL
text display*

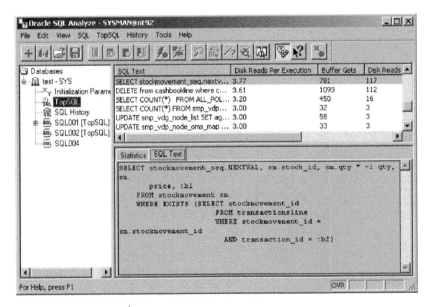

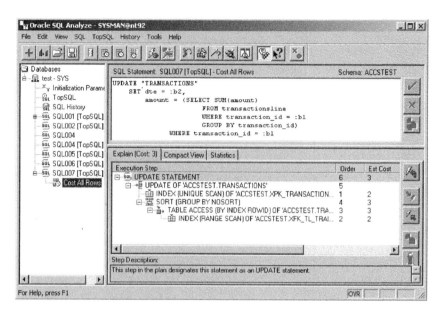

Figure 23.19 shows the EXPLAIN PLAN command query plan for an SQL statement.

Figure 23.20 shows the ability in SQL Analyze for index recommendations.

Figure 23.21 shows that a query plan can be assessed for all optimizer modes: RULE, FIRST_ROWS, ALL_ROWS, and CHOOSE. This allows testing of different modes of optimization.

Figure 23.22 shows menu access routes to the Virtual Index Wizard, the Hint Wizard, and the SQL Tuning Wizard. These tools are extremely useful for doing SQL code tuning, interactively and with ease of use.

Having used SQL Analyze quite extensively, I was rather enthused with its very rich capabilities. I am still noticing a few bugs, even in Oracle 9*i* Database, but nothing debilitating. SQL Analyze can be used to compare different versions of the same SQL statement, as shown in Figure 23.23. This multiple SQL statement functionality is completely interactive and changes as the SQL programmer changes things.

Figure 23.24 and Figure 23.25 show two query plans for a rather *busy* SQL join statement. Note the difference in cost between the ALL_ROWS and FIRST_ROWS Optimizer mode versions, respectively. The ALL_ROWS version is much lower in cost because the mutable join is retrieving all the rows in all the tables. This is more apparent when examin-

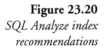

Figure 23.20
SQL Analyze index recommendations

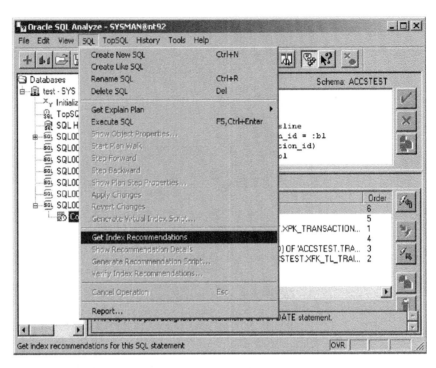

Figure 23.21
SQL Analyze query plan assessment

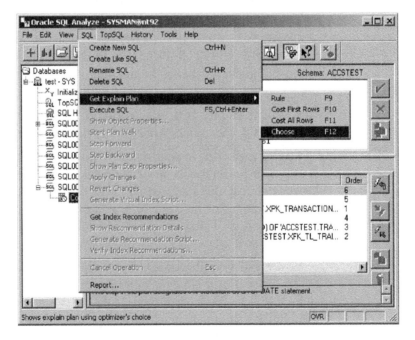

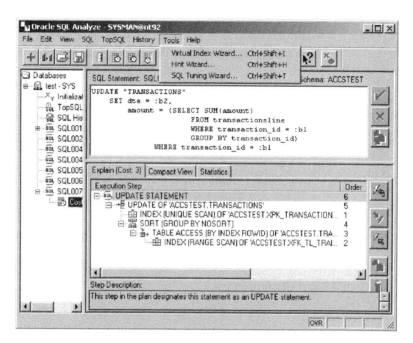

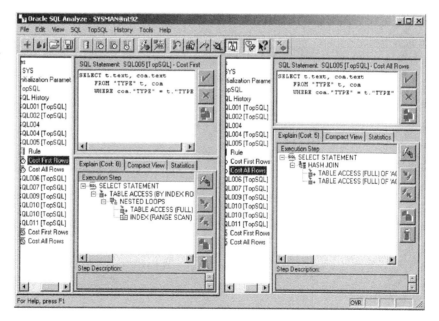

ing the query plans, showing that the FIRST_ROWS option in Figure 23.25 uses all nested loop joins with no hash joins. Hash joins are efficient for joining large row sets, and nested loop joins are better for joining a very small row set with another small or a large row set. Forcing FIRST_ROWS optimization as in Figure 23.25 makes the optimizer think it is not accessing many rows, and thus it defaults to nested loop joins.

Figure 23.24
An ALL_ROWS optimizer query plan

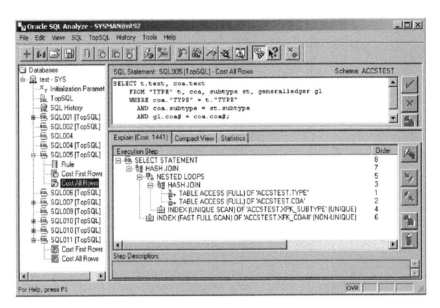

Figure 23.25
A FIRST_ROWS optimizer query plan

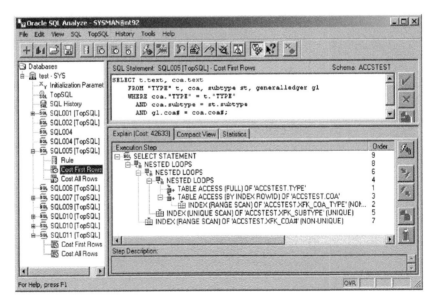

SQL Analyze is very rich in functionality. Spotlight and TOAD are non-Oracle tools of the same caliber with similar capabilities, but SQL

Analyze is a richer environment with respect to tuning SQL code. The only problem using any tool within Oracle Enterprise Manager is that you need to be a rocket scientist to set it up properly. Keep trying. Practice makes perfect! Parts of Oracle Enterprise Manager are extremely useful and informative.

Additionally, in the past Oracle Enterprise Manager using the Management Server has had serious security issues. In the past Oracle Enterprise Manager has been bug ridden and known to induce a certain amount of frustration, sometimes most immense frustration. These problems were mostly resolved by Release 2 of Oracle 9*i* Database.

What can SQL Analyze be used for in general?

- It can be used to search for and change poorly performing SQL code.

- It can be used to assess existing indexing.

- TopSQL can be used to show high-impact SQL statements from both current cache and historical SQL code. SQL code statements can be sorted on a large number of criteria, much like SQL Trace files can be sorted with TKPROF.

- A high-impact SQL statement can be selected. That selected statement can be analyzed in its entirety, including query plans. SQL statements can even be imported or typed in from scratch and tested.

- Query plans and execution statistics can be generated for all potential optimizer modes.

- A Hint Wizard allows suggested and tested alterations using hints.

- Virtual indexing and index-recommended alterations and additions can be utilized to produce varying query plans.

- There is some automated change capability in SQL Analyze. My experience with Oracle Enterprise Manager in general makes it necessary to recommend not executing any automation-type features, which change anything in the database without a database administrator being made aware of potential changes before changes are made.

- It allows comparisons between different query plans for the same SQL statement both in textual and graphical form. This is a really *cute* feature but not necessarily all that useful.

- It allows a step-by-step walk through of query plans giving a detailed, easy-to-understand explanation of each step.

23.1.2.2.3 Oracle Expert

Oracle Expert is a tool allowing recommendations and implementation of possible tuning approaches. This tool applies to SQL code tuning plus physical and configuration tuning. In this chapter, we will concentrate on the SQL code tuning aspects of Oracle Expert. As far as SQL code tuning is concerned, Oracle Expert can produce what is called an Optimal Index Analysis. An excerpt of one of these analyses executed on the Accounts schema is shown following:

```
-------------------------------------------------------------------
--  DROP Index Recommendations
-------------------------------------------------------------------
DROP INDEX ACCSTEST.XFK_CBL_CHEQUE;
DROP INDEX ACCSTEST.XFK_O_TYPE;
DROP INDEX ACCSTEST.XAK_O_TYPE_CUSTOMER;
DROP INDEX ACCSTEST.XFK_OL_ORDERS;
DROP INDEX ACCSTEST.XFK_TL_TRANSACTION;
```

Note that all the Oracle Expert has advised that I do is to drop foreign key indexes from the Accounts schema. Those foreign key indexes are not accessed by any SQL code. Shriek! That is definitely not an intelligent idea. Why? (1) Foreign key indexes will not necessarily be used by SQL code, and (2) removing indexes from foreign keys will create a lot of locking problems and probably result in some severe performance issues. Foreign key indexes are used by Oracle Database internal referential integrity checks. Those referential integrity checks are very likely ignored by Oracle Expert because no explicit SQL code is involved. This is not good. As already mentioned before in this chapter, be very careful using Oracle Expert in this particular respect.

The Oracle Expert on screen visual of the previous script is shown in Figure 23.26.

That's enough about Oracle Enterprise Manager. The best use of Oracle Enterprise Manager for physical and configuration tuning is diagnosis and analysis of potential bottlenecks using the GUI drilldown access paths into the Oracle Database Wait Event Interface. The Oracle Database Wait Event Interface will be covered in detail in the next chapter. Before that, we need to examine other tools, most especially use of the Database Control. The Database Control is a browser-based, very much updated version of the Oracle Enterprise Manager tool.

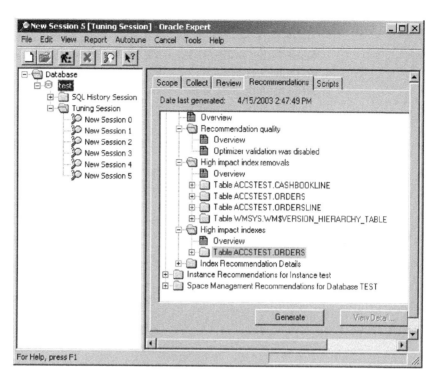

Figure 23.26
Oracle Expert recommendations for the Accounts schema

23.2 (10*g*) The Database Control

All the toys and tricks you have seen in the previous section (9*i*) Oracle Enterprise Manager) cover the equivalent of the Database Control in Oracle 9*i* Database. This section examines the same information, but using the updated Database Control browser-based GUI.

Note: (10*g*) The Oracle Enterprise Manager is now a client-only tool and is not installed with server software. Commercial DBAs are unlikely to use server software to manage their databases running on a server computer. Thus, the Oracle Enterprise Manager Console tool also no longer includes diagnostics and performance options in its menus.

Most important to note about the Database Control is that it is a tool run in a web interface. In other words, it runs in a browser across a network. So, how do we get the Database Control up and running? In Oracle 10*g* Database, use the following URL:

```
http://<hostname>:1158/em
```

Note: Other ports used may be 5500 and 5600. The port number depends on which release of Oracle 10*g* you have and how many Oracle databases exist on your database server computer. The portlist.ini configuration file contains port number settings for various tools, including iSQL*Plus and the Database Control.

The Database Control can be used to perform a multitude of functions against a database, including general administration, maintenance, performance, and even tasks such as backup and recovery. The main screens in the Database Control are the Home, Performance, Administration, and Maintenance screens.

The Home screen provides information about the database and the Oracle installation. Included are CPU usage, active database sessions, recovery capabilities, space usage efficiency, and diagnostics. This is all shown in Figure 23.27.

Figure 23.27
Database Control Home screen current database activity

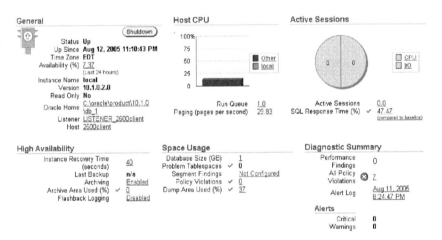

In addition, the Home screen contains alerts, indicating both critical alerts and less significant warnings. There are also various related links and drilldown options. All this is in shown Figure 23.28.

The Performance screen shows performance information, both good and bad, as shown in Figure 23.29. The objective is to indicate problem areas and allow acting to define a problem further, using drilldown links (the overlaid portion of Figure 23.29), such as TopSessions, TopSQL, and Database Locks.

Figure 23.28
*Database Control
Home screen alerts
and warnings*

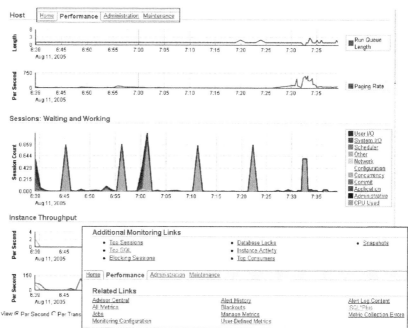

Figure 23.29
*Database Control
Performance screen*

The Administration screen provides a multitude of options for administration functionality, as shown in Figure 23.30.

The Maintenance screen provides comprehensive maintenance access to database utilities, backup, and recovery, plus deployment activities. This is all shown in Figure 23.31.

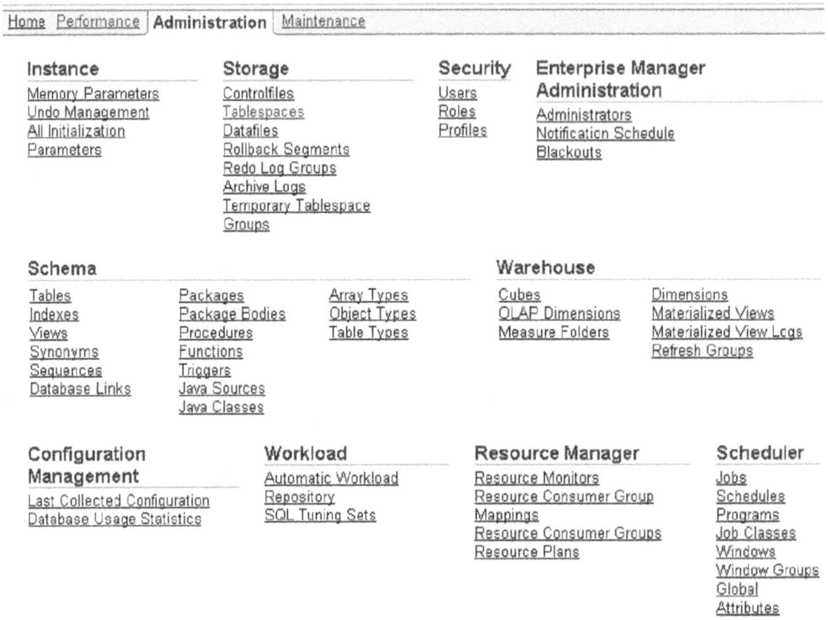

Figure 23.30
Database Control
Administration
screen

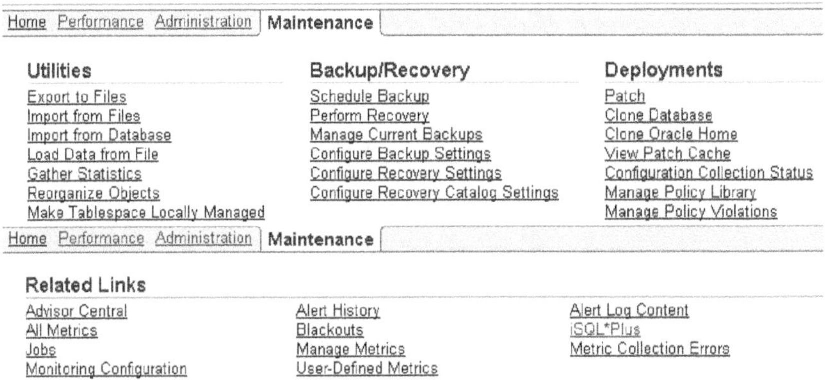

Home Performance | **Administration** | Maintenance

Instance   **Storage**   **Security**   **Enterprise Manager**
Memory Parameters   Controlfiles   Users   **Administration**
Undo Management   Tablespaces   Roles   Administrators
All Initialization   Datafiles   Profiles   Notification Schedule
Parameters   Rollback Segments   Blackouts
                         Redo Log Groups
                         Archive Logs
                         Temporary Tablespace
                         Groups

Schema   **Warehouse**

Tables   Packages   Array Types   Cubes   Dimensions
Indexes   Package Bodies   Object Types   OLAP Dimensions   Materialized Views
Views   Procedures   Table Types   Measure Folders   Materialized View Logs
Synonyms   Functions   Refresh Groups
Sequences   Triggers
Database Links Java Sources
                Java Classes

Configuration   **Workload**   **Resource Manager**   **Scheduler**
Management   Automatic Workload   Resource Monitors   Jobs
Last Collected Configuration Repository   Resource Consumer Group   Schedules
Database Usage Statistics SQL Tuning Sets   Mappings   Programs
                                                         Resource Consumer Groups   Job Classes
                                                         Resource Plans   Windows
                                                                                      Window Groups
                                                                                      Global
                                                                                      Attributes

Figure 23.31
Database Control
Maintenance
screen

Home Performance Administration | **Maintenance** |

Utilities   **Backup/Recovery**   **Deployments**
Export to Files   Schedule Backup   Patch
Import from Files   Perform Recovery   Clone Database
Import from Database   Manage Current Backups   Clone Oracle Home
Load Data from File   Configure Backup Settings   View Patch Cache
Gather Statistics   Configure Recovery Settings   Configuration Collection Status
Reorganize Objects   Configure Recovery Catalog Settings Manage Policy Library
Make Tablespace Locally Managed   Manage Policy Violations

Home Performance Administration | **Maintenance** |

Related Links

Advisor Central   Alert History   Alert Log Content
All Metrics   Blackouts   iSQL*Plus
Jobs   Manage Metrics   Metric Collection Errors
Monitoring Configuration   User-Defined Metrics

This book is a book about performance tuning, and so we will continue to focus on performance tuning.

One of the purposes of the Database Control is to attempt to automate, making the job of a DBA easier. Part of that automation process is that of building a small amount of artificial intelligence, in the form of an expert system, into the Database Control.

Note: An expert system is essentially the implementation of expert knowledge into a computer. Expert knowledge can be used to assess the state of a computer system, similar to the way that an expert could.

Some performance activities can be somewhat managed by the Database Control. However, the Database Control is a far cry from the experience of an expert-level Oracle Database performance tuner. What is interesting is that the Database Control is actually an attempt at what appears to be an expert system for automated performance tuning of an Oracle database. An apt expression for this technology would be "Watch this space!" and keep an eye on future developments. This stuff will improve gradually.

23.2.1 Proactive Maintenance

Once again, proactive maintenance is really all about setting up the Database Control to predict and track performance problems. The objective is to prevent critical problems before they occur and damage a database. This is contrary to reactive maintenance, which is reacting to a problem after it has occurred. Much of proactive activity is related to performance tuning a database in one way or another.

Proactive maintenance can be managed from within the Database Control, including areas such as warnings and alerts, metrics for determining thresholds of when and how warnings and alerts occur, and finally all sorts of advice from various Database Control tuning advisory tools. There is also a default configuration within the advisors and metrics provided when you create a database. For most databases, it is unlikely that you will ever need to change any of the defaults set up in the Database Control. Let's begin by examining the various advice tools, under the Advisor Central section within the Database Control.

23.2.2 Performance Architecture of the Database Control

The performance architecture of the Database Control is all about how to set up the Database Control to do stuff for you. That is all about metrics. Metrics are measures of desired performance and checks against those measures by the current state of a database. The Database Control will automatically monitor the state of your database against a desired performance target. If there are problems, or even expected problems, the Database Control will give you warnings and perhaps even indications of critical errors that require immediate attention.

23.2.2.1   Statistics Automation

Gathering of statistics is partially automated in Oracle 10*g* Database. Part of the reason for this is that it has to be, because the optimizer is now solely cost based. Cost-based optimization requires some statistical content to produce useful query plans.

Oracle 10*g* Database statistics gathering is intended to be centered around the Database Control. Much of the automation process is automatic SQL tuning. Automatic SQL tuning is new to Oracle 10*g* Database. The optimizer can be switched from normal mode into a tuning mode. That tuning mode can consume large amounts of resources and because of that is largely intended for use with complicated and long-running queries only. Automated SQL tuning can be performed manually using commands executed from within SQL*Plus, but it is recommended to use the Database Control. Using the Database Control is much easier. Automated SQL tuning involves the following parts:

- ***The AWR.*** The Automatic Workload Repository (AWR) is used for automatic collection of statistics.

- ***The ADDM.*** The Automatic Database Diagnostic Monitor (ADDM) is used for automatic performance diagnostics.

- (10*g*) The ADDM has replaced STATSPACK.

- ***Automatic SQL Tuning.*** Automatic SQL tuning uses the SQL tuning advisor, SQL tuning sets, and SQL profiles.

- ***SQL Access Advisor.*** SQL Access Advisor is used for data warehouses and materialized view analysis.

The AWR takes statistical snapshots of a database. The Statistics Management section, on the Administration screen, has a link called Automatic Workload Repository. Figure 23.32 shows the screen in the Database Control to manage the configuration of the AWR.

As shown in Figure 23.32, there is not really a need to explain all the little-bitty details in a book such as this. Essentially you can configure the AWR to collect statistics on a periodic basis. The AWR collects statistics,

Figure 23.32
Managing AWR configuration

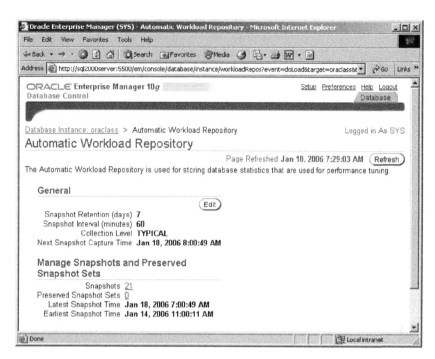

just like STATSPACK is used to periodically collect statistics in a scheduled job.

Snapshots collected by the AWR can be used by the ADDM to analyze and make assessments of what could or should be altered. The objective is to make the database more efficient. The ADDM does the same thing that the STATSPACK reporter does, comparing multiple snapshots with each other. The objective is to find bottlenecks that cause performance problems.

Statistics that are gathered by the AWR are as follows:

- *Object statistics*. These are objects such as tables and indexes.

- *Active session history (ASH)*. Use of the word history implies activity of recent sessions.

- *High-impact SQL*. These are SQL statements causing high impact on resources.

- *System statistics*. These are system-level statistics in V$SYSSTAT and V$SESSTAT performance views.

- *Time model system statistics*. These are V$SYS_TIME_MODEL and V$SESS_TIME_MODEL performance views.

The ADDM will then use snapshots taken by the AWR to make statistical comparisons and ultimately to produce reports from multiple AWR snapshots of the database. Execute the ADDM by clicking the Run ADDM Now button, found on the Performance screen. The ADDM is searching for these types of issues:

- *CPU time.* Excessive CPU activity can be for a variety of reasons.

- *Cache sizing.* The sizing of SGA and PGA buffers should be monitored. Arbitrarily increasing SGA sizes can tend to temporarily hide problems rather than resolve them.

- *Heavy I/O.* High I/O activity is not necessarily normal for an OLTP database but is normal for a data warehouse.

- *High-consumption SQL.* SQL statements can cause problems, or they can simply be doing a large amount of work. In other words, some SQL statements are expected to make heavy use of resources. This area would include PL/SQL and Java procedures, in addition to simple SQL queries, DML statements, and DDL statements.

- *Configuration issues.* Configuration is a large area, involving physical aspects such as file sizing and archives. There are also configuration issues where there may be inappropriate parameter settings, producing problems such as concurrency, hot blocking, and locking issues.

- *Anything busy.* Anything that is very busy is subject to scrutiny, but that could be normal for that specific installation.

Some 99% of what is returned by an ADDM report should be self-explanatory to someone reading a book such as this one. Figure 23.33 shows the screen resulting from the execution of an ADDM report. The Informational Findings section is what is important.

As you can see in Figure 23.33, my busy Accounts schema database has quite a few problems that the ADDM *thinks* should be addressed. Also notice that each of the issues shown in Figure 23.33 is links. You can drill-down directly into those links and get more specific information of what a problem is and what may be causing that particular problem, and perhaps it could be resolved. Figure 23.34 shows the drilldown screen from the link shown in Figure 23.33. The link in Figure 23.33 states that *SQL statements consuming significant database time were found.* As can be seen in Figure

Figure 23.33
The results of an ADDM report

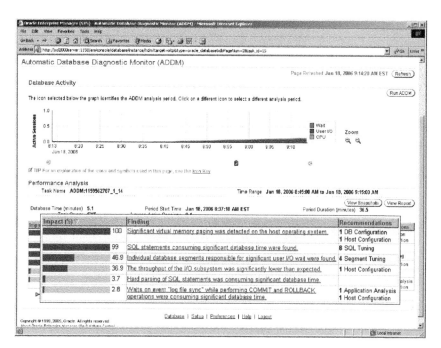

23.34, the drilldown gives you more detailed information with respect to this specific issue.

Figure 23.34
Drilldown in the ADDM report

As shown in Figure 23.34 there are links in this drilldown screen as well. This means you can drilldown even further.

Using the AWR and ADDM tools is mostly common sense. One of the really good points about the Database Control (and Oracle Enterprise Manager in the past) is the help files. Use the help files. They are an excellent training resource. STATSPACK will be examined in a later chapter, and then you will gain a detailed understanding of what is going on behind the scenes of the AWR and the ADDM in the Database Control.

23.2.2.2   Performance Metrics

The Database Control includes things called metrics. By definition, a metric is a measure of something. A metric has a threshold, where the threshold is the measure above which we do not want to see a statistic go. Statistics can be assessed against those metric thresholds. A statistic is a real picture of something in the database. A metric and its threshold are a picture of what we would like those statistics to be. If statistics are wildly different than a metric threshold, then it is assumed there is a problem. This is where the Database Control gets a little bit of artificial intelligence in the form of an expert system.

What is wonderful about the Database Control and Oracle 10*g* Database is that all the metrics, and their thresholds, are set up by default. They can be changed, but essentially there is an expert system already in place whenever a database is created. So, for a simple installation in a small company, the Database Control can provide a tremendous advantage. Problems can be spotted even before they occur, and warnings (or errors) are sent to the Home page of the Database Control (email and pagers can also be used). Administrators can then resolve issues before they occur, preferably without the expense of expert Oracle Database tuning help. The problem with not needing expert tuning help is that the Database Control can tell you what the problems are, but how to resolve those problems is another story. That may very well require expert-level help.

To view all the metrics in the Database Control, go to the bottom of the Performance page and click the All Metrics link. If you want to change threshold values (be very careful), click the Manage Metrics link. Thus, whenever some statistic or activity exceeds a threshold value, a warning or error will be returned to the Home screen of the Database Control.

Note: You have already read and hopefully understood the inner details of much of what is contained within the Database Control by reading the previous chapters in this book. This is why this chapter is toward the end of this book. The Database Control brings all this stuff together in place. The advantage of the Database Control is that it tells you that a problem exists. The disadvantage is that it doesn't necessarily tell you how to solve problems. Watch this space! It should improve.

One more thing about metrics: you can even create you own custom metrics for a database. There is a link at the bottom of the Performance screen called User-Defined Metrics.

23.2.2.2.1 Baseline Metrics

In addition to the default metrics set up for a database, there are also baseline metrics. What is a baseline metric? The answer is very simple. Multiple automated collections of statistics, over a period of time, when the database is stable, can be used to collect baseline metric values. Those baseline metric values become the actual metric measures for a specific database when that database is operating normally.

Note: Baseline metrics allow for customized measures to be measured against by the current statistical state of a database.

Metric baselines configuration can be arranged in various ways, including a moving window or a static period of time. A moving window will establish values relative to the current date. A static time slot will establish values once and then use those static metric baselines forever. A moving window is appropriate for most databases where data changes over time.

23.2.2.2.2 Metric Thresholds

Metrics work against thresholds. As already stated, a threshold is a value that, when exceeded, may indicate some kind of problem. Threshold values can be customized for specific environments. For example, if you have a Unix script that automatically destroys archive log files when an archive disk area is 95% full, there is not much point in a metric sending you a critical error when that same archive disk area is 80% full.

Thresholds can be either a specific value or a percentage. An alert can even be produced when there is insufficient data (the computer gets to guess). The detail of thresholds is very simple:

■ *Warning level*. The alert is a warning on the Home screen.

■ *Critical level*. The alert is a critical error on the Home screen. Do something about these issues quickly.

■ *Occurrences*. An alert can be allowed to occur a number of times before it is created as a warning or error in the Home screen.

23.2.3   Advice Performance Tools

The advice performance tools were available in past versions of Oracle Database as specialized views. These views were accessible using one of the SQL*Plus tools. In my opinion those tools in Oracle 9*i* Database were a little bit comical. They were not really useful at all. However, in Oracle 10*g* you can access advisors and find plenty of good advice by using the Database Control.

Get to the advisors by clicking the Advisor Central link at the bottom left of the Database Control Home page. The advisor central screen is shown in Figure 23.35, allowing access to numerous advisory tools.

Figure 23.35
Central Advisor screen access to all the advisor tools

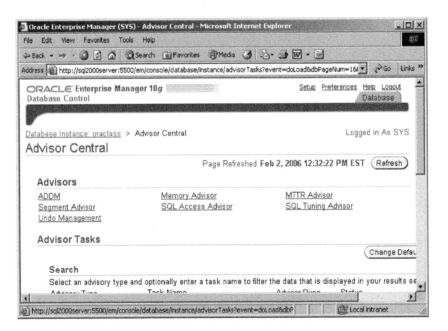

The different advisor tools can be briefly described as follows:

- *ADDM*. This advisor performs automated diagnostics by comparing multiple statistical snapshots taken against the database. The AWR collects those snapshots. Both the AWR and ADDM tools are covered in Chapter 13, so we won't go into them again in this chapter.

- *Segment Advisor*. This advisor searches for, automatically detects, and posts warnings and alerts for segment issues. A segment is essentially the purely physical I/O and disk aspects of a database object, such as a table.

- *Undo Management (Undo Advisor)*. This tool advises as to the optimal configuration of automated undo.

- *Memory Advisor*. This warns and alerts with respect to potential instance recovery, potential media recovery, and potential flashback recovery.

- *SQL Access Advisor*. This tool is generally used for materialized view analysis, usually in data warehouses.

- *SQL Tuning Advisor*. This performs automated SQL tuning activities using the SQL Tuning Advisor, SQL tuning sets, and SQL profiles.

- *Mean Time to Recovery (MTTR) Advisor*. This advises on the usage and sizing of the different memory buffers, including the entire SGA and session connection memory (the PGA).

23.2.3.1   The Segment Advisor

The Segment Advisor tells you about disk space, how it is used, how it should not be used, and what you might want to alter to help everything run smoothly. Of particular interest are shrinkage, fragmentation, growth, capacity planning, row chaining, and row migration. The primary focus is forecasting. Proactive maintenance is all about forecasting and perhaps preventing running out of disk space before it happens. Running out of disk space can crash a database because it has no space to write changes to disk.

The segment advisor consists of a number of separate steps:

- *Scope*. Scope allows definition of what you want advice on, such as tables or tablespaces.

- *Objects*. Having selected what kind of things to analyze (the scope of analysis), you can select exactly which tables to analyze. This of course assumes you selected tables as the scope of your selection.

- *Schedule*. You can schedule a segment advisory analysis to execute at a future point in time. You can also accept the default and execute the advisor immediately.

- *Review*. This step allows you to make sure that what you selected in the previous three steps is what you actually want to do.

Note: When a scheduled job is submitted, it is displayed as being in various states, such as CREATED or COMPLETED.

Get into the segment advisor by clicking the Segment Advisor link on the Central Advisor page. The steps listed here are all intuitive and easy enough to use and understand without need for further explanation and waffling on my part.

23.2.3.2   Undo Management (Undo Advisor)

The Undo Advisor works best with automated undo. The Undo Advisor will help you with the settings for automated undo configuration parameters, including retention and tablespace sizing.

Automated undo has removed the need for complex maintenance of manual rollback segments. Automated undo allows rollback of transactions, recovery of aborted and partly completed transactions, and some recovery. Additionally, undo space allows for read consistency. Read consistency implies that if one user makes a change without committing or rolling back, then only the user who made the change can see that change. Other users will see data the way it was before the change was made, until the change is committed. Most database engines function by making changes physically in the database as soon as the change is made. The execution of a COMMIT or ROLLBACK command simply removes the potential for rollback. This is the most efficient method of physical database update because it is assumed that far more data is committed than is ever rolled back. This is a perfectly sensible assumption. Thus, read consistency is very important to a relational database.

Click the Undo Management link on the Central Advisor page. The first page you get will be the Undo Management screen. To get advice on undo space, click the Undo Advisor button at the top right of the window. You will see a graphic as shown in Figure 23.36. This graphic will have textual callouts on it, with recommendations for changes to undo space configuration.

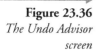

Figure 23.36
*The Undo Advisor
screen*

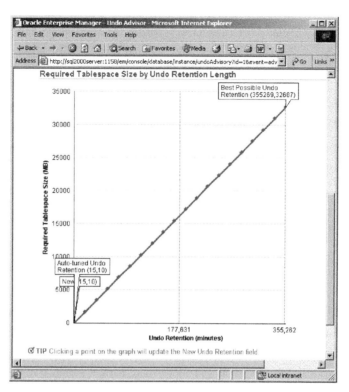

23.2.3.3 The Memory Advisor

The Memory Advisor page is split into advisors for both SGA memory and PGA memory. The SGA is made up of various buffers, including the shared pool and the database buffer cache. PGA is the session connection memory that is shared by connections to the database server. PGA manages memory operations on a database server, such as sorting, creating bitmaps, and creating hash tables.

Let's briefly remind ourselves about the contents of SGA and PGA memory areas. The SGA consists of the following configuration parameters:

- *Shared pool*. This contains the dictionary cache and the library cache. The dictionary of a relational database contains all system metadata plus application tables, indexes, materialized views, and so on. The library is all the preparsed SQL and PL/SQL code, which is reused when reexecuted within a reasonable period of time. Naming the shared pool as being *shared* describes the function of this buffer perfectly. The shared pool is essentially the most shareable memory buffer, providing concurrency for data and the database. The shared pool is usually the most critical buffer for any Oracle database. It cannot be too small because then it simply won't share enough of the most frequently used data. Consequently, it also cannot be sized too large because it can become too complex for Oracle Database to manage.

- *Database buffer cache*. This contains application data (the rows in your tables, indexes, and materialized views). As with the shared pool, if the database buffer cache is too small it won't provide fast enough access to highly shareable data. And yet again, as with the shared pool, if the database buffer cache is too big, it could be attempting to share data that is not frequently used.

- *Large pool*. This provides for processing requiring occasional large chunks of memory. This helps to prevent conflict for concurrency with other buffers by not pushing infrequently used data into memory. This buffer is used for odd tasks like backups and parallel processing.

- *Java pool*. This is memory space allocated for database-driven Java code. This pool can be set to zero if Java is not in use. Not doing so is a waste of memory resources.

- *Streams pool*. This is used for Oracle Streams and can be set to zero size if Oracle Streams is not in use. Memory resources should not be wasted. A stream is a little like a pipe in that it allows sharing of information between multiple databases by way of messages. Oracle Streams allows for distribution of data and can be an alternative to Oracle Replication.

- *SGA max size*. This is the sum total size that the SGA can be resized up to the maximum size setting. This limits the maximum size that any SGA-contained memory buffers can be resized up to when the Oracle instance is up and running. The objective is to inhibit *runaway* operations.

- *SGA target*. Setting this parameter to a value greater than zero enables automated SGA memory management. The following buffers will not need to be set at all as Oracle 10*g* Database does it all for you:

  - Shared pool (SHARED_POOL_SIZE)
  - Database buffer cache (DB_CACHE_SIZE)
  - Large pool (LARGE_POOL_SIZE)
  - Java pool (JAVA_POOL_SIZE)
  - Streams pool (STREAMS_POOL_SIZE)

These parameters are excluded from automated SGA management and the setting of the SGA_TARGET parameter:

- The log buffer (LOG_BUFFER_SIZE)
- All the database buffer cache buffers apart from the primary DB_CACHE_SIZE parameter; excluded parameters include all the keep and recycle pools (DB_KEEP_CACHE_SIZE, DB_RECYCLE_CACHE_SIZE, BUFFER_POOL_KEEP, BUFFER_POOL_RECYCLE), plus all the nondefault block size database buffer caches (DB_2K,4K,8K,16K,32K_CACHES_SIZE)

The PGA is controlled by the PGA_AGGREGATE_TARGET parameter. Setting this parameter to a value greater than zero enables automated PGA memory management. The PGA_AGGREGATE_TARGET parameter automates settings for all the *AREA_SIZE parameters, including the parameters BITMAP_MERGE_AREA_SIZE, CREATE_BITMAP_AREA_SIZE, HASH_AREA_SIZE, SORT_AREA_SIZE, and SORT_AREA_RETAINED_SIZE.

Note: There is no PGA_MAX_SIZE parameter—yet! This has been known to cause problems.

There are all sorts of options on the Memory Advisor screen. You can switch easily between automated SGA and manual SGA. You can also change all parameters from this point in the Database Control. Click any of the Advice options in the Memory Advisor window to get memory advice on specific cache areas.

Figure 23.37 shows the SGA Memory Advisor screen with automated SGA enabled. Figure 23.37 is very simple. All it is telling me is that if I make the SGA smaller, the database will become less efficient. Making the SGA larger will make no difference whatsoever. I am very much inclined to agree with the diagram in Figure 23.37.

Figure 23.38 shows a similar picture to that in Figure 23.37. However, in Figure 23.38, SGA memory is manually configured, and the PGA memory advisor is shown. Once again, changing the size of the shared pool is probably pointless. I disagree with making the database buffer cache larger because my data set (the size of my database) is extremely small, even if it is very busy. Advice on PGA memory size does not tell me anything at all.

Figure 23.37
*The Memory
Advisor screen with
automated SGA
enabled*

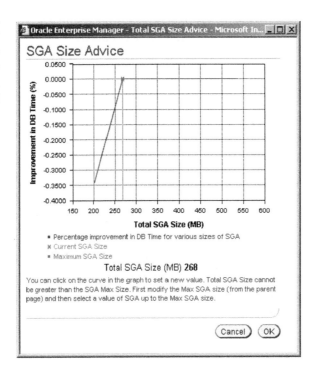

Figure 23.38
*The Memory
Advisor screen with
automated SGA
disabled*

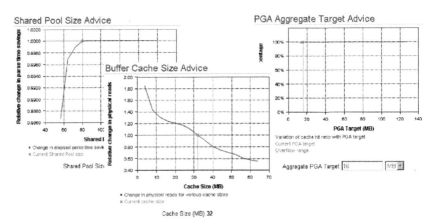

23.2.3.4   The SQL Access Advisor

The SQL Access Advisor allows you to analyze various database objects, such as indexes and materialized views, potentially making recommendations for improving performance. Get to the SQL Access Advisor by clicking the SQL Access Advisor link in the Advisor Central page. The various settings and options for this tool should be obvious and intuitive to some-one reading this book. Essentially you get to select various options:

- **_Templates_**. These are default templates for testing against.

- **_Workload source_**. Where will SQL coding come from? You could use current SQL activity, something in the past, or even a hypothetical scenario.

- **_Recommendation options_**. You can get recommendations as to whether you should create indexes, materialized views, or both.

- **_Schedule_**. You can schedule an advisory analysis to execute at a future point in time. You can also accept the default and execute the advisor immediately.

- **_Review_**. This step allows you to make sure that what you selected in the previous steps is what you actually want to do.

23.2.3.5   The SQL Tuning Advisor

The SQL Tuning Advisor is similar to the SQL Access Advisor but will ana-lyze SQL code, rather than database objects. This tool may make recom-mendations for improving performance. Get to the SQL Tuning Advisor by clicking the SQL Tuning Advisor link in the Central Advisor page. The SQL Tuning Advisor allows analysis of SQL statements and can make per-formance improvement recommendations. It can also be launched from various tools. Just click the Top Activity link to go into the SQL Tuning Advisor tool. Figure 23.39 shows a picture of what the SQL Tuning Advisor tool gives you as a TopActivity source execution. The right side of the graph shown in Figure 23.39 shows a sharp increase in general activity. The reason is because I started up my simulation code again just to show you what a lot of activity looks like.

As shown in Figure 23.39 you can click on the busiest SQL statements (TopSQL) or the busiest sessions (TopSessions). The graph at the top shows what is happening in the database with respect to the various wait event classifications (see Chapter 21). And you get pretty pictures as well, which are easy to read and decipher.

Other parts of the SQL Tuning Advisor tool are (1) the Period SQL tool, which allows you to look at potentially problematic SQL statements during a period of time, and (2) the SQL Tuning Sets, which allow compar-ison against a set of SQL statements that are present in a database.

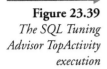

Figure 23.39
The SQL Tuning
Advisor TopActivity
execution

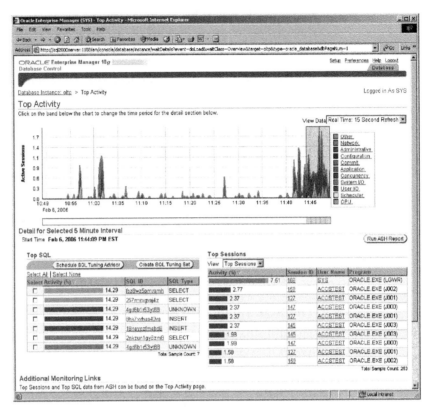

23.2.3.6   **The MTTR Advisor**

The MTTR Advisor in the Database Control allows you to monitor flash recovery. Get to the MTTR Advisor by clicking the MTTR Advisor link in the central advisor page. There is not really much to be said for this screen except that you can sacrifice up to the second recoverability by reducing the amount of real-time logging produced.

23.2.4   **Dealing with Locks**

From a purely technical perspective, handling locking situations is essentially an administration function. However, the occurrence of locks in a database can cause serious performance problems, even potentially halting a database and rendering it completely useless. The Instance Locks link, at the bottom of the Performance page, is an excellent and easily intuitive tool for managing locks. The tool is self-explanatory and it does not require demonstration in this book.

There are many other non-Oracle Corporation tools for monitoring and tuning Oracle databases. Spotlight is one of these tools.

23.3 ⑨ᵢ Spotlight

Spotlight on Oracle is an excellent tool for real-time monitoring and reactive, not predictive, tuning of busy production databases. With respect to physical tuning, Spotlight can do much, and its GUI is of excellent caliber. Spotlight can be used for SQL code tuning as well; however, it is best used as a monitoring and physical tuning advisory tool.

Note: ⑩g The last time I used Spotlight was with Oracle 9*i* Database. Its capabilities with Oracle 10*g* Database are unknown. Spotlight documentation and software does appear to have been upgraded for Oracle 10*g* Database, including use of all built-in advisors and automated memory management. The way the company manages trial software is too awkward to warrant updating this book at this point in time.

Figure 23.40 shows the primary screen in Spotlight on Oracle, used for monitoring a busy Oracle production database. Different colors represent different levels of alert: green is OK, red is serious—or just panic!

There are an enormous number of subset screens in Spotlight on Oracle for every aspect of Oracle Database tuning imaginable. Figure 23.41 shows a screen displaying real-time usage of the SGA for a database.

Figure 23.42 shows a mixture of various views from Spotlight with both textual and instantly recognizable graphic displays.

Spotlight is a very comprehensive tuning and monitoring tool for Oracle Database, especially in the area of real-time production database monitoring. As already stated, many third party (not Oracle Corporation)–produced Oracle database monitoring and tuning tools are available. Spotlight is the one of the most comprehensive and useful of those tools I have used in relation to its price.

23.4   Operating System Tools

Tools discussed in this section are the Performance Monitor for Windows 2000 and various Unix tools.

Figure 23.40
*Spotlight on Oracle
main monitoring
screen*

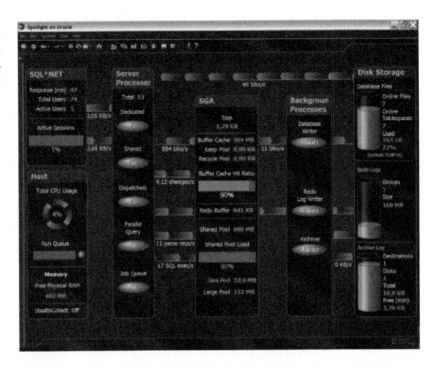

Figure 23.41
*Spotlight SGA
view*

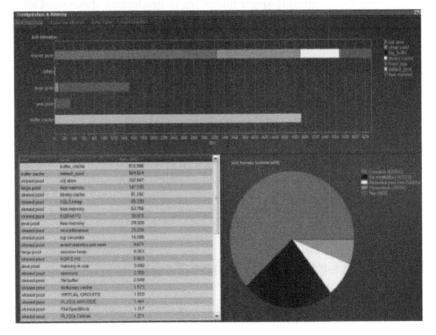

Figure 23.42
*Various Spotlight
views*

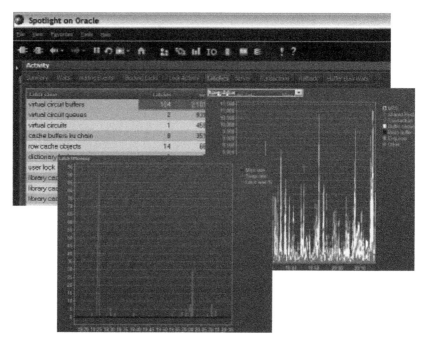

23.4.1 Windows Performance Monitor

The Windows Performance Monitor is useful for monitoring operating system–level performance. The GUI can be started up on a Windows 2000 server in the Administrative Tools icon on the Control Panel. This tool allows graphic display of all aspects of hardware and operating system–level activity. Figure 23.43 shows a picture of a dual CPU server displaying processors, memory, and network activity for a relatively idle database server.

Figure 23.44, on the other hand, shows the Windows Performance Monitor GUI for a highly active single CPU system. The Windows Task Manager snapshot is added to show how busy this system was when these screenshots were taken.

There are a multitude of command-line and GUI tools used for operating system monitoring and tuning in other operating systems, such as Unix or Linux.

Figure 23.43
*The Windows
Performance
Monitor*

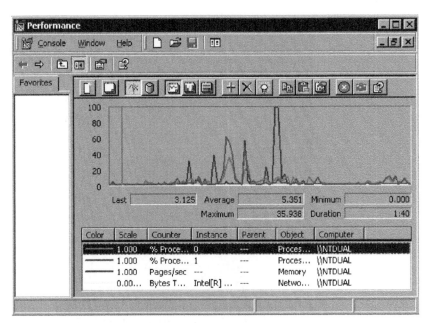

Figure 23.44
*This is a very busy
server*

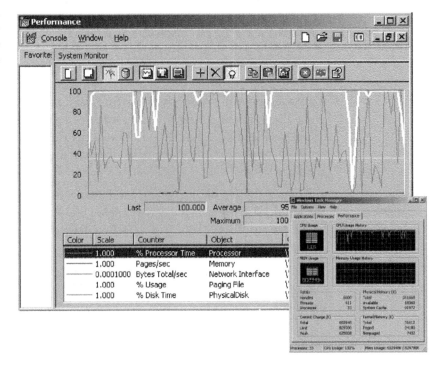

23.4.2 Unix Utilities

A plethora of command-line utilities and GUI-based monitoring tools can be used in all flavors of Unix and Linux operating systems. The following list includes some of the command-line monitoring tools used on Solaris:

- *CPU usage*: sar, vmstat, mpstat, iostat
- *Disk I/O activity*: sar, iostat
- *Memory usage*: sar, vmstat
- *Network usage*: netstat

I see no point in attempting to explain the detailed syntax and use of these tools. I am not an experienced systems administrator. There are plenty of other books written by SysAdmins that will give you precise information.

23.5 Other Utilities and Tools

Tools discussed in this section include import and export utilities, data pump technology, SQL*Loader, and STATSPACK. Various other architectural strategies and options are included here, all being solutions and assistants. STATSPACK is the only tuning tool in this section. Other tools and architectures can be tuned using specific methods within those tools. Or, architecturally, various options can make a database server perform better in general.

23.5.1 Data Pump, Import, Export, and SQL*Loader

The Export and SQL*Loader utilities can be executed in DIRECT mode. DIRECT mode implies that the SQL engine, executing INSERT statements, is completely bypassed and data is appended directly to datafiles on disk. DIRECT mode is much faster than passing through the SQL engine. Import and Export have a parameter called BUFFER, which limits chunks of rows processed. In very busy environments, using the BUFFER parameter can limit the impact on other database services.

Only use the Export utility to copy individual static tables you are absolutely sure will not change. Additionally, using a previously FULL exported backup file to import and then recreate a lost database is incredibly inefficient. I have seen a 200Gb database reconstructed using a FULL database export dump file. It took an entire weekend to rebuild the database. This particular database was also apparently destroyed by a junior DBA executing a script to drop all users in cascade mode, by mistake of course. Oops!

Note: The Import and Export utilities are inappropriate for backup and recovery.

23.5.1.1 (10g) **Data Pump Import and Export**

The Data Pump Import and Data Pump Export utilities have much better performance than the Import and Export utilities. Data pump technology allows for parallel execution, is apparently somewhat self-tuning, and does not require compression into a single extent. One would assume that compression might be performed automatically, if it is at all required.

SQL*Loader is an excellent tool for loading data into a database. SQL*Loader is very easy to use and can map data files in text format directly into database tables. Using SQL*Loader to load tables, as opposed to mass INSERT statements, can improve performance an order of magnitude in the thousands. SQL*Loader is also very easy to learn to use.

Note: (10g) SQL*Loader can now cache dates reducing conversions on duplicated date values.

23.5.2 **Resource Management and Profiling**

Resources can be managed and effectively shared in Oracle Database to create round robin–type queues. Hardware resources, such as CPU time, can be evenly distributed across multiple profiles. Profiles contain groups of users or functionality sets. Different activities can be given priority at different times of day. Perhaps OLTP activity can be favored during the daytime and backup or batch processing activities favored outside of normal business hours. This of course assumes you do not have to maintain a constant level of 24 × 7 database availability. There is a small amount of resource overhead with respect to Oracle Database internal implementation and execution of resource management.

23.5.3 Recovery Manager (RMAN)

RMAN is a vastly more powerful backup and recovery utility in comparison with such methods as backup mode tablespace datafile copies. RMAN essentially simplifies backup and recovery processing and DBA involvement. Additionally, performance with RMAN can be improved using parallel execution. RAMN can store scripting for backup management and automation, along with many other features.

23.5.4 Transportable Tablespaces

Transportable tablespaces can be used to copy entire physical tablespace and datafile structures between different databases, even on different platforms running different operating systems.

23.5.5 Oracle Streams

Oracle Streams has been utilized in the past for specialized types of replication processing where a stream (or pipe) can be used to send messages from one data to another. Oracle Streams can now be used with archive processing and general movement of data.

23.5.6 Oracle RAC and Oracle Grid

Oracle Real Application Clusters (RAC) can be used to speed up processing in general by dividing the processing performed by a database. The intention is to utilize the processing power of multiple database server computers.

23.5.7 (9i) STATSPACK

People have written and published entire books about STATSPACK. STATSPACK is a comprehensive statistics monitoring and tuning analysis tool. STATSPACK is the next generation offering from the UTLBSTAT.sql and UTLESTAT.sql tuning scripts. In addition, STATSPACK can be used to store statistical information in the database in a special repository. This special repository can be used for later comparison and analysis between different statistics set collections. When a performance problem occurs, a current snapshot can be compared against a previously obtained baseline snapshot. This allows for easy comparison and rapid diagnosis of the problem.

Note: STATSPACK is useful for analysis and detection of bottlenecks, but using the Oracle Database Wait Event Interface or the Database Control is better.

STATSPACK is very easy to install, configure, and use. The problem with it is that it produces enormous quantities of what could amount to superfluous information. Wading through all the mounds of information produced by STATSPACK could be somewhat daunting to the tuning novice—or even an expert who is trying to solve a problem in a hurry. Large amounts of information can even sometimes hide a smaller indicator of a problem, perhaps less noticeable among too much detail. The expression "trying to find a needle in a haystack" comes to mind.

STATSPACK is more useful for general performance tuning and analysis, as opposed to attempting to find specific bottlenecks. The Oracle Database Wait Event Interface is much more capable when isolating bottlenecks rapidly.

To use STATSPACK, a specific tablespace must be created:

```
CREATE TABLESPACE perfstat DATAFILE
'ORACLE_HOME/<SID>/perfstat01.dbf'
SIZE 25M AUTOEXTEND ON NEXT 1M MAXSIZE UNLIMITED
EXTENT MANAGEMENT LOCAL SEGMENT SPACE MANAGEMENT AUTO;
```

Do not create a user because the scripts will crash! Additionally, you might want to set the ORACLE_SID variable if your database server has multiple databases. The following script will create STATSPACK goodies:

```
@ORACLE_HOME/rdbms/admin/spcreate.sql;
```

If the installation completely freaks out, the following script will drop everything created by SPCREATE.SQL so that you can start all over again:

```
@ORACLE_HOME/rdbms/admin/spdrop.sql;
```

Once installed, take a snapshot of the database by executing these statements in SQL*Plus:

```
CONNECT perfstat/perfstat[@tnsname];
EXEC STATSPACK.SNAP;
```

The DBMS_JOBS package can be used to automate STATSPACK SNAP procedure executions on a periodic basis. In the following example script, a snapshot is executed every 5 minutes. Different snapshot levels can be used between 0 and 10. Using 0 is not enough. Using 10 is far too much. Using 5 is the default. Using 6 provides query execution plans. I would recommend starting at snapshot level 6 because the large majority of performance problems is caused by poorly written SQL code statements.

Snapshot levels are as follows:

- 0: simple performance statistics
- 5: include SQL statements—this is the default level
- 6: include SQL query plans
- 7: include segment statistics
- 10: include parent and child latches

Note: Running STATSPACK will affect performance, so do not leave it running constantly.

```
DECLARE
 jobno NUMBER;
 i INTEGER DEFAULT 1;
BEGIN
 DBMS_JOB.SUBMIT(jobno,' STATSPACK.SNAP(I_SNAP_LEVEL=>6);'
,SYSDATE,'SYSDATE+1/288');
COMMIT;
END;
/
```

Remove the jobs using an anonymous procedure such as this:

```
DECLARE
    CURSOR cJobs IS SELECT job FROM user_jobs;
BEGIN
    FOR rJob IN cJobs LOOP
```

```
        DBMS_JOB.REMOVE(rJob.job);
    END LOOP;
END;
/
COMMIT;
```

To remove a specific job, find the job number first.

Run a STATSPACK report using the following script. The script will prompt for two snapshots to execute between, comparing sets of statistics with each other:

```
@ORACLE_HOME/rdbms/admin/spreport.sql;
```

An SQL report can be executed on one SQL statement, searching for a bottleneck, where the hash value for the SQL code statement is found in the STATSPACK instance report:

```
@ORACLE_HOME/rdbms/admin/sprepsql.sql;
```

A number of other "SP*.SQL" STATSPACK scripts are used for various functions. Two of those scripts are SPPURGE.SQL and SPTRUNCATE.SQL. Purging allows the removal of a range of snapshots. If the database is bounced, then snapshots cannot be taken across the database restart. Truncate simply removes all STATSPACK data.

STATSPACK can also have threshold value settings such that characteristics below threshold values will be ignored. Default STATSPACK parameter settings including threshold values are stored in the STATS$STATSPACK_PARAMETER table.

This is enough information about physical tuning tools and use of utilities. The next chapter will look at physical and configuration tuning from the perspective of finding bottlenecks using the Oracle Database Wait Event Interface.

24

The Wait Event Interface

In the previous chapter, we briefly discussed some of the tools that can be used to aid in physical and configuration tuning, including what each tool can be used for. In this chapter, we will dig a little deeper into some very specific performance views containing database object facts and statistics. These details can be utilized to attempt to find what are commonly termed bottlenecks. After we have described a small portion of what is an absolute confusing plethora of performance views, we will once again revert to using tools ((9i) Oracle Enterprise Manager and the (10g) Database Control) to drilldown into the Oracle Database Wait Event Interface.

Note: (9i) Oracle Enterprise Manager and the (10g) Database Control will be henceforth in this chapter referred to simply as the GUI (graphical user interface).

24.1 What Is a Bottleneck?

A bottleneck is quite literally a small part of your installation (hardware or software), where too much processing is being funneled through a specific area. In other words, far too much is going on in one particular area of an installation, in comparison with any other part.

What are the causes of bottlenecks? Causes are numerous. More often than not, bottlenecks are a result of poorly designed SQL code or a poorly structured data model. Rarely is there a hardware issue. One of the most commonly occurring hardware performance issues is inappropriate disk structure for redo logs and archive logs. Hardware issues are generally out of the scope of this book and fall under the guise of systems administration. This book is all about tuning of Oracle databases and not about tuning at the operating system level. Therefore, any hardware or operating system aspects are not particularly relevant to this text.

Note: I am not a systems administrator, so my indulgence in that particular area would not be useful for the reader. It would not be prudent on my part either.

24.2 Detecting Potential Bottlenecks

So what can be done to detect potential bottlenecks? If you have read this entire book by now, you probably realize that multiple methods can be used to tune Oracle installations. I tend to approach tuning methods based on the skill sets of database administrators. Database administrators generally come from two main schools of thought: (1) a development background, or (2) a systems administration background. A systems administration background is the far more frequent of the two disciplines.

The point I am trying to make here is that there is a difference of approach between these two skill sets. Developers will take a top-down approach to tuning. Systems administrators will take a bottom-up approach to tuning. What does this mean? Developers will approach tuning from the application, leading down into the database. Systems administrators will approach a problem from the operating system and work upward. Obviously an assumption like this is not 100% true, but in my experience it is quite often the case.

Developers are more likely to move directly into the data model and particularly application SQL code. Systems administrators will more than likely look at the hardware and the operating system leading up into the database. The result is that developers are more likely to tune from the perspective of the first two parts of this book and that systems administrators will veer toward the third and fourth parts of this book.

What is the purpose of this chapter? It is to explain how to find performance problems by using Oracle database internal structures, namely database statistics in the Oracle Database Wait Event Interface, using performance views and *the GUI*.

Part II of this book gradually built up to tuning of SQL code, gradually describing the *how* and *with what* aspects of tuning SQL code. Part III and Part IV presented various fundamentals of physical and configuration tuning, as already mentioned. This chapter describes a method of tuning most likely to be used by systems administrators, but very useful for everyone, developers included. There has to be some complexity to promote understanding, but it is followed by easy solutions. This chapter covers what is often called the Oracle Database Wait Event Interface, or, quite simply, a bunch of performance views that enable drilling into wait events and all sorts of statistics, allowing for detection of potential bottlenecks. The objective is to tune by removing performance bottlenecks.

Using the Oracle Database Wait Event Interface is simply another tuning method or tool. It can often provide database administrators with enough ammunition to convince developers where SQL code can be altered to drastically improve performance. There are numerous steps database administrators can take to improve performance without involving or having to persuade developers to alter application code. However, there is a point where application-based SQL code simply must be changed if better performance is required. Quite often applications are written with encapsulated SQL code that might be very easy for developers to modify. Developers will be modifying SQL statements only, not surrounding application code.

The other aspect of using the Oracle Database Wait Event Interface for tuning Oracle installations is that it tends to be a reactive rather than a proactive tuning method. This means that wait event tuning is used to drill-down into problems as they occur. It is thus akin to putting out fires rather than preventing them. This is often the only available tuning method because of high time and cost limitations placed on the development process. Perhaps more planning and expense may appear to be required if tuning is done proactively. Proactive tuning means writing better SQL code and designing the database model for performance in the first place. However, this is often not possible. Therefore, reactive tuning is usually the only available approach.

24.3 **What Is the Wait Event Interface?**

The Wait Event Interface is a group of Oracle Database performance views that allow drilldown into various areas of activity occurring in an Oracle database installation. These activities are either summarized from the most recent database startup or maintained for the life of each session. The simplest way to present those views and their interrelated structure is to present them in steps. It should also be noted that drilling into wait events includes not only waits on events but deeper layers, such as latches and otherwise.

Note: (10*g*) Numerous Wait Event Model changes are made, including changes to various V$ performance views along with a number of additional V$ performance views.

Figure 24.1 shows a brief picture of various tools that can be used to drilldown into wait events. These tools can be used to allow easy access to underlying Oracle Database performance views. In this chapter, I want to begin by explaining the lowest level of application of the wait event interface using the performance views. Simply displaying how to use various tools or describing their output does not help to provide better understanding. When it comes to examples, the GUI will be used to drilldown into wait events as they occur.

Note: STATSPACK will be used in the next chapter in order to compare two different points in time for a database.

Figure 24.1
Tools for drilldown into the Oracle Database Wait Event Interface

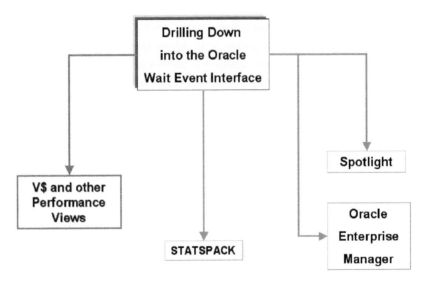

I like to divide the Wait Event Interface performance views into three layers: (1) the system aggregation layer, (2) the session layer, and (3) the third layer and beyond. The first layer I call the *system aggregation* layer because in its simplest form it contains a record of statistics collected by what I call the *session layer*, which is of course the second layer. The session layer contains statistics about sessions during the life of those sessions.

There is a deeper layer of the Wait Event Interface involving hooks through many other performance views. As already stated, I like to call this deeper layer *the third layer and beyond*, or perhaps even the *crazy about V$ views* layer. This third layer will not be examined in detail in this book, but only described briefly and then displayed by example using the GUI. There is too much complexity in the third layer to go into every detail. It is not worth explaining every nitty-gritty piece, possibly boring readers to tears.

24.3.1 The System Aggregation Layer

A brief overview of the system aggregation layer of the Wait Event Interface is shown in Figure 24.2. The V$EVENT_NAME view gives a list of all possible events. The V$SYSTEM_EVENT view contains an aggregation of existing wait events and total wait times for each. V$SYSTEM_EVENT view is cleared on database restart.

Note: The TIMED_STATISTICS parameter must be set to TRUE for V$SYSTEM_EVENT to contain information. Setting the TIMED_ STATISTICS parameter has minimum performance impact.

Note: (10*g*) By default the TIMED_STATISTICS is set to true.

The V$SYSTEM_EVENT view can be joined to the V$EVENT_ NAME view using the EVENT and NAME columns, respectively, as shown in Figure 24.2.

The V$EVENT_NAME view has information about hooks to drilldown into the third layer of potential bottleneck problems using the PARAMETER1, PARAMETER2, and PARAMETER3 parameter columns. These parameter columns contain information as to what event parameters in third-layer views, such as the V$LATCH view, will be pointed to from the V$SESSION_WAIT view.

Note: V$EVENT_NAME view parameter columns do not contain actual values, they contain only descriptions of what values are. The parameter values are contained in the session layer in the V$SESSION_WAIT performance view.

Figure 24.2
*The system
aggregation layer of
the Oracle
Database Wait
Event Interface*

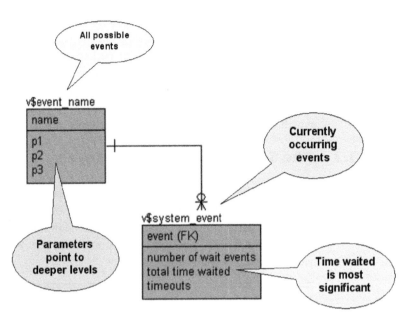

Some of the values in the V$EVENT_NAME view parameter columns
are as follows; there are a lot of them:

```
SELECT DISTINCT(parameter1) FROM v$event_name
WHERE parameter1 LIKE '%#%' ORDER BY 1;

PARAMETER1
----------------------------------------------------------------
block#
branch#
buffer#
by thread#
circuit#
copy latch #
end-point#
event #
file#
group#
log#
process#
segment#
session#
thread#
```

```
undo seg#|slot#
undo segment#

SELECT DISTINCT(parameter2) FROM v$event_name
WHERE parameter2 LIKE '%#%' ORDER BY 1;

PARAMETER2
-----------------------------------------------------------------
#bytes
0 or file #
Log #
QT_OBJ#
block#
chain#
disk group #
file #
file#
lms#
log # / thread id #
master object #
node#/parallelizer#
obj#
object #
our thread#
plan #
pool #
process#
table obj#
table space #
tablespace #
thread id #
transaction entry #
undo segment #
view object #
workspace #
wrap#

SELECT DISTINCT(parameter3) FROM v$event_name
WHERE parameter3 LIKE '%#%' ORDER BY 1;
```

```
PARAMETER3
----------------------------------------------------------------
Serial#
block#
bloom#
class#
file #
id#
object #
process#
relative file #
sequence #
sequence # / apply #
serial #
set-id#
undo segment # / other
workspace #
```

For instance, the combination of file# in PARAMETER1 and block# in PARAMETER2 can be used to drilldown into extents to find an offending segment. A segment is the equivalent of a table. The diagram shown in Figure 24.2 is appropriately adjusted in Figure 24.3.

Figure 24.3
Isolating segments using event parameters

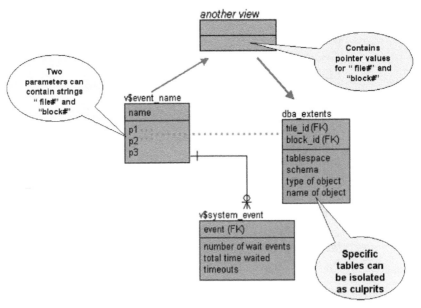

The following query shows how to join the various views for existing wait events. This query will not be executed in this chapter. A demonstration later on using Oracle Enterprise Manager will suffice.

```
SELECT de.segment_name, sw.event
FROM dba_extents de, (
    SELECT sw.event, sw.p1 AS file_id, sw.p2 AS block_id
    FROM v$session_wait sw WHERE IdleEvent(event) IS NOT NULL
AND sw.sid IN
(SELECT sid FROM v$session WHERE username = 'ACCOUNTS')
    AND sw.event != 'null event') sw
WHERE de.owner = 'ACCOUNTS'
AND de.file_id = sw.file_id AND de.block_id = sw.block_id;
```

By examining the DBA_EXTENTS view in detail from this perspective, we can see the different segment types:

```
SELECT DISTINCT(segment_type) FROM dba_extents ORDER BY 1;

SEGMENT_TYPE
------------------

CLUSTER
INDEX
INDEX PARTITION
LOB PARTITION
LOBINDEX
LOBSEGMENT
NESTED TABLE
ROLLBACK
TABLE
TABLE PARTITION
TABLE SUBPARTITION
TYPE2 UNDO
```

From another perspective, we can see table and index names.

```
SELECT DISTINCT(segment_name) FROM dba_extents
WHERE segment_type IN ('TABLE','INDEX') AND owner='ACCOUNTS'
ORDER BY 1;
```

```
SEGMENT_NAME
-----------------------------------------------------------
AK_GL_DTE
AK_SP_ZIP
AUDITSIM
CASHBOOK
CASHBOOKLINE
CATEGORY
COA
CUSTOMER
GENERALLEDGER
ORDERS
ORDERSLINE
PERIOD
PERIODSUM
PLAN_TABLE
POSTING
...
```

So we should be able see from the various queries already shown that potential wait event issues can be isolated to specific objects in the database. Let's look at some details. Let's start by listing the top currently occurring wait events. In this chapter, we are using queries from recent chapters (or slightly modified versions thereof). The emphasis is on attempting to find and solve existing problems, as opposed to architectural and configuration issues. The following query finds the top ten wait events:

```
COL event FORMAT a32;
COL percentage FORMAT 9999999990;
SELECT * FROM(
SELECT event "Event", total_waits "Waits", time_waited "Total
Time"
    ,TO_CHAR(
        (time_waited /
            (SELECT SUM(time_waited) FROM v$system_event
            WHERE IdleEvent(event) IS NOT NULL)
    )*100, 990.99) "Percentage"
FROM v$system_event WHERE IdleEvent(event) IS NOT NULL
ORDER BY 3 DESC) WHERE ROWNUM <= 10;
```

And following is the resulting top ten wait events based on the total amount of time the system spends waiting for each event. This is the result in my Oracle 9*i* Database:.

Event	Waits	Total Time	Percent
db file sequential read	623840	7542616	71.59
buffer busy waits	259455	2330819	22.12
enqueue	1944	566381	5.38
latch free	3996	49586	0.47
control file parallel write	4956	21016	0.20
db file parallel write	1102	7472	0.07
library cache pin	112	6666	0.06
control file sequential read	2156	6371	0.06
log file parallel write	1559	1621	0.02
library cache load lock	8	714	0.01

And this is the result in my Oracle 10*g* Database. Consistent with previous chapters, cache wait events such as buffer busy waits and library cache latches are no longer apparent. Enqueue waits indicating row locks are more prominent in Oracle 10*g* Database:

Event	Waits	Total Time	Percent
db file sequential read	72418	191664	59.26
read by other session	56948	41763	12.91
db file scattered read	17912	38701	11.97
enq: TM - contention	62	12396	3.83
log file parallel write	5985	6887	2.13
control file sequential read	2193	6388	1.98
log file sync	2874	5901	1.82
enq: TX - row lock contention	26	4954	1.53
db file parallel write	3272	3906	1.21
latch: enqueue hash chains	50	2946	0.91

The only thing to decide at this point is what is a significant event? Which event in the previous result is the most significant and can have the most profound effect on performance? Some knowledge of applications might be required at this stage because high incidence of some wait events could be normal, and thus acceptable, depending on applications.

The real problem with the preceding query is that the information obtained is a little too vague at this point. The db file sequential read event could indicate hot block issues but could also be normal. The same applies to buffer busy waits. The enqueue, latch free, and wait events in the library cache could have a more significant impact on performance.

24.3.2   The Session Layer

The session layer uses various performance views, such as V$SESSION_ EVENT and V$SESSION_WAIT. These session views contain information for a session only as long as that session exists and are shown in Figure 24.4.

Figure 24.4
Session level event and wait views

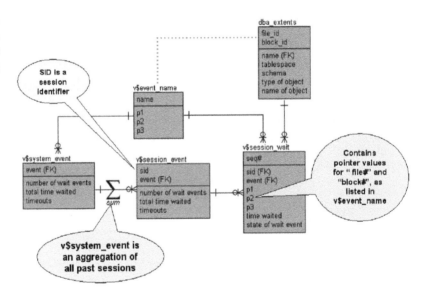

Note: The V$SYSTEM_EVENT contains an accumulated aggregation or summation of values in the V$SESSION_EVENT view, aggregated on termination of a session.

It is important to stress that using session-level performance views only finds wait events as they occur. If sessions are application controlled, or connections are shared, then using session-level wait event detection may be awkward to decipher without deeper analysis.

> **Note:** Snapshots may have to be taken over specified time periods, similar to the way in which STATSPACK and the Database Control AWR function.

Continual connecting and disconnecting to a database was common in client-server systems. This type of programming usually does not occur in OLTP database environments because sessions are often shared between connections in one form or another. The net result is that the specific nature of session-level wait event tracking can become somewhat blurred and possibly less useful, and perhaps even more akin to that of system-level event tracking. Session-level wait event detection may often be more appropriate to tracking down bad SQL code executed in ad hoc environments. Ad hoc SQL code is rare in mission-critical OLTP-type databases. This is because most OLTP databases are controlled by application coding—quite often custom-built application coding. In other words, end users cannot connect directly to the OLTP database at all; applications connect to the database for them.

The V$SESSION_EVENT performance view provides wait events for sessions for the entire life of a session. The V$SESSION_WAIT performance view provides the same information, but as each wait event occurs. Included in this structure is access to deeper layers using parameter pointer values, as shown in Figure 24.4. The V$SESSION_EVENT view is effectively an accumulation of wait events for sessions during the life of those sessions. Thus, V$SESSION_EVENT could be used to isolate sessions causing specific problems. The following query finds the worst ten events by session:

```
COL event FORMAT a32;
SELECT * FROM (
SELECT sid, event, total_waits "Waits", time_waited "Total
Time"
FROM v$session_event WHERE IdleEvent(event) IS NOT NULL
ORDER BY 4 DESC) WHERE ROWNUM <= 10;
```

This is the result in my Oracle 9*i* Database:

```
       SID EVENT                              Waits Total Time
---------- -------------------------------- ---------- ----------
        50 db file sequential read           8826      91390
         4 db file sequential read           3204      33929
```

```
17 enqueue                            94      28399
19 enqueue                            94      28398
25 enqueue                            93      28255
35 db file sequential read          6791      28112
40 buffer busy waits                3857      21593
45 buffer busy waits                3811      21338
 3 control file parallel write      2383      20054
37 db file sequential read          1493      17461
```

This is the result in my Oracle 10*g* Database. Again there are no cache wait events but also no row locks. This time it appears that Oracle 10*g* Database is indicating that my I/O subsystem is substandard. The database is of course, correct in that assumption:

```
SID EVENT                            Waits Total Time
---------- ------------------------------ ---------- ----------
164 db file sequential read         4649      20702
166 log file parallel write         6390       7047
167 db file parallel write          3692       4263
144 db file sequential read         1183       4054
161 db file sequential read          418       3854
147 db file sequential read          748       2552
159 db file sequential read          193       2131
147 control file sequential read     805       2078
165 control file parallel write     1566       1967
159 log file sync                    292       1954
```

The next query shows events causing the highest wait times. Total wait time is a measure of the amount of delay caused, which is more significant than frequency. The most frequently occurring events would be found by summing the number of waits:

```
COL event FORMAT a32;
SELECT * FROM (
SELECT event, SUM(time_waited) "Total Time"
FROM v$session_event WHERE IdleEvent(event) IS NOT NULL
GROUP BY event ORDER BY 2 DESC) WHERE ROWNUM <= 10;
```

This is the result in my Oracle 9*i* Database:

```
EVENT                                  Total Time
------------------------------------   ----------
db file sequential read                    489236
enqueue                                    360328
buffer busy waits                          292884
control file parallel write                 20653
db file parallel write                      10501
control file sequential read                 6169
latch free                                   3959
log file parallel write                      2306
LGWR wait for redo copy                       165
log file sequential read                       52
```

This is the result in my Oracle 10*g* Database with fewer cache issues, but also no row locks this time:

```
EVENT                                  Total Time
------------------------------------   ----------
db file sequential read                     37307
log file parallel write                      7174
db file parallel write                       4332
control file sequential read                 3413
log file sync                                2878
events in waitclass Other                    2796
control file parallel write                  2175
db file scattered read                       1718
os thread startup                            1028
library cache load lock                        65
```

Examining the V$SESSION_WAIT performance view will not only show wait events as they occur, but also allows us to use parameter value pointers to find specific details, such as database objects, as in the DBA_EXTENTS view query previously shown in this chapter. An accumulation on the V$SESSION_WAIT view is useful to get a better overall picture.

Note: This type of cumulative processing can be performed easily using a tool such as STATSPACK. At this stage, the objective is to explain and teach the basics rather than the syntax of a tool like STATSPACK.

The following procedure is a slight variation on a procedure introduced in a previous chapter. This procedure tries to find offending segments by using the file# and block# pointers, as found in the V$EVENT_NAME view:

```
DROP TABLE tmp;
CREATE TABLE tmp
  (sid NUMBER, event VARCHAR2(64), file_id NUMBER, block_id
NUMBER,
  wait_time NUMBER, seconds_in_wait NUMBER);
BEGIN
 FOR counter IN 1..1000 LOOP
  INSERT INTO tmp
   SELECT sw.sid, sw.event AS event, sw.p1 AS file_id,
    sw.p2 AS block_id, sw.wait_time, sw.seconds_in_wait
   FROM v$session_wait sw WHERE IdleEvent(sw.event) IS NOT
NULL
   AND sw.event IN (SELECT name FROM v$event_name
   WHERE parameter1 = 'file#' AND parameter2 = 'block#');
   COMMIT;
 END LOOP;
END;
/
```

And let's query the result:

```
COL event FORMAT a32;
SELECT * FROM (
SELECT sid, event, SUM(seconds_in_wait) "Current Wait Time"
FROM tmp
WHERE IdleEvent(event) IS NOT NULL
GROUP BY sid, event ORDER BY 2 DESC) WHERE ROWNUM <= 10;
```

This is the result of the previous query in Oracle 9*i* Database:

```
EVENT                             Current Wait Time
--------------------------------- -----------------
db file sequential read                        2670
buffer busy waits                               617
db file sequential read                         163
```

```
buffer busy waits                                    43
control file sequential read                          0
```

And this is the result in Oracle 10*g* Database, again somewhat consistent with respect to memory and I/O:

```
SID EVENT                                Current Wait Time
---------- -------------------------------- -----------------
   133 read by other session                               22
   138 read by other session                                0
   139 read by other session                                0
   145 read by other session                                0
   132 db file sequential read                              0
   133 db file sequential read                             33
   138 db file sequential read                              1
   139 db file sequential read                              0
   145 db file sequential read                              0
   147 db file sequential read                              0
```

Now let's take a step back and try to find the worst-performing sessions by querying the V$SESSION_EVENT view:

```
COL event FORMAT a32;
SELECT * FROM (
SELECT sid, SUM(time_waited) "Total Time"
FROM v$session_event WHERE IdleEvent(event) IS NOT NULL
GROUP BY sid ORDER BY 2 DESC) WHERE ROWNUM <= 10;
```

This is the result, and it doesn't really tell me anything at all. What is session identifier (SID) 50?

```
SID Total Time
---------- ----------
        50     124491
        17      54034
        19      54027
        25      52969
        40      52958
        45      52933
         4      41486
```

```
35      40264
41      34010
29      33403
```

We can find more information about SID 50 using the V$SESSION performance view. The real value of the session-level part of the Wait Event Interface (other than doing stuff like searching for offending database objects in the DBA_EXTENTS view) is the way in which the session identifier can be hooked up or linked to sessions in the V$SESSION view. Ultimately, that connection links to other views, including SQL code and optimizer query execution plans. Figure 24.5 shows the drilldown path of session level–executed SQL code and query plans. One of the primary factors causing database performance problems is poorly built SQL code.

Note: Sometimes data model problems can be isolated as a result of finding poorly performing SQL code.

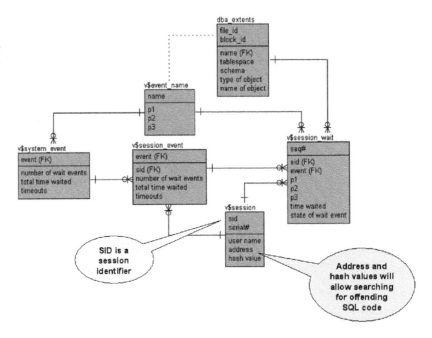

Figure 24.5
Hooking up wait events to sessions

So we could find the usernames (schemas) of offending sessions by joining the V$SESSION_EVENT or V$SESSION_WAIT views, with the V$SESSION performance view, as in the following query:

```
COL event FORMAT a32;
SELECT * FROM (
SELECT s.username, SUM(se.time_waited) "Total Time"
FROM v$session_event se, v$session s
WHERE IdleEvent(se.event) IS NOT NULL
GROUP BY s.username ORDER BY 2 DESC) WHERE ROWNUM <= 10;
```

USERNAME	Total Time
	889280
ACCOUNTS	166740
SYSMAN	166740
DBSNMP	166740
SYS	111160

Now let's add some of the various SQL code views, as shown in Figure 24.6.

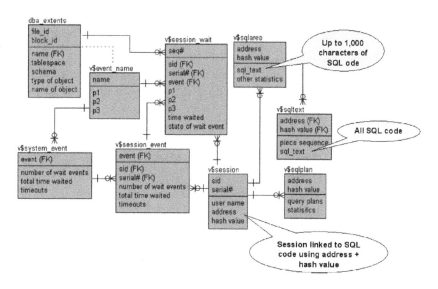

Figure 24.6
Find SQL code for sessions

The following query simply joins sessions and SQL code statements in order to find SQL code that is currently executing the most often:

```
SELECT * FROM (SELECT s.username, a.sql_text, a.executions
FROM v$session s, v$sqlarea a
WHERE s.sql_address = a.address AND s.sql_hash_value =
a.hash_value
ORDER BY 3 DESC) WHERE ROWNUM <= 10;
```

This is the result showing the top 10 SQL statements. The Transactions and Orders tables in my Accounts schema are both busy, which is expected. The first two queries have nothing to do with any particular schema. It is quite common that the most heavily executed queries are the simplest queries. This kind of thing may come as a surprise to developers:

```
USERNAME    SQL_TEXT
----------  -------------------------------------------------------------
            SELECT to_number(to_char(SYSTIMESTAMP,'FF3'))+1 from dual
            SELECT to_number(to_char(SYSTIMESTAMP,'FF3'))+1 from dual
ACCOUNTS    INSERT into transactions values(transactions_seq.nextval,'S'
ACCOUNTS    INSERT into transactions values(transactions_seq.nextval,'S'
ACCOUNTS    INSERT into transactions values(transactions_seq.nextval,'S'
ACCOUNTS    INSERT into transactions values(transactions_seq.nextval,'S'
ACCOUNTS    INSERT into transactions values(transactions_seq.nextval,'S'
ACCOUNTS    SELECT min(order_id),max(order_id) from orders
ACCOUNTS    SELECT min(order_id),max(order_id) from orders
ACCOUNTS    SELECT min(order_id),max(order_id) from orders
```

Similar join queries can be used to access both entire SQL code statements from the V$SQLTEXT view and stored query execution plans from the V$SQL_PLAN view. Joins can be constructed using the ADDRESS and HASH_VALUE columns.

24.3.3   **The Third Layer and Beyond**

From examination of the system aggregation and session layers, you should have noticed two general paths of drilldown that can be followed: (1) drilling into the parameters allows access to details about events and reasons they are causing issues, and (2) SQL code can be accessed directly using address and hash values. These two wait event drilldown access paths can be joined together because the SQL views are linked to a session. In turn, a session is linked to session wait events in the V$SESSION_WAIT performance view.

Let's take a look at a specific example of drilling down into the third layer, before we go on to show how the GUI does all this stuff! Let's take a look at latch free wait events. Figure 24.7 shows a pseudo-type structure for latch V$ performance views. There are numerous views, but we will simply look at the topmost part of the third layer, for latches only.

Figure 24.7
Drilling down into latches

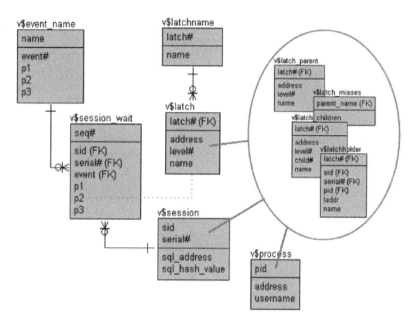

For latch free wait events, the LATCH# column on the V$LATCH-NAME view is contained in the PARAMETER2 column of the V$SESSION_WAIT view. This allows direct or indirect drilldown access into all of the various latch performance views. Let's take a look at current latch wait problems in order to demonstrate parameter-level drilldown into the third layer of the Oracle Database Wait Event Interface. First, check the parameter values:

```
SELECT parameter1||' '||parameter2||' '||parameter3
FROM v$event_name WHERE name = 'latch free';
```

This is the result:

```
PARAMETER1||''||PARAMETER2||''||PARAMETER3
-------------------------------------------
address number tries
```

PARAMETER2 contains a latch number, the equivalent of the LATCH# column in the V$LATCH performance view. The following query will not really tell us much, but it joins the V$LATCH and V$SESSION_WAIT performance views:

```
SELECT sw.sid, sw.event, sw.wait_time, sw.seconds_in_wait
,l.name, l.gets, l.misses, l.sleeps
FROM v$session_wait sw, v$latch l
WHERE sw.p2 = l.latch# AND IdleEvent(event) IS NOT NULL;
```

This is the result in my Oracle 10*g* Database:

```
SID EVENT                        WAIT_TIME SECONDS_IN_WAIT NAME
--- ---------------------------- --------- --------------- ----------------------
147 control file sequential read         0               0 post/wait queue
153 latch: library cache                 1              65 library cache
162 os thread startup                    0               0 event range base latch
133 log file sync                        0               2 event range base latch
```

We could quite obviously drill into the latches further, as can be seen in Figure 24.7. We can link to sessions, processes, SQL code, and query execution plans—the list goes on. The point to make now is as follows: There is a much easier way of drilling down into the Oracle Database Wait Event Interface—using the GUIs (Oracle Enterprise Manager and the Database Control). Similar functionality is available in tools such as Spotlight and STATSPACK. Before we move onto using the GUI to drilldown into the Oracle Database Wait Event Interface, we must digress a little into some Oracle Database 10*g* improvements to the Wait Event Interface.

24.4 (10*g*) **Oracle Database Wait Event Interface Improvements**

The following V$ performance views have been added to:

- **V$EVENT_NAME**. Class information is added, allowing classification and links to other V$ performance views containing class columns. A class is a classification or category for a wait event, as can be seen in the following query:

```
SELECT DISTINCT(wait_class) FROM v$event_name ORDER BY 1;

CLASS
----------------------------------------------------------
Administrative
Application
Cluster
Commit
Concurrency
Configuration
Idle
Network
Other
Scheduler
System I/O
User I/O
```

- ■ ***V$SESSION***. This has a lot more information in it, including class and parameter details for direct hooks to the third layer and beyond of the Oracle Database Wait Event Interface.

- ■ ***V$SESSION_WAIT***. This now includes wait event class columns.

These V$ performance views are new to Oracle Database 10*g*:

- ■ ***V$SYSTEM_WAIT_CLASS***. This is aggregation layer wait times for classes.

- ■ ***V$SESSION_WAIT_CLASS***. This is similar, but in the session layer.

- ■ ***V$EVENT_HISTOGRAM***. This is a waits and wait times event histogram.

- ■ ***V$FILE_HISTOGRAM and V$TEMP_HISTOGRAM***. These are single block read histograms for datafiles and temporary datafiles.

- ■ ***V$ACTIVE_SESSION_HISTORY***. This contains snapshots of wait event information, providing a history of wait event activity at the session level. This detail was previously aggregated into the system level (V$SYSTEM_EVENT) and is no longer available for the session level after disconnection of the session.

- *V$SYS_TIME_MODEL and V$SESS_TIME_MODEL*. These are wait event time accumulation statistics for the session level.

24.5   ⑨ᵢ Oracle Enterprise Manager and the Wait Event Interface

Oracle Enterprise Manager is an excellent tool for drilling down visually into the Oracle Database Wait Event Interface. Spotlight is best for real-time monitoring of a busy production database because it places all the important monitoring information in one place. However, Oracle Enterprise Manager is more visually palatable and easier to use as a drilldown tool.

We now have a basic understanding of the underlying V$ performance views allowing access into Oracle Database Wait Event Interface statistics. On that basis, I have abandoned any deeper layer drilldown into the Oracle Database Wait Event Interface using the Oracle Database V$ performance views. This is because Oracle Enterprise Manager is so much easier to use in this respect. Why make it difficult?

Some of the visual aspects of Oracle Enterprise Manager have already been covered in previous chapters of this book. It is assumed you know how to execute the console and log into a Management Server to allow access and drilldown into the Oracle Database Wait Event Interface for a particular database.

Note: Use of the Management Server is not an absolute requirement, but it does sometimes provide better functionality.

What I am going to do is to connect to my very busy database in the console (logged in through a Management Server) and then execute the Performance Overview option in the Diagnostics Pack, under the Tools menu. Then I will see if there are any problems with my database. If there are any problems, I will drilldown into those problem areas and attempt to locate something I can tune.

Looking at the Database Memory portion in the Database Health Overview chart, I notice something odd. The database buffer cache hit ratio is going up and down, vacillating between 60% and 90%, as shown in Figure 24.8. Depending on the application, this may not be a problem. However, since my application is mostly very small transactions, it seems a little odd.

Figure 24.8
Database Health Overview chart— Database Memory portion

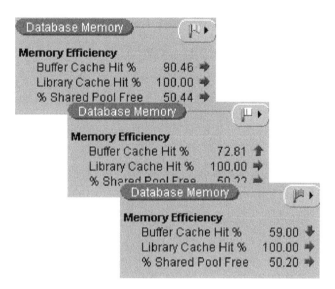

I am certainly not going to make my database buffer cache larger. Another clue is noticeable in that latch free wait events, as well as scattered reads, are much more prominent than sequential reads when the red flag is up, as seen in Figure 24.9.

Figure 24.9
Database Health Overview Chart— Database Memory portion

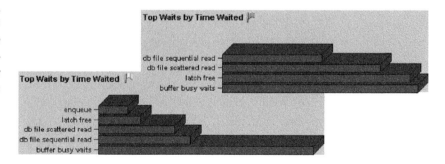

A large transaction is probably forcing highly used blocks out of the buffer. Consequently, those highly used blocks will probably be loaded back into the buffer. Let's drilldown. Looking at Figure 24.10, I drilldown into the *Top Objects By Physical Reads* and the *TopSQL (Physical Reads)*.

The two drilldown screens shown in Figure 24.10 tell me a lot. Note a number of points:

Figure 24.10
Top Objects and TopSQL

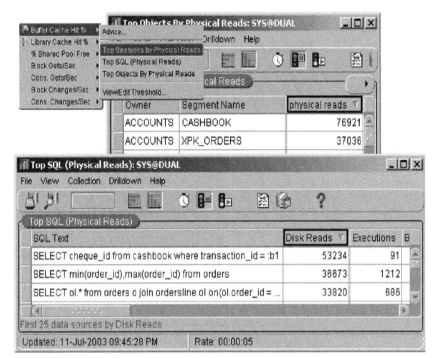

- The Cashbook table is at the top of both database objects and SQL in terms of data reads.

- The number of executions for the top SQL statement is relatively low.

- The physical reads for the Cashbook table is double the next object on the list, which is the Orders table primary key index.

- The really obvious part is that the Cashbook table is shown as being heavily active. An index on the Cashbook table is not being used.

By examining Figure 24.10 a little further, do I know what to look for yet? Yes, I do. The Cashbook table is probably being full table scanned when it should not be. Why? The SQL code statement on the Cashbook table has a WHERE clause against a foreign key index. I checked foreign key indexes on the Cashbook table. I found that the foreign key index on the Cashbook table TRANSACTION_ID column foreign key relation, to the Transactions table, was missing. The chances are, I dropped the index in error sometime during the course of writing this book. Or, it was never created. Let's create that index:

```
CREATE INDEX XFK_CB_TRANS ON cashbook(transaction_id)
TABLESPACE INDX ONLINE;
```

I then drilled down into the TopSQL and Top Objects tools again. I found that the Cashbook table was not even in the top 10 for both tools, as was evident in Figure 24.10. The problem was solved.

Any type of wait event can be drilled down into the lowest level of detail with a multitude of iterations of each tool using the Oracle Database Wait Event Interface, as implemented in the Oracle Enterprise Manager GUI. I would not recommend using the Oracle Database Wait Event Interface in any other way. Unless, of course, you have upgraded to Oracle 10*g* Database—then you can use the Database Control.

24.6 ⑩ The Database Control and the Wait Event Interface

What makes sense in this section is to do the same thing in the Database Control as I did with Oracle Enterprise Manager (for Oracle 9*i* Database). So, I do three things: (1) I watch the Database Control main screen with the index created, (2) I then drop the index and continue watching for a while, and (3) finally, I recreate the index and watch the Database Control again for a few minutes. The results of these three steps are shown in Figure 24.11.

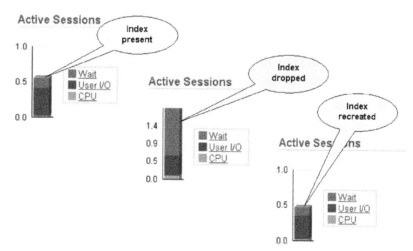

Figure 24.11

Active sessions in the Database Control

In Figure 24.11, I pulled out the graphic for the Active Sessions section for the different states of the index mentioned previously.

There is one thing wrong with this situation in that I know what the problem that I am looking for is. But never mind that for now. Figure 24.11 shows that when the index is dropped, wait events go up drastically. So, it makes sense to drop the index again, get the wait events up, and then drilldown into the wait events. I drilldown into wait events by clicking the Wait link in the Active Sessions section.

The index can be dropped using this statement:

```
DROP INDEX XFK_CB_TRANS;
```

And recreated using this statement:

```
CREATE INDEX XFK_CB_TRANS ON cashbook(transaction_id)
TABLESPACE INDX ONLINE;
```

Nothing else on the Database Control Home screen indicates any kind of problem with the database, other than the messages in the Performance Analysis section at the bottom of the screen (scroll down). The Performance Analysis section is shown in Figure 24.12.

Figure 24.12
Performance analysis in the Database Control

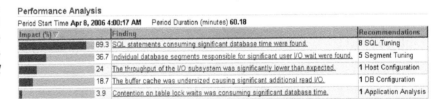

Performance Analysis

Period Start Time **Apr 8, 2006 4:00:17 AM**   Period Duration (minutes) **60.18**

Impact (%) ▽		Finding	Recommendations
	89.3	SQL statements consuming significant database time were found.	8 SQL Tuning
	36.7	Individual database segments responsible for significant user I/O wait were found.	5 Segment Tuning
	24	The throughput of the I/O subsystem was significantly lower than expected.	1 Host Configuration
	18.7	The buffer cache was undersized causing significant additional read I/O.	1 DB Configuration
	3.9	Contention on table lock waits was consuming significant database time.	1 Application Analysis

The performance analysis shown in Figure 24.12 tells me that SQL statements are causing some flag waving by the Database Control. Before examining SQL statements in detail, let's go back to Figure 24.11 and examine the database from the perspective of active sessions. I click on the Wait link in the Active Sessions section, as shown in Figure 24.11. The result I get is shown in Figure 24.13.

In Figure 24.13, the list of links on the right side is the various wait event classes. This book is printed in black and white (the Database Control uses lots of colors). So, you may not see this in the picture in the book, but probably 99% of the graph shown in Figure 24.13 is the color of the

Figure 24.13
Average sessions by wait event classification

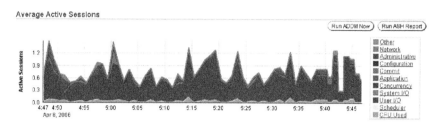

User I/O class wait events. That's events like scattered and sequential reads. When clicking the User I/O link classification as shown in Figure 24.13, the result as shown in Figure 24.14 is returned.

Figure 24.14
User I/O class wait events for active sessions

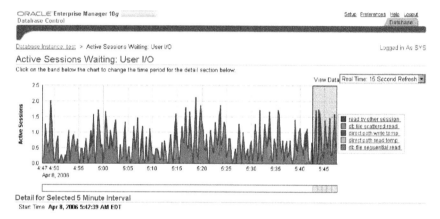

Once again, this book is printed in black and white, and the Database Control uses lots of different colors. So, I will tell you about it again. To the right side of Figure 24.14 is a list of user I/O classified wait events. The most frequent wait event indicated in the graph shown in Figure 24.14 is probably around 75% sequential reads (db file_sequential_read). High frequency of this wait event could indicate hot blocks in indexes and tables. This is very likely, considering the nature of the simulated application in the Accounts schema.

Figure 24.15 shows the drilldown from the link on the right side of Figure 24.14 for the db_file_sequential_read event.

Figure 24.16 is a drilldown from the SQL statements issue, as shown in Figure 24.12. Figure 24.16 shows SQL statements by TopSessions. What this means is that the busiest sessions are placed at the top of the list on the right side of Figure 24.16.

Figure 24.15
Sequential reads drilldown screen

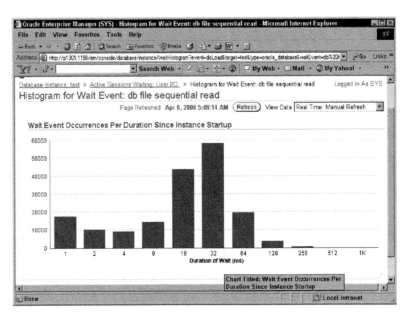

Figure 24.16
Drilldown in SQL statements by top session

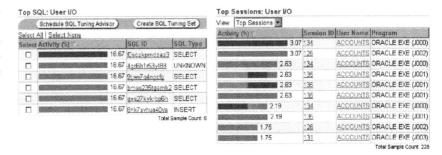

Figure 24.17 becomes a little more useful by changing Top Sessions to Top Objects. Now we can see that specific tables and indexes, in the Accounts schema, are much busier than everything else. This could indicate a number of problems with indexing. It is also quite possible that these problems might actually be the same problem but on different tables.

Again colors are an issue. Figure 24.14 has different colors applied to the different wait events listed on the right side of the graph. Now you may not be able to see this in the black and white print of Figure 24.17, but the bars across the table cell are made of the colors of the different wait events. The colors are related to the User I/O wait events because I have drilled down into the User I/O wait events. The bars are under the column called Activity (%). You can't see the colors so I will tell you about them a little. For

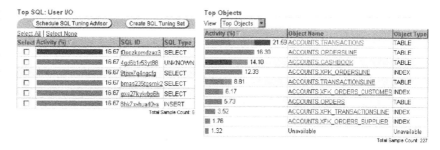

Figure 24.17
*Drilldown in SQL
statements by top
objects*

example, the Top Object indicated in Figure 24.17 is the Transactions table in the Accounts schema. The total user I/O wait event activity against the table is 21.59% of the total for all user I/O wait events. The bar has three colors: (1) blue for sequential reads, (2) brown for scattered reads, and (3) green for waiting for a consistent read by another session to complete. All this tells me is that the Transactions table is busy for both full read scans and index access. Index access includes both read and write activity. All I can sensibly conclude from this information is that the Transactions table is busy and that access is split between sequential and scattered activity. That is all normal for this table and this application.

The third item down the list on the right side of the picture in Figure 24.17 is the Cashbook table (we know this table is missing an index). The bar for the Cashbook table is different because it contains lots of green (read by another session), no blue whatsoever (no index reads), and lots of scattered reads (lots of full scanning). There's the missing index!

So I go back and recreate the missing foreign key index on the Cashbook table again. I then wait a few minutes and examine the Database Control again by Top Objects. And guess what? The Cashbook table disappears from the list shown on the right side of Figure 24.17. The problem is solved.

Objects are shown on the right side of Figure 24.17, and SQL statements are shown on the left side of Figure 24.17. All of these are links and can be drilled down into showing tables, structures, and indexes (we can drilldown into these further).

The only gripe I have with the information shown in Figure 24.17 is the query shown in the popup window in Figure 24.18. All the queries listed on the left side of Figure 24.18 are system-type queries and have absolutely nothing to do with my Accounts schema. This, of course, may indicate that my Accounts schema queries are efficient.

Figure 24.18
*Top SQL
statements in the
Database Control*

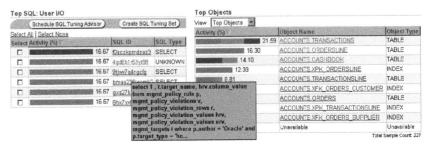

This chapter covered bottleneck isolation and identification using the Oracle Database Wait Event Interface. The next chapter looks at the command-line tuning tool STATSPACK.

25

$\textcircled{9i}$ *Tuning with STATSPACK*

STATSPACK has been discussed and referred to in this book on numerous occasions. STATSPACK is probably superceded by the Database Control AWR, and ADDM. However, it is quite possible that some DBAs still may prefer to use STATSPACK. Additionally, this book technically intends to cover all versions of Oracle Database from 9*i* through and including the latest version of 10*g*. Thus, inclusion of STATSPACK makes perfect sense.

25.1 Using STATSPACK

Chapter 23 included a brief description of how to set up STATSPACK, how to execute snapshots at different periods of time, and how to execute STATSPACK reports. As already stated in Chapter 23, STATSPACK is useful for analysis and detection of bottlenecks. In my opinion, Oracle Enterprise Manager and the Database Control (AWR and ADDM tools) are better at providing more focused and easy-to-use drilldown into the Wait Event Interface.

Note: $\textcircled{9i}$ STATSPACK was supposedly the official Oracle Corporation performance monitoring and tuning tool for Oracle 9*i* Database.

The easiest method of briefly explaining STATSPACK and its use is to display an example output report. Then we can describe the different sections step by step, as textual inserts into the report itself. The example used in this section is a range of ten level 6 snapshots, with the database in a consistent state of flux (intense simulated change activity) across all snapshots.

> **Note:** With the TIMED_STATISTICS parameter set to TRUE, events are listed in order of wait times, as opposed to the number of waits. Wait times are much more significant than number of waits.

25.1.1   An Example STATSPACK Report

This first section shows basic configuration and database instance information. This is a header for this chapter's STATSPACK report:

```
STATSPACK report for

DB Name        DB Id    Instance     Inst Num Release     Cluster Host
------------ ----------- ------------ -------- ----------- ------- ------------
TEST         1798396642 test               1 9.2.0.1.0   NO      2000SERVER


              Snap Id    Snap Time    Sessions Curs/Sess Comment
              ------- ------------------ -------- --------- --------------------
Begin Snap:       191 08-Aug-03 16:15:40      21       7.5
  End Snap:       200 08-Aug-03 16:31:04      21       7.1
  Elapsed:                 15.40 (mins)


Cache Sizes (end)
~~~~~~~~~~~~~~~~~
            Buffer Cache:        32M    Std Block Size:         8K
       Shared Pool Size:        64M        Log Buffer:       512K
```

The load profile section gives an overall health check and load information for the database server. The three most important things are *hard parses*, which should be as low as possible, *executions per second*, and *transactions per second*. Other values in this example report are all typical of an OLTP database, which the Accounts schema is attempting to simulate:

```
Load Profile
~~~~~~~~~~~~                      Per Second       Per Transaction
                                 ---------------   ---------------
            Redo size:              69,010.88          8,372.64
        Logical reads:               1,945.87            236.08
        Block changes:                 489.67             59.41
```

```
              Physical reads:              126.89              15.39
             Physical writes:               20.40               2.47
                  User calls:                8.54               1.04
                      Parses:               60.15               7.30
                Hard parses:                 0.02               0.00
                       Sorts:               27.41               3.33
                      Logons:                2.76               0.34
                   Executes:               120.65              14.64
               Transactions:                 8.24
```

```
% Blocks changed per Read:    25.16    Recursive Call %:    98.68
Rollback per transaction %:    0.33    Rows per Sort:       14.94
```

The instance efficiency section simply shows various ratios. Remember that ratios can be symptoms or indications of possible problems elsewhere. Do not attempt to tune ratios. The only possible problems in this case could be significant reparsing, and perhaps memory usage is a little low:

```
Instance Efficiency Percentages (Target 100%)
~~~~~~~~~~~~~~~~~~~~~~~~~~~~~~~~~~~~~~~~~~~~~~~~~
               Buffer Nowait %:    99.69        Redo NoWait %:   100.00
               Buffer  Hit   %:    93.65     In-memory Sort %:    99.85
               Library Hit   %:    99.99         Soft Parse %:    99.97
             Execute to Parse %:    50.15          Latch Hit %:   100.00
    Parse CPU to Parse Elapsd %:    66.64     % Non-Parse CPU:    97.37


    Shared Pool Statistics         Begin   End
                                   ------  ------
                 Memory Usage %:    32.76   33.78
          % SQL with executions>1:  73.04   88.26
       % Memory for SQL w/exec>1:   54.99   89.13
```

The top five timed wait events are those that can potentially affect performance most significantly. In this example report, sequential reads are much higher than scattered reads. This is normal for a small-sized transactional OTLP-type database. Buffer busy wait events are probably occurring due to conflict between many small transactions and a few large transactions, or as a result of lack of concurrency. The Accounts schema database has a small amount of reporting functionality executing on it as well as containing a heavy small transactional load:

Top 5 Timed Events

```
~~~~~~~~~~~~~~~~~~~                                            % Total
Event                                  Waits   Time (s) Ela Time
----------------------------------- ------------ ----------- --------
db file sequential read               79,028      7,261    80.74
db file scattered read                 3,325        424     4.71
buffer busy waits                      5,451        366     4.06
CPU time                                           286      3.18
direct path read                       1,513        205     2.28
                    -----------------------------------------------
```

Now we get a list of all wait events in order of wait time descending. Once again, the most significant wait time by far is for sequential reads. Sequential reads often indicate single block reads. High single block read wait times indicate concurrency issues at the block level, perhaps hot blocks; in the Accounts schema this very likely:

Wait Events for DB: TEST   Instance: test   Snaps: 191 –200
-> s – second
-> cs – centisecond -   100th of a second
-> ms – millisecond -   1000th of a second
-> us – microsecond - 1000000th of a second
-> **ordered by wait time desc, waits desc (idle events last)**

Event	Waits	Timeouts	Total Wait Time (s)	Avg wait (ms)	Waits /txn
db file sequential read	**79,028**	**0**	**7,261**	**92**	**10.4**
db file scattered read	3,325	0	424	127	0.4
buffer busy waits	5,451	0	366	67	0.7
direct path read	1,513	0	205	135	0.2
db file parallel write	820	408	105	128	0.1
enqueue	447	2	103	230	0.1
control file sequential read	610	0	66	108	0.1
log file sync	2,775	0	63	23	0.4
log file parallel write	7,017	4,957	57	8	0.9
control file parallel write	298	0	29	96	0.0
latch free	321	59	17	54	0.0
log file switch completion	9	1	8	873	0.0
direct path write	86	0	4	51	0.0

LGWR wait for redo copy	92	12	1	6	0.0
buffer deadlock	6	6	0	21	0.0
log file sequential read	2	0	0	11	0.0
log file single write	2	0	0	9	0.0
SQL*Net break/reset to clien	4	0	0	0	0.0
SQL*Net more data to client	3	0	0	0	0.0
wakeup time manager	29	29	858	29601	0.0
SQL*Net message from client	154	0	242	1569	0.0
SQL*Net more data from clien	22	0	0	0	0.0
SQL*Net message to client	154	0	0	0	0.0

The list of all wait events is followed by background processing wait events:

Background Wait Events for DB: TEST   Instance: test   Snaps: 191 –200
-> ordered by wait time desc, waits desc (idle events last)

				Avg	
			Total Wait	wait	Waits
Event	Waits	Timeouts	Time (s)	(ms)	/txn
db file parallel write	822	409	105	128	0.1
log file parallel write	7,021	4,959	57	8	0.9
control file parallel write	298	0	29	96	0.0
control file sequential read	136	0	18	129	0.0
db file scattered read	71	0	12	166	0.0
latch free	24	0	4	162	0.0
db file sequential read	28	0	4	133	0.0
LGWR wait for redo copy	92	12	1	6	0.0
direct path write	10	0	0	11	0.0
direct path read	10	0	0	8	0.0
log file sequential read	2	0	0	11	0.0
log file single write	2	0	0	9	0.0
buffer busy waits	1	0	0	9	0.0
rdbms ipc reply	4	0	0	2	0.0
rdbms ipc message	13,706	8,089	5,372	392	1.8
smon timer	3	2	782	#####	0.0

The next sections contain parsed SQL code ordered in various different ways. The first section orders SQL statements in descending database buffer gets order, where buffer gets exceed 10,000. It is my personal opinion that sequencing SQL code statements based on database buffer cache hits is not particularly useful to tuning in general, since it advocates *fiddling* with the size of the database buffer cache and shared pool.

> **Note:** Hash values can be used to access details of specific SQL code statements.

```
SQL ordered by Gets for DB: TEST  Instance: test  Snaps: 191 -200
-> End Buffer Gets Threshold:    10000
-> Note that resources reported for PL/SQL includes the resources used by
   all SQL statements called within the PL/SQL code.  As individual SQL
   statements are also reported, it is possible and valid for the summed
   total % to exceed 100
```

> **Note:** The number of executions is nearly always significant, regardless of how much a type of activity an SQL code statement is causing. A poorly tuned SQL code statement, even a simple statement, executed much more often than any other SQL code is always a problem.

```
                                                    CPU     Elapsd
 Buffer Gets    Executions  Gets per Exec  %Total Time (s)  Time (s) Hash Value
--------------- ------------ --------------- ------ -------- --------- ----------
   1,646,666       2,548         646.3      91.6   254.07   8266.96 1852168585
DECLARE job BINARY_INTEGER := :job; next_date DATE := :mydate;
broken BOOLEAN := FALSE; BEGIN SIMULATE; :mydate := next_date;
IF broken THEN :b := 1; ELSE :b := 0; END IF; END;

     235,786        468          503.8      13.1   132.43    871.74 2026502321
SELECT min(order_id),max(order_id) from orders

     136,975        251          545.7       7.6     6.43   1642.38 3111014165
SELECT tl.* from transactions t join transactionsline tl on(tl.t
ransaction_id = t.transaction_id) where t.supplier_id = :b1

     132,626       8,416          15.8       7.4     4.81     70.13 2781724698
INSERT into transactionsline values(:b4,:b3,:b2,:b1)

     132,557       8,415          15.8       7.4     5.06     62.82 1787838546
          -------------------------------------------------------------
```

> **Note:** All but the first five SQL code statements have been deleted from this section of this STATSPACK report. This avoids large amounts of superfluous text, an equally large quantity of paper, and a certain propensity to confusion on the part of the reader.

Ordering SQL code statements by descending physical reads—actual I/O activity—is much more useful than using descending buffer gets order. I/O activity can be a performance hog, but it can also be necessary depending on application and database type. For instance, full physical scans are preferable in data warehouses:

```
SQL ordered by Reads for DB: TEST  Instance: test  Snaps: 191 -200
-> End Disk Reads Threshold:     1000


                                                 CPU     Elapsd
Physical Reads   Executions  Reads per Exec %Total Time (s)  Time (s) Hash Value
--------------- ------------ --------------- ------ -------- --------- ----------
        111,203        2,548           43.6   94.8   254.07   8266.96 1852168585
DECLARE job BINARY_INTEGER := :job; next_date DATE := :mydate;
broken BOOLEAN := FALSE; BEGIN SIMULATE; :mydate := next_date; I
F broken THEN :b := 1; ELSE :b := 0; END IF; END;


         32,461          468           69.4   27.7   132.43    871.74 2026502321
SELECT min(order_id),max(order_id) from orders


         18,974          357           53.1   16.2     5.43   1622.03 3751280151
SELECT ol.* from orders o join ordersline ol on(ol.order_id = o.
order_id) where o.supplier_id = :b1


         18,891          251           75.3   16.1     6.43   1642.38 3111014165
SELECT tl.* from transactions t join transactionsline tl on(tl.t
ransaction_id = t.transaction_id) where t.supplier_id = :b1


          7,602          250           30.4    6.5     4.65    647.74   92829708
SELECT tl.* from transactions t join transactionsline tl on(tl.t
ransaction_id = t.transaction_id) where t.customer_id = :b1


          -------------------------------------------------------------
```

Note: Once again, all but the first five SQL code statements have been deleted from this section of this STATSPACK report.

In the next STATSPACK report snippet, SQL code statements have been sorted in descending order of execution. Ordering by number of executions is generally the most useful sorting option. The most useful method for detecting problems for highly active OLTP databases is usually a combination of executions and physical reads:

```
SQL ordered by Executions for DB: TEST   Instance: test  Snaps: 191 -200
-> End Executions Threshold:       100


                                             CPU per    Elap per
  Executions   Rows Processed   Rows per Exec   Exec (s)   Exec (s)  Hash Value
------------  ----------------  ----------------  -----------  ----------  ----------
      13,313           13,313              1.0        0.00        0.00 2489014428
SELECT to_number(to_char(SYSTIMESTAMP,'FF3'))+1 from dual

       8,416            8,416              1.0        0.00        0.01 2781724698
INSERT into transactionsline values(:b4,:b3,:b2,:b1)

       8,416            8,416              1.0        0.00        0.00 2822097328
INSERT into cashbookline values(:b3,:b2,:b1)

       8,415            8,415              1.0        0.00        0.01 1787838546
INSERT into ordersline values(:b4,:b3,:b2,:b1)

       8,413            8,413              1.0        0.00        0.01  52940216
INSERT into stockmovement values(stockmovement_seq.nextval,:b4,(
:b3*-1),:b2,:b1)    returning stockmovement_id  INTO :b0
          ----------------------------------------------------------------
```

The number of parse calls for an SQL code statement is relevant because it denotes how often SQL code statements are reparsed. Reparsing is inefficient because it costs significant CPU processing time:

```
SQL ordered by Parse Calls for DB: TEST   Instance: test  Snaps: 191 -200
-> End Parse Calls Threshold:       1000
```

```
                       % Total
Parse Calls   Executions   Parses   Hash Value
------------  ------------  -------  ----------
      3,612         3,612     6.50  3615375148
COMMIT


      2,571         2,558     4.63   493392946
update sys.job$ set this_date=:1 where job=:2


      2,570         2,570     4.62   990457800
select u1.user#, u2.user#, u3.user#, failures, flag, interval#,
   what, nlsenv, env, field1  from sys.job$ j, sys.user$ u1, sys
.user$ u2, sys.user$ u3  where job=:1 and (next_date < sysdate o
r :2 != 0)  and lowner = u1.name and powner = u2.name and cowner
 = u3.name


      2,570         2,557     4.62  3128358781
update sys.job$ set failures=0, this_date=null, flag=:1, last_da
te=:2,  next_date = greatest(:3, sysdate),  total=total+(sysdate
-nvl(this_date,sysdate)) where job=:4


      2,558         2,558     4.60  3013728279
select privilege#,level from sysauth$ connect by grantee#=prior
privilege# and privilege#>0 start with (grantee#=:1 or grantee#=
1) and privilege#>0
          -----------------------------------------------------------
```

The next section lists general instance activity statistics. There are a lot of different statistics to peruse. A large amount of information can be gathered from the instance activity statistics. Looking at the statistics we can see CPU usage, database writer process (DBWR) activity, buffers, enqueue locking, indexing, tables, I/O, logging, session activity, rollback and undo, and transactional activity, among many other indicators. The next output section is simply a list of all the instance activity statistics contained in a single section of the STATSPACK report. Two statistics shown in the STATSPACK report snippet shown here are called process last non-idle time and session connect time. These are both off the scale. The former statistic refers to the last time a process was executed. The latter statistic refers to session connection time. Both these statistics are irrelevant, based on the way in which my Accounts schema has OLTP activity executed against it:

Instance Activity Stats for DB: TEST   Instance: test   Snaps: 191 -200

Statistic	Total	per Second	per Trans
CPU used by this session	28,578	30.9	3.8
CPU used when call started	28,578	30.9	3.8
CR blocks created	644	0.7	0.1
DBWR buffers scanned	108,190	117.1	14.2
DBWR checkpoint buffers written	1,040	1.1	0.1
DBWR checkpoints	1	0.0	0.0
DBWR free buffers found	94,700	102.5	12.4
DBWR lru scans	429	0.5	0.1
DBWR make free requests	429	0.5	0.1
DBWR revisited being-written buff	0	0.0	0.0
DBWR summed scan depth	108,190	117.1	14.2
DBWR transaction table writes	51	0.1	0.0
DBWR undo block writes	3,800	4.1	0.5
SQL*Net roundtrips to/from client	151	0.2	0.0
active txn count during cleanout	6,271	6.8	0.8
background checkpoints completed	1	0.0	0.0
background checkpoints started	1	0.0	0.0
background timeouts	1,064	1.2	0.1
branch node splits	3	0.0	0.0
buffer is not pinned count	902,275	976.5	118.5
buffer is pinned count	130,645	141.4	17.2
bytes received via SQL*Net from c	138,570	150.0	18.2
bytes sent via SQL*Net to client	71,041	76.9	9.3
calls to get snapshot scn: kcmgss	194,194	210.2	25.5
calls to kcmgas	11,457	12.4	1.5
calls to kcmgcs	648	0.7	0.1
change write time	955	1.0	0.1
cleanout - number of ktugct calls	2,753	3.0	0.4
cleanouts and rollbacks - consist	184	0.2	0.0
cleanouts only - consistent read	141	0.2	0.0
cluster key scan block gets	241	0.3	0.0
cluster key scans	214	0.2	0.0
commit cleanout failures: block 1	113	0.1	0.0
commit cleanout failures: buffer	9	0.0	0.0
commit cleanout failures: callbac	57	0.1	0.0
commit cleanout failures: cannot	6	0.0	0.0
commit cleanouts	46,281	50.1	6.1

commit cleanouts successfully com	46,096	49.9	6.1
commit txn count during cleanout	5,998	6.5	0.8
consistent changes	2,968	3.2	0.4
consistent gets	1,101,924	1,192.6	144.7
consistent gets - examination	108,479	117.4	14.2
current blocks converted for CR	26	0.0	0.0
cursor authentications	82	0.1	0.0
data blocks consistent reads - un	2,363	2.6	0.3
db block changes	452,457	489.7	59.4
db block gets	696,070	753.3	91.4
deferred (CURRENT) block cleanout	10,492	11.4	1.4
dirty buffers inspected	1,266	1.4	0.2
enqueue conversions	4,213	4.6	0.6
enqueue deadlocks	1	0.0	0.0
enqueue releases	41,603	45.0	5.5
enqueue requests	41,610	45.0	5.5
enqueue timeouts	58	0.1	0.0
enqueue waits	423	0.5	0.1
exchange deadlocks	6	0.0	0.0
execute count	111,483	120.7	14.6
free buffer inspected	1,311	1.4	0.2
free buffer requested	120,649	130.6	15.8
hot buffers moved to head of LRU	34,312	37.1	4.5
immediate (CR) block cleanout app	325	0.4	0.0
immediate (CURRENT) block cleanou	5,150	5.6	0.7
index fast full scans (full)	463	0.5	0.1
index fetch by key	25,431	27.5	3.3
index scans kdiixs1	116,315	125.9	15.3
leaf node 90-10 splits	251	0.3	0.0
leaf node splits	547	0.6	0.1
logons cumulative	2,552	2.8	0.3
messages received	7,614	8.2	1.0
messages sent	7,614	8.2	1.0
no buffer to keep pinned count	0	0.0	0.0
no work - consistent read gets	858,628	929.3	112.7
opened cursors cumulative	54,152	58.6	7.1
parse count (failures)	1	0.0	0.0
parse count (hard)	18	0.0	0.0
parse count (total)	55,575	60.2	7.3
parse time cpu	753	0.8	0.1
parse time elapsed	1,130	1.2	0.2

physical reads	117,242	126.9	15.4
physical reads direct	3,116	3.4	0.4
physical writes	18,848	20.4	2.5
physical writes direct	3,125	3.4	0.4
physical writes non checkpoint	18,137	19.6	2.4
pinned buffers inspected	44	0.1	0.0
prefetched blocks	31,706	34.3	4.2
process last non-idle time	**2,692,317,558,691**	#############	############
recovery blocks read	0	0.0	0.0
recursive calls	590,362	638.9	77.5
recursive cpu usage	28,269	30.6	3.7
redo blocks written	132,490	143.4	17.4
redo buffer allocation retries	7	0.0	0.0
redo entries	229,257	248.1	30.1
redo log space requests	10	0.0	0.0
redo log space wait time	786	0.9	0.1
redo size	63,766,056	69,010.9	8,372.6
redo synch time	6,466	7.0	0.9
redo synch writes	2,663	2.9	0.4
redo wastage	1,924,580	2,082.9	252.7
redo write time	8,476	9.2	1.1
redo writer latching time	52	0.1	0.0
redo writes	7,004	7.6	0.9
rollback changes - undo records a	518	0.6	0.1
rollbacks only - consistent read	529	0.6	0.1
rows fetched via callback	17,855	19.3	2.3
session connect time	**2,692,317,558,691**	#############	############
session logical reads	1,797,981	1,945.9	236.1
session pga memory max	100,372	108.6	13.2
session uga memory	29,372,040	31,787.9	3,856.6
session uga memory max	268,212,120	290,272.9	35,216.9
shared hash latch upgrades - no w	76,480	82.8	10.0
shared hash latch upgrades - wait	1	0.0	0.0
sorts (disk)	38	0.0	0.0
sorts (memory)	25,287	27.4	3.3
sorts (rows)	378,384	409.5	49.7
summed dirty queue length	15,041	16.3	2.0
switch current to new buffer	997	1.1	0.1
table fetch by rowid	321,386	347.8	42.2
table fetch continued row	0	0.0	0.0
table scan blocks gotten	53,011	57.4	7.0

table scan rows gotten	9,862,509	10,673.7	1,295.0
table scans (long tables)	2	0.0	0.0
table scans (short tables)	24,593	26.6	3.2
transaction rollbacks	123	0.1	0.0
transaction tables consistent rea	13	0.0	0.0
transaction tables consistent rea	604	0.7	0.1
user calls	7,890	8.5	1.0
user commits	7,591	8.2	1.0
user rollbacks	25	0.0	0.0
write clones created in backgroun	1	0.0	0.0
write clones created in foregroun	41	0.0	0.0

The next two sections show tablespace and datafile physical read and write I/O statistics. In general, user application tables are contained within the DATA tablespace and related indexes in the INDX tablespace. Table reads should probably be higher than index reads because tables are read completely (full table scans) or as a result of index ROWID pointer searches and scans. Index writes are higher than table writes. This probably indicates many indexes for each table and high insertion activity. In fact, high row insertion activity is probably causing contention and thus the significant buffer wait events already seen. Other values in the following section indicate that temporary sort space on disk using the TEMP tablespace is possibly significant. Perhaps the sort area buffers, namely the SORT_AREA_SIZE and SORT_AREA_RETAINED SIZE parameters, could be increased in size. Rollback (automated undo) reads are likely caused by consistent transaction requirements. Write values for rollback space are much higher than those of read values. However, read values probably remain significant. However, in the Accounts schema, this type of rollback consistent requirement is normal for application and database type:

Tablespace IO Stats for DB: TEST   Instance: test   Snaps: 191 -200
->ordered by IOs (Reads + Writes) desc

Tablespace

	Reads	Av Reads/s	Av Rd(ms)	Av Blks/Rd	Writes	Av Writes/s	Buffer Waits	Av Buf Wt(ms)
--------------	-------	------	-------	------------	--------	----------	------	
DATA								
	42,865	46	101.1	1.0	3,280	4	1,287	66.2

INDX							
36,831	40	82.4	1.8	**7,106**	8	**4,145**	68.3
TEMP							
2,849	3	133.9	1.1	3,115	3	0	0.0
UNDOTBS1							
470	1	106.3	1.0	3,870	4	3	3.3
PERFSTAT							
1,721	2	130.7	1.0	1,367	1	0	0.0
SYSTEM							
453	0	131.1	2.6	95	0	75	43.2
OBJECTS							
1	0	170.0	1.0	1	0	0	0.0
TOOLS							
1	0	260.0	1.0	1	0	0	0.0
USERS							
1	0	260.0	1.0	1	0	0	0.0

With respect to datafiles, I/O activity appears to be spread well between the two datafiles for the DATA tablespace but not as well for the two datafiles in the INDX tablespace:

File IO Stats for DB: TEST   Instance: test   Snaps: 191 –200
->ordered by Tablespace, File

Tablespace   Filename
----------------------- ---

	Av	Av	Av		Av	Buffer	Av Buf
Reads	Reads/s	Rd(ms)	Blks/Rd	Writes	Writes/s	Waits	Wt(ms)
DATA			E:\ORACLE\ORADATA\TEST\DATA01.DBF				
21,460	23	103.4	1.0	1,606	2	549	65.1
			E:\ORACLE\ORADATA\TEST\DATA02.DBF				
21,405	23	98.8	1.1	1,674	2	738	67.0
INDX			E:\ORACLE\ORADATA\TEST\INDX01.DBF				
20,039	22	86.2	1.7	4,046	4	2,029	65.7
			E:\ORACLE\ORADATA\TEST\INDX02.DBF				
16,792	18	77.9	1.9	3,060	3	2,116	70.8
OBJECTS			E:\ORACLE\ORADATA\TEST\OBJECTS01.DBF				

1	0	170.0	1.0	1	0	0	

PERFSTAT   E:\ORACLE\ORADATA\TEST\PERFSTAT01.DBF

1,721	2	130.7	1.0	1,367	1	0	

SYSTEM   E:\ORACLE\ORADATA\TEST\SYSTEM01.DBF

453	0	131.1	2.6	95	0	75	43.2

TEMP   E:\ORACLE\ORADATA\TEST\TEMP01.DBF

2,849	3	133.9	1.1	3,115	3	0	

TOOLS   E:\ORACLE\ORADATA\TEST\TOOLS01.DBF

1	0	260.0	1.0	1	0	0	

UNDOTBS1   E:\ORACLE\ORADATA\TEST\UNDOTBS01.DBF

470	1	106.3	1.0	3,870	4	3	3.3

USERS   E:\ORACLE\ORADATA\TEST\USERS01.DBF

1	0	260.0	1.0	1	0	0	

Next we get database buffer cache statistics. Buffer busy waits are significant:

```
Buffer Pool Statistics for DB: TEST  Instance: test  Snaps: 191 -200
-> Standard block size Pools  D: default,  K: keep,  R: recycle
-> Default Pools for other block sizes: 2k, 4k, 8k, 16k, 32k
```

	Number of	Cache	Buffer	Physical	Physical	Free Buffer	Write Complete	Buffer Busy
P	Buffers	Hit %	Gets	Reads	Writes	Waits	Waits	Waits
---	----------	-----	----------	----------	----------	-------	--------	------
D	4,000	95.7	2,667,765	113,687	15,693	0	0	5,473

These are recovery requirement estimates:

```
Instance Recovery Stats for DB: TEST  Instance: test  Snaps: 191 -200
-> B: Begin snapshot,  E: End snapshot
```

	Targt MTTR (s)	Estd MTTR (s)	Recovery Estd IOs	Actual Redo Blks	Target Redo Blks	Log File Size Redo Blks	Log Ckpt Timeout Redo Blks	Log Ckpt Interval Redo Blks
B	35	27	496	25653	184320	184320	249736	
E	35	27	614	25742	184320	184320	221989	

This is the database buffer cache advisory. I did not find advisories particularly useful in Oracle 9*i* Database. They tended to encourage frequent upward resizing of the database buffer cache and shared pool. Resizing buffer pools upward does not solve problems but may sometimes alleviate symptoms of problems. It can even help to *obscure* significant performance problems:

Buffer Pool Advisory for DB: TEST   Instance: test   End Snap: 200
-> Only rows with estimated physical reads >0 are displayed
-> ordered by Block Size, Buffers For Estimate

P	Size for Estimate (M)	Size Factr	Buffers for Estimate	Est Physical Read Factor	Estimated Physical Reads
D	4	.1	500	4.83	8,118,743
D	8	.3	1,000	3.10	5,218,381
D	12	.4	1,500	1.99	3,340,086
D	16	.5	2,000	1.55	2,609,060
D	20	.6	2,500	1.35	2,275,264
D	24	.8	3,000	1.21	2,038,548
D	28	.9	3,500	1.10	1,851,173
D	32	1.0	4,000	1.00	1,681,112
D	36	1.1	4,500	0.91	1,533,069
D	40	1.3	5,000	0.83	1,401,561
D	44	1.4	5,500	0.76	1,281,701
D	48	1.5	6,000	0.70	1,171,290
D	52	1.6	6,500	0.64	1,070,867
D	56	1.8	7,000	0.58	979,671
D	60	1.9	7,500	0.53	892,039
D	64	2.0	8,000	0.48	808,529
D	68	2.1	8,500	0.44	737,110
D	72	2.3	9,000	0.40	673,978

D	76	2.4	9,500	0.37	618,692
D	80	2.5	10,000	0.34	569,011

Data block waits indicate hot block issues, common in highly active small transactional OLTP databases. Possible solutions are already well covered in this book:

```
Buffer wait Statistics for DB: TEST  Instance: test  Snaps: 191 -200
-> ordered by wait time desc, waits desc
```

		Tot Wait	Avg
Class	Waits	Time (s)	Time (ms)
data block	5,488	371	68
undo header	3	0	3

Enqueue activity is generally consistent with details covered already in this book. There is no need to reiterate:

```
Enqueue activity for DB: TEST  Instance: test  Snaps: 191 -200
-> Enqueue stats gathered prior to 9i should not be compared with 9i data
-> ordered by Wait Time desc, Waits desc
```

					Avg Wt	Wait
Eq	Requests	Succ Gets	Failed Gets	Waits	Time (ms)	Time (s)
TX	10,107	10,105	0	362	295.01	107
SQ	992	992	0	60	39.73	2
HW	69	69	0	1	.00	0

Rollback segment statistics show some wrapping, with, as already stated, possibly significant consistent transaction read requirements. In high concurrency, small transactional activity OLTP databases, this behavior is probably unavoidable. For automated undo, the UNDO_RETENTION parameter could be altered, for manual rollback segments create more, smaller rollback segments. Obviously, tuning rollback space does not solve the real problem but merely attempts to spread rollback more evenly. This may help to avoid rollback contention. The real problem is that the database is very busy. Possible solutions to this type of performance issue are better handling of concurrency at the block level by raising INITRANS values, using reverse key indexing, or perhaps even clustering:

Rollback Segment Stats for DB: TEST   Instance: test   Snaps: 191 -200
->A high value for "Pct Waits" suggests more rollback segments may be required
->RBS stats may not be accurate between begin and end snaps when using Auto Undo
  managment, as RBS may be dynamically created and dropped as needed

RBS No	Trans Table Gets	Pct Waits	Undo Bytes Written	Wraps	Shrinks	Extends
0	12.0	0.00	0	0	0	0
1	2,275.0	0.00	2,240,820	4	0	0
2	2,318.0	0.00	2,000,692	4	0	0
3	2,080.0	0.00	2,109,416	4	0	0
4	1,958.0	0.05	2,608,464	5	0	0
5	2,182.0	0.00	1,984,204	2	0	0
6	2,426.0	0.00	2,248,984	2	0	0
7	1,912.0	0.00	2,053,060	4	0	0
8	2,546.0	0.00	2,975,356	4	0	0
9	2,345.0	0.00	2,350,076	3	0	0
10	2,541.0	0.00	2,671,298	6	1	1

Rollback Segment Storage for DB: TEST   Instance: test   Snaps: 191 -200
->Optimal Size should be larger than Avg Active

RBS No	Segment Size	Avg Active	Optimal Size	Maximum Size
0	385,024	0		385,024
1	35,840,000	860,252		35,840,000
2	34,725,888	866,432		34,725,888
3	35,774,464	850,308		35,774,464
4	33,677,312	884,223		33,677,312
5	36,823,040	1,035,943		36,823,040
6	43,114,496	4,062,790		43,114,496
7	35,774,464	849,535		35,774,464
8	35,774,464	959,362		35,774,464

```
     9       35,774,464          987,376                    35,774,464
    10       32,759,808          697,641                    36,036,608
             -----------------------------------------------------------------
```

Undo Segment Summary for DB: TEST   Instance: test   Snaps: 191 -200
-> Undo segment block stats:
-> uS - unexpired Stolen,   uR - unexpired Released,   uU - unexpired reUsed
-> eS - expired   Stolen,   eR - expired   Released,   eU - expired   reUsed

Undo TS#	Undo Blocks	Num Trans	Max Qry Len (s)	Max Tx Concurcy	Snapshot Too Old	Out of Space	uS/uR/uU/ eS/eR/eU
1	5,291	452,288	196	3	0	0	0/0/0/0/0/0

```
             -----------------------------------------------------------------
```

Undo Segment Stats for DB: TEST   Instance: test   Snaps: 191 -200
-> ordered by Time desc

End Time	Undo Blocks	Num Trans	Max Qry Len (s)	Max Tx Concy	Snap Too Old	Out of Space	uS/uR/uU/ eS/eR/eU
08-Aug 16:36	2,378	157,059	196	2	0	0	0/0/0/0/0/0
08-Aug 16:26	2,334	150,680	169	2	0	0	0/0/0/0/0/0
08-Aug 16:16	579	144,549	28	3	0	0	0/0/0/0/0/0

```
             -----------------------------------------------------------------
```

Next is latch activity. There appear be significant issues with the data-base buffer cache and the library cache in the shared pool. These values are once again significant. The database buffer cache and shared pool are delib-erately set to low values in my database with my busy Accounts schema. This is done to create tunable problems:

Latch Activity for DB: TEST   Instance: test   Snaps: 191 -200
->"Get Requests", "Pct Get Miss" and "Avg Slps/Miss" are statistics for
  willing-to-wait latch get requests
->"NoWait Requests", "Pct NoWait Miss" are for no-wait latch get requests
->"Pct Misses" for both should be very close to 0.0

Latch	Get Requests	Pct Get Miss	Avg Slps /Miss	Wait Time (s)	NoWait Requests	Pct NoWait Miss
Consistent RBA	7,028	0.0		0	0	
FIB s.o chain latch	4	0.0		0	0	
FOB s.o list latch	57	0.0		0	0	
SQL memory manager worka	603	0.0		0	0	
active checkpoint queue	901	0.0		0	0	
archive control	12	0.0		0	0	
cache buffer handles	1,556	0.0		0	0	
cache buffers chains	4,761,717	0.0	1.0	0	154,473	0.0
cache buffers lru chain	153,530	0.0	1.0	0	84	0.0
channel handle pool latc	2	0.0		0	0	
channel operations paren	587	0.0		0	0	
checkpoint queue latch	66,578	0.0		0	15,155	0.0
child cursor hash table	293	0.0		0	0	
dml lock allocation	43,873	0.0	1.0	0	0	
dummy allocation	5,120	0.0		0	0	
enqueue hash chains	88,018	0.0	6.0	15	0	
enqueues	23,702	0.0	1.0	0	0	
event group latch	1	0.0		0	0	
file number translation	6,045	0.0		0	0	
hash table column usage	10	0.0		0	30	0.0
job workq parent latch	0			0	3,122	0.0
job_queue_processes para	375	0.0		0	0	
ktm global data	5	0.0		0	0	
kwqit: protect wakeup ti	29	0.0		0	0	
lgwr LWN SCN	7,029	0.0		0	0	
library cache	1,022,754	0.0	1.1	1	0	
library cache load lock	12	0.0		0	0	
library cache pin	630,683	0.0	1.0	0	0	
library cache pin alloca	323,891	0.0	1.1	0	0	
list of block allocation	8,313	0.0		0	0	
loader state object free	170	0.0		0	0	
longop free list parent	19	0.0		0	19	0.0
messages	35,912	0.0	1.0	0	0	
mostly latch-free SCN	7,031	0.0		0	0	
multiblock read objects	12,287	0.0		0	2	0.0
ncodef allocation latch	23	0.0		0	0	
post/wait queue	14,181	0.0		0	2,790	0.0

process allocation	1	0.0		0	1	0.0
process group creation	2	0.0		0	0	
redo allocation	242,912	0.0	1.1	0	0	
redo copy	60	1.7	2.0	0	228,845	0.1
redo writing	22,607	0.0		0	0	
row cache enqueue latch	29,914	0.0		0	0	
row cache objects	36,319	0.0		0	0	
sequence cache	57,781	0.0	1.0	0	0	
session allocation	68,320	0.0		0	0	
session idle bit	18,430	0.0		0	0	
session switching	23	0.0		0	0	
session timer	485	0.0		0	0	
shared pool	333,910	0.0	2.0	0	0	
sim partition latch	0			0	67	0.0
simulator hash latch	122,962	0.0		0	0	
simulator lru latch	12,525	0.0		0	118	0.0
sort extent pool	254	0.0		0	0	
transaction allocation	6,507	0.0		0	0	
transaction branch alloc	23	0.0		0	0	
undo global data	36,910	0.0	1.0	0	0	
user lock	5,096	0.0		0	0	

Latch sleeps are a result of missed latch acquisition. Missed latches are problematic for performance. Once again, significant issues are apparent in the database buffer cache and the library cache section of the shared pool:

Latch Sleep breakdown for DB: TEST   Instance: test   Snaps: 191 -200
-> ordered by misses desc

Latch Name	Get Requests	Misses	Sleeps	Spin & Sleeps 1->4
library cache	1,022,754	115	121	0/109/6/0/0
cache buffers chains	4,761,717	58	58	0/0/0/0/0
cache buffers lru chain	153,530	30	31	0/29/1/0/0
redo allocation	242,912	17	18	0/16/1/0/0
enqueue hash chains	88,018	9	54	0/3/0/6/0
library cache pin allocati	323,891	9	10	0/8/1/0/0
library cache pin	630,683	8	8	0/8/0/0/0
dml lock allocation	43,873	7	7	0/7/0/0/0

sequence cache	57,781	4	4 0/4/0/0/0
enqueues	23,702	3	3 0/3/0/0/0
undo global data	36,910	2	2 0/2/0/0/0
messages	35,912	1	1 0/1/0/0/0
redo copy	60	1	2 0/0/1/0/0
shared pool	**333,910**	**1**	**2 0/0/1/0/0**

The next section shows very deep-level sources of missed latches. From my perspective, this information is too excessive to be useful, considering the power of other tuning tools available:

Latch Miss Sources for DB: TEST   Instance: test   Snaps: 191 -200
-> only latches with sleeps are shown
-> ordered by name, sleeps desc

Latch Name	Where	NoWait Misses	Sleeps	Waiter Sleeps
cache buffers chains	kcbgtcr: kslbegin excl	0	21	24
cache buffers chains	kcbrls: kslbegin	0	13	9
cache buffers chains	kcbgcur: kslbegin	0	7	11
cache buffers chains	kcbchg: kslbegin: call CR	0	3	0
cache buffers chains	kcbget: exchange rls	0	3	0
cache buffers chains	kcbzwb	0	3	2
cache buffers chains	kcbget: exchange	0	2	0
cache buffers chains	kcbgtcr: fast path	0	2	3
cache buffers chains	kcbget: pin buffer	0	2	8
cache buffers chains	kcbchg: kslbegin: bufs not	0	1	0
cache buffers chains	kcbnlc	0	1	0
cache buffers lru chain	kcbzgb: wait	0	27	29
cache buffers lru chain	kcbbiop: lru scan	0	2	0
cache buffers lru chain	kcbbxsv: move to being wri	0	1	0
cache buffers lru chain	kcbzgb: posted for free bu	0	1	1
dml lock allocation	ktaiam	0	4	3
dml lock allocation	ktaidm	0	3	4
enqueue hash chains	ksqcmi: kslgpl	0	46	0
enqueue hash chains	ksqrcl	0	5	10
enqueue hash chains	ksqgtl3	0	2	35
enqueue hash chains	ksqcmi: get hash chain lat	0	1	9
enqueues	ksqgel: create enqueue	0	2	0

enqueues	ksqdel	0	1	2
library cache	kglupc: child	0	26	71
library cache	kglpndl: child: before pro	0	21	3
library cache	kglpndl: child: after proc	0	13	0
library cache	kgllkdl: child: cleanup	0	10	2
library cache	kglpin: child: heap proces	0	8	1
library cache	kglpnc: child	0	8	2
library cache	kglhdgc: child:	0	7	0
library cache	kglobpn: child:	0	7	1
library cache	kglget: child: KGLDSBRD	0	6	13
library cache	kglhdgn: child:	0	5	4
library cache	kglic	0	5	5
library cache	kglget: child: KGLDSBYD	0	3	0
library cache	kgldte: child 0	0	1	19
library cache	kglpin	0	1	0
library cache pin	kglpnal: child: alloc spac	0	4	2
library cache pin	kglpnc: child	0	4	0
library cache pin	kglpndl	0	2	0
library cache pin	kglupc	0	1	9
library cache pin alloca	kgllkdl	0	6	5
library cache pin alloca	kglpnal	0	4	5
messages	ksaamb: after wakeup	0	1	0
redo allocation	kcrfwr	0	16	11
redo allocation	kcrfwi: before write	0	1	2
redo allocation	kcrfwi: more space	0	1	5
redo copy	kcrfwr: nowait	0	2	0
sequence cache	kdnnxt: cached seq	0	3	0
sequence cache	kdnss	0	1	4
shared pool	kghalo	0	2	0
undo global data	ktubnd:child	0	1	1
undo global data	ktudba: KSLBEGIN	0	1	0

Next is another example of excessively deep-level analysis by STATSPACK, analyzing the row cache in the shared pool. More specifically, it is the data dictionary activity cache from the V$ROWCACHE performance view. The only interesting factor here is the occurrence of histograms. It appears that the ANALYZE command, used to compute statistics, generates histograms for all indexed columns by default in Oracle 9*i* Database, Release 2 (9.2) (on Windows 2000). This occurs when comput-

ing statistics on tables. At least it does on my database server. The occurrence of the high value for dc_histogram_defs is the result:

```
Dictionary Cache Stats for DB: TEST  Instance: test  Snaps: 191 -200
->"Pct Misses"  should be very low (< 2% in most cases)
->"Cache Usage" is the number of cache entries being used
->"Pct SGA"     is the ratio of usage to allocated size for that cache
```

Cache	Get Requests	Pct Miss	Scan Reqs	Pct Miss	Mod Reqs	Final Usage
dc_histogram_defs	98	80.6	0		0	194
dc_object_ids	76	2.6	0		0	293
dc_objects	212	0.0	0		0	447
dc_profiles	2,541	0.0	0		0	1
dc_rollback_segments	67	0.0	0		0	12
dc_segments	136	0.0	0		0	206
dc_sequences	931	0.0	0		931	8
dc_tablespace_quotas	5	0.0	0		5	4
dc_tablespaces	663	0.0	0		0	6
dc_user_grants	17	0.0	0		0	12
dc_usernames	25	0.0	0		0	4
dc_users	12,796	0.0	0		0	14

This section shows library cache activity based on object type. There is a
lot more SQL activity than anything else and a small number of reloads:

```
Library Cache Activity for DB: TEST  Instance: test  Snaps: 191 -200
->"Pct Misses"  should be very low
```

Namespace	Get Requests	Pct Miss	Pin Requests	Pct Miss	Reloads	Invali- dations
BODY	5,092	0.0	5,092	0.0	0	0
CLUSTER	2	0.0	3	0.0	0	0
INDEX	116	0.0	116	0.0	0	0
SQL AREA	**19,071**	**0.0**	**237,733**	**0.0**	**22**	**0**
TABLE/PROCEDURE	4,237	0.0	55,925	0.0	0	0
TRIGGER	7,547	0.0	7,547	0.0	0	0

Once again, a buffer area advisory, potentially encouraging excessive increased resizing of the shared pool, avoids solving and instead obscures underlying performance problems:

```
Shared Pool Advisory for DB: TEST  Instance: test  End Snap: 200
-> Note there is often a 1:Many correlation between a single logical object
   in the Library Cache, and the physical number of memory objects associated
   with it.  Therefore comparing the number of Lib Cache objects (e.g. in
   v$librarycache), with the number of Lib Cache Memory Objects is invalid
```

Shared Pool Size for Estim (M)	SP Size Factr	Estd Lib Cache Size (M)	Estd Lib Cache Mem Obj	Estd Lib Cache Time Saved (s)	Estd LC Time Saved Factr	Estd Lib Cache Mem Obj Hits
32	.5	11	2,813	35,757	1.0	2,269,393
40	.6	11	2,813	35,757	1.0	2,269,393
48	.8	11	2,813	35,757	1.0	2,269,393
56	.9	11	2,813	35,757	1.0	2,269,393
64	1.0	11	2,813	35,757	1.0	2,269,393
72	1.1	11	2,813	35,757	1.0	2,269,393
80	1.3	11	2,813	35,757	1.0	2,269,393
88	1.4	11	2,813	35,757	1.0	2,269,393
96	1.5	11	2,813	35,757	1.0	2,269,393
104	1.6	11	2,813	35,757	1.0	2,269,393
112	1.8	11	2,813	35,757	1.0	2,269,393
120	1.9	11	2,813	35,757	1.0	2,269,393
128	2.0	11	2,813	35,757	1.0	2,269,393

This is a summary of SGA sizes:

```
SGA Memory Summary for DB: TEST  Instance: test  Snaps: 191 -200
```

SGA regions	Size in Bytes
Database Buffers	33,554,432
Fixed Size	453,452
Redo Buffers	667,648
Variable Size	92,274,688
sum	126,950,220

The next section contains a breakdown of the SGA:

```
SGA breakdown difference for DB: TEST  Instance: test  Snaps: 191 -200

Pool   Name                         Begin value        End value   % Diff
------ --------------------------   ----------------   ----------------  -------
large  free memory                   8,388,608         8,388,608    0.00
shared 1M buffer                     2,098,176         2,098,176    0.00
shared Checkpoint queue               282,304           282,304    0.00
shared FileIdentificatonBlock         323,292           323,292    0.00
shared FileOpenBlock                  695,504           695,504    0.00
shared KGK heap                         3,756             3,756    0.00
shared KGLS heap                    1,766,080         1,788,664    1.28
shared KQR M PO                       451,100           492,572    9.19
shared KQR S PO                        58,940            58,940    0.00
shared KQR S SO                         3,072             3,072    0.00
shared KSXR large reply queue         166,104           166,104    0.00
shared KSXR pending messages que      841,036           841,036    0.00
shared KSXR receive buffers         1,033,000         1,033,000    0.00
shared MTTR advisory                   12,692            12,692    0.00
shared PL/SQL DIANA                 1,580,060         1,580,060    0.00
shared PL/SQL MPCODE                  497,840           507,844    2.01
shared PLS non-lib hp                   2,068             2,068    0.00
shared character set object           274,508           274,508    0.00
shared dictionary cache             1,610,880         1,610,880    0.00
shared enqueue                        171,860           171,860    0.00
shared event statistics per sess    1,718,360         1,718,360    0.00
shared fixed allocation callback          180               180    0.00
shared free memory                 56,403,656        55,548,136   -1.52
shared joxs heap init                   4,220             4,220    0.00
shared kgl simulator                  608,780           613,016    0.70
shared ksm_file2sga region            148,652           148,652    0.00
shared library cache                3,598,836         3,665,656    1.86
shared message pool freequeue         834,752           834,752    0.00
shared miscellaneous                4,250,564         4,250,564    0.00
shared parameters                      31,412            33,500    6.65
shared processes                      144,000           144,000    0.00
shared sessions                       410,720           410,720    0.00
shared sim memory hea                  25,400            25,400    0.00
shared sql area                     3,823,264         4,531,524   18.53
shared table definiti                   3,684             3,740    1.52
```

```
shared trigger defini                        6,732              6,732      0.00
shared trigger inform                          496                496      0.00
shared trigger source                          100                100      0.00
      buffer_cache                       33,554,432         33,554,432      0.00
      fixed_sga                             453,452            453,452      0.00
      log_buffer                            656,384            656,384      0.00

      -------------------------------------------------------------
```

And finally we get a listing of nondefault setting database configuration parameters:

init.ora Parameters for DB: TEST   Instance: test   Snaps: 191 –200

Parameter Name	Begin value	End value (if different)
aq_tm_processes	1	
background_dump_dest	E:\oracle\admin\test\bdump	
compatible	9.2.0.0.0	
control_files	E:\oracle\oradata\test\control01.	
core_dump_dest	E:\oracle\admin\test\cdump	
db_block_size	8192	
db_cache_size	33554432	
db_domain		
db_file_multiblock_read_count	16	
db_name	test	
fast_start_mttr_target	300	
hash_join_enabled	TRUE	
instance_name	test	
java_pool_size	0	
job_queue_processes	10	
large_pool_size	8388608	
open_cursors	300	
pga_aggregate_target	0	
processes	150	
query_rewrite_enabled	FALSE	
remote_login_passwordfile	EXCLUSIVE	
shared_pool_size	67108864	
sort_area_size	32768	
star_transformation_enabled	FALSE	
timed_statistics	TRUE	

```
undo_management              AUTO
undo_retention               10800
undo_tablespace              UNDOTBS1
user_dump_dest               E:\oracle\admin\test\udump
         ----------------------------------------------------------
```

End of Report

As you can now see, STATSPACK produces a large amount of information in a single report. This section on using STATSPACK is all a single STATSPACK report. Finding a very specific problem among all that detail is probably more difficult than using drilldown into the Oracle Database Wait Event Interface, especially when using Oracle Enterprise Manager or the Database Control. STATSPACK is best to get an overall picture of underlying physical structure. Using the Wait Event Interface is easier for isolating specific issues after having gained a general perspective using STATSPACK.

This chapter covering STATSPACK concludes the fourth part of this book on tuning everything at once for an Oracle database. This chapter also concludes this book. I hope you have enjoyed reading it as much as I have enjoyed writing it.

Appendix

Note: Please note that these scripts should be tested prior to use.

A.1   Database Schemas

Only schema entity relationship diagrams are included. There is little relevance with respect to tuning to include the schema creation scripting.

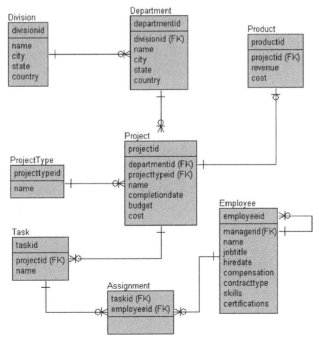

Figure A.1   *Employees Schema ERD Version One*

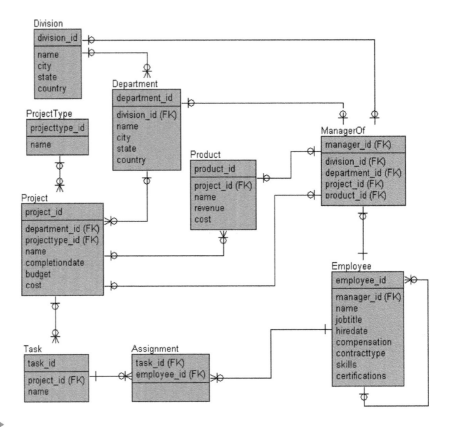

Figure A.2 · *Employees Schema ERD Version Two*

Inclusion of this highly normalized version of the Accounts schema is not strictly necessary. However, it is useful to show the vast difference between an overnormalized ERD and a fairly well denormalized ERD.

A.2   Accounts Schema Creation Scripting

This schema is best created in a new user name:

```
CREATE TABLE Type(
    type        CHAR(1) NOT NULL,
    text        VARCHAR2(32) NULL,
    CONSTRAINT XPK_Type PRIMARY KEY (type) USING INDEX TABLESPACE
INDX
) TABLESPACE DATA;
```

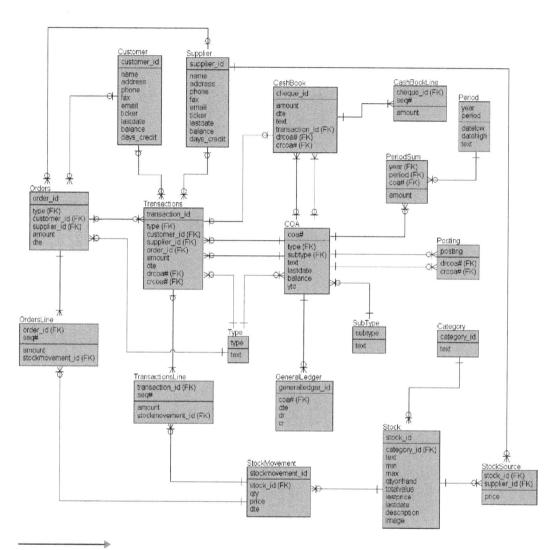

Figure A.3 *Accounts Schema ERD Denormalized Version*

```
CREATE TABLE SubType(
    subtype     CHAR(1) NOT NULL,
    text        VARCHAR2(32) NULL,
    CONSTRAINT XPK_SubType PRIMARY KEY (subtype) USING INDEX
TABLESPACE INDX
) TABLESPACE DATA;

CREATE TABLE COA(
    coa#        CHAR(5) NOT NULL,
    type        CHAR(1) NOT NULL,
    subtype     CHAR(1) NOT NULL,
```

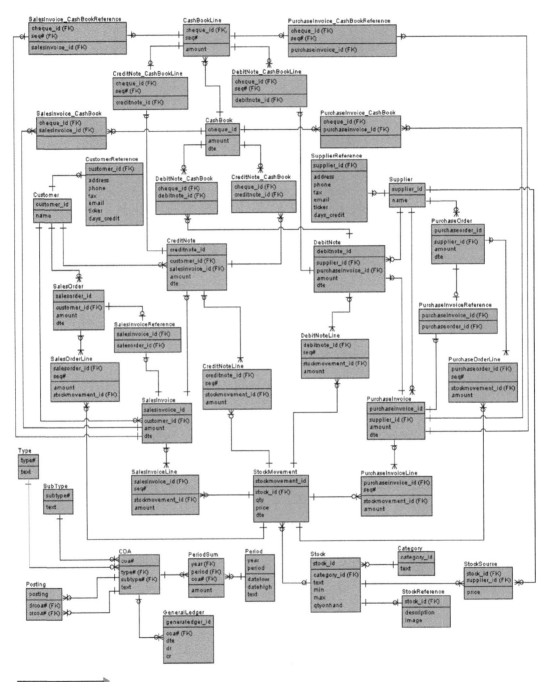

Figure A.4   *Accounts Schema ERD Normalized Version*

```
    text        VARCHAR2(32) NOT NULL,
    lastdate    DATE NULL,
    balance     NUMBER(20,2) NULL,
    ytd         NUMBER NULL,
    CONSTRAINT XPK_COA PRIMARY KEY (coa#) USING INDEX TABLESPACE
INDX,
    CONSTRAINT FK_COA_Type FOREIGN KEY (type) REFERENCES Type,
    CONSTRAINT FK_COA_Subtype FOREIGN KEY (subtype) REFERENCES
SubType,
    CONSTRAINT XAK_COA UNIQUE (text) USING INDEX TABLESPACE INDX
) TABLESPACE DATA;
CREATE INDEX XFK_COA_Type ON COA(type) TABLESPACE INDX;
CREATE INDEX XFK_COA_Subtype ON COA(subtype) TABLESPACE INDX;


CREATE TABLE Posting(
    posting     CHAR(32) NOT NULL,
    drcoa#      CHAR(5) NOT NULL,
    crcoa#      CHAR(5) NOT NULL,
    CONSTRAINT XPK_Posting PRIMARY KEY (posting) USING INDEX
TABLESPACE INDX,
    CONSTRAINT FK_Posting_DRCOA# FOREIGN KEY (drcoa#) REFERENCES
COA,
    CONSTRAINT FK_Posting_CRCOA# FOREIGN KEY (crcoa#) REFERENCES COA

) TABLESPACE DATA;
CREATE INDEX XFK_Posting_DRCOA# ON Posting(drcoa#) TABLESPACE INDX;
CREATE INDEX XFK_Posting_CRCOA# ON Posting(crcoa#) TABLESPACE INDX;


CREATE TABLE Customer(
    customer_id  NUMBER NOT NULL,
    name         VARCHAR2(64) NOT NULL,
    ticker       CHAR(10) NOT NULL,
    address      VARCHAR2(256) NULL,
    phone        VARCHAR2(20) NULL,
    fax          VARCHAR2(20) NULL,
    email        VARCHAR2(32) NULL,
    lastdate     DATE NULL,
    balance      NUMBER(10,2) NULL,
    days_credit  NUMBER NULL,
    CONSTRAINT   XPK_Customer PRIMARY KEY (customer_id) USING INDEX
TABLESPACE INDX,
    CONSTRAINT   AK_Customer_Name UNIQUE (name) USING INDEX
TABLESPACE INDX,
    CONSTRAINT   AK_Customer_Ticker UNIQUE (ticker) USING INDEX
TABLESPACE INDX
) TABLESPACE DATA;
```

```
CREATE TABLE Supplier(
   supplier_id  NUMBER NOT NULL,
   name         VARCHAR2(64) NOT NULL,
   ticker       CHAR(10) NOT NULL,
   address      VARCHAR2(256) NULL,
   phone        VARCHAR2(20) NULL,
   fax          VARCHAR2(20) NULL,
   email        VARCHAR2(32) NULL,
   lastdate     DATE NULL,
   balance      NUMBER(10,2) NULL,
   days_credit  NUMBER NULL,
   CONSTRAINT    XPK_Supplier PRIMARY KEY (supplier_id) USING INDEX
TABLESPACE INDX,
   CONSTRAINT    XAK_Supplier_Name UNIQUE (name) USING INDEX
TABLESPACE INDX,
   CONSTRAINT    XAK_Supplier_Ticker UNIQUE (ticker) USING INDEX
TABLESPACE INDX
) TABLESPACE DATA;

CREATE TABLE Orders(
   order_id     NUMBER NOT NULL,
   customer_id  NUMBER NULL,
   supplier_id  NUMBER NULL,
   type         CHAR(1) NOT NULL,
   amount       NUMBER(10,2) NOT NULL,
   dte          DATE NOT NULL,
   CONSTRAINT    XPK_Orders PRIMARY KEY (order_id) USING INDEX
TABLESPACE INDX,
   CONSTRAINT    FK_Orders_Type FOREIGN KEY (type) REFERENCES Type,
   CONSTRAINT    FK_Orders_Customer FOREIGN KEY (customer_id)
REFERENCES Customer,
   CONSTRAINT    FK_Orders_Supplier FOREIGN KEY (supplier_id)
REFERENCES Supplier
) TABLESPACE DATA;
CREATE INDEX XFK_Orders_Type ON Orders(type) TABLESPACE INDX;
CREATE INDEX XFK_Orders_Customer ON Orders(customer_id) TABLESPACE
INDX;
CREATE INDEX XFK_Orders_Supplier ON Orders(supplier_id) TABLESPACE
INDX;

CREATE TABLE Transactions(
   transaction_id NUMBER NOT NULL,
   type         CHAR(1) NOT NULL,
   customer_id  NUMBER NULL,
   supplier_id  NUMBER NULL,
   order_id     NUMBER NULL,
```

```
        amount          NUMBER(10,2) NOT NULL,
        dte             DATE NOT NULL,
        drcoa#          CHAR(5) NOT NULL,
        crcoa#          CHAR(5) NOT NULL,
     CONSTRAINT      XPK_Transactions PRIMARY KEY (transaction_id)
        USING INDEX TABLESPACE INDX,
     CONSTRAINT      FK_Trans_Type FOREIGN KEY (type) REFERENCES Type,

     CONSTRAINT       FK_Trans_DRCOA# FOREIGN KEY (drcoa#) REFERENCES
COA,
     CONSTRAINT       FK_Trans_CRCOA# FOREIGN KEY (crcoa#) REFERENCES
COA,
     CONSTRAINT       FK_Trans_Customer FOREIGN KEY (customer_id)
REFERENCES Customer,
     CONSTRAINT       FK_Trans_Supplier FOREIGN KEY (supplier_id)
REFERENCES Supplier,
     CONSTRAINT      FK_Trans_Orders FOREIGN KEY (order_id) REFERENCES
Orders
) TABLESPACE DATA;
CREATE INDEX XFK_Trans_Type ON Transactions(type) TABLESPACE INDX;
CREATE INDEX XFK_Trans_DRCOA# ON Transactions(drcoa#) TABLESPACE
INDX;
CREATE INDEX XFK_Trans_CRCOA# ON Transactions(crcoa#) TABLESPACE
INDX;
CREATE INDEX XFK_Trans_Customer ON Transactions(customer_id)
TABLESPACE INDX;
CREATE INDEX XFK_Trans_Supplier ON Transactions(supplier_id)
TABLESPACE INDX;
CREATE INDEX XFK_Trans_Orders ON Transactions(order_id) TABLESPACE
INDX;

CREATE TABLE CashBook(
     cheque_id       NUMBER NOT NULL,
     amount          NUMBER(10,2) NOT NULL,
     dte             DATE NOT NULL,
     text            VARCHAR2(32) NULL,
     drcoa#          CHAR(5) NOT NULL,
     crcoa#          CHAR(5) NOT NULL,
     CONSTRAINT      XPK_CashBook PRIMARY KEY (cheque_id) USING INDEX
TABLESPACE INDX,
     CONSTRAINT      FK_CashBook_DRCOA# FOREIGN KEY (drcoa#) REFERENCES
COA,
     CONSTRAINT      FK_CashBook_CRCOA# FOREIGN KEY (crcoa#) REFERENCES
COA
) TABLESPACE DATA;
CREATE INDEX XFK_CashBook_DRCOA# ON CashBook(drcoa#) TABLESPACE
INDX;
```

```
CREATE INDEX XFK_CashBook_CRCOA# ON CashBook(crcoa#) TABLESPACE
INDX;

CREATE TABLE CashBookLine(
    cheque_id       NUMBER NOT NULL,
    seq#            NUMBER NOT NULL,
    transaction_id NUMBER NULL,
    amount          NUMBER(10,2) NOT NULL,
    CONSTRAINT      XPK_CashBookLine PRIMARY KEY (cheque_id, seq#)
       USING INDEX TABLESPACE INDX,
    CONSTRAINT      FK_CBL_Transaction FOREIGN KEY (transaction_id)
       REFERENCES Transactions,
    CONSTRAINT      FK_CBL_CashBook FOREIGN KEY (cheque_id)
REFERENCES CashBook
) TABLESPACE DATA;
CREATE INDEX FK_CBL_Transaction ON CashBookLine(cheque_id)
TABLESPACE INDX;
CREATE INDEX FK_CBL_CashBook ON CashBookLine(transaction_id)
TABLESPACE INDX;

CREATE TABLE Category(
    category_id     NUMBER NOT NULL,
    text            VARCHAR2(32) NOT NULL,
    CONSTRAINT      XPK_Category PRIMARY KEY (category_id) USING
INDEX TABLESPACE INDX,
    CONSTRAINT      XAK_Category_text UNIQUE (text) USING INDEX
TABLESPACE INDX
) TABLESPACE DATA;

CREATE TABLE Stock(
    stock_id        NUMBER NOT NULL,
    category_id     NUMBER NOT NULL,
    text            VARCHAR2(128) NOT NULL,
    min             NUMBER NOT NULL,
    max             NUMBER NOT NULL,
    qtyonhand       NUMBER NULL,
    totalvalue      NUMBER(20,2) NULL,
    lastdate        DATE NULL,
    description     CLOB NULL,
    lastprice       NUMBER(10,2) NULL,
    image           BLOB NULL,
    CONSTRAINT      XPK_Stock PRIMARY KEY (stock_id) USING INDEX
TABLESPACE INDX,
    CONSTRAINT      FK_Stock_Category FOREIGN KEY (category_id)
REFERENCES Category,
```

```
        CONSTRAINT      AK_Stock_text UNIQUE (text) USING INDEX
TABLESPACE INDX
) TABLESPACE DATA;
CREATE INDEX XFK_Stock_Category ON Stock(category_id) TABLESPACE
INDX;


CREATE TABLE StockMovement(
   stockmovement_id NUMBER NOT NULL,
   stock_id         NUMBER NOT NULL,
   qty              NUMBER NOT NULL,
   price            NUMBER(10,2) NOT NULL,
   dte              DATE NOT NULL,
   CONSTRAINT       XPK_StockMovement PRIMARY KEY
(stockmovement_id)
      USING INDEX TABLESPACE INDX,
   CONSTRAINT       FK_SM_Stock FOREIGN KEY (stock_id) REFERENCES
Stock
) TABLESPACE DATA;
CREATE INDEX XFK_SM_Stock ON StockMovement(stock_id) TABLESPACE
INDX;


CREATE TABLE TransactionsLine(
   transaction_id   NUMBER NOT NULL,
   seq#             NUMBER NOT NULL,
   amount           NUMBER(10,2) NOT NULL,
   stockmovement_id NUMBER NOT NULL,
   CONSTRAINT       XPK_TransactionsLine PRIMARY KEY
(transaction_id, seq#)
      USING INDEX TABLESPACE INDX,
   CONSTRAINT       FK_TL_SM FOREIGN KEY (stockmovement_id)
REFERENCES StockMovement,
   CONSTRAINT       FK_TL_Trans FOREIGN KEY (transaction_id)
REFERENCES Transactions
) TABLESPACE DATA;
CREATE INDEX XFK_TL_SM ON TransactionsLine(stockmovement_id)
TABLESPACE INDX;
CREATE INDEX XFK_TL_Trans ON TransactionsLine(transaction_id)
TABLESPACE INDX;


CREATE TABLE OrdersLine(
   order_id         NUMBER NOT NULL,
   seq#             NUMBER NOT NULL,
   amount           NUMBER(10,2) NOT NULL,
   stockmovement_id NUMBER NOT NULL,
   CONSTRAINT       XPK_OrdersLine PRIMARY KEY (order_id, seq#)
      USING INDEX TABLESPACE INDX,
```

```
    CONSTRAINT        FK_OL_SM FOREIGN KEY (stockmovement_id)
REFERENCES StockMovement,
    CONSTRAINT        FK_OL_Orders FOREIGN KEY (order_id) REFERENCES
Orders
) TABLESPACE DATA;
CREATE INDEX XFK_OL_SM ON OrdersLine(stockmovement_id) TABLESPACE
INDX;
CREATE INDEX XFK_OL_Orders ON OrdersLine(order_id) TABLESPACE INDX;

CREATE TABLE Period(
    year          NUMBER NOT NULL,
    period        NUMBER NOT NULL,
    datelow       DATE NOT NULL,
    datehigh      DATE NOT NULL,
    text          VARCHAR2(32) NOT NULL,
    CONSTRAINT    XPK_Period PRIMARY KEY (year, period) USING INDEX
TABLESPACE INDX
) TABLESPACE DATA;

CREATE TABLE PeriodSum(
    year          NUMBER NOT NULL,
    period        NUMBER NOT NULL,
    coa#          CHAR(5) NOT NULL,
    amount        NUMBER(20,2) NULL,
    CONSTRAINT    XPK_PeriodSum PRIMARY KEY (year, period, coa#)
        USING INDEX TABLESPACE INDX,
    CONSTRAINT    FK_PeriodSum_COA# FOREIGN KEY (coa#) REFERENCES
COA,
    CONSTRAINT    FK_PeriodSum_YP FOREIGN KEY (year, period)
REFERENCES Period
) TABLESPACE DATA;
CREATE INDEX XFK_PeriodSum_COA# ON PeriodSum(year,period)
TABLESPACE INDX;
CREATE INDEX XFK_PeriodSum_YP ON PeriodSum(coa#) TABLESPACE INDX;

CREATE TABLE GeneralLedger(
    generalledger_id NUMBER NOT NULL,
    coa#             CHAR(5) NOT NULL,
    dr               NUMBER(10,2) NOT NULL,
    cr               NUMBER(10,2) NOT NULL,
    dte              DATE NOT NULL,
    CONSTRAINT       XPK_GeneralLedger PRIMARY KEY
(generalledger_id)
        USING INDEX TABLESPACE INDX,
    CONSTRAINT       FK_GL_COA# FOREIGN KEY (coa#) REFERENCES COA
) TABLESPACE DATA;
```

```
CREATE INDEX XFK_GL_COA# ON GeneralLedger(coa#) TABLESPACE INDX;
CREATE INDEX XAK_GL_COA#DTE ON GeneralLedger(coa#,dte) TABLESPACE
INDX;

CREATE TABLE Supplier_Stock (
    supplier_id       NUMBER NOT NULL,
    stock_id          NUMBER NOT NULL,
    price             NUMBER(10,2) NOT NULL,
    CONSTRAINT        XPK_Supplier_Stock PRIMARY KEY (supplier_id,
stock_id)
        USING INDEX TABLESPACE INDX,
    CONSTRAINT        FK_Supplier_Stock FOREIGN KEY (stock_id)
REFERENCES Stock,
    CONSTRAINT        FK_Supplier_Supplier FOREIGN KEY (supplier_id)
REFERENCES Supplier
) TABLESPACE DATA;
CREATE INDEX XFK_Supplier_Stock ON Supplier_Stock(supplier_id)
TABLESPACE INDX;
CREATE INDEX XFK_Supplier_Supplier ON Supplier_Stock(stock_id)
TABLESPACE INDX;


create sequence category_seq start with 1 increment by 1 nomaxvalue
nocycle;
create sequence customer_seq start with 1 increment by 1 nomaxvalue
nocycle;
create sequence supplier_seq start with 1 increment by 1 nomaxvalue
nocycle;
create sequence stock_seq start with 1 increment by 1 nomaxvalue
nocycle;
create sequence stockmovement_seq start with 1 increment by 1
nomaxvalue nocycle;
create sequence generalledger_seq start with 1 increment by 1
nomaxvalue nocycle;
create sequence orders_seq start with 1 increment by 1 nomaxvalue
nocycle;
create sequence transactions_seq start with 1 increment by 1
nomaxvalue nocycle;
create sequence cheque_seq start with 1 increment by 1 nomaxvalue
nocycle;
```

A.3   **Active Concurrent Database Scripting**

These scripts do not include trigger code. Use of triggers is easy but contradictory to performance tuning.

A.3.1   Internet OLTP Database Simulation

```
--every 1 second
declare
        jobno number;
        i integer default 1;
begin
        for j in 1..10 loop
        dbms_job.submit(jobno,'SIMULATE;',SYSDATE,'SYSDATE+1/
86400');
        end loop;
        commit;
end;
/

declare
        cursor cJobs is select job from user_jobs;
begin
        for rJob in cJobs loop
            dbms_job.remove(rJob.job);
        end loop;
end;
/
commit;

create or replace function random(n IN NUMBER DEFAULT 1) return
integer is
        random integer;
begin
        select to_number(to_char(SYSTIMESTAMP,'FF3'))+1 into random
from dual;
        random := (random/1000)*n;
        if random = 0 then random := 1; end if;
        return random;
exception when others then
        dbms_output.put_line('FUNC: random '||SQLERRM(SQLCODE));
end;
/
alter function random compile;

create or replace function getTime(ptime float default 0) return
float is
begin
        return to_number(to_char(systimestamp,'SSSSS.FF')) - ptime;
exception when others then
```

```
            dbms_output.put_line('FUNC: getTime '||SQLERRM(SQLCODE));
end;
/
alter function getTime compile;

create or replace procedure getPrice
(
        pstock_id IN integer default 0
        ,psupplier_id OUT integer
        ,pprice OUT float
) as
begin

        --find cheapest price for stock_id
        select a.supplier_id, a.price into psupplier_id, pprice
        from (
            select supplier_id, min(price) as price
            from stocksource
            where stock_id = pstock_id
            group by supplier_id
            order by price
        ) a where rownum = 1;
exception when others then
        dbms_output.put_line('PROC: getPrice '||SQLERRM(SQLCODE));
end;
/
alter procedure getprice compile;

create or replace procedure InsertSANDP (pdte IN date DEFAULT
SYSDATE) as
        vcustomer_id integer;
        vsupplier_id integer;
        vstock_id integer;
        vorder_id integer;
        vstockmovement_id integer;
        vtransaction_id integer;
        vcheque_id integer;
        vqty integer;
        vlines integer;
        vqtyonhand integer;
        vprice float;
        vamount float;
        vseq# integer;
        vmarkup float default 1.01;
        vtime float;
begin
```

```
        vtime := to_number(to_char(systimestamp,'SSSSS.FF'));

select max(customer_id) into vcustomer_id from customer;
vcustomer_id := random(vcustomer_id);
        select max(stock_id) into vstock_id from stock;
vstock_id := random(vstock_id);
        vqty := random(20); vlines := vqty;
        select qtyonhand into vqtyonhand from stock
where stock_id = vstock_id;

        if vqty - vqtyonhand > 0 then

            vqty := vqty - vqtyonhand; --vqty - vqtyonhand always
+ve
            getPrice(vstock_id,vsupplier_id,vprice);
            vamount := vqty * vprice;

            insert into orders values(orders_seq.nextval
,null,vsupplier_id,'P',(vamount*-1),pdte)
                returning order_id into vorder_id;

            insert into transactions
values(transactions_seq.nextval
,'P',null,vsupplier_id,vorder_id,(vamount*-1),pdte
                ,(select drcoa# from posting
where posting='PurchaseInvoice')
                ,(select crcoa# from posting
where posting='PurchaseInvoice'))
                returning transaction_id into vtransaction_id;

            insert into cashbook values(cheque_seq.nextval
,(vamount*-1),pdte,'Purchase Invoice
'||to_char(vtransaction_id)
                ,(select drcoa# from posting
where posting='PurchaseInvoice_CashBook')
                ,(select crcoa# from posting
where posting='PurchaseInvoice_CashBook')
                ,vtransaction_id)
                returning cheque_id into vcheque_id;

            for vseq# in 1..vlines loop

insert into stockmovement values(stockmovement_seq.nextval
,vstock_id,vqty,vprice,pdte)
```

```
                              returning stockmovement_id into vstockmovement_id;

                         insert into ordersline values(vorder_id,vseq#
,(vprice*-1),vstockmovement_id);

insert into transactionsline values(vtransaction_id,vseq#
,(vprice*-1),vstockmovement_id);

insert into cashbookline values(vcheque_id,vseq#,(vprice*-1));

            end loop;

            dbms_output.put_line('PROC: InsertSANDP
Purchase Complete '||to_char(getTime(vtime)));

        end if;

        --make sale, gen transaction and pay for it for vqty -
vqtyonhand

        getPrice(vstock_id,vsupplier_id,vprice);
        vprice := vprice * vmarkup;
        vamount := vqty * vprice;

        insert into orders values(orders_seq.nextval
,vcustomer_id,null,'S',vamount,pdte)
            returning order_id into vorder_id;

        insert into transactions values(transactions_seq.nextval
,'S',vcustomer_id,null,vorder_id,vamount,pdte
            ,(select drcoa# from posting where
posting='SalesInvoice')
            ,(select crcoa# from posting where
posting='SalesInvoice'))
            returning transaction_id into vtransaction_id;

        insert into cashbook values(cheque_seq.nextval
,vamount,pdte,'Sales Invoice '||to_char(vtransaction_id)
            ,(select drcoa# from posting
where posting='SalesInvoice_CashBook')
            ,(select crcoa# from posting
where posting='SalesInvoice_CashBook'),vtransaction_id)
            returning cheque_id into vcheque_id;

        for vseq# in 1..vlines loop
```

```
            insert into stockmovement
values(stockmovement_seq.nextval
,vstock_id,(vqty*-1),vprice,pdte)
                returning stockmovement_id into vstockmovement_id;

            insert into ordersline values(vorder_id
,vseq#,vprice,vstockmovement_id);

            insert into transactionsline values(vtransaction_id
,vseq#,vprice,vstockmovement_id);

            insert into cashbookline
values(vcheque_id,vseq#,vprice);

        end loop;

        dbms_output.put_line('PROC: InsertSANDP Sale Complete
'||to_char(getTime(vtime)));
        commit;
exception when others then
        dbms_output.put_line('PROC: InsertSANDP
'||SQLERRM(SQLCODE));
        rollback;
end;
/
alter procedure InsertSANDP compile;

create or replace procedure UpdateSORP (pdte IN date DEFAULT
SYSDATE) as
        vminorder_id integer;
        vmaxorder_id integer;
        vorder_id integer;
        vtransaction_id integer;
        vcheque_id integer;
        voption integer;
        vmod float;
        vtime float;
begin

        --not supposed to execute a stockmovement (too difficult)

        vtime := to_number(to_char(systimestamp,'SSSSS.FF'));

select min(order_id),max(order_id) into vminorder_id,vmaxorder_id
from orders;
```

```
        vorder_id := random(vmaxorder_id-
vminorder_id)+vminorder_id;
        select order_id into vorder_id from orders
where order_id = vorder_id;

        voption := random(2);
if voption <= 1 then vmod := 1.1;
else vmod := 0.9; end if;

        update ordersline set amount = amount*vmod
where order_id = vorder_id;
        update orders set dte = pdte, amount =
            (select sum(amount) from Ordersline
where order_id = vorder_id group by order_id)
        where order_id = vorder_id;

select transaction_id into vtransaction_id from transactions where
order_id = vorder_id;
        update transactionsline set amount = amount*vmod
where transaction_id = vtransaction_id;
        update transactions set dte = pdte, amount =
            (select sum(amount) from transactionsline
where transaction_id = vtransaction_id
group by transaction_id)
        where transaction_id = vtransaction_id;

        select cheque_id into vcheque_id from cashbook
where transaction_id = vtransaction_id;
        update cashbookline set amount = amount*vmod
where cheque_id = vcheque_id;
        update cashbook set dte = pdte, amount =
            (select sum(amount) from cashbookline
where cheque_id = vcheque_id group by cheque_id)
        where cheque_id = vcheque_id;

dbms_output.put_line('PROC: UpdateSORP Complete
'||to_char(getTime(vtime)));
        commit;

exception when others then
        dbms_output.put_line('PROC: UpdateSORP
'||SQLERRM(SQLCODE));
        rollback;
end;
/
alter procedure UpdateSORP compile;
```

```
create or replace procedure DeleteSORP(pdte IN DATE DEFAULT
SYSDATE) as
        vminorder_id integer;
        vmaxorder_id integer;
        vorder_id integer;
        vtransaction_id integer;
        vstockmovement_id integer;
        vstock_id integer;
        vcheque_id integer;
        vqty integer;
        vprice float;
        vid integer;
        vtime float;
        type tStockMovement is ref cursor return
StockMovement%rowtype;
        cStockMovements tStockMovement;
        rStockMovement StockMovement%rowtype;
begin

        vtime := to_number(to_char(systimestamp,'SSSSS.FF'));

select min(order_id),max(order_id) into vminorder_id,vmaxorder_id
from orders;
        vorder_id := random(vmaxorder_id-
vminorder_id)+vminorder_id;
        select order_id into vorder_id from orders
where order_id = vorder_id;
select transaction_id into vtransaction_id from transactions where
order_id = vorder_id;
        select cheque_id into vcheque_id from cashbook
where transaction_id = vtransaction_id;

        begin
            open cStockMovements for
                select stockmovement_seq.nextval, sm.stock_id
,(sm.qty*-1) as qty, sm.price, pdte
from stockmovement sm
                where exists(
                        select stockmovement_id from
transactionsline
where stockmovement_id = sm.stockmovement_id and transaction_id =
vtransaction_id);
            loop
                fetch cStockMovements into rStockMovement;
                exit when cStockMovements%NOTFOUND;
```

```
                    insert into stockmovement values
(rStockMovement.stockmovement_id
,rStockMovement.stock_id,rStockMovement.qty
,rStockMovement.price,rStockMovement.dte);
            end loop;
            close cStockMovements;
        exception when others then
            close cStockMovements;
        end;

        delete from cashbookline where cheque_id = vcheque_id;
        delete from cashbook where cheque_id = vcheque_id;
        delete from transactionsline
where transaction_id = vtransaction_id;
        delete from ordersline where order_id = vorder_id;
        delete from transactions where transaction_id =
vtransaction_id;
        delete from orders where order_id = vorder_id;

dbms_output.put_line('PROC: DeleteSORP Complete
'||to_char(getTime(vtime)));

        commit;

exception when others then
        dbms_output.put_line('PROC: DeleteSORP
'||SQLERRM(SQLCODE));
        rollback;
end;
/
alter procedure DeleteSORP compile;

create or replace procedure simulate as
        voption integer;
        vrange integer;
        vdte date default '01-MAR-03';
begin
        voption := random(10); vdte := vdte + random(366);
dbms_output.put_line('PROC: Simulate '||to_char(vdte)||'
'||to_char(voption));
        if voption in (1,2,3,4,5,6,7) then InsertSANDP(vdte);
        elsif voption in (8,9) then UpdateSORP(vdte);
        elsif voption in (10) then DeleteSORP(vdte);
        end if;
exception when others then
        dbms_output.put_line('PROC: Simulate '||SQLERRM(SQLCODE));
```

```
end;
/
alter procedure simulate compile;
```

A.3.2 Internet OLTP and Reporting Simulation

```
create or replace procedure Reports (popt IN integer) as
        vcustomer_id integer;
        vsupplier_id integer;
        vorder_id integer;
        vtransaction_id integer;
        vstock_id integer;
        vtime float;
        vcnt integer;

        type tOrders is ref cursor return Orders%rowtype;
        cOrders tOrders;
        rOrders Orders%rowtype;

        type tOrdersLine is ref cursor return OrdersLine%rowtype;
        cOrdersLine tOrdersLine;
        rOrdersLine OrdersLine%rowtype;

        type tTransactions is ref cursor return
Transactions%rowtype;
        cTransactions tTransactions;
        rTransactions Transactions%rowtype;

        type tTransactionsLine is ref cursor return
TransactionsLine%rowtype;
        cTransactionsLine tTransactionsLine;
        rTransactionsLine TransactionsLine%rowtype;

        type tCashbook is ref cursor return Cashbook%rowtype;
        cCashbook tCashbook;
        rCashbook Cashbook%rowtype;

        type tCashbookLine is ref cursor return
CashbookLine%rowtype;
        cCashbookLine tCashbookLine;
        rCashbookLine CashbookLine%rowtype;

        type tCOA is ref cursor return COA%rowtype;
        cCOA tCOA;
        rCOA COA%rowtype;
```

```
          type tStockMovement is ref cursor return
StockMovement%rowtype;
          cStockMovement tStockMovement;
          rStockMovement StockMovement%rowtype;

          voption integer;

begin

          vtime := to_number(to_char(systimestamp,'SSSSS.FF'));

          voption := rand(8);

          if voption = 1 then
              --print all orders
              select max(customer_id) into vcustomer_id from
customer;
vcustomer_id := rand(vcustomer_id);
              open cOrders for select * from orders
where customer_id = vcustomer_id;
              loop
                  fetch cOrders into rOrders;
                  exit when cOrders%notfound;
              end loop;
              select max(supplier_id) into vsupplier_id from
supplier;
vsupplier_id := rand(vsupplier_id);
              open cOrders for select * from orders
where supplier_id = vsupplier_id;
              loop
                  fetch cOrders into rOrders;
                  exit when cOrders%notfound;
              end loop;

          elsif voption = 2 then
              --print individual orders
              select max(customer_id) into vcustomer_id from
customer;
vcustomer_id := rand(vcustomer_id);
              select max(order_id) into vorder_id from orders
where customer_id = vcustomer_id;
vorder_id := rand(vorder_id);
              open cOrdersLine for select ol.* from orders o
join ordersline ol on(ol.order_id = o.order_id)
where o.customer_id = vcustomer_id;
```

```
                loop
                    fetch cOrdersLine into rOrdersLine;
                    exit when cOrdersLine%notfound;
                end loop;
                select max(supplier_id) into vsupplier_id from
supplier;
vsupplier_id := rand(vsupplier_id);
                select max(order_id) into vorder_id from orders
where supplier_id = vsupplier_id;
vorder_id := rand(vorder_id);
                open cOrdersLine for select ol.* from orders o
join ordersline ol on(ol.order_id = o.order_id)
where o.supplier_id = vsupplier_id;
                loop
                    fetch cOrdersLine into rOrdersLine;
                    exit when cOrdersLine%notfound;
                end loop;


        elsif voption = 3 then
                --print all transactions
                select max(customer_id) into vcustomer_id from
customer;
vcustomer_id := rand(vcustomer_id);
                open cTransactions for select * from transactions
where customer_id = vcustomer_id;
                loop
                    fetch cTransactions into rTransactions;
                    exit when cTransactions%notfound;
                end loop;
                select max(supplier_id) into vsupplier_id from
supplier;
vsupplier_id := rand(vsupplier_id);
                open cTransactions for select * from transactions
where supplier_id = vsupplier_id;
                loop
                    fetch cTransactions into rTransactions;
                    exit when cTransactions%notfound;
                end loop;


        elsif voption = 4 then
                --print individual transactions
                select max(customer_id) into vcustomer_id from
customer;
vcustomer_id := rand(vcustomer_id);
                select max(transaction_id) into vtransaction_id
```

```
from transactions where customer_id = vcustomer_id; vtransaction_id
:= rand(vtransaction_id);
          open cTransactionsLine for select tl.* from
transactions t
join transactionsline tl
on(tl.transaction_id = t.transaction_id)
where t.customer_id = vcustomer_id;
          loop
              fetch cTransactionsLine into rTransactionsLine;
              exit when cTransactionsLine%notfound;
          end loop;
          select max(supplier_id) into vsupplier_id from
supplier;
vsupplier_id := rand(vsupplier_id);
          select max(transaction_id) into vtransaction_id
from transactions where supplier_id = vsupplier_id; vtransaction_id
:= rand(vtransaction_id);
          open cTransactionsLine for select tl.* from
transactions t
join transactionsline tl
on(tl.transaction_id = t.transaction_id)
where t.supplier_id = vsupplier_id;
          loop
              fetch cTransactionsLine into rTransactionsLine;
              exit when cTransactionsLine%notfound;
          end loop;


      elsif voption = 5 then
          --print all invoices
          select max(customer_id) into vcustomer_id from
customer;
vcustomer_id := rand(vcustomer_id);
          select max(transaction_id) into vtransaction_id
from transactions where customer_id = vcustomer_id; vtransaction_id
:= rand(vtransaction_id);
          open cCashbook for select cb.* from transactions t
join cashbook cb
on(cb.transaction_id = t.transaction_id)
where t.customer_id = vcustomer_id;
          loop
              fetch cCashbook into rCashbook;
              exit when cCashbook%notfound;
          end loop;
          select max(supplier_id) into vsupplier_id from
supplier;
vsupplier_id := rand(vsupplier_id);
```

```
            select max(transaction_id) into vtransaction_id
from transactions where supplier_id = vsupplier_id;
vtransaction_id := rand(vtransaction_id);
            open cCashbook for select cb.* from transactions t
join cashbook cb
on(cb.transaction_id = t.transaction_id)
where t.supplier_id = vsupplier_id;
            loop
                fetch cCashbook into rCashbook;
                exit when cCashbook%notfound;
            end loop;

        elsif voption = 6 then
            --print individual invoices
            select max(customer_id) into vcustomer_id from
customer;
vcustomer_id := rand(vcustomer_id);
            select max(transaction_id) into vtransaction_id
from transactions where customer_id = vcustomer_id;
vtransaction_id := rand(vtransaction_id);
            open cCashbookLine for select cbl.* from transactions t

join transactionsline tl
on(tl.transaction_id = t.transaction_id)
join cashbook cb
on(cb.transaction_id = t.transaction_id)
join cashbookline cbl
on(cbl.cheque_id = cb.cheque_id)
where t.customer_id = vcustomer_id;
            loop
            fetch cCashbookLine into rCashbookLine;
                exit when cCashbookLine%notfound;
                end loop;
            select max(supplier_id) into vsupplier_id from
supplier;
vsupplier_id := rand(vsupplier_id);
            select max(transaction_id) into vtransaction_id
from transactions where supplier_id = vsupplier_id;
vtransaction_id := rand(vtransaction_id);
            open cCashbookLine for select cbl.* from transactions t

join transactionsline tl
on(tl.transaction_id = t.transaction_id)
join cashbook cb
on(cb.transaction_id = t.transaction_id)
join cashbookline cbl
```

```
                    on(cbl.cheque_id = cb.cheque_id)
          where t.supplier_id = vsupplier_id;
                    loop
                        fetch cCashbookLine into rCashbookLine;
                        exit when cCashbookLine%notfound;
                    end loop;

               elsif voption = 7 then
                    --coa
                    open cCOA for select c.* from coa c, type t, subtype s
          where c.type = t.type and c.subtype = s.subtype
          order by c.coa#, t.type, s.subtype;
                    loop
                        fetch cCOA into rCOA;
                        exit when cCOA%notfound;
                    end loop;

               elsif voption = 8 then
                    --stock
                    select max(stock_id) into vstock_id from stock;
          vstock_id := rand(vstock_id);
                    open cStockMovement for select sm.* from category c
          join stock s on(s.category_id = c.category_id)
          join stockmovement sm on(sm.stock_id = s.stock_id) where s.stock_id
          = vstock_id;
                    loop
                        fetch cStockMovement into rStockMovement;
                        exit when cStockMovement%notfound;
                    end loop;

               elsif voption in (9,10) then
                    --sorting
                    select count(*) into vcnt from
          (select * from customer order by address);
                    select count(*) into vcnt from
          (select drcoa#, sum(amount)
          from transactions group by drcoa#);
                        --selections from the generalledger and stockmovement
          --tables are avoided here due to reverse index primary keys

               end if;

               dbms_output.put_line('PROC: Reports Complete '
          ||to_char(getTime(vtime)));
               simAudit('PROCEDURE','Reports',getTime(vtime),popt);
```

```
exception when others then
        dbms_output.put_line('PROC: Reports '||SQLERRM(SQLCODE));
        rollback;
end;
/
alter procedure Reports compile;

create or replace procedure simulate as
        voption integer;
        vrange integer;
        vdte date default '01-MAR-03';
begin
        voption := rand(20); vdte := vdte + rand(366);
        dbms_output.put_line('PROC: Simulate
('||to_char(voption)||')'
||to_char(vdte)||' '||to_char(voption));
        if voption in (1,2,3,4,5,6,7,8,9,10) then Reports(voption);
        elsif voption in (11,12,13,14,15) then
InsertSANDP(vdte,voption);
        elsif voption in (16,17,18) then UpdateSORP(vdte,voption);
        elsif voption in (19,20) then DeleteSORP(vdte,voption);
        end if;
exception when others then
        dbms_output.put_line('PROC: Simulate '||SQLERRM(SQLCODE));
end;
/
alter procedure simulate compile;
```

Note: (9*i*) Procedures can be pinned into the shared pool using the DBMS_SHARED_POOL.KEEP.

A.4   Updating Summary Fields

```
create or replace procedure summaries as
        vtime float;
begin
        vtime := to_number(to_char(systimestamp,'SSSSS.FF'));

        --customer.balance
        update customer set balance =
        (
            select a.amount from
```

```
                    (
                        select customer_id, sum(t.amount-cb.amount) as
amount
                        from transactions t, cashbook cb
                        where t.transaction_id = cb.transaction_id
                        group by customer_id
                    ) a
                    where a.customer_id = customer.customer_id
                );
                commit;

                --customer.lastdate
                update customer set lastdate =
                (
                    select a.dte from
                    (
                        select customer_id, max(dte) as dte
                        from transactions
                        group by customer_id
                    ) a
                    where a.customer_id = customer.customer_id
                );
                commit;

                --supplier.balance
                update supplier set balance =
                (
                    select a.amount from
                    (
                        select supplier_id, sum(t.amount-cb.amount) as
amount
                        from transactions t, cashbook cb
                        where t.transaction_id = cb.transaction_id
                        group by supplier_id
                    ) a
                    where a.supplier_id = supplier.supplier_id
                );
                commit;

                --supplier.lastdate
                update supplier set lastdate =
                (
                    select a.dte from
                    (
                        select supplier_id, max(dte) as dte
```

```
            from transactions
            group by supplier_id
        ) a
        where a.supplier_id = supplier.supplier_id
    );
    commit;


    --coa.lastdate
    update coa set lastdate =
    (
        select a.dte from
        (
            select coa#, max(dte) as dte
            from generalledger
            group by coa#
        ) a
        where a.coa# = coa.coa#
    );
    commit;


    --periodsum
    insert into tmp_periodsum(year,period,coa#,amount)
        select to_number(to_char(dte,'IYYY')) as year
            ,to_number(to_char(dte,'MM')) as period
            ,coa# as coa
            ,abs(sum(dr-cr)) as amount
        from generalledger
        group by to_number(to_char(dte,'IYYY'))
,to_number(to_char(dte,'MM')), coa#;
    delete from periodsum;
    insert into periodsum
select * from tmp_periodsum where period in(1,2);
    delete from tmp_periodsum where period in(1,2);
    update periodsum set year=year-1,period=period+10;
    update tmp_periodsum set period=period-2;
    insert into periodsum select * from tmp_periodsum;
    commit;

    --coa.balance
    update coa set balance =
    (
        select amount from periodsum
        where year=2003 and period=1 and coa#=coa.coa#
    );
    commit;
```

```
update coa set ytd =
(
    select sum(amount) from periodsum
    where year=2003 and coa#=coa.coa#
);
commit;


--stock.lastdate
update stock set lastdate =
(
    select a.dte from
    (
        select stock_id, max(dte) as dte
        from stockmovement
        group by stock_id
    ) a
    where a.stock_id = stock.stock_id
);
commit;


--stock.qtyonhand
update stock set qtyonhand =
(
    select a.qty from
    (
        select stock_id, sum(qty) as qty
        from stockmovement
        group by stock_id
    ) a
    where a.stock_id = stock.stock_id
);
commit;


--stock.totalvalue
update stock set totalvalue =
(
    select a.amount from
    (
        select stock_id, sum(qty*price) as amount
        from stockmovement
        group by stock_id
    ) a
    where a.stock_id = stock.stock_id
);
```

```
            commit;

            dbms_output.put_line('PROC: UpdateSummaries Complete '
||to_char(getTime(vtime)));
            simAudit('PROCEDURE','UpdateSummaries',getTime(vtime),0);

   exception when others then
            dbms_output.put_line('PROC: UpdateSummaries
'||SQLERRM(SQLCODE));
            rollback;
   end;
   /
   alter procedure summaries compile;
   /
```

A.5   Partitioning Tablespace Creation

These commands create tablespaces for separate partitions created on the Accounts schema GeneralLedger table, used by partitioning examples in Chapter 17. Other examples in Chapter 17 creating partitions for other tables, use similar tablespace creation scripts. Not all scripts are included here:

```
--Execute in SQL*Plus logged in as SYSTEM or SYS
CREATE TABLESPACE DATAGLP1999 DATAFILE
'C:\ORACLE\PRODUCT\10.2.0\ORADATA\TEST\dataglp1999.dbf'
SIZE 6M AUTOEXTEND ON EXTENT MANAGEMENT LOCAL SEGMENT SPACE
MANAGEMENT AUTO;
CREATE TABLESPACE DATAGLP2000 DATAFILE
'D:\ORACLE\PRODUCT\10.2.0\ORADATA\TEST\dataglp2000.dbf'
SIZE 6M AUTOEXTEND ON EXTENT MANAGEMENT LOCAL SEGMENT SPACE
MANAGEMENT AUTO;
CREATE TABLESPACE DATAGLP2001 DATAFILE
'E:\ORACLE\PRODUCT\10.2.0\ORADATA\TEST\dataglp2001.dbf'
SIZE 6M AUTOEXTEND ON EXTENT MANAGEMENT LOCAL SEGMENT SPACE
MANAGEMENT AUTO;
CREATE TABLESPACE DATAGLP2002 DATAFILE
'F:\ORACLE\PRODUCT\10.2.0\ORADATA\TEST\dataglp2002.dbf'
SIZE 6M AUTOEXTEND ON EXTENT MANAGEMENT LOCAL SEGMENT SPACE
MANAGEMENT AUTO;
CREATE TABLESPACE INDXGLP1999 DATAFILE
'C:\ORACLE\PRODUCT\10.2.0\ORADATA\TEST\indexglp1999.dbf'
SIZE 6M AUTOEXTEND ON EXTENT MANAGEMENT LOCAL SEGMENT SPACE
MANAGEMENT AUTO;
CREATE TABLESPACE INDXGLP2000 DATAFILE
'D:\ORACLE\PRODUCT\10.2.0\ORADATA\TEST\indexglp2000.dbf'
```

```
SIZE 6M AUTOEXTEND ON EXTENT MANAGEMENT LOCAL SEGMENT SPACE
MANAGEMENT AUTO;
CREATE TABLESPACE INDXGLP2001 DATAFILE
'E:\ORACLE\PRODUCT\10.2.0\ORADATA\TEST\indexglp2001.dbf'
SIZE 6M AUTOEXTEND ON EXTENT MANAGEMENT LOCAL SEGMENT SPACE
MANAGEMENT AUTO;
CREATE TABLESPACE INDXGLP2002 DATAFILE
'F:\ORACLE\PRODUCT\10.2.0\ORADATA\TEST\indexglp2002.dbf'
SIZE 6M AUTOEXTEND ON EXTENT MANAGEMENT LOCAL SEGMENT SPACE
MANAGEMENT AUTO;
ALTER USER ACCOUNTS QUOTA UNLIMITED ON DATAGLP1999 QUOTA UNLIMITED
ON DATAGLP2000
QUOTA UNLIMITED ON DATAGLP2001 QUOTA UNLIMITED ON DATAGLP2002;
ALTER USER ACCOUNTS QUOTA UNLIMITED ON INDXGLP1999 QUOTA UNLIMITED
ON INDXGLP2000
QUOTA UNLIMITED ON INDXGLP2001 QUOTA UNLIMITED ON INDXGLP2002;


CREATE TABLESPACE DATATSP DATAFILE
'C:\ORACLE\PRODUCT\10.2.0\ORADATA\TEST\datasp.dbf'
SIZE 8M AUTOEXTEND ON EXTENT MANAGEMENT LOCAL SEGMENT SPACE
MANAGEMENT AUTO;
CREATE TABLESPACE DATATSS DATAFILE
'D:\ORACLE\PRODUCT\10.2.0\ORADATA\TEST\datass.dbf'
SIZE 2M AUTOEXTEND ON EXTENT MANAGEMENT LOCAL SEGMENT SPACE
MANAGEMENT AUTO;
CREATE TABLESPACE INDXTSP DATAFILE
'E:\ORACLE\PRODUCT\10.2.0\ORADATA\TEST\indxtsp.dbf'
SIZE 4M AUTOEXTEND ON EXTENT MANAGEMENT LOCAL SEGMENT SPACE
MANAGEMENT AUTO;
CREATE TABLESPACE INDXTSS DATAFILE
'F:\ORACLE\PRODUCT\10.2.0\ORADATA\TEST\indxtss.dbf'
SIZE 1M AUTOEXTEND ON EXTENT MANAGEMENT LOCAL SEGMENT SPACE
MANAGEMENT AUTO;
ALTER USER ACCOUNTS QUOTA UNLIMITED ON DATATSP QUOTA UNLIMITED ON
DATATSS;
ALTER USER ACCOUNTS QUOTA UNLIMITED ON INDXTSP QUOTA UNLIMITED ON
INDXTSS;


CREATE TABLESPACE DATAOL1 DATAFILE
'C:\ORACLE\PRODUCT\10.2.0\ORADATA\TEST\DATAOL1.DBF'
SIZE 5M AUTOEXTEND ON EXTENT MANAGEMENT LOCAL SEGMENT SPACE
MANAGEMENT AUTO;
CREATE TABLESPACE DATAOL2 DATAFILE
'D:\ORACLE\PRODUCT\10.2.0\ORADATA\TEST\DATAOL2.DBF'
SIZE 5M AUTOEXTEND ON EXTENT MANAGEMENT LOCAL SEGMENT SPACE
MANAGEMENT AUTO;
```

```
CREATE TABLESPACE DATAOL3 DATAFILE
'E:\ORACLE\PRODUCT\10.2.0\ORADATA\TEST\DATAOL3.DBF'
SIZE 5M AUTOEXTEND ON EXTENT MANAGEMENT LOCAL SEGMENT SPACE
MANAGEMENT AUTO;
CREATE TABLESPACE INDXOL1 DATAFILE
'C:\ORACLE\PRODUCT\10.2.0\ORADATA\TEST\INDXOL1.DBF'
SIZE 2M AUTOEXTEND ON EXTENT MANAGEMENT LOCAL SEGMENT SPACE
MANAGEMENT AUTO;
CREATE TABLESPACE INDXOL2 DATAFILE
'D:\ORACLE\PRODUCT\10.2.0\ORADATA\TEST\INDXOL2.DBF'
SIZE 2M AUTOEXTEND ON EXTENT MANAGEMENT LOCAL SEGMENT SPACE
MANAGEMENT AUTO;
CREATE TABLESPACE INDXOL3 DATAFILE
'E:\ORACLE\PRODUCT\10.2.0\ORADATA\TEST\INDXOL3.DBF'
SIZE 2M AUTOEXTEND ON EXTENT MANAGEMENT LOCAL SEGMENT SPACE
MANAGEMENT AUTO;

ALTER USER ACCOUNTS QUOTA UNLIMITED ON DATAOL1 QUOTA UNLIMITED ON
DATAOL2
QUOTA UNLIMITED ON DATAOL3;
ALTER USER ACCOUNTS QUOTA UNLIMITED ON INDXOL1 QUOTA UNLIMITED ON
INDXOL2
QUOTA UNLIMITED ON INDXOL3;
```

B

Appendix

Note: Please note that these scripts should be tested prior to use.

B.1   Interpreting EXPLAIN PLAN

All of these scripts SELECT rows from the PLAN_TABLE containing optimizer query plans generated by the EXPLAIN PLAN command:

```
explain plan set statement_id='TEST' for <SQL Statement>;

--a simple version
COL Cost FORMAT 9990;
COL Rows FORMAT 999990;
COL Bytes FORMAT 99999990;
COL Query FORMAT a64;
SELECT cost "Cost", cardinality "Rows", bytes "Bytes"
,operation||' '||options||' on '||object_name "Query"
FROM    plan_table ORDER BY id;

--for serial queries
COL Query FORMAT a48;
COL Pos FORMAT 990;
COL Cost FORMAT 990;
COL Rows FORMAT 999990;
COL Bytes FORMAT 99999990;
COL Sort FORMAT 99999990;
COL IO FORMAT 9999990;
COL CPU FORMAT 99999990;
SELECT TRIM(LEVEL)||'. '||LPAD (' ', LEVEL - 1)||operation
||' '||options||' on '||object_name "Query"
```

```
                 ,cost "Cost", cardinality "Rows", bytes "Bytes"
                 ,decode(level,1,0,position) "Pos", temp_space "Sort"
                 ,io_cost "IO", cpu_cost "CPU"
FROM     plan_table WHERE statement_id = 'TEST'
CONNECT BY prior id = parent_id AND prior statement_id =
statement_id
START WITH id = 0 AND statement_id = 'TEST' ORDER BY id;
delete from plan_table where statement_id='TEST';
commit;

--a parallel query version
COL Query FORMAT a60;
COL Pos FORMAT 990;
COL Cost FORMAT 990;
COL Rows FORMAT 999990;
COL Bytes FORMAT 99999990;
COL Sort FORMAT 99999990;
COL IO FORMAT 9999990;
COL CPU FORMAT 99999990;
SELECT TRIM(LEVEL)||'. '||LPAD (' ', LEVEL - 1)||operation||
' '||options||' on '||object_name||' '||other_tag||'
'||partition_start||' '||partition_stop "Query"
         ,cost "Cost", cardinality "Rows", bytes "Bytes"
         ,decode(level,1,0,position) "Pos"
         ,temp_space "Sort", io_cost "IO", cpu_cost "CPU"
FROM     plan_table WHERE statement_id = 'TEST'
CONNECT BY prior id = parent_id AND prior statement_id =
statement_id
START WITH id = 0 AND statement_id = 'TEST' ORDER BY id;
delete from plan_table where statement_id='TEST';
commit;

Using the DBMS_XPLAN package.

--serial
SELECT PLAN_TABLE_OUTPUT FROM
TABLE(DBMS_XPLAN.DISPLAY('plan_table',null,'serial'));

--parallel
SELECT * FROM TABLE(DBMS_XPLAN.DISPLAY());
```

B.2   Statistics Generation

Oracle recommends using the DBMS_STATS package to generate statistics with the latest version of Oracle. A similar type of script can be created using the DBMS_STATS package:

```
set termout off echo off feed off trimspool on head off pages 0;
spool c:\tmp\statistics.sql;
select 'analyze '||object_type||' '||object_name||'
compute statistics;'
from user_objects where object_type in ('TABLE','INDEX')
order by object_type,object_name;
spool off;
set termout on;
@@c:\tmp\statistics.sql;
exit;
```

B.3   Count Rows

```
set termout off echo off feed off trimspool on head off pages 0;
spool C:\temp\counts.log;
set column table_name format a16;
select 'SELECT '''||table_name||''',',
TO_CHAR(count(*),''999,999,990'') from '||table_name||';' from
user_tables;
spool off;
set termout on;
@@C:\temp\counts.log;
set termout on echo on feed on trimspool off head on pages 40;
```

B.4   Constraints

```
set wrap off linesize 132 pages 80;
column key format a10;
column pos format 990;
column col format a10;
column cons format a20;
column tab format a20;
column own format a10;
select decode(t.constraint_type,'P','Primary','R','Foreign'
,'U','Alternate','Unknown') "Key"
        ,t.table_name "Tab", t.constraint_name "Cons"
        ,c.column_name "Col", c.position "Pos"
```

```
from user_constraints t, user_cons_columns c
where t.constraint_type in ('P','R','U')
and t.table_name = c.table_name
and t.constraint_name = c.constraint_name
order by t.table_name, t.constraint_type, c.position;
```

B.5   Indexes

```
set wrap off linesize 132 pages 80;
column pos format 990;
column col format a10;
column ind format a25;
column tab format a25;
column typ format a20;
column tbs format a25;
select t.table_name "Tab"
        ,decode(t.index_type,'NORMAL','BTree','BITMAP','Bitmap'
,'FUNCTION-BASED NORMAL','Function-Based BTree'
,t.index_type) "Typ"
        ,t.index_name "Ind", c.column_name "Col", c.column_position
"Pos"
        ,t.tablespace_name "Tbs"
from user_indexes t, user_ind_columns c
where t.table_name = c.table_name
and t.index_name = c.index_name
and t.index_type not in ('IOT - TOP','LOB')
order by t.table_name, t.index_name, c.column_position;
```

B.6   Space in the Database

```
--database size
SELECT 'Database Size' "*****"
,round(sum(round(sum(nvl(fs.bytes/1024/1024,0)))) /
sum(round(sum(nvl(fs.bytes/1024/1024,0))) + round(df.bytes/1024/
1024 - sum(nvl(fs.bytes/1024/1024,0)))) * 100, 0) "%Free"
,round(sum(round(df.bytes/1024/1024 - sum(nvl(fs.bytes/1024/
1024,0)))) / sum(round(sum(nvl(fs.bytes/1024/1024,0))) +
round(df.bytes/1024/1024 - sum(nvl(fs.bytes/1024/1024,0)))) * 100,
0) "%Used"
        ,sum(round(sum(nvl(fs.bytes/1024/1024,0)))) "Mb Free"
        ,sum(round(df.bytes/1024/1024
- sum(nvl(fs.bytes/1024/1024,0)))) "Mb Used"
,sum(round(sum(nvl(fs.bytes/1024/1024,0))) + round(df.bytes/1024/
1024
- sum(nvl(fs.bytes/1024/1024,0)))) "Size"
```

```
FROM dba_free_space fs, dba_data_files df
WHERE  fs.file_id(+) = df.file_id
GROUP BY df.tablespace_name, df.file_id, df.bytes,
df.autoextensible
ORDER BY df.file_id;


--tablespace size
COL Tablespace FORMAT a16;
SELECT df.tablespace_name "Tablespace"
      ,round((sum(nvl(fs.bytes,0))/ (df.bytes)) * 100) "%Free"
      ,round(((df.bytes - sum(nvl(fs.bytes,0)))
 / (df.bytes) ) * 100) "%Used"
      ,round(sum(nvl(fs.bytes/1024/1024,0))) "Mb Free"
      ,round(df.bytes/1024/1024
 - sum(nvl(fs.bytes/1024/1024,0))) "Mb Used"
FROM dba_free_space fs, dba_data_files df
WHERE  fs.file_id(+) = df.file_id
GROUP BY df.tablespace_name, df.file_id, df.bytes,
df.autoextensible
ORDER BY df.file_id;


--extent size
COL Object FORMAT a24;
COL Type FORMAT a5;
SELECT segment_name "Object", segment_type "Type"
,ROUND(SUM(bytes)/1024/1024) "Mb", ROUND(SUM(bytes)/1024) "Kb"
,SUM(bytes) "Bytes", SUM(blocks) "Blocks"
FROM dba_extents
WHERE owner = 'ACCOUNTS' AND segment_type IN ('TABLE','INDEX')
GROUP BY segment_name, segment_type
ORDER BY segment_name, segment_type DESC;


--segment size
COL Object FORMAT a24;
COL Type FORMAT a5;
SELECT segment_name "Object", segment_type "Type"
,ROUND(bytes/1024/1024) "Mb", ROUND(bytes/1024) "Kb"
,bytes "Bytes", blocks "Blocks"
FROM dba_segments WHERE owner = 'ACCOUNTS'
AND segment_type IN ('TABLE','INDEX')
ORDER BY segment_name, segment_type DESC;
```

B.7   TKPROF Trace Files Interpretation Scripts

B.7.1   A Perl Wrapper Script

```perl
$source = shift; #a trace path and file name

open(trace,$source) || die "Cannot open file $source\n"; @lines =
<trace>; close (trace); $len = @lines;
@p = split("\\.",$source); $output = $p[0].".out";
open(output,">$output");

$x = 0; $i = 0; while ($i < $len)
{
        if (($lines[$i] =~ /^.*SELECT.*$/i)
|| ($lines[$i] =~ /^.*INSERT.*$/i)
|| ($lines[$i] =~ /^.*UPDATE.*$/i)
|| ($lines[$i] =~ /^.*DELETE.*$/i))
{ $x = $i; }

if ($lines[$i] =~ /^.*TABLE ACCESS FULL DUAL.*$/i)
{ $i++; next; }

if (($lines[$i] =~ /^.*SORT MERGE.*$/i)
|| ($lines[$i] =~ /^.*TABLE ACCESS FULL.*$/i))
    {
      $y = $i;
      while ($lines[$i] ne "\n") { $y = $i; $i++; }
      print output "--------------------------------------
----------------------------------------\n";
      for ($j = $x; $j <= $y; $j++)
      {
          if ($lines[$j] ne "\n")
          {
              if (
                      ($lines[$j] =~ /^call.*count.*$/)
                  || ($lines[$j] =~ /^Parse.*$/)
                  || ($lines[$j] =~ /^Execute .*$/)
                  || ($lines[$j] =~ /^Fetch.*$/)
                  || ($lines[$j] =~ /^total.*$/)
                  || ($lines[$j] =~ /^---.*$/)
                  || ($lines[$j] =~ /^Misses.*$/)
                  || ($lines[$j] =~ /^Optimizer.*$/)
                  || ($lines[$j] =~ /^Parsing.*$/)
              ) { next; }
              print output "$lines[$j]";
```

```
                    }
                }
            }
            $i++;
    }

    close(output);
```

B.7.2   The TKPROF Interpretation Script

```ksh
#!/bin/ksh

#execute profile - for example .cshrc

explain=$1 #set the explain variable to a non-null value if
required.

if [ -d /tmp/tkprof ]; then sleep 0; else mkdir /tmp/tkprof; fi

if [ -z "$explain" ]; then

ls -lat $ORACLE_TRACE/$ORACLE_SID*.trc\
| awk '{print $9}'\
| awk -F/ '{print $8}'\
| awk -F. '{\
printf("tkprof %s/%s.trc\ /tmp/tkprof/%s.prf\
n",oracle_trace,$1,$1)\
}' oracle_trace=$ORACLE_TRACE

else

ls -lat $ORACLE_TRACE/$ORACLE_SID*.trc\
| awk '{print $9}'\
| awk -F/ '{print $8}'\
| awk -F. '{\
printf("tkprof %s/%s.trc /tmp/tkprof/%s.prf\
explain=<owner>/<password> table=<owner>.plan_table\
sys=no record=/tmp/tkprof/%s.rec\n",oracle_trace,$1,$1,$1)\
}' oracle_trace=$ORACLE_TRACE

fi

ls -lat /tmp/tkprof/$ORACLE_SID*.prf\
| awk '{ printf("perl tkprof.pl %s\n",$9) }'

exit 0
```

C

Appendix

Syntax diagrams in this book use Backus-Naur Form syntax notation conventions. Backus-Naur Form has become the de facto standard for most computer texts:

- *Angle Brackets:* < ... >. Angle brackets are used to represent names of categories, also known as substitution variable representation. In this example, <table> will be replaced with a table name:

  ```
  SELECT * FROM <table>;
  ```
  Becomes:

  ```
  SELECT * FROM AUTHOR;
  ```

- *OR:* |. A pipe or | character represents an OR conjunction, meaning either can be selected. In this case all or some fields can be retrieved, some meaning one or more:

  ```
  SELECT { * | { <field>, … } } FROM <table>;
  ```

- *Optional:* [...]. In a SELECT statement, a WHERE clause is syntactically optional:

  ```
  SELECT * FROM <table> [ WHERE <field> = … ];
  ```

- *At Least One Of:* { ... | ... | ... }. For example, the SELECT statement must include one of *, or a list of one or more fields:

  ```
  SELECT { * | { <field>, … } } FROM <table>;
  ```

This is not a precise interpretation of Backus-Naur Form, where curly braces usually represent zero or more. In this book, curly braces represent one or more iterations, never zero.

D

Appendix

One of the most essential steps in performance tuning is the initial installation. For versions of Oracle Database prior to Oracle Database 10*g*, installation is very important. With the advent of automated locally managed tablespaces, and automated memory cache buffers in Oracle Database 10*g*, installing for performance is simple. It does not warrant a detailed explanation.

Note: In the first edition of this book, this section was in a chapter of its own. In this second edition, it is in an appendix and not a chapter for two reasons: (1) it covers Oracle Database 9*i* and not Oracle Database 10*g* (10*g* is too simple for all this), and (2) this appendix is not strictly all about performance tuning; some of it is configuration.

This appendix will be deleted in the next edition of this book. However, it does give you a brief picture of how all the underlying file and memory structures function.

D.1 Installing Oracle Database 9*i*

Oracle Database 9*i* software installs a lot of extra options if you let it. One way to install Oracle software without the extra options is to do a custom installation and select only the required options. Avoiding installing unwanted options will not necessarily help performance, but it can make administration, and ultimately tuning, a lot easier in the long run. However, this can cause problems because any missing components could have to be added at a later stage.

Note: ⬭10*g* The general trend is toward more automation, with installation, configuration, and the underlying physical architecture of an Oracle database. On the whole, Oracle Database 10*g* is very much simplified from Oracle Database 9*i*.

D.1.1 Different Editions of Oracle Database

The three different editions are Personal Oracle, Standard Edition, and Enterprise Edition. Personal Oracle is intended for use on a single machine, and Standard Edition is a trimmed-down, cheaper version of Enterprise Edition. There are also additional optional components available with Enterprise Edition, such as Oracle Partitioning. Some additional components require additional licensing fees. If you want the best and easiest to manage, the Enterprise Edition is well worth its slightly higher price tag.

There are a multitude of installable options, which can be added to an Oracle installation at the time of installation or at a later stage. Simply run the Oracle installation software again to add further Oracle Database binary options. Some options added into a database itself can be added at a later stage using scripts contained in the $ORACLE_HOME/rdbms/admin directory.

D.1.2 Oracle Enterprise Manager and the Database Control

What was Oracle Enterprise Manager in Oracle Database 9*i* is now the Database Control in Oracle Database 10*g*. Both of these tools are excellent Oracle Database management and tuning tools. Both contain very user-friendly interfaces. In Oracle Database 10*g*, what was the Oracle Enterprise Manager Console is now split between the client-side Console and the server-side Database Control. The Console in Oracle Database 10*g* is limited to purely client-side functionality and is largely application and development oriented. The Database Control runs in a browser, allowing total access to a database server, including performance tuning tools.

Search the Internet for a tool called Spotlight. Spotlight is perhaps better as a real-time monitoring tool for busy production databases. The Database Control in Oracle 10*g* is probably not quite as good as the database health screen in the Oracle 9*i* Enterprise Manager. The Oracle 9*i* version placed more information on the screen at once, and the drilldown process was a lot easier to use. With respect to the Database Control in Oracle 10*g*, I don't know if I could really say with confidence that finding problems is easier to use than something like Spotlight. However, that used to be the case in Oracle 9*i*. The Oracle 9*i* database health and drill-down capabilities allowed for a highly versatile interface, in finding problems with the Oracle Database Wait Event Interface. Oracle Enterprise Manager consists of the following parts:

- *Enterprise Manager Web Site*. This option allows Oracle Enterprise Manager functionality to be used over the Web.

- *Enterprise Manager Console and Client*. The console provides centralized access and control to all parts of Oracle Enterprise Manager.

- *Oracle Management Server and Agent Processes*. Some parts of Oracle Enterprise Manager require two extra processes, the Management Server and the Agent.

- *Add-on Packages*. Extra packages involve change management, diagnostics, and tuning capabilities. These add-on packages are extremely useful. The only point to note is that perhaps any automated functionality should be tested first before using in production.

D.2   Basic Configuration

Let's take a brief look at Oracle networking software configuration files and the Oracle instance configuration parameter file. Any details left out at this stage will be explained in the book. Oracle instance parameters are covered throughout this book but are described in some detail here. Let's start with the networking files since they are fairly simple.

D.2.1   Basic Network Files

The listener runs on the database server. It "listens" for requests from network processes, namely Oracle client processes. The database can be connected to a session using a tool such as SQL*Plus through a network protocol such as TCP/IP. A connection can be made on the server itself using something called the bequeath protocol, which is a direct connection to the database. The ORACLE_SID variable must be set to use the bequeath protocol. Using the bequeath protocol will probably be a little faster than passing the connection through TNS.

Configuring the Listener

The following file is an example listener configuration file. This file is installed in the $ORACLE_HOME/network/admin directory. Note that using the IP address instead of the hostname for the database server machine may be noticeably faster. However, subsequent changes to IP addresses on your network will require changing the listener configuration file and bouncing the listener. This is a problem if your database is not allowed any downtime.

```
LISTENER =
  (DESCRIPTION_LIST =
    (DESCRIPTION =
      (ADDRESS_LIST =
        (ADDRESS = (PROTOCOL = TCP)(HOST = <hostname>)(PORT = 1521))
      )
    )
  )

SID_LIST_LISTENER =
  (SID_LIST =
    (SID_DESC =
      (GLOBAL_DBNAME = <SID>)
      (ORACLE_HOME = /<path>/oracle/ora92)
      (SID_NAME = <SID>)
    )
  )
```

Start the listener by using the *lsnrctl* utility. Enter listener control commands within the utility or as a parameter to the utility. The command *lsnrctl start* starts the listener, and *lsnrctl stop* stops the listener. The command *lsnrctl status* will show the status of database services served by the listener. Typing *help* within the listener control utility will display a summary of all available listener control commands.

Configuring the Client

```
<TNS Name>  =
  (DESCRIPTION =
    (ADDRESS_LIST =
      (ADDRESS = (PROTOCOL = TCP)(HOST = <hostname>)(PORT = 1521))
    )
    (CONNECT_DATA =  (SERVICE_NAME = <SID>)
  )
)
```

Shown previously is a simple example tnsnames.ora file placed on a client machine. To test the connection with the database server, execute the command *tnsping <TNS Name>* from a shell on the client machine.

There is little "tuned" about these two network configuration files here. Much of tuning the performance of Oracle networking software involves tweaking these two and other configuration files, depending on configuration. Make sure all the parentheses match and are in the correct places, otherwise you will not be able to connect to the database. Other options such as Oracle Names and Connection Manager allow for scalability but not necessarily better performance.

D.2.2 The Parameter File

This section includes a simple example Oracle instance configuration parameter file with numerous comments. I use a file such as this when creating a database manually. The parameter file is usually placed in the $ORACLE_HOME/database directory or otherwise in the $ORACLE_BASE/admin/<SID>/pfile directory with a pointer file in the $ORACLE_HOME/database directory. This example is a text-format version of the parameter file, which in Oracle Database 9*i* and after can also be stored as a binary file called the SPFILE file. The SPFILE binary file was introduced in Oracle Database 9*i* and allows changing of many configuration parameters with the database online.

Note: The parameter file contains Oracle Database parameter values overriding default values. The parameter file is parsed and loaded when the Oracle instance is started up. If the parameter file contains errors, the database will not start!

Note: (10*g*) Configuration parameters have been simplified in Oracle Database 10*g* by categorizing them. For the simplest of configurations, only the basic parameters need to be changed. More advanced parameters can be altered for more complex and demanding environments. Many parameters have been greatly simplified, particularly the shared server parameters.

The following description of the parameter file contains descriptions of different variations for different types of databases, plus notes describing various settings. Comment out or delete the notes if you want to use this parameter file. There are many more configuration parameters in Oracle Database. The following query finds all the parameters and their settings:

```
SELECT name, value FROM v$parameter ORDER BY name;
```

Let's look at some of the configuration parameters.

Database Identification

```
db_name = "<SID>"
db_domain = ""
instance_name = <SID>
service_names = <SID>
```

Control Files

Place multiple control files onto different mount points to ensure that all control files are not lost. This is called multiplexing of control files and has negligible effect on performance.

```
control_files =
(
        "/<mp1>/oracle/oradata/<SID>/control01a.ctl"
       ,"/<mp1>/oracle/oradata/<SID>/control02a.ctl"
       ,"/<mp2>/oracle/oradata/<SID>/control01b.ctl"
       ,"/<mp2>/oracle/oradata/<SID>/control02b.ctl"
)
```

Block Size

OLTP databases are typically set to a block size of 8K. Increase the block size to 16K or even 32K for data warehouses and read-only type databases. Block sizes of 2K or 4K are not common, even for OLTP databases, except in older versions of Oracle Database.

```
db_block_size = 8192
```

Note: Available block sizes may vary for different operating systems.

Block checking can cause a performance overhead. It can help prevent data block-level corruption. Data corruption is more common when you have not spent enough money on disk storage media, like me. Using RAID arrays makes parameters such as this unnecessary.

```
db_block_checking = TRUE
```

Memory Buffers and I/O Behavior

The Database Buffer Cache

OracleDatabase 9*i* replaces the DB_BLOCK_BUFFERS parameter with the DB_CACHE_SIZE parameter. The database buffer cache should not be sized to a ridiculously high amount. A very high database buffer cache hit ratio is not an indicator of good performance. Very large database buffer cache sizes can actually hurt performance and sometimes be an indicator of poor performance.

```
db_cache_size = 80M
```

Note: Separate database buffer caches can also be set for tablespaces of non-standard database block size.

Thus, with a block size of 8K, DB_2K_CACHE_SIZE, DB_4K_ CACHE_SIZE, DB_16K_CACHE_SIZE, and DB_32K_ CACHE_SIZE parameters with their related tablespaces can be set.

```
db_2K_cache_size = 2M
db_4K_cache_size = 4M
db_16K_cache_size = 16M
db_32K_cache_size = 32M
```

Note: Available block sizes and thus DB_nK_CACHE_SIZE parameters may vary for different operating systems. A 32K block size is not available for Win2K SP3 running Oracle Database 9*i* Release 2 (9.2).

Multiple blocks can be read at once. Typically, OLTP databases are set to 8K or lower, and data warehouses are set to 16K or higher. Setting the DB_FILE_MULTIBLOCK_READ_COUNT parameter to 16 would read 16 blocks at once for every read of database buffer cache or disk. This parameter must remain small for OLTP databases because it can make full table scans more palatable to the optimizer. Multiple physically contiguous blocks (next to each other) are read at once. Data warehouses can benefit substantially from reading many blocks at once because they are more likely to have data physically sorted, depending on how tables are created. Obviously, reading large numbers of blocks at once in a highly active OLTP database could have ill effects; it is unlikely even when large chunks of data are required that everything will be physically contiguous.

```
db_file_multiblock_read_count = 8
```

The DB_KEEP_CACHE_SIZE and DB_RECYCLE_CACHE_SIZE parameters are parameters allowing forcing of MRU (most recently used) data to be retained and LRU (least recently used) data to be discarded with less interference from other data in the main database buffer cache. Depending on the size and function of the database, these parameters could be set at 5% and 25% of the DB_CACHE_SIZE parameter, respectively. These parameters must be a multiple of the standard block size, as defined by the DB_BLOCK_SIZE parameter.

```
db_keep_cache_size = 5M
db_recycle_cache_size 20M
```

The FAST_START_MTTR_TARGET parameter is a crash recovery parameter.

```
fast_start_mttr_target = 300
```

The Shared Pool

The shared pool contains the library cache, dictionary cache, language character set, and shared server queues. Shared server queues can contain some session connection memory. The library cache consists of parsed SQL code, optimization plans, and latches. The dictionary cache contains database metadata. Metadata is the data about the data. Like the database buffer cache, the shared pool is often sized much too large, often because of SQL code lacking bind variables. SQL code without use of bind variables forces constant reparsing, making reuse of SQL code nonexistent and increasing use of CPU time substantially.

```
shared_pool_size = 80M
```

A small portion of the shared pool can be reserved for large operations, creating a contiguous section of the buffer. This helps avoid defragmentation in the shared pool by large operations, minimizing latch problems and a lot of bouncing all over a large, possibly highly fragmented buffer. Typically, the SHARED_POOL_RESERVED_SIZE parameter is set to between 5% and 10% of the size of the shared pool, but it can be sized larger if circumstances and applications warrant it.

```
shared_pool_reserved_size = 8M
```

The processes parameter limits database connections, stored in the shared pool. Oracle Database 8*i* required a minimum of 55 processes with 200 processes required when using Oracle Enterprise Manager software. Oracle Database 9*i* and Oracle Database 10*g* values should be set higher as concurrent connections grow. The maximum processes for a dedicated server environment was recommended by Oracle Corporation at around 500. On the contrary, dedicated server environments can exceed 1000 concurrent connections and still function efficiently. To get an idea of processes, memory usage, there is one process per connection in a dedicated server environment. For 100 concurrent connections at 300K per connection, 30M of memory would be required. For 500 concurrent connections at 300K per connection, 150M of memory would be required. A shared server configuration may decrease the amount of connection memory required because there is sharing of resources with sharing of server processes.

```
processes = 500
```

Connection Memory Requirements

For dedicated servers, set the WORKAREA_SIZE_POLICY parameter to AUTO and set the PGA_AGGREGATE_TARGET parameter for automated session connection memory requirements. In the case of shared servers, the WORKAREA_SIZE_POLICY parameter must be set to MANUAL.

Setting the SORT_AREA_SIZE parameter to 1M with 1000 connections could claim 1Gb of memory if every connection was sorting at once. To reiterate, 1Gb of memory would only be claimed for sorting if every connection was performing an in-memory sort at the same time. This is unlikely, but it is possible depending on what applications do. Each user connection is allocated up to a SORT_AREA_SIZE parameter specified chunk of memory whenever a sort is performed. Do not make the SORT_AREA_SIZE parameter too large, because it will use a lot of memory if many concurrent connections are performing sorting. Reporting, lots of joins, bad SQL code, and data warehousing could very well cause lots of sorting.

```
sort_area_size = 256K
```

The SORT_AREA_RETAINED_SIZE parameter is recommended as set to 10% of SORT_AREA_SIZE when most transactions are small, and set equal to SORT_AREA_SIZE when many large transactions are the norm. A small portion of memory sort space is retained by the connection for queries containing multiple sorts. This parameter can potentially speed up some queries, probably complex, poorly tuned, or very large queries.

```
sort_area_retained_size = 6K
```

Other parameters in this group are as follows. These parameters are best not altered without proper planning and thought. Making the HASH_AREA_SIZE parameter larger tends to be useful when trying to persuade the optimizer to favor hash joins rather than nested loop joins. I do not see the point of that because I never assume that I am more intelligent than the optimizer unless statistics are completely useless, especially in Oracle Database 9*i* and beyond.

- *HASH_AREA_SIZE*. Used for SQL code optimizer hash joins on larger row sets
- *BITMAP_MERGE_AREA_SIZE*. Bitmap merges
- *CREATE_BITMAP_AREA_SIZE*. Creating bitmaps

The WORKAREA_SIZE_POLICY = AUTO and PGA_ AGGREGATE_ TARGET parameters are intended as replacements for the previous five parameters controlling session shared pool memory usage. Oracle Corporation recommends use of these parameters in Oracle Database 9*i* to automate PGA memory management.

Note: WORKAREA_SIZE_POLICY = AUTO will only function in a dedicated server, not a shared server environment.

The OPEN_CURSORS parameter sets a limit on the maximum number of open cursors allowed per session. Setting this parameter is application dependent, and being a limitation does not reserve space for each session.

```
open_cursors = 100
```

The Large Pool

The large pool is required for use of tools such as RMAN and parallel queries, and could be set to less than 200M, often much less. Shared server configuration pushes some connection session memory requirements from the shared pool into the large pool. Increase the large pool size to accommodate use of shared servers. The shared pool can be decreased accordingly.

```
large_pool_size = 200M
```

The Java Pool

The Java pool is used for the Oracle JVM if you choose to write stored procedures in Java. This parameter must be set if the Oracle JVM is installed into a database. Otherwise, this parameter can be set to 0 and is a complete waste of resources unless Java is being used to write stored procedures, apart from some specific tools and add-on options.

```
java_pool_size = 0
```

Note: (10*g*) JAVA_POOL_SIZE can be altered using the ALTER SYSTEM command and a binary parameter file, SPFILE.

The Redo Log Buffer Cache

Oracle Database 9*i* defaults the log buffer cache to 512K. This could be too high for low-activity OLTP databases, but it is not necessary to change the default. Perhaps set the LOG_BUFFER parameter higher for the biggest, highly concurrent databases or large transactional databases with a lot of throughput, and throughput changing rather than just reading data.

```
log_buffer = 524288
```

Small increases in the size of the log buffer can occasionally produce big increases in performance. However, I have seen databases with 500Mb log files and log buffer caches of 100Mb. Suffice it to say that these databases had serious performance problems, not only with little use of the log buffer cache but a lot of time spent copying redo log files to archive logs. The log buffer cache does not need to be enormous; it is recycled rapidly and written to disk.

Duplexing of redo logs is efficient, especially on servers with more than one CPU, and will generally not affect performance. It is always prudent to create multiple copies of redo logs no matter what your disk storage structure. Redo log files cannot be included in backups. Duplexing the redo logs provides for a second copy.

SQL Code Optimization

There are various parameters classifiable as influencing the optimizer:

- *CURSOR_SHARING*. This parameter is a temporary solution helping to alleviate performance problems when not using bind variables in SQL code. The CURSOR_SHARING parameter can be set to SIMILAR or FORCE, partially deteriorating the accuracy of statistics usage. The FORCE option will parse only the first SQL statement submitted. Because all literals are replaced with bind variables, subsequent submissions of similar SQL code may not match the current execution plan very well at all, depending on the structure of data. The SIMILAR option is the same as FORCE, except histograms are used to help tune the execution plan better than when using the FORCE option. Use CURSOR_SHARING settings of FORCE or SIMILAR in OLTP systems but not in data warehouses. A data warehouse database will perform better using exact matches on statistics with literal values in SQL code because data volumes are much greater. In a data warehouse environment perhaps, set the CURSOR_SHARING parameter to EXACT.

- *HASH_JOIN_ENABLED*. This parameter must be set to TRUE to allow use of hash joins in SQL code join optimization. It is extremely unlikely that any OLTP database would ever need to only use sort merge joins unless your OLTP database has very poorly tuned SQL join code or there is extensive reporting. If this parameter is not set to TRUE, inefficient sort merge joins will always be used in favor of hash joins. Sort merge joins are very bad for performance. Hash joins are potentially much faster than sort merge joins.

- *QUERY_REWRITE_ENABLED*. Set to TRUE to enable function-based indexing and query rewrites when using materialized views. Materialized views are generally only used in data warehouses or data marts.

- *QUERY_REWRITE_INTEGRITY*. Set to TRUSTED to enable function-based indexing.

- ***STAR_TRANSFORMATION_ENABLED***. Set to TRUE in data warehouses to enable star query transformations.

- ***PARALLEL_AUTOMATIC_TUNING***. Set to TRUE if you have more than one CPU. If there is only one CPU, this parameter can still help automate semi-parallel processed optimizer tuning. Rely on the optimizer; setting this parameter to TRUE helps the optimizer.

Note: (10*g*) The PARALLEL_AUTOMATIC_TUNING parameter is deprecated.

- ***COMPATIBLE***. Set to the version of Oracle Database installed to take advantage of newly introduced optimization features.

```
compatible = 9.2.0.1.0
```

Note: Some of the connection memory parameters, named as %_AREA_SIZE, could also be included here because they can affect optimizer behavior.

Auditing and Tracing

Auditing and tracing allows for tracking, auditing, and tuning of database use.

Auditing

Database auditing can be performed at the operating system, database, or even DML statement history levels. Switch auditing off if it is no longer required. It is a performance hog!

```
audit_trail = DB
```

Tracing

Tracing will affect performance drastically. I like to categorize levels of tracing into six groups:

1. ***No Tracing***

```
timed_statistics = TRUE
```

```
timed_os_statistics = 0
sql_trace = FALSE
```

Note: The overhead for setting the TIMED_STATISTICS = TRUE parameter is negligible.

2.   *Some Tracing*

```
timed_statistics = TRUE
timed_os_statistics = 5
sql_trace = FALSE
max_dump_file_size = 1M
statistics_level = BASIC or TYPICAL
```

3.   *SQL Tracing*

```
timed_statistics = TRUE
timed_os_statistics = 5
sql_trace = TRUE
max_dump_file_size = 1M
statistics_level = TYPICAL
```

4.   *Too Much Tracing*

```
timed_statistics = TRUE
timed_os_statistics = 5
sql_trace = TRUE
max_dump_file_size = 1M
statistics_level = ALL
```

5.   *Oracle Support Tracing.* You should never need this level of tracing. It produces a large amount of superfluous information and is utilized by setting the TRACE_ENABLED parameter to TRUE. This option is intended for the use of Oracle Corporation in analyzing potential bugs in Oracle software.

```
trace_enabled = FALSE
```

> **Note:** (10g) Oracle Trace and all ORACLE_TRACE_% parameters have
> been deprecated.

6. ***Session-Level Tracing***. Specific sessions can be traced. Tracing at
the session level can help remove tracing overhead from the database in general and focus on a specific session. However, the value
of session-level tracing is relative to how easy it is to track when
poorly performing SQL code occurs. It is true that instance-level
tracing is instantiated for the entire database and can hurt performance severely. Session-level tracing is easier to use in large transactional environments as opposed to sharing of sessions between
shared servers in an OLTP environment. Using the Oracle Database Wait Event Interface may provide better possibilities for
finding problems at this level of detail.

Archiving, Check Points, the Alert Log, and Trace Files

Archive Logs

```
log_archive_start=true
log_archive_dest_1='LOCATION=<mp1>/oracle/oradata/<SID>/archive'
log_archive_format=Arc_%s.arc
log_archive_start=false
```

Checkpointing

A checkpoint forces writing of all dirty buffer cache blocks to datafiles. Setting the LOG_CHECKPOINT_INTERVAL parameter to 0 will ignore
checkpoints altogether.

```
log_checkpoint_interval = 0
```

Checkpoints are executed every five minutes with this setting.

```
log_checkpoint_timeout = 300
```

The Alert Log and Trace Files

The BACKGROUND_DUMP_DEST parameter determines the location
of the alert log file and process trace files. User trace files are placed in the
directory specified in the USER_DUMP_DEST parameter.

```
background_dump_dest = /<mp1>/oracle/admin/<SID>/bdump
user_dump_dest = /<mp1>/oracle/admin/<SID>/udump
```

Rollback and Undo

Oracele Database 9*i* and beyond allows for automated undo in addition to manually configured rollback segments. My test database with my Accounts schema uses both manual and automated undo at different points in time. This book contains tuning information on both because many existing pre-Oracle Database 10*g* installations use manual rollback. Growth appears to be properly controlled using automated undo segments in highly active concurrent OLTP databases. Automated undo should be used, if possible, in Oracle Database 9*i*.

Manual Rollback Segments

OLTP databases require many small rollback segments. Many small rollback transactions for an OLTP database will increase database performance drastically for an OLTP database, because transactions will spread evenly across all online rollback segments. It may even be intelligent to make many rollback segments as small as 16K initial and next. Set optimal size depending on transaction size.

Note: Separate large rollback segments placed offline by default can be placed online and utilized for large transactions, and then placed offline on transaction completion.

OLTP databases can perform well with a large number of small rollback segments. The ROLLBACK_SEGMENTS parameter forces rollback segments online at database startup and is advisable even for public rollback segments. Otherwise, unused rollback segments may never be placed online and used. The number of rollback segments placed online at startup depends on potential transactions, not the sizes of rollback segments. When using large numbers of rollback segments, make sure that next extent values are very small to avoid rollback segments sharing too many transactions at once. The idea is to separate small transactions into separate rollback segments to reduce contention between different transactions using the same rollback segment.

```
max_rollback_segments 50
rollback_segments =
(
```

```
        RB00,RB01,RB02,RB03,RB04,RB05,RB06,RB07,RB08,RB09
,RB10,RB11,RB12,RB13,RB14,RB15,RB16,RB17,RB18,RB19
,RB20,RB21,RB22,RB23,RB24,RB25,RB26,RB27,RB28,RB29
,RB30,RB31,RB32,RB33,RB34,RB35,RB36,RB37,RB38,RB39
,RB40,RB41,RB42,RB43,RB44,RB45,RB46,RB47,RB48,RB49
)
```

Note: (10*g*) Manual rollback is deprecated.

Automated Undo Segments

Databases with small transactions can have lower values for the UNDO_RETENTION parameter.

```
undo_management = AUTO
undo_retention = 900
undo_tablespace = UNDOTBS
```

Note: (10*g*) The UNDO_SUPPRESS_ERRORS parameter is deprecated.

Resource Management

Resource management allows the distribution of resources such as CPU time between different groups of sessions. The RESOURCE_MANAGER_ PLAN parameter sets the default resource management plan or group. Resource plans can be altered depending on processing requirements during the course of a day, allowing for variable performance requirements. For instance, during high activity times, an OLTP grouping plan can be used allowing for fast reaction times, and during low activity times, a BACKUP or batch-type grouping could be used allowing for faster throughput.

```
resource_manager_plan = 'OLTP'
```

Job Scheduling

This parameter affects how many jobs can be scheduled and executed at once. I have some highly active code executed on my database using the DBMS_JOBS package to produce a tunable database for writing this book. This code kicks off between 10 and 100 jobs per second in order to produce highly concurrent activity. The intention was to create a tunable database. The default value for the JOB_QUEUE_PROCESSES parameter is 10.

```
job_queue_processes = 10
```

Networking

Networking parameters only affect Oracle shared servers (formerly MTS or Multi-Threaded Server). Shared servers allow for connection pooling, load balancing, and sharing of database connections. Shared servers perform the same function an application server or Web server would. A word of advice: If you can afford a connection pooling application server or Web server, avoid shared servers; it has not necessarily always been problematic but perhaps misused and misunderstood.

Note: Shared servers were called MTS or Multi-Threaded Server prior to Oracle Database 9*i*.

```
dispatchers = "(PROTOCOL=TCP) (DISPATCHERS=1) (POOL=ON)
(PORT=1521)"
shared_servers = 2
circuits = 10
shared_server_sessions = 10
max_dispatchers = 2
max_shared_servers = 5
```

Note: (10*g*) Shared server parameter configuration is simplified.

A simple explanation of shared servers is as shown in Figure D.1. In a dedicated server environment, client sessions connect directly to the database via a dedicated server process. In a shared server configuration, client processes can share connections to shared server processes, having messages passed between themselves and those shared server processes using dispatcher processes. Shared servers can therefore service a lot more connections because idle sessions are not always connected to the database, particularly when a client connection is idle. Idle connects through dedicated server processes waste resources that are better used otherwise. A shared server is more scalable than a dedicated server environment in terms of the number of concurrent connections to the database.

D.3   (9*i*) Creating a Database

Like initial Oracle binary software installation, well-structured and well-thought-out initial database creation is essential to a properly physically tuned Oracle database. There are two different methods of creating a database. The first is using the Database Configuration Assistant, and the sec-

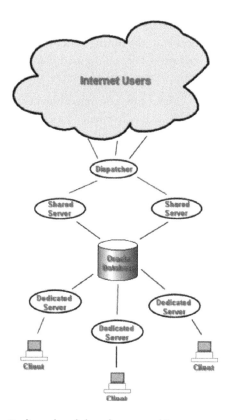

Figure D.1   *Dedicated and shared server architecture*

ond is manually using command-line scripts. The Database Configuration Assistant is easy to use and can be utilized to create a set of adjustable scripts. Let's look at the Database Configuration Assistant first.

D.3.1   The Database Configuration Assistant

I generally use the Database Configuration Assistant in two ways: (1) when creating a database initially using a new version of Oracle Database, and (2) as a database creation script generator.

Note: Selecting the New Database option, as shown in Figure D.2, will allow selection of explicit options for database creation, one of the most important being the removal of all the sample tablespaces as shown in Figure D.3. Extra options shown in Figure D.4, such as Oracle JVM and Intermedia, can also be removed later using $ORACLE_HOME/rdbms/admin scripts if so required.

Many of the steps involved in database creation are database administration and not tuning functions. However, in the interest of creating a properly physically configured database architecture, it is prudent to go through some of the steps of the Database Configuration Assistant.

Make sure you select the correct database creation template. An OLTP database is equivalent to a Transaction Processing database, as shown in Figure D.2. However, in order to create a database and remove the example schemas, it is best to select the New Database option.

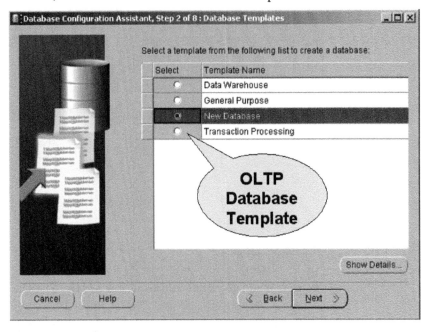

Figure D.2   *Choosing the appropriate database template.*

Figure D.3 shows various options, which can be removed from a database creation. All options can be retained. Bear in mind that general use of added options could incur higher Oracle software licensing fees.

Figure D.4 allows selection of standard included optional features. None of these options absolutely has to be retained; their selection depends on application requirements.

Even for highly active, concurrent, very large OLTP databases, dedicated servers are still commonly used, sometimes with as many as 1000 concurrent connections. A shared server configuration will ultimately be more scalable. Once again, if your database concurrency is high, it may be more cost effective in the long term to invest in a connection pooling appli-

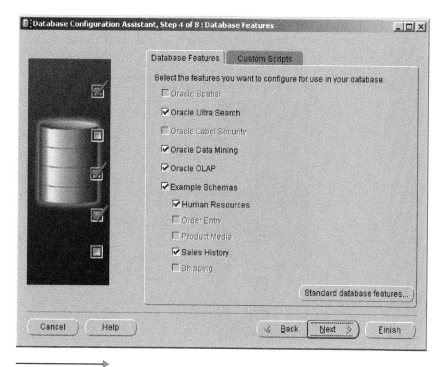

Figure D.3 *Options and examples when creating a database*

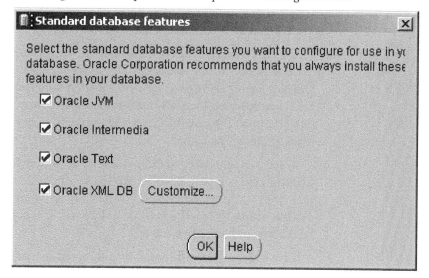

Figure D.4 *More optional database features*

cation or Web server machine, allowing more performance capacity for
your database. The choices of dedicated and shared server modes are shown
in Figure D.7.

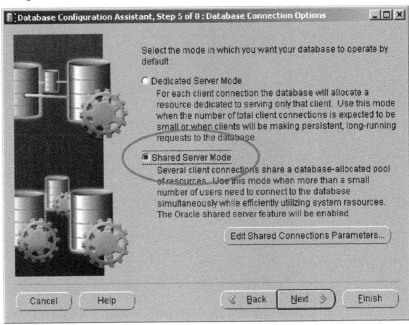

Figure D.5   *Choosing dedicated or shared servers*

Oracle Database tends to maximize the use of memory resources on a
database server, to the detriment of everything else on that server. Figure
D.6 and Figure D.7 show that I have altered buffer values to very low values. I am running Oracle Database on a low-powered, single CPU, Pen-
tium II, Intel Windows 2K box. Additionally, I have multiple databases
running on that machine.

Note in Figure D.6 that PGA is automatically entered. If this value is set
to 0, the tool will prompt to set the PGA value to an amount greater than
zero when clicking the next tab. Note that in Figure D.5, Shared Server
mode is selected. Shared Servers do not allow use of automatically managed
PGA cache in Oracle Database 9*i*.

I have two gripes with using this tool to create databases. My first gripe
is as shown in Figure D.8, showing the database creation tool creating a
large number of tablespaces containing numerous different examples and
Oracle options. These take up space, and too many tablespaces is simply
confusing. If you were to count all the users after creating a database with

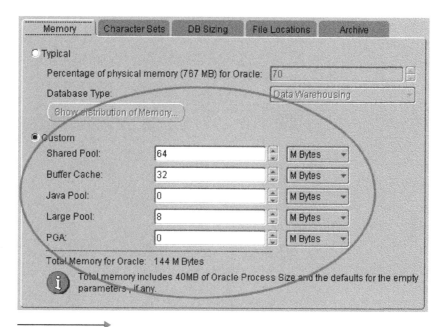

Figure D.6   *Oracle database memory buffer parameters*

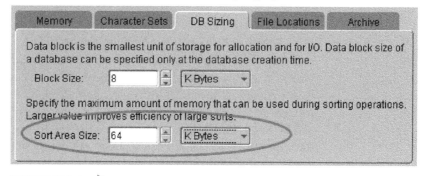

Figure D.7   *The sort buffer*

this tool, you should find that Oracle Database 9*i* Release 2 (9.2) creates almost 30 users, using all the extra tablespace datafiles shown in Figure D.8. The most essential usernames in a newly created Oracle database are SYS, SYSTEM, probably OUTLN, and perhaps DBSNMP and maybe RMAN. That's all!

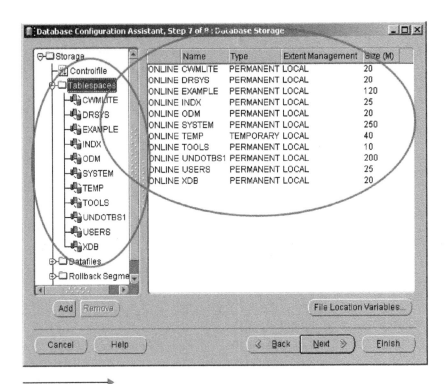

Figure D.8   *Creation of tablespaces and datafiles*

Note: (10*g*) My first gripe has been resolved by the addition of a system-level auxiliary tablespace. This is pleasing indeed. The SYSAUX tablespace will be created automatically, along with the SYSTEM tablespace. The SYSAUX tablespace contains options and tools, such as RMAN tools, Auditing, an Oracle Enterprise Manager repository (like the RMAN repository, best not to include with the production database), plus various add-on Oracle options such as OLAP, Data Mining, XML, and many others.

My second gripe with the Database Configuration Assistant is as shown in Figure D.9, where only three large redo log files are created. Rarely can an OLTP database survive with less than at least five and sometimes even as many as ten redo log files. Also, the redo logs are created at 100Mb each. This is a very big redo log file and can take time to archive, especially on a Windows box. A very active DML OLTP database with only three very large redo log files can result in the database periodically halting service while all redo log files are archived. Additionally, redo log files are not duplexed, and they probably should be for the sake of recoverability.

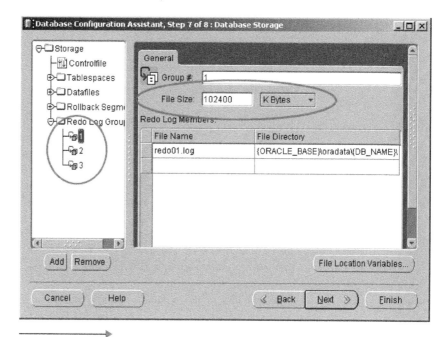

Figure D.9 *Creation of redo logs*

Current Trends

One particularly useful aspect of the Database Configuration Assistant is that it can be used to show current trends for Oracle Database creation. New things recently introduced definitely work properly when used for the SYSTEM tablespace. Some of these physical aspects affect much of the physical architecture, even to the level of logical objects such as tables and indexes. Orace Database 8*i* defaulted to creation of all tablespaces as dictionary managed except for the temporary sorting tablespace. Oracle 9*i* Release 1 (9.1) made all tablespaces locally managed except for the system tablespace. As can be seen in Figure D.10, the recommended physical structure in Oracle 9*i* Release 2 (9.2) is for all tablespaces to be locally managed with automatic allocation and automatic segment space management. This means it all works now.

Now let's look at manual database creation using command-line instructions and scripting.

D.3.2   Manual Database Creation

The best way to show how to create a database manually is to present a set of scripts and describe the pieces. These scripts are by no means executable

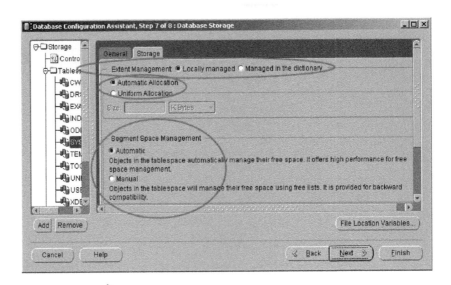

Figure D.10   *Physical datafile default structure*

as they are, as with any of the scripts in this book. However, these scripts should give you an overall picture of how to create a physically neat and properly structured database, which is easy to tune.

Note: Scripts presented here were originally built for a Solaris box Oracle 8*i* Release 2 (8.1.7) installation and upgraded for Oracle 9*i* Release 2 (9.2). The Database Configuration Assistant can be used to generate scripts like these, which can then be altered to suit your requirements. They are presented to merely show low-level physical structural details and are not necessarily applicable to the latest version of Oracle Database.

Create the Directory Structure

This script creates the directory structure for an Oracle database. It is generally in compliance with the Oracle Optimal Flexible Architecture (OFA). A few other bits and pieces are included, such as extra variables, SQL*Net configuration files, and most important, a preprepared configuration parameter file and the Oracle password file.

Note: Once again, scripts contained in this book are as is. Please do not simply type them in without testing them first, especially any UNIX or Perl scripting.

```ksh
#!/bin/ksh

ORACLE_BASE=/<mp1>/oracle
ORACLE_HOME=$ORACLE_BASE/ora92
TNS_ADMIN=/<mp1>/oracle/ora92/network/admin
ORACLE_SID=<SID>
ORACLE_DBF1=/<mp1>/oracle/oradata/$ORACLE_SID
ORACLE_DBF2=/<mp2>/oracle/oradata/$ORACLE_SID
ORACLE_BACKUPS=/<mp2>/backups
ORACLE_SBIN=$ORACLE_HOME/sbin
ORACLE_ALERT=$ORACLE_BASE/admin/$ORACLE_SID/bdump
PATH=/bin:/usr/bin:/etc:/usr/ccs/bin:/usr/openwin/bin:/usr/ucb:/
usr/local/bin:/usr/sbin:/usr/X/bin
PATH=${PATH}:$ORACLE_HOME/bin:$ORACLE_HOME/sbin:$JAVA_HOME

USAGE="$0: Incorrect arguments, Usage: $0 <password>"
if [ -z "$1" ]; then
        echo "$USAGE"
        exit 1
fi

if [ `/usr/ucb/whoami` != "oracle" ]; then
         echo "Must be oracle"
         exit 1
fi

orapwd file=$ORACLE_HOME/dbs/orapw$ORACLE_SID password=$1
entries=2
ln -s $ORACLE_BASE/admin/$ORACLE_SID/pfile/init$ORACLE_SID.ora
$ORACLE_HOME/dbs/init$ORACLE_SID.ora

mkdir $ORACLE_BASE/admin
mkdir $ORACLE_BASE/admin/$ORACLE_SID
mkdir $ORACLE_BASE/admin/$ORACLE_SID/adhoc
mkdir $ORACLE_BASE/admin/$ORACLE_SID/arch
mkdir $ORACLE_BASE/admin/$ORACLE_SID/bdump
mkdir $ORACLE_BASE/admin/$ORACLE_SID/cdump
mkdir $ORACLE_BASE/admin/$ORACLE_SID/create
mkdir $ORACLE_BASE/admin/$ORACLE_SID/exp
mkdir $ORACLE_BASE/admin/$ORACLE_SID/pfile
mkdir $ORACLE_BASE/admin/$ORACLE_SID/udump

mkdir $ORACLE_BASE/oradata
mkdir $ORACLE_BASE/oradata/$ORACLE_SID
mkdir $ORACLE_BASE/oradata/$ORACLE_SID/archive
```

```
mkdir /<mp2>/oracle/oradata
mkdir /<mp2>/oracle/oradata/$ORACLE_SID
mkdir $ORACLE_BACKUPS/$ORACLE_SID

cp ./listener.ora $TNS_ADMIN
cp ./tnsnames.ora $TNS_ADMIN
cp ./init$ORACLE_SID.ora $ORACLE_BASE/admin/$ORACLE_SID/pfile

$ORACLE_HOME/bin/lsnrctl start
```

Create the Database

This script creates a SYSTEM tablespace and a single set of five duplexed redo log files of 10Mb each. These redo log files are enough for a small-load OLTP database, perhaps even a little on the large size. A highly active large OLTP or data warehouse database would have many more, much larger redo logs.

Additionally, I am not using a binary parameter file (SPFILE) in this case. Using a binary parameter file is very useful for maintaining high availability because it allows for changing of parameters online using the ALTER SYSTEM command. A deeper discussion on the subject of the SPFILE is database administration, not tuning, and therefore inapplicable to this book. The only problem I have found using a binary parameter file is if the file gets lost. Some clients tend to forget to back up binary files or make textual parameter file copies. When something goes wrong with parameter settings, the clients sometimes forget what they have changed online using the ALTER SYSTEM command.

Lastly, I create a temporary rollback segment. I am not using automated undo segments on my test database at this point. My test database is a very old server and has a serious lack of disk space; manual rollback segments are easier to control in this respect. Both automated undo and manual rollback are being covered in this book because of the existence of many pre-Oracle Database 10*g* installations.

```
spool ../logs/system.log;
connect sys/<password> as sysdba
startup nomount pfile = "/<mp1>/oracle/admin/<SID>/pfile/
init<SID>.ora"

CREATE DATABASE "<SID>"
        maxdatafiles 400
        maxinstances 4
        maxlogfiles 16
```

```
              maxlogmembers 4
              maxloghistory 200
              character set US7ASCII
              national character set US7ASCII
              archivelog
DATAFILE '/<mp1>/oracle/oradata/<SID>/system01.dbf' SIZE 450M
AUTOEXTEND ON NEXT 1M MAXSIZE UNLIMITED
EXTENT MANAGEMENT LOCAL UNIFORM SIZE 1M
DEFAULT TEMPORARY TABLESPACE TEMP TEMPFILE
'/<mp1>/oracle/oradata/<SID>/temp01.dbf' SIZE 250M
AUTOEXTEND ON NEXT  1M MAXSIZE UNLIMITED
LOGFILE GROUP 1 ('/<mp1>/oracle/oradata/<SID>/redo01a.log',
'/<mp1>/oracle/oradata/<SID>/redo01b.log') SIZE 10M,
        GROUP 2 ('/<mp1>/oracle/oradata/<SID>/redo02a.log',
'/<mp1>/oracle/oradata/<SID>/redo02b.log') SIZE 10M,
        GROUP 3 ('/<mp1>/oracle/oradata/<SID>/redo03a.log',
'/<mp1>/oracle/oradata/<SID>/redo03b.log') SIZE 10M,
        GROUP 4 ('/<mp1>/oracle/oradata/<SID>/redo04a.log',
'/<mp1>/oracle/oradata/<SID>/redo04b.log') SIZE 10M;
        GROUP 5 ('/<mp1>/oracle/oradata/<SID>/redo05a.log',
'/<mp1>/oracle/oradata/<SID>/redo05b.log') SIZE 10M;

create rollback segment rbtemp tablespace system
storage (initial 64k next 64k minextents 2 maxextents 300);
alter rollback segment rbtemp online;

disconnect;
spool off;
```

Note: (9*i*) Manual rollback is deprecated.

If using automated undo, include the following command in the previous script immediately following the command creating the temporary tablespace:

```
UNDO TABLESPACE UNDOTBS1 DATAFILE
        '/<mp1>/oracle/oradata/<SID>/undotbs01.dbf' SIZE 250M
        AUTOEXTEND ON NEXT 1M MAXSIZE UNLIMITED
```

Tablespace and Rollback Creation

The script in this section creates a lot of tablespaces plus manual rollback segments. In general, I have created a tablespace structure based on an

expected rapid database growth rate rather than potential application functionality. This script is out of date intentionally to show the basics and is
commented inline for clarity.

```
spool ../logs/tbs.log;
connect sys/<password> as sysdba
```

In the latest version of Oracle Database 9*i*, all tablespaces are recommended as being locally managed. The following command assumes the
SYSTEM tablespace is dictionary managed.

Note: Creation of a logical standby database requires use of a backup Control file, which is problematic in Oracle Database 9*i* with a default temporary tablespace created for a database with a locally managed SYSTEM
tablespace.

Dictionary-managed tablespaces will be phased out in a future version
of Oracle Database, but if not then they still have potential uses for very
fine physical tuning. For both tablespace types, but more so for dictionary-
managed tablespaces, consistent sizes for all datafiles tend to minimize
wasted space by allowing reuse of freed extents. New larger extents will not
fit into smaller, older extents. This can result in a lot of wasted space
through fragmentation not even recoverable by coalescence. Even automatic extent allocation for locally managed tablespaces have default uniform sizes of 1M. I have not used automatic allocation of extents in these
scripts. Most OLTP databases grow rapidly. Small, variable extent sizes can
lead to huge numbers of extents in time. Smaller tables can be placed into
smaller extent-sized tablespaces if so desired.

```
alter tablespace system default storage
(initial 1M next 1M minextents 1 maxextents unlimited pctincrease
0);
alter tablespace system minimum extent 1M;
```

Temporary sort space is allocated to the database using the default temporary sort space. This is an Oracle Database 9*i* change and a very good one
at that. In the past, many databases used the SYSTEM tablespace for sorting. Many database administrators and developers were unaware of having
to assign a user a temporary tablespace for on-disk buffer overflow sorting
purposes when creating a user.

```
--Temporary sort
create temporary tablespace temp
tempfile '/<mp1>/oracle/oradata/<SID>/temp01.dbf'
size 300M autoextend on next 1M maxsize unlimited
extent management local uniform size 1M;
ALTER DATABASE DEFAULT TEMPORARY TABLESPACE TEMP;
```

Oracle Enterprise Manager requires its own tablespace. It is best to install the Oracle Enterprise Manager repository into a separate database on a separate machine, but licensing and security issues could make this a problem. Perhaps a development or a test database is a good place for an Oracle Enterprise Manager repository—or even in the same database as an RMAN repository. An RMAN repository should be in a database separate from that of a production database, and an RMAN database must be backed up separately from production databases. RMAN requires a backup of itself when not using a control file for the RMAN repository.

Note: (9*i*) The Oracle Enterprise Manager repository is included in the SYSAUX tablespace.

```
--Oracle Enterprise Manager
create tablespace oem datafile '/<mp1>/oracle/oradata/<SID>/
oem01.dbf'
size 500M
AUTOEXTEND ON NEXT 1M MAXSIZE UNLIMITED
EXTENT MANAGEMENT LOCAL UNIFORM SIZE 1M;

--Main rollbacks
create tablespace rbs1 datafile '/<mp1>/oracle/oradata/<SID>/
rbs01.dbf'
        size 300M
AUTOEXTEND ON NEXT 1M MAXSIZE UNLIMITED
EXTENT MANAGEMENT LOCAL UNIFORM SIZE 1M;
```

Note: (9*i*) Manual rollback is deprecated.

Note the different block size specifications of the next two large rollback and LOB tablespaces. A large block size would be relevant to the content of these tablespaces. The DB_32K_CACHE_SIZE parameter would have to be specified in the configuration parameter file, requiring bouncing of the database prior to creation of these tablespaces.

Note: A 32K block size is not available for Win2K SP3 running Oracle
Database 9*i* Release 2 (9.2).

```
---Batch rollbacks
create tablespace rbs2 datafile '/<mp1>/oracle/oradata/<SID>/
rbs02.dbf'
size 320M BLOCKSIZE 32K
AUTOEXTEND ON NEXT 1M MAXSIZE UNLIMITED
EXTENT MANAGEMENT LOCAL UNIFORM SIZE 8M;
```

Note: (9*i*) Manual rollback is deprecated.

```
--LOBs
create tablespace objects datafile '/<mp1>/oracle/oradata/<SID>/
objects01.dbf'
size 96M BLOCKSIZE 32K
AUTOEXTEND ON NEXT 1M MAXSIZE UNLIMITED
EXTENT MANAGEMENT LOCAL UNIFORM SIZE 4M;
```

RMAN functionality is often placed into a tablespace called Tools by the
Oracle Installer. As already stated, RMAN is always best installed into a
separate database on a separate server. Putting the RMAN repository onto a
production server in a production database can risk losing both production
database and backup recoverability. In other words, everything!

```
--Stored procedures
create tablespace tools datafile
'/<mp1>/oracle/oradata/<SID>/tools01.dbf'
size 100M
AUTOEXTEND ON NEXT 1M MAXSIZE UNLIMITED
EXTENT MANAGEMENT LOCAL UNIFORM SIZE 1M;
```

Small static data tables go into this tablespace. Note the nonstandard
block size of 2K. If the DB_2K_CACHE_SIZE parameter was not set, the
database may have to be bounced prior to the creation of this tablespace.
The tablespace cannot be created without the existence of a value in the
correct cache parameter.

```
--Static datafiles
create tablespace datastat datafile
```

```
'/<mp1>/oracle/oradata/<SID>/datastat01.dbf'
size 1M BLOCKSIZE 2K
AUTOEXTEND ON NEXT 32K MAXSIZE UNLIMITED
EXTENT MANAGEMENT LOCAL UNIFORM SIZE 32K;
```

Let's say that transaction datafiles are expected to grow rapidly and will need to reuse space. There are multiple transaction tablespaces shown following. The separation of these tablespaces is based on growth rates and not application functionality. Many Internet startup companies, using OLTP databases, never got past the starting post. The startup companies that did succeed often had physical storage structure problems within a short period of time, especially when their databases grew rapidly. Some companies had rapid growth from a few megabytes up to a few hundred gigabytes and even more.

There is one often forgotten fact: In the past, migration between versions of Oracle Database required exporting from the old version into the new version. The Oracle export and import utilities allow restructuring into a single extent for each datafile. It all depends on how fast a database grows. Is a database growing uncontrollably between new Oracle Database version releases?

Note: Oracle Database 9*i* and Oracle Database 10*g* have excellent interversion upgrade facilities.

```
--Transaction datafiles are separated based on expansion potential
create tablespace datatrn1 datafile
'/<mp1>/oracle/oradata/<SID>/datatrn101.dbf'
        size 50M
AUTOEXTEND ON NEXT 1M MAXSIZE UNLIMITED
EXTENT MANAGEMENT LOCAL UNIFORM SIZE 1M;

create tablespace datatrn2 datafile
'/<mp1>/oracle/oradata/<SID>/datatrn102.dbf'
size 100M
AUTOEXTEND ON NEXT 1M MAXSIZE UNLIMITED
EXTENT MANAGEMENT LOCAL UNIFORM SIZE 2M;

create tablespace datatrn4 datafile
'/<mp1>/oracle/oradata/<SID>/datatrn104.dbf'
size 200M
AUTOEXTEND ON NEXT 1M MAXSIZE UNLIMITED
EXTENT MANAGEMENT LOCAL UNIFORM SIZE 4M;
```

A tablespace such as this logging tablespace has rapid growth and generally involves only DML insertion and deletion activity, plus selection of data. Thus, its extent sizes are even larger than the transactional tablespaces.

```
create tablespace logs datafile
'/<mp1>/oracle/oradata/<SID>/logtrn01.dbf'
size 1000M BLOCKSIZE 16K
AUTOEXTEND ON NEXT 1M MAXSIZE UNLIMITED
EXTENT MANAGEMENT LOCAL UNIFORM SIZE 8M;
```

Tables and indexes should usually be separated into different tablespaces. Even when RAID arrays are used, index datafiles should be accessed sequentially, and table datafiles should be accessed mostly randomly from the index datafile. Some applications and database types require full scans of indexes. Potentially full-scanned indexes could be placed into randomly accessed storage media structures as long as you are sure those indexes are always accessed with physical fast full index scans.

The ratio between sizes of table and index tablespaces depends on how you index your data model with respect to referential integrity, use of sequence identifiers, and how much alternate indexing there is. A properly designed OLTP data model will have a minimum of indexing and will likely use much less space for indexing than for tables. A data warehouse— a more traditional or perhaps poorly designed OLTP database—could need a lot more index space than tablespace. Some data models have many indexes for each table, and most of those indexes are often composite column indexes. These types of data models will usually have much bigger index tablespaces than table tablespaces. This structure tends to partially negate the performance benefits of indexing. As a side issue, physical space problems are often common in OLTP databases using Bitmap and not BTree indexes.

Once again, the nonstandard block size of 2K is used. The DB_2K_CACHE_SIZE parameter is required.

```
--Static indexes
create tablespace indxstat datafile
'/<mp1>/oracle/oradata/<SID>/indxstat01.dbf'
size 1M BLOCKSIZE 2K
AUTOEXTEND ON NEXT 32K MAXSIZE UNLIMITED
EXTENT MANAGEMENT LOCAL UNIFORM SIZE 32K;

--Transactional indexes
```

```
create tablespace indxtrn1 datafile
'/<mp1>/oracle/oradata/<SID>/indxtrn101.dbf'
     size 50M
AUTOEXTEND ON NEXT 1M MAXSIZE UNLIMITED
EXTENT MANAGEMENT LOCAL UNIFORM SIZE 1M;

create tablespace indxtrn2 datafile
'/<mp1>/oracle/oradata/<SID>/indxtrn201.dbf'
     size 100M
AUTOEXTEND ON NEXT 1M MAXSIZE UNLIMITED
EXTENT MANAGEMENT LOCAL UNIFORM SIZE 2M;

create tablespace indxtrn4 datafile
'/<mp1>/oracle/oradata/<SID>/indxtrn401.dbf'
     size 200M
AUTOEXTEND ON NEXT 1M MAXSIZE UNLIMITED
EXTENT MANAGEMENT LOCAL UNIFORM SIZE 4M;
```

It is likely that a logging index tablespace will be smaller than a logging table tablespace. Thus, this tablespace has a smaller initial size and extent incremental size than the logging table tablespace.

```
create tablespace logsidx datafile
'/<mp1>/oracle/oradata/<SID>/logtidx01.dbf'
     size 200M
AUTOEXTEND ON NEXT 1M MAXSIZE UNLIMITED
EXTENT MANAGEMENT LOCAL UNIFORM SIZE 4M;

alter user sys temporary tablespace temp;
alter user system temporary tablespace temp;
```

In general, OLTP databases require many small rollback segments. Data warehouses and batch processing environments require a smaller number of much larger rollback segments. The larger the transactions are, the larger the rollback segments should be. Note that the MAXEXTENTS parameter is set for all rollback segments to prevent runaway transactions. If your customers are executing ad hoc queries or development is being done on a production database, this setting is prudent.

```
create public rollback segment rb00 tablespace rbs1 storage
(initial 256K next 256K optimal 512K minextents 2 maxextents 64);
create public rollback segment rb01 tablespace rbs1 storage
(initial 256K next 256K optimal 512K minextents 2 maxextents 64);
```

```
create public rollback segment rb02 tablespace rbs1 storage
(initial 256K next 256K optimal 512K minextents 2 maxextents 64);
.

.

.

create public rollback segment rb49 tablespace rbs1 storage
(initial 256K next 256K optimal 512K minextents 2 maxextents 64);
```

Explicitly force all rollback segments online to make sure that Oracle Database is more likely to spread transaction load across all of those rollback segments.

```
alter rollback segment rb00 online;
alter rollback segment rb01 online;
alter rollback segment rb02 online;
.

.

.

alter rollback segment rb49 online;
```

Creating large rollback segments can help separate small OLTP functionality from batch processing.

```
create public rollback segment large00 tablespace rbs2 storage
(initial 8M next 8M optimal 16M minextents 2 maxextents 32);
create public rollback segment large01 tablespace rbs2 storage
(initial 8M next 8M optimal 16M minextents 2 maxextents 32);
alter rollback segment large00 offline;
alter rollback segment large01 offline;

alter rollback segment rbtemp offline;
drop rollback segment rbtemp;

disconnect;
spool off;
```

Note: ⟨10*g*⟩ Manual rollback is deprecated.

The Catalog and the SPFILE

Creating the database catalog and the binary SPFILE parameter file is not directly relevant to tuning. A binary parameter file makes administration easier. The only danger is that it makes random *guesstimate* changes to configuration parameters easier to do. This is always dangerous. Research any changes first.

```
spool ../logs/catalog.log;
connect sys/<password> as sysdba;

--database creation of data dictionary views amongst many other
scripts
@/<mp1>/oracle/ora92/rdbms/admin/catalog.sql;

--oracle lock views
@/<mp1>/oracle/ora92/rdbms/admin/catblock.sql;

--database creation of PL/SQL
@/<mp1>/oracle/ora92/rdbms/admin/catproc.sql;

--export utility ovm_sys user
@/<mp1>/oracle/ora92/rdbms/admin/owminst.plb;

--pinning objects
@/<mp1>/oracle/ora92/rdbms/admin/dbmspool.sql;

--heterogeneous services
@/<mp1>/oracle/ora92/rdbms/admin/caths.sql;

--prepare database for direct path SQL*Loader
@/<mp1>/oracle/ora92/rdbms/admin/catldr.sql;

--audit trails views
@/<mp1>/oracle/ora92/rdbms/admin/cataudit.sql;

--parallel server views
@/<mp1>/oracle/ora92/rdbms/admin/catparr.sql;

--tkprof use
@/<mp1>/oracle/ora92/rdbms/admin/utltkprf.sql;

connect system/manager;
--sqlplus user help files @/<mp1>/oracle/ora92/sqlplus/admin/
pupbld.sql;

connect sys/<password> as sysdba;
--pl/sql recompilation
@/<mp1>/oracle/ora92/sqlplus/admin/utlrp.sql;
```

```
shutdown immediate;

create spfile='/<mp1>/oracle/database/spfile<SID>.ora' FROM
pfile='/<mp1>/oracle/admin/pfile/init<SID>.ora';

startup;
disconnect;
spool off;
```

The objective of providing these sample installation scripts, and particularly the variable physical sizes for the tablespaces, was for one reason only. Many of the client sites I have worked on in the past had serious problems with uncontrollable physical database growth. OLTP databases and data warehouses are becoming larger all the time. This is one possible approach. Your structure does not have to be the same. Additionally, many features and changes in the latest versions of Oracle Database will help with respect to rapid growth. Oracle Corporation generally responds vigorously to current industry commercial requirements of its software.

Note: Once again, scripts presented here were originally built for a Solaris box Oracle 8*i* Release 2 (8.1.7) installation and upgraded for Oracle 9*i* Release 2 (9.2). The Database Configuration Assistant can be used to generate scripts like these, which can then be altered to suit requirements. They are presented to merely show low-level physical structural details and are not necessarily applicable to the latest version of Oracle Database.

E

Appendix

- The author of this book can be contacted at the following email addresses:

    - oracledbaexpert@bellsouth.net
    - info@oracledbaexpert.com

- Oracle Technet at http://technet.oracle.com is an excellent source for entire Oracle reference documentation sets.

- Metalink at http://metalink.oracle.com is also excellent and a source of current information from support calls, questions, and answers placed by both Oracle users and Oracle support staff. The information on this site is well worth the Oracle licensing fees required.

- Search for a term such as *free buffer waits* in search engines, such as http://www.yahoo.com. Be aware that not all information will be current and might be incorrect. Verify it on Oracle Technet. If no results are found using Yahoo, try the full detailed listings on http://www.google.com.

- Try http://www.amazon.com and http://www.barnesandnoble.com where many Oracle titles can be found.

- Other titles by the same author:

    - *Beginning XML Databases* (ISBN: 0471791202)
    - *Oracle 10g Database Administrator* (ISBN: 1418836656)
    - *Beginning Database Design* (ISBN: 0764574906)
    - *Oracle Data Warehouse Tuning for 10g* (ISBN: 1555583350)
    - *Oracle 9i: SQL Exam Cram 2* (1Z0-007) (ISBN: 0789732483)
    - *Oracle SQL: Jumpstart with Examples* (ISBN: 1555583237)
    - *Oracle Performance Tuning for 9i and 10g* (1st *Edition*) (ISBN: 1555583059)
    - *ASP Scripting* (ISBN: 1932808450)

- *Oracle Performance Tuning* (ISBN: 1932808345)
- *Oracle Database Administration Fundamentals II* (ISBN: 1932072845)
- *Oracle Database Administration Fundamentals I* (ISBN: 1932072535)
- *Introduction to Oracle 9i and Beyond: SQL & PL/SQL* (ISBN: 1932072241)
- *Access 2007 Bible*

- Software accreditations:

  - Oracle 9*i* and Oracle 10*g* Relational Database
  - Microsoft Word, Powerpoint, Excel, Win2K
  - ERWin
  - Paintshop
  - Microsoft Access (MSAccess) Relational Database

Index

Printed and bound by CPI Group (UK) Ltd, Croydon, CR0 4YY

03/10/2024

01040343-0017